Basic Topics *in the* Philosophy of Language

Edited by

Robert M. Harnish
University of Arizona

HARVESTER
WHEATSHEAF

New York London Toronto Sydney Tokyo Singapore

First published 1994 by
Harvester Wheatsheaf
Campus 400, Maylands Avenue
Hemel Hempstead
Hertfordshire, HP2 7EZ
A division of
Simon & Schuster International Group

Typeset in 10pt Sabon
by The Midlands Book Typesetting Company, Loughborough

Printed and bound in Great Britain by
T.J. Press, Padstow, Cornwall

British Library Cataloguing in Publication Data

A catalogue record for this book is available from
the British Library

ISBN 0–7450–1358–9

---

1 2 3 4 5 97 96 95 94 93

For

Csilla, Thomas, Ágnes

Contents

Preface x
Introduction xi
Suggestions for Further Reading xv
Notes on the Selections xviii
Note to the Teacher xxiv
Notes xxv
References xxvi
Acknowledgements xxvii

Part I **Meaning, Speech Acts, and Communication**

Introduction **Kent Bach** 3

1 **Meaning** 21
H. P. Grice (1957)

2 **Locutionary, Illocutionary, Perlocutionary** 30
J. L. Austin (1962)

3 **Intention and Convention in Speech Acts** 40
P. F. Strawson (1964)

4 **Logic and Conversation** 57
H. P. Grice (1975)

5 **How Performatives Work** 74
J. R. Searle (1989)

Part II Sense and Reference

Introduction Nathan Salmon 99

6 **Of Names** 130
J. S. Mill (1843)

7 **On Sense and Reference** 142
G. Frege (1892)

8 **On Denoting** 161
B. Russell (1905)

9 **Reference and Definite Descriptions** 174
K. Donnellan (1966)

10 **Naming and Necessity** 192
S. Kripke (1980)

11 **The Meaning of 'Meaning'** 221
H. Putnam (1975)

12 **Demonstratives** 275
D. Kaplan (1977/89)

Part III Opacity and Attributions of Attitude

Introduction Graeme Forbes 323

13 **Referential Opacity** 338
W. Quine (1960)

14 **A Puzzle about Belief** 352
S. Kripke (1979)

15 **Individualism and the Mental** 393
T. Burge (1979)

16 **Frege's Puzzle** 447
N. Salmon (1986)

Part IV Meaning and Truth

Introduction **Scott Soames** 493

17 **The Thought: A Logical Inquiry** 517
G. Frege (1918)

18 **The Semantic Conception of Truth and the Foundations of Semantics** 536
A. Tarski (1944)

19 **Tarski's Theory of Truth** 571
H. Field (1972)

20 **Truth and Meaning** 598
D. Davidson (1967)

Afterword: Truth and Paradox **Vann McGee** 615

Preface

Although there are numerous textbooks available in the philosophy of language, my personal opinion is that there is no substitute for reading and confronting the original classics in our field. With rare exception, the original work has an excitement, a freshness of perception and depth of argumentation about it that no digest or commentary can match. Furthermore, students do need practice in reading and commenting on original works in the field. After a few courses they are usually on their own.

This anthology is the result of teaching philosophy of language for about twenty years. I have noticed that certain works are regularly discussed, criticized and built upon. I have also found many of these works hard to make available to students. Eleven of these selections are collected together for the first time. I hope that this anthology will also fill a gap in the selection of current books for teaching a first course in the philosophy of language. There are good anthologies available which invite the teacher and student to buy a large spectrum of articles from which one reads maybe half. The present anthology is more focused and attempts to give the student just about what he or she needs to get started. And of course, the instructor can supplement the anthology to taste.

A course based on this anthology will be an intense survey of some basic topics in the philosophy of language. These articles have all proven their accessibility and most have proven their staying power. Not every practitioner will agree with every choice, but few would disagree that almost all of these selections are central to the field, have definitely posed a central problem, pointed out important distinctions and directions for research, or introduced current terminology. As the secondary literature testifies, almost every selection has generated a comprehensive collection of commentary which all in all constitutes much of the best in recent philosophy of language.

Introduction

The philosophy of language broadly construed comprises virtually all philosophical theorizing about language. But in the last century it has evolved into a field concerned to solve a set of core philosophical problems arising out of language. Since problems are related, the core ramifies, and it is difficult to draw a principled distinction between some problems in the philosophy of language and problems in linguistics, logic, and the philosophy of logic. Here we will briefly set out some of the core problem areas in the philosophy of language and say a few words about how they relate to linguistics and logic. The introductions to each part will give a more complete survey of the relevant issues.

Meaning, reference and truth; these are core concepts in the philosophy of language. One of the distinguishing features of philosophical reflections on language is concern with how language relates to the world. In one way or another most other problems can be related to these, often as special cases. Three parts of this anthology are concerned with these notions respectively, and the ideas that they are related to.

Meaning

The word 'mean' and its cognates have a variety of uses in English. Some uses are just irrelevant to meaning theory in the philosophy of language:

1.

a That was no mean (insignificant) accomplishment.
b Those clouds mean (are a sign of) rain.
c This will mean (result in) the end of the regime.
d I mean (intend) to help if I can.

Others are close, and may be related:

2
a She didn't mean (believe) what she said.
b Keep off the grass; this means (refers to) you!
c Lucky Strike means (indicates) fine tobacco.

The core notions for the philosophy of language are speaker meaning and linguistic meaning:

3
a What did he mean by that remark?
b What does 'du jour' mean?

Notice that there are no obvious ways to paraphrase the word 'mean' in these occurrences. Part I analyses and systematizes the notion of meaning, and its connection with using language to state, question, order, etc. – to perform speech acts. Typically when such acts are successfully performed we also communicate something to someone. We want to trace the connections between meaning, speech acts and communication. Meaning also connects with reference and truth. These topics are taken up in Parts II and IV.

Reference

The concept of reference can also be applied to both speakers and to expressions in a language. There is a variety of terminology here: some authors distinguish speaker reference from semantic reference, others distinguish speaker reference from denotation or linguistic reference. Everyone agrees that we must distinguish these two species of reference if only because speakers can use words to refer to things that the words themselves do not refer to. To borrow an example from Donnellan, one might say 'The man drinking a martini is a famous poet,' and actually refer to somebody drinking ginger ale. What words mean and refer to is related to what speakers mean and refer to in uttering those expressions, so we may expect to find connections between Parts I and II. Utterances are also true or false depending on what is referred to, so we may expect to find connections with Part IV, Truth. The main referring devices of English (and related languages) are definite descriptions, proper names, natural kind terms, and indexicals (demonstratives). Each of the selections after Frege is devoted to one of these devices, and collectively this 'New Theory of Reference' poses the most serious challenge to date to (what was) Fregean orthodoxy.

Truth

We speak of many different kinds of things as true (and false): true statements, true propositions, true beliefs, and true sentences, just for starters. What is it for these to be true (or false)? Are any of these truth bearers basic in the sense that the truth (or falsehood) of the others can be defined in terms of it? And is it possible or desirable to give a theory of truth for a language? If so, what would it look like? Part IV analyses and systematizes the concept of truth, and its connection with meaning and reference. And there are such connections; we do not say that meaningless sounds and marks are true (or false), and the truth of what we say depends, in part, on what is being referred to. Even more interestingly, maybe the conditions under which a sentence is true are related to the meaning of the sentence so that a theory of truth for a language might be or be part of a theory of meaning for that language.

Opacity and attributions of attitude

Opacity and attributions of attitude is included because of its regular recurrence in theorizing since Frege, its obstinacy, and its centrality to recent work in the philosophy of language. Motivating its inclusion will take a little more discussion.

Frege noted that it is not immaterial to the truth of the sentence 'Columbus inferred from the roundness of the Earth that he could reach India by traveling towards the west,' whether we replace the phrase 'the Earth' with the co-referential phrase 'The planet which is accompanied by a moon whose diameter is greater than the fourth part of its own'. Although this last ponderous phrase also refers to the Earth, Columbus might not have thought of it this way, hence its inclusion in the sentence does not correctly characterize Columbus' travel plans.

Quine coined the phrase 'referential opacity' for the phenomenon of a sentence not preserving its truth value upon all substitution of co-referential constituent terms. How are we to account for such referentially 'opaque' contexts? If the sense and reference of a complex expression is determined by the sense and reference of its constituents, and their grammatical relations, then how can words retain their normal meaning and still occur opaquely?

Again, it was Frege who noted connections between these areas; he introduced the notion of sense by appealing to differences in the *cognitive significance* of statements such as 'Venus is the Morning Star' versus 'Venus is Venus'. Famously, he claimed that statements of the form ⌜a=a⌝ hold *a priori*, while statements of the form ⌜a=b⌝ can contain valuable extensions of knowledge and cannot always be established *a priori*. Thus, the notion of the sense of an expression is connected to the way the (purported) referent of the expression is presented to the language user who grasps it. Sense is objective cognitive content, and as such is often *reported* with sentences. According to Frege, reports of what someone thinks are opaque because one must substitute co-sensical expressions, not (just) co-referential expressions in order to preserve truth. This forges a connection between opaque and non-opaque sentences; sense is a constituent of the content of simple non-opaque sentences, and these senses are reported in attributions of attitude. One could, of course, analyse a fragment of a natural language which contained no opaque constructions. But natural languages are shot through with opacity, and it has proven almost impossible to separate the study of sense, reference and truth from it. Part III deals with these and related problems.

These sections represent the three and perhaps four core non-technical areas of philosophy of language, and the number of selections represent the relative attention devoted to these areas over the last few decades.

Linguistics and logic

How do these investigations relate to linguistics and logic? Linguistics is the scientific study of language. Its main non-historical branches are phonology (the study of speech sounds), morphology (the study of word structure), syntax (the study of sentence structure), semantics (the study of linguistic meaning and reference), and pragmatics (the study of language use in relation to language structure and context of utterance).[1] Clearly the concerns of semantics and pragmatics can overlap the philosophy of language and historically they have. Many ideas from the philosophy of language (such as model theory, speech act theory, and implicature) have found their way into semantics and pragmatics. There is no clear distinction between a linguistic study of these topics and a philosophical one. Linguistic studies construct hypotheses about language and test them against speaker's intuitions, just as philosophical theories do. Neither discipline makes much use of the numerical methodology (e.g. statistics) of the social and physical sciences. Probably the main difference is one of emphasis. Linguistic studies tend to be more systematic than philosophical studies in two senses. First, linguistic studies tend to be conducted from within a descriptive framework, theory, or model. Most linguists identify their work with some theoretical tradition such as Chomsky's Government and Binding (GB) Theory, or Montague Grammar. A theoretical framework allows the linguist to make predictions and give explanations for phenomena that are unavailable outside the framework. Second, linguistic studies tend to be more systematic in the sense that many cases are considered and related to each other via the general theory of language structure embodied in the framework. The emphasis is on patterns of phenomena and their relation to each other via language structure.

Philosophical studies, on the other hand, tend to be conducted outside of any detailed theory of language structure, and they also tend to contain analyses of fewer examples. More is made of general features of the phenomena independent of the details of a particular language. Put aphoristically, philosophical studies concentrate on features of language whereas linguistic studies concentrate on features of languages.

Logic was originally the study of principles of valid inference, but in the course of formalizing such principles the discipline has evolved into formal logic and informal logic (critical thinking). Formal logic is virtually a branch of mathematics, and there is no principled way of distinguishing advanced logic from foundations of mathematics. Indeed, Frege, who invented the core of current formal logic, did so in the course of working on the foundations of mathematics. The bridge between (formal) logic and the philosophy of language is the philosophy of logic, a sub-area that investigates philosophical issues arising out of logic. Again, logical investigations tend to differ from philosophical ones in their systematicity (and their technicality). Typically syntactic or semantic properties of some system (or class of systems) is under analysis, definitions are offered and theorems proved. And again as with linguistics, the divisions are not hard and fast; popular anthologies in the philosophy of logic share a number of papers with anthologies in the philosophy of language (see below).

In sum, it is hard to give a precise characterization of the philosophy of language either in terms of its domain or its method of investigation that clearly distinguish all its samples from linguistics and logic. The best way to get a feel for the subject is to read some of the best of it oneself, and this anthology is a good place to start.

Suggestions for Further Reading

Students interested in pursuing these topics further will profit from looking at any of the following works.

Texts in the Philosophy of Language

Alston, W. (1964), *The Philosophy of Language*, Englewood Cliffs, NJ: Prentice Hall.

Blackburn, S. (1984), *Spreading the Word*, New York: Oxford University Press.

Harrison, B. (1979), *An Introduction to the Philosophy of Language*, London: Macmillan.
Martin, R. (1987), *The Meaning of Language*, Cambridge, MA: Bradford/ MIT Press.
McCullogh, G. (1989), *The Game of the Name*, New York: Oxford University Press.
Platts, M. (1979), *Ways of Meaning*, London: Routledge and Kegan Paul.

Anthologies in the Philosophy of Language

Davidson, D. and G. Harman (eds) (1975), *The Logic of Grammar*, Encino, CA: Dickenson.
French, P., Vehling, P., Wettstein, H., (eds) (1979), *Contemporary Perspectives in the Philosophy of Language*, Minneapolis: University of Minnesota Press.
Garfield, J. and M. Kitely (eds) (1991), *Meaning and Truth*, New York: Paragon House.
Martinich, A. (ed.) (1990), *The Philosophy of Language*, second edition, New York: Oxford University Press.
Olshevsky, T. (ed.) (1969), *Problems in the Philosophy of Language*, New York: Holt, Rinehart and Winston.
Platts, M. (ed.) (1980), *Reference, Truth and Reality*, London: Routledge and Kegan Paul.
Rosenberg, J. and C. Travis (eds) (1971), *Readings in the Philosophy of Language*, Englewood Cliffs: Prentice Hall.
Searle, J. R. (ed.) (1971), *The Philosophy of Language*, New York: Oxford University Press.

Texts in Formal Semantics

Chierchia, G. and S. McConnell-Ginet (1990), *Meaning and Grammar*, Cambridge, MA: MIT Press.
Dowty, D., Wall, R. and S. Peters (1981), *Introduction to Montague Semantics*, Dordrecht: Reidel.

Anthologies in Semantics

Davidson, D. and G. Harman (eds) (1972), *Semantics of Natural Language*, Dordrecht: Reidel.
Keenan, E. (ed.) (1973), *Formal Semantics of Natural Language*, New York: Cambridge University Press.

Steinberg, D. and L. Jakobovits (eds) (1971), *Semantics*, New York: Cambridge University Press.
Zabeeh, F., Klemke E. and A. Jacobson (eds) (1974), *Readings in Semantics*, Chicago: University of Illinois Press.

Tests in Pragmatics

Blakemore, D. (1992), *Understanding Utterances*, Cambridge, MA: Blackwell.
Green, G. (1989), *Pragmatics and Natural Language Understanding*, Hillsdale, NJ: L. Erlbaum.
Leech, G. (1983), *Principles of Pragmatics*, Harlow: Longman.
Levinson, S. (1983), *Pragmatics*, New York: Cambridge University Press.

Anthologies in Pragmatics

Davis, S. (ed.) (1991), *Pragmatics: A Reader*, New York: Oxford University Press.
Katz, J., Bever, T. and T. Langendoen (eds) (1975), *An Integrated Theory of Linguistic Abilities*, New York: Crowell.

Texts in Philosophy of Logic

Putnam, H. (1971), *Philosophy of Logic*, New York: Harper and Row.
Quine, W. (1970), *Philosophy of Logic*, Englewood Cliffs, NJ: Prentice Hall.
Sainsbury, M. (1991), *Logical Forms*, Cambridge, MA: Blackwell.

Anthologies in Philosophy of Logic

Copi, I. and J. Gould (eds) (1978), *Contemporary Philosophical Logic*, New York: St. Martins.
Iseminger, G. (ed.) (1968), *Logic and Philosophy*, New York: Appleton Century Crofts.
Manicus, P. (ed.) (1971), *Logic as Philosophy*, New York: Van Nostrand.
Strawson, P. (ed.) (1967), *Philosophical Logic*, New York: Oxford University Press.

Notes on the Selections[2]

Philosophical substance, importance in and influence on the field, readability; these are the major criteria used in making these selections. Ask twenty philosophers of language for their top twenty, and you'll get twenty lists. However there will be significant overlap, and it is my intention that this anthology reflect that overlap.

Grice (1957) 'Meaning'

This short but influential paper initiated twenty-five years of work on the nature of meaning. It (versus the more sophisticated 1969 article) contains Grice's reasons for trying to connect semantic notions such as meaning with non-semantic notions such as belief and intention. It also argues for a certain structure to meaning intentions, one that has survived in its basic form to the present time. It is a highly readable no nonsense first selection in the philosophy of language.

Austin (1962) 'Locutionary, Illocutionary, Perlocutionary'

This selection gives Austin's original intuitions about the central trichotomy of speech acts: locutionary, illocutionary, perlocutionary. Austin himself began constructing a theory of these acts at the end of his life, and, as the secondary literature indicates, many others have continued this work continuing up to the present. Although there are highly readable introductions to speech act theory (see especially Searle 1965, 1969), the importance of this selection is that it fixes what these subsequent theories are supposed to be theories of.

Strawson (1964) 'Intention and Convention in Speech Acts'

This article performs the historically important function of bringing together Grice's original work on (speaker) meaning and Austin's work on illocutionary acts. The first few sections thus function as a concise and sophisticated review of the Grice and Austin selections. Strawson then argues for his influential revision of Grice's characterization of meaning and elaborates on Austin's notion of the role of conventions in speech acts.

Grice (1975) 'Logic and Conversation'

In this delightfully readable piece (sort of desert for Part I) Grice explores the ways in which something that is not said can be communicated (what is implicated). With this notion in hand Grice explores the possibility that some purported aspects of linguistic meaning might really be aspects of implicature. The methodological consequences of this move (so-called 'modified Occam's Razor': Don't multiply meanings without necessity) has had an enormous impact on the field of language study even outside philosophy.

Searle (1989) 'How Performatives Work'

This selection of Searle's brings us full circle in a way. Austin's opening wedge into the general theory of speech acts was the performative–constative distinction; the idea that some utterances (performatives) are primarily doings, not just sayings, whereas others (constative) were primarily true or false. Austin could not make this distinction work and eventually the dichotomy was dropped when performatives appropriated constatives as a special case. However Austin never explained how performatives work, regardless of how they are related to constatives. This selection makes it clear that performatives need an account on their own right. They are not a linguistic curiosity, rather many aspects of meaning and use come together in the performative, and understanding how they work will deepen our understanding of language structure and use in general.

Mill (1843) 'Of Names'

In this selection Mill articulates his controversial doctrine that 'a proper name is but an unmeaning mark'. This doctrine was criticized by Frege, flirted with by Russell, and has recently been revived by 'New Theorists of Reference'. We now regularly read of 'Millian' theories, so it is worth knowing what Mill actually said, and why.

Frege (1892) 'On Sense and Reference'

This is not an easy piece. It is rarely voted the most popular essay in the course. The issues seem obscure, the style is pedantic, the humor heavy. But Frege is the single most important philosopher of language and this is perhaps his single most influential article dealing as it does with the general theory of sense and reference. With guidance, the beginning student can, in my experience, be led through the article to an appreciation of (if not agreement with) the wonderful (and baroque) theory Frege constructed to deal with the many important philosophical phenomena he was the first (in our tradition at least) to uncover. As becomes clear from subsequent readings in this anthology, Frege is almost always a point of departure. Theories in the philosophy of language are constantly being measured against the Fregean standard. One simply cannot consider oneself educated in the philosophy of language without understanding Frege's views. (See also **Frege (1918)**).

Russell (1905) 'On Denoting'

'That paradigm of philosophy' wrote P. F. Ramsey. Not all students at the beginning of their studies agree. Definite descriptions (or their equivalent in other languages) appear to be a basic referring device, and Mill, Frege, and others treated them as such. Thus Russell's famous 'Theory of Descriptions' and its denial of the purported denoting function of descriptions constitutes an important alternative analysis. It is often counselled that we should read one of Russell's more 'accessible' expositions instead of this one. I think that this is a mistake for a number of reasons. First, of course, is the historical fact that it was this paper that started it all. Russell here first states and motivates the theory of descriptions. Second, here he develops his 'three puzzles' for a theory of denoting phrases. And finally, here he argues against the earlier theories of Meinong and Frege. The impression that this paper is so inaccessible is due almost entirely to the notorious 'Gray's Elegy' passage where Russell argues against Frege's theory of sense and reference. This passage is genuinely obscure and we have marked it off in the text. My advice to beginning students is just to read around it. For more advanced students it offers a unique exegetical challenge.

Donnellan (1966) 'Reference and Definite Descriptions'

In this paper Donnellan makes a distinction between referential and attributive uses of definite descriptions and goes on to argue that Russell's theory is adequate only for the second use. What exactly is this distinction? Is it semantic? What does it show against Russell? Can it be extended to other referring devices such as proper names and indexicals? These are all currently debated questions, but the fact that they are being debated is due primarily to this article.

Kripke (1972/80) 'Naming and Necessity'

Ever since these lectures were first given at Princeton in 1970, they have constituted one of the main challenges to the 'Fregean' doctrine that the sense of a proper name is a cluster of descriptive information an object must fit to be the referent. Kripke argues that proper names are rigid designators and among the consequences of these investigations is the contention that there are *a posteriori* necessary statements as well as *a priori* contingent statements. The philosophical significance of Kripke's work, combined with its intuitive, informal lecture style makes it a regular favorite with students.

Putnam (1975) 'The Meaning of "Meaning"'

There are numerous shorter extracts in print from this paper, but the various themes Putnam develops (Twin Earth, the indexicality of natural kind terms, the division of linguistic labor, theory of stereotypes, the normal form for the description of meaning and linguistic competence) all reinforce each other in a unique and compelling way in this single essay. My experience is that advanced students appreciate the unity of vision in the work, and beginning students appreciate the open, intuitive style of presentation. Some of the critical sections in the middle can be skimmed if time is short. Readers who want the shorter Putnam paper (1973) 'Meaning and reference' will find it contained in passages of the present work. These are marked in the text. The section on Davidson is most profitably read after **Davidson** (1967).

Kaplan (1977/89) 'Demonstratives'

For at least twelve years this paper was an underground classic, circulating in mimeographed form before its publication in 1989. The essay was effectively completed in 1971 and Kaplan's lectures from it in the 1970s account for the apparent anomaly of commentaries to a 1989 paper appearing in 1975. The title is misleading, as Kaplan acknowledges. Although demonstratives are the entering wedge, the essay explores a wide variety of referring expressions: indexicals, proper names, definite descriptions, natural kind terms, and pronouns. Like Kripke and Putnam, Kaplan is concerned to explore the relationship between the semantics of such terms and broader epistemological and metaphysical issues. He introduced the important notions of direct reference, singular proposition, character and content that are now so much a part of the current idiom in the philosophy of language.

Quine (1960) 'Referential Opacity'

Even though **Frege (1892)** first discovered the phenomena of referential opacity (in our tradition), Quine gave us its current terminology. Here he introduces the notions of a purely referential position (in a sentence and in a complex referring expression), the substitution of identity as a test for transparency, opacity, quotation (versus spelling), scope and propositional attitudes. All in Quine's distinctive style, which seems to be more accessible and hence more teachable here than in his widely reprinted (1956) article 'Quantifiers and Propositional Attitudes'.

Kripke (1979) 'A Puzzle About Belief'

Kripke's puzzle is still puzzling, despite numerous attempts to solve it. Although it focuses on attributions of attitude (here belief), it ranges over a wide range of issues in the philosophy of language. It may well be considered the fourth lecture for *Naming and Necessity*. As Kripke notes, in that work he advocated a Millian position for modal contexts but appeared to advocate a non-Millian account for epistemic contexts. How to resolve this tension? Unlike Frege and Russell, Kripke generates his puzzle without appealing to principles of substitution. Kripke's forceful, intuitive arguments makes it a regular favorite with students.

Burge (1979) 'Individualism and the Mental'

This paper is regularly cited as extending Putnam's twin earth critique of Fregean theories of reference to the social realm. Just as Putnam argues that traditional meaning theory leaves out the contribution of the physical world, Burge has been taken as arguing that traditional meaning theories have left out the contribution of the social world; the linguistic community plays a role in determining the objective content of thoughts ascribed in the language of that community. Burge's interpretation of his thought experiment is controversial, but the influence of this paper has been profound.

Salmon (1986) 'Frege's Puzzle'

Salmon takes Frege's argument for sense as his point of departure in this important discussion of the nature of the cognitive information content of declarative sentences. Since Salmon subscribes (in broad outline) to, and elaborates, Kaplan's theory of direct reference, Frege's puzzle becomes his. Salmon's answer that purported differences in sense (semantics) are really differences in implicature (pragmatics; **Grice, 1975**) is both ingenious and controversial. Indeed, a whole literature is developing around pragmatic solutions to Frege's puzzle.

Frege (1918) 'The Thought: A Logical Inquiry'

Although this paper of Frege's is primarily on thoughts (the senses of complete indicative sentences) and is included here in the section on truth and meaning, it contains insightful and important discussions of many topics relevant to other areas of the philosophy of language, including indexicals, proper names, mood and speech acts, and an anticipation of some of Grice's observations on implicature. There is even a fascinatingly contemporary discussion on solipsism, phenomenalism and the causal theory of perception. This paper nicely complements **Frege (1892)**.

Tarski (1944) 'The Semantic Conception of Truth and the Foundations of Semantics'

'It is probable that the content of the word "true" is unique and indefinable' wrote **Frege (1918)**. Tarski demurred. In this article he introduces the reader to some basic semantic terminology, the Liar Paradox, and then gives an informal but authoritative summary of his important technical work on the concept of truth in formalized languages. The article is clearly written and accessible to all students.

Field (1972) 'Tarski's Theory of Truth'

The theory of truth which is of interest to the philosophy of language is the 'semantic' conception of truth championed by **Tarski (1944)**. Intuitively, a sentence is true just in case the world is in fact the way the sentence represents it to be. The work of a theory of truth is establishing the proper connection between words and the world. **Davidson (1967)** enlists a 'Tarski type truth definition' for the service of giving a theory of meaning for a natural language. Tarski himself did not write an intermediate exposition of his highly technical early work on truth, and from reading **Tarski (1944)** one does not get a feeling for how a truth definition works, and how it could possibly fulfill the function Davidson wants it to fulfill. One of the many merits of Field's fine paper is that he sets out such structure in the course of challenging the broader philosophical implications Tarski drew from his own technical achievements.

Davidson (1967) 'Truth and Meaning'

This paper, like **Grice (1957)** launched a whole program in the philosophy of language, the program alluded to above of giving a Tarski type truth definition for a natural language as a theory of meaning for that language. Here Davidson argues for this approach over others, illustrates some of its virtues, and ends with a sketch of what needs to be done to bring this project to fruition. For twenty years many philosophers of language have been attempting to complete this program.

Clearly, in an anthology of twenty items, important works will have to be omitted. For instance, there is nothing by Wittgenstein. Why not? Because first, it is exceptionally hard coherently to excerpt Wittgenstein. Second, and more importantly, much of Wittgenstein's once radical doctrine has been so thoroughly absorbed into philosophy that it has colored almost everything that is written in the philosophy of language subsequently; one gets Wittgenstein automatically. Analogously for Strawson's 'On referring'. Other important works were not included because they were too technical either in substance or in style. Still other historically important pieces were not included because they succeeded so well in making their case that the dispute has quieted down (for the present). Quine on analyticity comes to mind. Still other classical papers concern issues that are not alive right now: the verifiability criterion of meaning, essentialism in modal logic, meaning and transformational grammar. Now we are concerned with causal historical chains of reference, rigid designation, Twin Earth, direct reference, singular propositions, cognitive significance, character and content. I am sure that in five years we will need new anthologies.

Note to the Teacher

A first course in the philosophy of language can be given at two importantly different levels. First, there is the course to sophomores and juniors – often, but not always, philosophy majors. On the whole they have had no formal logical training. The articles chosen for the most part make almost no explicit technical demands and when they do, it is inessential, the point being made non-technically as well. There is often a tension between work accessible to students and work influential in the field. The works collected here have passed both tests. What one can expect in this course is an audience of beginning philosophers and intellectually curious non-philosophers who, since the course is rarely required for anything, are taking it out of curiosity, interest or from word of mouth.

For this audience, problems in the philosophy of language are best motivated from problems they can already relate to. Starting with abstract issues in advanced philosophy of language (such as sense and reference or truth) first bewilders students, then intimidates them, then turns them off the subject. We begin with the most intuitive and accessible sub-area in the philosophy of language. Everyone has intuitions and opinions about meaning, speech acts and communication. This engages the student who may well be put off at the beginning by starting historically with, say Frege. Once these concepts are out, issues of sense, reference and truth can be developed naturally. Opacity is a bit different; it is almost a special topic, and other issues also have a claim to attention here.

Second, there is a course to seniors and graduate students. The introduction of graduate students into an upper-division philosophy class changes the character of the class considerably. Graduate students profit most from a more state of the art course on basic topics in the philosophy of language. They will also often have had some formal logic. Their formal and philosophical sophistication can often carry the class discussion quickly out of the reach of the audience of the first course.

Hence the structure of these readings. For the lower division undergraduate course I suggest concentrating on Parts I and II. For the upper division and graduate course I suggest all four parts, but selecting from the readings according to interest and competence. These works have been used successfully in both undergraduate and graduate courses.

Notes

1 See Akmajian, A., Demers, R., Farmer, A., Harnish, R., (1991), *Linguistics: An Introduction to Language and Communication*, MIT, for a recent introductory survey.
2 References in bold are to items in the present anthology.

References

Bach, K. (1987), *Thought and Reference*, New York: Oxford University Press.
Evans, G. (1973), 'The causal theory of reference', *Proceedings of the Aristotelian Society*, Supplementary Volume 47, The Aristotelian Society, London: Harrison & Sons Ltd.
Grice, H. P. (1969), 'Utterer's meaning and intentions', *Philosophical Review*, 78: 147–77.
Searle, J. (1965), 'What is a speech act?', in M. Black (ed.), *Philosophy in America*, London: George Allen & Unwin Ltd.
Searle, J. (1969), *Speech Acts*, New York: Cambridge University Press.
Strawson, P. (1950), 'On referring', *Mind*, 59: 320–44.

Acknowledgements

Numerous people have given me advice on this book, some of it unsolicited. I hereby thank them all, especially Kent Bach, Keith and Adrienne Lehrer and Nathan Salmon for their early encouragement and wise counsel. I also have a huge and undischargeable debt to my wife Csilla Pásztor for her support, not only in preparing this book. And to Thomas, who had to find someone else to beat in tennis; and to Ágnes, who had to find someone else to beat in chess.

The editor and publisher acknowledge with thanks permission granted to reproduce in this volume the following material previously published elsewhere. Every effort has been made to trace copyright holders, but if any have been inadvertently overlooked the publisher will be pleased to make the necessary arrangement at the first opportunity.

Part I

Austin, J. L. Selections reprinted by permission of the publishers from *How To Do Things With Words* by J. L. Austin, Cambridge, Mass.: Harvard University Press, copyright © 1962 the President and Fellows of Harvard College.

Grice, H. P. 'Logic and conversation', in P. Cole, and J. Morgan, (eds) *Syntax and Semantics* Vol. 3, London, Academic Press, 1975, copyright © 1988 Mrs K. B. Grice, reprinted by permission of Mrs K. B. Grice.

Searle, J. R. 'How performatives work', in *Linguistics and Philosophy*, 12, 1989, copyright © 1989 Kluwer Academic Publishers, reprinted by permission of Kluwer Academic Publishers.

Part II

Frege, G. 'On sense and reference', in P. Geach, and M. Black, (eds) *Translations from the Philosophical Writings of Gottlob Frege*, Second Edition, 1970, reprinted by permission of Blackwell Publishers.

Kaplan, D. Selections from 'Demonstratives', in J. Almog, *et al*, (eds) *Themes from Kaplan*, 1989, copyright © 1989 David Kaplan, reprinted by permission of the author.

Kripke, S. Selections reprinted by permission of the publishers from *Naming and Necessity* by Saul A. Kripke, Cambridge, Mass.: Harvard University Press, copyright © 1972, 1980 Saul A. Kripke.

Putnam, H. 'The meaning of "meaning"', in K. Gunderson, (ed.) *Language, Mind and Knowledge*, Minnesota Studies in Philosophy of Science Series, Vol. 7, 1975, copyright © 1975 University of Minnesota Press, reprinted by permission of the University of Minnesota Press and the author.

Russell, B. 'On denoting', in *Mind*, 14, 1905, copyright © 1905 Oxford University Press, reprinted by permission of Oxford University Press.

Part III

Burge, T. 'Individualism and the mental', in P. French *et al*, (eds) *Studies in Metaphysics*, Midwest Studies in Philosophy Series, Vol. 4, 1979, copyright © 1979 University of Minnesota Press, reprinted by permission of the University of Minnesota Press and the author.

Kripke, S. 'A puzzle about belief', in A. Margalit, (ed.) *Meaning and Use*, 1979, copyright © 1979 Saul A. Kripke, reprinted by permission of Kluwer Academic Publishers.

Quine, W. Selections from 'Referential Opacity', in *Word and Object*, 1960, copyright © 1960 The MIT Press, reprinted by permission of the The MIT Press.

Salmon, N. Selections from *Frege's Puzzle*, 1986, copyright © 1986, 1991 Nathan Salmon, reprinted by permission of Ridgeview Publishing Company and the author.

Part IV

Davidson, D. 'Truth and meaning', in *Synthese*, 17, 1967, copyright © 1967 D. Reidel Publishing Co., reprinted by permission of Kluwer Academic Publishers.

Field, H. 'Tarski's theory of truth', in *The Journal of Philosophy*, LXIX, 13, 1972, reprinted by permission of The Journal of Philosophy and the author.

Frege, G. 'The thought: A logical inquiry', translated by A. M. Quinton, and M. Quinton, in *Mind*, 65, 1956, and A. E. Blumberg, 'Correction to the translation of Frege's "The thought"', in *Mind*, 80, 1971, translation copyright © 1965 and 1971 Oxford University Press, reprinted by permission of Oxford University Press.

Tarski, A. 'The semantic conception of truth and the foundations of semantics', in *Philosophy and Phenomenological Research*, Vol. 4, 1944, copyright © 1992 the Estate of Alfred Tarski, reprinted by permission of Jan Tarski.

Part I

Meaning, Speech Acts, and Communication

Introduction

Kent Bach

There was a time when philosophy of language was concerned less with language and its use than with meanings and propositions. Meanings were abstracted from the linguistic items that have them, and (indicative) sentences were often equated with statements, which were in turn equated with propositions. It is no exaggeration to say that such philosophers as Frege, Russell, and the early Wittgenstein paid only lip service to natural languages, for they were more interested in deep and still daunting problems about representation, which they hoped to solve by studying the properties of ideal ('logically perfect') languages, where forms of sentences mirror the forms of what sentences symbolize. As Austin complains at the beginning of *How to Do Things with Words*, it was assumed by philosophers (he had the logical positivists in mind, like Schlick, Carnap, and Ayer) that 'the business of a [sentence] can only be to "describe" some state of affairs, or to "state some fact", which it must do either truly or falsely.' Austin and the later Wittgenstein changed all that. Austin made it abundantly clear that there are all sorts of 'speech acts' besides statements. And the Wittgenstein of the *Philosophical Investigations*, rebelling against his former self, came to think of language not primarily as a system of representation but as a vehicle for all sorts of social activity. 'Don't ask for the meaning, ask for the use,' he advised. Here he went too far, for there is good reason to separate the theory of linguistic meaning (semantics) from the theory of language use (pragmatics), not that they are unconnected.[1]

Linguistic Meaning and Speaker Meaning

Both words and people mean things. So we had better keep clear the difference between the meaning of a linguistic expression – a word, phrase, or sentence

– and what a person means in using it. Interestingly, although what an expression means is the meaning of the expression, we do not say that what a person means is the meaning of the person. Expressions have meanings; people do not. Expressions have meanings even when they are not being used,[2] but it is only in using expressions that a person means something.[3]

Various views have been held about linguistic meaning and its relationship to other semantic notions, such as reference, truth, mental content, synonymy, entailment, ambiguity, and vagueness. Some of these views will be presented in later parts of this book, so for the moment let us be neutral about the nature of linguistic meaning. I do not think that will affect our discussion of what it is for a speaker to mean something in using language and of the relationship between speaker meaning and linguistic meaning.[4] All we will assume about linguistic meaning itself is that it is a central part of the linguistic knowledge,[5] that speakers and hearers bring to bear to make themselves understood and to understand each other. This knowledge is taken for granted in ordinary conversations, where there is a mutual presumption among people that they speak the same language, specifically, that what a given expression means to one is the same as what it means to the other. Our discussion will rely on the very sort of knowledge of linguistic meaning on which we rely in everyday life when we communicate.

What we mean is generally connected to, though sometimes only remotely, to what our words mean. To appreciate this consider a case where there is no such connection. Suppose someone says to you, 'What's the frequency, Ken?' (the very words used by a man who mugged Dan Rather). By prearrangement he means that a certain meeting will take place that night. This is an exceptional case, for what the speaker means is not at all related to what his words mean. Ordinarily, what matters is the meaning of the words, not the words themselves. Even so, linguistic meaning does not in general determine what the speaker means. One way this can happen is because of ambiguity. A sentence can have more than one meaning because it contains an ambiguous expression, like 'pen' in

(1) Farmer Jones found his pen empty

or because it is, like (2), structurally ambiguous

(2) The chicken was ready to eat.

Because of the lexical ambiguity in (1), a speaker could be talking about a farmer looking for his animals or about a farmer wanting to write a letter. A user of the structurally ambiguous (2) could be talking about a hungry chicken or a broiled chicken. In each case only one linguistic meaning is relevant to what the speaker means.[6] Another way linguistic meaning can fail to determine what the speaker means is via non-literality. For instance, although sentence (3) means something analogous to what (4) means,

(3) Farmer Jones was up to his ears in debt
(4) Farmer Jones was up to his ears in mud

a speaker is likely to mean something quite different. What he means is related to but distinct from the linguistic meaning, since he means that Farmer Jones was only figuratively up to his ears in debt. In other cases, involving indirection, a speaker means what the sentence means but means something else as well. If a friend asks you for something to drink and you utter (5),

(5) There's some beer in the fridge

you mean not only that there is some beer there but that your friend may help himself to some. These various examples illustrate different ways in which what the speaker means can be distinct from what the sentence means. The speaker may mean one of the things the sentence means, as with (1) or (2), something quite distinct from anything it means, as with (3), or both, as with (5).

Now for a minor complication. We need to distinguish what a speaker means by an expression and what he means in using it.[7] The need for this distinction is evident from (6), for example,

(6) There was an explosion to Dr. Frankenstein's lavatory

where the speaker probably means laboratory by 'lavatory'. This distinction is also needed to handle utterances of ambiguous sentences such as (1) and (2), where what a speaker means by his words does not include each of the things that they mean. In these cases what the speaker means by his words determines which meaning is operative in his utterance of them. With (3), however, there is no linguistic ambiguity. Despite what a speaker would mean in using the words 'up to his ears' it is not clear that he means anything different by them than he would in uttering (4). The phrase does not seem to be ambiguous but rather to have both a literal and a figurative use, one tied to its single meaning and the other derived from it in a certain intuitively evident way. The speaker is exploiting the single (literal) meaning of his words in order to mean something else in using them. As for the case of (5) the speaker means both what the sentence means and something else as well. When he utters 'The beer is in the fridge,' he means by those words just what they mean. Yet in uttering (5) he means more than just that, namely that the hearer may help himself to some beer.

Speech Acts

So far we have identified various ways in which a speaker can mean something when uttering a meaningful sentence. Now let us look at utterances differently, as a kind of intentional action. With intentional action, what one intends can contribute to what one is doing. For instance, moving one's arm in a certain way can count not only as pushing away a bag of potato chips but also, partly because of one's intention, as trying to stay on one's diet and as trying to impress one's spouse. Notice here that a single bodily movement is involved in a multiplicity of actions.[8] This is what happens with ordinary utterances. In *How to Do Things with Words*, Austin identifies three distinct levels of action beyond the act of utterance itself. He distinguishes the act of saying something, what one does in saying it, and what one does by saying it, and dubs these the locutionary, the illocutionary, and the perlocutionary act. By the locutionary act Austin does not mean the act of utterance itself, the act of saying certain words that is reported by means of direct quotation, such as

(7) The President says, 'Inflation is not a problem.'

Rather, the locutionary act is what is reported by indirect quotation:

(8) The President says that inflation is not a problem.

The President does not have to use the words, 'Inflation is not a problem,' to say that inflation is not a problem. He does not even have to be speaking in English. Regardless of the means by which he says that inflation is not a problem, he could be performing the illocutionary act of assuring the public that prices and interest rates won't go up significantly and be thereby performing the perlocutionary act of assuaging their economic fears.

The sentence uttered does not in general determine the type of illocutionary act being performed. Just as we can do one of several different things in shaking hands – introduce ourselves, greet each other, seal a deal, or bid farewell – so we can use a given sentence in various ways. For example, you could use

(9) The police will break up the party

as a prediction, a warning, a promise, a threat, or even an order.[9] Now one obvious difference between sentence (9) and a handshake is that whereas the handshake means nothing in itself, the sentence does mean something independently of its various uses. Indeed, whereas the handshake just is a means for performing acts of various types, it is partly because of what the sentence means that it has its various uses. After all, the sentence expresses, at least relative to a given context of utterance, a proposition about what certain police will do with respect to a certain party. To be sure, the sentence doesn't specify which police or which party, but it is a linguistic fact about the sentence that an utterance of it, if taken literally, is about certain police and a certain party. Non-linguistic factors determine whether it counts as a prediction, a warning, a promise, a threat, or an order.

Performatives

Austin was astonished that philosophers generally assumed, or at least pretended, that sentences are essentially devices for making statements. After all, sentences can be marked grammatically for non-assertive use, as with the interrogative or imperative moods. Relying on his distinction between performatives and constatives, Austin claimed that even certain indicative sentences are marked for non-assertive use. These are utterances whereby we make explicit what we are doing by using a performative verb like 'promise', 'pronounce', 'apologize', or 'request' in a sentence beginning with 'I' followed by a performative verb in present tense and active voice, such as these:

(10) I promise you a new car
(11) I pronounce you husband and wife.

The first-person plural is possible too ('We apologize . . .'), as is the second-person passive,

(12) You're fired.

Austin contended that these explicit performative utterances, are, unlike statements, neither true nor false. For example, a performative promise is not, and does not involve, the statement that one is promising. It is an act of a distinctive sort, the very sort (promising) named by the performative verb. Now one can promise without doing so explicitly, without using the performative verb 'promise', but even if one does use it, according to Austin making explicit what one is doing is not describing what one is doing or stating that one is doing it. However, Austin never thought to ask what is said by someone who utters a sentence like (10). The speaker may be promising the hearer a new car, but offhand it seems that he is also saying (even if he is not stating) that he is promising the hearer a new car, in which case what he is saying *is* true or false. It is true just in case he is making that promise.

Strawson, in 'Intention and convention in speech acts,' quotes Austin's mysterious remark that the use of a sentence with a certain illocutionary force is 'conventional in the sense that at least it could be made explicit by the performative formula.' Austin must have thought that explicit performative utterances are conventional in some more straightforward sense. Perhaps he thought that a special explanation is needed for the fact that utterances of indicative sentences like (10) or (11) count as acts of types other than statements, and that this explanation resides in the distinctive nature of the performative formula. Since it is not part of the meaning of the word 'promise' that an utterance like (10) counts as a promise, perhaps there is some convention to that effect. If there is, presumably it is part of a general convention that covers all performative verbs. But is there such a convention?

Compare the situation with performatives with cases in which there clearly is a convention that an utterance of a certain form counts as the performance of an act of a certain sort. For instance, a jury foreman's pronouncement of 'Guilty' or 'Not guilty' counts as a verdict, an 'Aye' or a 'Nay' counts as a vote in a parliamentary session, and an umpire's cry of 'Y'er out' counts as calling a runner out. Indeed, even an utterance of the explicit performative (11), when uttered by a judge or a clergyman under the appropriate circumstances, counts as joining a couple in marriage. Similarly, a boss's 'You're fired' (12) to an employee can count as firing the employee. In all these cases there are specific, socially recognized circumstances in which a person with specific, socially recognized authority may perform an act of a certain sort by uttering words of a certain form.

Austin was interested enough in such cases to develop a theory of what it takes for these formalized utterances to be performed successfully and felicitously. He even classified the various things that can go wrong into 'flaws,' 'hitches,' and various other sorts of 'infelicities.' But, as Strawson shows, he was over-impressed by such cases. Strawson explains why conventional illocutionary acts constitute a special case. Most illocutionary acts involve not an intention to conform to an institutional convention but an intention to communicate something to the audience. There is no sense of the word 'conventional' in which the use of any given sentence with a certain illocutionary force is conventional, much less a sense having to do with the fact that this force can be 'made explicit by the performative formula.'

Although Austin did not abandon his view that performative utterances are neither true nor false, he came to realize that explicit constatives function like explicit performatives. For a statement can be made by using phrases like 'I assert . . .' or 'I predict . . .', just as a promise or a request can be made by means of 'I promise . . .' or 'I request . . .'. In later chapters of *How to Do Things with Words* the distinction between constative and performative utterances is superseded by the one between locutionary and illocutionary acts, and included among the latter are assertions, predictions, etc., for which Austin retains the term 'constative', along with promises, requests, etc. The newer nomenclature takes into account the fact that illocutionary acts need not be performed explicitly – you don't have to say 'I suggest . . .' to make a suggestion or 'I apologize . . .' to apologize.[10] So it would seem that an account of explicit performatives should not appeal, as Searle's elaborate account in 'How performatives work' does, to any special features of the performative formula.[11]

Communication

Strawson suggests that unlike those illocutionary acts confined to institutional contexts, most illocutionary acts are performed not with an intention to conform to a convention but with a communicative intention. But what is that? In 'Meaning' Grice characterizes the distinctively reflexive character of communicative intentions by proposing that a speaker means something by his utterance only if he intends his utterance 'to produce some effect in an audience by means of the recognition of this intention.'[12] If the rationale of this formulation is not clear from the various examples that lead up to it, consider the following games, which involve something like linguistic communication.

Take the game of charades, in which one player uses gestures and other bodily movements to help the other guess what she has in mind. Something like the reflexive intention involved in communication operates here, for part of what the first player intends the second player to take into account is the very fact that the first player intends her gestures etc., to enable him to guess what she has in mind. Nothing like this goes on in the game of twenty questions, where the second player uses answers to yes-or-no questions to narrow down the possibilities of what the first player has in mind. Here the only co-operation required is honest answers on the part of the first player. Compare twenty questions with the following game of tacit co-ordination: the first player selects and records an item in a certain specified category, such as a letter of the alphabet, a liquid, a mode of transportation, a city, and or a US president; the second player has one chance to guess what it is. Each player wins if and only if the second player guesses right without any help. Now what counts as guessing right depends entirely on what the first player has in mind, and that depends entirely on what she thinks the second player, taking into account that she wants him to guess right, will think she wants him to think. The second player guesses whatever he thinks she wants him to think. To appreciate how this co-operative guessing game works, play this game with a friend. Try additional categories too, and consider why some work better than others.

When players use the above categories, they almost always both pick the letter 'A'; water, cars, the city in which they are located; and the current president. It is not obvious what all these 'correct' choices have in common: each one stands out in a certain way from other members of the same category, but not in the same way. For example, being first (among letters of the alphabet), being the most common (among liquids), and being current (among presidents) are quite different ways of standing out. It is still not clear, in the many years since the question was first raised,[13] just what makes something uniquely salient in such situations. One suggestion is that it is the first item in the category that comes to mind, but this can't be right, since what first comes to the mind of one player may not be what first comes to the mind of the other.

Whatever the correct explanation of the meeting of the minds in successful communication, the basic insight underlying Grice's account of speaker meaning is that communication is like a game of tacit co-ordination: the speaker intends the hearer to reason in a certain way partly on the basis of being so intended. That is, the hearer is to take into account that he is intended to figure out the speaker's communicative intention. It is the meaning of the words uttered, of course, that provides the input to this inference, but what they mean does not determine what the speaker means (even if what he means is precisely what his words means, the fact that he is speaking literally is not determined by what they mean). What is loosely called 'context' encompasses whatever other considerations the hearer is to take into account in ascertaining the speaker's intention, partly on the basis that he is intended to do so.

Communication and Speech Acts

Now we are in a position to follow up on Strawson's suggestion that most illocutionary acts are performed not with an intention to conform to a convention but with a communicative intention. Pre-theoretically, we think of an act of communication, linguistic or otherwise, as an act of expressing oneself. This rather vague idea can be made more precise if we get more specific about what is being expressed. Take the case of an apology. If you utter, '[I'm] sorry I forgot your birthday' and intend this as an apology, you are expressing regret for something, in this case for forgetting the person's birthday. An apology just is the act of (verbally) expressing regret for, and thereby acknowledging, something one did that might have harmed or at least bothered the hearer. It is communicative because it is intended to be taken as expressing a certain attitude, in this case regret. It succeeds as such if it is so taken. This is what counts as making oneself understood. Using a special device such as the performative 'I apologize' may of course facilitate understanding (understanding is correlative with communicating), but in general this is unnecessary. Communicative success is achieved if the speaker chooses his words in such a way that the hearer will, under the circumstances of utterance, recognize his communicative intention. So, for example, if you spill some beer on someone and say 'Oops' in the right way, your utterance will be taken as an apology for having done that.

Now an utterance is generally more than just an act of communication. When you apologize, for example, you may intend not merely to express your regret but also to seek forgiveness. Seeking forgiveness is to be distinguished from apologizing, even though the one utterance is the performance of an act of both types. As an apology, the utterance succeeds if it is taken as expressing regret for the deed in question; as an act of seeking forgiveness, it succeeds if forgiveness is thereby obtained. Speech acts, being perlocutionary as well as illocutionary, generally have some ulterior purpose, but they are distinguished primarily by their illocutionary type, such as asserting, requesting, promising, and apologizing, which in turn may be distinguished by the type of attitude expressed. The perlocutionary act is essentially a matter of trying to get the hearer to form some correlative attitude. Here are some typical examples:

Illocutionary act	Attitude expressed	Intended hearer attitude
statement	belief that p	belief that p
request	desire for H to D	intention to D
promise	firm intention to D	belief that S will D
apology	regret for D-ing	forgiveness of S for D-ing

These are examples of the four major categories of communicative illocutionary acts, which may be called constatives, directives, commissives, and acknowledgements.[14]

If each type of act is distinguishable by the type of attitude expressed, there is no need to invoke the notion of convention to explain how it can succeed.[15] It can succeed if the hearer recognizes the attitude being expressed, such as a belief in the case of a statement and a desire in the case of a request.[16] Any further effect that it has on the hearer, such as being believed or being complied with or even being taken as sincere, is not essential to its being a statement or a request. Notice that an utterance can succeed as an act of communication even if the speaker does not possess the attitude he is expressing.[17] Communication is one thing, sincerity another. Sincerity is actually possessing the attitude one is expressing.[18]

Since communicating is the act of expressing an attitude (which one may or may not actually possess), so that the condition of its success is that one's audience infer the attitude from the utterance, one can appreciate why the intention to be performing such an act should have the reflexive character pinpointed by Grice. Considered as an act of communication rather than anything more, it is an attempt simply to get one's audience to recognize, partly on the basis that one so intends them, a certain attitude as being the one expressed. One is as it were putting a certain attitude on the table. The success of any further act has as its prerequisite that the audience recognize this attitude. Communication aims at a meeting of the minds not in the sense that the audience is to think what the speaker thinks but only in the sense that a certain attitude toward a certain proposition is to be recognized as being put forward for consideration.[19] For this reason, when Grice characterized meaning something as intending one's utterance 'to produce some effect in an audience by means of the recognition of this intention,' he should have imposed a tighter constraint on the kind of effect to be produced than that it be in the audience's control. As Strawson makes clear, the relevant effect is understanding or what Austin called 'uptake,' rather than a further (perlocutionary) effect, such as belief, desire, or even action on the part of the hearer.[20]

Conversational Implicature

In 'Logic and conversation' Grice coins the term 'implicature' for what a speaker means but does not say. Whereas what is said may imply something (Grice reserves the word 'implication' for what sentences imply), what a speaker implicates is a consequence of his saying it. For example, if I ask you what you think of my new car and you reply,

(13) Your car has a terrific stereo

you are implicating that my car is otherwise mediocre at best. The explanation for this implicature, and for my recognizing it, is essentially this: presumably you are giving an informative answer to my question, but saying something about my car's stereo, which is not an automotive feature, is on the face of it not an informative answer. However, you intend me to infer, and I do infer, partly on the basis that you intend me to infer, that you have nothing else to say in praise of my car. You are thereby implicating that it is mediocre at best (or something to that effect – implicatures can be vague). My making this inference (and your intending me to make it) relies on the supposition that despite appearances your answer really is informative, albeit tacitly so. Somewhat different inferences are required in the following cases,

(14) You won't need a car alarm

where you might be implicating that my car isn't worth stealing, and

(15) My car cost more than a Yugo

where I might be implicating that its price is none of your business.

Grice proposes a general 'co-operative principle' and specific 'maxims' – of quality, quantity, relation (relevance), and manner, as he calls them – to account for the rationale and success of conversational implicatures. However, it is arguable that being co-operative simply consists in being truthful and relevant, hence that there is no need for four separate maxims. For example, observing the maxim of quantity is just being relevantly informative. Also, it seems that the maxims might better be thought of as presumptions, for it is on the presumption that the speaker is being truthful and relevant that the hearer figures out what the speaker means over and above what he is saying.

Grice's philosophical purpose, beyond providing the framework for an account of rational co-operation in conversation, is to enforce a distinction between word meaning and speaker meaning in connection with certain words of special interest to philosophers, such as 'know,' 'seem,' 'good,' 'voluntary,' and logical connectives like 'if' and 'or.' His aim is to show that with such a distinction enforced, there is no need to impute to word meaning features that are really tied to use, so that analyses of word meanings can avoid needless commitments to ambiguity and other undue complications.[21] For example, it might seem that the word 'or' has both an inclusive and an exclusive sense, but the alleged exclusive sense can be explained away in Gricean terms. So if someone asks you where's the umbrella and you reply,

(16) It's with my raincoat or in the car

your words do not imply that it is not in both places (your raincoat could be in the car), but you are implying that it is in one place or the other and not both – and that you don't know which.

Conversational implicature is actually a kind of indirect speech act, a special case of performing one illocutionary act by way of performing another. Recall example (5) and consider (17) as well.

(5) There's some beer in the fridge
(17) The police are coming.

In uttering (5) you not only tell someone where the beer is but also suggest that they help themselves to some. Similarly, you might utter (17) not only to inform your guests that the police are coming but also to warn them to curtail their boisterous and illicit activities. The direct illocutionary act need not be a statement, as in the following examples. You might directly ask a question

(18) Do you know that you just got a parking ticket?

to inform someone indirectly that he just got a ticket, and you might make a suggestion

(19) Go to the hardware store

and thereby tell someone indirectly where they can find the tool they are looking for. In all these cases you have two communicative intentions, one corresponding to each illocutionary act, and you intend your audience to recognize one by way of recognizing the other. Most of Grice's examples of conversational implicature are special cases of indirection in which both the directly and the indirectly performed illocutionary acts are statements.

Grice confuses matters somewhat by counting as cases of implicature nonliteral utterances, such as irony

(20) That cut-rate lawyer was a real bargain

and metaphor

(21) Fired and divorced, I was thrown from the saddle of life.

Since he describes irony and metaphor as cases not of saying but merely 'making as if to say' something,[22] it is rather puzzling why he assimilates them to implicature. For one thinks of implicating as stating or meaning one thing and meaning something else as well, not as meaning something else instead.[23] Even so, the same sorts of inference processes are involved as in genuine implicatures, so that Grice's theory of conversational implicature may be generalized to cover not only indirect statements but also non-literal utterances, as well as indirect illocutionary acts besides statements.[24] For in general the hearer relies on the presumption that the speaker intends his communicative intention to be identifiable under the circumstances; if the speaker cannot plausibly be taken to mean what he says or just what he says, the hearer reasons that what the speaker does mean is inferable from what he is saying together with contextual information salient enough to have been expected to be taken into account.

What is Said and More

We need to say more about saying, the locutionary level of speech act, and the correlative notion of what is said. The notion of saying is needed for describing three kinds of cases: where the speaker means what he says and something else as well (implicature and indirect speech acts generally), where the speaker says one thing and means something else instead (non-literal utterances), and where the speaker says something and doesn't mean anything. The notion of what is said is needed for contrast with what is implicated (below we will see how it figures in Grice's notion of conventional as opposed to conversational implicature), and it is relevant to explaining what it is for an utterance to be literal, since in that case what is meant is identical to what is said. The notion of what is said is not as straightforward as it might seem, and lately some philosophers have suggested that it is more comprehensive than either Austin or Grice supposed.

Saying isn't just a matter of meaning what one's words mean. As Austin defines it, the locutionary act is the act of using words, 'as belonging to a certain vocabulary ... and as conforming to a certain grammar... with a certain more or less definite sense and reference.' And although what is said is, according to Grice, 'closely related to the conventional meaning of the ... sentence ... uttered,' it is not identical to conventional meaning because there can be ambiguity or context-dependent reference. Usually only one conventional (linguistic) meaning is operative in a given utterance, and linguistic meaning does not determine what the words 'she', 'this', and 'now' are used to refer to (see Part II). If someone utters, 'She wants this book,' he is saying that a certain woman wants a certain book, even though the words do not specify which woman and which book. So not just linguistic knowledge but (salient) contextual information can play a role in determining what is said.[25] Nevertheless, Grice gives the impression that the distinction between what is said and what is implicated is exhaustive. One problem, already noted, is that irony, metaphor, and other non-literal utterances do not seem to be cases of implicature, inasmuch as they are cases of saying one thing and meaning something else instead rather than in addition. There are two other kinds of cases to be considered, which were overlooked by Grice and have come to the fore only recently.

Lately it has been observed that there are many sentences whose standard uses are not strictly determined by their meanings but are not implicatures or figurative uses either. For example, if your child comes crying to you with a minor injury and you assure him,

(22) You're not going to die

you do not mean that he will never die (that is false and irrelevant) but merely that he won't die from that injury. And if someone wants you to join them for dinner and you say,

(23) I've already eaten

you do not mean you ate at some previous time (that is obviously true but irrelevant) but merely that you've had dinner that evening. In both cases you do not mean precisely what you are saying but something more specific.[26] On the other hand, what you do mean isn't an implicature either. The following two examples are somewhat different. If your spouse is honking the horn at you and you yell,

(24) I'm not ready

you mean that you are not ready to go with her in the car. And if your spouse yells back,

(25) We'll be late

she means that you will be late for a certain event that you are planning to attend. In neither case is there anything in the sentence that corresponds to the implicit reference. Although the speaker means something definite, the sentences themselves, even with the references of the indexicals 'I' and 'we' fixed, lack determinate truth conditions. As with (22) and (23), though for a different reason (semantic underdetermination), what the speaker means is more specific than what the sentence means. We might say that whereas what a user of (22) or (23) is an 'expansion' of the sentence meaning, what a user of (24) or (25) means is a 'completion' of the sentence meaning.[27]

Now several of Grice's critics have pointed out that expansions and completions are not related closely enough to conventional meaning to fall under Grice's notion of what is said but that they are too closely related to count as implicatures. Recanati suggests that the notion of what is said should be extended to cover such cases,[28] but clearly he is going beyond Grice's understanding of what is said as corresponding to the constituents of the sentence and their syntactic arrangement. Sperber and Wilson coin the word 'explicature' for this in-between category,[29] since part of what is meant explicates what is said. I propose calling what happens in these cases *impliciture*, since part of what is meant is not communicated not explicitly but implicitly, by way of expansion or completion.

Grice disallowed inexplicit saying, but he did recognize a category of explicit non-saying. For in his view there can be elements in what is meant that correspond directly to elements in the sentence uttered but do not enter into what is said. Because of this correspondence they lead to conventional rather than conversational implicatures, propositions which are merely 'indicated.' Grice's examples of 'problematic elements' are connectives, such as 'therefore' and 'but', which make a certain contribution to what the speaker means by indicating a certain relation between the two items they connect, e.g. that one is a consequence of the other or that there is a contrast between the two. Grice denies that this linguistically specified relation enters into what is said, evidently to allow for an element of literal content that is not truth-conditional. He denies that an utterance of (26), for example,

(26) He is an Englishman; he is, therefore, brave.

'would be, strictly speaking, false should the consequence in question fail to hold.' This may seem unintuitive – the speaker does seem to be saying that the second claim is a consequence of the first. Just because connectives like 'therefore' and 'but' are not truth-functional does not mean that they do not enter into truth conditions. Grice also suggests that conventional implicature is involved in the performance of what he calls 'non-central speech acts,'[30] such as qualifying, contrasting, or concluding. He has in mind the use of such expressions as 'loosely speaking', 'frankly', 'in contrast', 'to digress', 'if I may say so', and 'all in all', which are often used to comment on the very utterance in which they occur, as in the following examples,

(27) Frankly, you're making a big mistake
(28) In contrast, George would never do a thing like that.

However, it seems to me that it is not accurate to call these second-order speech acts (conventional) implicatures. The speaker of (27) or (28) is not implying that he is speaking frankly or is making a contrast. In using a locution like 'frankly' or 'in contrast', one is saying something about (providing a gloss or commentary on) one's utterance or its conversational role.

Summing up, we have reviewed a variety of ways in which what a speaker means can extend beyond what his words mean. Because of indexicality, ambiguity, underdetermination, non-literality, and indirection, sentences are not uniquely correlated with the attitudes they are used to express. Also, we have seen how the notion of speaker meaning can be incorporated into the theory of speech acts in so far as these are communicative rather than conventional in character. Communication is not a straightforward process of putting thoughts into words, nor is understanding the reverse but equally straightforward process of decoding those words. Communication is not essentially a matter of conveying linguistic meanings but of expressing attitudes, and understanding is a matter of recognizing the attitudes being expressed.

Notes

1. Many of the following notes not only give references but amplify or qualify points made in the text for the benefit of readers interested in pursuing them further. The text is self-contained, so that those new to the subject need not be distracted by these footnotes.
2. By 'expressions' I mean expression types, items that can be used over and over, not particular occurrences or tokens of them. For example, in the first sentence of this note the (one) word 'over' has two occurrences; there are two tokens of it in the token of that sentence that appears in each copy of this book.
3. Hereafter I will follow the usual graphophobic practice of referring to language users as speakers and those to whom uses are directed as hearers or as the audience.
4. There is the question, which I do not mean to be begging, of whether linguistic meaning can be reduced to speaker meaning. In 'Meaning' Grice suggests that it can be. He starts with the idea that for an expression to mean something is for people to mean something by it, and develops this idea in later articles (Grice 1968, 1969). Schiffer develops it still further in his 1972 book *Meaning*, but repudiates it in his 1987 book, *The Remnants of Meaning*. In my view meaning in a language reduces not to speaker meaning but to meaning in speaker's idiolects, to what words mean to speakers.
5. Knowledge of phonological (or orthographic) form and syntactic structure is needed too, in so far as meanings are correlated with forms and meanings of complex expressions depend on the structural relations as well as the meanings of their constituent expressions. We may suppose that, as a first approximation, the linguistic meaning of a sentence is what a language user knows about a sentence as a consequence of knowing the meanings of its constituents and of knowing how these constituents fit together syntactically.
6. There is such a thing as deliberate ambiguity, as in an easily imagined utterance of 'I'd like to see more of you,' but deliberate ambiguity is rare, at least outside of romance and politics.

7. This distinction was overlooked by Grice in 'Meaning,' the 1957 article reprinted here. He recognized it in his 1969 article, which avoided objections raised by Searle (1969, pp 44–5) and by Ziff (1967) to the earlier account.
8. For detailed discussion of this and other points in philosophical action theory, see Davis 1979.
9. For the case of ordering imagine a small-town mayor rattling off orders to various subordinates, including the police.
10. This raises a serious difficulty for Searle's theory in *Speech Acts*. Because it proposes to explain illocutionary forces by means of 'constitutive rules' (conventions) for using 'force-indicating' devices, such as performatives, it is incapable of explaining the presence of illocutionary forces in the absence of such devices.
11. In 'How performatives really work,' Harnish and I argue that Searle's account is based on a spurious distinction between having a communicative intention and being committed to having one (see note 19 below) and on a confusion between performativity and communicative success.
12. Partly because of certain alternative wordings, Grice's analysis is sometimes interpreted, by Strawson for example, as defining communicative intentions iteratively rather than reflexively. Recanati 1986 has pointed to certain problems with the iterative approach, but in reply I have argued (Bach 1987b) that these problems do not arise on the reflexive analysis.
13. This question was raised by Schelling (1960), who was the first to discuss games of tacit co-ordination (pp 54–8).
14. Harnish and I develop a detailed taxonomy in *Linguistic Communication and Speech Acts* Chapter 3), where each type of illocutionary act is individuated by the type of attitude expressed. In some cases there are constraints on the content as well. We borrow the terms 'constative' and 'commissive' from Austin and 'directive' from Searle. We adopt the term 'acknowledgment' rather than Austin's 'behabitive' or Searle's 'expressive' for apologies, greetings, thanks, congratulations, condolences, etc., which express an attitude to the hearer that is occasioned by some event that is thereby being acknowledged, often in satisfaction of a social expectation.
15. However, it is arguable that promises are conventional as well, because they create obligations and do not merely express firm intentions or commitments.
16. A common misconception is that the communicative theory of non-conventional illocutionary acts holds that the performance of such an act involves the communication of the type of act being performed. Blakemore (1991) suggests that this theory implies that, for example, to predict, even when no performative is used or when it is used only parenthetically, is to communicate not just what one is predicting but that one is predicting it. However, the theory does not imply this. It implies only that predicting is an act of communication and that an act of communication is the act of expressing an attitude, such as a belief about the future. The foregoing misconception about the communicative theory is part of the motivation for the opposing theory, so-called 'relevance theory,' put forth by Sperber and Wilson (1986) and for Blakemore's relevance-theoretic account of performatives.
17. The difference between expressing an attitude and actually possessing it is clear from the following definition: to express an attitude is reflexively to intend the hearer to take one's utterance as reason to think one has that attitude (Bach and Harnish 1979, p. 15). This reason need not be conclusive and if in the context

it is overridden, the hearer will, in order to identify the attitude being expressed, search for an alternative and perhaps nonliteral interpretation of the utterance. For discussion see *ibid.*, pp 57–9 and 289–91.

18. Correlatively, the hearer can understand the utterance without regarding it as sincere, e.g., take it as expressing regret without believing that the speaker regrets having done the deed in question. Getting one's audience to believe that one actually possesses the attitude one is expressing is not an illocutionary but a perlocutionary act.
19. If the hearer thinks the speaker actually possesses the attitude he is expressing, in effect she is taking him to be sincere in what he is communicating. But there is no question about his being sincere in the communicative intention itself, for this intention must be identified before the question of his sincerity (in having that attitude) can even arise. In other words, deceiving your audience about your real attitude presupposes successfully expressing some other attitude. You can be unsuccessful in conveying your communicative intention – by being too vague, ambiguous, or metaphorical, or even by being wrongly taken literally – but not insincere about it.
20. This is how Searle puts the point in *Speech Acts* (p. 47). Even though understanding is the intended effect of illocutionary acts, he does not regard them merely as acts of communication. In his view, there is more to the performance of an illocutionary act than the 'expression of its sincerity condition,' with the exception of cases like thanking and congratulating (p. 67). But his account of their 'essential conditions' does not make clear what this something more is.
21. Searle has a similar aim in 'Three fallacies in contemporary philosophy,' Chapter 6 of *Speech Acts.*
22. Grice is using 'say' idiosyncratically here, since for him saying something implies meaning it. This entails that someone who is not speaking literally is not saying anything. Evidently Grice uses 'say' not as a locutionary verb but as an illocutionary verb, to mean explicitly state. Interestingly, he originally (in Grice 1961) formulated the distinction between saying and implicating in terms of stating and implying.
23. That's what it is to speak non-literally – at least if one does it intentionally. One can also unintentionally not say what one means, owing to a slip of the tongue, misusing a word or phrase, or otherwise misspeaking. Also, one can say something without meaning anything at all, as in cases of translating, reciting, or rehearsing.
24. Harnish and I do just that in *Linguistic Communication and Speech Acts* (Chapter 4).
25. Indeed, as Grice points out, even on the linguistic side there is the assumption that the speaker is using standard English (or whatever the relevant language) and that he is using his words literally.
26. In Bach 1987a I describe such utterances as cases of sentence non-literality, because the words are being used literally but the sentence as a whole is being used loosely. Compare (22) and (23) with the similar sentences, 'Everybody is going to die' or 'I've already been in the Army', which are more likely to be used in a strictly literal way.
27. Semantic underdetermination is taken up in Sperber and Wilson 1986 and Bach 1987a.
28. Recanati 1989.

29. Sperber and Wilson 1986, p. 182.
30. In Grice 1968/1989, Chapter 6, p. 122. There is a straightforward explanation why these locutions do not fit comfortably into specifications of what is said: they are in construction syntactically but not semantically with the clauses they introduce. Syntactically they are sentence adverbials but they function as 'illocutionary adverbials' (Bach and Harnish 1979, pp 219–28), interpreted as modifying not the main clause but its utterance. The result is as it were a split-level utterance.

References

Bach, Kent (1987a), *Thought and Reference*, Oxford: Oxford University Press.

Bach, Kent (1987b), 'On communicative intentions: A reply to Recanati,' *Mind & Language* 2: 141–54.

Bach, Kent and Robert M. Harnish (1979), *Linguistic Communication and Speech Acts*, Cambridge, Mass.: MIT Press.

Bach, Kent and Robert M. Harnish (1992), 'How performatives really work: a reply to Searle,' *Linguistics and Philosophy*, 15: 93–110.

Blakemore, Diana (1991), 'Performatives and parentheticals,' *Proceedings of the Aristotelian Society*, 91: 197–213.

Davis, Lawrence H. (1979), *Theory of Action*, Englewood Cliffs, N.J.: Prentice-Hall.

Grice, H. P. (1961), 'The causal theory of perception,' *Proceedings of the Aristotelian Society, Supplementary Volume*, 35: 121–52; as abridged, Chapter 15 of Grice (1989), 224–47.

Grice, H. P. (1968), 'Utterer's meaning, sentence-meaning, and word meaning,' *Foundations of Language* 4: 225–42; Chapter 6 of Grice (1989).

Grice, H. P. (1969), 'Utterer's meaning and intentions,' *Philosophical Review*, 78: 147–77; Chapter 5 of Grice (1989).

Grice, Paul (1989), *Studies in the Ways of Words*, Cambridge, Mass.: Harvard University Press.

Recanati, Francois (1986), 'On defining communicative intentions,' *Mind & Language*, 1: 213–42.

Recanati, Francois (1989), 'The pragmatics of what is said,' *Mind & Language*, 4: 295–329.

Schelling, Thomas C. (1960), *The Strategy of Conflict*, Cambridge, Mass.: Harvard University Press.

Schiffer, Stephen R. (1972), *Meaning*, Oxford: Oxford University Press.

Schiffer, Stephen R. (1987), *The Remnants of Meaning*, Cambridge, Mass.: MIT Press.

Searle, John R. (1969), *Speech Acts: An Essay in the Philosophy of Language*, Cambridge, Eng.: Cambridge University Press.

Sperber, Dan and Deirdre Wilson (1986), *Relevance*, Cambridge, Mass.: Harvard University Press.

Ziff, Paul (1967), 'On H. P. Grice's account of meaning,' *Analysis*, 28: 1–8.

Chapter 1

Meaning

H. P. Grice

Consider the following sentences:

> Those spots mean (meant) measles.
> Those spots didn't mean anything to me, but to the doctor they meant measles.
> The recent budget means that we shall have a hard year.

I cannot say, 'Those spots meant measles, but he hadn't got measles,' and I cannot say, 'The recent budget means that we shall have a hard year, but we shan't have.' That is to say, in cases like the above, *x meant that p* and *x means that p* entail *p*.

I cannot argue from 'Those spots mean (meant) measles' to any conclusion about 'what is (was) meant by those spots'; for example, I am not entitled to say, 'What was meant by those spots was that he had measles.' Equally I cannot draw from the statement about the recent budget the conclusion 'What is meant by the recent budget is that we shall have a hard year.'

I cannot argue from 'Those spots meant measles' to any conclusion to the effect that somebody or other meant by those spots so-and-so. *Mutatis mutandis*, the same is true of the sentence about the recent budget.

For none of the above examples can a restatement be found in which the verb 'mean' is followed by a sentence or phrase in inverted commas. Thus 'Those spots meant measles' cannot be reformulated as 'Those spots meant "measles"' or as 'Those spots meant "he has measles."'

On the other hand, for all these examples an approximate restatement can be found beginning with the phrase 'The fact that . . .'; for example, 'The

First published in *The Philosophical Review*, July 1957, 66: 377–88.

fact that he had those spots meant that he had measles' and 'The fact that the recent budget was as it was means that we shall have a hard year.'

Now contrast the above sentences with the following:

> Those three rings on the bell (of the bus) mean that the 'bus is full.'
> That remark, 'Smith couldn't get on without his trouble and strife,' meant that Smith found his wife indispensable.

I can use the first of these and go on to say, 'But it isn't in fact full – the conductor has made a mistake'; and I can use the second and go on, 'But in fact Smith deserted her seven years ago.' That is to say, here *x means that p* and *x meant that p* do not entail *p*.

I can argue from the first to some statement about 'what is (was) meant' by the rings on the bell and from the second to some statement about 'what is (was) meant' by the quoted remark.

I can argue from the first sentence to the conclusion that somebody (viz., the conductor) meant, or at any rate should have meant, by the rings that the bus is full, and I can argue analogously for the second sentence.

The first sentence can be restated in a form in which the verb 'mean' is followed by a phrase in inverted commas, that is, 'Those three rings on the bell mean "the bus is full."' So also can the second sentence.

Such a sentence as 'The fact that the bell has been rung three times means that the bus is full' is not a restatement of the meaning of the first sentence. Both may be true, but they do not have, even approximately, the same meaning.

When the expressions 'means,' 'means something,' 'means that' are used in the kind of way in which they are used in the first set of sentences, I shall speak of the sense, or senses, in which they are used, as the *natural* sense, or senses, of the expressions in question. When the expressions are used in the kind of way in which they are used in the second set of sentences, I shall speak of the sense, or senses, in which they are used, as the *nonnatural* sense, or senses, of the expressions in question. I shall use the abbreviation 'means$_{NN}$' to distinguish the nonnatural sense or senses.

I propose, for convenience, also to include under the head of natural senses of 'mean' such senses of 'mean' as may be exemplified in sentences of the pattern '*A* means (meant) *to do* so-and-so (by *x*),' where *A* is a human agent. By contrast, as the previous examples show, I include under the head of nonnatural senses of 'mean' any senses of 'mean' found in sentences of the patterns '*A* means (meant) something by *x*' or '*A* means (meant) by *x* that . . .' (This is overrigid; but it will serve as an indication.)

I do not want to maintain that *all* our uses of 'mean' fall easily, obviously, and tidily into one of the two groups I have distinguished; but I think that in most cases we should be at least fairly strongly inclined to assimilate a use of 'mean' to one group rather than to the other. The question which now arises is this: 'What more can be said about the distinction between the cases where we should say that the word is applied in a natural sense and the cases where we should say that the word is applied in an nonnatural sense?' Asking this question will not of course prohibit us from trying to give an explanation of 'meaning$_{NN}$' in terms of one or another natural sense of 'mean.'

This question about the distinction between natural and nonnatural meaning is, I think, what people are getting at when they display an interest in a distinction between 'natural' and 'conventional' signs. But I think my formulation is better. For some things which can mean$_{NN}$ something are not signs (e.g., words are not), and some are not conventional in any ordinary sense (e.g., certain gestures); while some things which mean naturally are not signs of what they mean (cf. the recent budget example).

I want first to consider briefly, and reject, what I might term a causal type of answer to the question, 'What is meaning$_{NN}$?' We might try to say, for instance, more or less with C. L. Stevenson,[1] that for *x* to mean$_{NN}$ something, *x* must have (roughly) a tendency to produce in an audience some attitude (cognitive or otherwise) and a tendency, in the case of a speaker, to *be* produced *by* that attitude, these tendencies being dependent on 'an elaborate process of conditioning attending the use of the sign in communication.'[2] This clearly will not do.

Let us consider a case where an utterance, if it qualifies at all as meaning$_{NN}$ something, will be of a descriptive or informative kind and the relevant attitude, therefore, will be a cognitive one, for example, a belief. (I use 'utterance' as a neutral word to apply to any candidate for meaning$_{NN}$; it has a convenient act-object ambiguity.) It is no doubt the case that many people have a tendency to put on a tail coat when they think they are about to go to a dance, and it is no doubt also the case that many people, on seeing someone put on a tail coat, would conclude that the person in question was about to go to a dance. Does this satisfy us that putting on a tail coat means$_{NN}$ that one is about to go to a dance (or indeed means$_{NN}$ anything at all)? Obviously not. It is no help to refer to the qualifying phrase 'dependent on an elaborate process of conditioning. . . .' For if all this means is that the response to the sight of a tail coat being put on is in some way learned or acquired, it will not exclude the present case from being one of meaning$_{NN}$. But if we have to take seriously the second part of the qualifying phrase ('attending the use of the sign in communication'), then the account of meaning$_{NN}$ is obviously circular. We might just as well say, '*X* has meaning$_{NN}$ if it is used in communication,' which, though true, is not helpful.

If this is not enough, there is a difficulty – really the same difficulty, I think – which Stevenson recognizes: how we are to avoid saying, for example, that 'Jones is tall' is part of what is meant by 'Jones is an athlete,' since to tell someone that Jones is an athlete would tend to make him believe that Jones is tall. Stevenson here resorts to invoking linguistic rules, namely, a permissive rule of language that 'athletes may be nontall.' This amounts to saying that we are not prohibited by rule from speaking of 'nontall athletes.' But why are we not prohibited? Not because it is not bad grammar, or is not impolite, and so on, but presumably because it is not meaningless (or, if this is too strong, does not in any way violate the rules of meaning for the expressions concerned). But this seems to involve us in another circle. Moreover, one wants to ask why, if it is legitimate to appeal here to rules to distinguish what is meant from what is suggested, this appeal was not made earlier, in the case of groans, for example, to deal with which Stevenson originally introduced the qualifying phrase about dependence on conditioning.

A further deficiency in a causal theory of the type just expounded seems to be that, even if we accept it as it stands, we are furnished with an analysis only of statements about the *standard* meaning, or the meaning in general, of a 'sign.' No provision is made for dealing with statements about what a particular speaker or writer means by a sign on a particular occasion (which may well diverge from the standard meaning of the sign); nor is it obvious how the theory could be adapted to make such provision. One might even go further in criticism and maintain that the causal theory ignores the fact that the meaning (in general) of a sign needs to be explained in terms of what users of the sign do (or should) mean by it on particular occasions; and so the latter notion, which is unexplained by the causal theory, is in fact the fundamental one. I am sympathetic to this more radical criticism, though I am aware that the point is controversial.

I do not propose to consider any further theories of the 'causal-tendency' type. I suspect no such theory could avoid difficulties analogous to those I have outlined without utterly losing its claim to rank as a theory of this type.

I will now try a different and, I hope, more promising line. If we can elucidate the meaning of

> 'x meant_{NN} something (on a particular occasion)' and
> 'x meant_{NN} that so-and-so (on a particular occasion)'

and of

> 'A meant_{NN} something by x (on a particular occasion)' and
> 'A meant_{NN} by x that so-and-so (on a particular occasion),'

this might reasonably be expected to help us with

> 'x means_{NN} (timeless) something (that so-and-so),'
> 'A means_{NN} (timeless) by x something (that so-and-so),'

and with the explication of 'means the same as,' 'understands,' 'entails,' and so on. Let us for the moment pretend that we have to deal only with utterances which might be informative or descriptive.

A first shot would be to suggest that '*x* meant_{NN} something' would be true if *x* was intended by its utterer to induce a belief in some 'audience' and that to say what the belief was would be to say what *x* meant_{NN}. This will not do. I might leave *B*'s handkerchief near the scene of a murder in order to induce the detective to believe that *B* was the murderer; but we should not want to say that the handkerchief (or my leaving it there) meant_{NN} anything or that I had meant_{NN} by leaving it that *B* was the murderer. Clearly we must at least add that for *x* to have meant_{NN} anything, not merely must it have been 'uttered' with the intention of inducing a certain belief but also the utterer must have intended an 'audience' to recognize the intention behind the utterance.

This, though perhaps better, is not good enough. Consider the following cases:

(1) Herod presents Salome with the head of St. John the Baptist on a charger.
(2) Feeling faint, a child lets its mother see how pale it is (hoping that she may draw her own conclusions and help).
(3) I leave the china my daughter has broken lying around for my wife to see.

Here we seem to have cases which satisfy the conditions so far given for meaning_{NN}. For example, Herod intended to make Salome believe that St. John the Baptist was dead and no doubt also intended Salome to recognize that he intended her to believe that St. John the Baptist was dead. Similarly for the other cases. Yet I certainly do not think that we should want to say that we have here cases of meaning_{NN}.

What we want to find is the difference between, for example, 'deliberately and openly letting someone know' and 'telling' and between 'getting someone to think' and 'telling.'

The way out is perhaps as follows. Compare the following two cases:

(1) I show Mr. *X* a photograph of Mr. *Y* displaying undue familiarity to Mrs. *X*.
(2) I draw a picture of Mr. *Y* behaving in this manner and show it to Mr. *X*.

I find that I want to deny that in (1) the photograph (or my showing it to Mr. *X*) meant_{NN} anything at all; while I want to assert that in (2) the picture (or my drawing and showing it) meant_{NN} something (that Mr. *Y* had been unduly unfamiliar), or at least that I had meant_{NN} by it that Mr. *Y* had been unduly familiar. What is the difference between the two cases? Surely that in case (1) Mr. *X*'s recognition of my intention to make him believe that there is something between Mr. *Y* and Mrs. *X* is (more or less) irrelevant to the production of this effect by the photograph. Mr. *X* would be led by the photograph at least to suspect Mrs. *X* even if instead of showing it to him I had left it in his room by accident; and I (the photograph shower) would not be unaware of this. But it will make a difference to the effect of my picture on Mr. *X* whether or not he takes me to be intending to inform him (make him believe something) about Mrs. *X*, and not to be just doodling or trying to produce a work of art.

But now we seem to be landed in a further difficulty if we accept this account. For consider now, say, frowning. If I frown spontaneously, in the ordinary course of events, someone looking at me may well treat the frown as a natural sign of displeasure. But if I frown deliberately (to convey my displeasure), an onlooker may be expected, provided he recognizes my intention, *still* to conclude that I am displeased. Ought we not then to say, since it could not be expected to make any difference to the onlooker's reaction whether he regards my frown as spontaneous or as intended to be informative, that my frown (deliberate) does *not* mean$_{NN}$ anything? I think this difficulty can be met; for though in general a deliberate frown may have the same effect (as regards inducing belief in my displeasure) as a spontaneous frown, it can be expected to have the same effect only *provided* the audience takes it as intended to convey displeasure. That is, if we take away the recognition of intention, leaving the other circumstances (including the recognition of the frown as deliberate), the belief-producing tendency of the frown must be regarded as being impaired or destroyed.

Perhaps we may sum up what is necessary for *A* to mean something by *x* as follows. *A* must intend to induce by *x* a belief in an audience, and he must also intend his utterance to be recognized as so intended. But these intentions are not independent; the recognition is intended by *A* to play its part in inducing the belief, and if it does not do so something will have gone wrong with the fulfillment of *A*'s intentions. Moreover, *A*'s intending that the recognition should play this part implies, I think, that he assumes that there is some chance that it will in fact play this part, that he does not regard it as a foregone conclusion that the belief will be induced in the audience whether or not the intention behind the utterance is recognized. Shortly, perhaps, we may say that '*A* meant$_{NN}$ something by *x*' is roughly equivalent to '*A* uttered *x* with the intention of inducing a belief by means of the recognition of this intention.' (This seems to involve a reflexive paradox, but it does not really do so.)

Now perhaps it is time to drop the pretense that we have to deal only with 'informative' cases. Let us start with some examples of imperatives or quasi-imperatives. I have a very avaricious man in my room, and I want him to go; so I throw a pound note out of the window. Is there here any utterance with a meaning$_{NN}$? No, because in behaving as I did, I did not intend his recognition of my purpose to be in any way effective in getting him to go. This is parallel to the photograph case. If on the other hand I had pointed to the door or given him a little push, then my behavior will be held to constitute a meaningful$_{NN}$ utterance, just because the recognition of my intention would be intended by me to be effective in speeding his departure. Another pair of cases would be (1) a policeman who stops a car by standing in its way and (2) a policeman who stops a car by waving.

Or, to turn briefly to another type of case, if as an examiner I fail a man, I may well cause him distress or indignation or humiliation; and if I am vindictive, I may intend this effect and even intend him to recognize my intention. But I should not be inclined to say that my failing him meant$_{NN}$ anything. On the other hand, if I cut someone in the street I do feel inclined to assimilate this to the cases of meaning$_{NN}$, and this inclination seems to me dependent on the fact that I could not reasonably expect him to be distressed (indignant, humiliated) unless he recognized my intention to affect him in this way. (Cf., if my college stopped my salary altogether I should accuse them of ruining me; if they cut it by 2/6d I might accuse them of insulting me; with some intermediate amounts I might not know quite what to say.)

Perhaps then we may make the following generalizations:

'*A* meant$_{NN}$ something by *x*' is (roughly) equivalent to '*A* intended the utterance of *x* to produce some effect in an audience by means of the recognition of this intention'; and we may add that to ask what *A* meant is to ask for a specification of the intended effect (though, of course, it may not always be possible to get a straight answer involving a 'that' clause, for example, 'a belief that . . .').

'*x* meant something' is (roughly) equivalent to 'Somebody meant$_{NN}$ something by *x*.' Here again there will be cases where this will not quite work. I feel inclined to say that (as regards traffic lights) the change to red meant$_{NN}$ that the traffic was to stop; but it would be very unnatural to say, 'Somebody (e.g., the Corporation) meant$_{NN}$ by the red-light change that the traffic was to stop.' Nevertheless, there seems to be *some* sort of reference to somebody's intentions.

'*x* means$_{NN}$ (timeless) that so-and-so' might as a first shot be equated with some statement or disjunction of statements about what 'people' (vague) intend (with qualifications about 'recognition') to effect by *x*. I shall have a word to say about this.

Will any kind of intended effect do, or may there be cases where an effect is intended (with the required qualifications) and yet we should not want to talk of meaning$_{NN}$? Suppose I discovered some person so constituted that, when I told him that whenever I grunted in a special way I wanted him to blush or to incur some physical malady, thereafter whenever he recognized the grunt (and with it my intention), he did blush or incur the malady. Should we then want to say that the grunt meant$_{NN}$ something? I do not think so. This points to the fact that for *x* to have meaning$_{NN}$, the intended effect must be something which in some sense is within the control of the audience, or that in some sense of 'reason' the recognition of the intention behind *x* is for the audience a reason and not merely a cause. It might look as if there is a sort of pun here ('reason for believing' and 'reason for doing'), but I do not think this is serious. For though no doubt from one point of view questions about reasons for believing are questions about evidence and so quite different from questions about reasons for doing, nevertheless to recognize an utterer's intention in uttering *x* (descriptive utterance), to have a reason for believing that so-and-so, is at least quite like 'having a motive for' accepting so-and-so. Decisions 'that' seem to involve decisions 'to' (and this is why we can 'refuse to believe' and also be 'compelled to believe'). (The 'cutting' case needs slightly different treatment, for one cannot in any straight-forward sense 'decide' to be offended; but one can refuse to be offended.) It looks then as if the intended effect must be something within the control of the audience, or at least the *sort* of thing which is within its control.

One point before passing to an objection or two. I think it follows that from what I have said about the connection between meaning$_{NN}$ and recognition of intention that (insofar as I am right) only what I may call the primary intention of an utterer is relevant to the meaning$_{NN}$ of an utterance. For if I utter *x*, intending (with the aid of the recognition of this intention) to induce an effect *E*, and intend this effect *E* to lead to a further effect *F*, then insofar as the occurrence of *F* is thought to be dependent solely on *E*, I cannot regard *F* as in the least dependent on recognition of my intention to induce *E*. That is, if (say) I intend to get a man to do something by giving him some information, it cannot be regarded as relevant to the meaning$_{NN}$ of my utterance to describe what I intend him to do.

Now some question may be raised about my use, fairly free, of such words as 'intention' and 'recognition.' I must disclaim any intention of peopling all our talking life with armies of complicated psychological occurrences. I do not hope to solve any philosophical puzzles about intending, but I do want briefly to argue that no special difficulties are raised by my use of the word 'intention' in connection with meaning. First, there will be cases where an utterance is accompanied or preceded by a conscious 'plan,' or explicit formulation of intention (e.g., I declare how I am going to use *x*, or ask myself how to 'get something across'). The presence of such an explicit 'plan' obviously counts fairly heavily in favor of the utterer's intention (meaning) being as 'planned'; though it is not, I think, conclusive; for example, a speaker who has declared an intention to use a familiar expression in an unfamiliar way may slip into the familiar use. Similarly in nonlinguistic cases: if we are asking about an agent's intention, a previous expression counts heavily; nevertheless, a man might plan to throw a letter in the dustbin and yet take it to the post; when lifting his hand he might 'come to' and say *either* 'I didn't intend to do this at all' *or* 'I suppose I must have been intending to put it in.'

Explicitly formulated linguistic (or quasi-linguistic) intentions are no doubt comparatively rare. In their absence we would seem to rely on very much the same kinds of criteria as we do in the case of nonlinguistic intentions where there is a general usage. An utterer is held to intend to convey what is normally conveyed (or normally intended to be conveyed), and we require a good reason for accepting that a particular use diverges from the general usage (e.g., he never knew or had forgotten the general usage). Similarly in nonlinguistic cases: we are presumed to intend the normal consequences of our actions.

Again, in cases where there is doubt, say, about which of two or more things an utterer intends to convey, we tend to refer to the context (linguistic or otherwise) of the utterance and ask which of the alternatives would be relevant to other things he is saying or doing, or which intention in a particular situation would fit in with some purpose he obviously has (e.g., a man who calls for a 'pump' at a fire would not want a bicycle pump). Nonlinguistic parallels are obvious: context is a criterion in settling the question of why a man who has just put a cigarette in his mouth has put his hand in his pocket; relevance to an obvious end is a criterion in settling why a man is running away from a bull.

In certain linguistic cases we ask the utterer afterward about his intention, and in a few of these cases (the very difficult ones, like a philosopher asked to explain the meaning of an unclear passage in one of his works), the answer is not based on what he remembers but is more like a decision, a decision about how what he said is to be taken. I cannot find a nonlinguistic parallel here; but the case is so special as not to seem to contribute a vital difference.

All this is very obvious; but surely to show that the criteria for judging linguistic intentions are very like the criteria for judging nonlinguistic intentions is to show that linguistic intentions are very like nonlinguistic intentions.

Notes

1. *Ethics and Language* (New Haven, 1944), ch. iii.
2. *Ibid.*, p. 57.

Chapter 2

Locutionary, Illocutionary, Perlocutionary

J. L. Austin

Lecture VII

[· · ·]

We want to reconsider more generally the senses in which to say something may be to do something, or in saying something we do something (and also perhaps to consider the different case in which *by* saying something we do something). Perhaps some clarification and definition here may help us out of our tangle. For after all, 'doing something' is a very vague expression. When we issue any utterance[1] whatsoever, are we not 'doing something'? Certainly the ways in which we talk about 'action' are liable here, as elsewhere, to be confusing. For example, we may contrast men of words with men of action, we may say they *did* nothing, only talked or *said* things: yet again, we may contrast *only* thinking something with *actually* saying it (out loud), in which context saying it *is* doing something.

It is time to refine upon the circumstances of 'issuing an utterance'.[2] To begin with, there is a whole group of senses, which I shall label (A), in which to say anything must always be to do something, the group of senses which together add up to 'saying' something, in the full sense of 'say'. We may agree, without insisting on formulations or refinements, that to say anything is

(A.*a*) always to perform the act of uttering certain noises (a 'phonetic' act), and the utterance is a phone;

From Austin, J. L. (1975) *How To Do Things with Words*, second edition, Cambridge, MA: Harvard University Press.

(A.*b*) always to perform the act of uttering certain vocables or words, i.e. noises of certain types belonging to *and as* belonging to a certain vocabulary, in a certain construction, i.e. conforming to and as conforming to a certain grammar, with a certain intonation, &c. This act we may call a 'phatic' act, and the utterance which it is the act of uttering a 'pheme' (as distinct from the phememe of linguistic theory); and

(A.*c*) generally to perform the act of using that pheme or its constituents with a certain more or less definite 'sense' and a more or less definite 'reference' (which together are equivalent to 'meaning'). This act we may call a 'rhetic' act, and the utterance which it is the act of uttering a 'rheme'.

Lecture VIII

In embarking on a programme of finding a list of explicit performative verbs, it seemed that we were going to find it not always easy to distinguish performative utterances from constative, and it therefore seemed expedient to go farther back for a while to fundamentals – to consider from the ground up how many senses there are in which to say something *is* to do something, or *in* saying something we do something, and even *by* saying something we do something. And we began by distinguishing a whole group of senses of 'doing something' which are all included together when we say, what is obvious, that to say something is in the full normal sense to do something – which includes the utterance of certain noises, the utterance of certain words in a certain construction, and the utterance of them with a certain 'meaning' in the favourite philosophical sense of that word, i.e. with a certain sense and with a certain reference.

The act of 'saying something' in this full normal sense I call, i.e. dub, the performance of a locutionary act, and the study of utterances thus far and in these respects the study of locutions, or of the full units of speech. Our interest in the locutionary act is, of course, principally to make quite plain what it is, in order to distinguish it from other acts with which we are going to be primarily concerned. Let me add merely that, of course, a great many further refinements would be possible and necessary if we were to discuss it for its own sake – refinements of very great importance not merely to philosophers but to, say, grammarians and phoneticians.

We had made three rough distinctions between the phonetic act, the phatic act, and the rhetic act. The phonetic act is merely the act of uttering certain noises. The phatic act is the uttering of certain vocables or words, i.e. noises of certain types, belonging to and as belonging to, a certain vocabulary, conforming to and as conforming to a certain grammar. The rhetic act is the performance of an act of using those vocables with a certain more-or-less definite sense and reference. Thus 'He said "The cat is on the mat"', reports a phatic act, whereas 'He said that the cat was on the mat' reports a rhetic act. A similar contrast is illustrated by the pairs:

> He said 'The cat is on the mat', He said (that) the cat was on the mat;
> He said 'I shall be there', He said he would be there;
> He said 'Get out', He told me to get out;
> He said 'Is it in Oxford or Cambridge?'; He asked whether it was in Oxford or Cambridge.

To pursue this for its own sake beyond our immediate requirements, I shall mention some general points worth remembering:

1. Obviously, to perform a phatic I must perform a phonetic act, or, if you like, in performing one I am performing the other (not, however, that phatic acts are a sub-class of phonetic acts; we defined the phatic act as the uttering of vocables *as* belonging to a certain vocabulary): but the converse is not true, for if a monkey makes a noise indistinguishable from 'go' it is still not a phatic act.
2. Obviously in the definition of the phatic act two things were lumped together: vocabulary and grammar. So we have not assigned a special name to the person who utters, for example, 'cat thoroughly the if' or 'the slithy toves did gyre'. Yet a further point arising is the intonation as well as grammar and vocabulary.
3. The phatic act, however, like the phonetic, is essentially mimicable, reproducible (including intonation, winks, gestures &c). One can mimic not merely the statement in quotation marks 'She has lovely hair', but also the more complex fact that he said it like this: 'She has lovely *hair*' (shrugs).

This is the 'inverted commas' use of 'said' as we get it in novels: every utterance can be just reproduced in inverted commas, or in inverted commas with 'said he' or, more often, 'said she', &c., after it.

But the rhetic act is the one we report, in the case of assertions, by saying 'He said that the cat was on the mat', 'He said he would go', 'He said I was to go' (his words were 'You are to go'). This is the so-called 'indirect speech'. If the sense or reference is *not* being taken as clear, then the whole or part is to be in quotation marks. Thus I might say: 'He said I was to go to "the minister", but he did not say which minister' or 'I said that he was behaving badly and he replied that "the higher you get the fewer"'. We cannot, however, always use 'said that' easily: we would say 'told to', 'advise to', &c., if he used the imperative mood, or such equivalent phrases as 'said I was to', 'said I should', &c. Compare such phrases as 'bade me welcome' and 'extended his apologies'.

I add one further point about the rhetic act: of course sense and reference (naming and referring) themselves are here ancillary acts performed in performing the rhetic act. Thus we may say 'I meant by "bank" . . .' and we say 'by "he" I was referring to . . .' Can we perform a rhetic act without referring or without naming? In general it would seem that the answer is that we cannot, but there are puzzling cases. What is the reference in 'all triangles have three sides'? Correspondingly, it is clear that we can perform a phatic act which is not a rhetic act, though not conversely. Thus we may repeat someone else's remark or mumble over some sentence, or we may read a Latin sentence without knowing the meaning of the words.

The question when one pheme or one rheme is the *same* as another, whether in the 'type' or 'token' sense, and the question what is one single pheme or rheme, do not so much matter here. But, of course, it is important to remember that the same pheme, e.g., sentence, that is, tokens of the same type, may be used on different occasions of utterance with a different sense or reference, and so be a different rheme. When different phemes are used with the same sense and reference, we might speak of rhetically equivalent acts ('the same statement' in one sense) but not of the same rheme or rhetic acts (which are the same statement in another sense which involves using the same words).

The pheme is a unit of *language*: its typical fault is to be nonsense – meaningless. But the rheme is a unit of *speech*; its typical fault is to be vague or void or obscure, &c.

But though these matters are of much interest, they do not so far throw any light at all on our problem of the constative as opposed to the performative utterance. For example, it might be perfectly possible, with regard to an utterance, say 'It is going to charge', to make entirely plain 'what we were saying' in issuing the utterance, in all the senses so far distinguished, and yet not at all to have cleared up whether or not in issuing the utterance I was performing the act of *warning* or not. It may be perfectly clear what I mean by 'It is going to charge' or 'Shut the door', but not clear whether it is meant as a statement or warning, etc.

To perform a locutionary act is in general, we may say, also and *eo ipso* to perform an *illocutionary* act, as I propose to call it. Thus in performing a locutionary act we shall also be performing such an act as:

asking or answering a question,
giving some information or an assurance or a warning,
announcing a verdict or an intention,
pronouncing sentence,
making an appointment or an appeal or a criticism,
making an identification or giving a description,

and the numerous like. (I am not suggesting that this is a clearly defined class by any means.) There is nothing mysterious about our *eo ipso* here. The trouble rather is the number of different senses of so vague an expression as 'in what way are we using it' – this may refer even to a locutionary act, and, further to perlocutionary acts to which we shall come in a minute. When we perform a locutionary act, we use speech: but in what way precisely are we using it on this occasion? For there are very numerous functions of or ways in which we use speech, and it makes a great difference to our act in some sense – sense (B) – in which way and which *sense* we were on this occasion 'using' it. It makes a great difference whether we were advising, or merely suggesting, or actually ordering, whether we were strictly promising or only announcing a vague intention, and so forth. These issues penetrate a little but not without confusion into grammar (see above), but we constantly do debate them, in such terms as whether certain words (a certain locution) *had the force of* a question, or *ought to have been taken as* an estimate and so on.

I explained the performance of an act in this new and second sense as the performance of an 'illocutionary' act, i.e. performance of an act *in* saying something as opposed to performance of an act *of* saying something; I call the act performed an 'illocution' and shall refer to the doctrine of the different types of function of language here in question as the doctrine of 'illocutionary forces'.

It may be said that for too long philosophers have neglected this study, treating all problems as problems of 'locutionary usage', and indeed that the 'descriptive fallacy' mentioned in Lecture I commonly arises through mistaking a problem of the former kind for a problem of the latter kind. True, we are now getting out of this; for some years we have been realizing more and more clearly that the occasion of an utterance matters seriously, and that the words used are to some extent to be 'explained' by the 'context' in which they are designed to be or have actually been spoken in a linguistic interchange. Yet still perhaps we are too prone to give these explanations in terms of 'the meaning of words'. Admittedly we can use 'meaning' also with reference to illocutionary force – 'He meant it as an order', &c. But I want to distinguish *force* and meaning in the sense in which meaning is equivalent to sense and reference, just as it has become essential to distinguish sense and reference.

Moreover, we have here an illustration of the different uses of the expression, 'uses of language', or 'use of a sentence', &c. – 'use' is a hopelessly ambiguous or wide word, just as is the word 'meaning', which it has become customary to deride. But 'use', its supplanter, is not in much better case. We may entirely clear up the 'use of a sentence' on a particular occasion, in the sense of the locutionary act, without yet touching upon its use in the sense of an *illocutionary* act.

Before refining any further on this notion of the illocutionary act, let us contrast both the locutionary *and* the illocutionary act with yet a third kind of act.

There is yet a further sense (C) in which to perform a locutionary act, and therein an illocutionary act, may also be to perform an act of another kind.

Saying something will often, or even normally, produce certain consequential effects upon the feelings, thoughts, or actions of the audience, or of the speaker, or of other persons: and it may be done with the design, intention, or purpose of producing them; and we may then say, thinking of this, that the speaker has performed an act in the nomenclature of which reference is made either (C.*a*), only obliquely, or even (C.*b*), not at all, to the performance of the locutionary or illocutionary act. We shall call the performance of an act of this kind the performance of a 'perlocutionary' act, and the act performed, where suitable – essentially in cases falling under (C.*a*) – a 'perlocution'. Let us not yet define this idea any more carefully – of course it needs it – but simply give examples:

(E.1)

Act (A) or Locution
He said to me 'Shoot her!' meaning by 'shoot' shoot and referring by 'her' to *her*.

Act (B) or Illocution
He urged (or advised, ordered, &c.) me to shoot her.

Act (C.*a*) or Perlocution
He persuaded me to shoot her.

Act (C.*b*)
He got me to (or made me, &c.) shoot her.

(E.2)

Act (A) or Locution
He said to me, 'You can't do that'

Act (B) or Illocution
He protested against my doing it.

Act (C.*a*) or Perlocution
He pulled me up, checked me.

Act (C.*b*)
He stopped me, he brought me to my senses, &c.
He annoyed me.

We can similarly distinguish the locutionary act 'he said that . . .' from the illocutionary act 'he argued that . . .' and the perlocutionary act 'he convinced me that . . .'

It will be seen that the 'consequential effects' here mentioned (see C.*a* and C.*b*) do not include a particular kind of consequential effects, those achieved, e.g., by way of committing the speaker as in promising, which come into the illocutionary act. Perhaps restrictions need making, as there is clearly a difference between what we feel to be the real production of real effects and what we regard as mere conventional consequences; we shall in any case return later to this.

We have here then roughly distinguished three kinds of acts – the locutionary, the illocutionary, and the perlocutionary. Let us make some general comments on these three classes, leaving them still fairly rough. The first three points will be about 'the use of language' again.

Our interest in these lectures is essentially to fasten on the second, illocutionary act and contrast it with the other two. There is a constant tendency in philosophy to elide this in favour of one or other of the other two. Yet it is distinct from both. We have already seen how the expressions 'meaning' and 'use of sentence' can blur the distinction between locutionary and illocutionary acts. We now notice that to speak of the 'use' of language can likewise blur the distinction between the illocutionary and perlocutionary act – so we will distinguish them more carefully in a minute. Speaking of the 'use of "language" for arguing or warning' looks just like speaking of 'the use of "language" for persuading, rousing, alarming'; yet the former may, for rough contrast, be said to be *conventional*, in the sense that at least it could be made explicit by the performative formula; but the latter could not. Thus we can say 'I argue that' or 'I warn you that' but we cannot say 'I convince you that' or 'I alarm you that'. Further, we may entirely clear up whether someone was arguing or not without touching on the question whether he was convincing anyone or not.

To take this farther, let us be quite clear that the expression 'use of language' can cover other matters even more diverse than the illocutionary and perlocutionary acts and obviously quite diverse from any with which we are here concerned. For example, we may speak of the 'use of language' *for* something, e.g. for joking; and we may use 'in' in a way different from the illocutionary 'in', as when we say 'in saying "p" I was joking' or 'acting a part' or 'writing poetry'; or again we may speak of 'a poetical use of language' as distinct from 'the use of language in poetry'. These references to 'use of language' have nothing to do with the illocutionary act. For example, if I say 'Go and catch a falling star', it may be quite clear what both the meaning and the force of my utterance is, but still wholly unresolved which of these other kinds of things I may be doing. There are aetiolations, parasitic uses, etc., various 'not serious' and 'not full normal' uses. The normal conditions of reference may be suspended, or no attempt made at a standard perlocutionary act, no attempt to make you do anything, as Walt Whitman does not seriously incite the eagle of liberty to soar.

Furthermore, there may be some things we 'do' in some connexion with saying something which do not seem to fall, intuitively at least, exactly into any of these roughly defined classes, or else seem to fall vaguely into more than one; but any way we do not at the outset feel so clear that they are as remote from our three acts as would be joking or writing poetry. For example, *insinuating*, as when we insinuate something in or by issuing some utterance, seems to involve some convention, as in the illocutionary act; but we cannot *say* 'I insinuate . . .', and it seems like implying to be a clever effect rather than a mere act. A further example is evincing emotion. We may evince emotion in or by issuing an utterance, as when we swear; but once again we have no use here for performative formulas and the other devices of illocutionary acts. We might say that we use swearing[3] *for* relieving our feelings. We must notice that the illocutionary act is a conventional act: an act done as conforming to a convention.

The next three points that arise do so importantly because our acts are *acts*.

Acts of all our three kinds necessitate, since they are the performing of actions, allowance being made for the ills that all action is heir to. We must systematically be prepared to distinguish between 'the act of doing *x*', i.e. achieving *x*, and 'the act of attempting to do *x*'.

In the case of illocutions we must be ready to draw the necessary distinction, not noticed by ordinary language except in exceptional cases, between

(*a*) the act of attempting or purporting (or affecting or professing or claiming or setting up or setting out) to perform a certain illocutionary act, and
(*b*) the act of successfully achieving or consummating or bringing off such an act.

This distinction is, or should be, a commonplace of the theory of our language about 'action' in general. But attention has been drawn earlier to its special importance in connexion with performatives: it is always possible, for example, to try to thank or inform somebody yet in different ways to fail, because he doesn't listen, or takes it as ironical, or wasn't responsible for whatever it was, and so on. This distinction will arise, as over any act, over locutionary acts too; but failures here will not be unhappinesses as there, but rather failures to get the words out, to express ourselves clearly, etc.

Since our acts are actions, we must always remember the distinction between producing effects or consequences which are intended or unintended; and (i) when the speaker intends to produce an effect it may nevertheless not occur, and (ii) when he does not intend to produce it or intends not to produce it it may nevertheless occur. To cope with complication (i) we invoke as before the distinction between attempt and achievement; to cope with complication (ii) we invoke the normal linguistic devices of disclaiming (adverbs like 'unintentionally' and so on) which we hold ready for general use in all cases of doing actions.[4]

Furthermore, we must, of course, allow that as actions they may be things that we do not exactly *do*, in the sense that we did them, say, under duress or in any other such way. Other ways besides in which we may not fully do the action are given in (2) above. We may, perhaps, add the cases given in (5) where we produce consequences by mistake, did not intend to do so.

Finally we must meet the objection about our illocutionary and perlocutionary acts – namely that the notion of an act is unclear – by a general doctrine about action. We have the idea of an 'act' as a fixed physical thing that we do, as distinguished from conventions and as distinguished from consequences. But

(*a*) the illocutionary act and even the locutionary act too involve conventions: compare with them the act of doing obeisance. It is obeisance only because it is conventional and it is done only because it is conventional. Compare also the distinction between kicking a wall and kicking a goal;

(*b*) the perlocutionary act always includes some consequences, as when we say 'By doing *x* I was doing *y*': we do bring in a greater or less stretch of 'consequences' always, some of which may be 'unintentional'. there is no restriction to the minimum physical act at all. That we can import an arbitrarily long stretch of what might also be called the 'consequences' of our act into the nomenclature of the act itself is, or should be, a fundamental commonplace of the theory of our language about all 'action' in general. Thus if asked 'What did he do?', we may reply either 'He shot the donkey' or 'He fired a gun' or 'He pulled the trigger' or 'He moved his trigger finger', and all may be correct. So, to shorten the nursery story of the endeavours of the old woman to drive her pig home in time to get her old man's supper, we may in the last resort say that the cat drove or got the pig, or made the pig get, over the stile. If in such cases we *mention* both a B act (illocution) and a C act (perlocution) we shall say '*by* B-ing he C-ed' rather than '*in*-B-ing . . .' This is the reason for calling C a *per*locutionary act as distinct from an illocutionary act.

Next time we shall revert to the distinction between our three kinds of act, and to the expressions 'in' and 'by doing *x* I am doing *y*', with a view to getting the three classes and their members and non-members somewhat clearer. We shall see that just as the locutionary act embraces doing many things at once to be complete, so may the illocutionary and perlocutionary acts.

Notes

1. I use 'utterance' only as equivalent to *utteratum*: for *utteratio* I use 'the issuing of an utterance'.

2. We shall not always mention but must bear in mind the possibility of 'etiolation' as it occurs when we use speech in acting, fiction and poetry, quotation and recitation.
3. 'Swearing' is ambiguous: 'I swear by Our Lady' *is* to swear by Our Lady: but 'Bloody' is not to swear by Our Lady.
4. This complication (ii), it may be pointed out, can of course also arise in the cases of both locutionary and illocutionary acts. I may say something or refer to something without meaning to, or commit myself unintentionally to a certain undertaking; for example, I may order someone to do something, when I did not intend to order him to do so. But it is in connexion with perlocution that it is most prominent, as is also the distinction between attempt and achievement.

Chapter 3

Intention and Convention in Speech Acts

P. F. Strawson

I

In this paper I want to discuss some questions regarding J. L. Austin's notions of the illocutionary force of an utterance and of the illocutionary act which a speaker performs in making an utterance.[1]

There are two preliminary matters I must mention, if only to get them out of the way. Austin contrasts what he calls the 'normal' or 'serious' use of speech with what he calls 'etiolated' or 'parasitical' uses. His doctrine of illocutionary force relates essentially to the normal or serious use of speech and not, or not directly, to etiolated or parasitical uses; and so it will be with my comments on his doctrine. I am not suggesting that the distinction between the normal or serious use of speech and the secondary uses which he calls etiolated or parasitical is so clear as to call for no further examination; but I shall take it that there is such a distinction to be drawn and I shall not here further examine it.

My second preliminary remark concerns another distinction, or pair of distinctions, which Austin draws. Austin distinguishes the illocutionary force of an utterance from what he calls its 'meaning' and distinguishes between the illocutionary and the locutionary acts performed in issuing the utterance. Doubts may be felt about the second term of each of these distinctions. It may be felt that Austin has not made clear just what abstractions from the total speech act he intends to make by means of his notions of meaning and of locutionary act. Although this is a question on which I have views, it is not what the present paper is about. Whatever doubts may be entertained about Austin's notions of meaning and of locutionary act, it is enough for

First published in *The Philosophical Review*, Oct 1964, 439–60.

present purposes to be able to say, as I think we clearly can, the following about their relation to the notion of illocutionary force. The meaning of a (serious) utterance, as conceived by Austin, always embodies some limitation on its possible force, and sometimes – as, for example, in some cases where an explicit performative formula, like 'I apologize,' is used – the meaning of an utterance may exhaust its force; that is, there may be no more to the force than there is to the meaning; but very often the meaning, though it limits, does not exhaust, the force. Similarly, there may sometimes be no more to say about the illocutionary force of an utterance than we already know if we know what locutionary act has been performed; but very often there is more to know about the illocutionary force of an utterance than we know in knowing what locutionary act has been performed.

So much for these two preliminaries. Now I shall proceed to assemble from the text some indications as to what Austin means by the force of an utterance and as to what he means by an illocutionary act. These two notions are not so closely related that to know the force of an utterance is the same thing as to know what illocutionary act was actually performed in issuing it. For if an utterance with the illocutionary force of, say, a warning is not understood in this way (that is, as a warning) by the audience to which it is addressed, then (it is held) the illocutionary act of warning cannot be said to have been actually performed. 'The performance of an illocutionary act involves the securing of uptake'; that is, it involves 'bringing about the understanding of the meaning and of the force of the locution' (pp. 115–116).[2] Perhaps we may express the relation by saying that to know the force of an utterance is the same thing as to know what illocutionary act, *if any*, was actually performed in issuing it. Austin gives many examples and lists of words which help us to form at least a fair intuitive notion of what is meant by 'illocutionary force' and 'illocutionary act.' Besides these, he gives us certain general clues to these ideas, which may be grouped, as follows, under four heads:

1. Given that we know (in Austin's sense) the meaning of an utterance, there may still be a further question as to *how what was said was meant* by the speaker, or as to *how the words spoken were used*, or as to *how the utterance was to be taken* or *ought to have been taken* (pp. 98–99). In order to know the illocutionary force of the utterance, we must know the answer to this further question.
2. A locutionary act is an act *of* saying something; an illocutionary act is an act we perform *in* saying something. It is what we *do, in* saying what we *say*. Austin does not regard this characterization as by any means a satisfactory test for identifying kinds of illocutionary acts since, so regarded, it would admit many kinds of acts which he wishes to exclude from the class (p. 99 and Lecture X).
3. It is a sufficient, though not, I think, a necessary, condition of a verb's being the name of a *kind* of illocutionary act that it can figure, in the first

person present indicative, as what Austin calls an explicit performative. (This latter notion I shall assume to be familiar and perspicuous.)

4. The illocutionary act is 'a conventional act; an act done as conforming to a convention' (p. 105). As such, it is to be sharply contrasted with the producing of certain effects, intended or otherwise, by means of an utterance. This producing of effects, though it too can often be ascribed *as an act* to the speaker (his *perlocutionary* act), is in no way a conventional act (pp. 120–121). Austin reverts many times to the 'conventional' nature of the illocutionary act (pp. 103, 105, 108, 115, 120, 121, 127) and speaks also of 'conventions of illocutionary force' (p. 114). Indeed, he remarks (pp. 120–121) that though acts which can properly be called by the same names as illocutionary acts – for example, acts of warning – can be brought off nonverbally, without the use of words, yet in order to be properly called by these names, such acts must be *conventional* nonverbal acts.

II

I shall assume that we are clear enough about the intended application of Austin's notions of illocutionary force and illocutionary act to be able to criticize, by reference to cases, his general doctrines regarding those notions. It is the general doctrine I listed last above – the doctrine that an utterance's having such and such a force is a matter of convention – that I shall take as the starting point of inquiry. Usually this doctrine is affirmed in a quite unqualified way. But just once there occurs an interestingly qualified statement of it. Austin says, of the use of language with a certain illocutionary force, that 'it may . . . be said to be *conventional* in the sense that at least it could be made explicit by the performative formula' (p. 103). The remark has a certain authority in that it is the first explicit statement of the conventional nature of the illocutionary act. I shall refer to it later.

Meanwhile let us consider the doctrine in its unqualified form. Why does Austin say that the illocutionary act is a conventional act, an act done as conforming to a convention? I must first mention, and neutralize, two possible sources of confusion. (It may seem an excess of precaution to do so. I apologize to those who find it so.) First, we may agree (or not dispute) that any speech act is, as such, at least in part a conventional act. The performance of any *speech* act involves at least the observance or exploitation of some *linguistic* conventions, and every illocutionary act is a speech act. But it is absolutely clear that this is not the point that Austin is making in declaring the illocutionary act to be a conventional act. We must refer, Austin would say, to linguistic conventions to determine what *locutionary* act has been performed in the making of an utterance, to determine what the *meaning* of the utterance is. The doctrine now before us is the further doctrine that where force is *not* exhausted by meaning, the fact that an utterance has the further unexhausted force it has is also a matter of convention; or, where it is exhausted by meaning, the fact *that* it is, is a matter of convention. It is not just as being a speech act that an illocutionary act – for example, of warning – is conventional. A nonverbal act of warning is, Austin maintains, conventionally such in just the same way as an illocutionary – that is, verbal – act of warning is conventionally such.

Second, we must dismiss as irrelevant the fact that it can properly be said to be a matter of convention that an act of, for example, warning is correctly called by this name. For if this were held to be a ground for saying that illocutionary acts were conventional acts, then any describable act whatever would, as correctly described, be a conventional act.

The contention that illocutionary force is a matter of convention is easily seen to be correct in a great number of cases. For very many kinds of human transaction involving speech are governed and in part constituted by what we easily recognize as established conventions of procedure additional to the conventions governing the *meanings* of our utterances. Thus the fact that the word 'guilty' is pronounced by the foreman of the jury in court at the proper moment constitutes his utterance as the act of bringing in a verdict; and that this is so is certainly a matter of the conventional procedures of the law. Similarly, it is a matter of convention that if the appropriate umpire pronounces a batsman 'out,' he thereby performs the act of *giving the man out*, which no player or spectator shouting 'Out!' can do. Austin gives other examples, and there are doubtless many more which could be given, where there clearly exist statable conventions, relating to the circumstances of utterance, such that an utterance with a certain meaning, pronounced by the appropriate person in the appropriate circumstances, has the force it has *as* conforming to those conventions. Examples of illocutionary acts of which this is true can be found not only in the sphere of social institutions which have a legal point (like the marriage ceremony and the law courts themselves) or of activities governed by a definite set of rules (like cricket and games generally) but in many other relations of human life. The act of *introducing*, performed by uttering the words 'This is Mr. Smith,' may be said to be an act performed as conforming to a convention. The act of surrendering, performed by saying '*Kamerad*!' and throwing up your arms when confronted with a bayonet, may be said to be (to have become) an act performed as conforming to an accepted convention, a conventional act.

But it seems equally clear that, although the circumstances of utterance are always relevant to the determination of the illocutionary force of an utterance, there are many cases in which it is not as conforming to an accepted *convention* of any kind (other than those linguistic conventions which help to fix the meaning of the utterance) that an illocutionary act is performed. It seems clear, that is, that there are many cases in which the illocutionary force of an utterance, though not exhausted by its meaning, is not owed to any *conventions* other than those which help to give it its meaning. Surely there may be cases in which to utter the words 'The ice over there is very thin' to a skater is to issue a warning (is to say something with the *force* of a warning) without its being the case that there is any statable convention at all (other than those which bear on the nature of the *locutionary* act) such that the speaker's act can be said to be an act done as conforming to that convention.

Here is another example. We can readily imagine circumstances in which an utterance of the words 'Don't go' would be correctly described not as a request or an order, but as an entreaty. I do not want to deny that there may be conventional postures or procedures for entreating: one can, for example, kneel down, raise one's arms and *say*, 'I entreat you.' But I do want to deny that an act of entreaty can be performed only as conforming to some such conventions. What makes *X*'s words to *Y* an *entreaty* not to go is something – complex enough, no doubt – relating to *X*'s situation, attitude to *Y*, manner, and current intention. There are questions here which we must discuss later. But to suppose that there is always and necessarily a convention conformed to would be like supposing that there could be no love affairs which did not proceed on lines laid down in the *Roman de la Rose* or that every dispute between men must follow the pattern specified in Touchstone's speech about the countercheck quarrelsome and the lie direct.

Another example. In the course of a philosophical discussion (or, for that matter, a debate on policy) one speaker *raises an objection* to what the previous speaker has just said. *X* says (or proposes) that *p* and *Y objects* that *q*. *Y*'s utterance has the force of an objection to *X*'s assertion (or proposal) that *p*. But where is the *convention* that constitutes it an objection? That *Y*'s utterance has the force of an objection may lie partly in the character of the dispute and of *X*'s contention (or proposal) and it certainly lies partly, in *Y*'s *view* of these things, in the bearing which he takes the proposition that *q* to have on the doctrine (or proposal) that *p*. But although there may be, there does not have to be, any convention involved other than those linguistic conventions which help to fix the meanings of utterances.

I do not think it necessary to give further examples. It seems perfectly clear that, if at least we take the expressions 'convention' and 'conventional' in the most natural way, the doctrine of the conventional nature of the illocutionary act does not hold generally. Some illocutionary acts are conventional; others are not (except in so far as they are locutionary acts). Why then does Austin repeatedly affirm the contrary? It is unlikely that he has made the simple mistake of generalizing from some cases to all. It is much more likely that he is moved by some further, and fundamental, feature of illocutionary acts, which it must be our business to discover. Even though we may decide that the description 'conventional' is not appropriately used, we may presume it worth our while to look for the reason for using it. Here we may recall that oddly qualified remark that the performance of an illocutionary act, or the use of a sentence with a certain illocutionary force, 'may be said to be conventional in the sense that at least it *could* be made explicit by the performative formula' (p. 103). On this we may first, and with justice, be inclined to comment that there is no such *sense* of 'being conventional,' that if this is a *sense* of anything to the purpose, it is a sense of 'being *capable* of being conventional.' But although this is a proper comment on the remark, we should not simply dismiss the remark with this comment. Whatever it is that leads Austin to call illocutionary acts in general 'conventional' must be closely connected with whatever it is about such acts as warning, entreating, apologizing, advising, that accounts for the fact that *they* at least *could* be made explicit by the use of the corresponding first-person performative form. So we must ask what it is about them that accounts for this fact. Obviously it will not do to answer simply that they are acts which can be performed by the use of words. So are many (perlocutionary) acts, like convincing, dissuading, alarming, and amusing, for which, as Austin points out, there is no corresponding first-person *performative* formula. So we need some further explanation.

III

I think a concept we may find helpful at this point is one introduced by H. P. Grice in his valuable article on *Meaning (Philosophical Review*, LXVII, 1957), namely, the concept of *someone's nonnaturally meaning something by an utterance.* The concept does not apply only to speech acts – that is, to cases where that by which someone nonnaturally means something is a *linguistic* utterance. It is of more general application. But it will be convenient to refer to that by which someone, *S*, nonnaturally means something as *S*'s *utterance.* The explanation of the introduced concept is given in terms of the concept of intention. *S* nonnaturally means something by an utterance x if *S* intends (i_1) to produce by uttering x a certain response (r) in an audience *A* and intends (i_2) that *A* shall recognize *S*'s intention (i_1) and intends (i_3) that this recognition on the part of *A* of *S*'s intention (i_1) shall function as *A*'s reason, or a part of his reason, for his response r. (The word 'response,' though more convenient in some ways than Grice's 'effect,' is not ideal. It is intended to cover cognitive and affective states or attitudes as well as actions.) It is, evidently, an important feature of this definition that the securing of the response r is intended to be mediated by the securing of another (and always cognitive) effect in *A*; namely, recognition of *S*'s intention to secure response r.

Grice's analysis of his concept is fairly complex. But I think a little reflection shows that it is not quite complex enough for his purpose. Grice's analysis is undoubtedly offered as an analysis of a situation in which one person is trying, in a sense of the word 'communicate' fundamental to any theory of meaning, to communicate with another. But it is possible to imagine a situation in which Grice's three conditions would be satisfied by a person *S* and yet, in this important sense of 'communicate,' it would not be the case that *S* could be said to be trying to communicate by means of his production of *x* with the person *A* in whom he was trying to produce the response *r*. I proceed to describe such a situation.

S intends by a certain action to induce in *A* the belief that *p*; so he satisfies condition (i_1). He arranges convincing-looking 'evidence' that *p*, in a place where *A* is bound to see it. He does this, knowing that *A* is watching him at work, but *knowing also that* A *does not know that* S *knows that* A *is watching him at work*. He realizes that *A* will not take the *arranged* 'evidence' as genuine or natural evidence that *p*, but realizes, and indeed intends, that *A* will take his arranging of it as grounds for thinking that he, *S*, intends to induce in *A* the belief that *p*. That is, he intends *A* to recognize his (i_1) intention. So *S* satisfies condition (i_2). He knows that *A* has general grounds for thinking that *S* would not wish to make him, *A*, think that *p* unless it were known to *S* to be the case that *p*; and hence that *A*'s recognition of his (*S*'s) intention to induce in *A* the belief that *p* will in fact seem to *A* a sufficient reason for believing that *p*. And he intends that *A*'s recognition of his intention (i_1) should function in just this way. So he satisfies condition (i_3).

S, then, satisfies all Grice's conditions. But this is clearly not a case of attempted *communication* in the sense which (I think it is fair to assume) Grice is seeking to elucidate. *A* will indeed take *S* to be trying to bring it about that *A* is aware of some fact; but he will not take *S* as trying, in the colloquial sense, to 'let him know' something (or to 'tell' him something). But unless *S* at least brings it about that *A* takes him (*S*) to be trying to let him (*A*) know something, he has not succeeded in communicating with *A*; and if, as in our example, he has not even *tried* to bring this about, then he has not even *tried* to communicate with *A*. It seems a minimum further condition of his trying to do this that he should not only intend *A* to recognize his intention to get *A* to think that *p*, but that he should also *intend* A *to recognize his intention to get* A *to recognize his intention* to get *A* to think that *p*.

We might approximate more closely to the communication situation if we changed the example by supposing it not only clear to both *A* and *S* that *A* was watching *S* at work, but also clear to them both that it *was* clear to them both. I shall content myself, however, with drawing from the actually considered example the conclusion that we must add to Grice's conditions the further condition that *S* should have the further intention (i_4) that *A* should recognize his intention (i_2). It is possible that further argument could be produced to show that even adding this condition is not *sufficient* to constitute the case as one of attempted communication. But I shall rest content for the moment with the fact that this addition at least is necessary.

Now we might have expected in Grice's paper an account of what it is for *A* to *understand* something by an utterance *x*, an account complementary to the account of what is is for *S* to *mean* something by an utterance *x*. Grice in fact gives no such account, and I shall suggest a way of at least partially supplying this lack. I say 'at least partially' because the uncertainty as to the sufficiency of even the modified conditions for *S*'s nonnaturally *meaning* something by an utterance *x* is reflected in a corresponding uncertainty in the sufficiency of conditions for *A*'s understanding. But again we may be content for the moment with necessary conditions. I suggest, then, that for *A* (in the appropriate sense of 'understand') to understand *something* by utterance *x*, it is necessary (and perhaps sufficient) that there should be *some* complex intention of the (i_2) form, described above, which *A* takes *S* to have, and that for *A* to understand the utterance correctly, it is necessary that *A* should take *S* to have *the* complex intention of the (i_2) form which *S* does have. In other words, if *A* is to understand the utterance correctly, *S*'s (i_4) intention and hence his (i_2) intention must be fulfilled. Of course it does not follow from the fulfillment of these intentions that his (i_1) intention is fulfilled; nor, consequently, that his (i_3) intention is fulfilled.

It is at this point, it seems, that we may hope to find a possible point of connection with Austin's terminology of 'securing uptake.' If we do find such a point of connection, we also find a possible starting point for an at least partial analysis of the notions of illocutionary force and of the illocutionary act. For to secure uptake is to secure understanding of (meaning and) illocutionary force; and securing understanding of illocutionary force is said by Austin to be an essential element in bringing off the illocutionary act. It is true that this doctrine of Austin's may be objected to.[3] For surely a man may, for example, actually have made such and such a bequest, or gift, even if no one ever reads his will or instrument of gift. We may be tempted to say instead that at least *the aim, if not the achievement*, of securing uptake is an essential element in the performance of the illocutionary act. To this, too, there is an objection. Might not a man really have made a gift, in due form, and take some satisfaction in the thought, even if he had no expectations of the fact ever being known? But this objection at most forces on us an amendment to which we are in any case obliged[4]: namely, that the aim, if not the achievement, of securing uptake is essentially *a standard, if not an invariable*, element in the performance of the illocutionary act. So the analysis of the aim of securing uptake remains an essential element in the analysis of the notion of the illocutionary act.

IV

Let us, then, make a tentative identification – to be subsequently qualified and revised – of Austin's notion of uptake with that at least partially analyzed notion of understanding (on the part of an audience) which I introduced just now as complementary to Grice's concept of somebody nonnaturally meaning something by an utterance. Since the notion of audience understanding is introduced by way of a fuller (though partial) analysis than any which Austin gives of the notion of uptake, the identification is equivalent to a tentative (and partial) analysis of the notion of uptake and hence of the notions of illocutionary act and illocutionary force. If the identification were correct, then it would follow that to say something with a certain illocutionary force is at least (in the standard case) to have a certain complex intention of the (i_4) form described in setting out and modifying Grice's doctrine.

Next we test the adequacy and explanatory power of this partial analysis by seeing how far it helps to explain other features of Austin's doctrine regarding illocutionary acts. There are two points at which we shall apply this test. One is the point at which Austin maintains that the production of an utterance with a certain illocutionary force is a conventional act in that unconventional sense of 'conventional' which he glosses in terms of general suitability for being made explicit with the help of an explicitly performative formula. The other is the point at which Austin considers the possibility of a general characterization of the illocutionary act as what we *do, in* saying what we say. He remarks on the unsatisfactoriness of this characterization in that it would admit as illocutionary acts what are not such; and we may see whether the suggested analysis helps to explain the exclusion from the class of illocutionary acts of those acts falling under this characterization which Austin wishes to exclude. These points are closely connected with each other.

First, then, we take the point about the general suitability of an illocutionary act for performance with the help of the explicitly performative formula for that act. The explanation of this feature of illocutionary acts has two phases; it consists of, first, a general, and then a special, point about intention. The first point may be roughly expressed by saying that in general, a man can speak of his intention in performing an action with a kind of authority which he cannot command in predicting its outcome. What he intends in doing something is up to him in a way in which the results of his doing it are not, or not only, up to him. But we are concerned not with just any intention to produce any kind of effect by acting, but with a very special kind of case. We are concerned with the case in which there is not simply an intention to produce a certain response in an audience, but an intention to produce that response by means of recognition on the part of the audience of the intention to produce that response, this recognition to serve as part of the reason that the audience has for its response, and the intention that this recognition should occur being itself intended to be recognized. The speaker, then, not only has the general authority on the subject of his intention that any agent has; he also has a motive, inseparable from the nature of his act, for making that intention clear. For he will not have secured understanding of the illocutionary force of his utterance, he will not have performed the act of communication he sets out to perform, unless his complex intention is grasped. Now clearly, for the enterprise to be possible at all, there must exist, or he must find, means of making the intention clear. If there exists any conventional linguistic means of doing so, the speaker has both a right to use, and a motive for using, those means. One such means, available sometimes, which comes very close to the employment of the explicit performative form, would be to attach, or subjoin, to the substance of the message what looks like a force-elucidating *comment* on it, which may or may not have the form of a self-ascription. Thus we have phrases like 'This is only a suggestion' or 'I'm only making a suggestion'; or again 'That was a warning' or 'I'm warning you.' For using such phrases, I repeat, the speaker has the *authority* that anyone has to speak on the subject of his intentions and the *motive* that I have tried to show is inseparable from an act of communication.

From such phrases as these – which have, *in appearance*, the character of comments on utterances other than themselves – to the explicit performative formula the step is only a short one. My reason for *qualifying* the remark that such phrases have the character of comments on utterances other than themselves is this. We are considering the case in which the subjoined quasi-comment is addressed to the same audience as the utterance on which it is a quasi-comment. Since it is *part* of the speaker's audience-directed intention to make clear the character of his utterance as, for example, a warning, and since the subjoined quasi-comment directly subserves this intention, it is better to view the case, appearances notwithstanding, *not* as a case in which we have two utterances, one commenting on the other, but as a case of a single unitary speech act. Crudely, the addition of the quasi-comment 'That was a warning' is *part* of the total act of warning. The effect of the short step to the explicitly performative formula is simply to bring appearances into line with reality. When that short step is taken, we no longer have, even in appearance, two utterances, one a comment on the other, but a single utterance in which the first-person performative verb *manifestly* has that peculiar logical character of which Austin rightly made so much, and which we may express in the present context by saying that the verb serves not exactly to *ascribe* an intention to the speaker but rather, in Austin's phrase, to *make explicit* the type of communication intention with which the speaker speaks the type of force which the utterance has.

The above might be said to be a deduction of the general possibility and utility of the explicitly performative formula for the cases of illocutionary acts not essentially conventional. It may be objected that the deduction fails to show that the intentions rendered explicit by the use of performative formulae *in general* must be of just the complex form described, and hence fails to justify the claim that just this kind of intention lies at the core of all illocutionary acts. And indeed we shall see that this claim would be mistaken. But before discussing why, we shall make a further application of the analysis at the second testing point I mentioned. That is, we shall see what power it has to explain why some of the things we may be *doing, in* saying what we say, are not illocutionary acts and could not be rendered explicit by the use of the performative formula.

Among the things mentioned by Austin which we might be doing in saying things, but which are not illocutionary acts, I shall consider the two examples of (1) showing off and (2) insinuating. Now when we show off, we are certainly trying to produce an effect on the audience: we talk, indeed, for effect; we try to impress, to evoke the response of admiration. But it is no part of the intention to secure the effect *by means of* the recognition of the intention to secure it. It is no part of our total intention to secure recognition of the intention to produce the effect at all. On the contrary: recognition of the intention might militate against securing the effect and promote an opposite effect, for example, disgust.

This leads on to a further general point not explicitly considered by Austin, but satisfactorily explained by the analysis under consideration. In saying to an audience what we do say, we very often intend not only to produce the primary response *r* by means of audience recognition of the intention to produce that response, but to produce further effects by means of the production of the primary response *r*. Thus my further purpose in informing you that *p* (that is, aiming to produce in you the primary cognitive response of knowledge or belief that *p*) may be to bring it about thereby that you adopt a certain line of conduct or a certain attitude. In saying what I say, then, part of what I am *doing* is trying to influence your attitudes or conduct in a certain way. Does this part of what I am doing in saying what I say contribute to determining the character of the illocutionary act I perform? And if not, why not? If we take the first question strictly as introduced and posed, the answer to it is 'No.' The reason for the answer follows from the analysis. We have no complex intention (i_4) that there should be recognition of an intention (i_2) that there should be recognition of an intention (i_1) that the further effect should be produced; for it is no part of our intention that the further effect should be produced by way of recognition of our intention that it should be; the production in the audience of belief that *p* is intended to be itself the means whereby his attitude or conduct is to be influenced. We secure uptake, perform the act of communication that we set out to perform, if the audience understands us as *informing* him that *p*. Although it is true that, in saying what we say, we are in fact *trying* to produce the further effect – this is part of what we are doing, whether we succeed in producing the effect or not – yet this does not enter into the characterization of the illocutionary act. With this case we have to contrast the case in which, instead of aiming at a primary response and a further effect, the latter to be secured through the former alone, we aim at a complex primary response. Thus in the case where I do not simply inform, but warn, you that *p*, among the intentions I intend you to recognize (and intend you to recognize as intended to be recognized) are not only the intention to secure your belief that *p*, but the intention to secure that you are on your guard against *p*-perils. The difference (one of the differences) between showing off and warning is that your recognition of my intention to put you on your guard may well contribute to putting you on your guard, whereas your recognition of my intention to impress you is not likely to contribute to my impressing you (or not in the way I intended).[5]

Insinuating fails, for a different reason, to be a type of illocutionary act. An essential feature of the intentions which make up the illocutionary complex is their overtness. They have, one might say, essential avowability. This is, in one respect, a logically embarrassing feature. We have noticed already how we had to meet the threat of a counterexample to Grice's analysis of the communicative act in terms of three types of intention – (i_1), (i_2), and (i_3) – by the addition of a further intention (i_4) that an intention (i_2) should be recognized. We have no proof, however, that the resulting enlarged set of conditions is a complete analysis. Ingenuity might show it was not; and the way seems open to a regressive series of intentions that intentions should be recognized. While I do not think there is anything necessarily objectionable in this, it does suggest that the complete and rounded-off set of conditions aimed at in a conventional analysis is not easily and certainly attainable in these terms. That is why I speak of the feature in question as logically embarrassing. At the same time it enables us easily to dispose of insinuating as a candidate for the status of a type of illocutionary act. The whole point of insinuating is that the audience is to *suspect*, but not more than suspect, the intention, for example, to induce or disclose a certain belief. The intention one has in insinuating is essentially nonavowable.

Now let us take stock a little. We tentatively laid it down as a necessary condition of securing understanding of the illocutionary force of an utterance that the speaker should succeed in bringing it about that the audience took him, in issuing his utterance, to have a complex intention of a certain kind, namely the intention that the audience should recognize (and recognize as intended to be recognized) his intention to induce a certain response in the audience. The suggestion has, as we have just seen, certain explanatory merits. Nevertheless we cannot claim general application for it as even a partial analysis of the notions of illocutionary force and illocutionary act. Let us look at some reasons why not.

V

I remarked earlier that the words 'Don't go' may have the force, *inter alia*, either of a request or of an entreaty. In either case the primary intention of the utterance (if we presume the words to be uttered with the *sense* 'Don't go *away*') is that of inducing the person addressed to stay where he is. His staying where he is is the primary response aimed at. But the only other intentions mentioned in our scheme of partial analysis relate directly or indirectly to recognition of the primary intention. So how, in terms of that scheme, are we to account for the variation in illocutionary force between requests and entreaties?

This question does not appear to raise a major difficulty for the scheme. The scheme, it seems, merely requires supplementing and enriching. *Entreaty*, for example, is a matter of trying to secure the primary response not merely through audience recognition of the intention to secure it, but through audience recognition of a complex attitude of which this primary intention forms an integral part. A wish that someone should stay may be held in different ways: passionately or lightly, confidently or desperately; and it may, for different reasons, be part of a speaker's intention to secure recognition of *how* he holds it. The most obvious reason, in the case of entreaty, is the belief, or hope, that such a revelation is more likely to secure the fulfillment of the primary intention.

But one may not only request and entreat; one may *order* someone to stay where he is. The words 'Don't go' may have the illocutionary force of an order. Can we so simply accommodate in our scheme *this* variation in illocutionary force? Well, we can accommodate it; though not so simply. We can say that a man who issues an order typically intends his utterance to secure a certain response, that he intends this intention to be recognized, and its recognition to be a reason for the response, that he intends the utterance to be recognized as issued in a certain social context such that certain social rules or conventions apply to the issuing of utterances in this context and such that certain consequences may follow in the event of the primary response not being secured, that he intends *this* intention too to be recognized, and finally that he intends the recognition of these last features to function as an element in the reasons for the response on the part of the audience.

Evidently, in this case, unlike the case of entreaty, the scheme has to be extended to make room for explicit reference to social convention. It can, with some strain, be so extended. But as we move further into the region of institutionalized procedures, the strain becomes too much for the scheme to bear. On the one hand, one of its basic features – namely, the reference to an intention to secure a definite response in an audience (over and above the securing of uptake) – has to be dropped. On the other, the reference to social conventions of procedure assumes a very much greater importance. Consider an umpire giving a batsman out, a jury bringing in a verdict of guilty, a judge pronouncing sentence, a player redoubling at bridge, a priest or a civil officer pronouncing a couple man and wife. Can we say that the umpire's primary intention is to secure a certain response (say, retiring to the pavilion) from a certain audience (say, the batsman), the jurymen's to secure a certain response (say, the pronouncing of sentence) from a certain audience (say, the judge), and then build the rest of our account around this, as we did, with some strain, in the case of the order? Not with plausibility. It is not even possible, in other than a formal sense, to isolate, among all the participants in the procedure (trial, marriage, game) to which the utterance belongs, a particular audience to whom the utterance can be said to be addressed.

Does this mean that the approach I suggested to the elucidation of the notion of illocutionary force is entirely mistaken? I do not think so. Rather, we must distinguish types of case; and then see what, if anything, is common to the types we have distinguished. What we initially take from Grice – with modifications – is an at least partially analytical account of an act of communication, an act which might indeed be performed nonverbally and yet exhibit all the essential characteristics of a (nonverbal) equivalent of an illocutionary act. We gain more than this. For the account enables us to understand how such an act may be linguistically conventionalized right up to the point at which illocutionary force is exhausted by meaning (in Austin's sense); and in this understanding the notion of wholly overt or essentially avowable intention plays an essential part. Evidently, in these cases, the illocutionary act itself is not *essentially* a conventional act, an act done as conforming to a convention; it may be that the act is conventional, done as conforming to a convention, only in so far as *the means used to perform it* are conventional. To speak only of those conventional means which are also *linguistic* means, the extent to which the act is one done as conforming to conventions may depend solely on the extent to which conventional linguistic meaning exhausts illocutionary force.

At the other end of the scale – the end, we may say, from which Austin began – we have illocutionary acts which *are* essentially conventional. The examples I mentioned just now will serve – marrying, redoubling, giving out, pronouncing sentence, bringing in a verdict. Such acts could have no existence outside the rule- or convention-governed practices and procedures of which they essentially form parts. Let us take the standard case in which the participants in these procedures know the rules and their roles, and are trying to play the game and not wreck it. Then they are presented with occasions on which they have to, or may, perform an illocutionary act which forms part of, or furthers, the practice or procedure as a whole; and sometimes they have to make a decision within a restricted range of alternatives (for example, to pass or redouble, to pronounce sentence of imprisonment for some period not exceeding a certain limit). Between the case of such acts as these and the case of the illocutionary act not essentially conventional, there is an important likeness and an important difference. The likeness resides in the fact that, in the case of an utterance belonging to a convention-governed practice or procedure, the speaker's utterance is standardly *intended* to further, or affect the course of, the practice in question in some one of the alternative ways open, and intended to be recognized as so intended. I do not mean that such an act could *never* be performed *unintentionally*. A player might let slip the word 'redouble' without *meaning* to redouble; but if the circumstances are appropriate and the play strict, then he *has* redoubled (or he may be *held* to have redoubled). But a player who continually did this sort of thing would not be asked to play again, except by sharpers. Forms can take charge, in the absence of appropriate intention; but when they do, the case is *essentially* deviant or nonstandard. There is present in the standard case, that is to say, the same element of wholly overt and avowable intention as in the case of the act not essentially conventional.

The difference is a more complicated affair. We have, in these cases, an act which is conventional in two connected ways. First, if things go in accordance with the rules of the procedure in question, the act of furthering the practice in the way intended is an act required or permitted by those rules, an act done as falling under the rules. Second, the act is identified as the act it is just because it is performed by the utterance of a form of words conventional for the performance of that act. Hence the speaker's utterance is not only *intended* to further, or affect the course of, the practice in question in a certain conventional way; in the absence of any breach of the conventional conditions for furthering the procedure in this way, it cannot fail to do so.

And here we have the contrast between the two types of case. In the case of an illocutionary act of a kind not essentially conventional, the act of communication is performed if *uptake* is secured, if the utterance is taken to be issued with the complex overt intention with which it is issued. But even though the act of communication is performed, the wholly overt intention which lies at the core of the intention complex may, *without any breach of rules or conventions*, be frustrated. The audience response (belief, action, or attitude) may simply not be forthcoming. It is different with the utterance which forms part of a wholly convention-governed procedure. Granted that uptake is secured, then any frustration of the wholly overt intention of the utterance (the intention to further the procedure in a certain way) must be attributable to a breach of rule or conventions. The speaker who abides by the conventions can avowably have the intention to further the procedure in the way to which his current linguistic act is conventionally appropriated *only* if he takes it that the conventional conditions for so furthering it are satisfied and hence takes it *that his utterance will not only reveal his intentions but give them effect*. There is nothing parallel to this in the case of the illocutionary act of a kind not essentially conventional. In both cases, we may say, speakers assume the responsibility for making their intentions overt. In one case (the case of the convention-constituted procedure) the speaker who uses the explicitly performative form also explicitly assumes the responsibility for making his overt intention effective. But in the other case the speaker cannot, in the speech act itself, explicitly assume any such responsibility. For there are no conditions which can conventionally guarantee the effectiveness of his overt intention. Whether it is effective or not is something that rests with his audience. In the one case, therefore, the explicitly performative form *may* be the name of the very act which is performed if and only if the speaker's overt intention is effective; but in the other case it cannot be the name of this act. But of course – and I shall recur to this thought – the sharp contrast I have here drawn between two extreme types of case must not blind us to the existence of intermediate types.

Acts belonging to convention-constituted procedures of the kind I have just referred to form an important part of human communication. But they do not form the whole nor, we may think, the most fundamental part. It would be a mistake to take them as the model for understanding the notion of illocutionary force in general, as Austin perhaps shows some tendency to do when he both insists that the illocutionary act is essentially a conventional act and connects this claim with the possibility of making the act explicit by the use of the performative formula. It would equally be a mistake, as we have seen, to generalize the account of illocutionary force derived from Grice's analysis; for this would involve holding, falsely, that the complex overt intention manifested in any illocutionary act always includes the intention to secure a certain definite response or reaction in an audience over and above that which is necessarily secured if the illocutionary force of the utterance is understood. Nevertheless, we can perhaps extract from our consideration of two contrasting types of case something which is common to them both and to all the other types which lie between them. For the illocutionary force of an utterance is essentially something that is intended to be understood. And the understanding of the force of an utterance in all cases involves recognizing what may be called broadly an audience-directed intention and recognizing it as wholly overt, as intended to be recognized. It is perhaps this fact which lies at the base of the general possibility of the explicit performative formula; though, as we have seen, extra factors come importantly into play in the case of convention-constituted procedures.

Once this common element in all illocutionary acts is clear, we can readily acknowledge that the types of audience-directed intention involved may be very various and, also, that different types may be exemplified by one and the same utterance.

I have set in sharp contrast those cases in which the overt intention is simply to forward a definite and convention-governed practice (for example, a game) in a definite way provided for by the conventions or rules of the practice and those cases in which the overt intention includes that of securing a definite response (cognitive or practical) in an audience over and above that which is necessarily secured if uptake is secured. But there is something misleading about the sharpness of this contrast; and it would certainly be wrong to suppose that all cases fall clearly and neatly into one or another of these two classes. A speaker whose job it is to do so may offer information, instructions, or even advice, and yet be overtly indifferent as to whether or not his information is accepted as such, his instructions followed, or his advice taken. His wholly overt intention may amount to no more than that of making available – in a 'take it or leave it' spirit – to his audience the information or instructions or opinion in question; though again, in some cases, he may be seen as the mouthpiece, merely, of another agency to which may be attributed at least general intentions of the kind that can scarcely be attributed, in the particular case, to him. We should not find such complications discouraging;

for we can scarcely expect a general account of linguistic communication to yield more than schematic outlines, which may also be lost to view when every qualification is added which fidelity to the facts requires.

Notes

1. All references, unless otherwise indicated, are to *How To Do Things with Words* (Oxford, 1962).
2. I refer later to the need for qualification of this doctrine.
3. I owe the objections which follow to Professor Hart.
4. For an illocutionary act *may* be performed *altogether* unintentionally. See the examples about redoubling at bridge, p. 59 below.
5. Perhaps trying to impress might sometimes have an illocutionary character. For I might try to impress you with my *effrontery*, intending you to recognize this intention and intending your recognition of it to function as part of your reason for being impressed, and so forth. But then I am not *merely* trying to impress you; I am *inviting* you to be impressed. I owe this point to Mr. B. F. McGuinness.

Chapter 4

Logic and Conversation

H. P. Grice

It is a commonplace of philosophical logic that there are, or appear to be, divergences in meaning between, on the one hand, at least some of what I shall call the *formal* devices – $\sim$. $\wedge$, $\vee$, $\supset$, (x), $\exists(x)$, ιx (when these are given a standard two-valued interpretation) – and, on the other, what are taken to be their analogs or counterparts in natural language – such expressions as *not, and, or, if, all, some* (or *at least one*), *the*. Some logicians may at some time have wanted to claim that there are in fact no such divergences; but such claims, if made at all, have been somewhat rashly made, and those suspected of making them have been subjected to some pretty rough handling.

Those who concede that such divergences exist adhere, in the main, to one or the other of two rival groups, which for the purposes of this article I shall call the formalist and the informalist groups. An outline of a not uncharacteristic formalist position may be given as follows: Insofar as logicians are concerned with the formulation of very general patterns of valid inference, the formal devices possess a decisive advantage over their natural counterparts. For it will be possible to construct in terms of the formal devices a system of very general formulas, a considerable number of which can be regarded as, or are closely related to, patterns of inferences the expression of which involves some or all of the devices: Such a system may consist of a certain set of simple formulas that must be acceptable if the devices have the meaning that has been assigned to them, and an indefinite number of further formulas, many of them less obviously acceptable, each of which can be shown to be acceptable if the members of the original set are acceptable. We have, thus, a way of handling dubiously acceptable patterns of inference, and if, as is

From Cole and Morgan (eds) *Syntax and Semantics*, Vol. 3, Speech Acts. Academic Press, 1975.

sometimes possible, we can apply a decision procedure, we have an even better way. Furthermore, from a philosophical point of view, the possession by the natural counterparts of those elements in their meaning, which they do not share with the corresponding formal devices, is to be regarded as an imperfection of natural languages; the elements in question are undesirable excrescences. For the presence of these elements has the result that the concepts within which they appear cannot be precisely/clearly defined, and that at least some statements involving them cannot, in some circumstances, be assigned a definite truth value; and the indefiniteness of these concepts is not only objectionable in itself but leaves open the way to metaphysics – we cannot be certain that none of these natural language expressions is metaphysically 'loaded'. For these reasons, the expressions, as used in natural speech, cannot be regarded as finally acceptable, and may turn out to be, finally, not fully intelligible. The proper course is to conceive and begin to construct an ideal language, incorporating the formal devices, the sentences of which will be clear, determinate in truth value, and certifiably free from metaphysical implications; the foundations of science will now be philosophically secure, since the statements of the scientist will be expressible (though not necessarily actually expressed) within this ideal language. (I do not wish to suggest that all formalists would accept the whole of this outline, but I think that all would accept at least some part of it.)

To this, an informalist might reply in the following vein. The philosophical demand for an ideal language rests on certain assumptions that should not be conceded; these are, that the primary yardstick by which to judge the adequacy of a language is its ability to serve the needs of science, that an expression cannot be guaranteed as fully intelligible unless an explication or analysis of its meaning has been provided, and that every explication or analysis must take the form of a precise definition that is the expression/assertion of a logical equivalence. Language serves many important purposes besides those of scientific inquiry; we can know perfectly well what an expression means (and so a fortiori that it is intelligible) without knowing its analysis, and the provision of an analysis may (and usually does) consist in the specification, as generalized as possible, of the conditions that count for or against the applicability of the expression being analyzed. Moreover, while it is no doubt true that the formal devices are especially amenable to systematic treatment by the logician, it remains the case that there are very many inferences and arguments, expressed in natural language and not in terms of these devices, that are nevertheless recognizably valid. So there must be a place for an unsimplified, and so more or less unsystematic, logic of the natural counterparts of these devices; this logic may be aided and guided by the simplified logic of the formal devices but cannot be supplanted by it; indeed, not only do the two logics differ, but sometimes they come into conflict; rules that hold for a formal device may not hold for its natural counterpart.

Now, on the general question of the place in philosophy of the reformation of natural language, I shall, in this article, have nothing to say. I shall confine myself to the dispute in its relation to the alleged divergences mentioned at the outset. I have, moreover, no intention of entering the fray on behalf of either contestant. I wish, rather, to maintain that the common assumption of the contestants that the divergences do in fact exist is (broadly speaking) a common mistake, and that the mistake arises from an inadequate attention to the nature and importance of the conditions governing conversation. I shall, therefore, proceed at once to inquire into the general conditions that, in one way or another, apply to conversation as such, irrespective of its subject matter.

Implicature

Suppose that A and B are talking about a mutual friend C, who is now working in a bank. A asks B how C is getting on in his job, and B replies, *Oh quite well, I think; he likes his colleagues, and he hasn't been to prison yet.* At this point, A might well inquire what B was implying, what he was suggesting, or even what he meant by saying that C had not yet been to prison. The answer might be any one of such things as that C is the sort of person likely to yield to the temptation provided by his occupation, that C's colleagues are really very unpleasant and treacherous people, and so forth. It might, of course, be quite unnecessary for A to make such an inquiry of B, the answer to it being, in the context, clear in advance. I think it is clear that whatever B implied, suggested, meant, etc., in this example, is distinct from what B said, which was simply that C had not been to prison yet. I wish to introduce, as terms of art, the verb *implicate* and the related nouns *implicature* (cf. *implying*) and *implicatum* (cf. *what is implied*). The point of this maneuver is to avoid having, on each occasion, to choose between this or that member of the family of verbs for which *implicate* is to do general duty. I shall, for the time being at least, have to assume to a considerable extent an intuitive understanding of the meaning of *say* in such contexts, and an ability to recognize particular verbs as members of the family with which *implicate* is associated. I can, however, make one or two remarks that may help to clarify the more problematic of these assumptions, namely, that connected with the meaning of the word *say*.

In the sense in which I am using the word *say*, I intend what someone has said to be closely related to the conventional meaning of the words (the sentence) he has uttered. Suppose someone to have uttered the sentence *He is in the grip of a vice*. Given a knowledge of the English language, but no knowledge of the circumstances of the utterance, one would know something about what the speaker had said, on the assumption that he was speaking standard English, and speaking literally. One would know that he had said, about some particular male person or animal *x*, that at the time of the utterance (whatever that was), either (1) *x* was unable to rid himself of a certain kind of bad character trait or (2) some part of *x*'s person was caught in a certain kind of tool or instrument (approximate account, of course). But for a full identification of what the speaker had said, one would need to know (a) the identity of *x*, (b) the time of utterance, and (c) the meaning, on the particular occasion of utterance, of the phrase *in the grip of a vice* [a decision between (1) and (2)]. This brief indication of my use of *say* leaves it open whether a man who says (today) *Harold Wilson is a great man* and another who says (also today) *The British Prime Minister is a great man* would, if each knew that the two singular terms had the same reference, have said the same thing. But whatever decision is made about this question, the apparatus that I am about to provide will be capable of accounting for any implicatures that might depend on the presence of one rather than another of these singular terms in the sentence uttered. Such implicatures would merely be related to different maxims.

In some cases the conventional meaning of the words used will determine what is implicated, besides helping to determine what is said. If I say (smugly), *He is an Englishman; he is, therefore, brave*, I have certainly committed myself, by virtue of the meaning of my words, to its being the case that his being brave is a consequence of (follows from) his being an Englishman. But while I have said that he is an Englishman, and said that he is brave, I do not want to say that I have *said* (in the favored sense) that it follows from his being an Englishman that he is brave, though I have certainly indicated, and so implicated, that this is so. I do not want to say that my utterance of this sentence would be, *strictly speaking*, false should the consequence in question fail to hold. So *some* implicatures are conventional, unlike the one with which I introduced this discussion of implicature.

I wish to represent a certain subclass of nonconventional implicatures, which I shall call *conversational* implicatures, as being essentially connected with certain general features of discourse; so my next step is to try to say what these features are.

The following may provide a first approximation to a general principle. Our talk exchanges do not normally consist of a succession of disconnected remarks, and would not be rational if they did. They are characteristically, to some degree at least, cooperative efforts; and each participant recognizes in them, to some extent, a common purpose or set of purposes, or at least a mutually accepted direction. This purpose or direction may be fixed from the start (e.g., by an initial proposal of a question for discussion), or it may evolve during the exchange; it may be fairly definite, or it may be so indefinite as to leave very considerable latitude on the participants (as in a casual conversation). But at each stage, *some* possible conversational moves would be excluded as conversationally unsuitable. We might then formulate a rough general principle which participants will be expected (ceteris paribus) to observe, namely: Make your conversational contribution such as is required, at the stage at which it occurs, by the accepted purpose or direction of the talk exchange in which you are engaged. One might label this the *Cooperative Principle.*

On the assumption that some such general principle as this is acceptable, one may perhaps distinguish four categories under one or another of which will fall certain more specific maxims and submaxims, the following of which will, in general, yield results in accordance with the Cooperative Principle. Echoing Kant, I call these categories Quantity, Quality, Relation, and Manner. The category of *Quantity* relates to the quantity of information to be provided, and under it fall the following maxims:

1. Make your contribution as informative as is required (for the current purposes of the exchange).
2. Do not make your contribution more informative than is required.

(The second maxim is disputable; it might be said that to be overinformative is not a transgression of the CP but merely a waste of time. However, it might be answered that such overinformativeness may be confusing in that it is liable to raise side issues; and there may also be an indirect effect, in that the hearers may be misled as a result of thinking that there is some particular *point* in the provision of the excess of information. However this may be, there is perhaps a different reason for doubt about the admission of this second maxim, namely, that its effect will be secured by a later maxim, which concerns relevance.)

Under the category of *Quality* falls a supermaxim – 'Try to make your contribution one that is true' – and two more specific maxims:

1. Do not say what you believe to be false.
2. Do not say that for which you lack adequate evidence.

Under the category of *Relation* I place a single maxim, namely, 'Be relevant.' Though the maxim itself is terse, its formulation conceals a number of problems that exercise me a good deal: questions about what different kinds and focuses of relevance there may be, how these shift in the course of a talk exchange, how to allow for the fact that subjects of conversation are legitimately changed, and so on. I find the treatment of such questions exceedingly difficult, and I hope to revert to them in a later work.

Finally, under the category of *Manner*, which I understand as relating not (like the previous categories) to what is said but, rather, to *how* what is said is to be said, I include the supermaxim – 'Be perspicuous' – and various maxims such as:

1. Avoid obscurity of expression.
2. Avoid ambiguity.

3. Be brief (avoid unnecessary prolixity).
4. Be orderly.

And one might need others.

It is obvious that the observance of some of these maxims is a matter of less urgency than is the observance of others; a man who has expressed himself with undue prolixity would, in general, be open to milder comment than would a man who has said something he believes to be false. Indeed, it might be felt that the importance of at least the first maxim of Quality is such that it should not be included in a scheme of the kind I am constructing; other maxims come into operation only on the assumption that this maxim of Quality is satisfied. While this may be correct, so far as the generation of implicatures is concerned it seems to play a role not totally different from the other maxims, and it will be convenient, for the present at least, to treat it as a member of the list of maxims.

There are, of course, all sorts of other maxims (aesthetic, social, or moral in character), such as 'Be polite', that are also normally observed by participants in talk exchanges, and these may also generate nonconventional implicatures. The conversational maxims, however, and the conversational implicatures connected with them, are specially connected (I hope) with the particular purposes that talk (and so, talk exchange) is adapted to serve and is primarily employed to serve. I have stated my maxims as if this purpose were a maximally effective exchange of information; this specification is, of course, too narrow, and the scheme needs to be generalized to allow for such general purposes as influencing or directing the actions of others.

As one of my avowed aims is to see talking as a special case or variety of purposive, indeed rational, behavior, it may be worth noting that the specific expectations or presumptions connected with at least some of the foregoing maxims have their analogues in the sphere of transactions that are not talk exchanges. I list briefly one such analog for each conversational category.

1. **Quantity.** If you are assisting me to mend a car, I expect your contribution to be neither more nor less than is required; if, for example, at a particular stage I need four screws, I expect you to hand me four, rather than two or six.
2. **Quality.** I expect your contributions to be genuine and not spurious. If I need sugar as an ingredient in the cake you are assisting me to make, I do not expect you to hand me salt; if I need a spoon, I do not expect a trick spoon made of rubber.
3. **Relation.** I expect a partner's contribution to be appropriate to immediate needs at each stage of the transaction; if I am mixing ingredients for a cake, I do not expect to be handed a good book, or even an oven cloth (though this might be an appropriate contribution at a later stage).

4. **Manner.** I expect a partner to make it clear what contribution he is making, and to execute his performance with reasonable dispatch.

These analogies are relevant to what I regard as a fundamental question about the CP and its attendant maxims, namely, what the basis is for the assumption which we seem to make, and on which (I hope) it will appear that a great range of implicatures depend, that talkers will in general (ceteris paribus and in the absence of indications to the contrary) proceed in the manner that these principles prescribe. A dull but, no doubt at a certain level, adequate answer is that it is just a well-recognized empirical fact that people *do* behave in these ways; they have learned to do so in childhood and not lost the habit of doing so; and, indeed, it would involve a good deal of effort to make a radical departure from the habit. It is much easier, for example, to tell the truth than to invent lies.

I am, however, enough of a rationalist to want to find a basis that underlies these facts, undeniable though they may be; I would like to be able to think of the standard type of conversational practice not merely as something that all or most do *in fact* follow but as something that it is *reasonable* for us to follow, that we *should not* abandon. For a time, I was attracted by the idea that observance of the CP and the maxims, in a talk exchange, could be thought of as a quasi-contractual matter, with parallels outside the realm of discourse. If you pass by when I am struggling with my stranded car, I no doubt have some degree of expectation that you will offer help, but once you join me in tinkering under the hood, my expectations become stronger and take more specific forms (in the absence of indications that you are merely an incompetent meddler); and talk exchanges seemed to me to exhibit, characteristically, certain features that jointly distinguish cooperative transactions:

1. The participants have some common immediate aim, like getting a car mended; their ultimate aims may, of course, be independent and even in conflict – each may want to get the car mended in order to drive off, leaving the other stranded. In characteristic talk exchanges, there is a common aim even if, as in an over-the-wall chat, it is a second-order one, namely, that each party should, for the time being, identify himself with the transitory conversational interests of the other.
2. The contributions of the participants should be dovetailed, mutually dependent.
3. There is some sort of understanding (which may be explicit but which is often tacit) that, other things being equal, the transaction should continue in appropriate style unless both parties are agreeable that it should terminate. You do not just shove off or start doing something else.

But while some such quasi-contractual basis as this may apply to some cases, there are too many types of exchange, like quarreling and letter writing, that it fails to fit comfortably. In any case, one feels that the talker who is irrelevant or obscure has primarily let down not his audience but himself. So I would like to be able to show that observance of the CP and maxims is reasonable (rational) along the following lines: that any one who cares about the goals that are central to conversation/communication (e.g., giving and receiving information, influencing and being influenced by others) must be expected to have an interest, given suitable circumstances, in participation in talk exchanges that will be profitable only on the assumption that they are conducted in general accordance with the CP and the maxims. Whether any such conclusion can be reached, I am uncertain; in any case, I am fairly sure that I cannot reach it until I am a good deal clearer about the nature of relevance and of the circumstances in which it is required.

It is now time to show the connection between the CP and maxims, on the one hand, and conversational implicature on the other.

A participant in a talk exchange may fail to fulfill a maxim in various ways, which include the following:

1. He may quietly and unostentatiously *violate* a maxim; if so, in some cases he will be liable to mislead.
2. He may *opt out* from the operation both of the maxim and of the CP; he may say, indicate, or allow it to become plain that he is unwilling to cooperate in the way the maxim requires. He may say, for example, *I cannot say more; my lips are sealed.*
3. He may be faced by a *clash*: He may be unable, for example, to fulfill the first maxim of Quantity (Be as informative as is required) without violating the second maxim of Quality (Have adequate evidence for what you say).
4. He may *flout* a maxim; that is, he may *blatantly* fail to fulfill it. On the assumption that the speaker is able to fulfill the maxim and to do so without violating another maxim (because of a clash), is not opting out, and is not, in view of the blatancy of his performance, trying to mislead, the hearer is faced with a minor problem: How can his saying what he did say be reconciled with the supposition that he is observing the overall CP? This situation is one that characteristically gives rise to a conversational implicature; and when a conversational implicature is generated in this way, I shall say that a maxim is being *exploited.*

I am now in a position to characterize the notion of conversational implicature. A man who, by (in, when) saying (or making as if to say) that *p* has implicated that *q*, may be said to have conversationally implicated that *q*, *provided that* (1) he is to be presumed to be observing the conversational maxims, or at least the cooperative principle; (2) the supposition that he is aware that, or thinks that, *q* is required in order to make his saying or making as if to say *p* (or doing so in *those* terms) consistent with this presumption;

and (3) the speaker thinks (and would expect the hearer to think that the speaker thinks) that it is within the competence of the hearer to work out, or grasp intuitively, that the supposition mentioned in (2) *is* required. Apply this to my initial example, to B's remark that C has not yet been to prison. In a suitable setting A might reason as follows: '(1) B has apparently violated the maxim 'Be relevant' and so may be regarded as having flouted one of the maxims conjoining perspicuity, yet I have no reason to suppose that he is opting out from the operation of the CP; (2) given the circumstances, I can regard his irrelevance as only apparent if, and only if, I suppose him to think that C is potentially dishonest; (3) B knows that I am capable of working out step (2). So B implicates that C is potentially dishonest.'

The presence of a conversational implicature must be capable of being worked out; for even if it can in fact be intuitively grasped, unless the intuition is replaceable by an argument, the implicature (if present at all) will not count as a *Conversational* implicature; it will be a *Conventional* implicature. To work out that a particular conversational implicature is present, the hearer will rely on the following data: (1) the conventional meaning of the words used, together with the identity of any references that may be involved; (2) the CP and its maxims; (3) the context, linguistic or otherwise, of the utterance; (4) other items of background knowledge; and (5) the fact (or supposed fact) that all relevant items falling under the previous headings are available to both participants and both participants know or assume this to be the case. A general pattern for the working out of a conversational implicature might be given as follows: 'He has said that *p*; there is no reason to suppose that he is not observing the maxims, or at least the CP; he could not be doing this unless he thought that *q*; he knows (and knows that I know that he knows) that I can see that the supposition that he thinks that *q is* required; he has done nothing to stop me thinking that *q*; he intends me to think, or is at least willing to allow me to think, that *q*; and so he has implicated that *q*.'

Examples

I shall now offer a number of examples, which I shall divide into three groups.

Group A: Examples in which no maxim is violated, or at least in which it is not clear that any maxim is violated

A is standing by an obviously immobilized car and is approached by B; the following exchange takes place:

(1) A: I am out of petrol.
B: There is a garage round the corner.

(Gloss: B would be infringing the maxim 'Be relevant' unless he thinks, or thinks it possible, that the garage is open, and has petrol to sell; so he implicates that the garage is, or at least may be open, etc.)

In this example, unlike the case of the remark *He hasn't been to prison yet*, the unstated connection between B's remark and A's remark is so obvious that, even if one interprets the supermaxim of Manner, 'Be perspicuous,' as applying not only to the expression of what is said but also to the connection of what is said with adjacent remarks, there seems to be no case for regarding that supermaxim as infringed in this example. The next example is perhaps a little less clear in this respect:

(2) A: Smith doesn't seem to have a girlfriend these days.
B: He has been paying a lot of visits to New York lately.

B implicates that Smith has, or may have, a girlfriend in New York. (A gloss is unnecessary in view of that given for the previous example.)

In both examples, the speaker implicates that which he must be assumed to believe in order to preserve the assumption that he is observing the maxim of relation.

Group B: An example in which a maxim is violated, but its violation is to be explained by the supposition of a clash with another maxim

A is planning with B an itinerary for a holiday in France. Both know that A wants to see his friend C, if to do so would not involve too great a prolongation of his journey:

(3) A: Where does C live?
B: Somewhere in the South of France.

(Gloss: There is no reason to suppose that B is opting out; his answer is, as he well knows, less informative than is required to meet A's needs. This infringement of the first maxim of Quantity can be explained only by the supposition that B is aware that to be more informative would be to say something that infringed the maxim of Quality, 'Don't say what you lack adequate evidence for', so B implicates that he does not know in which town C lives.)

Group C: Examples that involve exploitation, that is, a procedure by which a maxim is flouted for the purpose of getting in a conversational implicature by means of something of the nature of a figure of speech

In these examples, though some maxim is violated at the level of what is said, the hearer is entitled to assume that that maxim, or at least the overall Cooperative Principle, is observed at the level of what is implicated.

(1a) A flouting of the first maxim of Quantity

A is writing a testimonial about a pupil who is a candidate for a philosophy job, and his letter reads as follows: 'Dear Sir, Mr. X's command of English is excellent, and his attendance at tutorials has been regular. Yours, etc.' (Gloss: A cannot be opting out, since if he wished to be uncooperative, why write at all? He cannot be unable, through ignorance, to say more, since the man is his pupil; moreover, he knows that more information than this is wanted. He must, therefore, be wishing to impart information that he is reluctant to write down. This supposition is tenable only on the assumption that he thinks Mr. X is no good at philosophy. This, then, is what he is implicating.)

Extreme examples of a flouting of the first maxim of Quantity are provided by utterances of patent tautologies like *Women are women* and *War is war*. I would wish to maintain that at the level of what is said, in my favored sense, such remarks are totally noninformative and so, at that level, cannot but infringe the first maxim of Quantity in any conversational context. They are, of course, informative at the level of what is implicated, and the hearer's identification of their informative content at this level is dependent on his ability to explain the speaker's selection of this *particular* patent tautology.

(3b) An infringement of the second maxim of Quantity, 'Do not give more information than is required', on the assumption that the existence of such a maxim should be admitted

A wants to know whether *p*, and B volunteers not only the information that *p*, but information to the effect that it is certain that *p*, and that the evidence for its being the case that *p* is so-and-so and such-and-such.

B's volubility may be undesigned, and if it is so regarded by A it may raise in A's mind a doubt as to whether B is as certain as he says he is ('Methinks the lady doth protest too much'). But if it is thought of as designed, it would be an oblique way of conveying that it is to some degree controversial whether or not *p*. It is, however, arguable that such an implicature could be explained by reference to the maxim of Relation without invoking an alleged second maxim of Quantity.

(2a) Examples in which the first maxim of Quality is flouted

1. **Irony.** X, with whom A has been on close terms until now, has betrayed a secret of A's to a business rival. A and his audience both know this. A says '*X is a fine friend*'. (Gloss: It is perfectly obvious to A and his audience that what A has said or has made as if to say is something he does not believe, and the audience knows that A knows that this is obvious to the audience. So, unless A's utterance is entirely pointless, A

must be trying to get across some other proposition than the one he purports to be putting forward. This must be some obviously related proposition; the most obviously related proposition is the contradictory of the one he purports to be putting forward.)

2. **Metaphor.** Examples like *You are the cream in my coffee* characteristically involve categorial falsity, so the contradictory of what the speaker has made as if to say will, strictly speaking, be a truism; so it cannot be *that* that such a speaker is trying to get across. The most likely supposition is that the speaker is attributing to his audience some feature or features in respect of which the audience resembles (more or less fancifully) the mentioned substance.

   It is possible to combine metaphor and irony by imposing on the hearer two stages of interpretation. I say *You are the cream in my coffee*, intending the hearer to reach first the metaphor interpretant 'You are my pride and joy' and then the irony interpretant 'You are my bane.'
3. **Meiosis.** Of a man known to have broken up all the furniture, one says *He was a little intoxicated.*
4. **Hyperbole.** Every nice girl loves a sailor.

(**2b**) Examples in which the second maxim of Quality, 'Do not say that for which you lack adequate evidence', is flouted are perhaps not easy to find, but the following seems to be a specimen. I say of X's wife, *She is probably deceiving him this evening.* In a suitable context, or with a suitable gesture or tone of voice, it may be clear that I have no adequate reason for supposing this to be the case. My partner, to preserve the assumption that the conversational game is still being played, assumes that I am getting at some related proposition for the acceptance of which I *do* have a reasonable basis. The related proposition might well be that she is given to deceiving her husband, or possibly that she is the sort of person who would not stop short of such conduct.

(3) *Examples in which an implicature is achieved by real, as distinct from apparent, violation of the maxim of Relation* are perhaps rare, but the following seems to be a good candidate. At a genteel tea party, A says *Mrs. X is an old bag.* There is a moment of appalled silence, and then B says *The weather has been quite delightful this summer, hasn't it?* B has blatantly refused to make what *he* says relevant to A's preceding remark. He thereby implicates that A's remark should not be discussed and, perhaps more specifically, that A has committed a social gaffe.

(4) Examples in which various maxims falling under the supermaxim 'be perspicuous' are flouted

1. *Ambiguity*. We must remember that we are concerned only with ambiguity that is deliberate, and that the speaker intends or expects to be recognized by his hearer. The problem the hearer has to solve is why a speaker should, when still playing the conversational game, go out of his way to choose an ambiguous utterance. There are two types of cases:
   (a) Examples in which there is no difference, or no striking difference, between two interpretations of an utterance with respect to straightforwardness; neither interpretation is notably more sophisticated, less standard, more recondite or more far-fetched than the other. We might consider Blake's lines: 'Never seek to tell thy love, Love that never told can be.' To avoid the complications introduced by the presence of the imperative mood, I shall consider the related sentence, *I sought to tell my love, love that never told can be.* There may be a double ambiguity here. *My love* may refer to either a state of emotion or an object of emotion, and *love that never told can be* may mean either 'Love that cannot be told' or 'love that if told cannot continue to exist.' Partly because of the sophistication of the poet and partly because of internal evidence (that the ambiguity is kept up), there seems to be no alternative to supposing that the ambiguities are deliberate and that the poet is conveying both what he would be saying if one interpretation were intended rather than the other, and vice versa; though no doubt the poet is not explicitly *saying* any one of these things but only conveying or suggesting them (cf. 'Since she [nature] pricked thee out of women's pleasure, mine be thy love, and thy love's use their treasure.)
   (b) Examples in which one interpretation is notably less straightforward than another. Take the complex example of the British General who captured the town of Sind and sent back the message *Peccavi.* The ambiguity involved ('I have Sind'/'I have sinned') is phonemic, not morphemic; and the expression actually used is unambiguous, but since it is in a language foreign to speaker and hearer, translation is called for, and the ambiguity resides in the standard translation into native English.

   Whether or not the straightforward interpretant ('I have sinned') is being conveyed, it seems that the nonstraightforward must be. There might be stylistic reasons for conveying by a sentence merely its nonstraightforward interpretant, but it would be pointless, and perhaps also stylistically objectionable, to go to the trouble of finding an expression that nonstraightforwardly conveys that *p*, thus imposing on an audience the effort involved in finding this interpretant, if this interpretant were otiose so far as communication was concerned. Whether the straightforward interpretant is also being conveyed seems to depend on whether such a supposition would conflict with other conversational requirements, for example, would it be relevant, would it be something the speaker could be supposed to accept, and so on. If such requirements are not satisfied, then the straightforward interpretant is not being conveyed. If they are, it is. If the author of *Peccavi* could naturally be supposed to think that he had committed some kind of transgression, for example, had disobeyed his orders in capturing Sind, and if reference to such a transgression would be relevant to the presumed interests of the audience, then he would have been conveying both interpretants; otherwise he would be conveying only the nonstraightforward one.

2. *Obscurity.* How do I exploit, for the purposes of communication, a deliberate and overt violation of the requirement that I should avoid obscurity? Obviously, if the Cooperative Principle is to operate, I must intend my partner to understand what I am saying despite the obscurity I import into my utterance. Suppose that A and B are having a conversation in the presence of a third party, for example, a child, then A might be deliberately obscure, though not too obscure, in the hope that B would understand and the third party not. Furthermore, if A expects B to see that A is being deliberately obscure, it seems reasonable to suppose that, in making his conversational contribution in this way, A is implicating that the contents of his communication should not be imparted to the third party.
3. *Failure to be brief or succinct.* Compare the remarks:

   (a) Miss X sang 'Home sweet home'
   (b) Miss X produced a series of sounds that corresponded closely with the score of 'Home sweet home'.

   Suppose that a reviewer has chosen to utter (b) rather than (a). (Gloss: Why has he selected that rigmarole in place of the concise and nearly synonymous *sang?* Presumably, to indicate some striking difference between Miss X's performance and those to which the word *singing* is usually applied. The most obvious supposition is that Miss X's performance suffered from some hideous defect. The reviewer knows that this supposition is what is likely to spring to mind, so that is what he is implicating.)

I have so far considered only cases of what I might call particularized conversational implicature – that is to say, cases in which an implicature is carried by saying that *p* on a particular occasion in virtue of special features of the context, cases in which there is no room for the idea that an implicature of this sort is *normally* carried by saying that *p*. But there are cases of generalized conversational implicature. Sometimes one can say that the use of a certain form of words in an utterance would normally (in the *absence* of special circumstances) carry such-and-such an implicature or type of implicature. Noncontroversial examples are perhaps hard to find, since it is all too easy to treat a generalized conversational implicature as if it were a conventional implicature. I offer an example that I hope may be fairly noncontroversial.

Anyone who uses a sentence of the form *X is meeting a woman this evening* would normally implicate that the person to be met was someone other than X's wife, mother, sister, or perhaps even close platonic friend. Similarly, if I were to say *X went into a house yesterday and found a tortoise inside the front door*, my hearer would normally be surprised if some time later I revealed that the house was X's own. I could produce similar linguistic phenomena involving the expressions *a garden, a car, a college,* and so on. Sometimes, however, there would normally be no such implicature ('I have been sitting in a car all morning'), and sometimes a reverse implicature ('I broke a finger yesterday'). I am inclined to think that one would not lend a sympathetic ear to a philosopher who suggested that there are three senses of the form of expression *an X*: one in which it means roughly 'something that satisfies the conditions defining the word *X*,' another in which it means approximately 'an X (in the first sense) that is only remotely related in a certain way to some person indicated by the context,' and yet another in which it means 'an X (in the first sense) that is closely related in a certain way to some person indicated by the context.' Would we not much prefer an account on the following lines (which, of course, may be incorrect in detail): When someone, by using the form of expression *an X*, implicates that the X does not belong to or is not otherwise closely connected with some identifiable person, the implicature is present because the speaker has failed to be specific in a way in which he might have been expected to be specific, with the consequence that it is likely to be assumed that he is not in a position to be specific. This is a familiar implicature situation and is classifiable as a failure, for one reason or another, to fulfill the first maxim of Quantity. The only difficult question is why it should, in certain cases, be presumed, independently of information about particular contexts of utterance, that specification of the closeness or remoteness of the connection between a particular person or object and a further person who is mentioned or indicated by the utterance should be likely to be of interest. The answer must lie in the following region: Transactions between a person and other persons or things closely connected with him are liable to be very different as regards their concomitants and results from the same sort of transactions involving only remotely connected persons or things; the concomitants and results, for instance, of my finding a hole in *my* roof are likely to be very different from the concomitants and results of my finding a hole in someone else's roof. Information, like money, is often given without the giver's knowing to just what use the recipient will want to put it. If someone to whom a transaction is mentioned gives it further consideration, he is likely to find himself wanting the answers to further questions that the speaker may not be able to identify in advance; if the appropriate specification will be likely to enable the hearer to answer a considerable variety of such questions for himself, then there is a presumption that the speaker should include it in his remark; if not, then there is no such presumption.

Finally, we can now show that, conversational implicature being what it is, it must possess certain features:

1. Since to assume the presence of a conversational implicature, we have to assume that at least the Cooperative Principle is being observed, and since it is possible to opt out of the observation of this principle, it follows that a generalized conversational implicature can be canceled in a particular case. It may be explicitly canceled, by the addition of a clause that states or implies that the speaker has opted out, or it may be contextually canceled, if the form of utterance that usually carries it is used in a context that makes it clear that the speaker *is* opting out.
2. Insofar as the calculation that a particular conversational implicature is present requires, besides contextual and background information, only a knowledge of what has been said (or of the conventional commitment of the utterance), and insofar as the manner of expression plays no role in the calculation, it will not be possible to find another way of saying the same thing, which simply lacks the implicature in question, except where some special feature of the substituted version is itself relevant to the determination of an implicature (in virtue of one of the maxims of Manner). If we call this feature *nondetachability*, one may expect a generalized conversational implicature that is carried by a familiar, nonspecial locution to have a high degree of nondetachability.
3. To speak approximately, since the calculation of the presence of a conversational implicature presupposes an initial knowledge of the conventional force of the expression the utterance of which carries the implicature, a conversational implicatum will be a condition that is not included in the original specification of the expression's conventional force. Though it may not be impossible for what starts life, so to speak, as a conversational implicature to become conventionalized, to suppose that this is so in a given case would require special justification. So, initially at least, conversational implicata are not part of the meaning of the expressions to the employment of which they attach.
4. Since the truth of a conversational implicatum is not required by the truth of what is said (what is said may be true – what is implicated may be false), the implicature is not carried by what is said, but only by the saying of what is said, or by 'putting it that way.'
5. Since, to calculate a conversational implicature is to calculate what has to be supposed in order to preserve the supposition that the Cooperative Principle is being observed, and since there may be various possible

specific explanations, a list of which may be open, the conversational implicatum in such cases will be disjunction of such specific explanations; and if the list of these is open, the implicatum will have just the kind of indeterminacy that many actual implicata do in fact seem to possess.

Chapter 5

How Performatives Work[1]

J. R. Searle

The notion of a performative is one that philosophers and linguists are so comfortable with that one gets the impression that somebody must have a satisfactory theory. But I have not seen such a theory and in this article I want to address the question: how exactly do performatives work? I believe that answering that question is not just a fussy exercise in linguistic analysis but can give us insights into the nature of language and the relation between speech acts and actions generally. Some people who have written about performatives[2] seem to think that it is just a semantic fact about certain verbs that they have performative occurrences, but the puzzle is: how could any verbs have such remarkable properties just as a matter of semantics? I can't fix the roof by saying, 'I fix the roof' and I can't fry an egg by saying, 'I fry an egg,' but I can promise to come and see you just by saying, 'I promise to come and see you' and I can order you to leave the room just by saying, 'I order you to leave the room.' Now why the one and not the other? And, to repeat, how exactly does it work? Perhaps the most widely accepted current view is the following: performative utterances are really just statements with truth values like any other statements, and Austin was wrong to contrast performative utterances with some other kind.[3] The only special feature of the performative statement is that the speaker can perform some other speech act indirectly by making the statement. And the task of a theory of performatives is to explain how the speaker can intend and the hearer can understand a second speech act from the making of the first speech act, the statement.

I have not seen an account of performatives that I thought was satisfactory. Therefore, in this paper I will attempt to:

First published in *Linguistics and Philosophy*, 12: 535–58, 1989.

1. Characterize performatives in a way that will enable us to give a (fairly) precise statement of the problem;
2. State the conditions of adequacy on any solution;
3. Show that certain analyses of performatives fail;
4. Introduce the elements of the apparatus necessary to solve the problem; and
5. Suggest a solution.

What Exactly is a Performative?

The word 'performative' has had a very confusing history and I need to make clear at the start how I am using it. Austin originally introduced the notion of *performatives* to contrast them with *constatives*; and his idea was that performatives were *actions*, such as making a promise or giving an order; and constatives were *sayings*, such as making a statement or giving a description. Constatives, but not performatives, could be true or false. But that distinction didn't work, because stating and describing are just as much actions as promising and ordering, and some performatives, such as warnings, can be true or false. Furthermore statements can be made with explicit performative verbs, as in 'I hereby state that it is raining.' So it looked for a while as if he would have to say that every utterance was a performative, and that would render the notion useless. Another distinction which didn't work is that between explicit and implicit performatives, e.g., the distinction between 'I promise to come' (explicit) and 'I intend to come' (implicit). This distinction doesn't work because in the sense in which the explicit performatives are performatives the implicit cases aren't performative at all. If I say, 'I intend to come.' I have literally just made a statement about my intention. (Though, of course, in making such a statement, I might also indirectly be making a promise.)

I believe the correct way to situate the notion of performatives within a general theory of speech acts is as follows: some illocutionary acts can be performed by uttering a sentence containing an expression that names the type of speech act, as in for example, 'I order you to leave the room.' These utterances, and only these, are correctly described as performative utterances. On my usage, the only performatives are what Austin called 'explicit performatives.' Thus, though every utterance is indeed a *performance*, only a very restricted class are *performatives*.

If we adopt this usage, it now becomes essential to distinguish between performative utterances, performative sentences, and performative verbs. As I shall use these expressions a *performative sentence* is a sentence whose literal utterance in appropriate circumstances constitutes the performance of an illocutionary act named by an expression in that very sentence in virtue of the occurrence of that expression. A *performative utterance* is an utterance of a performative sentence token, such that the utterance constitutes the performance of the act named by the performative expression in the sentence. A *performative verb* is simply a verb that can occur as the main verb in performative sentences. When such a verb occurs in such a sentence in a performative utterance I shall speak of the *performative use* of the sentence and the verb. An utterance of

(1) Leave the room!

can constitute the *performance of* making of an order, but it is not *performative*, whereas an utterance of

(2) I *order* you to leave the room.

would normally be performative.

Furthermore not every sentence containing a performative verb in the first person present indicative is a performative sentence.

(3) I *promise* to come on Wednesday.

is a performative sentence, but

(4) I *promise* too many things to too many people.

is not a performative sentence. In English most, but not all, performative utterances contain occurrences in the first person present singular indicative of the performative verb. There are also some occurrences in the present continuous, e.g.,

(5) I am *asking* you to do this for me, Henry, I am *asking* you to do it for me and Cynthia and the children.

and some performative utterances use verbs in the plural, e.g.,

(6) We *pledge* our lives, our fortunes and our sacred honor.

Furthermore, some performative sentences are in the passive:

(7) Passengers are hereby *advised* that all flights to Phoenix have been cancelled.

Sometimes the performative expression is not a verb and it may be in a separate clause or sentence, as in

(8) I'll come to see you next week, and that's a *promise.*

Not every occurrence of a performative sentence is a performative use. Thus, e.g., (3) could be used to report a habitual practice: 'Whenever I see you on Tuesday I always do the same thing: I promise to come and see you on Wednesday.'[4]

What Exactly is the Problem About Performatives?

Put at its most naive (and in a preliminary formulation we will later have to revise), the puzzle about performatives is simply this: how can there be a class of sentences whose meaning is such that we can perform the action named by the verb just by saying literally we are performing it? How can meaning determine that saying is doing? How does the saying *constitute* the doing? There are other questions related to this: why is the class of verbs restricted in the way that it seems to be? As I mentioned, I can promise by saying 'I hereby promise,' but I can't fry an egg, by saying 'I hereby fry an egg.' Furthermore, how can one and the same unambiguous sentence have both a literal performative and a literal nonperformative use?

Another crucial question is why is it that in some sense I can't lie or be mistaken or utter a falsehood with the performative part of the performative utterance, in the way that statements normally can be lies, falsehoods or mistakes. This question has to be stated precisely. When I say, 'Bill promised to come and see you last week' that utterance can be a lie, a mistake, or some other form of falsehood, just as any statement can. But when I say 'I promise to come and see you next week' that utterance could be insincere (if I don't intend to do the act represented by the propositional content) and it can fail to be a promise if certain of the presuppositions fail to obtain (e.g. if the person I take myself to be addressing is not a person but a fence post) but I can't be lying or mistaken about it's having the *force* of a promise, because, in some sense that we need to explain, my uttering the sentence and meaning literally what I say gives it the force of a promise. Just to have a name I will call this the 'self-guaranteeing' character of performative utterances.

Finally, there is a problem about the semantic analysis of performative verbs. Are we to be forced to say that these verbs have two meanings, one performative and one not? Or two senses? Or what?

Condition of Adequacy

What are the constraints that we would like to achieve on our analysis of performatives? Well first we would like the analysis to fit into an overall account of language. Ideally performatives should not just stick out as some oddity or anomaly, but it should seem necessary that these verbs, sentences, and utterances would have these properties given the rest of our account of language. In this connection we would like to preserve the intuition that performative sentences are ordinary sentences in the indicative and that as such they are used to make statements that have truth values, even when uttered performatively. Also, we would like to avoid having to postulate ambiguities; especially since we have independent linguistic evidence that performative verbs are not ambiguous between a performative and a nonperformative sense. For example, we can get something like conjunction reduction in examples of the following sort: the sentence, 'John promises to come and see you next week, and I promise to come and see you next week,' can be paraphrased as 'John promises to come and see you next week and so do I.' We need further to explain the occurrence of 'hereby' in performative sentences. But the hard problem is that we need to meet these constraints in a way that accounts for the special character of performatives, especially the self-guaranteeing feature that I mentioned earlier.

Just so we can see what the problems are, I will simply list the main features that I would like to be able to account for.

1. Performative utterances are performances of the act named by the main verb (or other performative expression) in the sentence.
2. Performative utterances are self-guaranteeing in the sense that the speaker cannot be lying, insincere, or mistaken about the type of act being performed (even though he or she can be lying, insincere, or mistaken about the propositional content of the speech act and he or she can fail to perform the act if certain other conditions fail to obtain.)
3. Performative utterances achieve features (1) and (2) in virtue of the literal meaning of the sentence uttered.
4. They characteristically take 'hereby' as in 'I hereby promise that I will come and see you.'
5. The verbs in question are not ambiguous between a performative and a non-performative sense, even though the verbs have both performative and non-performative literal occurrences.
6. Performative utterances are not indirect speech acts, in the sense in which an utterance of 'Can you pass the salt?' can be an indirect speech act of requesting the hearer to pass the salt.
7. Performative utterances in virtue of their literal meaning are statements with truth values.
8. Performative sentences typically use an unusual tense in English, the so called 'dramatic present.'

Previous Analyses

I am not sure that all these conditions can be met, and perhaps some of them are incorrect, but in any case none of the discussions I have read and heard of performatives meets all of them. Let me review my own earlier writings on this subject. In *Speech Acts* (Searle, 1969) and other writings I pointed out that in general, illocutionary acts have the structure F(p), where the 'F' stands for the illocutionary force, and the '(p)' stands for the propositional content. If communication is to be successful, the hearer has to be able to figure out from hearing the sentence what is the illocutionary force and what is the propositional content. So there will in general be in the syntax of sentences an illocutionary force indicating device and a representation of the propositional content. In the sentence, 'It's raining,' the propositional content expressed is: that it is raining, and the illocutionary force of a statement is indicated by such things as word order, intonation contour, mood of the verb and punctuation.

Now on this account, I argued in *Speech Acts* that the performative prefix is just an indicator of illocutionary force like any other. In 'I state that it is raining' and 'I order you to leave the room' the performative prefixes 'I state' and 'I order' function to make explicit the illocutionary force of the utterance of the sentence. As far as it goes, I think that account is right, but incomplete in that it doesn't explain how performatives work. In particular, it doesn't so far explain how the same syntactical sequence can occur in some cases as an indicator of illocutionary force and in others as part of propositional content. So the present task can be described in part as an attempt to complete the account I began in *Speech Acts*.

In *Foundations of Illocutionary Logic*, (Searle and Vanderveken, 1985) Daniel Vanderveken and I argued that performative utterances were all cases of declarations. Declarations, just to remind you, are speech acts such as for example, 'The meeting is adjourned' or 'War is hereby declared' where the illocutionary point of the speech act is to change the world in such a way that the propositional content matches the world, because the world has been changed to match the propositional content. In a declaration of the form F(p) the successful performance of the speech act changes the world to make it the case that p. Declarations thus have simultaneously both the word-to-world and the world-to-word directions of fit.[5] Now on this account of performative utterances, just as I can declare the meeting to be adjourned, so I can declare a promise to be made or an order to be issued, and I use a performative prefix to do these things. If we just read off the structure of the speech act from the surface structure of the sentence that account seems obviously right. The propositional content, e.g. that I order you to leave the room, is made true by the utterance of the sentence 'I order you to leave the room;' and such an utterance differs from an utterance of the sentence, 'Leave the room;' because though an utterance of 'Leave the room' also makes it the case that I ordered you to leave the room; it does not do so by declaration. It does not do so by representing it as being the case, and thus it differs from a performative.

This analysis of performatives as declarations has the consequence that the illocutionary structure of 'I order you to leave the room' is:

Declare (that I order(that you leave the room)).

The propositional content of the declaration is: that I order that you leave the room, even though the propositional content of the order is: that you leave the room.

I think it is correct to say that all performatives are declarations, but that does not really answer our original question, 'How do performatives work' it only extends it into 'How do declarations work?' Also it has consequences of the sort that make philosophers nervous, e.g., What about the use of 'I declare' as a performative prefix for a declaration?[6] Is that used to make a declaration of a declaration? And if so how far can such a regress go?

Most recent attempts at analysing performatives have treated them as statements[7] from which some other speech act can be derived; and many, though not all of these accounts treat them as a type of indirect speech act. I said earlier that intuitively performatives did not seem to be indirect speech acts, but there is something very appealing about any approach that treats them as statements because it takes seriously the fact that a performative sentence is grammatically an ordinary sentence in the indicative mood. Typical attempts to try to make this approach work treat performative utterances as indirect speech acts on analogy with such cases as 'Can you pass the salt?' used to request somebody to pass the salt or 'It's hot in here' used to request somebody to open the window. The idea is that the literal speech act is a statement and then by some mechanism of Gricean implicature the hearer is supposed to infer the intent to perform some other speech act. I do not think these accounts are adequate; but just to consider the best I have seen, I will briefly review the account given by Bach and Harnish.

According to Bach and Harnish, 'in the case of performative utterances, even those without the use of 'hereby,' normally the hearer could reason, and could be intended to reason as follows:

(1) He is saying 'I order you to leave.'
(2) He is stating that he is ordering me to leave.
(3) If his statement is true, then he must be ordering me to leave.
(4) If he is ordering me to leave, it must be his utterance that constitutes the order. (What else could it be?)
(5) Presumably, he is speaking the truth.
(6) Therefore, in stating that he is ordering me to leave he is ordering me to leave.[8]

I believe this account is unsatisfactory, because it fails to meet even the most uncontroversial of our conditions of adequacy. Specifically, it fails to explain the performative character and the self-guaranteeing character of performative utterances. It fails to meet conditions (1) and (2). The phenomenon that we are trying to explain is how a statement *could* constitute an order, and on this account, it is just blandly asserted in (4) that it does constitute an order. The fact we were trying to explain is left unexplained by the Bach-Harnish account. Furthermore, we were trying to explain the self-guaranteeing character which performatives have, but other statements do not have. Now, if we are right in thinking that performatives are self-guaranteeing, then it is redundant to suppose that we need an extra presumption that the speaker is telling the truth (their step (5)) because as far as the illocutionary force is concerned, there is no way he could fail to speak the truth.

Their account takes it as given that the utterance can constitute an order, but if we are allowed to assume that utterances can constitute states of affairs described by the utterance, then we do not have an account that explains the differences between sentences which work as performatives and sentences which do not, such as e.g., 'I am the King of Spain.' They offer no explanation of why their analysis works for ordering but wouldn't work for the following:

(1) He is saying 'I am the King of Spain.'
(2) He is stating that he is the King of Spain.
(3) If his statement is true, then he must be the King of Spain.
(4) If he is the King of Spain, it must be his utterance that constitutes his being the King of Spain. (What else could it be?)
(5) Presumably, he is speaking the truth.
(6) Therefore, in stating that he is the King of Spain, he is being the King of Spain.

I think it is obvious that 'I order you to leave' can be used performatively and 'I am the King of Spain' cannot, but there is nothing in the Bach-Harnish account that explains the difference. Why does the one work and not the other? Another way to state the same objection is to point out that they are relying on our understanding of how the sentence 'I order you to leave' can be used performatively and not explaining how it can be so used.

Still, there is something very appealing about the idea that performative utterances are statements from which the performative is somehow derived. We have only to look at the syntax of these sentences to feel the appeal. So let's try to make the strongest case for it that we can. What we are trying to explain in the first instance is how the literal meaning of the indicative sentence is such that its serious and literal utterance is (or can be) the performance of the very act named by the main verb.

Performatives as Assertives

Notice first that the 'hereby' marks a self reference. Whether the 'hereby' occurs explicitly or not, the performative utterance is about itself. In 'I order you to leave' or 'I hereby order you to leave,' the speaker in some sense says that that very utterance is an order. Such utterances are no more and no less self referential than, e.g., 'This statement is being made in English.'[9]

Now, if we were going to take seriously the idea that performatives work by way of being statements to the effect that one performs a certain speech act, we would have to show how the characteristics of such self-referential statements were sufficient to be constitutive of the performance of the speech act named by the performative verb. In the formal mode we could say that we need to show how (assuming certain contextual conditions are satisfied) the statement: 'John made a self-referential statement to the effect that his utterance was a promise that *p*' entails, as a matter of logic, 'John made a promise that *p*.' Well, what are the characteristics of such statements and what are the characteristics of performatives and what are the relations between them? The characteristics in question are these:

1. A statement is an intentionally undertaken commitment to the truth of the expressed propositional content.
2. Performative statements are self-referential.
3. An essential constitutive feature of any illocutionary act is the intention to perform that act. It is a constitutive feature of a promise, for example, that the utterance should be intended as a promise.

Now our question is a little more precise. Can we show how the first two characteristics combine to guarantee the presence of the third? Can we show how the fact that one made a self-referential statement to the effect that one was making a promise that *p* is sufficient to guarantee that one had the intention to make a promise that *p*? I used to think this was possible, and in fact when I completed an earlier version of this paper I thought I had a pretty good demonstration of how it worked. I now think that it can't be made to work, but I believe its failure is instructive, so let's go through the steps. I will try to set out in some detail an argument designed to show that a self-referential statement to the effect that the utterance is a promise that *p* necessarily has the force of a promise; and then I will try to show why the argument doesn't work.

Step 1. Suppose someone makes a statement literally uttering the sentence, 'I promise to come and see you next week.' Well, as such it is a statement; and a statement is a commitment to the truth of the proposition, so the speaker is committed to the truth of the proposition that he promises to come to see the hearer next week.

But in general, the making of a statement does not guarantee that it is true or even that the speaker intends that it be true. For even though the statement commits him to its truth, he might lie or he might be mistaken. So from the mere fact that the utterance is a statement that he promises, we cannot derive that it is a promise.

Step 2. The statement is self-referential. It isn't just *about* a promise but it says of itself that it is a promise. It might be paraphrased as 'This very utterance is the making of a promise to come and see you next week.'

But the addition of self-referentiality by itself is still not enough to guarantee that it is a promise or even that it is intended as a promise. If I say 'This very utterance is being made in French' there is nothing in the fact that a self-referential statement has been made that guarantees that it is true or even that it is intended to be true.

Step 3. In the utterance of the sentence, the speaker has made a self-referential truth claim to the effect that his utterance is a promise. But what would make it true, in what would its truth consist? Well obviously its truth would consist in its being a promise. But in what does its being a promise consist? Given that the preparatory and other conditions are satisfied, *its being a promise consists in its being intended as a promise*. Given that everything else is all right with the speech act, if it is intended as a promise then it is a promise. So now our question narrows down to this: How do the other features guarantee the intention to make a promise?

Step 4. The main feature of its being a promise is that it is intended as a promise. But now, and this is the crucial point, if the utterance is self-referential and if the intended truth conditions are that it be a promise and if the main component in those truth conditions actually being satisfied is the intention that it be a promise, then the intention to make the self-referential statement that the utterance is a promise is sufficient to guarantee the presence of the intention that it be a promise and therefore sufficient to guarantee that it is a promise. Why?

Step 5. The intention to label the utterance as a promise is sufficient for the intention to be a promise, because the intention to label it as a promise carries a commitment. The commitment in assertives is that the proposition is true. But now, the commitment to its truth, intentionally undertaken, already carries a commitment to the intention that it be a promise. But that intention, in the appropriate circumstances, is sufficient for its being a promise.

So on this account, though statements in general do not guarantee their own truth, performative statements are exceptions for two reasons, first they are self-referential and second the self-reference is to the other speech act being performed in that very utterance. Notice that the self-referentiality is crucial here. If I assert that I will promise or that I have promised, such assertions do not carry the commitments of the actual promise in a way that the assertion 'This very speech act is a promise' does carry the commitments both of the assertion and thereby of the promise.

This, I believe, is the best argument to show that performatives are primarily statements. What is wrong with it? For a long time it seemed right to me, but it now seems to me that it contains a mistake. And any mistake, once you see it, is an obvious mistake. The mistake is that the argument confuses *being committed to having an intention* with actually *having the intention*. If I characterize my utterance as a promise, I am committed to that utterance's having been made with the intention that it be a promise, but this is not enough to guarantee that it was actually made with that intention. I thought this objection could be evaded by the self-referentiality, but it can't be. Just self-referentially describing one of my own utterances as a promise is not enough to guarantee that it is made with the intention that it be a promise, even though it is enough to commit me to having made it with that intention.

The point is a fairly subtle one, but I have reluctantly come to the conclusion that it is decisive. So, I will repeat it: The intention to assert self-referentially of an utterance that it is an illocutionary act of a certain type, say a promise, is simply not sufficient to guarantee the existence of an intention in that utterance to make a promise. Such an assertion does indeed *commit* the speaker to the existence of the intention, but the commitment to having the intention doesn't guarantee the *actual presence* of the intention. And that was what we needed to show. We needed to show that the assertion somehow guaranteed the presence of the performative intention, when the assertion was a self-referential assertion to the effect that it was an illocutionary act named by the performative verb.

It now turns out that the effort to show that performatives are a species of assertion fails. The performative character of an utterance cannot be derived from its literal features as an assertion. I have come to the unfortunate conclusion that any attempt to derive performatives from assertives is doomed to failure because assertives fail to produce the self-guaranteeing feature of performatives, and in failing to account for the self-guaranteeing feature, the analysis fails to account for performativity. The failure to satisfy condition (2) automatically produces a failure to satisfy condition (1). In order to derive the performative from the assertive, we would have to show that given the statement S of certain conditions on the speech act, the conjunction of S and the proposition '*x* made the self-referential assertion that he promised that *p*' entails '*x* promised that *p*'; and this cannot be done because the assertive intention by itself does not guarantee the presence of the performative intention.

Performatives as Declarations

Now we have to go back to the drawing board. We were trying to derive the declarational character of performatives from their assertive character and it didn't work. So let's reconsider what is implied by the view that performatives are declarations. We saw earlier that, trivially, performatives are declarations because they satisfy the definition of a declaration. The definition is that an utterance is a declaration if the successful performance of the speech act is sufficient to bring about the fit between words and world, to make the propositional content true. Declarations thus have the double direction of fit ↕ whereas assertives have the word-to-world direction of fit ↓.[10] One way to characterize our failure so far is to say that my effort to derive the double direction of fit from the assertive direction of fit was a failure. I thought I could do it with self referentiality plus the lexical meaning of some peculiar verbs, but it turned out that the apparatus was too weak.

So let us now ask 'How do declarations work in general?', and we can then use the answer to that question to locate the special features of performatives.

In order intentionally to produce changes in the world through our actions, normally our bodily movements have to set off a chain of ordinary physical causation. If, for example, I am trying to hammer a nail into a board or start the car, my bodily movements – e.g., swinging my arm while holding the hammer, turning my wrist while holding the key in the ignition – will cause certain desired effects.

But there is an important class of actions where intention, bodily movement and desired effect are not related by physical causation in this way. If somebody says, 'The meeting is adjourned,' 'I pronounce you husband and wife,' 'War is declared,' or 'You're fired,' he may succeed in changing the world in the ways specified in these utterances just by performing the relevant speech acts. How is that possible? Well, notice that the literal utterance of the appropriate sentences is not enough. For two reasons; first, for many of these utterances someone might utter the same sentence speaking literally and just be making a report. If the chairman says, 'The meeting is adjourned' as a way of adjourning the meeting, I might report to my neighbor at the meeting, 'The meeting is adjourned' and my speaker meaning includes the same literal sentence meaning as did the speaker meaning of the chairman, but he and not I performed the declaration. Second, even if I say, 'The meeting is adjourned' intending thereby to adjourn the meeting, I will not succeed because I lack the authority. How is it that the chairman succeeds and I do not? In general, these sorts of declarations require the following four features:

1. An extra-linguistic institution.
2. A special position by the speaker, and sometimes by the hearer, within the institution.
3. A special convention that certain literal sentences of natural languages count as the performances of certain declarations within the institution.
4. The intention by the speaker in the utterance of those sentences that his utterance has a declarational status, that it creates a fact corresponding to the propositional content.

As a general point, the difference between pounding a nail and adjourning a meeting is that in the case of adjourning the meeting the intention to perform the action, as manifested in the appropriate bodily movement (in this case the appropriate utterances) performed by a person duly authorized, and recognized by the audience, is constitutive of bringing about the desired change. When I say in such cases that the intention is constitutive of the action, I mean that the manifestation of the intention in the utterance does not require any further causal effects of the sort we have in hammering a nail or starting a car. It simply requires recognition by the audience.

The more formal the occasion, the more condition (3) is required. The speaker must utter the right expressions or the utterance does not count as marrying you, adjourning the meeting, etc. But often on informal occasions, there is no special ritual phrase. I can give you my watch just by saying, 'It's yours,' 'You can have it,' 'I give it to you,' etc.

The most prominent exceptions to the claim that declarations require an extra-linguistic institution are supernatural declarations. When God says, 'Let there be light!', that I take it is a declaration. It is not a promise; it doesn't mean, 'When I get around to it, I'll make light for you.' And it is not an order; it doesn't mean, 'Sam over there, turn on the lights.' It makes it the case by fiat that light exists. Fairy stories, by the way, are full of declarations performed by witches, wizards, magicians, etc. We ordinary humans do not have the ability to perform supernatural declarations, but we do have a quasi-magical power nonetheless of bringing about changes in the world through our utterances; and we are given this power by a kind of human agreement. All of these institutions in question are social institutions, and it is only as long as the institution is recognized that it can continue to function to allow for the performance of declarations.

When we turn to performatives such as 'I promise to come and see you,' 'I order you to leave the room,' 'I state that it is raining,' etc., we find that these, like our earlier declarations, also create new facts, but in these cases, the facts created are linguistic facts; the fact that a promise has been made, an order given, a statement issued, etc. To mark these various distinctions, let's distinguish between *extra-linguistic* declarations – such as adjourning the meeting, pronouncing somebody man and wife, declaring war, etc. – and *linguistic* declarations – such as promising, ordering, and stating by way of declaration. Both linguistic and extra-linguistic declarations are speech acts, and in that sense they are both linguistic. In the examples we have considered, they are all performed by way of performative utterances. Naively the best way to think of the distinction is this: A declaration is a speech act whose point is to create a new fact corresponding to the propositional content. Sometimes those new facts are themselves speech acts such as promises, statements, orders, etc. These I am calling linguistic declarations. Sometimes the new facts are not further speech acts, but wars, marriages, adjournments, light, property transfers, etc. These I am calling extralinguistic declarations.

When the chairman says, 'The meeting is adjourned,' he performs a linguistic *act*, but the *fact* he creates, that the meeting is adjourned, is not a *linguistic fact*. On the other hand, when I say, 'I order you to leave the room,' I create a new fact, the fact that I have ordered you to leave the room, but that fact is a linguistic fact.

Since the facts created by linguistic declarations are linguistic facts, we don't need an extralinguistic institution to perform them. Language is itself an institution, and it is sufficient to empower speakers to perform such declarations as promising to come and see someone or ordering someone to leave the room. Of course, extralinguistic facts may also be required for the performance of the linguistic declaration. For example, I have to be in a position of power or authority in order to issue orders to you. And such facts as that I am in a position of power are not facts of language. Nonetheless, they are conditions required by the rules of linguistic acts. No non-linguistic institution is necessary for me to give an order, and the rules of ordering already specify the extralinguistic features of the world that are necessary in order to perform a successful and non-defective order.[11]

All performative utterances are declarations. Not all declarations are performatives for the trivial reason that not all declarations contain a performative expression, e.g., 'Let there be light!' does not. But every declaration that is not a performative could have been one: e.g., 'I hereby decree that there be light!' The important distinction is not between those declarations which are performatives and those which are not, but between those declarations which create a linguistic entity, a speech act such as an order, promise, or statement; and those which create a nonlinguistic entity such as a marriage, a war, or an adjournment. The important distinction is between, e.g., 'I promise to come and see you,' and 'War is hereby declared.'

Traditionally in speech act theory we have regarded the nonlinguistic cases as prototypical of declarations but it is also important to see how much nonlinguistic apparatus they require. Consider 'divorce.' I am told that in certain Moslem countries a man can divorce his wife by uttering three times the performative sentence, 'I divorce you.' This is a remarkable power for a speech act, but it adds nothing to the meaning of 'divorce' or its translations. The ability to create divorces through declarational speech acts derives from legal/theological powers and not from semantics.

Performatives and Literal Meaning

Since ordinary linguistic declarations are encoded in performative sentences such as, 'I order you to leave the room' or 'Leave, and that's an order,' they do not require an extralinguistic institution. The literal meaning of the sentence is enough. But now the question arises: how could it be enough? How can the literal meaning of an ordinary indicative sentence encode the actual performance of an action named by the main verb? And how can the literal meaning both encode the performative and the assertive meaning without being ambiguous? It is not enough to say that in the one case the speaker intends the utterance as a performative and in the other as an assertion. The question is: how could one and the same literal meaning accommodate both intentions?

With these questions we come to the crux of the argument of this paper. I believe it is the failure to see an answer to these questions – or even to see the questions – that has led to the currently fashionable views that performatives are some kind of indirect speech act where the supposedly non-literal performative is somehow derived from the literal assertion by Gricean mechanisms. On my view, the performative utterance is literal. The speaker utters the sentence and means it literally. If the boss says to me, 'I hereby order you to leave the room,' I don't have to *infer* that he has made an order, nor do I think that he hasn't quite said exactly what he meant. It is not at all like, 'Would you mind leaving the room?' said as an order to leave.

The apparatus necessary for answering these questions includes at least the following three elements:

First, we need to recognize that there is a class of actions where the manifestation of the intention to perform the action, in an appropriate context, is sufficient for the performance of the action.

Second, we need to recognize the existence of a class of verbs which contain the notion of intention as part of their meaning. To say that a person performed the act named by the verb implies that he or she did it intentionally, that if it wasn't intentional, then the agent didn't do it under that description. Illocutionary verbs characteristically have this feature. I cannot, e.g., promise unintentionally. If I didn't intend it as a promise, then it wasn't a promise.

Third, we need to recognize the existence of a class of literal utterances which are self referential in a special way, they are not only *about* themselves, but they also operate on themselves. They are both *self-referential* and *executive*.

Now if you put all these three together you can begin to see how performative sentences can be uttered as linguistic declarations. The first step is to see that for any type of action you can perform, the question naturally arises: how do you do it? By what means do you do it? For some actions you can do it solely by manifesting the intention to do it, and in general speech acts fall within this class. Typically we perform a type of illocutionary act by uttering a type of sentence that encodes the intention to perform an act of that type, e.g., we perform directive speech acts by uttering sentences in the imperative mood. But another way to manifest the intention to perform an illocutionary act is to utter a performative sentence. Such sentences are self-referential and their meaning encodes the intention to perform the act named in the sentence by the utterance of that very sentence. Such a sentence is 'I hereby order you to leave.' And an utterance of such a sentence functions as a performative, and hence as a declaration because (a) the verb 'order' is an intentional verb, (b) ordering is something you can do by manifesting the intention to do it, and (c) the utterance is both self-referential and executive, as indicated by the word 'hereby' in a way that I will now explain.

Normally it is a bit pompous to stick in 'hereby.' It is sufficient to say 'I order you . . .' or even 'That's an order.' Such sentences can be used either just to make assertions or as performatives, without being ambiguous. The sentence uttered as an assertion and uttered as a performative mean exactly the same thing. Nonetheless, when they are uttered as performatives the speaker's intention is different from when uttered as assertives. Performative speaker meaning includes sentence meaning but goes beyond it. In the case of the performative utterance, the intention is that the utterance should constitute the performance of the act named by the verb. The word 'hereby' makes this explicit, and with the addition of this word, sentence meaning and performative speaker meaning coincide. The 'here' part is the self referential part. The 'by' part is the executive part. To put it crudely, the whole expression means 'by-this-here-very-utterance.' Thus, if I say, 'I hereby order you to leave the room,' the whole thing means, 'By this here very utterance I make it the case that I order you to leave the room.' And it is possible to succeed in making it the case just by saying so, because, to repeat, the utterance is a manifestation (and not just a description or expression) of the intention to order you to leave the room, by making that very utterance. The whole thing implies, 'This very utterance is intended as an order to you to leave the room' where that implication is to be taken not just as the description of an intention but as its manifestation. And the manifestation of that intention, as we have seen, is sufficient for its being an order.

It is perhaps important to emphasize again a point I made earlier, namely, that the self-referential *assertive* intention is not enough to do the job. Just intending to assert that the utterance is an order or even that it is intended as an order doesn't guarantee the intention to issue an order. But intending that the utterance *make it the case* that it is an order is sufficient to guarantee the intention to issue an order. *And that intention can be encoded in the meaning of a sentence when the sentence encodes executive self-referentiality over an intentional verb.*

To show how the analysis works in more detail, let us go through a derivation from the hearer's point of view. We should *en passant* be able to show how the utterance of a performative sentence constitutes both a declaration and, by derivation, an assertion.

(1) S uttered the sentence 'I hereby order you to leave' (or he uttered 'I order you to leave' meaning 'I hereby order you to leave').
(2) The literal meaning of the utterance is such that by that very utterance the speaker *intends* to make it the case that he orders me to leave.
(3) Therefore, in making the utterance *S manifested an intention* to make it the case by that utterance that he ordered me to leave.
(4) Therefore, in making the utterance S manifested an intention to *order* me to leave by that very utterance.
(5) Orders are a class of actions where the manifestation of the intention to perform the action is sufficient for its performance, given that certain other conditions are satisfied.
(6) We assume those other conditions are satisfied.
(7) S ordered me to leave, by that utterance.
(8) S both said that he ordered me to leave and made it the case that he ordered me to leave. Therefore he made a true statement.

This last step explains how the performative utterance can also be a true statement: Declarations, by definition, make their propositional content true. That's what a successful declaration is. It is an utterance that changes the world in such a way as to bring about the truth of its propositional content. If I say, 'The meeting is adjourned,' and succeed in my declaration, then I make it the case that what I said is true; similarly with 'I order you to leave the room.' But it is important to emphasize, contrary to the hypothesis that I considered earlier, that the truth of the statement derives from the declarational character of the utterance and not conversely. In the case of performative utterances, the assertion is derived from the declaration and not the declaration from the assertion.

Now this whole analysis has a somewhat surprising result. If we ask what are the special semantic properties of performativity within the class of intentional verbs which enable a subclass of them to function as performative verbs; the answer seems to be, roughly speaking, there are none. If God decides to fry an egg by saying, 'I hereby fry an egg,' or to fix the roof by saying, 'I hereby fix the roof,' He is not misusing English. It is just a fact about how the world works, and not part of the semantics of English verbs, that we humans are unable to perform these acts by declaration. But there is nothing in the semantics of such verbs that prevents us from intending them performatively; it is just a fact of nature that it won't work. If I now say, 'I hereby end all wars and produce the eternal happiness of mankind,' my attempted declaration will fail, but my failure is not due to semantic limitations. It is due to the facts of nature that in real life, performatives are restricted to those verbs which name actions where the manifestation of the intention is constitutive of the action, and (religious and supernatural cases apart) those verbs are confined to linguistic and institutional declarations.

There are a number of semantic features which *block* a performative occurrence. So for example, famously, 'hint,' 'insinuate,' and 'boast' cannot be used performatively, because they imply that the act was performed in a way that was not explicit and overt and performative utterances are completely explicit and overt. But there is no special *semantic* property of performativity which attaches to verbs and thereby *enables* them to be used performatively. As far as the literal meaning of the verb is concerned, unless there is some sort of block, any verb that describes an intentional action could be used performatively. There is nothing linguistically wrong with the utterance, 'I hereby make it the case that all swans are purple.' The limitation, to repeat, is not in the semantics, it is in the world. Similarly with the perlocutionary verbs. What is wrong with 'I hereby convince (persuade, annoy, amuse, etc.) you' is not their semantics but their presumption. The limitation on performatives is provided by the fact that only a very tiny number of changes can be brought about in the world solely by saying that one is making those changes by that very utterance. For nonsupernaturally endowed humans beings,[12] these fall into two classes: the creation of purely linguistic institutional facts – such as those created by saying, 'I hereby promise to come and see you,' 'I order you to leave the room,' etc. – and extra-linguistic institutional facts – such as, 'The meeting is adjourned,' 'I pronounce you husband and wife,' etc. But the special semantic property of performativity simply dissolves. There is nothing there. What we find instead are human conventions, rules, and institutions that enable certain utterances to function to create the state of affairs represented in the propositional content of the utterance. These new facts are essentially social, and the act of creating them can succeed only if there is successful communication between speaker and hearer. Thus the connection between the literal meaning of the sentence uttered and the institutional fact created by its utterance. 'I promise' creates a promise; 'The meeting is adjourned' creates an adjournment.

Summary and Conclusion

The analysis I am proposing runs dead counter to most of the current ways of thinking about this issue and counter to the view I myself held until recently, so it is perhaps useful to summarize the argument so far.

Our problem is to explain how the literal utterance of certain ordinary indicative sentences can constitute, and not merely describe, the acts named by the main verb (or some other performative expression) in that very sentence. It turns out under investigation that that question is the same question as how the literal utterance of these sentences can necessarily manifest the intention to perform those acts; since we discovered for such acts, the manifestation of the intention is constitutive of the performance. So our puzzle was: how can the literal utterance of 'I hereby order you to leave the room' constitute an order as much as the literal utterance of 'Leave the room' constitutes a directive in general, when the first is obviously an ordinary indicative sentence, apparently purporting to describe some behavior on the part of the speaker?

We found that it was impossible to derive the performative from the assertion because the assertion by itself wasn't sufficient to guarantee the presence of the intention in question. The difference between the assertion that you promise and the making of a promise is that in the making of a promise you have to intend your utterance as a promise, and there is no way that an assertion by itself can guarantee the presence of that intention. The solution to the problem came when we saw that the self-guaranteeing character of these actions derives from the fact that not only are these utterances self-referential, but they are self-referential to a verb which contains the notion of an intention as part of its meaning, and the acts in question can be performed by manifesting the intention to perform them. You can perform any of these acts by an utterance because the utterance can be the manifestation (and not just a commitment to the existence) of the relevant intention. But you can, furthermore, perform them by a performative utterance because the performative utterance is self-referential to a verb which contains the notion of the intention which is being manifested in that very utterance. The literal utterance of 'I hereby order you to leave' is – in virtue of its literal meaning – a manifestation of the intention to order you to leave. And this in turn explains why as far as illocutionary force is concerned the speaker cannot lie or be mistaken: assuming the other conditions on the speech act are satisfied, if he intends his utterance to have the force of an order, then it has that force; because the manifested intention is constitutive of that force.

I have so far tried to give an account which will satisfy all but one of our conditions of adequacy, i.e. to show:

1. How performative utterances can be performances of the act named by the performative verb.
2. How they are self-guaranteeing in the sense explained.
3. How they have features (1) and (2) in virtue of their literal meaning.
4. Why they characteristically take 'hereby.'
5. How they can achieve all of this without being ambiguous between a performative and a non-performative sense.
6. How they work without being indirect speech acts.
7. How it is that they can be statements with truth values.

It remains only to answer:

8. Why do they take that peculiar tense, the dramatic present?

This tense is used to mark events which are, so to speak, to be construed as instantaneous with the utterance. Thus, the chemistry professor says while giving the demonstration,

> I pour the sulphuric acid into the test tube. I then add five grams of pure carbon. I heat the resulting mixture over the Bunsen burner.

In these cases, the sentence describes an event that is simultaneous with its utterance, and for that reason Julian Boyd (in conversation) calls this tense 'the present present.' Similarly, though less obviously, with the written text of a play. We are to think of sentences such as, 'John sits' or 'Sally raises the glass to her lips,' not as reporting a previously occurring set of events nor as predicting what will happen on the stage, but as providing an isomorphic model, a kind of linguistic mirror of a sequence of events. Now, because the performative utterance is both self-referential and executive, the present present is ideally suited to it. 'I promise to come and see you' marks an event which is right then and there, simultaneous with the utterance, because the event is achieved by way of making the utterance.

Our analysis had two unexpected consequences, or at least consequences that run counter to the current ways of thinking about these matters. First, most contemporary analyses try to derive the performative from the assertion; but on my proposal, the performative, the declaration, is primary; the assertion is derived. Secondly, it turns out that there is no such thing as a semantic property which defines performative verbs. Unless there is some special feature of the verb which implies nonperformativity (as with 'hint,' 'insinuate' and 'boast') any verb at all which names an intentional action could be uttered performatively. The limitations on the class that determine which will succeed and which will fail derive from facts about how the world works, not from the meanings of the verbs.

If one looks at the literature on this subject, one finds two apparently absolutely inconsistent and firmly held sets of linguistic intuitions. One set, exemplified powerfully by Austin (1962), insists roundly that performatives are not statements, but rather, performances of some other kind. Another set insists, equally roundly, that all performatives are obviously statements. One of my aims has been to show the truth in both of these intuitions. Austin was surely right in thinking that the primary purpose of saying, 'I promise to come and see you' is not to make a statement or a description, but to make a promise. His critics are surely right in claiming that, all the same, when one says, 'I promise to come and see you,' one does make a statement. What my argument attempts to show is how the statement is derivative from the promise and not conversely.

Notes

1. An earlier version of this paper was delivered as a forum address to the Linguistics Society of America Summer Institute at Stanford, 1987. I am indebted to several people for helpful comments and criticism, and I especially want to thank J. Boyd, Y. Matsumoto, T. B. Nguyen, D. Searle and E. Sweetser.

There is now a vast literature on the subject of performatives, and I am, of course, indebted to the authors whose works I have read. Specifically, I wish to acknowledge my indebtedness to J. Austin, K. Bach, M. Bierwisch, C. Ginet, R. Harnish, I. Hedenius, J. Lemmon, J. McCawley, F. Récanati, J. Sadock, J. Urmson, and G. Warnock. (See bibliography.)

2. E.g., McCawley (1979)
3. I believe the earliest version of this view is in Lemmon (1962). For another early statement see also Hedenius (1963).
4. Notice that I have restricted the definition of performatives to illocutionary acts. On my definition utterances of 'I am now speaking' or 'I am shouting' (said in a loud voice) are not performative utterances.
5. For an explanation of all these notions see Searle (1979), Chapter one.
6. 'Declare' in English also functions as an assertive prefix, as in 'I declare that the contents of this document are true and complete.'
7. E.g. Lewis (1972), Bach (1975), Ginet (1979), and Bach and Harnish (1979).
8. Bach and Harnish (1979), p. 208.
9. Many authors have remarked on this self-referential feature. Perhaps the first was Åqvist (1972).
10. See Searle (1979), Chapter 1 for further discussion of the notion of direction of fit.
11. Suppose somebody rigs up a transducer device sensitive to acoustic signals which is such that if he stands next to his car and says, 'I hereby start the car,' the car will start. Has he performed a declaration? Well, obviously not. Why not? *Because the semantic properties played no role.* The acoustic properties are irrelevant except insofar as they are an expression or an encoding of the semantics. Another way to put the same point is to say that declarations can be performed in any language, and there is no set of physical properties that any given declaration has in all and only its occurrences. You can't define the declaration physically.
12. Again, I am ignoring the religious cases such as blessing, cursing, damning, etc.

References

Åqvist, L.: 1972, 'Performatives and Verifiability by the Use of Language', *Filosofiska Studier* **14**, University of Uppsala.

Austin, J. L.: 1962, *How to do Things with Words*, Harvard University Press, Cambridge, Mass.

Bach, K.: 1975, 'Performatives Are Statements Too', in *Philosophical Studies* **28**, 229–36.

Bach, K. and R. Harnish: 1979, *Linguistic Communication and Speech Acts*, MIT Press, Cambridge, Mass.

Bierwisch, M: 1980, 'Semantic Structure and Illocutionary Force', in J. R. Searle, F. Kiefer and M. Bierwisch (eds.), *Speech Act Theory and Pragmatics*, pp. 1–36. D. Reidel Publishing Company, Dordrecht.

Ginet, C.: 1979, 'Performativity', *Linguistics and Philosophy* **3**, 245–65

Hedenius, I.: 1963,'Performatives'. *Theoria* **29**, 115–36.

Lemmon, J. E.: 1962, 'Sentences Verifiable by Their Use', *Analysis* **12**, 86–9.

Lewis, D.: 1972, 'General Semantics', in D. Davidson and G. Harman (eds.). *Semantics of Natural Language*, pp. 169–218. D. Reidel Publishing Company, Dordrecht.
McCawley, James D.: 1979, 'Remarks on the Lexicography of Performative Verbs', in *Adverbs, Vowels, and Other Objects of Wonder*, pp. 161–173, University of Chicago Press, Chicago and London.
Récanati, F.: 1980, 'Some Remarks on Explicit Performatives, Indirect Speech Acts, Locutionary Meaning and Truth-value'. in J. R. Searle, F. Kiefer and M. Bierwisch (eds.), pp. 205–220, D. Reidel Publishing Company, Dordrecht.
Sadock. J.: 1974, *Toward a Linguistic Theory of Speech Acts*, Academic Press, New York.
Searle, J.R.: 1969, *Speech Acts: An Essay in the Philosophy of Language*, Cambridge University Press, Cambridge.
Searle, J. R.: 1979, *Expression and Meaning: Studies in the Theory of Speech Acts*, Cambridge University Press, Cambridge.
Searle, J. R. and D. Vanderveken: 1985, *Foundations of Illocutionary Logic*, Cambridge University Press, Cambridge.
Urmson, J.: 1977, 'Performative Utterances', *Midwest Studies in Philosophy* 2, 120–27.
Warnock, G. J.: 1973, 'Some Types of Performative Utterance', in I. Berlin *et al.* (eds), *Essays on J. L. Austin*, pp. 69–89, Clarendon Press, Oxford.

Part II

Sense and Reference

Introduction

Nathan Salmon

Reference and Semantic Content

A French speaker in uttering the words 'La neige est blanche' asserts the same thing as an English speaker uttering the words 'Snow is white'. The thing asserted is a proposition, the proposition that snow is white. The fundamental semantic role of a declarative sentence is to encode, or 'express' a proposition. A declarative sentence is said to contain the proposition it encodes, and that proposition is described as the semantic content of the sentence.[1]

Propositions are ontologically complex; they have components. This is apparent from consideration of distinct propositions having components in common. The proposition that Socrates is ingenious has some component in common with the proposition that Socrates is ingenuous, since both of these are directly about Socrates, and some other component again in common with the proposition that Plato is ingenious, since both of these directly ascribe ingenuity. These two proposition components are separately semantically correlated with the two major syntactic components of the sentence – the name 'Socrates' and the predicate 'is ingenious'. Let us call the proposition component semantically correlated with an expression the semantic content of the expression. The systematic method by which it is secured which proposition is semantically contained in which sentence is, very roughly, that a sentence semantically contains that proposition whose components are the semantic contents of the sentence parts, with these semantic contents combined in a manner parallel to that in which the sentence parts are themselves combined to form the sentence.[2] In order to analyse the proposition contained in a sentence

Portions of my books *Reference and Essence* (1981) and *Frege's Puzzle* (1986) and of my article 'Reference and information content: Names and descriptions' have been incorporated into the present article by permission of Princeton University Press/Basil Blackwell, the MIT Press, and D. Reidel, respectively.

into its components, one simply decomposes the sentence into its semantically contentful parts, and the semantic contents thereof are the components of the contained proposition. In this way, declarative sentences not only encode, but also codify, propositions.

The articles in Part II are concerned with the question of the semantic content for certain sorts of terms, particularly ordinary proper names, demonstratives, and singular definite descriptions – ie., singular noun phrases formed from the definite article 'the' or from a possessive adjective, such as 'the oldest living American', 'your first wife', etc. Terms of this sort are commonly classified as singular terms. A singular term is an expression whose semantic function, when used in a particular context, is to *refer to*, ie. to stand for, a single individual thing.

The Naive Theory

One natural and elegantly simple theory identifies the semantic content of a singular term (as used in particular context) with its referent (in that context), that is, with the object or individual referred to (with respect to that context). Likewise, the semantic content of the predicate 'is tall' might be identified with the property of being tall, and the semantic content of the predicate 'is taller than' might be identified with the binary relation of being greater in height.[3] This may be called the Naive Theory of semantic content. Its central theses are: (*i*) The semantic content of any singular term is its referent; (*ii*) Any semantically contentful expression may be thought of as referring to its semantic content; and (*iii*) The semantic content of a sentence is a complex, ordered entity (something like a sequence) whose constituents are semantically correlated systematically with expressions making up the sentence, typically the simple (non-compound) component expressions. (Exceptions arise in connection with quotation marks, and similar devices.) On the naive theory the proposition contained in a simple atomic subject-predicate sentence such as 'Socrates is ingenious' is what David Kaplan in Chapter 12 calls a singular proposition – a complex abstract entity consisting partly of things like properties, relations, and concepts, and partly of the very individuals the proposition is about. By contrast, a (purely) general proposition is made up entirely of the former sorts of entities (in a certain way). On the Naive Theory, a sentence is a means for referring to its semantic content, by specifying the components that make it up.

The Naive Theory is both powerful and cogent. The theory yields a plausible rendering of the observation that the proposition that Socrates is ingenious is proposition about or concerning Socrates: Socrates is an individual constituent of it. The Naive Theory gives substance to the oft-repeated slogan that to give (or to know, etc.) the semantic content or 'meaning' of a sentence of statement is to give (know, etc.) its truth conditions. Its notion of semantic content is exemplary of the kind of notion of content that is needed in connection with the notions of so-called *de re* modality and *de re* propositional attitudes. Perhaps the most important thing to be said for the Naive Theory is its cogency and intuitive appeal as a theory of assertion. When you utter 'Socrates is ingenious', your speech act divides into two parts: You pick someone out, Socrates, and you ascribe something to him, ingenuity. These two component speech acts – reference and ascription – correspond to two components of what you assert when you assert that Socrates is ingenious.

Mill's Theory

Unfortunately, the Naive Theory's central theses apparently come into conflict with regard to definite descriptions. According to the Naive Theory, the semantic content of a phrase like 'the individual who wrote *Begriffsschrift*' is simply its referent, Frege. Consequently, the proposition semantically contained in 'The individual who wrote *Begriffsschrift* is ingenious' is to be the singular proposition about Frege that he is ingenious. But the definite description is a phrase which, like a sentence, has parts with identifiable semantic contents – for example the singular term (work title) '*Begriffsschrift*', as well as the predicate 'wrote *Begriffsschrift*'. These semantically contentful components of the definite description are *ipso facto* semantically contentful components of the sentence. If the semantic content of a sentence is made up of the semantic contents of its semantically contentful parts, the semantic contents of these description components must also go in to make up part of the proposition that the author of *Begriffsschrift* is ingenious. Thus, instead of identifying the semantic content of 'the individual who wrote *Begriffsschrift*' with its referent, one should look instead for some complex entity made up partly of something like the relational property of having written *Begriffsschrift* at some time earlier than *t*, where *t* is the time of utterance, and partly of whatever serves as the semantic content of the definite description operator 'the'. On this modified version of the Naive Theory, the proposition that the author of *Begriffsschrift* is ingenious is not the singular proposition about Frege that he is ingenious, but a different proposition composed of something involving the property of authorship of *Begriffsschrift* in place of Frege himself.

One extremely important wrinkle in this modification of the Naive Theory is that a definite description ⌜the φ⌝, unlike other sorts of singular terms, is seen as having a two-tiered semantics. On the one hand, there is the description's referent, which is the individual that satisfies the description's constituent φ, if there is only one such individual, and is nothing otherwise. On the other hand, there is the description's semantic content. This is a complex made up, in part, of the semantic content of φ. By contrast, a proper name or other simple singular term is seen as having a one-tiered semantics: its semantic content (with respect to a particular context) is just its referent (with respect to that context). From the point of view of the modified Naive Theory, the original Naive Theory errs by treating definite descriptions on the model of a simple individual constant (proper name). Definite descriptions are not single words but phrases, and therefore have a richer semantic structure.

It can be demonstrated that if a notion of reference is to be extended to expressions other than singular terms, then an expression of any variety is best regarded as referring to its semantic extension.[4] Thus, an n-ary predicate is best regarded as referring to the set of n-tuples to which it applies, a sentence to its truth-value, and so on. Accordingly, the central theses of the Modified Naive Theory are: *(i′)* The semantic content of any simple (non-compound) singular term is its referent; *(ii′)* Any expression may be thought of as referring to its extension; and *(iii′)* The semantic content of a typical contentful compound expression (including both definite descriptions as well as sentences) is a complex, ordered entity (something like a sequence) whose constituents are semantically correlated systematically with expressions making up the compound expression, typically the simple (non-compound) component expressions.[5]

Thesis *(ii′)* involves a significant departure from the original Naive Theory with regard to simple predicates, such as ‘flies’. The Naive Theory identifies the semantic content of ‘flies’ with its referent, and both with the property of flying (at t). Instead, the Modified Naive Theory casts the class of all things having flight as the analogue to reference for ‘flies’, and reserves the property of having flight for the separate role of semantic content. Thus the Modified Naive Theory attributes a two-tiered semantics to some simple expressions in addition to compound expressions. The theory retains the principle that the semantic content of a compound contentful expression is typically made up of the semantic contents of its contentful parts, but by attributing a two-tiered semantics to simple predicates, this involves abandoning the original naive-theoretical principle that the semantic content of a compound expression is made up of the referents of its simple components.

The theory proffered by John Stuart Mill in Chapter 6 is a variant of the Modified Naive Theory. Mill distinguished two possible semantic attributes of a term, which he called ‘denotation’ and ‘connotation’. In the case of singular terms, Mill’s use of ‘denotation’ corresponds with the term ‘referent’, as used here. In addition, a general term (‘concrete general name’) is said to ‘denote’ the class of individuals to which the term applies ie., the extension of the term. Mill uses the term ‘connotation’, in effect, for a special kind of semantic content consisting of attributes or properties. All general terms were held by Mill to have both denotation and connotation. Among singular terms, according to Mill, definite descriptions also have both connotation and (typically) denotation as well, whereas proper names never have connotation.[6]

The Puzzles

There are at least four well-known puzzles that arise on both the Naive Theory and the Modified Naive Theory. The articles in Parts II and III below are concerned in one way or another with one or more of the four puzzles. Each of the puzzles has been put forward as a refutation of the theory on which it arises. First, there is Frege's Puzzle involving the informativeness of identity sentences. The sentence 'Hesperus is Phosphorus' (or 'The evening star is the morning star') is informative; its semantic content apparently extends knowledge. The sentence 'Hesperus is Hesperus' ('The evening star is the evening star') is uninformative; its semantic content is a 'given.' According to both the Naive Theory and the Modified Naive Theory, the semantic content of 'Hesperus is Hesperus' consists of the planet Venus, taken twice, and the relation of identity (or the relation of identity-at-*t*, where *t* is the time of utterance). Yet the semantic content of 'Hesperus is Phosphorus', according to these theories, is made of precisely the same components, and apparently in precisely the same way.[7] Assuming a plausible principle of compositionality for propositions the Naive Theory and the Modified Naive Theory ascribe precisely the same semantic content to both sentences. This flies in the face of the fact that the two sentences differ dramatically in their informativeness.

In his early work *Begriffsschrift*, Gottlob Frege proposed solving this puzzle by reading the identity predicate, '=' or 'is' in the sense of 'is one and the very same object as' (the 'is' of identity), as covertly metalinguistic: It was held that the sentence 'Hesperus is Phosphorus' contains a proposition not about the planet Venus, but about the very names 'Hesperus' and 'Phosphorus' themselves, to the effect that they are co-referential. It is, of course, trivial that 'Hesperus' is co-referential with itself, but then this is a transparently different proposition from the proposition that 'Hesperus' is co-referential with 'Phosphorus', since the latter concerns the name 'Phosphorus'. It is no wonder, therefore, that the sentences 'Hesperus is Hesperus' and 'Hesperus is Phosphorus' differ in informativeness. There are a number of serious difficulties with this account, and Frege himself later came to reject it (Chapter 7). Frege's criticism was that the account misrepresents the proposition contained in the sentence 'Hesperus is Phosphorus' as something which, if true, is made so entirely by virtue of arbitrary linguistic convention or decision, whereas the proposition that Hesperus is Phosphorus is actually made true by virtue of a certain celestial state of affairs, quite independently of human convention. There are also technical difficulties with the account. It renders the identity predicate a non-extensional device similar to quotation marks. This makes quantification in (as for example in 'For every x and every y, if x and y are both natural satellites of the Earth, then $x = y$') impossible, or at least highly problematic. Moreover, the account fails to solve the general problem of which Frege's Puzzle is only a special case: whereas we are told how the sentence 'Hesperus is Hesperus' can differ in informativeness from the sentence 'Hesperus is Phosphorus', unless the theory is only part of a much more sweeping proposal concerning the semantic contents of all expressions and not just that of the identity predicate, we are given no explanation for the analogous difference in informativeness between such pairs of sentences as 'Hesperus is a planet if Hesperus is' and 'Hesperus is a planet if Phosphorus is.[8] In any event, the account does not even address the remaining problems with the Naive Theory and the Modified Naive Theory.

The second puzzle is, from one point of view, a generalization of the first, though it can arise on any of a wide variety of semantic theories. This is the apparent failure of substitutivity of co-referential names or other (simple) singular terms in certain contexts, especially in propositional-attitude contexts. If Jones has learned the names 'Hesperus' and 'Phosphorus' but remains unaware that they refer to the same heavenly body, he may sincerely and reflectively assent to the sentence 'Hesperus appears in the evening' and sincerely and reflectively dissent from the sentence 'Phosphorus appears in the evening', while understanding both sentences perfectly, ie., while fully grasping their semantic content. It seems, then, that Jones believes that Hesperus appears in the evening, but does not believe, indeed disbelieves, that Phosphorus appears in the evening. This presents a serious problem for any semantic theory, since it appears to violate a classical logical rule of inference, commonly called *the Substitutivity of Equality* or *Leibniz's Law*. This inference rule permits the substitution of an occurrence of any singular term b for an occurrence of any singular term a in a sentence, given $\ulcorner a = b \urcorner$. Of course, classical Substitutivity of Equality is subject to certain well-known restrictions. Most notably, the inference rule does not extend to contexts involving quotation marks and similar devices. Failure of substitutivity in propositional–attitude contexts, however, poses an especially pressing difficulty for both the Naive Theory and the Modified Naive Theory. These theories are unable to accommodate the apparent fact about Jones that he believes the proposition contained in the sentence 'Hesperus appears in the evening' but does not believe the proposition contained in the sentence 'Phosphorus appears in the evening', since the theories ascribe precisely the same semantic content to both sentences. Hence, the Naive Theory requires the validity of Substitutivity of Equality in propositional–attitude contexts, and the Modified Naive Theory requires the validity of a restricted but apparently equally objectionable version of the same.

Failure of substitutivity involving definite descriptions in modal contexts presents a similar difficulty. One example, due to W. V. O. Quine, effectively refutes the Naive Theory: The sentences 'It is mathematically necessary that nine is odd' and 'The number of planets is nine' are both true, but the sentence 'It is mathematically necessary that the number of planets is odd' is false, since there might have been ten planets rather than 9.[9] Modality creates no like difficulty for the Modified Naive Theory, which requires the validity of substitutivity of co-referential names and other simple singular terms in modal contexts (eg., 'It is a necessary truth that . . .'), but does not require the validity of substitutivity of all co-referential singular terms, including definite descriptions, in such contexts.

Third, there is the puzzle of true negative existentials, such as 'The present king of France does not exist' (Russell) and 'Donald Duck does not exist'. These sentences are true if and only if the singular term in subject position does not refer to anything. Yet on any of a variety of semantic theories, including the Naive Theory, a sentence involving a singular term can be true only if the term has a referent. In the case of a negative existential, the ascribed property is that of non-existence (at *t*) – a property for which it is impossible that there should exist something (at *t*) that has it.

In fact, on the (Modified) Naive Theory the semantic content of any sentence involving a (simple) singular term will lack a necessary component if any contained (simple) singular term lacks a referent. This presents a fourth and more general puzzle concerning any meaningful sentence involving non-referring singular terms, such as Russell's problematic sentence 'The present king of France is bald' and sentences from fiction, eg., 'Donald Duck wears a blue hat'. Such sentences clearly have content. But how can they, according to the Naive Theory? It seems clear, moreover, that such a sentence as 'The present king of France is bald' cannot be counted true. Should it then be counted false? If so, one should be able to say that the present king of France is *not bald*, yet this is no better than saying that he is bald. There seems to be a violation of the classical Law of Excluded Middle: either *p* or not-*p*.

Russell's Theory

Inspired by his new theory of logical analysis, Bertrand Russell promoted his (post-1904) theory of semantic content explicitly on the grounds of its ability to handle the four puzzles (Chapter 8). Russell's theory augments, and slightly modifies, the central theses of the Naive Theory. The primary departure is the replacement of attributes with propositional functions. A propositional function is a function that assigns to any objects in its domain, in singular proposition concerning those objects.

Russell handled the apparent inconsistency of the Naive Theory in the case of definite descriptions and other such phrases (which he called 'denoting phrases'), and the four puzzles, via his so-called Theory of Descriptions. The latter has both a special and general form. The General Theory of Descriptions concerns the logico-semantic status of restricted universal quantifier phrases, such as 'every man', and restricted existential quantifier phrases (sometimes called 'indefinite descriptions'), such as 'some dog', and 'an anthropologist', etc. We consider first restrictive universal sentences of the form $\ulcorner\Pi(\ldots, \text{every } \varphi, \ldots)\urcorner$ (or $\ulcorner\Pi(\ldots, \text{any } \varphi, \ldots)\urcorner$, $\ulcorner\Pi(\ldots, \text{each } \varphi, \ldots)\urcorner$, $\ulcorner\Pi(\ldots, \text{all } \varphi, \ldots)\urcorner$, etc.) built from an *n*-place predicate Π together with the restricted universal quantifier phrase ⌜every φ⌝ instead of a singular term in one (or more) of the *n* singular-term positions. On the general theory, such a sentence is analysed as

> Everything is an individual β such that, if β is φ, then Π(. . . , β, . . .).

(We may let β be the first variable, in some ordering of the variables, that does not occur in ⌜Π(. . . , every φ, . . .)⌝.) A restricted existential sentence of the form ⌜Π(. . . , some φ, . . .)⌝ (or ⌜Π(. . . , a φ, . . .)⌝) is analysed instead as

> Something is an individual β such that β is φ and Π(. . . , β, . . .).

An extremely important aspect of Russell's General Theory of Descriptions concerns the matter of scope. Such constructions as 'every man', 'some dog', etc., often yield syntactic scope ambiguities in surface structure when embedded within more complex sentential context, as for example 'Every man is not an island' or 'Some treasurer must be found'. The two readings of the latter sentence correspond to two ways of extending the Russellian analysis of ⌜Π(. . . , some φ, . . .)⌝ to ⌜OΠ(. . . , some φ, . . .)⌝, where *O* creates a sentential context. One way is simply to embed the analysis of ⌜Π. . . , some φ, . . .)⌝ within the context O, as in

> It must be that: something is both a treasurer and found.

On this reading the phrase 'some treasurer' is said to have narrow scope, or to have its secondary occurrence. The other way of extending the Russellian analysis is to imitate the treatment for the atomic case, treating the extended singular term context ⌜OΠ(. . . , ——, . . .)⌝ as if it were a simple, unstructured monadic predicate

> Something is both a treasurer and such that it must be that he/she is found.

On this reading the phrase 'some treasurer' has wide scope, or its primary occurrence. Further embeddings within sentential contexts yield further scope ambiguities, one additional reading for each additional context-embedding. For example, the sentence 'Some treasurer must not be needy' will have three readings: 'It must not be that: some treasurer is needy' (narrow scope); 'It must be that: some treasurer is such that he or she is not needy' (intermediate scope); 'Some treasurer is such that he or she must not be needy' (wide scope).

On the General Theory of Descriptions, the phrase 'some logician' occurring in the sentence 'Some logician is ingenious' corresponds to the essentially incomplete string 'Something both is a logician and . . .'. Indeed, Russell called such phrases as 'some logician', 'every treasurer', etc. incomplete symbols, and asserted that they are without semantic content (or without 'meaning in isolation').[10] It is natural and plausible on this theory to regard the word 'something' as a second-order predicate, while regarding the remainder of the sentence as a long-winded version of the compound first-order predicate 'is an ingenious logician'. The sentence 'Some logician is ingenious' would thus be construed as having a semantic content made up of the second-order propositional function that is the semantic content of 'something' and the first-order propositional function that is the semantic content of 'is an ingenious logician'. This is nothing that the phrase 'some logician' contributes on its own to this proposition – although the determiner 'some' may be regarded as contributing its semantic content and the semantic content of 'logician' figures indirectly in the construction of the semantic content of 'is both a logician and ingenious'. Exactly analogous results obtain in connection with the phrase 'every logician'. On the General Theory of Descriptions, the determiner component of such a phrase (a word like 'every', 'some', etc.) may be regarded as making a separate contribution to the semantic content of the sentence in which the description occurs. The rest of the description makes no contribution of its own but joins with the surrounding sentential context to yield something that does. In this way, such phrases form part of a larger construction whose semantically contentful components exclude, but overlap with, the phrase.

Russell's Special Theory of Descriptions concerns singular definite descriptions, and treats them as indefinite descriptions of a particular kind, in accordance with the General Theory. A sentence having the surface structure of a subject-predicate sentence, $\ulcorner \Pi(\ldots, \text{the } \varphi, \ldots \urcorner$, consisting of an *n*-place predicate and containing a complete definite description $\ulcorner \text{the } \varphi \urcorner$ among its *n* occurrences of singular terms, is analysed into a conjunction of three sentences

> There is at least one φ (The existence condition)
> There is at most one φ (The uniqueness condition) and
> $\Pi(\ldots, \text{every } \varphi, \ldots)$ (The subsumption condition).

The process is to be repeated until all definite-description occurrences have undergone an application of the procedure. A definite description $\ulcorner \text{the } \varphi \urcorner$ is said to be proper when the first two conditions both obtain (ie. if there is exactly one individual that answers to it), and is said to be improper otherwise. None of the sentences making up the analysans is logically subject-predicate; each is a quantificational generalization containing no definite descriptions. The Russellian analysis is thus said to be a method of eliminating definite descriptions, replacing an apparently subject-predicate sentence by a conjunction of quantificational generalizations.

Equivalently, $\ulcorner \Pi(\ldots, \text{the } \varphi, \ldots) \urcorner$ may be analysed by means of a single complex generalization: Something is an individual β such that β, and only

β, is φ, and $\Pi(\ldots, \beta, \ldots)$. This version of the analysis illustrates the central tenet of the Special Theory of Descriptions: a complete definite description such as 'the author of *Begriffsschrift*' is regarded as semantically equivalent to the corresponding uniqueness-restricted existential quantifier, 'some unique author of *Begriffsschrift*' (or 'a unique author of *Begriffsschrift*'), which falls under the purview of the General Theory of Descriptions.

This central tenet of the Special Theory of Descriptions has several important consequences. First, the theory predicts scope ambiguities in cases where definite descriptions are embedded within sentential contexts, one additional reading for each additional embedding. Most important for present purposes are the consequences of conjoining the Special Theory of Descriptions with the Naive Theory. The former's central tenet distinguishes it from semantic theories that accord definite descriptions the logico-semantic status of singular terms. The Special Theory of Descriptions enables Russell to maintain both of the original naive-theoretical theses (*i*) and (*ii*).[11] (This distinguishing characteristic of Russell's theory is obscured by the fact that he misleadingly and artificially extended Mill's term 'denotation' to the semantic relation that obtains between a uniqueness-restricted existential quantifier ⌜some unique φ⌝, which the theory regards as not forming a semantically self-contained unit, and the individual, if any, that uniquely satisfies φ. For example, although the definite description 'the author of *Begriffsschrift*' is not a semantically significant unit on Russell's theory, it is nevertheless said by Russell to 'denote' Frege. Thus Russell verbally mimics Mill's version of the Modified Naive Theory, while retaining the term 'meaning' for the semantic notion here called 'semantic content'.)

As with the Modified Naive Theory, on Russell's theory such a sentence as 'The author of *Begriffsschrift* is ingenious' does not contain the singular proposition about Frege that he is ingenious. Frege does not 'occur as a constituent' of the contained proposition; the sentence is only indirectly about him. Rather, the sentence is regarded as being directly about the conceptually complex propositional function (or property), being both *a unique author of Begriffsschrift* and *ingenious*, to the effect that it is instantiated. Thus the sentence does not directly concern any individual, but only a certain propositional function. This is critical to Russell's solutions to the four puzzles that arise in connection with the Naive Theory.

The four puzzles arise primarily from the identification of the semantic content of a singular term with the term's referent. Since the Modified Naive Theory and the Special Theory of Descriptions distinguish the semantic content of a definite description from the individual that uniquely answers to it, those theories are able to solve the puzzles in the special case where the singular terms involved are all definite descriptions, but the problems remain in the case where the terms involved are proper names, demonstratives, or pronouns. Russell handled these remaining difficulties by combining his Special Theory of Descriptions with the thesis that terms ordinarily regarded as proper names are ordinarily used not as 'genuine names' (singular terms) for individuals. Instead they are 'disguised,' 'concealed,' 'truncated,' or 'abbreviated' definite descriptions. This thesis has the effect of reducing to the previous case the special problems that arise in connection with proper names and indexicals.

Russell's treatment of the puzzle of the failure of substitutivity in propositional-attitude contexts is complicated by the fact that, on his theory, a propositional-attitude attribution such as 'Jones believes that Hesperus appears in the evening' is ambiguous. It has both a narrow-scope and a wide-scope reading. On the wide-scope reading, the sentence attributes to Jones a belief of the singular proposition about the planet Venus that it appears in the evening. Given the further premise 'Hesperus = Phosphorus', the wide-scope reading of the sentence 'Jones believes that Phosphorus appears in the evening' does indeed follow. It is only on the narrow-scope reading that Substitutivity of Equality fails. Russell's theory solves the puzzle of failure of substitutivity in narrow-scope propositional-attitude contexts by reading the complement clause, 'Hesperus appears in the evening', as referring to a different proposition from that referred to by 'Phosphorus appears in the evening'. Substitutivity of Equality licenses the substitution of co-referential singular terms (including variables). According to Russell's theory, definite descriptions, concealed or not, do not have the logical status of singular terms, and hence the traditional rule of Substitutivity of Equality does not apply to them. However, when it is given that two propositional-function expressions φ and ψ are satisfied by exactly the same individuals, restricted quantifiers of the same sort constructed from φ and ψ, such as $\ulcorner$some $\varphi\urcorner$ and $\ulcorner$some $\psi\urcorner$, will usually be interchangeable on other logical grounds. In the special case where it is given that there is something that uniquely satisfies φ and also uniquely satisfies ψ, the uniqueness-restricted existential quantifiers $\ulcorner$some unique $\varphi\urcorner$ and $\ulcorner$some unique $\psi\urcorner$, and hence the definite descriptions $\ulcorner$the $\varphi\urcorner$ and $\ulcorner$the $\psi\urcorner$, will be interchangeable in most contexts on logical grounds (which include the Substitutivity of Equality as applied to variables). It is for this reason that Substitutivity is upheld in the wide-scope reading of propositional-attitude attributions. But since $\ulcorner$some unique $\varphi\urcorner$ and $\ulcorner$some unique $\psi\urcorner$ may still contribute differently to the semantic contents of sentences in which they occur, they need not be interchangeable when occurring within the scope of operators, such as those of propositional attitude, that are sensitive to semantic content. An exactly analogous solution is available for the problems of failure of substitutivity in modal contexts.

The remaining two puzzles are solved in a similar manner, by reading sentences involving improper definite descriptions as encoding propositions about the corresponding propositional functions. In particular, the negative-existential 'The present king of France does not exist' is ambiguous on the Special Theory of Descriptions, with a true narrow-scope reading and a contradictory wide-scope reading. An unmodified sentence involving an improper definite description (concealed or not), such as 'The present king of

France is bald', will in general be false, since part of what it asserts is that there is a unique present king of France. Its apparent negation, 'The present king of France is not bald', is ambiguous on the Special Theory of Descriptions. Its narrow-scope reading yields the genuine negation of the original sentence. Its wide-scope reading is perhaps the more natural reading, but on this reading the sentence is false, for the same reason as with the original sentence. The Law of Excluded Middle is preserved in the case of 'Either the present king of France is bald, or the present king of France is not bald', provided both occurrences of the description 'the present king of France' are given narrow scope. Other readings of this ambiguous sentence are not proper instances of the law.

Russell's thesis that proper names and demonstratives are ordinarily used as disguised definite descriptions, together with his Special Theory of Descriptions, has the effect of purging (closed) simple singular terms from the language. It might seem, therefore, that Russell ultimately solves the philosophical problems that beset the Naive Theory by denying the existence of all singular terms other than individual variables. However, Russell acknowledged the possibility of 'logically proper names' or 'names in the strict, logical sense,' which are semantically simple and unstructured, and which therefore function in accordance with the Naive Theory. The class of possible semantic contents for genuine names was severely limited by Russell's Principle of Acquaintance: every proposition that one can grasp must be composed entirely of constituents with respect to which one has a special sort of intimate and direct epistemic access, 'direct acquaintance.' Because the semantic content of a genuine name is to be its referent, the only genuine names of individuals that one could grasp, according to Russell, were generally the demonstrative 'this', used deictically by a speaker to refer to mental items presently (or at least very recently) contained in his or her consciousness, and perhaps the first-person pronoun 'I' used with introspective deictic reference to oneself.[12]

Though Russell acknowledged the possibility of genuine names, for which semantic content coincides with reference, his restriction on admissible referents seems sufficient to prevent the four puzzles from arising. True identity sentences involving genuine names for an item of direct acquaintance are all equally uninformative, and all co-referential genuine names are validly intersubstitutable in propositional-attitude contexts. Russell did not countenance genuine names lacking a referent; the remaining two puzzles are thus blocked.[13]

Frege's Theory of Sense and Reference

Frege's later theory of meaning, though superficially similar to Russell's in certain respects, is fundamentally different. In his classic '*Über Sinn und Bedeutung*' (Chapter 7), Frege proposed abandoning the Naive Theory in favor of a different and richly elegant philosophy of semantics. Whereas the Modified Naive Theory attributes a two-tiered semantics to definite descriptions and predicates, Frege further extended two-tiered semantics to include all meaningful expressions, even sentences. Frege distinguished between the *Bedeutung* of an expression and its *Sinn*. The former corresponds in the case of singular terms to what is here called the 'referent'. The latter, standardly translated by the English 'sense', is the expression's semantic content. Frege's conception of sense is similar to Mill's notion of connotation, except that all meaningful expressions, including proper names, are held to have a sense. The sense of an expression is something like a purely conceptual representation, by means of which a referent for the expression is secured.[14] An expression's sense is a conception of something, and the expression's referent, if there is one, is whoever of whatever uniquely fits the concept. Since the sense of a singular term secures the term's referent, strictly synonymous expressions (ie. expressions having the very same sense) must have the same referent – although different expressions having the same referent may differ in sense. An expression is said to express its sense, and its sense, in turn, (typically) determines an object. The reference relation is simply the relative product of the relation of expressing between an expression and its sense, and the relation of determining between a sense and the object that uniquely fits it. In the special case of a sentence, Frege called its sense a 'thought' ('*Gedanke*').

The clearest examples of expressions exhibiting something like Frege's distinction between sense and referent are certain definite descriptions. (Like Mill and unlike Russell, Frege counted definite descriptions as genuine singular terms.) One of Frege's illustrations involves descriptions in the language of geometry: if *a*, *b*, and *c* are the three medians of a triangle, then the expressions 'the point of intersection of *a* and *b*' and 'the point of intersection of *b* and *c*' both refer to the centroid of the triangle, but they do so by presenting that point to the mind's grasp in different ways, by means of different aspects of the point. The descriptions thus share a common referent, but differ in sense. The senses are the semantic contents of the two expressions, and it is in virtue of this difference in sense that the sentence 'The point of intersection of *a* and *b* is the point of intersection of *b* *c*' contains different, and more valuable, information than that contained in the sentence 'The point of intersection of *a* and *b* is the point of intersection of *a* and *b*'.

Frege illustrates what the sense of a proper name is by means of carefully chosen definite descriptions. The observation that proper names have this sort of conceptual content as well as a referent, together with Frege's doctrine that this conceptual content and not the referent serves the role of semantic content, immediately solves the puzzle about the informativeness of identity sentences involving two names for the same individual. The distinction between sense and referent also immediately solves the problem of how sentences involving non-referring singular terms can have content.

Crucial to Frege's theory are a pair of principles concerning the referent and sense of complex expressions. These are the Principle of Compositionality (Interchange) of Reference and the analogous Principle of Compositionality (Interchange) of Sense. They hold that the referent or sense of a complex expression is a function only of the referents or senses, respectively, of the constituent expressions. In the latter case Frege often spoke (explicitly metaphorically) of the sense of a constituent expression as a *part* of the sense of the complex expression. Thus, if a constituent expression is replaced by one having the same referent but differing in sense, the referent of the whole is preserved, but not the sense. If a constituent expression is replaced by something strictly synonymous, both the sense and the referent of the whole are preserved. In particular, Frege held as a special case of the Compositionality of Reference that a compound expression having a non-referring part must itself be non-referring. Relying on the Compositionality of Reference, Frege argued that the 'cognitive value' (*Erkenntniswerte*) of a sentence is not the referent of the sentence, but is (or is at least fixed by) its sense or 'thought' content, and that the referent of a sentence is simply its truth value, either truth or falsehood ('the True' or 'the False').[15]

The Compositionality of Reference thus solves the problem of the truth value of sentences involving non-referring singular terms. Since a sentence refers to its truth value, and a sentence involving a non-referring singular term itself refers to nothing, such as a sentence as 'The present king of France is bald' is neither true nor false; it lacks truth value. The same holds for its negation, 'The present king of France is not bald'. Frege held that the 'thoughts' (propositions) expressed by these sentences do not assert, but merely presuppose, that there is a unique present king of France and that the expression 'the present king of France' has a referent. Thus Frege's theory does not preserve an unrestricted Law of Excluded Middle, nor any other law of logic. The laws of logic must be restricted to sentences whose presuppositions are fulfilled.

Whereas the Compositionality of Reference solves one of the puzzles, it also issues in the problems of failure of substitutivity and of true negative existentials. Since on Frege's theory sentences refer to their truth values, and the referent of a sentence is a function of the referents of its constituents, the theory requires the universal validity of Substitutivity of Equality – even in quotational contexts. Furthermore, since on Frege's theory sentences involving non-referring singular terms are neither true nor false, the theory appears unable to accommodate the truth of the negative existential 'The present king of France does not exist'.

Frege explicitly considered the problems of failure of substitutivity in quotational and propositional-attitude contexts, treating both in a like manner. Quotation marks and the sentential operator 'that' associated with propositional-attitude operators (eg. 'Jones believes that'), according to Frege, create a special context in which expressions take on a different referent from their customary referent. Whereas the expression 'Hesperus' customarily refers to the planet Venus, when occurring within quotation marks, as in the sentence 'The expression "Hesperus" is a string of eight letters', it instead refers to itself. Such is the case when someone's remarks are reported in 'direct discourse,' that is, when quoting the very words used by the speaker, as in 'Jones said "Hesperus appears in the evening"'. Analogously, when occurring in a 'that'-clause in a propositional-attitude attribution, as in 'Jones believes that Hesperus appears in the evening', the name 'Hesperus' occurs in an *ungerade* (indirect, oblique) context, referring there neither to its customary referent nor to itself but to its customary sense. Similarly, the entire embedded sentence 'Hesperus appears in the evening', when occurring within the 'that'-operator refers to its customary sense rather than to its customary referent. Such is the case when someone's remarks are reported in 'indirect discourse,' that is, when reporting the content of his or her remarks, as in 'Jones said that Hesperus appears in the evening', rather than the very words used. The principle of Compositionality of Reference is to be understood as requiring the validity of substituting for the name 'Hesperus' in such a position any expression having the same referent as 'Hesperus' in that position. This validates the substitution of any expression having the same customary sense as 'Hesperus'; it does not validate the substitution of an expression merely having the same customary referent. Similarly, the Compositionality of Reference does not validate any substitution within quotation marks. Thus Frege's theory gives central importance to a relativized semantic notion of an expression *e* expressing a sense *s* (or referring to an object *o*) as occurring in a particular position *p* within a sentence – or equivalently, to a notion of an expression occurrence (within a sentence) referring to an object or expressing a sense – rather than the more standard notion in contemporary semantics of an expression referring to (denoting) an object ('in isolation'). The latter Frege called 'customary' reference.

Since all reference on Frege's theory is mediated by sense, an occurrence of an expression standing within a single occurrence of a propositional-attitude operator (eg. the occurrence of 'Hesperus' in 'Jones believes that Hesperus appears in the evening') must refer to its customary sense by expressing some further sense that is also associated with the expression and that determines the expression's customary sense in the usual way that sense determines reference. This Frege called the '*ungerade Sinn*' (indirect sense) of the expression. He explained this notion by observing that the *ungerade Sinn* of a sentence such as 'Socrates is wise' is just the customary sense of the phrase 'the proposition (thought) that Socrates is wise'. Just as an occurrence of a single propositional-attitude operator induces a shift in the reference of expression occurrences standing within its scope from customary referent to customary sense, so an occurrence of an expression standing within the embedding of one occurrence of a propositional-attitude operator within another (eg. the occurrence of 'Hesperus' in 'Smith doubts that Jones believes that Hesperus appears in the evening') refers not to its customary sense but to its *ungerade Sinn*. This would have to be accomplished by means of some yet third sense associated with the expression – a doubly indirect sense – which determines the expression's (singly) indirect sense. Since there is no limit in principle to the number of allowable embeddings of operators ('Brown realizes that Smith doubts that Jones believes that . . .'), it is generally acknowledged that Frege admitted the existence of an infinite hierarchy of senses associated with each meaningful expression.

Frege did not explicitly consider the problem of failure of substitutivity in modal contexts, nor that of true negative existentials. It is in the spirit of Frege's theory, though, to regard modal operators as creating further *ungerade* contexts in which expressions refer to their customary sense, as in the sentence 'It is necessary that nine is odd' since it is not the truth value of the embedded sentence 'nine is odd' that is said to be necessary, but rather its proposition or 'thought' content, the proposition that nine is odd.[16] Scattered remarks in Frege's posthumously published writings suggest that he might have applied his doctrine of reference-shifting also to the problem of true negative-existentials, treating a sentence like 'The present king of France does not exist' as making the metalinguistic assertion that the phrase 'the present king of France' is non-referring.

The Orthodox Theory

The theories of Russell and Frege have been extremely influential in contemporary philosophy. Although Russell's is essentially a supplement to the Naive Theory whereas Frege's involves a total abandonment of the Naive Theory (and any modification thereof), there is considerable common ground, especially in regard to ordinary proper names. This area of agreement between the two theories has ascended to the status of orthodoxy. The orthodox theory can be explained as follows. Let us say that an expression *e*, as used in a particular possible context, is *descriptional* if there is a set of properties semantically associated with *e* in such a way as to generate a semantic relation, which may be called 'denotation' or 'reference', and which correlates with *e* (with respect to such semantic parameters as a possible world *w* and a time *t*) whoever or whatever uniquely has all (or at least sufficiently and appropriately many) of these properties (in *w* at *t*), if there is a unique such individual, and nothing otherwise.[17] A descriptional term is one that denotes by way of properties. It is a term that expresses a way of conceiving something, and its 'denotation' (with respect to a possible world and time) is secured indirectly by means of this conceptual content. Definite descriptions, such as 'the author of *Begriffsschrift*', are descriptional. A non-descriptional singular term is one whose reference is not semantically mediated by associated conceptual content. The paradigm of a non-descriptional singular term is the individual variable. The referent or 'denotation' of a variable under an assignment of value (with respect to a possible world and time) is semantically determined directly by the value assignment, and not by extracting a conceptual 'mode of presentation' from the variable.

Frege and Russell held a strong version of the theory that an ordinary proper name, as used in a particular context, is descriptional. On their view, if a name such as 'St Anne' is analysable as 'the mother of Mary', it must be in some sense analysable even further, since the name 'Mary' is also supposed to be descriptional. But even 'the mother of the mother of Jesus' must be in this sense further analysable, in view of the occurrence of the name 'Jesus', and so on. Let α be a non-descriptional singular term referring to Socrates. Then the definite description ⌜the wife of α⌝, though descriptional, is not thoroughly so. The property expressed is an intrinsically relational property directly involving Socrates, the property of being *his* wife. We may say that the description is only relationally descriptional, and that it is descriptional relative to Socrates. A thoroughly descriptional term, then, is one that is descriptional but not relationally descriptional.[18]

The orthodox theory is the theory that proper names, demonstratives, and such terms as 'you', 'he', etc., as used in a particular possible context, are either thoroughly descriptional or descriptional relative only to items of 'direct acquaintance,' such as sensations, visual images, and the like. Frege held the very strong version of this theory that all such terms are thoroughly descriptional. Only if a term is thoroughly descriptional can there be something that counts as a genuine Fregean sense for the term. The reason for this is that the Fregean conception of sense is a compilation or conflation of at least three distinct linguistic attributes. First, the sense of an expression is a purely conceptual mode of presentation. Individuals that are not themselves senses, such as persons and their sensations, cannot form part of a genuine Fregean sense. Second, the sense of a singular term is the mechanism by which its referent is secured and semantically determined. Third, the sense of an expression is its semantic content. Nothing counts as the sense of a term, as Frege intended the notion, unless it is all three at once. Frege supposed that the purely conceptual content of any singular term is also its semantic content, which also secures its referent. This three-way identification constitutes a very strong theoretical claim. A descriptional singular term is precisely one whose mode of securing a referent is its descriptive content, which also serves as its semantic content. Only if the term is thoroughly descriptional, however, can this be identified with a purely conceptual (or a purely qualitatively descriptive) content. Strictly speaking, even a Russellian term descriptional relative only to items of direct acquaintance (if there exist any such terms) does not have a genuine Fregean sense. Any departure from this thesis would constitute a rejection of fundamental Fregean theory.

The Theory of Direct Reference

Beginning around the mid-1960s the orthodox theory was forcefully challenged by some philosophers, notably by Keith Donnellan (Chapter 9), David Kaplan (Chapter 12), Saul Kripke (Chapter 10), and Hilary Putnam (Chapter 11). They held the opposing theory that ordinary proper names and single-word indexical singular terms are non-descriptional. Donnellan, in particular, extended the thesis even to what is probably the most common use of definite descriptions – the so-called referential, as opposed to attributive, use. Since their view denies that the reference of names and some other terms is mediated by a descriptive concept, it has come to be called 'the theory of direct reference'. This title may be misleading, however, since it suggests the obviously false thesis that reference is entirely unmediated. Also misleading, though literally correct, is the characterization of the direct-reference theory as the doctrine that names and indexicals have reference but not sense. In denying that proper names are descriptional, the direct-reference theory is not denying that a use of a particular proper name may exhibit any or all of the three aspects of a Fregean sense mentioned in the previous section. What the direct-reference theory denies is that the conceptual content associated with an individual constant is what secures the referent. Thus, for example, the direct-reference theory would hold that the proper name 'Shakespeare' is not shorthand for any description or cluster of descriptions, such as 'England's greatest bard', 'the author of *Romeo and Juliet*', etc. But the central thesis of the direct reference theory is significantly stronger than a simple denial of Russell's doctrine that ordinary names are concealed definite descriptions. The direct-reference theory holds that ordinary names are not even similar to definite descriptions. According to the orthodox theory, ordinary names are either thoroughly descriptional or descriptional relative only to items of 'direct acquaintance.' Against this, the direct-reference theorists argue that names and single-word indexical singular terms, as ordinarily used, are not descriptional at all. An immediate consequence is that a great many definite descriptions fail to be thoroughly descriptional, or descriptional relative only to items of direct acquaintance, since so many contain proper names or indexicals referring to ordinary individuals.

A number of arguments have been advanced in favor of the central thesis of the direct-reference theory. Although the arguments are many and varied, most of them may be seen as falling under one of three main kinds: modal arguments, epistemological arguments, and semantic arguments. The modal arguments are due chiefly to Kripke. Consider the name 'Shakespeare' as used to refer to the famous English dramatist. Consider now the properties that someone might associate with the name as forming its conceptual content on a particular occasion. These properties might include Shakespeare's distinguishing characteristics – such properties as that of being a famous

English poet and playwright of the late sixteenth and early seventeenth centuries; authorship of several classic plays including *Hamlet, Macbeth*, and *Romeo and Juliet*; partnership in the Globe Theatre; and so on. Suppose for simplicity that the name 'Shakespeare' simply means 'the English playwright who wrote *Hamlet, Macbeth* and *Romeo and Juliet*.' Consider now the following sentences

> Shakespeare, if he exists, wrote *Hamlet, Macbeth*, and *Romeo and Juliet*. If anyone is an English playwright who is sole author of *Hamlet, Macbeth*, and *Romeo and Juliet*, then he is Shakespeare.

If the orthodox theory of names is correct, then by substituting for the name its longhand synonym we find that these two sentences taken together simply mean: someone is the English playwright who wrote *Hamlet, Macbeth*, and *Romeo and Juliet* if and only if he is the English playwright who wrote *Hamlet, Macbeth*, and *Romeo and Juliet*. This is, if the orthodox theory is correct, the sentences displayed above should express *logical truths* – indeed they should be *analytic* in the traditional sense – and should therefore express necessary truths, propositions true with respect to all possible worlds. But surely, the argument continues, it is not at all necessary that someone is Shakespeare if and only if he is an English playwright who wrote *Hamlet, Macbeth*, and *Romeo and Juliet*. In the first place, it might have come to pass that Shakespeare elected to enter a profession in law instead of becoming a writer and dramatist. Hence, the first sentence displayed above does not express a necessary truth. Furthermore, assuming Shakespeare had gone into law instead of drama, it could have come to pass that some Englishman other than Shakespeare, say, Francis Bacon, should go on to write these plays. Hence even the second sentence displayed above expresses only a contingent truth. It follows that the name 'Shakespeare' is not descriptional in terms of the properties mentioned.

The intuition that the two sentences displayed above are false with respect to certain possible worlds is supported by a complementary intuition concerning reference: that the name 'Shakespeare' continues to refer to the same person even with respect to counterfactual situations in which this individual lacks all of the distinguishing characteristics that we actually use to identify him. In particular, the name 'Shakespeare' continues to refer to the same individual even in discourse about a counterfactual situation in which not he but some other Englishman wrote *Hamlet, Macbeth*, and *Romeo and Juliet*, whereas the definite description 'the English playwright who wrote *Hamlet, Macbeth*, and *Romeo and Juliet*' will refer in such discourse to the other Englishmen. Consequently, the two sentences displayed above must be false in such discourse. Thus the main intuition behind the modal arguments is intimately connected with a related linguistic intuition concerning the reference of proper names and indexical singular terms, in contrast to definite descriptions, with respect to other possible worlds. The orthodox theory comes into conflict with this intuition; the direct-reference theorists offer an alternative that conforms with this intuition. One important consequence of the theory of direct reference is that such expressions as proper names and single-word indexical singular terms are rigid designators (Kripke). An expression is a rigid designator if it designates the same thing with respect to every possible world in which that thing exists (and does not designate anything else with respect to other possible worlds).

The epistemological arguments against the orthodox theory, also due chiefly to Kripke, are similar to the modal arguments. Consider again the two sentences displayed above. Assuming that the orthodox theory is correct, these sentences should contain propositions that are knowable a priori, ie. knowable solely by reflection on the concepts involved and without recourse to experience. But it is not difficult to imagine circumstances in which it is discovered that, contrary to popular belief, Shakespeare did not write *Hamlet*, *Macbeth*, *Romeo and Juliet*, or any other work commonly attributed to him. Since this possibility is not automatically precluded by reflection on the concepts involved, it follows that the first sentence displayed above contains a proposition that is knowable only a posteriori, ie. knowable only by recourse to experience. One can even imagine circumstances in which it is discovered that we have been the victims of a massive hoax, and that, though Shakespeare is not responsible for any of these great works, some other Englishman (say, Bacon) wrote every one of the plays and sonnets commonly attributed to Shakespeare. This means that even the second sentence displayed above is not analytic or true by definition, as alleged, but contains an a posteriori posposition.

The most direct and persuasive of the three kinds of arguments for the direct-reference theory are the semantic arguments. One example is Donnellan's argument concerning Thales. Suppose that the sense or conceptual content of 'Thales' is determined by the description 'the Greek philosopher who held that all is water'. Suppose now that, owing to some error or fraud, the man referred to by writers such as Aristotle and Herodotus, from whom our use of the name 'Thales' derives, never genuinely believed that all is water. Suppose further that by a very strange coincidence there was indeed a Greek hermit-philosopher who did in fact hold this bizarre view, though he was unknown to them and bears no historical connection to us. To which of these two philosophers would our name 'Thales' refer? Clearly to the first of the two; our use of the name would bear no significant connection to the second character whatsoever. It is only by way of a comical accident that he enters into the story at all.

This example is not to be confused with the corresponding modal or epistemological arguments ('Thales might not have been the Greek philosopher who held that all is water'). In the modal and epistemological arguments, the main question is what the truth value of such a sentence as 'Thales is the Greek philosopher who held that all is water', which is alleged to be analytic, becomes when the sentence is evaluated with respect to certain imagined circumstances The strategy in the semantic arguments is more direct. The issue here is not whom the name *actually* refers to *with respect to* the imagined circumstances; the issue is whom the name *would have* referred to if the circumstances described above *had* obtained. The modal arguments are indirectly related to the question of what a particular term refers to *with respect to another possible world*; the semantic arguments are directly concerned with the non-modal question of reference *simpliciter*. The key phrase in the definition of a descriptional singular term is not 'correlated with respect to a possible world', but 'whoever or whatever uniquely has the properties'.

The theory of direct reference should not be misunderstood as involving the thesis that no descriptive concepts or properties are ever semantically associated with names or indexicals. Proponents of the direct-reference theory allow that some non-descriptional terms may be introduced into a language or idiolect by way of descriptional expressions. In this special kind of definition the descriptional expression serves only to assign a referent to the term being introduced, and does not simultaneously bequeath its descriptionality to the new term. To use Kripke's apt phrase, the descriptional expression is used only to 'fix the reference' of the non-descriptional term.

This admission is generally coupled with the observation that there are almost always non-descriptional contextual elements at work in fixing the referent of a name. The semantic arguments reveal that the way the referent is determined is not a purely conceptual matter; external factors enter into it. The surrounding settings in which speakers find themselves are crucial to determining the referents of the names and other terms they use. This is true not only of the extra-linguistic setting in which the referent is to be found, but also of the linguistic setting in which the term is used or was learned by the speaker, ie. the history of the use of the name leading up to the speaker's learning it. In a word, the securing of a referent for a proper name is a contextual phenomenon. Donnellan and Kripke have provided accounts of the securing of a referent for a proper name by means of such historical chains of communication. Putnam has given a similar account of certain terms designating something by means of a 'division of linguistic labor' and a 'structured co-operation between experts and nonexperts.' In virtue of these accounts the theory of direct reference is often called the 'causal' theory of reference. It would be better to call the theory the contextual theory of reference, thereby including standard accounts of such indexicals as 'I' and 'now'. The contextual accounts provided by direct-reference theorists are usually sketchy and incomplete. Though there have been attempts to work out the details of how the referent of a proper name or demonstrative, as used in a particular context, is secured, there is much that remains to be done in this area.

The Modified Naive Theory Reconsidered

The direct-reference theory is concerned primarily to distinguish two of the three aspects of a name conflated by the Fregean conception of sense: the conceptual content and what secures the referent. We are still left, then, with a pressing question concerning the third aspect of sense: What is the semantic content of a proper name? If the direct-reference theory is correct, it cannot be the sense of the name, for there is none.

A tempting answer to our question is that the semantic content of a name is simply its associated conceptual content, its 'mode of presentation' of its referent. This identification does not require the further identification with the manner of securing a referent. This idea thus preserves a good deal, but not all, of Frege's point of view without positing full-blown Fregean senses for names.

Many of the considerations that count against the orthodox theory (the modal arguments for example) extend also to this simpler theory. To use a variant of the semantic argument, there could be two distinct individuals, *A* and *B*, such that the descriptive content individual *C* associates with *A*'s name is exactly the same as that associated by individual *D* with *B*'s name. (This could happen for any number of reasons. Perhaps *A* and *B* are very much like one another, or one or both of *C* and *D* is mistaken, etc.) Hence according to the proposed theory, *A*'s name has the same semantic content for *C* that *B*'s name has for *D*. This conflicts with the fact that when *C* uses *A*'s name to ascribe something to *A* – say, that he weighs exactly 175 pounds – and *D* uses *B*'s name to ascribe the very same thing to *B*, *C* asserts a proposition concerning *A* (and does not assert any proposition concerning *B*) whereas *D* asserts a proposition concerning *B* (and does not assert any proposition concerning *A*). The two assertions may even differ in truth value.

It might be proposed, then, that the semantic content of a name is constituted partly by associated descriptive or conceptual content, and partly by something else, say the context that secures the referent, or perhaps the referent itself. But any proposal that identifies the semantic content of a name even only partly with descriptive or conceptual associations faces some of the same difficulties as the orthodox theory – for example, the epistemological arguments. There is always a possibility of error and inaccuracy in conceptual or descriptive associations. The descriptive content one associates with the name 'Frege' may be riddled with misattribution and misdescription, enough so as to befit someone else, say Russell, far better than Frege. Nevertheless, the sentence 'Frege wrote *Begriffsschrift*' contains a proposition that is entirely accurate and error-free. Hence, the descriptive associations that attach to the name cannot be even only a part of the name's semantic content.[19]

There is a more general difficulty which these and other alternatives to the Naive Theory and the Modified Naive Theory. Recall the argument from Frege's Puzzle about the informativeness of identity statements. An exactly similar argument can be mounted against any of a wide variety of theories of semantic content, including Frege's own. For example, Hilary Putnam confesses that he does not have the slightest idea what characteristics differentiate beech trees from elm trees, other than the fact that the English term for beeches is 'beech' and the English term for elms is 'elm'. The purely conceptual content that Putnam attaches to the term 'beech' is the same that he attaches to the term 'elm', and it is a pretty meager one at that. Nevertheless, an utterance of the sentence 'Elm wood is beech wood' would (under the right circumstances) be highly informative for him. In fact, he knows that elm wood is not beech wood. By an argument exactly analogous to the one constructed from Frege's Puzzle, we should conclude that the semantic content of 'elm' or 'beech' is not the conceptual content.[20] This argument employs the same general strategy and mostly the same premises as the original Fregean argument in connection with 'Hesperus' and 'Phosphorus'. The generalized Fregean strategy may be applied against virtually any minimally plausible and substantive theory of semantic content. In this particular application of the generalized strategy, the relevant informative identity statement is not even true, but that does not matter to the general strategy. The truth of an informative identity statement is required only in the application of the general argument against theories that locate semantic content, at least in part, in reference. In the general case, only informativeness is required. False identity statements are always informative – so informative, in fact, as to be misinformative. Thus, virtually any substantive theory of semantic content imaginable reintroduces a variant of Frege's Puzzle, or else it is untenable on independent grounds (modal arguments, epistemological arguments, the argument from error, etc.).

The sheer range of applicability of the generalized Fregean strategy would seem to indicate that the strategy involves some error. The fact that the generalized strategy is indeed flawed might be demonstrated through an application of the generalized strategy to a situation involving straightforward (strict) synonyms for which it is uncontroversial that semantic content is preserved. Suppose that foreign-born Sasha learns the words 'ketchup' and 'catsup' not by being taught that they are perfect synonyms, but by actually consuming the condiment and reading the labels on the bottles. Suppose further that, in Sasha's idiosyncratic experience, people typically have the condiment called 'catsup' with their eggs and hash browns at breakfast, whereas they routinely have the condiment called 'ketchup' with their hamburgers at lunch. This naturally leads Sasha to conclude, erroneously, that ketchup and catsup are different condiments that happen to share a similar taste, color, consistency, and name. Whereas the sentence 'Ketchup is ketchup' is uninformative for Sasha, the sentence 'Catsup is ketchup' is every bit as informative as 'Hesperus is Phosphorus'. Applying the generalized Fregean strategy, we would conclude that the terms 'catsup' and 'ketchup' differ in semantic content for Sasha. But this is clearly wrong. The terms 'ketchup' and 'catsup' are perfect synonyms in English. Some would argue that they are merely two different spellings of the very same English word. Most of us who have learned these words (or these spellings of the single word) probably learned one of them in an ostensive definition of some sort, and the other as a strict synonym (or as an alternative spelling) of the first. Some of us learned 'ketchup' first and 'catsup' second; for others the order was the reverse. Obviously, it does not matter which is learned first and which second. If either may be learned by ostensive definition then both may be. Indeed, Sasha has learned both words (spellings) in much the same way that nearly everyone else has learned at least one of them: by means of a sort of ostensive definition. This manner of acquiring the two words (spellings) is unusual, but not impossible. Sasha's acquisition of these words (spellings) prevented him from learning at the outset that they are perfect synonyms, but the claim that he therefore has not learned both is highly implausible. Each word (spelling) was learned by Sasha in much the same way that some of us learned it. Even in Sasha's idiolect, then, the two words (spellings) are perfectly synonymous, and therefore share the same semantic content. This discredits the original Fregean argument against the Naive Theory and the Modified Naive Theory in connection with 'Hesperus' and 'Phosphorus'. (See Chapter 16 below for related discussion.)

Further argumentation is needed if the Modified Naive Theory is to be properly assessed. One important consideration favoring the Modified Naive Theory over the orthodox theory comes by way of the paradigms of non-descriptional singular terms, individual variables. A related consideration involves pronouns. Consider the following so-called *de re* (as opposed to *de dicto*), or *relational* (as opposed to *notional*), propositional-attitude attribution, expressed by way of abstraction into the *ungerade* context created by the non-extensional operator 'believes that'

(1) Venus is an individual x such that Jones believes that x is a star.

Such a *de re* locution may be expressed less formally in colloquial English as

(1′) Jones believes of the planet Venus that it is a star.

What is characteristic of these *de re* locutions is that they do not specify how Jones conceives of the planet Venus in believing it to be a star. It is left open whether he is thinking of Venus as the first heavenly body visible at dusk, or as the last heavenly body visible at dawn, or instead as the heavenly body he sees at time *t*, or none of the above. The orthodox theorist contends that this lack of specificity is precisely a result of the fact that the (allegedly descriptional) name 'Venus' is positioned outside of the scope of the *ungerade* context created by the non-extensional operator 'believes that', where it is open to substitution of co-referential singular terms and to existential generalization. What is more significant, however, is that another, non-descriptional singular term is positioned within the scope of the non-extensional context: the last occurrence of the variable '*x*' in (1), the pronoun 'it' in (1′). Consider first the quasi-formal sentence (1). It follows by the principles of conventional formal semantics that (1) is true if and only if its component open sentence

(2) Jones believes that *x* is a star

is true under the assignment of the planet Venus as value for the variable '*x*' – or in the terminology of Tarski, if and only if Venus *satisfies* (2). The open sentence (2) is true under the assignment of Venus as value of '*x*' if and only if Jones believes the proposition that is the semantic content of the complement open sentence

(3) *x* is a star

under the same assignment of Venus as the value of '*x*'.

A parallel derivation proceeds from the colloquial *de re* attribution (1′). Sentence

(1′) is true if and only if its component sentence
(2′) Jones believes that it is a star

is true under the anaphoric assignment of Venus as referent for the pronoun 'it'. As with the open sentence (2), sentences (2′) is true under the assignment of Venus as the referent of 'it' if an only if Jones believes the semantic content of

(3′) It is a star

under this same assignment.

Now, the fundamental characteristic of a variable with an assigned value, or of a pronoun with a particular referent, is precisely that its semantic content is just its referent. There is nothing else for it to contribute to the semantic content of sentences like (3) or (3′) in which it figures. In fact, this is precisely the point of using a variable or a pronoun rather than a definite description (like 'the first heavenly body visible at dusk') within the scope of an attitude verb in a *de re* attribution. A variable with an assigned value, or a pronoun with a particular referent cannot have, in addition to its referent, a Fregean sense – a conceptual representation that it contributes to semantic content. If it had, (3) and (3′) would contain specific general propositions, under these assignments, and (2) and (2′) would thus be notional rather than relational. If (1) and (1′) are to be relational – if they are to fail to specify how Jones conceives of Venus – the content of (3) or (3′) under the assignment of Venus to '*x*' or 'it' can only be the singular proposition about Venus that it is a star, the sort of proposition postulated by the Modified Naive Theory. This means that the semantic content of either the variable or the pronoun must be its referent.

What is good for the individual variable under an assigned value is good for the individual constant. Indeed, the only difference between a variable and a constant is that the variable varies where the constant stands fast. The semantics for a given language fixes the reference of its individual constants. Individual variables are singular terms that would be individual constants but for their promiscuity. Conversely, then, individual constants are singular terms that would be variables but for their monogamy. The variability of a variable has nothing whatsoever to do with the separate feature that the variable's semantic content, under an assignment of a referent, is just the assigned referent. It is the simplicity of the variable that gives it the latter feature; the variability only guarantees that the semantic content also varies. Once the variable is assigned a particular value, the variable becomes, for all intents and purposes pertaining to that assignment, a constant. Hence, if the open sentence (3), under the assignment of Venus as the value of '*x*', contains the singular proposition about Venus that it is a star, then the closed sentence

a is a star,

where '*a*' is an individual constant that refers to Venus, contains this same proposition.

There is a great deal more to be said both against and in favor of the Modified Naive Theory. In particular, there are the arguments that derive from the remaining three puzzles. It is important to note in this connection that at least some aspects of these puzzles would arise even in a language for which it was stipulated – say, by an authoritative linguistic committee that legislates the grammar and semantics of the language, and to which all speakers of the language give their co-operation and consent – that the Modified Naive Theory is correct. Suppose, for example, that such a committee decreed that individual names are to function exactly like the mathematician's variables '*x*', '*y*', and '*z*', except that they are to remain constant. Almost certainly, ordinary speakers would continue to regard co-referential names as not always interchangeable in propositional-attitude attributions. English speakers who use 'ketchup' and 'catsup' as exact synonyms but who do not reflect philosophically on the matter, and even some who do reflect philosophically, may be inclined to assent to the sentence 'Sasha believes that ketchup is a sandwich condiment, but he does not believe that catsup is'. On reflection, however, it emerges that this sentence expresses a logical impossibility, since the proposition that catsup is a sandwich condiment just is the proposition that ketchup is a sandwich condiment. Similarly, speakers who agree to abide by the legislative committee's decree about proper names and variables, especially if these speakers do not reflect philosophically on the implications of the decree in connection with such constructions as (1), might for independent pragmatic reasons be led to utter or assent to such sentences as 'Jones believes that Hesperus appears in the evening, but he does not believe that Phosphorus does'. Perhaps speakers would be led to utter this sentence, for example, in order to convey the complex fact that Jones agrees to the proposition about Venus that it appears in the evening when he takes it in the way it is presented to him by the sentence 'Hesperus appears in the evening' but not when he takes it in the way it is presented to him by the sentence 'Phosphorus appears in the evening.'[21] In so far as the same phenomena that give rise to the puzzles would arise even in the case of a language for which the Modified Naive Theory was true by fiat and unanimous consent (and do in fact arise with respect to such straightforward strict synonyms as 'ketchup' and 'catsup'), the puzzles cannot be taken as evidence against the Modified Naive Theory.[22]

The puzzles arising from non-referring names involve a complex nest of further issues that cannot be discussed here. A deeper understanding is needed of all four of the puzzles that gave rise to the present situation in the theory of reference, as well as a re-examination of the Modified Naive Theory in light of this deeper understanding. Until this is achieved, it is premature to reject the Modified Naive Theory solely on the basis of the puzzles.[23]

Notes

1. The notion of semantic content is the same as that for which the phrase 'information value' is used in Chapter 16 of this anthology. Throughout this article the verb 'contain' is used in such a way that an unambiguous declarative sentence semantically contains a *single* proposition (with respect to a given possible context). This proposition is referred to by the result of prefixing the phrase 'the proposition that' to the sentence. A declarative sentence may contain two or more propositions (with respect to the same context), but if it does so, it is ambiguous. Propositions contained by the proper logical consequences of an unambiguous sentence are not themselves contained, in this sense, by the sentence.
2. The latter clause is needed in order to distinguish 'John loves Marsha' from 'Marsha loves John', where the sequential order of composition is crucial. A complication arises in connection with such quantificational locutions as 'someone' in 'Someone is ingenious'. Whereas grammatically 'someone' is

combined with 'is ingenious' in just the same way that 'Socrates' combines with 'is ingenious', the semantic contents of 'someone' and 'is ingenious' are combined very differently from the way the semantic contents of 'Socrates' and 'is ingenious' are combined. A perhaps more important qualification arises in connection with quotation marks and similar devices – since the semantic content of the numeral '9' is no part of the semantic content of the sentence 'The numeral '9' is a singular term'. Yet another important qualification concerns overlaid quantifiers. For details, see (Salmon 1986), pp. 143–51.

3. A sophisticated version of this theory identifies the semantic content of a predicate, as used on a particular occasion, with a corresponding temporally-indexed (and spatially-indexed, if necessary) attribute, for example the property of being tall at *t*, where *t* is the time of the utterance. This yields a more plausible notion of proposition. For further details, see Salmon 1986, pp 24–43.
4. The argument is due, in its essentials, to Alonzo Church and independently to Kurt Godel. For details see Church 1943; Church 1956, pp 24–5; Godel 1944, pp 128–9; Salmon 1981, pp 48–52; and Salmon 1986, pp 22–3.
5. Here again, exceptions arise in connection with quotation marks and similar devices. A further exception arises in connection with compound predicates. The semantic contents of these are best regarded as attributes, or something similar, rather than as complexes made from the semantic contents of the parts.
6. Mill actually held a somewhat complex theory of semantic content, according to which the proposition contained in such a sentence as 'Socrates is ingenious' has two components: the proposition about Socrates that he has the property of ingenuity, and the metalinguistic proposition about the expressions 'Socrates' and 'ingenious' that the individual denoted by the former has the property connoted by the latter, and is therefore among the things denoted by the latter. In the special case of an identity sentence, such as 'Hesperus is Phosphorus', Mill held that the first component was null, so that the proposition contained reduces to the metalinguistic truth that the name 'Hesperus' denotes the same thing as the name 'Phosphorus'.
7. But see Putnam 1954, and Salmon 1986, pp 164–5*n*4.
8. See Chapter 16 below for an analysis of Frege's puzzle.
9. Temporal contexts give rise to analogous failures of substitution: Although the sentences 'In 1978, George Bush was a Republican' and 'George Bush is the US President' are both true at the time of the writing of the present article, the sentence 'In 1978, the US President was a Republican' is false, since in 1978 a Democrat was US President.
10. The Naive Theory may take the semantic content of the phrase 'some logician' to be the (second-order) property of being a (first-order) property possessed by at least one logician. Using Russell's preferred notion of a propositional function, the description 'some logician' might be regarded as having as its semantic content the second-order propositional function *f* that assigns to any one-place first-order propositional function *F* the proposition that at least one logician instantiates *F* (where an individual *x* is said to *instantiate* a one-place propositional function *F* if the proposition obtained by applying *F* to *x* is true). The proposition that some logician is ingenious would then be regarded as made up of the second-order propositional function *f* and the first-order propositional function *being ingenious*. Alternatively, the determiner 'some' is

plausibly regarded as a two-place quantifier, so that the phrase 'some logician' would be seen as an incomplete string that is formed by attaching a two-place second-order predicate to a single first-order predicate, and that stands in need of completion by a second first-order predicate. The general theory of descriptions conflicts with both of these theories concerning the logico-semantic status of 'some logician'.

11. The special theory conflicts with one of the assumptions used in the Church-Gödel argument for the replacement of thesis (*ii*) of the Naive Theory by these (*ii'*) of the Modified Naive Theory. (See note 4 above.)
12. Russell held that uses of genuine names for oneself or one's own mental items were rare, since the singular proposition contained in a sentence involving such a name would be apprehended by the speaker of the sentence only very briefly, and never by anyone else. Even if a speaker were to use a genuine name, his or her audience would be forced to understand the name as a disguised definite description for the intended referent. Since communication using genuine names must be circumvented in this way, even when speaking about oneself or one's own present experiences one might typically employ definite descriptions, disguised or not, in lieu of genuine names. Genuine names of individuals are expedient only when conversing with oneself about oneself.
13. Russell claimed that singular existential or negative existential statements involving genuine names are without content, in part, because the semantic content of the unrestricted existential quantifier, 'something', is seen to be a higher-order propositional function that applies only to propositional functions of individuals, and not to the individuals themselves. This observation overlooks the fact that the unrestricted existential quantifier together with the identity predicate defines (something equivalent to) a first-order existence predicate: 'Something is identical with ____'. It would have been better to say that singular existentials and negative existentials involving genuine names have content, but are always trivially true and trivially false, respectively.
14. In characterizing the sense of an expression as a purely conceptual entity, I intend the word 'concept' with a more or less ordinary meaning and not with that of Frege's special use of '*Begriff*'. Senses are neither empirically observed (as are external, concrete objects) nor 'had' in the way that sensations or other private experiences are had, but are abstract entities that are 'grasped' or 'apprehended' by the mind. In addition, I intend the term 'pure' to exclude concepts that include non-conceptual elements as constituents. A genuine sense may involve reference to an object, but it must do so by including a conceptual representation of the object in place of the object itself.
15. The Church-Gödel argument mentioned in note 4 above was inspired by Frege's arguments, and was offered independently by both Church and Gödel on Frege's behalf.
16. Frege explicitly considered certain temporal contexts – specifically the phenomenon of tense as well as such temporal indexicals as 'yesterday'. From his treatment of these it is possible to extract a solution to the problem of failure of substitutivity in temporal contexts. A tensed or temporally indexical sentence, according to Frege, is incomplete and must be supplemented by a time-specification before it can properly express a thought and refer to a truth value. Whenever such a sentence is uttered, the very time of utterance is relied upon as the needed

time-specification, a specification of itself. Analogously, a definite description whose referent may vary with the time of utterance may be regarded as an operator that forms a complete singular term only when joined with a time-specification, as may be provided by the time of the utterance itself. Thus, although the definite description 'the US President', supplemented by the time of the writing of the present article, refers to the same individual as the name 'George Bush', the description 'the US President' cannot be substituted for the name 'George Bush' in the sentence 'In 1978, George Bush was a Republican', since this sentence already includes a verbal time-specification, 'in 1978', which supersedes the time of utterance in completing any expressions occurring within its scope in need of completion by a time-specification. (A similar solution is possible for such complex constructions as 'When I lived in Princeton, George Bush was a Republican' and for quantificational temporal operators, such as 'always', in place of specific time-indicators.) It should be noted that the solution here is significantly different from that for quotational and propositional-attitude contexts. The time-specification 'in 1978' is seen not as creating an *ungerade* context inducing a reference shift, but as providing a component needed to complete the singular term so that it may properly refer to an individual, relative to its position in the sentence. Once completed by the time-specification, its referent, as occurring at that position, is just its customary referent.

The present article concerns singular terms. A full account of Frege's theory of meaning, not undertaken here, would require consideration of Frege's further doctrines concerning functions and their role in the semantics of predicates, connectives, quantifiers, and operators.

17. Frege and Russell wrote before the advent of modern intensional semantics, and consequently neither spoke of reference or truth *with respect to a possible world* or *with respect to a time*, but only of reference ('meaning') or truth (in a language) *simpliciter*. The parenthetical phrase 'with respect to a possible world in a time' indicates the natural and usual extensions of their account to modal and temporal semantics. It must be noted, however, that both Frege and Russell treated the phenomenon of tense and other temporal operators differently from the usual treatment today, and neither clearly distinguished tense from the distinct phenomenon of indexicality.
18. See Salmon 1981, pp 14–21, 43–4, 54–5) for a more detailed discussion of these notions.
19. For further difficulties with this and other proposed alternatives to the Modified Naive Theory, see Salmon 1986, pp 63–75.
20. It may be objected that Putnam's concept of elm trees includes the concept of being called 'elms' in English, and perhaps even the concept of being a different genus from the things called 'beeches' in English, making the purely conceptual contents different after all. There are compelling reasons, however, for denying that any concept like that of being called such-and-such in English can be part of the semantic content of terms like 'elm' and 'beech'. See Kripke 1972, pp 68–70; Chapter 14 below; and Salmon 1986, pp 163–4*n*2.
21. Such a position is sketched in some detail in Chapter 16 below.
22. This general strategy employed in this argument is developed in Kripke (1979), where is applied to Donnellan's claims supporting his referential-attributive distinction. I do not know whether Kripke would endorse this application of

the general strategy to the purported failure of substitutivity of proper names in propositional-attitude contexts.

23. A comprehensive survey of the topics of this article is provided in Salmon (1989).

References

Church, A. (1943), Review of Carnap's *Introduction to Semantics*, in *The Philosophical Review*, 52, pp 298–304.

Church, A. (1956), *Introduction to Mathematical Logic I* (Princeton, NJ: Princeton University Press).

Godel, K. (1944), 'Russell's mathematical logic,' in Paul A. Schilpp, (ed.), *The Philosophy of Bertrand Russell*, (La Salle, Illinois: Open Court), pp 125–53.

Kripke, S. (1972), *Naming and Necessity*, (Cambridge, Mass.: Harvard University Press).

Kripke, S. (1979), 'Speaker's reference and semantic reference,' in P. French, T. Uehling, and H. Wettstein (eds), *Contemporary Perspectives in the Philosophy of Language*, (Mineappolis: University of Minnesota Press), pp 6–27.

Putnam, H. (1954) 'Synonymy and the analysis of belief sentences,' in Salmon and Soames, 1988, pp 149–58.

Salmon, N. (1981), *Reference and Essence*, (Princeton, NJ: Princeton University Press and Basil Blackwell).

Salmon, N. (1989), 'Reference and information content: Names and descriptions,' in D. Gabbay and F. Guenthner (eds), *Handbook of Philosophical Logic IV: Topics in the Philosophy of Language* (Dordrecht: D. Reidel), pp 409–61.

Salmon, N. (1990), 'A Millian heir rejects the wages of *Sinn*,' in C. Anthony Anderson and J. Owens (eds), *Propositional Attitudes: The Role of Content in Logic, Language, and Mind*, (Stanford, Ca: Center for the Study of Language and Information), pp 215–47.

Salmon, N. (1991), *Frege's Puzzle*, (Atascadero, California: Ridgeview).

Salmon, N. and S. Soames (1988), *Propositions and Attitudes* (Oxford: Oxford University Press).

Chapter 6

Of Names

J. S. Mill

§1 'A name,' says Hobbes,[1] 'is a word taken at pleasure to serve for a mark which may raise in our mind a thought like to some thought we had before, and which being pronounced to others, may be to them a sign of what thought the speaker had[2] before in his mind.' This simple definition of a name, as a word (or a set of words) serving the double purpose of a mark to recall to ourselves the likeness of a former thought, and a sign to make it known to others, appears unexceptionable. Names, indeed, do much more than this; but whatever else they do, grows out of, and is the result of this; as will appear in its proper place.

Are names more properly said to be the names of things, or of our ideas of things?

[. . .]

It seems proper to consider a word as the *name* of that which we intend to be understood by it when we use it; of that which any fact that we assert of it is to be understood of; that, in short, concerning which, when we employ the word, we intend to give information. Names, therefore, shall always be spoken of in this work as the names of things themselves, and not merely of our ideas of things.

But the question now arises, of what things? and to answer this it is necessary to take into consideration the different kinds of names.

§3 All names are names of something, real or imaginary; but all things have not names appropriated to them individually. For some individual objects we require, and consequently have, separate distinguishing names; there is a name

From J. S. Mill (1843), *A System of Logic*

for every person, and for every remarkable place. Other objects, of which we have not occasion to speak so frequently, we do not designate by a name of their own; but when the necessity arises for naming them, we do so by putting together several words, each of which, by itself, might be and is used for an indefinite number of other objects; as when I say, *this stone:* 'this' and 'stone' being, each of them, names that may be used of many other objects besides the particular one meant, though the only object of which they can both be used at the given moment, consistently with their signification, may be the one of which I wish to speak.

Were this the sole purpose for which names, that are common to more things than one, could be employed; if they only served, by mutually limiting each other, to afford a designation for such individual objects as have no names of their own: they could only be ranked among contrivances for economizing the use of language. But it is evident that this is not their sole function. It is by their means that we are enabled to assert *general* propositions; to affirm or deny any predicate of an indefinite number of things at once. The distinction, therefore, between *general* names, and *individual* or *singular* names, is fundamental; and may be considered as the first grand division of names.

A general name is familiarly defined, a name which is capable of being truly affirmed, in the same sense, of each of an indefinite number of things. An individual or singular name is a name which is only capable of being truly affirmed, in the same sense, of one thing.

Thus, *man* is capable of being truly affirmed of John, George, Mary, and other persons without assignable limit; and it is affirmed of all of them in the same sense; for the word man expresses certain qualities, and when we predicate it of those persons, we assert that they all possess those qualities. But *John* is only capable of being truly affirmed of one single person, at least in the same sense. For, though there are many persons who bear that name, it is not conferred upon them to indicate any qualities, or anything which belongs to them in common; and cannot be said to be affirmed of them in any *sense* at all, consequently not in the same sense. 'The king who succeeded William the Conqueror,' is also an individual name. For, that there cannot be more than one person of whom it can be truly affirmed, is implied in the meaning of the words. Even '*the* king,' when the occasion or the context defines the individual of whom it is to be understood, may justly be regarded as an individual name.

It is not unusual, by way of explaining what is meant by a general name, to say that it is the name of a *class*. But this, though a convenient mode of expression for some purposes, is objectionable as a definition, since it explains the clearer of two things by the more obscure. It would be more logical to reverse the proposition, and turn it into a definition of the word *class*: 'A class is the indefinite multitude of individuals denoted by a general name.'

It is necessary to distinguish *general* from *collective* names. A general name is one which can be predicated of *each* individual of a multitude; a collective name cannot be predicated of each separately, but only of all taken together. 'The 76th regiment of foot in the British army,' which is a collective name, is not a general but an individual name; for though it can be predicated of a multitude of individual soldiers taken jointly, it cannot be predicated of them severally. We may say, Jones is a soldier, and Thompson is a soldier, and Smith is a soldier, but we cannot say, Jones is the 76th regiment, and Thompson is the 76th regiment, and Smith is the 76th regiment. We can only say, Jones, and Thompson, and Smith, and Brown, and so forth (enumerating all the soldiers), are the 76th regiment.

'The 76th regiment' is a collective name, but not a general one: 'a regiment' is both a collective and a general name. General with respect to all individual regiments, of each of which separately it can be affirmed: collective with respect to the individual soldiers of whom any regiment is composed.

§4 The second general division of names is into *concrete* and *abstract*. A concrete name is a name which stands for a thing; an abstract name is a name which stands for an attribute of a thing. Thus *John, the sea, this table,* are names of things. *White*, also is the name of a thing, or rather of things. Whiteness, again, is the name of a quality or attribute of those things. Man is a name of many things; humanity is a name of an attribute of those things. *Old* is a name of things; *old age* is a name of one of their attributes.

I have used the words concrete and abstract in the sense annexed to them by schoolmen, who, notwithstanding the imperfections of their philosophy, were unrivalled in the construction of technical language, and whose definitions, in logic at least, though they never went more than a little way into the subject, have seldom, I think, been altered but to be spoiled. A practice, however, has grown up in more modern times, which, if not introduced by Locke, has gained currency chiefly from his example, of applying the expression 'abstract name' to all names which are the result of abstraction or generalisation, and consequently to all general names, instead of confining it to the names of attributes. The metaphysicians of the Condillac school, – whose admiration of Locke, passing over the profoundest speculations of that truly original genius, usually fastens with peculiar eagerness upon his weakest points, – have gone on imitating him in this abuse of language, until there is now some difficulty in restoring the word to its original signification. A more wanton alteration in the meaning of a word is rarely to be met with: for the expression *general name*, the exact equivalent of which exists in all languages I am acquainted with, was already available for the purpose to which *abstract* has been misappropriated, while the misappropriation leaves that important class of words, the names of attributes, without any compact distinctive appellation. The old acceptation, however, has not gone so completely out of use, as to deprive those who still adhere to it of all chance of being understood. By *abstract*, then, I shall always, in Logic proper, mean the opposite of *concrete;* by an abstract name, the name of an attribute; by a concrete name, the name of an object.

Do abstract names belong to the class of general, or to that of singular names? Some of them are certainly general. I mean those which are names not of one single and definite attribute, but of a class of attributes. Such as the word *colour*, which is a name common to whiteness, redness &c. Such is even the word whiteness, in respect of the different shades of whiteness to which it is applied in common: the word magnitude, in respect of the various degrees of magnitude and the various dimensions of space; the word weight, in respect of the various degrees of weight. Such also is the word *attribute* itself, the common name of all particular attributes. But when only one attribute, neither variable in degree nor in kind, is designated by the name; as visibleness; tangibleness; equality; squareness; milkwhiteness; then the name can hardly be considered general; for though it denotes an attribute of many different objects, the attribute itself is always conceived as one, not many.[3] To avoid needless logomachies, the best course would probably be to consider these names as neither general nor individual, and to place them in a class apart.

It may be objected to our definition of an abstract name, that not only the names which we have called abstract, but adjectives, which we have placed in the concrete class, are names of attributes; that *white*, for example, is as much the name of the colour as *whiteness* is. But (as before remarked) a word ought to be considered as the name of that which we intend to be understood by it when we put it to its principal use, that is, when we employ it in predication. When we say snow is white, milk is white, linen is white, we do not mean it to be understood that snow, or linen, or milk, is a colour. We mean that they are things having the colour. The reverse is the case with the word whiteness; what we affirm to *be* whiteness is not snow, but the colour of snow. Whiteness, therefore, is the name of the colour exclusively: white is a name of all things whatever having the colour; a name, not of the quality of whiteness, but of every white object. It is true, this name was given to all those various objects on account of the quality; and we may therefore say, without impropriety, that the quality forms part of its signification; but a name can only be said to stand for, or to be a name of, the things of which it can be predicated. We shall presently see that all names which can be said to have any signification, all names by applying which to an individual we give any information respecting that individual, may be said to *imply* an attribute of some sort; but they are not names of the attribute; it has its own proper abstract name.

§5 This leads to the consideration of a third great division of names, into *connotative* and *non-connotative*, the latter sometimes, but improperly, called *absolute*. This is one of the most important distinctions which we shall have occasion to point out, and one of those which go deepest into the nature of language.

A non-connotative term is one which signifies a subject only, or an attribute only. A connotative term is one which denotes a subject, and implies an attribute. By a subject is here meant anything which possesses attributes. Thus John, or London, or England, are names which signify a subject only. Whiteness, length, virtue, signify an attribute only. None of these names, therefore, are connotative. But *white, long, virtuous*, are connotative. The word white, denotes all white things, as snow, paper, the foam of the sea, &c., and implies, or in the language of the schoolmen, *connotes*,[4] the attribute *whiteness*. The word white is not predicated of the attribute, but of the subjects, snow, &c.; but when we predicate it of them, we convey the meaning that the attribute whiteness belongs to them. The same may be said of the other words above cited. Virtuous, for example, is the name of a class, which includes Socrates, Howard, the Man of Ross, and an undefinable number of other individuals, past, present, and to come. These individuals, collectively and severally, can alone be said with propriety to be denoted by the word: of them alone can it properly be said to be a name. But it is a name applied to all of them in consequences of an attribute which they are supposed to possess in common, the attribute which has received the name of virtue. It is applied to all beings that are considered to possess this attribute; and to none which are not so considered.

All concrete general names are connotative. The word *man*, for example, denotes Peter, Jane, John, and an indefinite number of other individuals, of whom, taken as a class, it is the name. But it is applied to them, because they possess, and to signify that they possess, certain attributes. These seem to be, corporeity, animal life, rationality, and a certain external form, which for distinction we call the human. Every existing thing, which possessed all these attributes, would be called a man; and anything which possessed none of them, or only one, or two, or even three of them without the fourth, would not be so called. For example, if in the interior of Africa there were to be discovered a race of animals possessing reason equal to that of human beings, but with the form of an elephant, they would not be called men. Swift's Houyhnhnms would not be so called. Or if such newly-discovered beings possessed the form of man without any vestige of reason, it is probable that some other name than that of man would be found for them. How it happens that there can be any doubt about the matter, will appear hereafter. The word *man*, therefore, signifies all these attributes, and all subjects which possess these attributes. But it can be predicated only of the subjects. What we call men, are the subjects, the individual Stiles and Nokes; not the qualities by which their humanity is constituted. The name, therefore, is said to signify the subjects *directly*, the attributes *indirectly*; it *denotes* the subjects, and implies, or involves, or indicates, or as we shall say henceforth *connotes*, the attributes. It is a connotative name.

Connotative[5] names have hence been also called *denominative*, because the subject which they denote is denominated by, or receives a name from, the attribute which they connote. Snow, and other objects, receive the name white, because they possess the attribute which is called whiteness; Peter, James, and others receive the name man because they possess the attributes which are considered to constitute humanity. The attribute, or attributes, may therefore be said to denominate those objects, or to give them a common name.

It has been seen that all concrete general names are connotative. Even abstract names, though the names only of attributes, may in some instances be justly considered as connotative; for attributes themselves may have attributes ascribed to them; and a word which denotes attributes may connote an attribute of those attributes. Of this description, for example, is such a word as *fault*; equivalent to *bad* or *hurtful quality*. This word is a name common to many attributes, and connotes hurtfulness, an attribute of those various attributes. When, for example, we say that slowness, in a horse, is a fault, we do not mean that the slow movement, the actual change of place of the slow horse, is a bad thing, but that the property or peculiarity of the horse, from which it derives that name, the quality of being a slow mover, is an undesirable peculiarity.

In regard to those concrete names which are not general but individual, a distinction must be made.

Proper names are not connotative: they denote the individuals who are called by them; but they do not indicate or imply any attributes as belonging to those individuals. When we name a child by the name of Paul, or a dog by the name Cæsar, these names are simply marks used to enable those individuals to be made subjects of discourse. It may be said, indeed, that we must have had some reason for giving them those names rather than any others; and this is true; but the name, once given, is independent of the reason. A man may have been named John, because that was the name of his father; a town may have been named Dartmouth, because it is situated at the mouth of the Dart. But it is no part of the signification of the word John, that the father of the person so called bore the same name; nor even of the word Dartmouth, to be situated at the mouth of the Dart. If sand should choke up the mouth of the river, or an earthquake change its course, and remove it to a distance from the town, the name of the town would not necessarily be changed. The fact, therefore, can form no part of the signification of the word; for otherwise, when the fact confessedly ceased to be true, no one would any longer think of applying the name. Proper names are attached to the objects themselves, and are not dependent on the continuance of any attribute of the object.

But there is another kind of names, which, although they are individual names, that is, predictable only of one object, are really connotative. For, though we may give to an individual a name utterly unmeaning, which we call a proper name, – a word which answers the purpose of showing what thing it is we are talking about, but not of telling anything about it; yet a name peculiar to an individual is not necessarily of this description. It may be significant of some attribute, or some union of attributes, which, being possessed by no object but one, determines the name exclusively to that individual. 'The sun' is a name of this description; 'God,' when used by a monotheist, is another. These, however, are scarcely examples of what we are not attempting to illustrate, being, in strictness of language, general, not individual names: for, however they may be *in fact* predictable only of one object, there is nothing in the meaning of the words themselves which implies this: and, accordingly, when we are imagining and not affirming, we may speak of many suns; and the majority of mankind have believed, and still believe, that there are many gods. But it is easy to produce words which are real instances of connotative individual names. It may be part of the meaning of the connotative name itself, that there can exist but one individual possessing the attribute which it connotes: as for instance, 'the *only* son of John Stiles;' 'the *first* emperor of Rome.' Or the attribute connoted may be a connexion with some determinate event, and the connexion may be of such a kind as only one individual could have; or at least be such as only one individual actually had; and this may be implied in the form of the expression. 'The father of Socrates' is an example of the one kind (since Socrates could not have had two fathers); 'the author of the Iliad,' 'the murderer of Henri Quatre,' of the second. For, though it is conceivable that more persons than one might have participated in the authorship of the Iliad, or in the murder of Henri Quatre, the employment of the article *the* implies that, in fact, this was not the case. What is here done by the word *the*, is done in other cases by the context: thus, 'Cæsar's army' is an individual name, if it appears from the context that the army meant is that which Cæsar commanded in a particular battle. The still more general expressions, 'the Roman army,' or 'the Christian army,' may be individualised in a similar manner. Another case of frequent occurrence has already been noticed; it is the following. The name, being a many-worded one, may consist, in the first place, of a *general* name, capable therefore in itself of being affirmed of more things than one, but which is, in the second place, so limited by other words joined with it, that the entire expression can only be predicated of one object, consistently with the meaning of the general term. This is exemplified in such an instance as the following: 'the present Prime Minister of England.' Prime Minister of England is a general name; the attributes which it connotes may be possessed by an indefinite number of persons: in succession however, not simultaneously; since the meaning of the name itself imports (among other things) that there can be only one such person at a time. This being the case, and the application of the name being afterwards limited by the article and the word *present*, to such individuals as possess the attributes at one indivisible point of time, it becomes applicable only to one individual. And as this appears from the meaning of the name, without any extrinsic proof, it is strictly an individual name.

From the preceding observations it will easily be collected, that whenever the names given to objects convey any information, that is, whenever they have properly any meaning, the meaning resides not in what they *denote*, but in what they *connote*. The only names of objects which connote nothing are *proper* names; and these have, strictly speaking, no signification.[6]

If, like the robber in the Arabian Nights, we make a mark with chalk on a house to enable us to know it again, the mark has a purpose, but it has not properly any meaning. The chalk does not declare anything about the house; it does not mean, This is such a person's house, or This is a house which contains booty. The object of making the mark is merely distinction. I say to myself, All these houses are so nearly alike that if I lose sight of them I shall not again be able to distinguish that which I am now looking at, from any of the others; I must therefore contrive to make the appearance of this one house unlike that of the others, that I may hereafter know when I see the mark – not indeed any attribute of the house – but simply that it is the same house which I am now looking at. Morgiana chalked all the other houses in a similar manner, and defeated the scheme: how? simply by obliterating the difference of appearance between that house and the others. The chalk was still there, but it no longer served the purpose of a distinctive mark.

When we impose a proper name, we perform an operation in some degree analogous to what the robber intended in chalking the house. We put a mark, not indeed upon the object itself, but, so to speak, upon the idea of the object. A proper name is but an unmeaning mark which we connect in our minds with the idea of the object, in order that whenever the mark meets our eyes or occurs to our thoughts, we may think of that individual object. Not being attached to the thing itself, it does not, like the chalk, enable us to distinguish the object when we see it; but it enables us to distinguish it when it is spoken of, either in the records of our own experience, or in the discourse of others; to know that what we find asserted in any proposition of which it is the subject, is asserted of the individual thing with which we were previously acquainted.

When we predicate of anything its proper name; when we say, pointing to a man, this is Brown or Smith, or pointing to a city, that it is York, we do not, merely by so doing, convey to the reader any information about them, except that those are their names. By enabling him to identify the individuals, we may connect them with information previously possessed by him; by saying, This is York, we may tell him that it contains the Minster. But this is in virtue of what he has previously heard concerning York; not by anything implied in the name. It is otherwise when objects are spoken of by connotative names. When we say, The town is built of marble, we give the hearer what may be entirely new information, and this merely by the signification of the many-worded connotative name, 'built of marble.' Such names are not signs of the mere objects, invented because we have occasion to think and speak of those objects individually; but signs which accompany an attribute: a kind of livery in which the attribute clothes all objects which are recognised as possessing it. They are not mere marks, but more, that is to say, significant marks; and the connotation is what constitutes their significance.

As a proper name is said to be the name of the one individual which it is predicated of, so (as well from the importance of adhering to analogy, as for the other reasons formerly assigned) a connotative name ought to be considered a name of all the various individuals which it is predicable of, or in other words *denotes*, and not of what it connotes. But by learning what things it is a name of, we do not learn the meaning of the name: for to the same thing we may, with equal propriety, apply many names, not equivalent in meaning. Thus, I call a certain man by the name Sophroniscus: I call him by another name, The father of Socrates. Both these are names of the same individual, but their meaning is altogether different; they are applied to that individual for two different purposes: the one, merely to distinguish him from other persons who are spoken of; the other to indicate a fact relating to him, the fact that Socrates was his son. I further apply to him these other expressions: a man, a Greek, an Athenian, a sculptor, an old man, an honest man, a brave man. All these are, or may be, names of Sophroniscus, not indeed of him alone, but of him and each of an indefinite number of other human beings. Each of these names is applied to Sophroniscus for a different reason, and by each whoever understands its meaning is apprised of a distinct fact or number of facts concerning him; but those who knew nothing about the names except that they were applicable to Sophroniscus, would be altogether ignorant of their meaning. It is even possible that I might know every single individual of whom a given name could be with truth affirmed, and yet could not be said to know the meaning of the name. A child knows who are its brothers and sisters, long before it has any definite conception of the nature of the facts which are involved in the signification of those words.

In some cases it is not easy to decide precisely how much a particular word does or does not connote; that is, we do not exactly know (the case not having arisen) what degree of difference in the object would occasion a difference in the name. Thus, it is clear that the word man, besides animal life and rationality, connotes also a certain external form; but it would be impossible to say precisely what form; that is, to decide how great a deviation from the form ordinarily found in the beings whom we are accustomed to call men, would suffice in a newly-discovered race to make us refuse them the name of man. Rationality, also, being a quality which admits of degrees, it has never been settled what is the lowest degree of that quality which would entitle any creature to be considered a human being. In all such cases, the meaning of the general name is so far unsettled and vague; mankind have not come to any positive agreement about the matter. When we come to treat of Classification, we shall have occasion to show under what conditions this vagueness may exist without practical inconvenience; and cases will appear in which the ends of language are better promoted by it than by complete precision; in order that, in natural history for instance, individuals or species of no very marked character may be ranged with those more strongly characterised individual or species, to which, in all their properties taken together, they bear the nearest resemblance.

But this partial uncertainty in the connotation of names can only be free from mischief when guarded by strict precautions. One of the chief sources, indeed, of lax habits of thought, is the custom of using connotative terms without a distinctly ascertained connotation, and with no more precise notion of their meaning than can be loosely collected from observing what objects they are used to denote. It is in this manner that we all acquire, and inevitably so, our first knowledge of our vernacular language. A child learns the meaning of the words *man*, or *white*, by hearing them applied to a variety of individual objects, and finding out, by a process of generalization and analysis which he could not himself describe, what those different objects have in common. In the case of these two words the process is so easy as to require not assistance from culture; the objects called human beings, and the objects called white, differing from all others by qualities of a peculiarly definite and obvious character. But in many other cases, objects bear a general resemblance to one another, which leads to their being familiarly classed together under a common name, while, without more analytic habits than the generality of mankind possess, it is not immediately apparent what are the particular attributes, upon the possession of which in common by them all, their general resemblance depends. When this is the case, people use the name without any recognised connotation, that is, without any precise meaning; they talk, and consequently think, vaguely, and remain contented to attach only the same degree of significance to their own words, which a child three years old attaches to the words brother and sister. The child at least is seldom puzzled by the starting up of new individuals, on whom he is ignorant whether or not to confer the title; because there is usually an authority close at hand competent to solve all doubts. But a similar resource does not exist in the generality of cases; and new objects are continually presenting themselves to men, women, and children, which they are called upon to class *proprio motu*. They, accordingly, do this on no other principle than that of superficial similarity, giving to each new object the name of that familiar object, the idea of which it most readily recalls, or which, on a cursory inspection, it seems to them most to resemble: as an unknown substance found in the ground will be called, according to its texture, earth, sand, or a stone. In this manner, names creep on from subject to subject, until all traces of a common meaning sometimes disappear, and the word comes to denote a number of things not only independently of any common attribute, but which have actually no attribute in common; or none but what is shared by other things to which the name is capriciously refused.[7] Even scientific writers have aided in this perversion of general language from its purpose; sometimes because, like the vulgar, they knew no better; and sometimes in deference to that aversion to admit new words, which induces mankind, on all subjects not considered technical to attempt to make the original stock of names serve with but little augmentation to express a constantly increasing number of objects and distinctions, and, consequently, to express them in a manner progressively more and more imperfect.

To what a degree this loose mode of classing and denominating objects has rendered the vocabulary of mental and moral philosophy unfit for the purposes of accurate thinking, is best known to whoever has most meditated on the present condition of those branches of knowledge. Since, however, the introduction of a new technical language as the vehicle of speculations on subjects belonging to the domain of daily discussion, is extremely difficult to effect, and would not be free from inconvenience even if effected, the problem for the philosopher, and one of the most difficult which he has to resolve, is, in retaining the existing phraseology, how best to alleviate its imperfections. This can only be accomplished by giving to every general concrete name which there is frequent occasion to predicate, a definite and fixed connotation; in order that it may be known what attributes, when we call an object by that name, we really mean to predicate of the object. And the question of most nicety is, how to give this fixed connotation to a name, with the least possible change in the objects which the name is habitually employed to denote; with the least possible disarrangement, either by adding or subtracting, of the group of objects which, in however imperfect a manner, it serves to circumscribe and hold together; and with the least vitiation of the truth of any propositions which are commonly received as true.

This desirable purpose, of giving a fixed connotation where it is wanting, is the end aimed at whenever any one attempts to give a definition of a general name already in use; every definition of a connotative name being an attempt either merely to declare, or to declare and analyse, the connotation of the name. And the fact, that no questions which have arisen in the moral sciences have been subjects of keener controversy than the definitions of almost all the leading expressions, is a proof how great an extent the evil to which we have adverted has attained.

Names with indeterminate connotation are not to be confounded with names which have more than one connotation, that is to say, ambiguous words. A word may have several meanings, but all of them fixed and recognised ones; as the word *post*, for example, or the word *box*, the various senses of which it would be endless to enumerate. And the paucity of existing names, in comparison with the demand for them, may often render it advisable and even necessary to retain a name in this multiplicity of acceptations, distinguishing these so clearly as to prevent their being confounded with one another. Such a word may be considered as two or more names, accidentally written and spoken alike.

[. . .]

Notes

1. *Computation or Logic*, chap. ii.
2. In the original 'had, *or had not*.' These last words, as involving a subtlety foreign to our present purpose, I have forborne to quote.
3. Vide infra, note at the end of § 3, book ii, chap. ii.
4. *Notare*, to mark; *Con*notare, to mark *along with*; to mark one thing *with* or *in addition* to another.
5. Archbishop Whately, who, in the later editions of his *Elements of Logic*, aided in reviving the important distinction treated of in the text, proposes the term 'Attributive' as a substitute for 'Connotative' (p 22, 9th ed.). The expression is, in itself, appropriate; but as it has not the advantage of being connected with any verb, of so markedly distinctive a character as 'to connote,' it is not, I think, fitted to supply the place of the word Connotative in scientific use.
6. A writer who entitles his book *Philosophy; or, The Science of Truth*, charges me in his very first page (referring at the foot of it to this passage) with asserting that *general* names have properly no signification. And he repeats this statement many times in the course of his volume, with comments, not at all flattering, thereon. It is well to be now and then reminded to how great a length perverse misquotation (for, strange as it appears, I do not believe that the writer is dishonest) can sometimes go. It is a warning to readers when they see an author accused, with volume and page referred to, and the apparent guarantee of inverted commas, of maintaining something more than commonly absurd, not to give implicit credence to the assertion without verifying the reference.
7. 'Take the familiar term Stone. It is applied to mineral and rocky materials, to the kernels of fruit, to the accumulations in the gall-bladder and in the kidney; while it is refused to polished minerals (called gems), to rocks that have the cleavage suited for roofing (slates), and to baked clay (bricks). It occurs in the designation of the magnetic oxide of iron (loadstone), and not in speaking of other metallic ores. Such a term is wholly unfit for accurate reasoning, unless hedged round on every occasion by other phrases; as building stone, precious stone, gall stone, etc. Moreover, the methods of definition are baffled for want of sufficient community to ground upon. There is no quality uniformly present in the cases where it is applied, and uniformly absent where it is not applied; hence the definer would have to employ largely the licence of striking off existing applications, and taking in new ones.' – Bain, *Logic*, ii. 172.

Chapter 7

On Sense and Reference

G. Frege

Equality[1] gives rise to challenging questions which are not altogether easy to answer. Is it a relation? A relation between objects or between names or signs of objects? In my *Begriffsschrift*[2] I assumed the latter. The reasons which seem to favour this are the following: $a=a$ and $a=b$ are obviously statements of differing cognitive value; $a=a$ holds *a priori* and, according to Kant, is to be labelled analytic, while statements of the form $a=b$ often contain very valuable extensions of our knowledge and cannot always be established *a priori*. The discovery that the rising sun is not new every morning, but always the same, was one of the most fertile astronomical discoveries. Even to-day the identification of a small planet or a comet is not always a matter of course. Now if we were to regard equality as a relation between that which the names 'a' and 'b' designate, it would seem that $a=b$ could not differ from $a=a$ (i.e. provided $a=b$ is true). A relation would thereby be expressed of a thing to itself, and indeed one in which each thing stands to itself but to no other thing. What is intended to be said by $a=b$ seems to be that the signs or names 'a' and 'b' designate the same thing, so that those signs themselves would be under discussion; a relation between them would be asserted. But this relation would hold between the names or signs only in so far as they named or designated something. It would be mediated by the connexion of each of the two signs with the same designated thing. But this is arbitrary. Nobody can be forbidden to use any arbitrarily producible event or object as a sign for something. In that case the sentence $a=b$ would no longer refer to the subject matter, but only to its mode of designation; we would express no proper knowledge by its mean. But in many cases this is just what we want to do. If the sign 'a' is

From P. Geach and M. Black (1970), *Translations from the Philosophical Writings of Gottlob Frege*, second edition, Oxford: Blackwell.

distinguished from the sign '*b*' only as object (here, by means of its shape), not as sign, (i.e. not by the manner in which it designates something), the cognitive value of $a=a$ becomes essentially equal to that of $a=b$, provided $a=b$ is true. A difference can arise only if the difference between the signs corresponds to a difference in the mode of presentation of that which is designated. Let *a*, *b*, *c* be the lines connecting the vertices of a triangle with the midpoints of the opposite sides. The point of intersection of *a* and *b* is then the same as the point of intersection of *b* and *c*. So we have different designations for the same point, and these names ('point of intersection of *a* and *b*,' 'point of intersection of *b* and *c*') likewise indicate the mode of presentation; and hence the statement contains actual knowledge.

It is natural, now, to think of there being connected with a sign (name, combination of words, letter), besides that to which the sign refers, which may be called the reference of the sign, also what I should like to call the *sense* of the sign, wherein the mode of presentation is contained. In our example, accordingly, the reference of the expressions 'the point of intersection of *a* and *b*' and 'the point of intersection of *b* and *c*' would be the same, but not their senses. The reference of 'evening star' would be the same as that of 'morning star,' but not the sense.

It is clear from the context that by 'sign' and 'name' I have here understood any designation representing a proper name, which thus has as its reference a definite object (this word taken in the widest range), but not a concept or a relation, which shall be discussed further in another article.[3] The designation of a single object can also consist of several words or other signs. For brevity, let every such designation be called a proper name.

The sense of a proper name is grasped by everybody who is sufficiently familiar with the language or totality of designations to which it belongs;[4] but this serves to illuminate only a single aspect of the reference, supposing it to have one. Comprehensive knowledge of the reference would require us to be able to say immediately whether any given sense belongs to it. To such knowledge we never attain.

The regular connexion between a sign, its sense, and its reference is of such a kind that to the sign there corresponds a definite sense and to that in turn a definite reference, while to a given reference (an object) there does not belong only a single sign. The same sense has different expressions in different languages or even in the same language. To be sure, exceptions to this regular behaviour occur. To every expression belonging to a complete totality of signs, there should certainly correspond a definite sense; but natural languages often do not satisfy this condition, and one must be content if the same word has the same sense in the same context. It may perhaps be granted that every grammatically well-formed expression representing a proper name always has a sense. But this is not to say that to the sense there also corresponds a reference. The words 'the celestial body most distant from the Earth' have a sense, but it is very doubtful if they also have a reference. The expression 'the least rapidly convergent series' has a sense but demonstrably has no reference, since for every given convergent series, another convergent, but less rapidly convergent, series can be found. In grasping a sense, one is not certainly assured of a reference.

If words are used in the ordinary way, what one intends to speak of is their reference. It can also happen, however, that one wishes to talk about the words themselves or their sense. This happens, for instance, when the words of another are quoted. One's own words then first designate words of the other speaker, and only the latter have their usual reference. We then have signs of signs. In writing, the words are in this case enclosed in quotation marks. Accordingly, a word standing between quotation marks must not be taken as having its ordinary reference.

In order to speak of the sense of an expression 'A' one may simply use the phrase 'the sense of the expression "A"'. In reported speech one talks about the sense, e.g., of another person's remarks. It is quite clear that in this way of speaking words do not have their customary reference but designate what is usually their sense. In order to have a short expression, we will say: In reported speech, words are used *indirectly* or have their *indirect* reference. We distinguish accordingly the *customary* from the *indirect* reference of a word; and its *customary* sense from its *indirect* sense. The indirect reference of a word is accordingly its customary sense. Such exceptions must always be borne in mind if the mode of connexion between sign, sense, and reference in particular cases is to be correctly understood.

The reference and sense of a sign are to be distinguished from the associated idea. If the reference of a sign is an object perceivable by the senses, my idea of it is an internal image,[5] arising from memories of sense impressions which I have had and acts, both internal and external, which I have performed. Such an idea is often saturated with feeling; the clarity of its separate parts varies and oscillates. The same sense is not always connected, even in the same man, with the same idea. The idea is subjective: one man's idea is not that of another. There result, as a matter of course, a variety of differences in the ideas associated with the same sense. A painter, a horseman, and a zoologist will probably connect different ideas with the name 'Bucephalus.' This constitutes an essential distinction between the idea and the sign's sense, which may be the common property of many and therefore is not a part or a mode of the individual mind. For one can hardly deny that mankind has a common store of thoughts which is transmitted from one generation to another.[6]

In the light of this, one need have no scruples in speaking simply of *the* sense, whereas in the case of an idea one must, strictly speaking, add to whom it belongs and at what time. It might perhaps be said: Just as one man connects this idea, and another that idea, with the same word, so also one man can associate this sense and another that sense. But there still remains a difference in the mode of connexion. They are not prevented from grasping the same sense; but they cannot have the same idea. *Si duo idem faciunt, non est idem.* If two persons picture the same thing, each still has his own idea. It is indeed sometimes possible to establish differences in the ideas, or even in the sensations, of different men; but an exact comparison is not possible, because we cannot have both ideas together in the same consciousness.

The reference of a proper name is the object itself which we designate by its means; the idea, which we have in that case, is wholly subjective; in between lies the sense, which is indeed no longer subjective like the idea, but is yet not the object itself. The following analogy will perhaps clarify these relationships. Somebody observes the Moon through a telescope. I compare the Moon itself to the reference; it is the object of the observation, mediated by the real image projected by the object glass in the interior of the telescope, and by the retinal image of the observer. The former I compare to the sense, the latter is like the idea or experience. The optical image in the telescope is indeed one-sided and dependent upon the standpoint of observation; but it is still objective, inasmuch as it can be used by several observers. At any rate it could be arranged for several to use it simultaneously. But each one would have his own retinal image. On account of the diverse shapes of the observers' eyes, even a geometrical congruence could hardly be achieved, and an actual coincidence would be out of the question. This analogy might be developed still further, by assuming A's retinal image made visible to B; or A might also see his own retinal image in a mirror. In this way we might perhaps show how an idea can itself be taken as an object, but as such is not for the observer what it directly is for the person having the idea. But to pursue this would take us too far afield.

We can now recognize three levels of difference between words, expressions, or whole sentences. The difference may concern at most the ideas, or the sense but not the reference, or, finally, the reference as well. With respect to the first level, it is to be noted that, on account of the uncertain connexion of ideas with words, a difference may hold for one person, which another does not find. The difference between a translation and the original text should properly not overstep the first level. To the possible differences here belong also the colouring and shading which poetic eloquence seeks to give to the sense. Such colouring and shading are not objective, and must be evoked by each hearer or reader according to the hints of the poet or the speaker. Without some affinity in human ideas art would certainly be impossible; but it can never be exactly determined how far the intentions of the poet are realized.

In what follows there will be no further discussion of ideas and experiences; they have been mentioned here only to ensure that the idea aroused in the hearer by a word shall not be confused with its sense or its reference.

To make short and exact expressions possible, let the following phraseology be established:

> A proper name (word, sign, sign combination, expression) *expresses* its sense, *stands for* or *designates* its reference. By means of a sign we express its sense and designate its reference.

Idealists or sceptics will perhaps long since have objected: 'You talk, without further ado, of the Moon as an object; but how do you know that the name 'the Moon' has any reference? How do you know that anything whatsoever has a reference?' I reply that when we say 'the Moon,' we do not intend to speak of our idea of the Moon, nor are we satisfied with the sense alone, but we presuppose a reference. To assume that in the sentence 'The Moon is smaller than the Earth' the idea of the Moon is in question, would be flatly to misunderstand the sense. If this is what the speaker wanted, he would use the phrase 'my idea of the Moon.' Now we can of course be mistaken in the presupposition, and such mistakes have indeed occurred. But the question whether the presupposition is perhaps always mistaken need not be answered here; in order to justify mention of the reference of a sign it is enough, at first, to point out our intention in speaking or thinking. (We must then add the reservation: provided such reference exists.)

So far we have considered the sense and reference only of such expressions, words, or signs as we have called proper names. We now inquire concerning the sense and reference for an entire declarative sentence. Such a sentence contains a thought.[7] Is this thought, now to be regarded as its sense or its reference? Let us assume for the time being that the sentence has reference. If we now replace one word of the sentence by another having the same reference, but a different sense, this can have no bearing upon the reference of the sentence. Yet we can see that in such a case the thought changes; since, e.g., the thought in the sentence 'The morning star is a body illuminated by the Sun' differs from that in the sentence 'The evening star is a body illuminated by the Sun.' Anybody who did not know that the evening star is the morning star might hold the one thought to be true, the other false. The thought, accordingly, cannot be the reference of the sentence, but must rather be considered as the sense. What is the position now with regard to the reference? Have we a right even to inquire about it? Is it possible that a sentence as a whole has only a sense, but no reference? At any rate, one might expect that such sentences occur, just as there are parts of sentences having sense but no reference. And sentences which contain proper names without reference will be of this kind. The sentence 'Odysseus was set ashore at Ithaca while sound asleep' obviously has a sense. But since it is doubtful whether the name 'Odysseus,' occurring therein, has reference, it is also doubtful whether the whole sentence has one. Yet it is certain, nevertheless, that anyone who seriously took the sentence to be true or false would ascribe to the name 'Odysseus' a reference, not merely a sense; for it is of the reference of the name that the predicate is affirmed or denied. Whoever does not admit the name has reference can neither apply nor withhold the predicate. But in that case it would be superfluous to advance to the reference of the name; one could be satisfied with the sense, if one wanted to go no further than the thought. If it were a question only of the sense of the sentence, the thought, it would be unnecessary to bother with the reference of a part of the sentence; only the sense, not the reference, of the part is relevant to the sense of the whole sentence. The thought remains the same whether 'Odysseus' has reference or not. The fact that we concern ourselves at all about the reference of a part of the sentence indicates that we generally recognize and expect a reference for the sentence itself. The thought loses value for us as soon as we recognize that the reference of one of its parts is missing. We are therefore justified in not being satisfied with the sense of a sentence, and in inquiring also as to its reference. But now why do we want every proper name to have not only a sense, but also a reference? Why is the thought not enough for us? Because and to the extent that, we are concerned with its truth value. This is not always the case. In hearing an epic poem, for instance, apart from the euphony of the language we are interested only in the sense of the sentences and the images and feelings thereby aroused. The question of truth would cause us to abandon aesthetic delight for an attitude of scientific investigation. Hence it is a matter of no concern to us whether the name 'Odysseus,' for instance, has reference, so long as we accept the poem as a work of art.[8] It is the striving for truth that drives us always to advance from the sense to the reference.

We have seen that the reference of a sentence may always be sought, whenever the reference of its components is involved; and that this is the case when and only when we are inquiring after the truth value.

We are therefore driven into accepting the *truth value* of a sentence as constituting its reference. By the truth value of a sentence I understand the circumstance that it is true or false. There are no further truth values. For brevity I call the one the True, and the other the False. Every declarative sentence concerned with the reference of its words is therefore to be regarded as a proper name, and its reference, if it has one, is either the True or the False. These two objects are recognized, if only implicitly, by everybody who judges something to be true – and so even by a sceptic. The designation of the truth values as objects may appear to be an arbitrary fancy or perhaps a mere play upon words, from which no profound consequences could be drawn. What I mean by an object can be more exactly discussed only in connexion with concept and relation. I will reserve this for another article.[9] But so much should already be clear, that in every judgment,[10] no matter how trivial, the step from the level of thoughts to the level of reference (the objective) has already been taken.

One might be tempted to regard the relation of the thought to the True not as that of sense to reference, but rather as that of subject to predicate. One can, indeed, say: 'The thought, that 5 is a prime number, is true.' But closer examination shows that nothing more has been said than in the simple sentence '5 is a prime number.' The truth claim arises in each case from the form of the declarative sentence, and when the latter lacks its usual force, e.g., in the mouth of an actor upon the stage, even the sentence 'The thought that 5 is a prime number is true' contains only a thought, and indeed the same thought as the simple '5 is a prime number.' It follows that the relation of the thought to the True may not be compared with that of subject to predicate. Subject and predicate (understood in the logical sense) are indeed elements of thought; they stand on the same level for knowledge. By combining subject and predicate, one reaches only a thought, never passes from sense to reference, never from a thought to its truth value. One moves at the same level but never advances from one level to the next. A truth value cannot be a part of a thought, any more than, say, the Sun can, for it is not a sense but an object.

If our supposition that the reference of a sentence is its truth value is correct, the latter must remain unchanged when a part of the sentence is replaced by an expression having the same reference. And this is in fact the case. Liebniz gives the definition: '*Eadem sunt, quae sibi mutuo substitui possunt, salva veritate.*' What else but the truth value could be found, that belongs quite generally to every sentence if the reference of its components is relevant, and remains unchanged by substitutions of the kind in question?

If now the truth value of a sentence is its reference, then on the one hand all true sentences have the same reference and so, on the other hand, do all false sentences. From this we see that in the reference of the sentence all that is specific is obliterated. We can never be concerned only with the reference of a sentence; but again the mere thought alone yields no knowledge, but only the thought together with its reference, i.e. its truth value. Judgments can be regarded as advances from a thought to a truth value. Naturally this cannot be a definition. Judgment is something quite peculiar and incomparable. One might also say that judgments are distinctions of parts within truth values. Such distinction occurs by a return to the thought. To every sense belonging to a truth value there would correspond its own manner of analysis. However, I have here used the word 'part' in a special sense. I have in fact transferred the relation between the parts and the whole of the sentence to its reference, by calling the reference of a word part of the reference of the sentence, if the word itself is a part of the sentence. This way of speaking can certainly be attacked, because the whole reference and one part of it do not suffice to determine the remainder, and because the word 'part' is already used in another sense of bodies. A special term would need to be invented.

The supposition that the truth value of a sentence is its reference shall now be put to further test. We have found that the truth value of a sentence remains unchanged when an expression is replaced by another having the same reference: but we have not yet considered the case in which the expression to be replaced is itself a sentence. Now if our view is correct, the truth value of a sentence containing another as part must remain unchanged when the part is replaced by another sentence having the same truth value. Exceptions are to be expected when the whole sentence or its part is direct or indirect quotation; for in such cases, as we have seen, the words do not have the customary reference. In direct quotation, a sentence designates another sentence, and in indirect quotation a thought.

We are thus led to consider subordinate sentences or clauses. These occur as parts of a sentence complex, which is, from the logical standpoint, likewise a sentence – a main sentence. But here we meet the question whether it is also true of the subordinate sentence that its reference is a truth value. Of indirect quotation we already know the opposite. Grammarians view subordinate clauses as representatives of parts of sentences and divide them accordingly into noun clauses, adjective clauses, adverbial clauses. This might generate the supposition that the reference of a subordinate clause was not a truth value but rather of the same kind as the reference of a noun or adjective or adverb – in short, of a part of a sentence, whose sense was not a thought but only a part of a thought. Only a more thorough investigation can clarify the issue. In so doing, we shall not follow the grammatical categories strictly, but rather group together what is logically of the same kind. Let us first search for cases in which the sense of the subordinate clause, as we have just supposed, is not an independent thought.

The case of an abstract[11] noun clause, introduced by 'that,' includes the case of indirect quotation, in which we have seen the words to have their indirect reference coinciding with what is customarily their sense. In this case, then, the subordinate clause has for its reference a thought, not a truth value; as sense not a thought, but the sense of the words 'the thought, that . . . ,' which is only a part of the thought in the entire complex sentence. This happens after 'say', 'hear,' 'be of the opinion,' 'be convinced,' 'conclude,' and similar words.[12] There is a different, and indeed somewhat complicated, situation after words like 'perceive,' 'know,' 'fancy,' which are to be considered later.

That in the cases of the first kind the reference of the subordinate clause is in fact the thought can also be recognized by seeing that it is indifferent to the truth of the whole whether the subordinate clause is true or false. Let us compare, for instance, the two sentences 'Copernicus believed that the planetary orbits are circles' and 'Copernicus believed that the apparent motion of the sun is produced by the real motion of the Earth.' One subordinate clause can be substituted for the other without harm to the truth. The main clause and the subordinate clause together have as their sense only a single thought, and the truth of the whole includes neither the truth nor the untruth of the subordinate clause. In such cases it is not permissible to replace one expression in the subordinate clause by another having the same customary reference, but only by one having the same indirect reference, i.e. the same customary sense. If somebody were to conclude: The reference of a sentence is not its truth value, for in that case it could always be replaced by another sentence of the same truth value; he would prove too much; one might just as well claim that the reference of 'morning star' is not Venus, since one may not always say 'Venus' in place of 'morning star.' One has the right to conclude only that the reference of a sentence is not *always* its truth value, and that 'morning star' does not always stand for the planet Venus, viz. when the word has its indirect reference. An exception of such a kind occurs in the subordinate clause just considered which has a thought as its reference.

If one says 'It seems that . . .' one means 'It seems to me that . . .' or 'I think that . . .' We therefore have the same case again. The situation is similar in the case of expressions such as 'to be pleased,' 'to regret,' 'to approve,' 'to blame,' 'to hope,' 'to fear.' If, toward the end of the battle of Waterloo,[13] Wellington was glad that the Prussians were coming, the basis for his joy was a conviction. Had he been deceived, he would have been no less pleased so long as his illusion lasted; and before he became so convinced he could not have been pleased that the Prussians were coming – even though in fact they might have been already approaching.

Just as a conviction or a belief is the ground of a feeling, it can, as in inference, also be the ground of a conviction. In the sentence: 'Columbus inferred from the roundness of the Earth that he could reach India by travelling towards the west,' we have as the reference of the parts two thoughts, that the Earth is round, and that Columbus by travelling to the west could reach India. All that is relevant here is that Columbus was convinced of both, and that the one conviction was a ground for the other. Whether the Earth is really round and Columbus could really reach India by travelling west, as he thought, is immaterial to the truth of our sentence; but it is not immaterial whether we replace 'the Earth' by 'the planet which is accompanied by a moon whose diameter is greater than the fourth part of its own.' Here also we have the indirect reference of the words.

Adverbial final clauses beginning 'in order that' also belong here; for obviously the purpose is a thought; therefore: indirect reference for the words, subjunctive mood.

A subordinate clause with 'that' after 'command,' 'ask,' 'forbid,' would appear in direct speech as an imperative. Such a clause has no reference but only a sense. A command, a request, are indeed not thoughts, yet they stand on the same level as thoughts. Hence in subordinate clauses depending upon 'command,' 'ask,' etc., words have their indirect reference. The reference of such a clause is therefore not a truth value but a command, a request, and so forth.

The case is similar for the dependent question in phrases such as 'doubt whether,' 'not to know what.' It is easy to see that here also the words are to be taken to have their indirect reference. Dependent clauses expressing questions and beginning with 'who,' 'what,' 'where,' 'when,' 'how,' 'by what means,' etc., seem at times to approximate very closely to adverbial clauses in which words have their customary references. These cases are distinguished linguistically [in German] by the mood of the verb. With the subjunctive, we have a dependent question and indirect reference of the words, so that a proper name cannot be general be replaced by another name of the same object.

In the cases so far considered the words of the subordinate clauses had their indirect reference, and this made it clear that the reference of the subordinate clause itself was indirect, i.e. not a truth value but a thought, a command, a request, a question. The subordinate clause could be regarded as a noun, indeed one could say: as a proper name of that thought, that command, etc., which it represented in the context of the sentence structure.

We now come to other subordinate clauses, in which the words do have their customary reference without however a thought occurring as sense and a truth value as reference. How this is possible is best made clear by examples.

> Whoever discovered the elliptic form of the planetary orbits died in misery.

If the sense of the subordinate clause were here a thought, it would have to be possible to express it also in a separate sentence. But this does not work, because the grammatical subject 'whoever' has no independent sense and only mediates the relation with the consequent clause 'died in misery.' For this reason the sense of the subordinate clause is not a complete thought, and its reference is Kepler, not a truth value. One might object that the sense of the whole does contain a thought as part, viz. that there was somebody who first discovered the elliptic form of the planetary orbits; for whoever takes the whole to be true cannot deny this part. This is undoubtedly so; but only because otherwise the dependent clause 'whoever discovered the elliptic form of the planetary orbits' would have no reference. If anything is asserted there is always an obvious presupposition that the simple or compound proper names used have reference. If one therefore asserts 'Kepler died in misery,' there is a presupposition that the name 'Kepler' designates something; but it does not follow that the sense of the sentence 'Kepler died in misery' contains the thought that the name 'Kepler' designates something. If this were the case the negation would have to run not

> Kepler did not die in misery

but

> Kepler did not die in misery, or the name 'Kepler' has no reference.

That the name 'Kepler' designates something is just as much a presupposition for the assertion

> Kepler died in misery

as for the contrary assertion. Now languages have the fault of containing expressions which fail to designate an object (although their grammatical form seems to qualify them for that purpose) because the truth of some sentence is a prerequisite. Thus it depends on the truth of the sentence:

> There was someone who discovered the elliptic form of the planetary orbits

whether the subordinate clause

> Whoever discovered the elliptic form of the planetary orbits

really designates an object or only seems to do so while having in fact no reference. And thus it may appear as if our subordinate clause contained as a part of its sense the thought that there was somebody who discovered the elliptic form of the planetary orbits. If this were right the negation would run:

> Either whoever discovered the elliptic form of the planetary orbits did not die in misery or there was nobody who discovered the elliptic form of the planetary orbits.

This arises from an imperfection of language, from which even the symbolic language of mathematical analysis is not altogether free; even there combinations of symbols can occur that seem to stand for something but have (at least so far) no reference, e.g. divergent infinite series. This can be avoided, e.g., by means of the special stipulation that divergent infinite series shall stand for the number 0. A logically perfect language (*Begriffsschrift*) should satisfy the conditions, that every expression grammatically well constructed as a proper name out of signs already introduced shall in fact designate an object, and that no new sign shall be introduced as a proper name without being secured a reference. The logic books contain warnings against logical mistakes arising from the ambiguity of expressions. I regard as no less pertinent a warning against apparent proper names having no reference. The history of mathematics supplies errors which have arisen in this way. This lends itself to demagogic abuse as easily as ambiguity – perhaps more easily. 'The will of the people' can serve as an example; for it is easy to establish that there is at any rate no generally accepted reference for this expression. It is therefore by no means unimportant to eliminate the source of these mistakes, at least in science, once and for all. Then such objections as the one discussed above would become impossible, because it could never depend upon the truth of a thought whether a proper name had a reference.

With the consideration of these noun clauses may be coupled that of types of adjective and adverbial clauses which are logically in close relation to them.

Adjective clauses also serve to construct compound proper names, though, unlike noun clauses, they are not sufficient by themselves for this purpose. These adjective clauses are to be regarded as equivalent to adjectives. Instead of 'the square root of 4 which is smaller than 0,' one can also say 'the negative square root of 4.' We have here the case of a compound proper name constructed from the expression for a concept with the help of the singular definite article. This is at any rate permissible if the concept applies to one and only one single object.[14]

Expressions for concepts can be so constructed that marks of a concept are given by adjective clauses as, in our example, by the clause 'which is smaller than 0.' It is evident that such an adjective clause cannot have a thought as sense or a truth value as reference, any more than the noun clause could. Its sense, which can also be expressed in many cases by a single adjective, is only a part of a thought. Here, as in the case of the noun clause, there is no independent subject and therefore no possibility of reproducing the sense of the subordinate clause in an independent sentence.

Places, instants, stretches of time, are, logically considered, objects; hence the linguistic designation of a definite place, a definite instant, or a stretch of time is to be regarded as a proper name. Now adverbial clauses of place and time can be used for the construction of such a proper name in a manner similar to that which we have seen in the case of noun and adjective clauses. In the same way, expressions for concepts bringing in places, etc., can be constructed. It is to be noted here also that the sense of these subordinate clauses cannot be reproduced in an independent sentence, since an essential component, viz. the determination of place or time, is missing and is only indicated by a relative pronoun or a conjunction.[15]

In conditional clauses, also, there may usually be recognized to occur an indefinite indicator, having a similar correlate in the dependent clause. (We have already seen this occur in noun, adjective, and adverbial clauses.) In so far as each indicator refers to the other, both clauses together form a connected whole, which as a rule expresses only a single thought. In the sentence

> If a number is less than 1 and greater than 0, its square is less than 1 and greater than 0

the component in question is 'a number' in the conditional clause and 'its' in the dependent clause. It is by means of this very indefiniteness that the sense acquires the generality expected of a law. It is this which is responsible for the fact that the antecedent clause alone has no complete thought as its sense and in combination with the consequent clause expresses one and only one thought, whose parts are no longer thoughts. It is, in general, incorrect to say that in the hypothetical judgment two judgments are put in reciprocal relationship. If this or something similar is said, the word 'judgment' is used in the same sense as I have connected with the word 'thought,' so that I would use the formulation: 'A hypothetical thought establishes a reciprocal relationship between two thoughts.' This could be true only if an indefinite indicator is absent,[16] but in such a case there would also be no generality.

If an instant of time is to be indefinitely indicated in both conditional and dependent clauses, this is often achieved merely by using the present tense of the verb, which in such a case however does not indicate the temporal present. This grammatical form is then the indefinite indicator in the main and subordinate clauses. An example of this is: 'When the Sun is in the tropic of Cancer, the longest day in the northern hemisphere occurs.' Here, also, it is impossible to express the sense of the subordinate clause in a full sentence, because this sense is not a complete thought. If we say: 'The Sun is in the tropic of Cancer,' this would refer to our present time and thereby change the sense. Just as little is the sense of the main clause a thought; only the whole, composed of main and subordinate clauses, has such a sense. It may be added that several common components in the antecedent and consequent clauses may be indefinitely indicated.

It is clear that noun clauses with 'who' or 'what' and adverbial clauses with 'where,' 'when,' 'wherever,' 'whenever' are often to be interpreted as having the sense of conditional clauses, e.g. 'who touches pitch, defiles himself.'

Adjective clauses can also take the place of conditional clauses. Thus the sense of the sentence previously used can be given in the form 'The square of a number which is less than 1 and greater than 0 is less than 1 and greater than 0.'

The situation is quite different if the common component of the two clauses is designated by a proper name. In the sentence:

> Napoleon, who recognized the danger to his right flank, himself led his guards against the enemy position

two thoughts are expressed:

1. Napoleon recognized the danger to his right flank
2. Napoleon himself led his guards against the enemy position.

When and where this happened is to be fixed only by the context, but is nevertheless to be taken as definitely determined thereby. If the entire sentence is uttered as an assertion, we thereby simultaneously assert both component sentences. If one of the parts is false, the whole is false. Here we have the case that the subordinate clause by itself has a complete thought as sense (if we complete it by indication of place and time). The reference of the subordinate clause is accordingly a truth value. We can therefore expect that it may be replaced, without harm to the truth value of the whole, by a sentence having the same truth value. This is indeed the case;

but it is to be noticed that for purely grammatical reasons, its subject must be 'Napoleon,' for only then can it be brought into the form of an adjective clause belonging to 'Napoleon.' But if the demand that it be expressed in this form be waived, and the connexion be shown by 'and,' this restriction disappears.

Subsidiary clauses beginning with 'although' also express complete thoughts. This conjunction actually has no sense and does not change the sense of the clause but only illuminates it in a peculiar fashion.[17] We could indeed replace the concessive clause without harm to the truth of the whole by another of the same truth value; but the light in which the clause is placed by the conjunction might then easily appear unsuitable, as if a song with a sad subject were to be sung in a lively fashion.

In the last cases the truth of the whole included the truth of the component clauses. The case is different if a conditional clause expresses a complete thought by containing, in place of an indefinite indicator, a proper name or something which is to be regarded as equivalent. In the sentence

If the Sun has already risen, the sky is very cloudy

the time is the present, that is to say, definite. And the place is also to be thought of as definite. Here it can be said that a relation between the truth values of conditional and dependent clauses has been asserted, viz. such that the case does not occur in which the antecedent stands for the True and the consequent for the False. Accordingly, our sentence is true if the Sun has not yet risen, whether the sky is very cloudy or not, and also if the Sun has risen and the sky is very cloudy. Since only truth values are here in question, each component clause can be replaced by another of the same truth value without changing the truth value of the whole. To be sure, the light in which the subject appears would usually be unsuitable; the thought might easily seem distorted; but this has nothing to do with its truth value. One must always take care not to clash with the subsidiary thoughts, which are however not explicitly expressed and therefore should not be reckoned in the sense. Hence, also, no account need be taken of their truth values.[18]

The simple cases have now been discussed. Let us review what we have learned.

The subordinate clause usually has for its sense not a thought, but only a part of one, and consequently no truth value as reference. The reason for this is either that the words in the subordinate clause have indirect reference, so that the reference, not the sense, of the subordinate clause is a thought; or else that, on account of the presence of an indefinite indicator, the subordinate clause is incomplete and expresses a thought only when combined with the main clause. It may happen, however, that the sense of the subsidiary clause is a complete thought, in which case it can be replaced by another of the same truth value without harm to the truth of the whole – provided there are no grammatical obstacles.

An examination of all the subordinate clauses which one may encounter will soon provide some which do not fit well into these categories. The reason, so far as I can see, is that these subordinate clauses have no such simple sense. Almost always, it seems, we connect with the main thoughts expressed by us subsidiary thoughts which, although not expressed, are associated with our words, in accordance with psychological laws, by the hearer. And since the subsidiary thought appears to be connected with our words of its own accord, almost like the main thought itself, we want it also to be expressed. The sense of the sentence is thereby enriched, and it may well happen that we have more simple thoughts than clauses. In many cases the sentence must be understood in this way, in others it may be doubtful whether the subsidiary thought belongs to the sense of the sentence or only accompanies it.[19] One might perhaps find that the sentence

> Napoleon, who recognized the danger to his right flank, himself led his guards against the enemy position

expresses not only the two thoughts shown above, but also the thought that the knowledge of the danger was the reason why he led the guards against the enemy position. One may in fact doubt whether this thought is merely slightly suggested or really expressed. Let the question be considered whether our sentence be false if Napoleon's decision had already been made before he recognized the danger. If our sentence could be true in spite of this, the subsidiary thought should not be understood as part of the sense. One would probably decide in favour of this. The alternative would make for a quite complicated situation: We would have more simple thoughts than clauses. If the sentence

> Napoleon recognized the danger to his right flank

were now to be replaced by another having the same truth value, e.g.

> Napoleon was already more than 45 years old

not only would our first thought be changed, but also our third one. Hence the truth value of the latter might change – viz. if his age was not the reason for the decision to lead the guards against the enemy. This shows why clauses of equal truth value cannot always be substituted for one another in such cases.

The clause expresses more through its connexion with another than it does in isolation.

Let us now consider cases where this regularly happens. In the sentence:

> Bebel fancies that the return of Alsace-Lorraine would appease France's desire for revenge

two thought are expressed, which are not however shown by means of antecedent and consequent clauses, viz.:

> (1) Bebel believes that the return of Alsace-Lorraine would appease France's desire for revenge
> (2) the return of Alsace–Lorraine would not appease France's desire for revenge.

In the expression of the first thought, the words of the subordinate clause have their indirect reference, while the same words have their customary reference in the expression of the second thought. This shows that the subordinate clause in our original complex sentence is to be taken twice over, with different reference, standing once for a thought, once for a truth value. Since the truth value is not the whole reference of the subordinate clause, we cannot simply replace the latter by another of equal truth value. Similar considerations apply to expressions such as 'know,' 'discover,' 'it is known that.'

By means of a subordinate causal clause and the associated main clause we express several thoughts, which however do not correspond separately to the original clauses. In the sentence: 'Because ice is less dense than water, it floats on water' we have

1. Ice is less dense than water;
2. If anything is less dense than water, it floats on water;
3. Ice floats on water.

The third thought, however, need not be explicitly introduced, since it is contained in the remaining two. On the other hand, neither the first and third nor the second and third combined would furnish the sense of our sentence. It can now be seen that our subordinate clause

> because ice is less dense than water

expresses our first thought, as well as a part of our second. This is how it comes to pass that our subsidiary clause cannot be simply replaced by another of equal truth value; for this would alter our second thought and thereby might well alter its truth value.

The situation is similar in the sentence

If iron were less dense than water, it would float on water.

Here we have the two thoughts that iron is not less dense than water, and that something floats on water if it is less dense than water. The subsidiary clause agains expresses one thought and a part of the other.

If we interpret the sentence already considered

> After Schleswig-Holstein was separated from Denmark, Prussia and Austria quarrelled

in such a way that it expresses the thought that Schleswig-Holstein was once separated from Denmark, we have first this thought, and secondly the thought that at a time, more closely determined by the subordinate clause, Prussia and Austria quarrelled. Here also the subordinate clause expresses not only one thought but also a part of another. Therefore it may not in general be replaced by another of the same truth value.

It is hard to exhaust all the possibilities given by language; but I hope to have brought to light at least the essential reasons why a subordinate clause may not always be replaced by another of equal truth value without harm to the truth of the whole sentence structure. These reasons arise:

1. when the subordinate clause does not stand for a truth value, inasmuch as it expresses only a part of a thought;
2. when the subordinate clause does stand for a truth value but is not restricted to so doing, inasmuch as its sense includes one thought and part of another.

The first case arises:

1. in indirect reference of words
2. if a part of the sentence is only an indefinite indicator instead of a proper name.

In the second case, the subsidiary clause may have to be taken twice over, viz. once in its customary reference, and the other time in indirect reference; or the sense of a part of the subordinate clause may likewise be a component of another thought, which, taken together with the thought directly expressed by the subordinate clause, makes up the sense of the whole sentence.

It follows with sufficient probability from the foregoing that the cases where a subordinate clause is not replaceable by another of the same value cannot be brought in disproof of our view that a truth value is the reference of a sentence having a thought as its sense.

Let us return to our starting point.

When we found '$a=a$' and '$a=b$' to have different cognitive values, the explanation is that for the purpose of knowledge, the sense of the sentence, viz., the thought expressed by it, is no less relevant than its reference, i.e. its truth value. If now $a=b$, then indeed the reference of 'b' is the same as that of 'a,' and hence the truth value of '$a=b$' is the same as that of '$a=a$.' In spite of this, the sense of 'b' may differ from that of 'a', and thereby the thought expressed in '$a=b$' differs from that of '$a=a$'. In that case the two sentences do not have the same cognitive value. If we understand by 'judgment' the advance from the thought to its truth value, as in the above paper, we can only say that the judgments are different.

Notes

1. I use this word in the sense of identity and understand '$a=b$' to have the sense of '*a* is the same as *b*' or '*a* and *b* coincide.'
2. The reference is to Frege's *Begriffsschrift, eine der arithmetischen nachgebildete Formelsprache des reinen Denkens* (Halle, 1879). [Editor's note]
3. See his 'Ueber Begriff und Gegenstand' *(Vierteljahrsschrift für wissenschaftliche Philosophie* XVI [1892], 192–205). [Editor's note]
4. In the case of an actual proper name such as 'Aristotle' opinions as to the sense may differ. It might, for instance, be taken to be the following: the pupil of Plato and teacher of Alexander the Great. Anybody who does this will attach another sense to the sentence 'Aristotle was born in Stagira' than will a man who takes as the sense of the name: the teacher of Alexander the Great who was born in Stagira. So long as the reference remains the same, such variations of sense may be tolerated, although they are to be avoided in the theoretical structure of a demonstrative science and ought not to occur in a perfect language.
5. We can include with ideas the direct experiences in which sense-impressions and acts themselves take the place of the traces which they have left in the mind. The distinction is unimportant for our purpose, especially since memories of sense-impressions and acts always go along with such impressions and acts themselves to complete the perceptual image. One may on the other hand understand direct experience as including any object, in so far as it is sensibly perceptible or spatial.
6. Hence it is inadvisable to use the word 'idea' to designate something so basically different.
7. By a thought I understand not the subjective performance of thinking but its objective content, which is capable of being the common property of several thinkers.
8. It would be desirable to have a special term for signs having only sense. If we name them, say, representations, the words of the actors on the stage would be representations; indeed the actor himself would be a representation.
9. See his 'Ueber Begriff und Gegenstand' *(Vierteljahrsschrift für wissenschaftliche Philosphie* XVI [1892], 192–205. [Editor's note]
10. A judgment, for me is not the mere comprehension of a thought, but the admission of its truth.

11. A literal translation of Frege's 'abstracten Nennsätzen' whose meaning eludes me.
12. In 'A lied in saying he had seen B,' the subordinate clause designates a thought which is said (1) to have been asserted by A (2) while A was convinced of its falsity.
13. Frege uses the Prussian name for the battle – 'Belle Alliance.'
14. In accordance with what was said above, an expression of the kind in question must actually always be assured of reference, by means of a special stipulation, e.g. by the convention that 0 shall count as its reference, when the concept applies to no object or to more than one.
15. In the case of these sentences, various interpretations are easily possible. The sense of the sentence, 'After Schleswig-Holstein was separated from Denmark, Prussia, and Austria quarrelled' can also be rendered in the form 'After the separation of Schleswig-Holstein from Denmark, Prussia and Austria quarrelled.' In this version, it is surely sufficiently clear that the sense is not to be taken as having as a part the thought that Schleswig-Holstein was once separated from Denmark, but that this is the necessary presupposition in order for the expression 'after the separation of Schleswig-Holstein from Denmark' to have any reference at all. To be sure, our sentence can also be interpreted as saying that Schleswig-Holstein was once separated from Denmark. We then have a case which is to be considered later. In order to understand the difference more clearly, let us project ourselves into the mind of a Chinese who, having little knowledge of European history, believes it to be false that Schleswig-Holstein was ever separated from Denmark. He will take our sentence, in the first version, to be neither true nor false but will deny it to have any reference, on the ground of absence of reference for its subordinate clause. This clause would only apparently determine a time. If he interpreted our sentence in the second way, however, he would find a thought expressed in it which he would take to be false, beside a a part which would be without reference for him.
16. At times an explicit linguistic indication is missing and must be read off from the entire context.
17. Similarly in the case of 'but,' 'yet.'
18. The thought of our sentence might also be expressed thus: 'Either the Sun has not risen yet or the sky is very cloudy' – which shows how this kind of sentence connexion is to be understood.
19. This may be important for the question whether an assertion is a lie, or an oath a perjury.

Chapter 8

On Denoting

B. Russell

BY a 'denoting phrase' I mean a phrase such as any one of the following: a man, some man, any man, every man, all men, the present King of England, the present King of France, the centre of mass of the solar system at the first instant of the twentieth century, the revolution of the earth round the sun, the revolution of the sun round the earth. Thus a phrase is denoting solely in virtue of its *form*. We may distinguish three cases: (1) A phrase may be denoting, and yet not denote anything; e.g., 'the present King of France'. (2) A phrase may denote one definite object; e.g., 'the present King of England' denotes a certain man. (3) A phrase may denote ambiguously; e.g., 'a man' denotes not many men, but an ambiguous man. The interpretation of such phrases is a matter of considerably difficulty; indeed, it is very hard to frame any theory not susceptible of formal refutation. All the difficulties with which I am acquainted are met, so far as I can discover, by the theory which I am about to explain.

The subject of denoting is of very great importance, not only in logic and mathematics, but also in theory of knowledge. For example, we know that the centre of mass of the solar system at a definite instant is some definite point, and we can affirm a number of propositions about it; but we have no immediate *acquaintance* with this point, which is only known to us by description. The distinction between *acquaintance* and *knowledge about* is the distinction between the things we have presentations of, and the things we only reach by means of denoting phrases. It often happens that we know that a certain phrase denotes unambiguously, although we have no acquaintance with what it denotes; this occurs in the above case of the centre of mass. In perception we have acquaintance with the objects

From Marsh, R., (ed.) (1956), *B. Russell, Logic and Knowledge*, London: George Allen and Unwin.

of perception, and in thought we have acquaintance with objects of a more abstract logical character; but we do not necessarily have acquaintance with the objects denoted by phrases composed of words with whose meanings we are acquainted. To take a very important instance: there seems no reason to believe that we are ever acquainted with over people's minds, seeing that these are not directly perceived; hence what we know about them is obtained through denoting. All thinking has to start from acquaintance; but it succeeds in thinking *about* many things with which we have no acquaintance.

The course of my argument will be as follows. I shall begin by stating the theory I intend to advocate;[1] I shall then discuss the theories of Frege and Meinong, showing why neither of them satisfies me; then I shall give the grounds in favour of my theory; and finally I shall briefly indicate the philosophical consequences of my theory.

My theory, briefly, is as follows. I take the notion of the *variable* as fundamental; I use '$C(x)$' to mean a proposition[2] in which x is a constituent, where x, the variable, is essentially and wholly undetermined. Then we can consider the two notions '$C(x)$ is always true' and '$C(x)$ is sometimes true'.[3] Then *everything* and *nothing* and *something* (which are the most primitive of denoting phrases) are to be interpreted as follows:

> C (everything) means '$C(x)$ is always true';
> C (nothing) means ' "$C(x)$ is false" is always true';
> C (something) means 'It is false that "$C(x)$ is false" is always true'.[4]

Here the notion '$C(x)$ is always true' is taken as ultimate and indefinable, and the others are defined by means of it. *Everything, nothing*, and *something* are not assumed to have any meaning in isolation, but a meaning is assigned to *every* proposition in which they occur. This is the principle of the theory of denoting I wish to advocate: that denoting phrases never have any meaning in themselves, but that every proposition in whose verbal expression they occur has a meaning. The difficulties concerning denoting are, I believe, all the result of a wrong analysis of propositions whose verbal expressions contain denoting phrases. The proper analysis, if I am not mistaken, may be further set forth as follows.

Suppose now we wish to interpret the proposition, 'I met a man'. If this is true, I met some definite man; but that is not what I affirm. What I affirm is, according to the theory I advocate:

> ' "I met x, and x is human" is not always false'.

Generally, defining the class of men as the class of objects having the predicate *human*, we say that:

> 'C (a man)' means ' "$C(x)$ and x is human" is not always false'.

This leaves 'a man', by itself, wholly destitute of meaning, but gives a meaning to every proposition in whose verbal expression 'a man' occurs.

Consider next the proposition 'all men are mortal'. This proposition[5] is really hypothetical and states that *if* anything is a man, it is mortal. That is, it states that if x is a man, x is mortal, whatever x may be. Hence, substituting 'x is human' for 'x is a man', we find:

> 'All men are mortal' means ' "If x is human, x is mortal" is always true'.

This is what is expressed in symbolic logic by saying that 'all men are mortal' means ' "x is human" implies "x is mortal" for all values of x'. More generally, we say:

> 'C (all men)' means ' "If x is human, then C (x) is true" is always true'.

Similarly

> 'C (no men)' means ' "If x is human, then C (x) is false" is always true'.
> 'C (some men)' will mean the same as 'C (a man)',[6] and
> 'C (a man)' means 'It is false that "C (x) and x is human" is always false'.
> 'C (every man)' will mean the same as 'C (all men)'.

It remains to interpret phrases containing *the*. These are by far the most interesting and difficult of denoting phrases. Take as an instance 'the father of Charles II was executed'. This asserts that there was an x who was the father of Charles II and was executed. Now *the*, when it is strictly used, involves uniqueness; we do, it is true, speak of '*the* son of So-and-so' even when So-and-so has several sons, but it would be more correct to say '*a* son of So-and-so'. Thus for our purposes we take *the* as involving uniqueness. Thus when we say 'x was *the* father of Charles II' we not only assert that x had a certain relation to Charles II, but also that nothing else had this relation. The relation in question, without the assumption of uniqueness, and without any denoting phrases, is expressed by 'x begat Charles II'. To get an equivalent of 'x was the father of Charles II', we must add, 'If y is other than x, y did not beget Charles II', or, what is equivalent, 'If y begat Charles II, y is identical with x'. Hence 'x is the father of Charles II' becomes: 'x begat Charles II; and "if y begat Charles II, y is identical with x" is always true of y'.

> Thus 'the father of Charles II was executed' becomes: 'It is not always false of x that x begat Charles II and that x was executed

> and that "if y begat Charles II, y is identical with x" is always true of y'.

This may seem a somewhat incredible interpretation; but I am not at present giving reasons, I am merely *stating* the theory.

To interpret 'C (the father of Charles II)', where C stands for any statement about him, we have only to substitute C (x) for 'x was executed' in the above. Observe that, according to the above interpretation whatever statement C may be, 'C (the father of Charles II)' implies:

> 'It is not always false of x that "if y begat Charles II, y is identical with x" is always true of y',

which is what is expressed in common language by 'Charles II had one father and no more'. Consequently if this condition fails, *every* proposition of the form 'C (the father of Charles II)' is false. Thus e.g. every proposition of the form 'C (the present King of France)' is false. This is a great advantage in the present theory. I shall show later that it is not contrary to the law of contradiction, as might be at first supposed.

The above gives a reduction of all propositions in which denoting phrases occur to forms in which no such phrases occur. Why it is imperative to effect such a reduction, the subsequent discussion will endeavour to show.

The evidence for the above theory is derived from the difficulties which seem unavoidable if we regard denoting phrases as standing for genuine constituents of the propositions in whose verbal expressions they occur. Of the possible theories which admit such constituents the simplest is that of Meinong.[7] This theory regards any grammatically correct denoting phrase as standing for an *object*. Thus 'the present King of France', 'the round square', etc., are supposed to be genuine objects. It is admitted that such objects do not *subsist*, but nevertheless they are supposed to be objects. This is in itself a difficult view; but the chief objection is that such objects, admittedly, are apt to infringe the law of contradiction. It is contended, for example, that the existent present King of France exists, and also does not exist; that the round square is round, and also not round, etc. But this is intolerable; and if any theory can be found to avoid this result, it is surely to be preferred.

The above breach of the law of contradiction is avoided by Frege's theory. He distinguishes, in a denoting phrase, two elements, which we may call the *meaning* and the *denotation*.[8] Thus 'the centre of mass of the solar system at the beginning of the twentieth century' is highly complex in *meaning*, but its *denotation* is a certain point, which is simple. The solar system, the twentieth century, etc., are constituents of the *meaning*; but the *denotation* has no constituents at all.[9] One advantage of this distinction is that it shows why it is often worth while to assert identity. If we say 'Scott is the author of *Waverley*', we assert an identity of denotation with a difference of meaning.

I shall, however, not repeat the grounds in favour of this theory, as I have urged its claims elsewhere (loc. cit.), and am now concerned to dispute those claims.

One of the first difficulties that confront us, when we adopt the view that denoting phrases *express* a meaning and *denote* a denotation,[10] concerns the cases in which the denotation appears to be absent. If we say 'the King of England is bald', that is, it would seem, not a statement about the complex *meaning* 'the King of England', but about the actual man denoted by the meaning. But now consider 'the King of France is bald'. By parity of form, this also ought to be about the denotation of the phrase 'the King of France'. But this phrase, though it has a *meaning* provided 'the King of England' has a meaning, has certainly no denotation, at least in any obvious sense. Hence one would suppose that 'the King of France is bald' ought to be nonsense; but it is not nonsense, since it is plainly false. Or again consider such a proposition as the following: 'If u is a class which has only one member, then that one member is a member of u', or, as we may state it, 'If u is a unit class, *the* u is a u'. This proposition ought to be *always* true, since the conclusion is true whenever the hypothesis is true. But 'the u' is a denoting phrase, and it is the denotation, not the meaning, that is said to be a u. Now if u is *not* a unit class, 'the u' seems to denote nothing; hence our proposition would seem to become nonsense as soon as u is not a unit class.

Now it is plain that such propositions do *not* become nonsense merely because their hypotheses are false. The King in *The Tempest* might say, 'If Ferdinand is not drowned, Ferdinand is my only son'. Now 'my only son' is a denoting phrase, which, on the face of it, has a denotation when, and only when, I have exactly one son. But the above statement would nevertheless have remained true if Ferdinand had been in fact drowned. Thus we must either provide a denotation in cases in which it is at first sight absent, or we must abandon the view that the denotation is what is concerned in propositions which contain denoting phrases. The latter is the course that I advocate. The former course may be taken, as by Meinong, by admitting objects which do not subsist, and denying that they obey the law of contradiction; this, however, is to be avoided if possible. Another way of taking the same course (so far as our present alternative is concerned) is adopted by Frege, who provides by definition some purely conventional denotation for the cases in which otherwise there would be none. Thus 'the King of France', is to denote the null-class; 'the only son of Mr. So-and-so' (who has a fine family of ten), is to denote the class of all his sons; and so on. But this procedure, though it may not lead to actual logical error, is plainly artificial, and does not give an exact analysis of the matter. Thus if we allow that denoting phrases, in general, have the two sides of meaning and denotation, the cases where there seems to be no denotation cause difficulties both on the assumption that there really is a denotation and on the assumption that there really is none.

A logical theory may be tested by its capacity for dealing with puzzles, and it is a wholesome plan, in thinking about logic, to stock the mind with as many puzzles as possible, since these serve much the same purpose as is served by experiments in physical science. I shall therefore state three puzzles which a theory as to denoting ought to be able to solve; and I shall show later that my theory solves them.

1. If *a* is identical with *b*, whatever is true of the one is true of the other, and either may be substituted for the other in any proposition without altering the truth or falsehood of that proposition. Now George IV wished to know whether Scott was the author of *Waverley*; and in fact Scott *was* the author of *Waverley*. Hence we may substitute *Scott* for *the author of 'Waverley'*, and thereby prove that George IV wished to know whether Scott was Scott. Yet an interest in the law of identity can hardly be attributed to the first gentleman of Europe.
2. By the law of excluded middle, either '*A* is *B*' or '*A* is not *B*' must be true. Hence either 'the present King of France is bald' or 'the present King of France is not bald' must be true. Yet if we enumerated the things that are bald, and then the things that are not bald, we should not find the present King of France in either list. Hegelians, who love a synthesis, will probably conclude that he wears a wig.
3. Consider the proposition '*A* differs from *B*'. If this is true, there is a difference between *A* and *B*, which fact may be expressed in the form 'the difference between *A* and *B* subsists'. But if it is false that *A* differs from *B*, then there is no difference between *A* and *B*, which fact may be expressed in the form 'the difference between *A* and *B* does not subsist'. But how can a non-entity be the subject of a proposition? 'I think, therefore I am' is no more evident than 'I am the subject of a proposition, therefore I am', provided 'I am' is taken to assert subsistence or being,[11] not existence. Hence, it would appear, it must always be self-contradictory to deny the being of anything; but we have seen, in connexion with Meinong, that to admit being also sometimes leads to contradictions. Thus if *A* and *B* do not differ, to suppose either that there is, or that there is not, such an object as 'the difference between *A* and *B*' seems equally impossible.

The relation of the meaning to the denotation involves certain rather curious difficulties, which seem in themselves sufficient to prove that the theory which leads to such difficulties must be wrong.

When we wish to speak about the *meaning* of a denoting phrase, as opposed to its *denotation*, the natural mode of doing so is by inverted commas. Thus we say:

> The centre of mass of the solar system is a point, not a denoting complex;

'The centre of mass of the solar system' is a denoting complex, not a point.

*Or again,

The first line of Gray's Elegy states a proposition.

'The first line of Gray's Elegy' does not state a proposition. Thus taking any denoting phrase, say C, we wish to consider the relation between C and 'C', where the difference of the two is of the kind exemplified in the above two instances.

We say, to begin with, that when C occurs it is the *denotation* that we are speaking about; but when 'C' occurs, it is the *meaning*. Now the relation of meaning and denotation is not merely linguistic through the phrase: there must be a logical relation involved, which we express by saying that the meaning denotes the denotation. But the difficulty which confronts us is that we cannot succeed in *both* preserving the connexion of meaning and denotation *and* preventing them from being one and the same; also that the meaning cannot be got at except by means of denoting phrases. This happens as follows.

The one phrase C was to have both meaning and denotation. But if we speak of 'the meaning of C', that gives us the meaning (if any) of the denotation. 'The meaning of the first line of Gray's Elegy' is the same as 'The meaning of "The curfew tolls the knell of parting day",' and is not the same as 'The meaning of "the first line of Gray's Elegy".' Thus in order to get the meaning we want, we must speak not of 'the meaning of C', but of 'the meaning of "C",' which is the same as 'C' by itself. Similarly 'the denotation of C' does not mean the denotation we want, but means something which, if it denotes at all, denotes what is denoted by the denotation we want. For example, let 'C' be 'the denoting complex occurring in the second of the above instances'. Then

C = 'the first line of Gray's Elegy', and

the denotation of C = The curfew tolls the knell of parting day. But what we *meant* to have as the denotation was 'the first line of Gray's Elegy'. Thus we have failed to get what we wanted.

The difficulty in speaking of the meaning of a denoting complex may be stated thus: The moment we put the complex in a proposition, the proposition is about the denotation; and if we make a proposition in which the subject is 'the meaning of C', then the subject is the meaning (if any) of the denotation,

*Editor's note: The passage enclosed within rules is famously obscure.

which was not intended. This leads us to say that, when we distinguish meaning and denotation, we must be dealing with the meaning: the meaning has denotation and is a complex, and there is not something other than the meaning, which can be called the complex, and be said to *have* both meaning and denotation. The right phrase, on the view in question, is that some meanings have denotations.

But this only makes our difficulty in speaking of meanings more evident. For suppose *C* is our complex; then we are to say that *C* *is* the meaning of the complex. Nevertheless, whenever C occurs without inverted commas, what is said is not true of the meaning, but only of the denotation, as when we say: The centre of mass of the solar system is a point. Thus to speak of C itself, i.e., to make a proposition about the meaning, our subject must not be C, but something which denotes C. Thus 'C', which is what we use when we want to speak of the meaning, must be not the meaning, but something which denotes the meaning. And C must not be a constituent of this complex (as it is of 'the meaning of C'); for if C occurs in the complex, it will be its denotation, not its meaning, that will occur, and there is no backward road from denotations to meanings, because every object can be denoted by an infinite number of different denoting phrases.

Thus it would seem that 'C' and C are different entities, such that 'C' denotes C; but this cannot be an explanation, because the relation of 'C' to C remains wholly mysterious; and where are we to find the denoting complex 'C' which is to denote C? Moreover, when C occurs in a proposition, it is not *only* the denotation that occurs (as we shall see in the next paragraph); yet, on the view in question, C is only the denotation, the meaning being wholly relegated to 'C'. This is an inextricable tangle, and seems to prove that the whole distinction of meaning and denotation has been wrongly conceived.

That the meaning is relevant when a denoting phrase occurs in a proposition is formally proved by the puzzle about the author of *Waverley*. The proposition 'Scott was the author of *Waverley*' has a property not possessed by 'Scott was Scott', namely the property that George IV wished to know whether it was true. Thus the two are not identical propositions; hence the meaning of 'the author of *Waverley*' must be relevant as well as the denotation, if we adhere to the point of view to which this distinction belongs. Yet, as we have just seen, so long as we adhere to this point of view, we are compelled to hold that only the denotation can be relevant. Thus the point of view in question must be abandoned.

It remains to show how all the puzzles we have been considering are solved by the theory explained at the beginning of this article.

According to the view which I advocate, a denoting phrase is essentially *part* of a sentence, and does not, like most single words, have any significance on its own account. If I say 'Scott was a man', that is a statement of the form '*x* was a man', and it has 'Scott' for its subject. But if I say 'the author of *Waverley* was a man', that is not a statement of the form '*x* was a man', and does not have 'the author of *Waverley*' for its subject. Abbreviating the statement made at the beginning of this article, we may put, in place of 'the author of *Waverley* was a man', the following: 'One and only one entity wrote *Waverley*, and that one was a man'. (This is not so strictly what is meant as what was said earlier; but it is easier to follow.) And speaking generally, suppose we wish to say that the author of *Waverley* had the property ϕ, what we wish to say is equivalent to 'One and only one entity wrote *Waverley*, and that one had the property ϕ'.

The explanation of *denotation* is now as follows. Every proposition in which 'the author of *Waverley*' occurs being explained as above, the proposition 'Scott was the author of *Waverley*' (i.e. 'Scott was identical with the author of *Waverley*') becomes 'One and only one entity wrote *Waverley*, and Scott was identical with that one'; or, reverting to the wholly explicit form: 'It is not always false of x that x wrote *Waverley*, that it is always true of y that if y wrote *Waverley* y is identical with x, and that Scott is identical with x'. Thus if '*C*' is a denoting phrase, it may happen that there is one entity x (there cannot be more than one) for which the proposition 'x is identical with *C*' is true, this proposition being interpreted as above. We may then say that the entity x is the denotation of the phrase '*C*'. Thus Scott is the denotation of 'the author of *Waverley*'. The '*C*' in inverted commas will be merely the *phrase*, not anything that can be called the *meaning*. The phrase *per se* has no meaning, because in any proposition in which it occurs the proposition, fully expressed, does not contain the phrase, which has been broken up.

The puzzle about George IV's curiosity is now seen to have a very simple solution. The proposition 'Scott was the author of *Waverley*', which was written out in its unabbreviated form in the preceding paragraph, does not contain any constituent 'the author of *Waverley*' for which we could substitute 'Scott'. This does not interfere with the truth of inferences resulting from making what is *verbally* the substitution of 'Scott' for 'the author of *Waverley*', so long as 'the author of *Waverley*' has what I call a *primary* occurrence in the proposition considered. The difference of primary and secondary occurrences of denoting phrases is as follows:

When we say: 'George IV wished to know whether so-and-so', or when we say 'So-and-so is surprising' or 'So-and-so is true', etc., the 'so-and-so' must be a proposition. Suppose now that 'so-and-so' contains a denoting phrase. We may either eliminate this denoting phrase from the subordinate proposition 'so-and-so', or from the whole proposition in which 'so-and-so' is a mere constituent. Different propositions result according to which we do. I have heard of a touchy owner of a yacht to whom a guest, on first seeing it, remarked, 'I thought your yacht was larger than it is'; and the owner replied, 'No, my yacht is not larger than it is'. What the guest meant was, 'The size that I thought your yacht was is greater than the size your yacht is'; the meaning attributed to him is, 'I thought the size of your yacht was greater than the size of your yacht'. To return to George IV and *Waverley*, when we say, 'George IV wished to know whether Scott was the author of *Waverley*', we normally mean 'George IV wished to know whether one and only one man wrote *Waverley* and Scott was that man'; but we *may* also mean: 'One and only one man wrote *Waverley*, and George IV wished to know whether Scott was that man'. In the latter, 'the author of *Waverley*' has a *primary* occurrence; in the former, a *secondary*. The latter might be expressed by 'George IV wished to know, concerning the man who in fact wrote *Waverley*, whether he was Scott'. This would be true, for example, if George IV had seen Scott at a distance, and had asked 'Is that Scott?'. A *secondary* occurrence of a denoting phrase may be defined as one in which the phrase occurs in a proposition *p* which is a mere constituent of the proposition we are considering, and the substitution for the denoting phrase is to be effected in *p*, not in the whole proposition concerned. The ambiguity as between primary and secondary occurrences is hard to avoid in language; but it does no harm if we are on our guard against it. In symbolic logic it is of course easily avoided.

The distinction of primary and secondary occurrences also enables us to deal with the question whether the present King of France is bald or not bald, and generally with the logical status of denoting phrases that denote nothing. If '*C*' is a denoting phrase, say 'the term having the property *F*', then

> '*C* has the property ϕ' means 'one and only one term has the property *F*, and that one has the property ϕ'.[12]

If now the property *F* belongs to no terms, or to several, it follows that '*C* has the property ϕ' is false for *all* values of ϕ. Thus 'the present King of France is bald' is certainly false; and 'the present King of France is not bald' is false if it means

> 'There is an entity which is now King of France and is not bald',

but is true if it means

> 'It is false that there is an entity which is now King of France and is bald'.

That is, 'the King of France is not bald' is false if the occurrence of 'the King of France' is *primary*, and true if it is *secondary*. Thus all propositions in which 'the King of France' has a primary occurrence are false; the denials of such propositions are true, but in them 'the King of France' has a secondary occurrence. Thus we escape the conclusion that the King of France has a wig.

We can now see also how to deny that there is such an object as the difference between *A* and *B* in the case when *A* and *B* do not differ. If *A* and *B* do differ, there is one and only one entity *x* such that '*x* is the difference between *A* and *B*' is a true proposition; if *A* and *B* do not differ, there is no such entity *x*. Thus according to the meaning of denotation lately explained, 'the difference between *A* and *B*' has a denotation when *A* and *B* differ, but not otherwise. This difference applies to true and false propositions generally. If '*a R b*' stands for '*a* has the relation *R* to *b*', then when *a R b* is true, there is such an entity as the relation *R* between *a* and *b*; when *a R b* is false, there is no such entity. Thus out of any proposition we can make a denoting phrase, which denotes an entity if the proposition is true, but does not denote an entity if the proposition is false. E.g., it is true (at least we will suppose so) that the earth revolves round the sun, and false that the sun revolves round the earth; hence 'the revolution of the earth round the sun' denotes an entity, while 'the revolution of the sun round the earth' does not denote an entity.[13]

The whole realm of non-entities, such as 'the round square', 'the even prime other than 2', 'Apollo', 'Hamlet', etc., can now be satisfactorily dealt with. All these are denoting phrases which do not denote anything. A proposition about Apollo means what we get by substituting what the classical dictionary tells us is meant by Apollo, say 'the sun-god'. All propositions in which Apollo occurs are to be interpreted by the above rules for denoting phrases. If 'Apollo' has a primary occurrence, the proposition containing the occurrence is false; if the occurrence is secondary, the proposition may be true. So again 'the round square is round' means 'there is one and only one entity *x* which is round and square, and that entity is round', which is a false proposition, not, as Meinong maintains, a true one. 'The most perfect Being has all perfections; existence is a perfection; therefore the most perfect Being exists' becomes:

'There is one and only one entity *x* which is most perfect; that one has all perfections; existence is a perfection; therefore that one exists'. As a proof, this fails for want of a proof of the premiss 'there is one and only one entity *x* which is most perfect'.[14]

Mr. MacColl (*Mind*, N.S., No. 54, and again No. 55, page 401) regards individuals as of two sorts, real and unreal; hence he defines the null-class as the class consisting of all unreal individuals. This assumes that such phrases as 'the present King of France', which do not denote a real individual, do, nevertheless, denote an individual, but an unreal one. This is essentially Meinong's theory, which we have seen reason to reject because it conflicts with the law of contradiction. With our theory of denoting, we are able to hold that there are no unreal individuals; so that the null-class is the class containing no members, not the class containing as members all unreal individuals.

It is important to observe the effect of our theory on the interpretation of definitions which proceed by means of denoting phrases. Most mathematical definitions are of this sort; for example '$m - n$ means the number which, added to n, gives m'. Thus $m - n$ is defined as meaning the same as a certain denoting phrase; but we agreed that denoting phrases have no meaning in isolation. Thus what the definition really ought to be is: 'Any proposition containing $m - n$ is to mean the proposition which results from substituting for "$m - n$" "the number which, added to n, gives m".' The resulting proposition is interpreted according to the rules already given for interpreting propositions whose verbal expression contains a denoting phrase. In the case where m and n are such that there is one and only one number x which, added to n, gives m, there is a number x which can be substituted for $m - n$ in any proposition containing $m - n$ without altering the truth or falsehood of the proposition. But in other cases, all propositions in which '$m - n$' has a primary occurrence are false.

The usefulness of *identity* is explained by the above theory. No one outside a logic-book ever wishes to say 'x is x', and yet assertions of identity are often made in such forms as 'Scott was the author of *Waverley*' or 'thou art the man'. The meaning of such propositions cannot be stated without the notion of identity, although they are not simply statements that Scott is identical with another term, the author of *Waverley*, or that thou art identical with another term, the man. The shortest statement of 'Scott is the author of *Waverley*' seems to be 'Scott wrote *Waverley*; and it is always true of y that if y wrote *Waverley*, y is identical with Scott'. It is in this way that identity enters into 'Scott is the author of *Waverley*'; and it is owing to such uses that identity is worth affirming.

One interesting result of the above theory of denoting is this: when there is anything with which we do not have immediate acquaintance, but only definition by denoting phrases, then the propositions in which this thing is introduced by means of a denoting phrase do not really contain this thing as a constituent, but contain instead the constituents expressed by the several words of the denoting phrase. Thus in every proposition that we can apprehend (i.e. not only in those whose truth or falsehood we can judge of, but in all that we can think about), all the constituents are really entities with which we have immediate acquaintance. Now such things as matter (in the sense in which matter occurs in physics) and the minds of other people are known to us only by denoting phrases, i.e. we are not *acquainted* with them, but we know them as what has such and such properties. Hence, although we can form propositional functions $C(x)$ which must hold of such and such a material particle, or of So-and-so's mind, yet we are not acquainted with the propositions which affirm these things that we know must be true, because we cannot apprehend the actual entities concerned. What we know is 'So-and-so has a mind which has such and such properties' but we do not know 'A has such and such properties', where A *is* the mind in question. In such a case, we know the properties of a thing without having acquaintance with the thing itself, and without, consequently, knowing any single proposition of which the thing itself is a constituent.

Of the many other consequences of the view I have been advocating, I will say nothing. I will only beg the reader not to make up his mind against the view – as he might be tempted to do, on account of its apparently excessive complication – until he has attempted to construct a theory of his own on the subject of denotation. This attempt, I believe, will convince him that, whatever the true theory may be, it cannot have such a simplicity as one might have expected beforehand.

Notes

1. I have discussed this subject in *Principles of Mathematics*, Chap. V, and § 476. The theory there advocated is very nearly the same as Frege's, and is quite different from the theory to be advocated in what follows.
2. More exactly, a propositional function.
3. The second of these can be defined by means of the first, if we take it to mean, 'It is not true that "$C(x)$ is false" is always true'.
4. I shall sometimes use, instead of this complicated phrase, the phrase '$C(x)$ is not always false', or '$C(x)$ is sometimes true', supposed *defined* to mean the same as the complicated phrase.
5. As has been ably argued in Mr. Bradley's *Logic*, Book I, Chap. II.
6. Psychologically 'C (a man)' has a suggestion of *only one*, and 'C (some men)' has a suggestion of *more than one*; but we may neglect these suggestions in a preliminary sketch.
7. See *Untersuchungen zur Gegenstandstheorie und Psychologie* (Leipzig, 1904) the first three articles (by Meinong, Ameseder and Mally respectively).
8. See his 'Ueber Sinn und Bedeutung', *Zeitschrift für Phil. und Phil. Kritik*, Vol. 100.
9. Frege distinguishes the two elements of meaning and denotation everywhere, and not only in complex denoting phrases. Thus it is the *meanings* of the constituents of a denoting complex that enter into its *meaning*, not their *denotation*. In the proposition 'Mont Blanc is over 1,000 metres high', it is, according to him, the *meaning* of 'Mont Blanc', not the actual mountain, that is a constituent of the *meaning* of the proposition.
10. In this theory, we shall say that the denoting phrase *expresses* a meaning; and we shall say both of the phrase and of the meaning that they *denote* a denotation. In the other theory, which I advocate, there is no *meaning*, and only sometimes a *denotation*.
11. I use these as synonyms.
12. This is the abbreviated, not the stricter, interpretation.
13. The propositions from which such entities are derived are not identical either with these entities or with the propositions that these entities have being.
14. The argument can be made to prove validly that all members of the class of most perfect Beings exist; it can also be proved formally that this class cannot have *more* than one member; but, taking the definition of perfection as possession of all positive predicates, it can be proved almost equally formally that the class does not have even one member.

Chapter 9

Reference and Definite Description

K. Donnellan

I

DEFINITE descriptions, I shall argue, have two possible functions. They are used to refer to what a speaker wishes to talk about, but they are also used quite differently. Moreover, a definite description occurring in one and the same sentence may, on different occasions of its use, function in either way. The failure to deal with this duality of function obscures the genuine referring use of definite descriptions. The best-known theories of definite descriptions, those of Russell and Strawson, I shall suggest, are both guilty of this. Before discussing this distinction in use, I will mention some features of these theories to which it is especially relevant.

On Russell's view a definite description may denote an entity: 'if "*C*" is a denoting phrase [as definite descriptions are by definition], it may happen that there is one entity *x* (there cannot be more than one) for which the proposition "*x* is identical with *C*" is true. . . . We may then say that the entity *x* is the denotation of the phrase "*C*".'[2] In using a definite description, then, a speaker may use an expression which denotes some entity, but this is the only relationship between that entity and the use of the definite description recognized by Russell. I shall argue, however, that there are two uses of definite descriptions. The definition of denotation given by Russell is applicable to both, but in one of these the definite description serves to do something more. I shall say that in this use the speaker uses the definite description to *refer* to something, and call this use the 'referential use' of a definite description. Thus, if I am right, referring is not the same as denoting and the referential use of definite description is not recognized on Russell's view.

First published in *The Philosophical Review*, 75: 281–304.

Furthermore, on Russell's view the type of expression that comes closest to performing the function of the referential use of definite descriptions turns out, as one might suspect, to be a proper name (in 'the narrow logical sense'). Many of the things said about proper names by Russell can, I think be said about the referential use of definite descriptions without straining senses unduly. Thus the gulf Russell thought he saw between names and definite descriptions is narrower than he thought.

Strawson, on the other hand, certainly does recognize a referential use of definite definitions. But what I think he did not see is that a definite description may have a quite different role – may be used nonreferentially, even as it occurs in one and the same sentence. Strawson, it is true, points out nonreferential uses of definite descriptions,[3] but which use a definite description has seems to be for him a function of the kind of sentence in which it occurs; whereas, if I am right, there can be two possible uses of a definite description in the same sentence. Thus, in 'On Referring,' he says, speaking of expressions used to refer, 'Any expression of any of these classes [one being that of definite descriptions] can occur as the subject of what would traditionally be regarded as a singular subject-predicate sentence; and would, so occurring, exemplify the use I wish to discuss.'[4] so the definite description in, say, the sentence 'The Republican candidate for president in 1968 will be a conservative' presumably exemplifies the referential use. But if I am right, we could not say this of the sentence in isolation from some particular occasion on which it is used to state something; and then it might or might not turn out that the definite description has a referential use.

Strawson and Russell seem to me to make a common assumption here about the question of how definite descriptions function: that we can ask how a definite description functions in some sentence independently of a particular occasion upon which it is used. This assumption is not really rejected in Strawson's arguments against Russell. Although he can sum up his position by saying, ' "Mentioning" or "referring" is not something an expression does; it is something that someone can use an expression to do,'[5] he means by this to deny the radical view that a 'genuine' referring expression *has* a referent, functions to refer, independent of the context of some use of the expression. The denial of this view, however, does not entail that definite descriptions cannot be identified as referring expressions in a sentence unless the sentence is being used. Just as we can speak of a function of a tool that is not at the moment performing its function, Strawson's view, I believe, allows us to speak of the referential function of a definite description in a sentence even when it is not being used. This, I hope to show, is a mistake.

A second assumption shared by Russell's and Strawson's account of definite descriptions is this. In many cases a person who uses a definite description can be said (in some sense) to presuppose or imply that something fits the description.[6] If I state that the king is on his throne, I presuppose or imply that there is a king. (At any rate, this would be a natural thing to say for anyone who doubted that there is a king.) Both Russell and Strawson assume that where the presupposition or implication is false, the truth value of what the speaker says is affected. For Russell the statement made is false; for Strawson it has no truth value. Now if there are two uses of definite descriptions, it may be that the truth value is affected differently in each case by the falsity of the presupposition or implication. This is what I shall in fact argue. It will turn out, I believe, that one or the other of the two views, Russell's or Strawson's, may be correct about the nonreferential use of definite descriptions, but neither fits the referential use. This is not so surprising about Russell's view, since he did not recognize this use in any case, but it is surprising about Strawson's since the referential use is what he tries to explain and defend. Furthermore, on Strawson's account, the result of there being nothing which fits the description is a failure of reference.[7] This too, I believe, turns out not to be true about the referential use of definite descriptions.

II

There are some uses of definite descriptions which carry neither any hint of a referential use nor any presupposition or implication that something fits the description. In general, it seems, these are recognizable from the sentence frame in which the description occurs. These uses will not interest us, but it is necessary to point them out if only to set them aside.

An obvious example would be the sentence 'The present kind of France does not exist,' used, say, to correct someone's mistaken impression that de Gaulle is the king of France.

A more interesting example is this. Suppose someone were to ask, 'Is de Gaulle the king of France?' This is the natural form of words for a person to use who is in doubt as to whether de Gaulle is king or president of France. Given this background to the question, there seems to be no presupposition or implication that someone is the king of France. Nor is the person attempting to refer to someone by using the definite description. On the other hand, reverse the name and description in the question and the speaker probably would be thought to presuppose or imply this. 'Is the king of France de Gaulle?' is the natural question for one to ask who wonders whether it is de Gaulle rather than someone else who occupies the throne of France.[8]

Many times, however, the use of a definite description does carry a presupposition or implication that something fits the description. If definite descriptions do have a referring role, it will be here. But it is a mistake, I think, to try, as I believe both Russell and Strawson do, to settle this matter without further ado. What is needed, I believe, is the distinction I will now discuss.

III

I will call the two uses of definite descriptions I have in mind the attributive use and the referential use. A speaker who uses a definite description attributively in an assertion states something about whoever or whatever is the so-and-so. A speaker who uses a definite description referentially in an assertion, on the other hand, uses the description to enable his audience to pick out whom or what he is talking about and states something about that person or thing. In the first case the definite description might be said to occur essentially, for the speaker wishes to assert something about whatever or whoever fits that description; but in the referential use the definite description is merely one tool for doing a certain job – calling attention to a person or thing – and in general any other device for doing the same job, another description or a name, would do as well. In the attributive use, the attribute of being the so-and-so is all important, while it is not in the referential use.

To illustrate this distinction, in the case of a single sentence, consider the sentence, 'Smith's murderer is insane.' Suppose first that we come upon poor Smith foully murdered. From the brutal manner of the killing and the fact that Smith was the most lovable person in the world, we might exclaim, 'Smith's murderer is insane.' I will assume, to make it a simpler case, that in a quite ordinary sense we do not know who murdered Smith (though this is not in the end essential to the case). This, I shall say, is an attributive use of the definite description.

The contrast with such a use of the sentence is one of those situations in which we expect and intend our audience to realize whom we have in mind when we speak of Smith's murderer and, most importantly, to know that it is this person about whom we are going to say something.

For example, suppose that Jones has been charged with Smith's murder and has been placed on trial. Imagine that there is a discussion of Jones's odd behavior at his trial. We might sum up our impression of his behavior by saying, 'Smith's murderer is insane.' If someone asks to whom we are referring, by using this description, the answer here is 'Jones.' This, I shall say, is a referential use of the definite description.

That these two uses of the definite description in the same sentence are really quite different can perhaps best be brought out by considering the consequences of the assumption that Smith had no murderer (for example, he in fact committed suicide). In both situations, in using the definite description 'Smith's murderer,' the speaker in some sense presupposes or implies that there is a murderer. But when we hypothesize that the presupposition or implication is false, there are different results for the two uses. In both cases we have used the predicate 'is insane,' but in the first case, if there is no murderer, there is no person of whom it could be correctly said that we attributed insanity to him. Such a person could be identified (correctly) only in case someone fitted the description used. But in the second case, where the definite description is simply a means of identifying the person we want to talk about, it is quite possible for the correct identification to be made even though no one fits the description we used.[9] We were speaking about Jones even though he is not in fact Smith's murderer and, in the circumstances imagined, it was his behavior we were commenting upon. Jones might, for example, accuse us of saying false things of him in calling him insane and it would be no defense, I should think, that our description, 'the murderer of Smith,' failed to fit him.

It is, moreover, perfectly possible for our audience to know to whom we refer, in the second situation, even though they do not share our presupposition. A person hearing our comment in the context imagined might know we are talking about Jones even though he does not think Jones guilty.

Generalizing from this case, we can say, I think, that there are two uses of sentences of the form, 'The ϕ is ψ.' In the first, if nothing is the ϕ then nothing has been said to be ψ. In the second, the fact that nothing is the ϕ does not have this consequence.

With suitable changes the same difference in use can be formulated for uses of language other than assertions Suppose one is at a party and, seeing an interesting-looking person holding a martini glass, one asks, 'Who is the man drinking a martini?' If it should turn out that there is only water in the glass, one has nevertheless asked a question about a particular person, a question that it is possible for someone to answer. Contrast this with the use of the same question by the chairman of the local Teetotalers Union. He has just been informed that a man is drinking a martini at their annual party. He responds by asking his informant, 'Who is the man drinking a martini?' In asking the question the chairman does not have some particular person in mind about whom he asks the question; if no one is drinking a martini, if the information is wrong, no person can be singled out as the person about whom the question was asked, Unlike the first case, the attribute of being the man drinking a martini is all-important, because if it is the attribute of no one, the chairman's question has no straightforward answer.

This illustrates also another difference between the referential and the attributive use of definite descriptions. In the one case we have asked a question about a particular person or thing even though nothing fits the description we used; in the other this is not so. But also in the one case our question can be answered; in the other it cannot be. In the referential use of a definite description we may succeed in picking out a person or thing to ask a question about even though he or it does not really fit the description; but in the attributive use if nothing fits the description, no straightforward answer to the question can be given.

This further difference is also illustrated by commands or orders containing definite descriptions. Consider the order, 'Bring me the book on the table.' If 'the book on the table' is being used referentially, it is possible to fulfill the order even though there is no book on the table. If, for example, there is a book *beside* the table, though there is none *on* it, one might bring that book back and ask the issuer of the order whether this is 'the book you meant.' And it may be. But imagine we are told that someone has laid a book on our prize antique table, where nothing should be put. The order, 'Bring me the book on the table' cannot now be obeyed unless there is a book that has been placed on the table. There is no possibility of bringing back a book which was never on the table and having it be the one that was meant, because there is no book that in that sense was 'meant.' In the one case the definite description was a device for getting the other person to pick the right book; if he is able to pick the right book even though it does not satisfy the description, one still succeeds in his purpose. In the other case, there is, antecedently, no 'right book' except one which fits the description; the attribute of being the book on the table is essential. Not only is there no book about which an order was issued, if there is no book on the table, but the order itself cannot be obeyed. When a definite description is used attributively in a command or question and nothing fits the description, the command cannot be obeyed and the question cannot be answered. This suggests some analogous consequence for assertions containing definite descriptions used attributively. Perhaps the analogous result is that the assertion is neither true nor false: this is Strawson's view of what happens when the presupposition of the use of a definite description is false. But if so, Strawson's view works not for definite descriptions used referentially, but for the quite different use, which I have called the attributive use.

I have tried to bring out the two uses of definite descriptions by pointing out the different consequences of supposing that nothing fits the description used. There are still other differences. One is this: when a definite description is used referentially, not only is there in some sense a presupposition or implication that someone or something fits the description, as there is also in the attributive use, but there is a quite different presupposition; the speaker presupposes of some *particular* someone or something that he or it fits the description. In asking, for example, 'Who is the man drinking a martini?' where we mean to ask a question about that man over there, we are presupposing that that man over there is drinking a martini – not just that *someone* is a man drinking a martini. When we say, in a context where it is clear we are referring to Jones, 'Smith's murderer is insane,' we are presupposing that Jones is Smith's murderer. No such presupposition is present in the attributive use of definite descriptions. There is, of course, the presupposition that someone *or other* did the murder, but the speaker does not presuppose of someone in particular – Jones or Robinson, say – that he did it. What I mean by this second kind of presupposition that someone or something in particular fits the description – which is present in a referential use but not in an attributive use – can perhaps be seen more clearly by considering a member of the speaker's audience who believes that Smith was not murdered at all. Now in the case of the referential use of the description, 'Smith's murderer,' he could accuse the speaker of mistakenly presupposing both that someone or other is the murderer and that also Jones is the murderer, for even though he believes Jones not to have done the deed, he knows that the speaker was referring to Jones. But in the case of the attributive use, he can accuse the speaker of having only the first, less specific presupposition; he cannot pick out some person and claim that the speaker is presupposing that that person is Smith's murderer. Now the more particular presuppositions that we find present in referential uses are clearly not ones we can assign to a definite description in some particular sentence in isolation from a context of use. In order to know that a person presupposes that Jones is Smith's murderer in using the sentence 'Smith's murderer is insane,' we have to know that he is using the description referentially and also to whom he is referring. The sentence by itself does not tell us any of this.

IV

From the way in which I set up each of the previous examples it might be supposed that the important difference between the referential and the attributive use lies in the beliefs of the speaker. Does he believe of some particular person or thing that he or it fits the description used? In the Smith murder example, for instance, there was in the one case no belief as to who did the deed, whereas in the contrasting case it was believed that Jones did it. But this is, in fact, not an essential difference. It is possible for a definite description to be used attributively even though the speaker (and his audience) believes that a certain person or thing fits the description. And it is possible for a definite description to be used referentially where the speaker believes that nothing fits the description. It is true – and this is why, for simplicity, I set up the examples the way I did – that if a speaker does not believe that anything fits the description or does not believe that he is in a position to pick out what does fit the description, it is likely that he is not using it referentially. It is also true that if he and his audience would pick out some particular thing or person as fitting the description, then a use of the definite description is very likely referential. But these are only presumptions and not entailments.

To use the Smith murder case again, suppose that Jones is on trial for the murder and I and everyone else believe him guilty. Suppose that I comment that the murderer of Smith is insane, but instead of backing this up, as in the example previously used, by citing Jones's behavior in the dock, I go on to outline reasons for thinking that *anyone* who murdered poor Smith in that particularly horrible way must be insane. If now it turns out that Jones was not the murderer after all, but someone else was, I think I can claim to have been right if the true murderer is after all insane. Here, I think, I would be using the definite description attributively, even though I believe that a particular person fits the description.

It is also possible to think of cases in which the speaker does not believe that what he means to refer to by using the definite description fits the description, or to imagine cases in which the definite description is used referentially even though the speaker believes *nothing* fits the description. Admittedly, these cases may be parasitic on a more normal use; nevertheless, they are sufficient to show that such beliefs of the speaker are not decisive as to which use is made of a definite description.

Suppose the throne is occupied by a man I firmly believe to be not the king, but a usurper. Imagine also that his followers as firmly believe that he is the king. Suppose I wish to see this man. I might say to his minions, 'Is the king in his countinghouse?' I succeed in referring to the man I wish to refer to without myself believing that he fits the description. It is not even necessary, moreover, to suppose that his followers believe him to be the king. If they are cynical about the whole thing, know he is not the king, I may still succeed in referring to the man I wish to refer to. Similarly, neither I nor the people I speak to may suppose that *anyone* is the king and, finally, each party may know that the other does not so suppose and yet the reference may go through.

V

Both the attributive and the referential use of definite descriptions seem to carry a presupposition or implication that there is something which fits the description. But the reasons for the existence of the presupposition or implication are different in the two cases.

There is a presumption that a person who uses a definite description referentially believes that what he wishes to refer to fits the description. Because the purpose of using the description is to get the audience to pick out or think of the right thing or person, one would normally choose a description that he believes the thing or person fits. Normally a misdescription of that to which one wants to refer would mislead the audience. Hence, there is a presumption that the speaker believes *something* fits the description – namely, that to which he refers.

When a definite description is used attributively, however, there is not the same possibility of misdescription. In the example of 'Smith's murderer' used attributively, there was not the possibility of misdescribing Jones or anyone else; we were not referring to Jones nor to anyone else by using the description. The presumption that the speaker believes *someone* is Smith's murderer does not arise here from a more specific presumption that he believes Jones or Robinson or someone else whom he can name or identify is Smith's murderer.

The presupposition or implication is borne by a definite description used attributively because if nothing fits the description the linguistic purpose of the speech act will be thwarted. That is, the speaker will not succeed in saying something true, if he makes an assertion; he will not succeed in asking a question that can be answered, if he has asked a question; he will not succeed in issuing an order that can be obeyed, if he has issued an order. If one states that Smith's murderer is insane, when Smith has no murderer, and uses the definite description nonreferentially, then one fails to say anything *true*. If one issues the order 'Bring me Smith's murderer' under similar circumstances, the order cannot be obeyed; nothing would count as obeying it.

When the definite description is used referentially, on the other hand, the presupposition or implication stems simply from the fact that normally a person tries to describe correctly what he wants to refer to because normally this is the best way to get his audience to recognize what he is referring to. As we have seen, it is possible for the linguistic purpose of the speech act to be accomplished in such a case even though nothing fits the description; it is possible to say something true or to ask a question that gets answered or to issue a command that gets obeyed. For when the definite description is used referentially, one's audience may succeed in seeing to what one refers even though neither it nor anything else fits the description.

VI

The result of the last section shows something to be wrong with the theories of both Russell and Strawson; for though they give differing accounts of the implication or presupposition involved, each gives only one. Yet, as I have argued, the presupposition or implication is present for a quite different reason, depending upon whether the definite description is used attributively or referentially, and exactly what presuppositions or implications are involved is also different. Moreover, neither theory seems a correct characterization of the referential use. On Russell's there is a logical entailment: 'The ϕ is ψ' entails 'There exists one and only one ϕ.' Whether or not this is so for the attributive use, it does not seem true of the referential use of the definite description. The 'implication' that something is the ϕ, as I have argued, does not amount to an entailment; it is more like a presumption based on what is *usually* true of the use of a definite description to refer. In any case, of course, Russell's theory does not show – what is true of the referential use – that the implication that *something* is the ϕ comes from the more specific implication that *what is being referred to* is the ϕ. Hence, as a theory of definite descriptions, Russell's view seems to apply, if at all, to the attributive use only.

Russell's definition of denoting (a definite description denotes an entity if that entity fits the description uniquely) is clearly applicable to either use of definite descriptions. Thus whether or not a definite description is used referentially or attributively, it may have a denotation. Hence, denoting and referring, as I have explicated the latter notion, are distinct and Russell's view recognizes only the former. It seems to me, moreover, that this is a welcome result, that denoting and referring should not be confused. If one tried to maintain that they are the same notion, one result would be that a speaker might be referring to something without knowing it. If someone said, for example, in 1960 before he had any idea that Mr. Goldwater would be the Republican nominee in 1964, 'The Republican candidate for president in 1964 will be a conservative,' (perhaps on the basis of an analysis of the views of party leaders) the definite description here would *denote* Mr. Goldwater. But would we wish to say that the speaker had referred to, mentioned, or talked about Mr. Goldwater? I feel these terms would be out of place. Yet if we identify referring and denoting, it ought to be possible for it to turn out (after the Republican Convention) that the speaker had, unknown to himself, referred in 1960 to Mr. Goldwater. On my view, however, while the definite description used did *denote* Mr. Goldwater (using Russell's definition), the speaker used it *attributively* and did not *refer* to Mr. Goldwater.

Turning to Strawson's theory, it was supposed to demonstrate how definite descriptions are referential. But it goes too far in this direction. For there are nonreferential uses of definite descriptions also, even as they occur in one and the same sentence. I believe that Strawson's theory involves the following propositions:

1. If someone asserts that the ϕ is ψ he has not made a true or false statement if there is no ϕ.[10]
2. If there is no ϕ then the speaker has failed to refer to anything.[11]
3. The reason he has said nothing true or false is that he has failed to refer.

Each of these propositions is either false or, at best, applies to only one of the two uses of definite descriptions.

Proposition (1) is possibly true of the attributive use. In the example in which 'Smith's murderer is insane' was said when Smith's body was first discovered, an attributive use of the definite description, there was no person to whom the speaker referred. If Smith had no murderer, nothing true was said. It is quite tempting to conclude, following Strawson, that nothing true *or* false was said. But where the definite description is used referentially, something true may well have been said. It is possible that something true was said of the person or thing referred to.[12]

Proposition (2) is, as we have seen, simply false. Where a definite description is used referentially it is perfectly possible to refer to something though nothing fits the description used.

The situation with proposition (3) is a bit more complicated. It ties together, on Strawson's view, the two strands given in (1) and (2). As an account of why, when the presupposition is false, nothing true or false has been stated, it clearly cannot work for the attributive use of definite descriptions, for the reason it supplies is that reference has failed. It does not then give the reason why, if indeed this is so, a speaker using a definite description attributively fails to say anything true or false if nothing fits the description. It does, however, raise a question about the referential use. Can reference fail when a definite description is used referentially?

I do not fail to refer merely because my audience does not correctly pick out what I am referring to. I can be referring to a particular man when I use the description 'the man drinking a martini,' even though the people to whom I speak fail to pick out the right person or any person at all. Nor, as we have stressed, do I fail to refer when nothing fits the description. But perhaps I fail to refer in some extreme circumstances, when there is nothing that *I* am willing to pick out as that to which I referred.

Suppose that I think I see at some distance a man walking and ask, 'Is the man carrying a walking stick the professor of history?' We should perhaps distinguish four cases at this point. (a) There is a man carrying a walking stick; I have then referred to a person and asked a question about him that can be answered if my audience has the information. (b) The man over there is not carrying a walking stick, but an umbrella; I have still referred to someone and asked a question that can be answered, though if my audience sees that it is an umbrella and not a walking stick, they may also correct my apparently mistaken impression. (c) It is not a man at all, but a rock that looks like one; in this case, I think I still have referred to something, to the thing over there that happens to be a rock but that I took to be a man. But in this case it is not clear that my question can be answered correctly. This, I think, is not because I have failed to refer, but rather because, given the true nature of what I referred to, my question is not appropriate. A simple 'No, that is not the professor of history' is at least a bit misleading if said by someone who realizes that I mistook a rock for a person. It may, therefore, be plausible to conclude that in such a case I have not asked a question to which there is a straightforwardly correct answer. But if this is true, it is not because nothing fits the description I used, but rather because what I referred to is a rock and my question has no correct answer when asked of a rock. (d) There is finally the case in which there is nothing at all where I thought there was a man with a walking stick; and perhaps here we have a genuine failure to refer at all, even though the description was used for the purpose of referring. There is no rock, nor anything else, to which I meant to refer; it was, perhaps, a trick of light that made me think there was a man there. I cannot say of anything, 'That is what I was referring to, though I now see that it's not a man carrying a walking stick.' This failure of reference, however, requires circumstances much more radical than the mere nonexistence of anything fitting the description used. It requires that there be nothing of which it can be said, 'That is what he was referring to.' Now perhaps also in such cases, if the speaker has asserted something, he fails to state anything true or false if there is nothing that can be identified as that to which he referred. But if so, the failure of reference and truth value does not come about merely because nothing fits the description he used. So (3) may be true of some cases of the referential use of definite descriptions; it may be true that a failure of reference results in a lack of truth value. But these cases are of a much more extreme sort than Strawson's theory implies.

I conclude, then, that neither Russell's nor Strawson's theory represents a correct account of the use of definite descriptions – Russell's because it ignores altogether the referential use, Strawson's because it fails to make the distinction between the referential and the attributive and mixes together truths about each (together with some things that are false).

VII

It does not seem possible to say categorically of a definite description in a particular sentence that it is a referring expression (of course, one could say this if he meant that it *might* be used to refer). In general, whether or not a definite description is used referentially or attributively is a function of the speaker's intentions in a particular case. 'The murderer of Smith' may be used either way in the sentence 'The murderer of Smith is insane.' It does not appear plausible to account for this, either, as an ambiguity in the sentence. The grammatical structure of the sentence seems to me to be the same whether the description is used referentially or attributively: that is, it is not syntactically ambiguous. Nor does it seem at all attractive to suppose an ambiguity in the meaning of the words; it does not appear to be semantically ambiguous. (Perhaps we could say that the sentence is pragmatically ambiguous: the distinction between roles that the description plays is a function of the speaker's intentions.) These, of course, are intuitions; I do not have an argument for these conclusions. Nevertheless, the burden of proof is surely on the other side.

This, I think, means that the view, for example, that sentences can be divided up into predicates, logical operators, and referring expressions is not generally true. In the case of definite descriptions one cannot always assign the referential function in isolation from a particular occasion on which it is used.

There may be sentences in which a definite description can be used only attributively or only referentially. A sentence in which it seems that the definite description could be used only attributively would be 'Point out the man who is drinking my martini,' I am not so certain that any can be found in which the definite description can be used only referentially. Even if there are such sentences, it does not spoil the point that there are many sentences, apparently not ambiguous either syntactically or semantically, containing definite descriptions that can be used either way.

If it could be shown that the dual use of definite descriptions can be accounted for by the presence of an ambiguity, there is still a point to be made against the theories of Strawson and Russell. For neither, so far as I can see, has anything to say about the possibility of such an ambiguity and, in fact, neither seems compatible with such a possibility. Russell's does not recognize the possibility of the referring use, and Strawson's, as I have tried to show in the last section, combines elements from each use into one unitary account. Thus the view that there is an ambiguity in such sentences does not seem any more attractive to these positions.

VIII

Using a definite description referentially, a speaker may say something true even though the description correctly applies to nothing. The sense in which he may say something true is the sense in which he may say something true about someone or something. This sense is, I think, an interesting one that needs investigation. Isolating it is one of the by-products of the distinction between the attributive and referential uses of definite descriptions.

For one thing, it raises questions about the notion of a statement. This is brought out by considering a passage in a paper by Leonard Linsky in which he rightly makes the point that one can refer to someone although the definite description used does not correctly describe the person:

> ... said of a spinster that 'Her husband is kind to her' is neither true nor false. But a speaker might very well be referring to someone using these words, for he may think that someone is the husband of the lady (who in fact is a spinster). Still, the statement is neither true nor false, for it presupposes that the lady has a husband, which she has not. This last refutes Strawson's thesis that if the presupposition of existence is not satisfied, the speaker has failed to refer.[13]

There is much that is right in this passage. But because Linsky does not make the distinction between the referential and the attributive uses of definite descriptions, it does not represent a wholly adequate account of the situation. A perhaps minor point about this passage is that Linsky apparently thinks it sufficient to establish that the speaker in his example is referring to someone by using the definite description 'her husband,' that he *believe* that someone is her husband. This will only approximate the truth provided that the 'someone' in the description of the belief means 'someone in particular' and is not merely the existential quantifier, 'there is someone or other.' For in both the attributive and the referential use the belief that someone *or other* is the husband of the lady is very likely to be present. If, for example, the speaker has just met the lady and, noticing her cheerfulness and radiant good health, makes his remark from his conviction that these attributes are always the result of having good husbands, he would be using the definite description attributively. Since she has no husband, there is no one to pick out as the person to whom he was referring. Nevertheless, the speaker believed that *someone or other* was her husband. On the other hand, if the use of 'her husband' was simply a way of referring to a man the speaker has just met whom he assumed to be the lady's husband, he would have referred to that man even though neither he nor anyone else fits the description. I think it is likely that in this passage Linsky did mean by 'someone,' in his description of the belief, 'someone in particular.' But even then, as we have seen, we have neither a sufficient nor a necessary condition for a referential use of the definite description. A definite description can be used attributively even when the speaker believes that some particular thing or person fits the description, and it can be used referentially in the absence of this belief.

My main point, here, however, has to do with Linsky's view that because the presupposition is not satisfied, the *statement* is neither true nor false. This seems to me possibly correct *if* the definite description is thought of as being used attributively (depending upon whether we go with Strawson or Russell). But when we consider it as used referentially, this categorical assertion is no longer clearly correct. For the man the speaker referred to may indeed be kind to the spinster; the speaker may have said something true about that man. Now the difficulty is in the notion of 'the statement.' Suppose that we know that the lady is a spinster, but nevertheless know that the man referred to by the speaker is kind to her. It seems to me that we shall, on the one hand, want to hold that the speaker said something true, but be reluctant to express this by 'It is true that her husband is kind to her.'

This shows, I think, a difficulty in speaking simply about 'the statement' when definite descriptions are used referentially. For the speaker stated something, in this example, about a particular person, and his statement, we may suppose, was true. Nevertheless, we should not like to agree with his statement by using the sentence he used; we should not like to identify the true statement via the speaker's words. The reason for this is not so hard to find. If we say, in this example, 'It is true that her husband is kind to her,' *we* are now using the definite description either attributively or referentially. But we should not be subscribing to what the original speaker truly said if we use the description attributively, for it was only in its function as referring to a particular person that the definite description yields the possibility of saying something true (since the lady has no husband). Our reluctance, however, to endorse the original speaker's statement by using the definite description referentially to refer to the same person stems from quite a different consideration. For if we too were laboring under the mistaken belief that this man was the lady's husband, we could agree with the original speaker using his exact words. (Moreover, it is possible, as we have seen, deliberately to use a definite description to refer to someone we believe not to fit the description.) Hence, our reluctance to use the original speaker's words does not arise from the fact that if we did we should not succeed in stating anything true or false. It rather stems from the fact that when a definite description is used referentially there is a presumption that the speaker believes that what he refers to fits the description. Since we, who know the lady to be a spinster, would not normally want to give the impression that we believe otherwise, we would not like to use the original speaker's way of referring to the man in question.

How then would we express agreement with the original speaker without involving ourselves in unwanted impressions about our beliefs? The answer shows another difference between the referential and attributive uses of definite descriptions and brings out an important point about genuine referring.

When a speaker says, 'The ϕ is ψ,' where 'the ϕ' is used attributively, if there is no ϕ, we cannot correctly report the speaker as having said *of* this or that person or thing that it is ψ. But if the definite description is used referentially we can report the speaker as having attributed ψ to something. And *we* may refer to what the speaker referred to, using whatever description or name suits our purpose. Thus, if a speaker says, 'Her husband is kind to her,' referring to the man he was just talking to, and if that man is Jones, we may report him as having said *of Jones* that he is kind to her. If Jones is also the president of the college, we may report the speaker as having said *of the president of the college* that he is kind to her. And finally, if we are talking to Jones, we may say, referring to the original speaker, 'He said of you that *you* are kind to her.' It does not matter here whether or not the woman has a husband or whether, if she does, Jones is her husband. If the original speaker referred to Jones, he said of him that he is kind to her. Thus where the definite description is used referentially, but does not fit what was referred to, we can report what a speaker said and agree with him by using a description or name which does fit. In doing so we need not, it is important to note, choose a description or name which the original speaker would agree fits what he was referring to. That is, we can report the speaker in the above case to have said truly of Jones that he is kind to her even if the original speaker did not know that the man he was referring to is named Jones or even if he thinks he is not named Jones.

Returning to what Linsky said in the passage quoted, he claimed that, were someone to say 'Her husband is kind to her,' when she has no husband, *the statement* would be neither true nor false. As I have said, this is a likely view to hold if the definite description is being used attributively. But if it is being used referentially it is not clear what is meant by 'the statement.' If we think about what the speaker said about the person he referred to, then there is no reason to suppose he has not said something true or false about him, even though he is not the lady's husband. And Linsky's claim would be wrong. On the other hand, if we do not identify the statement in this way, what is the statement that the speaker made? To say that the statement he made was that her husband is kind to her lands us in difficulties. For we have to decide whether in using the definite description here in the identification of the statement, we are using it attributively or referentially. If the former, then we misrepresent the linguistic performance of the speaker; if the latter, then we are ourselves referring to someone and reporting the speaker to have said something of that person, in which case we are back to the possibility that he did say something true or false of that person.

I am thus drawn to the conclusion that when a speaker uses a definite description referentially he may have stated something true or false even if nothing fits the description, and that there is not a clear sense in which he has made a statement which is neither true nor false.

IX

I want to end by a brief examination of a picture of what a genuine referring expression is that one might derive from Russell's views. I want to suggest that this picture is not so far wrong as one might suppose and that strange as this may seem, some of the things we have said about the referential use of definite descriptions are not foreign to this picture.

Genuine proper names, in Russell's sense, would refer to something without ascribing any properties to it. They would, one might say, refer to the thing itself, not simply the thing in so far as it falls under a certain description.[14] Now this would seem to Russell something a definite description could not do, for he assumed that if definite descriptions were capable of referring at all, they would refer to something only in so far as that thing satisfied the description. Not only have we seen this assumption to be false, however, but in the last section we saw something more. We saw that when a definite description is used referentially, a speaker can be reported as having said something *of* something. And in reporting what it was of which he said something we are not restricted to the description he used, or synonyms of it; we may ourselves refer to it using any descriptions, names, and so forth, that will do the job. Now this seems to give a sense in which we are concerned with the thing itself and not just the thing under a certain description, when we report the linguistic act of a speaker using a definite description referentially. That is, such a definite description comes closer to performing the function of Russell's proper names than certainly be supposed.

Secondly, Russell thought, I believe, that whenever we use descriptions, as opposed to proper names, we introduce an element of generality which ought to be absent if what we are doing is referring to some particular thing. This is clear from his analysis of sentences containing definite descriptions. One of the conclusions we are supposed to draw from that analysis is that such sentences express what are in reality completely general propositions: there is a ϕ and only one such and any ϕ is ψ. We might put this in a slightly different way. If there is anything which might be identified as reference here, it is reference in a very weak sense – namely, reference to *whatever* is the one and only one ϕ, if there is any such. Now this is something we might well say about the attributive use of definite descriptions, as should be evident from the previous discussion. But this lack of particularity is absent from the referenial use of definite descriptions precisely because the description is here merely a device for getting one's audience to pick out or think of the thing to be spoken about, a device which may serve its function even if the description is incorrect. More importantly perhaps, in the referential use as opposed to the attributive, there is a *right* thing to be picked out by the audience and its being the right thing is not simply a function of its fitting the description.

Notes

1. I should like to thank my colleagues, John Canfield, Sydney Shoemaker, and Timothy Smiley, who read an earlier draft and gave me helpful suggestions. I also had the benefit of the valuable and detailed comments of the referee for the paper, to whom I wish to express my gratitude.
2. 'On Denoting,' reprinted in *Logic and Knowledge*, ed. By Robert C. Marsh (London, 1956), p. 51.
3. 'On Referring,' reprinted in *Philosophy and Ordinary Language*, cd. by Charles C. Caton (Urbana, 1963), pp. 162–163.
4. *Ibid*., p. 162.
5. *Ibid*., p. 170.
6. Here and elsewhere I use the disjunction 'presuppose or imply' to avoid taking a stand that would side me with Russell or Strawson on the issue of what the relationship involved is. To take a stand here would be beside my main point as well as being misleading, since later on I shall argue that the presupposition or implication arises in a different way depending upon the use to which the definite description is put. This last also accounts for my use of the vagueness indicator, 'in some sense.'
7. In a footnote added to the original version of 'On Referring' (*op. cit*., p. 181) Strawson seems to imply that where the presupposition is false, we still succeed in referring in a 'secondary' way, which seems to mean 'as we could be said to refer to fictional or make-believe things.' But his view is still that we cannot refer in such a case in the 'primary' way. This is, I believe, wrong. For a discussion of this modification of Strawson's view see Charles C. Caton, 'Strawson on Referring,' *Mind*, LXVIII (1959), 539–544.
8. This is an adaptation of an example (used for a somewhat different purpose) given by Leonard Linsky in 'Reference and Referents,' in *Philosophy and Ordinary Language*, p. 80.
9. In 'Reference and Referents' (pp. 74–75, 80), Linsky correctly points out that one does not fail to refer simply because the description used does not in fact fit anything (or fits more than one thing). Thus he pinpoints one of the difficulties in Strawson's view. Here, however, I use this fact about referring to make a distinction I believe he does not draw, between two uses of definite descriptions. I later discuss the second passage from Linsky's paper.
10. In 'A Reply to Mr. Sellars,' *Philosophical Review*, LXIII (1954), 216–231, Strawson admits that we do not always refuse to ascribe truth to what a person says when the definite description he uses fails to fit anything (or fits more than one thing). To cite one of his examples, a person who said, 'The United States

Chamber of Deputies contains representatives of two major parties,' would be allowed to have said something true even though he had used the wrong title. Strawson thinks that does not constitute a genuine problem for his view. He thinks that what we do in such cases, 'where the speaker's intended reference is pretty clear, is simply to amend his statement in accordance with his guessed intentions and assess the amended statement for truth or falsity; we are not awarding a truth value at all to the original statement' (p. 230).

The notion of an 'amended statement,' however, will not do. We may note, first of all, that the sort of case Strawson has in mind could arise only when a definite description is used referentially. For the 'amendment' is made by seeing the speaker's intended reference. But this could happen only if the speaker had an intended reference, a particular person or thing in mind, independent of the description he used. The cases Strawson has in mind are presumably not cases of slips of the tongue or the like; presumably they are cases in which a definite description is used because the speaker believes, though he is mistaken, that he is describing correctly what he wants to refer to. We supposedly amend the statement by knowing to what he intends to refer. But what description is to be used in the amended statement? In the example, perhaps, we could use 'the United States Congress.' But this description might be one the speaker would not even accept as correctly describing what he wants to refer to, because he is misinformed about the correct title. Hence, this is not a case of deciding what the speaker meant to say as opposed to what he in fact said, for the speaker did not mean to say 'the United States Congress.' If this is so, then there is no bar to the 'amended' statement containing any description that does correctly pick out what the speaker intended to refer to. It could be, e.g., 'The lower house of the United States Congress.' But this means that there is no one unique 'amended' statement to be assessed for truth value. And, in fact, it should now be clear that the notion of the amended statement really plays no role anyway. For if we can arrive at the amended statement only by first knowing to what the speaker intended to refer, we can assess the truth of what he said simply by deciding whether what he intended to refer to has the properties he ascribed to it.

11. As noted earlier (n. 7), Strawson may allow that one has possibly referred in a 'secondary' way, but, if I am right, the fact that there is no ϕ does not preclude one from having referred in the same way one does if there is a ϕ.
12. For a further discussion of the notion of saying something true *of* someone or something, see sec. VIII.
13. 'Reference and Referents,' p. 80. It should be clear that I agree with Linsky in holding that a speaker may refer even though the 'presupposition of existence' is not satisfied. And I agree in thinking this an objection to Strawson's view. I think, however, that this point, among others, can be used to define two distinct uses of definite descriptions which, in turn, yields a more general criticism of Strawson. So, while I develop here a point of difference, which grows out of the distinction I want to make, I find myself in agreement with much of Linsky's article.
14. Cf. 'The Philosophy of Logical Atomism,' reprinted in *Logic and Knowledge*, p. 200.

Chapter 10

Naming and Necessity

S. Kripke

Lecture I: January 20, 1970[1]

I hope that some people see some connection between the two topics in the title. If not, anyway, such connections will be developed in the course of these talks. Furthermore, because of the use of tools involving reference and necessity in analytic philosophy today, our views on these topics really have wide-ranging implications for other problems in philosophy that traditionally might be thought far-removed, like arguments over the mind-body problem or the so-called 'identity thesis'. Materialism, in this form, often now gets involved in very intricate ways in questions about what is necessary or contingent in identity of properties – questions like that. So, it is really very important to philosophers who may want to work in many domains to get clear about these concepts.

[· · ·]

The first topic in the pair of topics is naming. By a name here I will mean a proper name, i.e., the name of a person, a city, a country, etc. It is well known that modern logicians also are very interested in definite descriptions: phrases of the form 'the x such that φx', such as 'the man who corrupted Hadleyburg'. Now, if one and only one man ever corrupted Hadleyburg, then that man is the referent, in the logician's sense, of that description. We will use the term 'name' so that it does *not* include definite descriptions of that sort, but only those things which in ordinary language would be called 'proper names'. If we want a common term to cover names and descriptions, we may use the term 'designator'.

It is a point, made by Donnellan,[3] that under certain circumstances a particular speaker may use a definite description to refer, not to the proper referent, in the sense that I've just defined it, of that description, but to something else which he wants to single out and which he thinks is the proper referent of the description, but which in fact isn't. So you may say, 'The man over there with the champagne in his glass is happy', though he actually only has water in his glass. Now, even though there is no champagne in his glass, and there may be another man in the room who does have champagne in his glass, the speaker *intended* to refer, or maybe, in some sense of 'refer', *did* refer, to the man he thought had the champagne in his glass. Nevertheless, I'm just going to use the term 'referent of the description' to mean the object uniquely satisfying the conditions in the definite description. This is the sense in which it's been used in the logical tradition. So, if you have a description of the form 'the x such that φx' and there is exactly one x such that φx, that is the referent of the description.

Now, what is the relation between names and descriptions? There is a well known doctrine of John Stuart Mill, in his book *A System of Logic*, that names have denotation but not connotation. To use one of his examples, when we use the name 'Dartmouth' to describe a certain locality in England, it may be so called because it lies at the mouth of the Dart. But even, he says, had the Dart (that's a river) changed its course so that Dartmouth no longer lay at the mouth of the Dart, we could still with propriety call this place 'Dartmouth', even though the name may suggest that it lies at the mouth of the Dart. Changing Mill's terminology, perhaps we should say that a name such as 'Dartmouth' *does* have a 'connotation' to some people, namely, it *does* connote (not to me – I never thought of this) that any place called 'Dartmouth' lies at the mouth of the Dart. But then in some way it doesn't have a 'sense'. At least, it is not part of the *meaning* of the name 'Darmouth' that the town so named lies at the mouth of the Dart. Someone who said that Dartmouth did not lie at the Dart's mouth would not contradict himself.

It should not be thought that every phrase of the form 'the x such that Fx' is always used in English as a description rather than a name. I guess everyone has heard about The Holy Roman Empire, which was neither holy, Roman nor an empire. Today we have The United Nations. Here it would seem that since these things can be so-called even though they are not Holy Roman United Nations, these phrases should be regarded not as definite descriptions, but as names. In the case of some terms, people might have doubts as to whether they're names or descriptions; like 'God' – does it describe God as the unique divine being or is it a name of God? But such cases needn't necessarily bother us.

Now here I am making a distinction which is certainly made in language. But the classical tradition of modern logic has gone very strongly against Mill's view. Frege and Russell both thought, and seemed to arrive at these conclusions independently of each other, that Mill was wrong in a very strong sense: really a proper name, properly used, simply was a definite description abbreviated or disguised. Frege specifically said that such a description gave the sense of the name.[4]

Now the reasons against Mill's view and in favor of the alternative view adopted by Frege and Russell are really very powerful; and it is hard to see – though one may be suspicious of this view because names don't seem to be disguised descriptions – how the Frege-Russell view, or some suitable variant, can fail to be the case.

Let me give an example of some of the arguments which seem conclusive in favor of the view of Frege and Russell. The basic problem for any view such as Mill's is how we can determine what the referent of a name, as used by a given speaker, is. According to the description view, the answer is clear. If 'Joe Doakes' is just short for 'the man who corrupted Hadleyburg', then whoever corrupted Hadleyburg uniquely is the referent of the name 'Joe Doakes'. However, if there is *not* such a descriptive content to the name, then how do people ever use names to refer to things at all? Well, they may be in a position to point to some things and thus determine the references of certain names ostensively. This was Russell's doctrine of acquaintance, which he thought the so-called genuine or proper names satisfied. But of course ordinary names refer to all sorts of people, like Walter Scott, to whom we can't possibly point. And our reference here seems to be determined by our knowledge of them. Whatever we know about them determines the referent of the name as the unique thing satisfying those properties. For example, if I use the name 'Napoleon', and someone asks, 'To whom are you referring?', I will answer something like, 'Napoleon was emperor of the French in the early part of the nineteenth century; he was eventually defeated at Waterloo', thus giving a uniquely identifying description to determine the referent of the name. Frege and Russell, then, appear to give the natural account of how reference is determined here; Mill appears to give none.

There are subsidiary arguments which, though they are based on more specialized problems, are also motivations for accepting the view. One is that sometimes we may discover that two names have the same referent, and express this by an identity statement. So, for example (I guess this is a hackneyed example), you see a star in the evening and it's called 'Hesperus'. (That's what we call it in the evening, is that right? – I hope it's not the other way around.) We see a star in the morning and call it 'Phosphorus'. Well, then, in fact we find that it's not a star, but is the planet Venus and that Hesperus and Phosphorus are in fact the same. So we express this by 'Hesperus is Phosphorus'. Here we're certainly not just saying of an object that it's identical with itself. This is something that we discovered. A very natural thing to say is that the real content [is that] the star which we saw in the evening is the star which we saw in the morning (or, more accurately, that the thing which we saw in the evening is the thing which we saw in the morning). This, then, gives the real meaning of the identity statement in question; and the analysis in terms of descriptions does this.

Also we may raise the question whether a name has any reference at all when we ask, e.g., whether Aristotle ever existed. It seems natural here to think that what is questioned is not whether this *thing* (man) existed. Once we've *got* the thing, we know that it existed. What really is queried is whether anything answers to the properties we associate with the name – in the case of Aristotle, whether any one Greek philosopher produced certain works, or at least a suitable number of them.

It would be nice to answer all of these arguments. I am not entirely able to see my way clear through every problem of this sort than can be raised. Furthermore, I'm pretty sure that I won't have time to discuss all these questions in these lectures. Nevertheless, I think it's pretty certain that the view of Frege and Russell is false.[5]

Many people have said that the theory of Frege and Russell is false, but, in my opinion, they have abandoned its letter while retaining its spirit, namely, they have used the notion of a cluster concept. Well, what is this? The obvious problem for Frege and Russell, the one which comes immediately to mind, is already mentioned by Frege himself. He said,

> In the case of genuinely proper names like 'Aristotle' opinions as regards their sense may diverge. As such may, e.g., be suggested: Plato's disciple and the teacher of Alexander the Great. Whoever accepts this sense will interpret the meaning of the statement 'Aristotle was born in Stagira', differently from one who interpreted the sense of 'Aristotle' as the Stagirite teacher of Alexander the Great. As long as the nominatum remains the same, these fluctuations in sense are tolerable. But they should be avoided in the system of a demonstrative science and should not appear in a perfect language.[6]

So, according to Frege, there is some sort of looseness or weakness in our language. Some people may give one sense to the name 'Aristotle', others may give another. But of course it is not only that; even a single speaker when asked 'What description are you willing to substitute for the name?' may be quite at a loss. In fact, he may know many things about him; but any particular thing that he knows he may feel clearly expresses a contingent property of the object. If 'Aristotle' meant *the man who taught Alexander the Great*, then saying 'Aristotle was a teacher of Alexander the Great' would be a mere tautology. But surely it isn't; it expresses the fact that Aristotle taught Alexander the Great, something we could discover to be false. So, *being the teacher of Alexander the Great* cannot be part of [the sense of] the name.

The most common way out of this difficulty is to say 'really it is not a weakness in ordinary language that we can't substitute a *particular* description for the name; that's all right. What we really associate with the name is a *family* of descriptions.' A good example of this is (if I can find it) in *Philosophical Investigations*, where the idea of family resemblances is introduced and with great power.

> Consider this example. If one says, 'Moses did not exist', this may mean various things. It may mean: the Israelites did not have a *single* leader when they withdrew from Egypt – or: their leader was not called Moses – or: there cannot have been anyone who accomplished all that the Bible relates of Moses – . . . But when I make a statement about Moses, – am I always ready to substitute some *one* of those descriptions for 'Moses'? I shall perhaps say: by 'Moses' I understand the man who did what the Bible relates of Moses, or at any rate, a good deal of it. But how much? Have I decided how much must be proved false for me to give up my proposition as false? Has the name 'Moses' got a fixed and unequivocal use for me in all possible cases?[7]

According to this view, and a *locus classicus* of it is Searle's article on proper names,[8] the referent of a name is determined not by a single description but by some cluster or family. Whatever in some sense satisfies enough or most of the family is the referent of the name. I shall return to this view later. It may seem, as an analysis of ordinary language, quite a bit more plausible than that of Frege and Russell. It may seem to keep all the virtues and remove the defects of this theory.

Let me say (and this will introduce us to another new topic before I really consider this theory of naming) that there are two ways in which the cluster concept theory, or even the theory which requires a single description, can be viewed. One way of regarding it says that the cluster or the single description actually gives the meaning of the name; and when someone says 'Walter Scott', he means *the man such that such and such and such and such*.

Now another view might be that even though the description in some sense doesn't give the *meaning* of the name, it is what *determines it reference* and although the phrase 'Walter Scott' isn't *synonymous* with 'the man such that such and such and such and such', or even maybe with the family (if something can be synonymous with a family), the family or the single description is what is used to determine to whom someone is referring when he says 'Walter Scott'. Of course, if when we hear his beliefs about Walter Scott we find that they are actually much more nearly true of Salvador Dali, then according to this theory the reference of this name is going to be Mr. Dali, not Scott. There are writers, I think, who explicitly deny that names have meaning at all even more strongly than I would but still use this picture of how the referent of the name gets determined. A good case in point is Paul Ziff, who says, very emphatically, that names don't have meaning at all, [that] they are not a part of language in some sense. But still, when he talks about how we determine what the reference of the name was, then he gives this picture. Unfortunately I don't have the passage in question with me, but this is what he says.[9]

The difference between using this theory as a theory of meaning and using it as a theory of reference will come out a little more clearly later on. But some of the attractiveness of the theory is lost if it isn't supposed to give the meaning of the name; for some of the solutions of problems that I've just mentioned will not be right, or at least won't clearly be right, if the description doesn't give the meaning of the name. For example, if someone said 'Aristotle does not exist' *means* 'there is no man doing such and such', or in the example from Wittgenstein, 'Moses does not exist', *means* 'no man did such and such', that might depend (and in fact, I think, does depend) on taking the theory in question as a theory of the meaning of the name 'Moses', not just as a theory of its reference. Well, I don't know. Perhaps all that is immediate now is the other way around: if 'Moses' means the same as 'the man who did such and such' then to say that Moses did not exist is to say that the man who did such and such did not exist, that is, that no one person did such and such. If, on the other hand, 'Moses' is not synonymous with any description, then even if its reference is in some sense determined by a description, statements containing the name cannot in general be *analyzed* by replacing the name by a description, though they may be materially equivalent to statements containing a description. So the analysis of singular existence statements mentioned above will have to be given up, unless it is established by some special argument, independent of a general theory of the meaning of names; and the same applies to identity statements. In any case, I think it's false that 'Moses exists' means that at all. So we won't have to see if such a special argument can be drawn up.[10]

Before I go any further into this problem, I want to talk about another distinction which will be important in the methodology of these talks. Philosophers have talked (and, of course, there has been considerable controversy in recent years over the meaningfulness of these notions) [about] various categories of truth, which are called '*a priori*', 'analytic', 'necessary' – and sometimes even 'certain' is thrown into this batch. The terms are often used as if *whether* there are things answering to these concepts is an interesting question, but we might as well regard them all as meaning the same thing. Now, everyone remembers Kant (a bit) as making a distinction between '*a priori*' and 'analytic'. So maybe this distinction is still made. In contemporary discussion very few people, if any, distinguish between the concepts of statements being *a priori* and their being necessary. At any rate I shall *not* use the terms '*a priori*' and 'necessary' interchangeably here.

Consider what the traditional characterizations of such terms as '*a priori*' and 'necessary' are. First the notion of a prioricity is a concept of epistemology. I guess the traditional characterization from Kant goes something like: *a priori* truths are those which can be known independently of any experience. This introduces another problem before we get off the ground, because there's another modality in the characterization of '*a priori*', namely, it is supposed to be something which *can* be known independently of any experience. That means that in some sense it's *possible* (whether we do or do not in fact know it independently of any experience) to know this independently of any experience. And possible for whom? For God? For the Martians? Or just for people with minds like ours? To make this all clear might [involve] a host of problems all of its own about what sort of possibility is in question here. It might be best therefore, instead of using the phrase '*a priori* truth', to the extent that one uses it at all, to stick to the question of whether a particular person or knower knows something *a priori* or believes it true on the basis of *a priori* evidence.

I won't go further too much into the problems that might arise with the notion of a prioricity here. I will say that some philosophers somehow change the modality in this characterization from *can* to *must*. They think that if something belongs to the realm of *a priori* knowledge, it couldn't possibly be known empirically. This is just a mistake. Something may belong in the realm of such statements that *can* be known *a priori* but still may be known by particular people on the basis of experience. To give a really common sense example: anyone who has worked with a computing machine knows that the computing machine may give an answer to whether such and such a number is prime. No one has calculated or proved that the number is prime; but the machine has given the answer: this number is prime. We, then, if we believe that the number is prime, believe it on the basis of our knowledge of the laws of physics, the construction of the machine, and so on. We therefore do not believe this on the basis of purely *a priori* evidence. We believe it (if anything is *a posteriori* at all) on the basis of *a posteriori* evidence. Nevertheless, maybe this could be known *a priori* by someone who made the requisite calculations. So '*can* be known *a priori*' doesn't mean '*must* be known *a priori*'.

The second concept which is in question is that of necessity. Sometimes this is used in an epistemological way and might then just mean *a priori*. And of course, sometimes it is used in a physical way when people distinguish between physical and logical necessity. But what I am concerned with here is a notion which is not a notion of epistemology but of metaphysics, in some (I hope) nonpejorative sense. We ask whether something might have been true, or might have been false. Well, if something is false, it's obviously not necessarily true. If it is true, might it have been otherwise? It is possible that, in this respect, the world should have been different from the way it is? If the answer is 'no', then this fact about the world is a necessary one. If the answer is 'yes', then this fact about the world is a contingent one. This in and of itself has nothing to do with anyone's knowledge of anything. It's certainly a philosophical thesis, and not a matter of obvious definitional equivalence, either that everything *a priori* is necessary or that everything necessary is *a priori*. Both concepts may be vague. That may be another problem. But at any rate they are dealing with two different domains, two different areas, the epistemological and the metaphysical. Consider, say, Fermat's last theorem – or the Goldbach conjecture. The Goldbach conjecture says that an even number greater than 2 must be the sum of two prime numbers. If this is true, it is presumably necessary, and, if it is false, presumably necessarily false. We are taking the classical view of mathematics here and assume that in mathematical reality it is either true or false.

If the Goldbach conjecture is false, then there is an even number, n, greater than 2, such that for no primes p_1 and p_2, both $< n$, does $n = p_1 + p_2$. This fact about n, if true, is verifiable by direct computation, and thus is necessary if the results of arithmetical computations are necessary. On the other hand, if the conjecture is true, then every even number exceeding 2 is the sum of two primes. Could it then be the case that, although in fact every such even number is the sum of two primes, there might have been such an even number which was not the sum of two primes? What would that mean? Such a number would have to be one of 4, 6, 8, 10, . . .; and, by hypothesis, since we are assuming Goldbach's conjecture to be true, each of these can be shown, again by direct computation, to be the sum of two primes. Goldbach's conjecture, then, cannot be contingently true or false; whatever truth-value it has belongs to it by necessity.

But what we can say, of course, is that right now, as far as we know, the question can come out either way. So, in the absence of a mathematical proof deciding this question, none of us has any *a priori* knowledge about this question in either direction. We don't know whether Goldbach's conjecture is true or false. So right now we certainly don't know anything *a priori* about it.

[· · ·]

The terms 'necessary' and '*a priori*', then, as applied to statements, are *not* obvious synonyms. There may be a philosophical argument connecting them, perhaps even identifying them; but an argument is required, not simply the observation that the two terms are clearly interchangeable. (I will argue below that in fact they are not even coextensive – that necessary *a posteriori* truths, and probably contingent *a priori* truths, both exist.)

[· · ·]

Another term used in philosophy is 'analytic'. Here it won't be too important to get any clearer about this in this talk. The common examples of analytic statements, nowadays, are like 'bachelors are unmarried'. Kant (someone just pointed out to me) gives as an example 'gold is a yellow metal', which seems to me an extraordinary one, because it's something I think that can turn out to be false. At any rate, let's just make it a matter of stipulation that an analytic statement is, in some sense, true by virtue of its meaning and true in all possible worlds by virtue of its meaning. Then something which is analytically true will be both necessary and *a priori*. (That's sort of stipulative.)

Another category I mentioned was that of certainty. Whatever certainty is, it's clearly not obviously the case that everything which is necessary is certain. Certainty is another epistemological notion. Something can be known, or at least rationally believed, *a priori*, without being quite certain. You've read a proof in the math book; and, though you think it's correct, maybe you've made a mistake. You often do make mistakes of this kind. You've made a computation, perhaps with an error.

[· · ·]

Let's use some terms quasi-technically. Let's call something a *rigid designator* if in every possible world it designates the same object, *a nonrigid* or *accidental designator* if that is not the case. Of course we don't require that the objects exist in all possible worlds. Certainly Nixon might not have existed if his parents had not gotten married, in the normal course of things. When we think of a property as essential to an object we usually mean that it is true of that object in any case where it would have existed. A rigid designator of a necessary existent can be called *strongly rigid*.

One of the intuitive theses I will maintain in these talks is that *names* are rigid designators. Certainly they seem to satisfy the intuitive test mentioned above: although someone other than the U.S. President in 1970 might have been the U.S. President in 1970 (e.g., Humphrey might have), no one other than Nixon might have been Nixon. In the same way, a designator rigidly designates a certain object if it designates that object wherever the object exists; if, in addition, the object is a necessary existent, the designator can be called *strongly rigid*. For example, 'the President of the U.S. in 1970' designates a certain man, Nixon; but someone else (e.g., Humphrey) might have been the President in 1970, and Nixon might not have; so this designator is not rigid.

In these lectures, I will argue, intuitively, that proper names are rigid designators, for although the man (Nixon) might not have been the President, it is not the case that he might not have been Nixon (though he might not have been *called* 'Nixon'). Those who have argued that to make sense of the notion of rigid resignator, we must antecedently make sense of 'criteria of transworld identity' have precisely reversed the cart and the horse; it is *because* we can refer (rigidly) to Nixon, and stipulate that we are speaking of what might have happened to *him* (under certain circumstances), that 'transworld identifications' are unproblematic in such cases.[16]

The tendency to demand purely qualitative descriptions of counterfactual situations has many sources. One, perhaps, is the confusion of the epistemological and the metaphysical, between a prioricity and necessity. If someone identifies necessity with a prioricity, and thinks that objects are named by means of uniquely identifying properties, he may think that it is the properties used to identify the object which, being known about it *a priori*, must be used to identify it in all possible worlds, to find out which object is Nixon. As against this, I repeat: (1) Generally, things aren't 'found out' about a counterfactual situation, they are stipulated; (2) possible worlds need not be given purely qualitatively, as if we were looking at them through a telescope.

[· · ·]

Above I said that the Frege-Russell view that names are introduced by description could be taken either as a theory of the meaning of names (Frege and Russell seemed to take it this way) or merely as a theory of their reference. Let me give an example, not involving what would usually be called a 'proper name,' to illustrate this. Suppose someone stipulates that 100 degrees centigrade is to be the temperature at which water boils at sea level. This isn't completely precise because the pressure may vary at sea level. Of course, historically, a more precise definition was given later. But let's suppose that this were the definition. Another sort of example in the literature is that one meter is to be the length of *S* where *S* is a certain stick or bar in Paris. (Usually people who like to talk about these definitions then try to make 'the length of' into an 'operational' concept. But it's not important.)

Wittgenstein says something very puzzling about this. He says: 'There is one thing of which one can say neither that it is one meter long nor that it is not one meter long, and that is the standard meter in Paris. But this is, of course, not to ascribe any extraordinary property to it, but only to mark its peculiar role in the language game of measuring with a meter rule.'[19] This seems to be a very 'extraordinary property', actually, for any stick to have. I think he must be wrong. If the stick is a stick, for example, 39.37 inches long (I assume we have some different standard for inches), why isn't it one meter long? Anyway, let's suppose that he is wrong and that the stick is one meter long. Part of the problem which is bothering Wittgenstein is, of course, that this stick serves as a standard of length and so we can't attribute length to it. Be this as it may (well, it may not be), is the statement 'stick *S* is one meter long', a necessary truth? Of course its length might vary in time. We could make the definition more precise by stipulating that one meter is to be the length of *S* at a fixed time t_0. It is then a necessary truth that stick *S* is one meter long at time t_0? Someone who thinks that everything one knows *a priori* is necessary might think: 'This is the *definition* of a meter. By definition, stick *S* is one meter long at t_0. That's a necessary truth.' But there seems to me to be no reason so to conclude, even for a man who uses the stated definition of 'one meter'. For he's using this definition not to *give the meaning* of what he called the 'meter', but to *fix the reference*. (For such an abstract thing as a unit of length, the notion of reference may be unclear. But let's suppose it's clear enough for the present purposes.) He uses it to fix a reference. There is a certain length which he wants to mark out. He marks it out by an accidental property, namely that there is a stick of that length. Someone else might mark out the same reference by another accidental property. But in any case, even though he uses this to fix the reference of his standard of length, a meter, he can still say, 'if heat had been applied to this stick S at t_0, then at t_0 stick S would not have been one meter long.'

[· · ·]

Lecture II: January 22, 1970

Last time we ended up talking about a theory of naming which is given by a number of theses here on the board.

1. To every name or designating expression 'X', there corresponds a cluster of properties, namely the family of those properties φ such that A believes 'φX'.
2. One of the properties, or some conjointly, are believed by A to pick out some individual uniquely.
3. If most, or a weighted most, of the φ's are satisfied by one unique object y, then y is the referent of 'X'.
4. If the vote yields no unique object, 'X' does not refer.
5. The statement, 'If X exists, then X has most of the φ's' is known *a priori* by the speaker.
6. The statement, 'If X exists, then X has most of the φ's' expresses a necessary truth (in the idiolect of the speaker).

C. For any successful theory, the account must not be circular. The properties which are used in the vote must not themselves involve the notion of reference in such a way that it is ultimately impossible to eliminate.

C is not a thesis but a condition on the satisfaction of the other theses. In other words, Theses 1–6 cannot be satisfied in a way which leads to a circle, in a way which does not lead to any independent determination of reference. The example I gave last time of a blatantly circular attempt to satisfy these conditions was a theory of names mentioned by William Kneale. I was a little surprised at the statement of the theory when I was reading what I had copied down, so I looked it up again. I looked it up in the book to see if I'd copied it down accurately. Kneale *did* use the past tense. He said that though it is not trifling to be told that Socrates was the greatest philosopher of ancient Greece, it is trifling to be told that Socrates was called 'Socrates'. Therefore, he concludes, the name 'Socrates' must simply mean 'the individual called "Socrates"'. Russell, as I've said, in some places gives a similar analysis. Anyway, as stated using the past tense, the condition wouldn't be circular, because one certainly could decide to use the term 'Socrates' to refer to whoever was called 'Socrates' by the Greeks. But, of course, in that sense it's not at all trifling to be told that Socrates was called 'Socrates'. If this is any kind of fact, it might be false. Perhaps we know that *we* call him 'Socrates'; that hardly shows that the Greeks did so. In fact, of course, they may have pronounced the name differently. It may be, in the case of this particular name, that transliteration from the Greek is so good that the English version is not pronounced *very* differently from the Greek. But that won't be so in the general case. Certainly it is not trifling to be told that Isaiah was called 'Isaiah'. In fact, it is false to be told that Isaiah was called 'Isaiah'; the prophet wouldn't have recognized this name at all. And of course the Greeks didn't call their country anything like 'Greece'. Suppose we amend the thesis so that it reads: it's trifling to be told that Socrates is called 'Socrates' by us, or at least, by me, the speaker. Then in some sense this is fairly trifling. I don't think it is necessary or analytic. In the same way, it is trifling to be told that horses are called 'horses', without this leading to the conclusion that the word 'horse', simply *means* 'the animal called a "horse" '. As a theory of the reference of the name 'Socrates' it will lead immediately to a vicious circle. If one was determining the referent of a name like 'Glunk' to himself and made the following decision, 'I shall use the term "Glunk" to refer to the man that I call "Glunk" ', this would get one nowhere. One had better have some independent determination of the referent of 'Glunk'. This is a good example of blatantly circular determination. Actually sentences like 'Socrates is called "Socrates" ' are very interesting and one can spend, strange as it may seem, hours talking about their analysis. I actually did, once, do that. I won't do that, however, on this occasion. (See how high the seas of language can rise. And at the lowest points too.) Anyway this is a useful example of a violation of the noncircularity condition. The theory will satisfy all of these statements, perhaps, but it satisfies them only because there is some independent way of determining the reference independently of the particular condition: being the man called 'Socrates'.

I have already talked about, in the last lecture, Thesis 6. Theses 5 and 6, by the way, have converses. What I said for Thesis 5 is that the statement that if X exists, X has most of the φ's, is *a priori* true for the speaker. It will also be true under the given theory that certain converses of this statement hold true also *a priori* for the speaker, namely: if any unique thing has most of the properties φ in the properly weighted sense, it is X. Similarly a certain converse to this will be *necessarily* true, namely: if anything has most of the properties φ in the properly weighted sense, it is X. So really one can say that it is both *a priori* and necessary that something is X if and only if it uniquely has most of the properties φ. This really comes from the previous Theses 1–4, I suppose. And 5 and 6 really just say that a sufficiently reflective speaker grasps this theory of proper names. Knowing this, he therefore sees that 5 and 6 are true. The objections to Theses 5 and 6 will *not* be that some speakers are unaware of this theory and therefore don't know these things.

What I talked about in the last lecture is Thesis (6). It's been observed by many philosophers that, if the cluster of properties associated with a proper name is taken in a very narrow sense, so that only one property is given any weight at all, let's say one definite description to pick out the referent – for example, Aristotle was the philosopher who taught Alexander the Great – then certain things will seem to turn out to be necessary truths which are not necessary truths – in this case, for example, that Aristotle taught Alexander the Great. But as Searle said, it is not a necessary truth but a contingent one that Aristotle ever went into pedagogy. Therefore, he concludes that one must drop the original paradigm of a single description and turn to that of a cluster of descriptions.

To summarize some things that I argued last time, this is not the correct answer (whatever it may be) to this problem about necessity. For Searle goes on to say,

> Suppose we agree to drop 'Aristotle' and use, say, 'the teacher of Alexander', then it is a necessary truth that the man referred to is Alexander's teacher – but it is a contingent fact that Aristotle ever went into pedagogy, though I am suggesting that it is a necessary fact that Aristotle has the logical sum, inclusive disjunction, of properties commonly attributed to him. . . .[31]

This is what is not so. It just is not, in any intuitive sense of necessity, a necessary truth that Aristotle had the properties commonly attributed to him. There is a certain theory, perhaps popular in some views of the philosophy of history, which might both be deterministic and yet at the same time assign a great role to the individual in history. Perhaps Carlyle would associate with the meaning of the name of a great man his achievements. According to such a view it will be necessary, once a certain individual is born, that he is destined to perform various great tasks and so it will be part of the very nature of Aristotle that he should have produced ideas which had a great influence on the western world. Whatever the merits of such a view may be as a view of history or the nature of great men, it does not seem that it should be trivially true on the basis of a theory of proper names. It would seem that it's a contingent fact that Aristotle ever did *any* of the things commonly attributed to him today, *any* of these great achievements that we so much admire.

[. . .]

To clear up one thing which some people have asked me: When I say that a designator is rigid, and designates the same thing in all possible worlds, I mean that, as used in *our* language, it stands for that thing, when *we* talk about counterfactual situations. I don't mean, of course, that there mightn't be counterfactual situations in which in the other possible worlds people actually spoke a different language. One doesn't say that 'two plus two equals four' is contingent because people might have spoken a language in which 'two plus two equals four' meant that seven is even. Similarly, when we speak of a counterfactual situation, we speak of it in English, even if it is part of the description of that counterfactual situation that we were all speaking German in that counterfactual situation. We say, 'suppose we had all been speaking German' or 'suppose we had been using English in a nonstandard way'. Then we are describing a possible world or counterfactual situation in which people, including ourselves, did speak in a certain way different from the way we speak. But still, in describing that world, we use *English* with *our* meanings and *our* references. It is in this sense that I speak of a rigid designator as having the same reference in all possible worlds. I also don't mean to imply that the thing designated exists in all possible worlds, just that the name refers rigidly to that thing. If you say 'suppose Hitler had never been born' then 'Hitler' refers here, still rigidly, to something that would not exist in the counterfactual situation described.

Given these remarks, this means we must cross off Thesis 6 as incorrect. The other theses have nothing to do with necessity and can survive. In particular Thesis 5 has nothing to do with necessity and it can survive. If I use the name 'Hesperus' to refer to a certain planetary body when seen in a certain celestial position in the evening, it will not therefore be a necessary truth that Hesperus is ever seen in the evening. That depends on various contingent facts about people being there to see and things like that. So even if I should say to myself that I will use 'Hesperus' to name the heavenly body I see in the evening in yonder position of the sky, it will not be necessary that Hesperus was ever seen in the evening. But it may be *a priori* in that this is how I have determined the referent. If I have determined that Hesperus is the thing that I saw in the evening over there, then I will know, just from making that determination of the referent, that if there is any Hesperus at all it's the thing I saw in the evening. This at least survives as far as the arguments we have given up to now go.

How about a theory where Thesis 6 is eliminated? Theses 2, 3, and 4 turn out to have a large class of counterinstances. Even when Theses 2–4 are true, Thesis 5 is usually false; the truth of Theses 3 and 4 is an empirical 'accident', which the speaker hardly knows *a priori*. That is to say, other principles really determine the speaker's reference, and the fact that the referent coincides with that determined by 2–4 is an 'accident', which we were in no position to know *a priori*. Only in a rare class of cases, usually initial baptisms, are all of 2–5 true.

What picture of naming do these Theses (1–5) give you? The picture is this. I want to name an object. I think of some way of describing it uniquely and then I go through, so to speak, a sort of mental ceremony: By 'Cicero' I shall mean the man who denounced Catiline; and that's what the reference of 'Cicero' will be. I will use 'Cicero' to designate rigidly the man who (in fact) denounced Catiline, so I can speak of possible worlds in which he did not. But still my intentions are given by first, giving some condition which uniquely determines an object, then using a certain word as a name for the object determined by this condition. Now there may be some cases in which we actually do this. Maybe, if you want to stretch and call it description, when you say: I shall call that heavenly body over there 'Hesperus'.[33] That is really a case where the theses not only are true but really even give a correct picture of how the reference is determined. Another case, if you want to call this a name, might be when the police in London use the name 'Jack' or 'Jack the Ripper' to refer to the man, whoever he is, who committed all these murders, or most of them. Then they are giving the reference of the name by a description.[34] But in many or most cases, I think the theses are false. So let's look at them.[35]

Thesis 1, as I say, is a definition. Thesis 2 says that one of the properties believed by *A* of the object, or some conjointly, are believed to pick out some individual uniquely. A sort of example people have in mind is just what I said: I shall use the term 'Cicero' to denote the man who denounced Catiline (or first denounced him in public, to make it unique). This picks out an object uniquely in this particular reference. Even some writers such as Ziff in *Semantic Analysis*, who don't believe that names have meaning in any sense, think that this is a good picture of the way reference can be determined.

Let's see if Thesis 2 is true. It seems, in some *a priori* way, that it's got to be true, because if you don't think that the properties you have in mind pick out anyone uniquely – let's say they're all satisfied by two people – then how can you say which one of them you're talking about? There seem to be no grounds for saying you're talking about the one rather than about the other. Usually the properties in question are supposed to be some famous deeds of the person in question. For example, Cicero was the man who denounced Catiline. The average person, according to this, when he refers to Cicero, is saying something like 'the man who denounced Catiline' and thus has picked out a certain man uniquely. It is a tribute to the education of philosophers that they have held this thesis for such a long time. In fact, most people, when they think of Cicero, just think of *a famous Roman orator*, without any pretension to think either that there was only one famous Roman orator or that one must know something else about Cicero to have a referent for the name. Consider Richard Feynman, to whom many of us are able to refer. He is a leading contemporary theoretical physicist. Everyone *here* (I'm sure!) can state the contents of one of Feynman's theories so as to differentiate him from Gell-Mann. However, the man in the street, not possessing these abilities, may still use the name 'Feynman'. When asked he will say: well he's a physicist or something. He may not think that this picks out anyone uniquely. I still think he uses the name 'Feynman' as a name for Feynman.

But let's look at some of the cases where we do have a description to pick out someone uniquely. Let's say, for example, that we know that Cicero was the man who first denounced Catiline. Well, that's good. That really picks someone out uniquely. However, there is a problem, because this description contains another name, namely 'Catiline'. We must be sure that we satisfy the conditions in such a way as to avoid violating the noncircularity condition here. In particular, we must not say that Catiline was the man denounced by Cicero. If we do this, we will really not be picking out anything uniquely, we will simply be picking out a pair of objects *A* and *B*, such that *A* denounced *B*. We do not think that this was the only pair where such denunciations ever occurred; so we had better add some other conditions in order to satisfy the uniqueness condition.

If we say Einstein was the man who discovered the theory of relativity, that certainly picks out someone uniquely. One can be sure, as I said, that everyone *here* can make a compact and independent statement of this theory and so pick out Einstein uniquely; but many people actually don't know enough about this stuff, so when asked what the theory of relativity is, they will say: 'Einstein's theory', and thus be led into the most straightforward sort of vicious circle.

So Thesis 2, in a straightforward way, fails to be satisfied when we say Feynman is a famous physicist without attributing anything else to Feynman. In another way it may not be satisfied in the proper way even when it is satisfied: If we say Einstein was 'the man who discovered relativity theory', that does pick someone out uniquely; but it may not pick him out in such a way as to satisfy the noncircularity condition, because the theory of relativity may in turn be picked out as 'Einstein's theory'. So Thesis 2 seems to be false.

[· · ·]

Let's go on to Thesis 3: If most of the φ's, suitably weighted, are satisfied by a unique object *y*, then *y* is the referent of the name for the speaker. Now, since we have already established that Thesis 2 is wrong, why should any of the rest work? The whole theory depended on always being able to specify unique conditions which are satisfied. But still we can look at the other theses. The picture associated with the theory is that only by giving some unique properties can you know who someone is and thus know what the reference of your name is. Well, I won't go into the question of knowing who someone is. It's really very puzzling. I think you *do* know who Cicero is if you just can answer that he's a famous Roman orator. Strangely enough, if you know that Einstein discovered the theory of relativity and nothing about that theory, you can both know who Einstein is, namely the discoverer of the theory of relativity, and who discovered the theory of relativity, namely Einstein, on the basis of this knowledge. This seem to be a blatant violation of some sort of noncircularity condition; but it is the way we talk. It therefore would seem that a picture which suggests this condition must be the wrong picture.

Suppose most of the φ's are in fact satisfied by a unique object. Is that object necessarily the referent of '*X*' for *A*? Let's suppose someone says that Gödel is the man who proved the incompleteness of arithmetic, and this man is suitably well educated and is even able to give an independent account of the incompleteness theorem. He doesn't just say, 'Well, that's Gödel's theorem', or whatever. He actually states a certain theorem, which he attributes to Gödel as the discoverer. Is it the case, then, that if most of the φ's are satisfied by a unique object *y*, then *y* is the referent of the name '*X*' for *A*? Let's take a simple case. In the case of Gödel that's practically the only thing many people have heard about him – that he discovered the incompleteness of arithmetic. Does it follow that whoever discovered the incompleteness of arithmetic is the referent of 'Gödel'?

Imagine the following blatantly fictional situation. (I hope Professor Gödel is not present.) Suppose that Gödel was not in fact the author of this theorem. A man named 'Schmidt', whose body was found in Vienna under mysterious circumstances many years ago, actually did the work in question. His friend Gödel somehow got hold of the manuscript and it was thereafter attributed to Gödel. On the view in question, then, when our ordinary man uses the name 'Gödel', he really means to refer to Schmidt, because Schmidt is the unique person satisfying the description, 'the man who discovered the incompleteness of arithmetic'. Of course you might try changing it to 'the man who *published* the discovery of the incompleteness of arithmetic'. By changing the story a little further one can make even this formulation false. Anyway, most people might not even know whether the thing was published or got around by word of mouth. Let's stick to 'the man who discovered the incompleteness of arithmetic'. So, since the man who discovered the incompleteness of arithmetic is in fact Schmidt, we, when we talk about 'Gödel', are in fact always referring to Schmidt. But it seems to me that we are not. We simply are not. One reply, which I will discuss later, might be: You should say instead, 'the man to whom the incompleteness of arithmetic is commonly attributed', or something like that. Let's see what we can do with that later.

But it may seem to many of you that this is a very odd example, or that such a situation occurs rarely. This also is a tribute to the education of philosophers. Very often we use a name on the basis of considerable misinformation. The case of mathematics used in the fictive example is a good case in point. What do we know about Peano? What many people in this room may 'know' about Peano is that he was the discoverer of certain axioms which characterize the sequence of natural numbers, the so-called 'Peano axioms'. Probably some people can even state them. I have been told that these axioms were not first discovered by Peano but by Dedekind. Peano was of course not a dishonest man. I am told that his footnotes include a credit to Dedekind. Somehow the footnote has been ignored. So on the theory in question the term 'Peano', as we use it, really refers to – now that you've heard it you see that you were really all the time talking about – Dedekind. But you were not. Such illustrations could be multiplied indefinitely.

Even worse misconceptions, of course, occur to the layman. In a previous example I supposed people to identify Einstein by reference to his work on relativity. Actually, I often used to hear that Einstein's most famous achievement was the invention of the atomic bomb. So when we refer to Einstein, we refer to the inventor of the atomic bomb. But this is not so. Columbus was the first man to realize that the earth was round. He was also the first European to land in the western hemisphere. Probably none of these things are true, and therefore, when people use the term 'Columbus' they really refer to some Greek if they use the roundness of the earth, or to some Norseman, perhaps, if they use the 'discovery of America'. But they don't. So it does not seem that if most of the φ's are satisfied by a unique object *y*, then *y* is the referent of the name. This seems simply to be false.[36]

Thesis 4: If the vote yields no unique object the name does not refer. Really this case has been covered before – has been covered in my previous examples. First, the vote may not yield a *unique* object, as in the case of Cicero or Feynman. Secondly, suppose it yields *no* object, that nothing satisfies most, or even any, substantial number of the φ's. Does that mean the name doesn't refer? No: in the same way that you may have false beliefs about a person which may actually be true of someone else, so you may have false beliefs which are true of absolutely no one. And these may constitute the totality of your beliefs. Suppose, to vary the example about Gödel, no one had discovered the incompleteness of arithmetic – perhaps the proof simply materialized by a random scattering of atoms on a piece of paper – the man Gödel being lucky enough to have been present when this improbable event occurred. Further, suppose arithmetic is in fact complete. One wouldn't really expect a random scattering of atoms to produce a correct proof. A subtle error, unknown through the decades, has still been unnoticed – or perhaps not actually unnoticed, but the friends of Gödel. . . . So even if the conditions are not satisfied by a unique object the name may still refer. I gave you the case of Jonah last week. Biblical scholars, as I said, think that Jonah really existed. It isn't because they think that someone ever was swallowed by a big fish or even went to Nineveh to preach. These conditions may be true of no one whatsoever and yet the name 'Jonah' really has a referent. In the case above of Einstein's invention of the bomb, possibly no one really deserves to be called the 'inventor' of the device.

Thesis 5 says that the statement 'If *X* exists, then *X* has most of the φ's', is *a priori* true for *A*. Notice that even in a case where 3 and 4 *happen* to be true, a typical speaker hardly knows *a priori* that they are, as required by the theory. I *think* that my belief about Gödel *is* in fact correct and that the 'Schmidt' story is just a fantasy. But the belief hardly constitutes *a priori* knowledge.

[. . .]

Someone, let's say, a baby, is born; his parents call him by a certain name. They talk about him to their friends. Other people meet him. Through various sorts of talk the name is spread from link to link as if by a chain. A speaker who is on the far end of this chain, who has heard about, say Richard Feynman, in the market place or elsewhere, may be referring to Richard Feynman even though he can't remember from whom he first heard of Feynman or from whom he ever heard of Feynman. He knows that Feynman is a famous physicist. A certain passage of communication reaching ultimately to the man himself does reach the speaker. He then is referring to Feynman even though he can't identify him uniquely. He doesn't know what a Feynman diagram is, he doesn't know what the Feynman theory of pair production and annihilation is. Not only that: he'd have trouble distinguishing between Gell-Mann and Feynman. So he doesn't have to know these things, but, instead, a chain of communication going back to Feynman himself has been established, by virtue of his membership in a community which passed the name on from link to link, not by a ceremony that he makes in private in his study: 'By "Feynman" I shall mean the man who did such and such and such and such'.

[. . .]

On our view, it is not how the speaker thinks he got the reference, but the actual chain of communication, which is relevant.

I think I said the other time that philosophical theories are in danger of being false, and so I wasn't going to present an alternative theory. Have I just done so? Well, in a way; but my characterization has been far less specific than a real set of necessary and sufficient conditions for reference would be. Obviously the name is passed on from link to link. But of course not every sort of causal chain reaching from me to a certain man will do for me to make a reference. There may be a causal chain from our use of the term 'Santa Claus' to a certain historical saint, but still the children, when they use this, by this time probably do not refer to that saint. So other conditions must be satisfied in order to make this into a really rigorous theory of reference. I don't know that I'm going to do this because, first, I'm sort of too lazy at the moment; secondly, rather than giving a set of necessary and sufficient conditions which will work for a term like reference, I want to present just a *better picture* than the picture presented by the received views.

Haven't I been very unfair to the description theory? Here I have stated it very precisely – more precisely, perhaps, than it has been stated by any of its advocates. So then it's easy to refute. Maybe if I tried to state mine with sufficient precision in the form of six or seven or eight theses, it would also turn out that when you examine the theses one by one, they will all be false. That might even be so, but the difference is this. What I think the examples I've given show is not simply that there's some technical error here or some mistake there, but that the whole picture given by this theory of how reference is determined seems to be wrong from the fundamentals. It seems to be wrong to think that we give ourselves some properties which somehow qualitatively uniquely pick out an object and determine our reference in that manner. What

I am trying to present is a better picture – a picture which, if more details were to be filled in, might be refined so as to give more exact conditions for reference to take place.

One might never reach a set of necessary and sufficient conditions. I don't know, I'm always sympathetic to Bishop Butler's 'Everything is what it is and not another thing' – in the nontrivial sense that philosophical analyses of some concept like reference, in completely different terms which make no mention of reference, are very apt to fail. Of course in any particular case when one is given an analysis one has to look at it and see whether it is true or false. One can't just cite this maxim to oneself and then turn the page. But more cautiously, I want to present a better picture without giving a set of necessary and sufficient conditions for reference. Such conditions would be very complicated, but what is true is that it's in virtue of our connection with other speakers in the community, going back to the referent himself, that we refer to a certain man.

There may be some cases where the description picture is true, where some man really gives a name by going into the privacy of his room and saying that the referent is to be the unique thing with certain identifying properties. 'Jack the Ripper' was a possible example which I gave. Another was 'Hesperus'. Yet another case which can be forced into this description is that of meeting someone and being told his name. Except for a belief in the description theory, in its importance in other cases, one probably wouldn't think that that was a case of giving oneself a description, i.e., 'the guy I'm just meeting now'. But one can put it in these terms if one wishes, and if one has never heard the name in any other way. Of course, if you're introduced to a man and told, 'That's Einstein', you've heard of him before, it may be wrong, and so on. But maybe in some cases such a paradigm works – especially for the man who first gives someone or something a name. Or he points to a star and says, 'That is to be Alpha Centauri'. So he can really make himself this ceremony: 'By "Alpha Centauri" I shall mean the star right over there with such and such coordinates'. But in general this picture fails. In general our reference depends not just on what we think ourselves, but on other people in the community, the history of how the name reached one, and things like that. It is by following such a history that one gets to the reference.

[. . .]

A rough statement of a theory might be the following: An initial 'baptism' takes place. Here the object may be named by ostension, or the reference of the name may be fixed by a description.[42] When the name is 'passed from link to link', the receiver of the name must, I think, intend when he learns it to use it with the same reference as the man from whom he heard it. If I hear the name 'Napoleon' and decide it would be a nice name for my pet aardvark, I do not satisfy this condition.[43] (Perhaps it is some such failure to keep the reference fixed which accounts for the divergence of present uses of 'Santa Claus' from the alleged original use.)

Notice that the preceding outline hardly *eliminates* the notion of reference; on the contrary, it takes the notion of intending to use the same reference as a given. There is also an appeal to an initial baptism which is explained in terms either of fixing a reference by a description, or ostension (if ostension is not to be subsumed under the other category).[44] (Perhaps there are other possibilities for initial baptisms.) Further, the George Smith case casts some doubt as to the sufficiency of the conditions. Even if the teacher does refer to his neighbor, is it clear that he has passed on his reference to the pupils? Why shouldn't their belief be about any other man named 'George Smith'? If he says that Newton was hit by an apple, somehow his task of transmitting a reference is easier, since he has communicated a common misconception about Newton.

To repeat, I may not have presented a theory, but I do think that I have presented a better picture than that given by description theorists.

I think the next topic I shall want to talk about is that of statements of identity. Are these necessary or contingent? The matter has been in some dispute in recent philosophy. First, everyone agrees that descriptions can be used to make contingent identity statements. If it is true that the man who invented bifocals was the first Postmaster General of the United States – that these were one and the same – it's contingently true. That is, it might have been the case that one man invented bifocals and another was the first Postmaster General of the United States. So certainly when you make identity statements using descriptions – when you say 'the x such that φx and the x such that ψx are one and the same' – that can be a contingent fact. But philosophers have been interested also in the question of identity statements between names. When we say 'Hesperus is Phosphorus' or 'Cicero is Tully', is what we are saying necessary or contingent? Further, they've been interested in another type of identity statement, which comes from scientific theory. We identify, for example, light with electromagnetic radiation between certain limits of wavelengths, or with a stream of photons. We identify heat with the motion of molecules; sound with a certain sort of wave disturbance in the air; and so on. Concerning such statements the following thesis is commonly held. First, that these are obviously contingent identities: we've found out that light is a stream of photons, but of course it might not have been a stream of photons. Heat is in fact the motion of molecules; we found that out, but heat might not have been the motion of molecules. Secondly, many philosophers feel damned lucky that these examples are around. Now, why? These philosophers, whose views are expounded in a vast literature, hold to a thesis called 'the identity thesis' with respect to some psychological concepts. They think, say, that pain is just a certain material state of the brain or of the body, or what have you – say the stimulation of C-fibers. (It doesn't matter what.) Some people have then objected, 'Well, look, there's perhaps a *correlation* between pain and these states of the body; but this must just be a contingent correlation between two different things, because it was an empirical discovery that this correlation ever held. Therefore, by "pain" we must mean something different from this state of the body or brain; and, therefore, they must be two different things.'

Then it's said, 'Ah, but you see, this is wrong! Everyone knows that there can be contingent identities.' First, as in the bifocals and Postmaster General case, which I have mentioned before. Second, in the case, believed closer to the present paradigm, of theoretical identifications, such as light and a stream of photons, or water and a certain compound of hydrogen and oxygen. These are all contingent identities. They might have been false. It's no surprise, therefore, that it can be true as a matter of contingent fact and not of any necessity that feeling pain, or seeing red, is just a certain state of the human body. Such psychophysical identifications can be contingent facts just as the other identities are contingent facts. And of course there are widespread motivations – ideological, or just not wanting to have the 'nomological dangler' of mysterious connections not accounted for by the laws of physics, one to one correlations between two different kinds of thing, material states, and things of an entirely different kind, which lead people to want to believe this thesis.

I guess the main thing I'll talk about first is identity statements between names.

[. . .]

Let's suppose we refer to the same heavenly body twice, as 'Hesperus' and 'Phosphorus'. We say: Hesperus is that star over there in the evening; Phosphorus is that star over there in the morning. Actually, Hesperus is Phosphorus. Are there really circumstances under which Hesperus wouldn't have been Phosphorus? Supposing that Hesperus is Phosphorus, let's try to describe a possible situation in which it would not have been. Well, it's easy. Someone goes by and he calls two *different* stars 'Hesperus' and 'Phosphorus'. It may even be under the same conditions as prevailed when we introduced the names 'Hesperus' and 'Phosphorus'. But are those circumstances in which Hesperus is not Phosphorus or would not have been Phosphorus? It seems to me that they are not.

Now, of course I'm committed to saying that they're not, by saying that such terms as 'Hesperus' and 'Phosphorus', when used as names, are rigid designators. They refer in every possible world to the planet Venus. Therefore, in that possible world too, the planet Venus is the planet Venus and it doesn't matter what any other person has said in this other possible world. How should *we* describe this situation? He can't have pointed to Venus twice, and in the one case called it 'Hesperus' and in the other 'Phosphorus', as we did. If he did so, then 'Hesperus is Phosphorus' would have been true in that situation too. He pointed maybe neither time to the planet Venus – at least one time he didn't point to the planet Venus, let's say when he pointed to the body he called 'Phosphorus'. Then in that case we can certainly say that the name 'Phosphorus' might not have referred to Phosphorus. We can even say that in the very position when viewed in the morning that we found Phosphorus, it might have been the case that Phosphorus was not there – that something else was there, and that even, under certain circumstances it would have been *called* 'Phosphorus'. But that still is not a case in which Phosphorus was not Hesperus. There might be a possible world in which, a possible counterfactual situation in which, 'Hesperus' and 'Phosphorus' weren't names of the things they in fact are names of. Someone, if he did determine their reference by identifying descriptions, might even have used the very identifying descriptions we used. But still that's not a case in which Hesperus wasn't Phosphorus. For there couldn't have been such a case, given that Hesperus is Phosphorus.

Now this seems very strange because in advance, we are inclined to say, the answer to the question whether Hesperus is Phosphorus might have turned out either way. So aren't there really two possible worlds – one in which Hesperus was Phosphorus, the other in which Hesperus wasn't Phosphorus – in advance of our discovering that these were the same? First, there's one sense in which things might turn out either way, in which it's clear that that doesn't imply that the way it finally turns out isn't necessary. For example, the four color theorem might turn out to be true and might turn out to be false. It might turn out either way. It still doesn't mean that the way it turns out is not necessary. Obviously, the 'might' here is purely 'epistemic' – it merely expresses our present state of ignorance, or uncertainty.

But it seems that in the Hesperus-Phosphorus case, something even stronger is true. The evidence I have before I know that Hesperus is Phosphorus is that I see a certain star on a certain heavenly body in the evening and call it 'Hesperus', and in the morning and call it 'Phosphorus'. I know these things. There certainly is a possible world in which a man should have seen a certain star at a certain position in the evening and called it 'Hesperus' and a certain star in the morning and called it 'Phosphorus'; and should have concluded – should have found out by empirical investigation – that he names two different stars, or two different heavenly bodies. At least one of these stars or heavenly bodies was not Phosphorus, otherwise it couldn't have come out that way. But that's true. And so it's true that given the evidence that someone has antecedent to his empirical investigation, he can be placed in a sense in exactly the same situation, that is a qualitively identical epistemic situation, and call two heavenly bodies 'Hesperus' and 'Phosphorus', without their being identical. So in that sense we can say that it might have turned out either way. Not that it might have turned out either way as to Hesperus's being Phosphorus. Though for all we knew in advance, Hesperus wasn't Phosphorus, that couldn't have turned out any other way, in a sense. But being put in a situation where we have exactly the same evidence, qualitatively speaking, it could have turned out that Hesperus was not Phosphorus; that is, in a counterfactual world in which 'Hesperus' and 'Phosphorus' were not used in the way that we use them, as names of this planet, but as names of some other objects, one could have had qualitatively identical evidence and concluded that 'Hesperus' and 'Phosphorus' named two different objects.[48] But we, using the names as we do right now, can say in advance, that if Hesperus and Phosphorus are one and the same, then in no other possible world can they be different. We use 'Hesperus' as the name of a certain body and 'Phosphorus' as the name of a certain body. We use them as names of those bodies in all possible worlds. If, in fact, they are the *same* body, then in any other possible world we have to use them as a name of that object. And so in any other possible world it will be true that Hesperus is Phosphorus. So two things are true: first, that we do not know *a priori* that Hesperus is Phosphorus, and are in no position to find out the answer except empirically. Second, this is so because we could have evidence qualitatively indistinguishable from the evidence we have and determine the reference of the two names by the positions of two planets in the sky, without the planets being the same.

Of course, it is only a contingent truth (not true in every other possible world) that the star seen over there in the evening is the star seen over there in the morning, because there are possible worlds in which Phosphorus was not visible in the morning. But that contingent truth shouldn't be identified with the statement that Hesperus is Phosphorus. It could only be so identified if you thought that it was a necessary truth that Hesperus is visible over there in the evening or that Phosphorus is visible over there in the morning. But neither of those are necessary truths even if that's the way we pick out the planet. These are the contingent marks by which we identify a certain planet and give it a name.

Notes

1. In January of 1970, I gave three talks at Princeton University transcribed here. As the style of the transcript makes clear, I gave the talks without a written text, and, in fact, without notes. The present text is lightly edited from the *verbatim* transcript; an occasional passage has been added to expand the thought, an occasional sentence has been rewritten, but no attempt has been made to change the informal style of the original. Many of the footnotes have been added to the original, but a few were originally spoken asides in the talks themselves.

   I hope the reader will bear these facts in mind as he reads the text. Imagining it spoken, with proper pauses and emphases, may occasionally facilitate comprehension. I have agreed to publish the talks in this form with some reservations. The time allotted, and the informal style, necessitated a certain amount of compression of the argument, inability to treat certain objections, and the like. Especially in the concluding sections on scientific identities and the mind-body problem thoroughness had to be sacrificed. Some topics essential to a full presentation of the viewpoint argued here, especially that of existence statements and empty names, had to be omitted altogether. Further, the informality of the presentation may well have engendered a sacrifice of clarity at certain points. All these defects were accepted in the interest of early publication. I hope that perhaps I will have the chance to do a more thorough job later. To repeat, I hope the reader will bear in mind that he is largely reading informal lectures, not only when he encounters repetitions or infelicities, but also when he encounters irreverence or corn.

[· · ·]

3. Keith Donnellan, 'Reference and Definite Descriptions', *Philosophical Review* 75 (1966), pp. 281–304. See also Leonard Linsky, 'Reference and Referents', in *Philosophy and Ordinary Language* (ed. Caton), University of Illinois Press, Urbana, 1963. Donnellan's distinction seems applicable to names as well as to descriptions. Two men glimpse someone at a distance and think they recognize him as Jones. 'What is Jones doing?' 'Raking the leaves'. If the distant leaf-raker is actually Smith, then in some sense they are *referring* to Smith, even though they both use 'Jones' *as a name of* Jones. In the text, I speak of the 'referent' of a name to mean the thing named by the name – e.g., Jones, not Smith – even thought a speaker may sometimes properly be said to use the name to refer to someone else. Perhaps it would have been less misleading to use a technical term, such as 'denote' rather than 'refer'. My use of 'refer' is such as to satisfy the schema, 'The referent of "*X*" is *X*', where '*X*' is replaceable by any name or description. I am tentatively inclined to believe, in opposition to Donnellan, that his remarks about reference have little to do with semantics or truth-conditions, though they may be relevant to a theory of speech-acts. Space limitations do not permit me to explain what I mean by this, much less defend the view, except for a brief remark: Call the referent of a name or description in my sense the 'semantic referent'; for a name, this is the thing named, for a description, the thing uniquely satisfying the description.

   Then the speaker may *refer* to something other than the semantic referent if he has appropriate false beliefs. I think this is what happens in the naming (Smith-Jones) cases and also in the Donnellan 'champagne' case; the one requires no theory that names are ambiguous, and the other requires no modification of Russell's theory of descriptions.
4. Strictly speaking, of course, Russell says that the names don't abbreviate descriptions and don't have any sense; but then he also says that, just because the things that we call 'names' do abbreviate descriptions, they're not really names. So, since 'Walter Scott', according to Russell, does abbreviate a description, 'Walter Scott' is not a name; and the only names that really exist in ordinary language are, perhaps, demonstratives such as 'this' or 'that', used on a particular occasion to refer to an object with which the speaker is 'acquainted' in Russell's sense. Though we won't put things the way Russell does, we could describe Russell as saying that names, as they are ordinarily called, *do* have sense. They have sense in a strong way, namely, we should be able to give a definite description such that the

referent of the name, by definition, is the object satisfying the description. Russell himself, since he eliminates descriptions from his primitive notation, seems to hold in 'On Denoting' that the notion of 'sense' is illusory. In reporting Russell's views, we thus deviate from him in two respects. First, we stipulate that 'names' shall be names as ordinarily conceived, not Russell's 'logically proper names'; second, we regard descriptions, and their abbreviations, as having sense.

5. When I speak of the Frege-Russell view and its variants, I include only those versions which give a substantive theory of the reference of names. In particular, Quine's proposal that in a 'canonical notation' a name such as 'Socrates' should be replaced by a description 'the Socratizer' (where 'Socratizes' is an invented predicate), and that the description should then be eliminated by Russell's method, was not intended as a theory of reference for names but as a proposed reform of language with certain advantages. The problems discussed here will all apply, *mutatis mutandis*, to the reformed language; in particular, the question, 'How is the reference of "Socrates" determined?' yields to the question, 'How is the extension of "Socratizes" determined?' Of course I do not suggest that Quine has ever claimed the contrary.
6. Gottlob Frege, 'On Sense and Nominatum', translated by Herbert Feigl in *Readings in Philosophical Analysis* (ed. by Herbert Feigl and Wilfrid Sellars), Appleton Century Crofts, 1949, p. 86.
7. Ludwig Wittgenstein, *Philosophical Investigations*, translated by G. E. M. Anscombe, MacMillan, 1953, § 79.
8. John R. Searle, 'Proper Names', *Mind* 67 (1958), 166–73.
9. Ziff's most detailed statement of his version of the cluster-of-descriptions theory of the reference of names is in 'About God', reprinted in *Philosophical Turnings*, Cornell University Press, Ithaca, and Oxford University Press, London, 1966, pp. 94–96. A briefer statement is in his *Semantic Analysis*, Cornell University Press, Ithaca, 1960, pp. 102–05 (esp. pp. 103–04). The latter passage suggests that names of things with which we are acquainted should be treated somewhat differently (using ostension and baptism) from names of historical figures, where the reference is determined by (a cluster of) associated descriptions. On p. 93 of *Semantic Analysis* Ziff states that 'simple strong generalization(s) about proper names' are impossible; 'one can only say what is so for the most part . . .' Nevertheless Ziff clearly states that a cluster-of-descriptions theory is a reasonable such rough statement, at least for historical figures. For Ziff's view that proper names ordinarily are not words of the language and ordinarily do not have meaning, see pp. 85–89 and 93–94 of *Semantic Analysis*.
10. Those determinists who deny the importance of the individual in history may well argue that had Moses never existed, someone else would have arisen to achieve all that he did. Their claim cannot be refuted by appealing to a correct philosophical theory of the meaning of 'Moses exists'.

[. . .]

16. Of course I don't imply that language contains a name for every object. Demonstratives can be used as rigid designators, and free variables can be used as rigid designators of unspecified objects. Of course when we specify a

counterfactual situation, we do not describe the whole possible world, but only the portion which interests us.

[. . .]

19. *Philosophical Investigations*, § 50.

[. . .]

31. Searle, 'Proper Names', in Caton, op. cit., p. 160.

[. . .]

33. An even better case of determining the reference of a name by description, as opposed to ostension, is the discovery of the planet Neptune. Neptune was hypothesized as the planet which caused such and such discrepancies in the orbits of certain other planets. If Leverrier indeed gave the name 'Neptune' to the planet before it was ever seen, then he fixed the reference of 'Neptune' by means of the description just mentioned. At that time he was unable to see the planet even through a telescope. At this stage, an *a priori* material equivalence held between the statements 'Neptune exists' and 'some one planet perturbing the orbit of such and such other planets exists in such and such a position', and also such statements as 'if such and such perturbations are caused by a planet, they are caused by Neptune' had the status of *a priori* truths. Nevertheless, they were not *necessary* truths, since 'Neptune' was introduced as a name rigidly designating a certain planet. Leverrier could well have believed that if Neptune had been knocked off its course one million years earlier, it would have caused no such perturbations and even that some other object might have caused the perturbations in its place.
34. Following Donnellan's remarks on definite descriptions, we should add that in some cases, an object may be identified, and the reference of a name fixed, using a description which may turn out to be false of its object. The case where the reference of 'Phosphorus' is determined as the 'morning star', which later turns out not to be a star, is an obvious example. In such cases, the description which fixes the reference clearly is in no sense known *a priori* to hold of the object, though a more cautious substitute may be. If such a more cautious substitute is available, it is really the substitute which fixes the reference in the sense intended in the text.
35. Some of the theses are sloppily stated in respect of fussy matters like use of quotation marks and related details. (For example, Theses (5) and (6), as stated, presuppose that the speaker's language is English.) Since the purport of the theses is clear, and they are false anyway, I have not bothered to set these things straight.
36. The cluster-of-descriptions theory of naming would make 'Peano discovered the axioms for number theory' express a trivial truth, not a misconception, and

similarly for other misconceptions about the history of science. Some who have conceded such cases to me have argued that there are *other* uses of the same proper names satisfying the cluster theory. For example, it is argued, if we say, 'Gödel proved the incompleteness of arithmetic,' we are, of course, referring to Gödel, not to Schmidt. But, if we say, 'Gödel relied on a diagonal argument in this step of the proof,' don't we here, perhaps, refer to *whoever proved the theorem*? Similarly, if someone asks, 'What did Aristotle (or Shakespeare) have in mind here?', isn't he talking about the author of the passage in question, whoever he is? By analogy to Donnellan's usage for descriptions, this might be called an 'attributive' use of proper names. If this is so, then assuming the Gödel-Schmidt story, the sentence 'Gödel proved the incompleteness theorem' is false, but 'Gödel used a diagonal argument in the proof' is (at least in some contexts) true, and the reference of the name 'Gödel' is ambiguous. Since some counterexamples remain, the cluster-of-descriptions theory would still, in general, be false, which was my main point in the text; but it would be applicable in a wider class of cases than I thought. I think, however, that no such ambiguity need be postulated. It is, perhaps, true that sometimes when someone uses the name 'Gödel', his main interest is in whoever proved the theorem, and *perhaps*, in some sense, he 'refers' to him. I do not think that this case is different from the case of Smith and Jones in n. 3. If I mistake Jones for Smith, I may *refer* (in an appropriate sense) to Jones when I say that Smith is raking the leaves; nevertheless I do not use 'Smith' ambiguously, as a name sometimes of Smith and sometimes of Jones, but univocally as a name of Smith. Similarly, if I erroneously think that Aristotle wrote such-and-such passage. I may perhaps sometimes use 'Aristotle' to *refer* to the actual author of the passage, even though there is no ambiguity in my use of the name. In both cases, I will withdraw my original statement, and my original use of the name, if apprised of the facts. Recall that, in these lectures, 'referent' is used in the technical sense of the thing named by a name (or uniquely satisfying a description), and there should be no confusion.

[. . .]

42. A good example of a baptism whose reference was fixed by means of a description was that of naming Neptune in n. 33. The case of a baptism by ostension can perhaps be subsumed under the description concept also. Thus the primary applicability of the description theory is to cases of initial baptism. Descriptions are also used to fix a reference in cases of designation which are similar to naming except that the terms introduced are not usually called 'names'. The terms 'one meter', '100 degrees Centigrade', have already been given as examples, and other examples will be given later in these lectures. Two things should be emphasized concerning the case of introducing a name via a description in an initial baptism. First, the description used is not synonymous with the name it introduces but rather fixes its reference. Here we differ from the usual description theorists. Second, most cases of initial baptism are far from those which originally inspired the description theory. Usually a baptizer is acquainted in some sense with the object he names and is able to name is ostensively. Now the inspiration of the description theory lay in the fact that we can often use names of famous figures

of the past who are long dead and with whom no living person is acquainted; and it is precisely these cases which, on our view, cannot be correctly explained by a description theory.

43. I can transmit the name of the aardvark to other people. For each of these people, as for me, there will be a certain sort of causal or historical connection between my use of the name and the Emperor of the French, but not one of the required type.

44. Once we realize that the description used to fix the reference of a name is not synonymous with it, then the description theory can be regarded as presupposing the notion of naming or reference. The requirement I made that the description used not itself involve the notion of reference in a circular way is something else and is crucial if the description theory is to have any value at all. The reason is that the description theorist supposes that each speaker essentially uses the description he gives in an initial act of naming to determine his reference. Clearly, if he introduces the name 'Cicero' by the determination, 'By "Cicero" I shall refer to the man I call "Cicero",' he has by this ceremony determined no reference at all.

    Not all description theorists thought that they were eliminating the notion of reference altogether. Perhaps some realized that some notion of ostension, or primitive reference, is required to back it up. Certainly Russell did.

[. . .]

48. There is a more elaborate discussion of this point in the third lecture, where its relation to a certain sort of counterpart theory is also mentioned.

Chapter 11

The Meaning of 'Meaning'

H. Putnam

Language is the first broad area of human cognitive capacity for which we are beginning to obtain a description which is not exaggeratedly oversimplified. Thanks to the work of contemporary transformational linguists,[1] a very subtle description of at least some human languages is in the process of being constructed. Some features of these languages appear to be *universal.* Where such features turn out to be 'species-specific' – 'not explicable on some general grounds of functional utility or simplicity that would apply to arbitrary systems that serve the functions of language' – they may shed some light on the structure of mind. While it is extremely difficult to say to what extent the structure so illuminated will turn out to be a universal structure of *language*, as opposed to a universal structure of innate general learning strategies,[2] the very fact that this discussion can take place is testimony to the richness and generality of the descriptive material that linguists are beginning to provide, and also testimony to the depth of the analysis, insofar as the features that appear to be candidates for 'species-specific' features of language are in no sense surface or phenomenological features of language, but lie at the level of deep structure.

The most serious drawback to all of this analysis, as far as a philosopher is concerned, is that it does not concern the meaning of words. Analysis of the deep structure of linguistic forms gives us an incomparably more powerful description of the *syntax* of natural languages than we have ever had before. But the dimension of language associated with the word 'meaning' is, in spite of the usual spate of heroic if misguided attempts, as much in the dark as it ever was.

In this essay, I want to explore why this should be so. In my opinion, the reason that so-called semantics is in so much worse condition than syntactic

From K. Gunderson (Ed) (1975), 131–93. *Language, Mind & Knowledge*, Minneapolis, MW: University of Minnesota Press.

theory is that the *prescientific* concept on which semantics is based – the prescientific concept of *meaning* – is itself in much worse shape than the prescientific concept of syntax. As usual in philosophy, skeptical doubts about the concept do not at all help one in clarifying or improving the situation any more than dogmatic assertions by conservative philosophers that all's really well in this best of all possible worlds. The reason that the prescientific concept of meaning is in bad shape is not clarified by some general skeptical or nominalistic argument to the effect that meanings don't exist. Indeed, the upshot of our discussion will be that meanings don't exist in quite the way we tend to think they do. But electrons don't exist in quite the way Bohr thought they did, either. There is all the distance in the world between this assertion and the assertion that meanings (or electrons) 'don't exist.'

I am going to talk almost entirely about the meaning of words rather than about the meaning of sentences because I feel that our concept of word-meaning is more defective than our concept of sentence-meaning. But I will comment briefly on the arguments of philosophers such as Donald Davidson who insist that the concept of word-meaning *must* be secondary and that study of sentence-meaning must be primary. Since I regard the traditional theories about meaning as myth-eaten (notice that the topic of 'meaning' is the one topic discussed in philosophy in which there is literally nothing but 'theory' – literally nothing that can be labelled or even ridiculed as the 'common sense view'), it will be necessary for me to discuss and try to disentangle a number of topics concerning which the received view is, in my opinion, wrong. The reader will give me the greatest aid in the task of trying to make these matters clear if he will kindly assume that *nothing* is clear in advance.

Meaning and Extension

Since the Middle Ages at least, writers on the theory of meaning have purported to discover an ambiguity in the ordinary concept of meaning, and have introduced a pair of terms – *extension* and *intension*, or *Sinn* and *Bedeutung*, or whatever – to disambiguate the notion. The *extension* of a term, in customary logical parlance, is simply the set of things the term is true of. Thus, 'rabbit,' in its most common English sense, is true of all and only rabbits, so the extension of 'rabbit' is precisely the set of rabbits. Even this notion – and it is the *least* problematical notion in this cloudy subject – has its problems, however. Apart from problems it inherits from its parent notion of *truth*, the foregoing example of 'rabbit' *in its most common English sense* illustrates one such problem: strictly speaking, it is not a term, but an ordered pair consisting of a term and a 'sense' (or an occasion of use, or something else that distinguishes a term in one sense from the same term used in a different sense) that has an extension. Another problem is this: a 'set,' in the mathematical sense, is a 'yes-no' object; any given object either definitely belongs to *S* or definitely does not belong to *S*, if *S* is a set. But words in a natural language are not generally 'yes-no': there are things of which the description 'tree' is clearly true and things of which the description 'tree' is clearly false, to be sure, but there are a host of borderline cases. Worse, the line between the clear cases and the borderline cases is itself fuzzy. Thus the idealization involved in the notion of *extension* – the idealization involved in supposing that there is such a thing as the set of things of which the term 'tree' is true – is actually very severe.

Recently some mathematicians have investigated the notion of a *fuzzy set* – that is, of an object to which other things belong or do not belong with a given probability or to a given degree, rather than belong 'yes-no'. If one really wanted to formalize the notion of extension as applied to terms in a natural language, it would be necessary to employ 'fuzzy sets' or something similar rather than sets in the classical sense.

The problem of a word's having more than one sense is standardly handled by treating each of the senses as a different word (or rather, by treating the word as if it carried invisible subscripts, thus: 'rabbit_1' – animal of a certain kind; 'rabbit_2' – coward; and as if 'rabbit_1' and 'rabbit_2' or whatever were different words entirely). This again involves two very severe idealizations (at least two, that is): supposing that words have discretely many senses, and supposing that the entire repertoire of senses is fixed once and for all. Paul Ziff has recently investigated the extent to which both of these suppositions distorts the actual situation in natural language;[3] nevertheless, we will continue to make these idealizations here.

Now consider the compound terms 'creature with a heart' and 'creature with a kidney.' Assuming that every creature with a heart possesses a kidney and vice versa, the extension of these two terms is exactly the same. But they obviously differ in meaning. Supposing that there is a sense of 'meaning' in which meaning = extension, there must be another sense of 'meaning' in which the meaning of a term is not its extension but something else, say the 'concept' associated with the term. Let us call this 'something else' the *intension* of the term. The concept of a creature with a heart is clearly a different concept from the concept of a creature with a kidney. Thus the two terms have different intension. When we say they have different 'meaning,' meaning = intension.

Intension and Extension

Something like the preceding paragraph appears in every standard exposition of the notions 'intension' and 'extension.' But it is not at all satisfactory. Why it is not satisfactory is, in a sense, the burden of this entire essay. But some points can be made at the very outset: first of all, what evidence is there that 'extension' *is* a sense of the word 'meaning'? The canonical explanation of the notions 'intension' and 'extension' is very much like 'in one sense "meaning" means *extension* and in the other sense "meaning" means *meaning*.' The fact is that while the notion of 'extension' is made quite precise, relative to the fundamental logical notion of *truth* (and under the severe idealizations remarked above), the notion of intension is made no more precise than the vague (and, as we shall see, misleading) notion 'concept.' It is as if someone explained the notion 'probability' by saying: 'in one sense "probability" means frequency, and in the other sense it means *propensity*. 'Probability' *never* means 'frequency', and 'propensity' is at least as unclear as 'probability.'

*Unclear as it is, the traditional doctrine that the notion 'meaning' possesses the extension/intension ambiguity has certain typical consequences. Most traditional philosophers thought of concepts as something *mental*. Thus the doctrine that the meaning of a term (the meaning 'in the sense of intension,' that is) is a concept carried the implication that meanings are mental entities. Frege and more recently Carnap and his followers, however, rebelled against this 'psychologism,' as they termed it. Feeling that meanings are *public* property – that the *same* meaning can be 'grasped' by more than one person and by persons at different times – they identified concepts (and hence 'intensions' or meanings) with abstract entities rather than mental entities. However, 'grasping' these abstract entities was still an individual psychological act. None of these philosophers doubted that understanding a word (knowing its intension) was just a matter of being in a certain psychological state (somewhat in the way in which knowing how to factor numbers in one's head is just a matter of being in a certain very complex psychological state).

Secondly, the timeworn example of the two terms 'creature with a kidney' and 'creature with a heart' does show that two terms can have the same extension and yet differ in intension. But it was taken to be obvious that the reverse is impossible: two terms cannot differ in extension and have the same intension. Interestingly, no argument for this impossibility was ever offered. Probably it reflects the tradition of the ancient and medieval philosophers who assumed that the concept corresponding to a term was just a conjunction of predicates, and hence that the concept corresponding to a term must *always* provide a necessary and sufficient condition for falling into the extension of the term.[4] For philosophers like Carnap, who accepted the verifiability theory of meaning, the concept corresponding to a term provided (in the ideal case, where the term had 'complete meaning') a *criterion* for belonging to the extension (not just

*Editors note: The material enclosed within rules on this and later pages constitutes the content of Putnam (1973).

in the sense of 'necessary and sufficient condition,' but in the strong sense of *way of recognizing* if a given thing falls into the extension or not). Thus these positivistic philosophers were perfectly happy to retain the traditional view on this point. So theory of meaning came to rest on two unchallenged assumptions:

1. That knowing the meaning of a term is just a matter of being in a certain psychological state (in the sense of 'psychological state' in which states of memory and psychological dispositions are 'psychological states'; no one thought that knowing the meaning of a word was a continuous state of consciousness, of course).
2. That the meaning of a term (in the sense of 'intension') determines its extension (in the sense that sameness of intension entails sameness of extension).

I shall argue that these two assumptions are not jointly satisfied by *any* notion, let alone any notion of meaning. The traditional concept of meaning is a concept which rests on a false theory.

'Psychological State' and Methodological Solipsism

In order to show this, we need first to clarify the traditional notion of a psychological state. In one sense a state is simply a two-place predicate whose arguments are an individual and a time. In this sense, *being five feet tall, being in pain, knowing the alphabet*, and even *being a thousand miles from Paris* are all states. (Note that the *time* is usually left implicit or 'contextual'; the full form of an atomic sentence of these predicates would be 'x is five feet tall at time t,' 'x is in pain at time t,' etc.) In science, however, it is customary to restrict the term state to properties which are defined in terms of the parameters of the individual which are fundamental from the point of view of the given science. Thus, being five feet tall is a state (from the point of view of physics); being in pain is a state (from the point of view of mentalistic psychology, at least); knowing the alphabet might be a state (from the point of view of cognitive psychology), although it is hard to say; but being a thousand miles from Paris would *not* naturally be called a *state*. In one sense, a psychological state is simply a state which is studied or described by psychology. In this sense it may be trivially true that, say, *knowing the meaning of the word 'water'* is a 'psychological state' (viewed from the standpoint of cognitive psychology). But this is not the sense of psychological state that is at issue in the above assumption 1.

When traditional philosophers talked about psychological states (or 'mental' states), they made an assumption which we may call the assumption of methodological solipsism. This assumption is the assumption that no psychological state, properly so called, presupposes the existence of any individual other than the subject to whom that state is ascribed. (In fact, the assumption was that no psychological state presupposes the existence of the subject's *body* even: if *P* is a psychological state, properly so called, then it must be logically possible for a 'disembodied mind' to be in *P*.) This assumption is pretty explicit in Descartes, but it is implicit in just about the whole of traditional philosophical psychology. Making this assumption is, of course, adopting a *restrictive program* – a program which deliberately limits the scope and nature of psychology to fit certain mentalistic preconceptions or, in some cases, to fit an idealistic reconstruction of knowledge and the world. Just *how* restrictive the program is, however, often goes unnoticed. Such common or garden variety psychological states as *being jealous* have to be reconstructed, for example, if the assumption of methodological solipsism is retained. For, in its ordinary use, *x is jealous of y* entails that *y* exists, and *x is jealous of y's regard for z* entails that both *y* and *z* exist (as well as *x*, of course). Thus *being jealous* and *being jealous of someone's regard for someone else* are not psychological states permitted by the assumption of methodological solipsism. (We shall call them 'psychological states in the wide sense' and refer to the states which are permitted by methodological solipsism as 'psychological states in the narrow sense.') The reconstruction required by methodological solipsism would be to reconstrue *jealousy* so that I can be jealous of my own hallucinations, or of figments of my imagination, etc. Only if we assume that psychological states in the narrow sense have a significant degree of causal closure (so that restricting ourselves to psychological states in the narrow sense will facilitate the statement of psychological *laws*) is there any point to engaging in this reconstruction, or in making the assumption of methodological solipsism. But the three centuries of failure of mentalistic psychology is tremendous evidence against this procedure, in my opinion.

Be that as it may, we can now state more precisely what we claimed at the end of the preceding section. Let *A* and *B* be any two terms which differ in extension. By assumption 2 they must differ in meaning (in the sense of 'intension'). By assumption 1, *knowing the meaning of A* and *knowing the meaning of B* are psychological states *in the narrow sense* – for this is how we shall construe assumption 1. *But these psychological states must determine the extension of the terms A and B just as much as the meanings ('intensions') do.*

To see this, let us try assuming the opposite. Of course, there cannot be two terms *A* and *B* such that *knowing the meaning of A* is the same state as *knowing the meaning of B* even though *A* and *B* have different extensions. For *knowing the meaning of A* isn't just 'grasping the intension' of *A*, whatever that may come to; it is also knowing that the 'intension' that one has 'grasped' *is* the intension of *A*. (Thus, someone who knows the meaning of 'wheel' presumably 'grasps the intension' of its German synonym 'Rad';

but if he doesn't know that the 'intension' in question is the intension of *Rad*, he isn't said to 'know the meaning of *Rad*.') If *A* and *B* are different terms, then *knowing the meaning of A* is a different state from *knowing the meaning of B* whether the meanings of *A* and *B* be themselves the same or different. But by the same argument, if I_1 and I_2 are different *intensions* and *A* is a term, then *knowing that* I_1 *is the meaning of A* is a different psychological state from *knowing that* I_2 *is the meaning of A*. Thus, there cannot be two different logically possible worlds L_1 and L_2 such that, say, Oscar is in the *same* psychological state (in the narrow sense) in L_1 and L_2 (in all respects), but in L_1 Oscar understands *A* as having the meaning I_1 and in L_2 Oscar understands *A* as having the meaning I_2. (For, if there were, then in L_1 Oscar would be in the psychological state *knowing that* I_1 *is the meaning of A* and in L_2 Oscar would be in the psychological state *knowing that* I_2 *is the meaning of A*, and these are different and even – assuming that *A* has just one meaning for Oscar in each world – incompatible psychological states in the narrow sense.)

In short, if *S* is the sort of psychological state we have been discussing – a psychological state of the form *knowing that I is the meaning of A*, where *I* is an 'intension' and *A* is a term – then the *same* necessary and sufficient condition for falling into the extension of *A* 'works' in *every* logically possible world in which the speaker is in the psychological state *S*. For the state *S* *determines* the intension *I*, and by assumption 2 the intension amounts to a necessary and sufficient condition for membership in the *extension*.

If our interpretation of the traditional doctrine of intension and extension is fair to Frege and Carnap, then the whole psychologism/Platonism issue appears somewhat a tempest in a teapot, as far as meaning-theory is concerned. (Of course, it is a very important issue as far as general philosophy of mathematics is concerned.) For even if meanings are 'Platonic' entities rather than 'mental' entities on the Frege-Carnap view, 'grasping' those entities is presumably a psychological state (in the narrow sense). Moreover, the psychological state uniquely determines the 'Platonic' entity. So whether one takes the 'Platonic' entity or the psychological state as the 'meaning' would appear to be somewhat a matter of convention. And taking the psychological state to be the meaning would hardly have the consequence that Frege feared, that meanings would cease to be public. For psychological states are 'public' in the sense that different people (and even people in different epochs) can be in the *same* psychological state. Indeed, Frege's argument against psychologism is only an argument against identifying concepts with mental particulars, not with mental entities in general.

The 'public' character of psychological states entails, in particular, that if Oscar and Elmer understand a word *A* differently, then they must be in *different* psychological states. For the state of *knowing the intension of A to be, say I, is the same* state whether Oscar or Elmer be in it. Thus two speakers cannot be in the same psychological state in all respects and understand the term *A* differently; the psychological state of the speaker determines the intension (and hence, by assumption 2, the extension) of *A*.

It is this last consequence of the joint assumptions 1, 2 that we claim to be false. We claim that it is possible for two speakers to be in exactly the *same* psychological state (in the narrow sense), even though the extension of the term *A* in the idiolect of the one is different from the extension of the term *A* in the idiolect of the other. Extension is *not* determined by psychological state.

This will be shown in detail in later sections. If this is right, then there are two courses open to one who wants to rescue at least one of the traditional assumptions: to give up the idea that psychological state (in the narrow sense) determines *intension*, or to give up the idea that intension determines extension. We shall consider these alternatives later.

Are Meanings in the Head?

That psychological state does not determine extension will now be shown with the aid of a little science fiction. For the purpose of the following science-fiction examples, we shall suppose that somewhere in the galaxy there is a planet we shall call Twin Earth. Twin Earth is very much like Earth; in fact, people on Twin Earth even speak *English*. In fact, apart from the differences we shall specify in our science-fiction examples, the reader may suppose that Twin Earth is *exactly* like Earth. He may even suppose that he has a *Doppelgänger* – an identical copy – on Twin Earth, if he wishes, although my stories will not depend on this.

Although some of the people on Twin Earth (say, the ones who call themselves 'Americans' and the ones who call themselves 'Canadians' and the ones who call themselves 'Englishmen,' etc.) speak English, there are, not surprisingly, a few tiny differences which we will now describe between the dialects of English spoken on Twin Earth and Standard English. These differences themselves depend on some of the peculiarities of Twin Earth.

One of the peculiarities of Twin Earth is that the liquid called 'water' is not H_2O but a different liquid whose chemical formula is very long and complicated. I shall abbreviate this chemical formula simply as XYZ. I shall suppose that XYZ is indistinguishable from water at normal temperatures and pressures. In particular, it tastes like water and it quenches thirst like water. Also, I shall suppose that the oceans and lakes and seas of Twin Earth contain XYZ and not water, that it rains XYZ on Twin Earth and not water, etc.

If a spaceship from Earth ever visits Twin Earth, then the supposition at first will be that 'water' has the same meaning on Earth and on Twin Earth. This supposition will be corrected when it is discovered that 'water' on Twin Earth is XYZ, and the Earthian spaceship will report somewhat as follows:

'On Twin Earth the word "water" means XYZ.'

(It is this sort of use of the word 'means' which accounts for the doctrine that extension is one sense of 'meaning,' by the way. But note that although 'means' does mean something like *has an extension in* this example, one would *not say*

'On Twin Earth the meaning of the word "water" is XYZ'

unless, possibly, the fact that 'water is XYZ' was known to every adult speaker of English on Twin Earth. We can account for this in terms of the theory of meaning we develop below; for the moment we just remark that although the verb 'means' sometimes means 'has as extension,' the nominalization 'meaning' *never* means 'extension.')

Symmetrically, if a spaceship from Twin Earth ever visits Earth, then the supposition at first will be that the word 'water' has the same meaning on Twin Earth and on Earth. This supposition will be corrected when it is discovered that 'water' on Earth is H_2O, and the Twin Earthian spaceship will report:

'On Earth[5] the word "water" means H_2O.'

Note that there is no problem about the extension of the term 'water.' The word simply has two different meanings (as we say): in the sense in which it is used on Twin Earth, the sense of $water_{TE}$, what we call 'water' simply isn't water; while in the sense in which it is used on Earth, the sense of $water_E$, what the Twin Earthians call 'water' simply isn't water. The extension of 'water' in the sense of $water_E$ is the set of all wholes consisting of H_2O molecules, or something like that; the extension of water in the sense of $water_{TE}$ is the set of all wholes consisting of XYZ molecules, or something like that.

Now let us roll the time back to about 1750. At that time chemistry was not developed on either Earth or Twin Earth. The typical Earthian speaker of English did not know water consisted of hydrogen and oxygen, and the typical Twin Earthian speaker of English did not know 'water' consisted of XYZ. Let $Oscar_1$ be such a typical Earthian English speaker, and let $Oscar_2$ be his counterpart on Twin Earth. You may suppose that there is no belief that $Oscar_1$ had about water that $Oscar_2$ did not have about 'water.' If you like, you may even suppose that $Oscar_1$ and $Oscar_2$ were exact duplicates in appearance, feelings, thoughts, interior monologue, etc. Yet the extension of the term 'water' was just as much H_2O on Earth in 1750 as in 1950; and the extension of the term 'water' was just as much XYZ on Twin Earth in 1750 as in 1950. $Oscar_1$ and $Oscar_2$ understood the term 'water' differently in 1750 *although they were in the same psychological state*, and although, given the state of science at the time, it would have taken their scientific communities about fifty years to discover that they understood the term 'water' differently. Thus the extension of the term 'water' (and, in fact, its 'meaning' in the intuitive preanalytical usage of that term) is *not* a function of the psychological state of the speaker by itself.

But, it might be objected, why should we accept it that the term 'water' had the same extension in 1750 and in 1950 (on both Earths)? The logic of natural-kind terms like 'water' is a complicated matter, but the following is a sketch of an answer. Suppose I point to a glass of water and say 'this liquid is called water' (or 'this is called water,' if the marker 'liquid' is clear from the context). My 'ostensive definition' of water has the following empirical presupposition: that the body of liquid I am pointing to bears a certain sameness relation (say, *x is the same liquid as y*, or *x is the same*$_L$ *as y*) to most of the stuff I and other speakers in my linguistic community have on other occasions called 'water.' If this presupposition is false because, say, I am without knowing it pointing to a glass of gin and not a glass of water, then I do not intend my ostensive definition to be accepted. Thus the ostensive definition conveys what might be called a defeasible necessary and sufficient condition: the necessary and sufficient condition for being water is bearing the relation $same_L$ to the stuff in the glass; but this is the necessary and sufficient condition only if the empirical presupposition is satisfied. If it is not satisfied, then one of a series of, so to speak, 'fallback' conditions becomes activated.

The key point is that the relation $same_L$ is a *theoretical* relation: whether something is or is not the same liquid as *this* may take an indeterminate amount of scientific investigation to determine. Moreover, even if a 'definite' answer has been obtained either through scientific investigation or through the application of some 'common sense' test, the answer is *defeasible*: future investigation might reverse even the most 'certain' example. Thus, the fact that an English speaker in 1750 might have called XYZ 'water,' while he or his successors would not have called XYZ water in 1800 or 1850 does not mean that the 'meaning' of 'water' changed for the average speaker in the interval. In 1750 or in 1850 or in 1950 one might have pointed to, say, the liquid in Lake Michigan as an example of 'water.' What changed was that in 1750 we would have mistakenly thought that XYZ bore the relation $same_L$ to the liquid in Lake Michigan, while in 1800 or 1850 we would have known that it did not (I am ignoring the fact that the liquid in Lake Michigan was only dubiously water in 1950, of course).

Let us now modify our science-fiction story. I do not know whether one can make pots and pans out of molybdenum; and if one can make them out of molybdenum, I don't know whether they could be distinguished easily from aluminum pots and pans. (I don't know any of this even though I have acquired the word 'molybdenum.') So I shall suppose that molybdenum pots and pans *can't* be distinguished from aluminum pots and pans save by an expert. (To emphasize the point, I repeat that this could be true for all I know, and a fortiori it could be true for all I know by virtue of 'knowing the meaning' of the words *aluminum and molybdenum.*) We will now suppose that molybdenum is as common on Twin Earth as aluminum is on Earth, and that aluminum is as rare on Twin Earth as molybdenum is on Earth. In particular, we shall assume that 'aluminum' pots and pans are made of molybdenum on Twin Earth. Finally, we shall assume that the words 'aluminum' and 'molybdenum' are *switched* on Twin Earth: 'aluminum' is the name of *molybdenum* and 'molybdenum' is the name of *aluminum.*

This example shares some features with the previous one. If a spaceship from Earth visited Twin Earth, the visitors from Earth probably would not suspect that the 'aluminum' pots and pans on Twin Earth were not made of aluminum, especially when the Twin Earthians said they were. But there is one important difference between the two cases. An Earthian metallurgist could tell very easily that 'aluminum' was molybdenum, and a Twin Earthian metallurgist could tell equally easily that aluminum was 'molybdenum.' (The shudder quotes in the preceding sentence indicate Twin Earthian usages.) Whereas in 1750 no one on either Earth or Twin Earth could have distinguished water from 'water,' the confusion of aluminum with 'aluminum' involves only a part of the linguistic communities involved.

The example makes the same point as the preceding one. If $Oscar_1$ and $Oscar_2$ are standard speakers of Earthian English and Twin Earthian English respectively, and neither is chemically or metallurgically sophisticated, then there may be no difference at all in their psychological state when they use the word 'aluminum'; nevertheless we have to say that 'aluminum' has the extension *aluminum* in the idiolect of $Oscar_1$ and the extension *molybdenum* in the idiolect of $Oscar_2$. (Also we have to say that $Oscar_1$ and $Oscar_2$ mean different things by 'aluminum,' that 'aluminum' has a different meaning on Earth than it does on Twin Earth, etc.) Again we see that the psychological state of the speaker does *not* determine the extension (or the 'meaning,' speaking preanalytically) of the word.

Before discussing this example further, let me introduce a *non*-science-fiction example. Suppose you are like me and cannot tell an elm from a beech tree. We still say that the extension of 'elm' in my idiolect is the same as the extension of 'elm' in anyone else's, viz., the set of all elm trees, and that the set of all beech trees is the extension of 'beech' in *both* of our idiolects. Thus 'elm' in my idiolect has a different extension from 'beech' in your idiolect (as it should). Is it really credible that this difference in extension is brought about by some difference in our *concepts*? My *concept* of an elm tree is exactly the same as my concept of a beech tree (I blush to confess). (This shows that the identification of meaning 'in the sense of intension' with *concept* cannot be correct, by the way.) If someone heroically attempts to maintain that the difference between the extension of 'elm' and the extension of 'beech' in *my* idiolect is explained by a difference in my psychological state, then we can always refute him by constructing a 'Twin Earth' example – just let the words 'elm' and 'beech' be switched on Twin Earth (the way 'aluminum' and 'molybdenum' were in the previous example). Moreover, suppose I have a *Doppelgänger* on Twin Earth who is molecule for molecule 'identical' with me (in the sense in which two neckties can be 'identical'). If you are a dualist, then also suppose my *Doppelgänger* thinks the same verbalized thoughts I do, has the same sense data, the same dispositions, etc. It is absurd to think *his* psychological state is one bit different from mine: yet he 'means' *beech* when he says 'elm' and *I* 'mean' *elm* when I say elm. Cut the pie any way you like, 'meanings' just ain't in the *head*!

A Socio-linguistic Hypothesis

The last two examples depend upon a fact about language that seems, surprisingly, never to have been pointed out: that there is *division of linguistic labor.* We could hardly use such words as 'elm' and 'aluminum' if no one possessed a way of recognizing elm trees and aluminum metal; but not everyone to whom the distinction is important has to be able to make the distinction. Let us shift the example: consider *gold.* Gold is important for many reasons: it is a precious metal, it is a monetary metal, it has symbolic value (it is important to most people that the 'gold' wedding ring they wear *really* consist of gold and not just *look* gold), etc. Consider our community as a 'factory': in this 'factory' some people have the 'job' of *wearing gold wedding rings*, other people have the 'job' of selling gold wedding rings, still other people have the job of *telling whether or not something is really gold.* It is not at all necessary or efficient that everyone who wears a gold ring (or a gold cuff link, etc.), or discusses the 'gold standard,' etc., engage in buying and selling gold. Nor is it necessary or efficient that everyone who buys and sells gold be able to tell whether or not something is really gold in a society where this form of dishonesty is uncommon (selling fake gold) and in which one can easily consult an expert in case of doubt. And it is *certainly* not necessary or efficient that everyone who has occasion to buy or wear gold be able to tell with any reliability whether or not something is really gold.

The foregoing facts are just examples of mundane division of labor (in a wide sense). But they engender a division of linguistic labor: everyone to whom gold is important for any reason has to acquire the word 'gold'; but he does not have to acquire the *method of recognizing* if something is or is not gold. He can rely on a special subclass of speakers. The features that are generally thought to be present in connection with a general name – necessary and sufficient conditions for membership in the extension, ways of recognizing if something is in the extension ('criteria'), etc. – are all present in the linguistic community *considered as a collective body*; but that collective body divides the 'labor' of knowing and employing these various parts of the 'meaning' of 'gold.'

This division of linguistic labor rests upon and presupposes the division of *non*-linguistic labor, of course. If only the people who know how to tell if some metal is really gold or not have any reason to have the word 'gold' in their vocabulary, then the word 'gold' will be as the word 'water' was in 1750 with respect to that subclass of speakers, and the other speakers just won't acquire it at all. And some words do not exhibit any division of linguistic labor: 'chair,' for example. But with the increase of division of labor in the society and the rise of science, more and more words begin to exhibit this kind of division of labor. 'Water,' for example, did not exhibit it at all prior to the rise of chemistry. Today it is obviously necessary for every speaker to be able to recognize water (reliably under normal conditions), and probably every adult speaker even knows the necessary and sufficient condition 'water is H_2O,' but only a few adult speakers could distinguish water from liquids which superficially resembled water. In case of doubt, other speakers would rely on the judgment of these 'expert' speakers. Thus the way of recognizing possessed by these 'expert' speakers is also, through them, possessed by the collective linguistic body, even though it is not possessed by each individual member of the body, and in this way the most recherché fact about water may become part of the *social* meaning of the word while being unknown to almost all speakers who acquire the word.

It seems to me that this phenomenon of division of linguistic labor is one which it will be very important for sociolinguistics to investigate. In connection with it, I should like to propose the following hypothesis:

> **Hypothesis of the Universality of the Division of Linguistic Labor:**
>
> Every linguistic community exemplifies the sort of division of linguistic labor just described, that is, possesses at least some terms whose associated 'criteria' are known only to a subset of

> the speakers who acquire the terms, and whose use by the other speakers depends upon a structured co-operation between them and the speakers in the relevant subsets.

It would be of interest, in particular, to discover if extremely primitive peoples were sometimes exceptions to this hypothesis (which would indicate that the division of linguistic labor is a product of social evolution), or if even they exhibit it. In the latter case, one might conjecture that division of labor, including linguistic labor, is a fundamental trait of our species.

It is easy to see how this phenomenon accounts for some of the examples given above of the failure of the assumptions 1, 2. Whenever a term is subject to the division of linguistic labor, the 'average' speaker who acquires it does not acquire anything that fixes its extension. In particular, his individual psychological state *certainly* does not fix its extension; it is only the sociolinguistic state of the collective linguistic body to which the speaker belongs that fixes the extension.

We may summarize this discussion by pointing out that there are two sorts of tools in the world: there are tools like a hammer or a screwdriver which can be used by one person; and there are tools like a steamship which require the cooperative activity of a number of persons to use. Words have been thought of too much on the model of the first sort of tool.

Indexicality and Rigidity[6]

The first of our science-fiction examples – 'water' on Earth and on Twin Earth in 1750 – does not involve division of linguistic labor, or at least does not involve it in the same way the examples of 'aluminum' and 'elm' do. There were not (in our story, anyway) any 'experts' on water on Earth in 1750, nor any experts on 'water' on Twin Earth. (The example *can* be construed as involving division of labor *across time*, however. I shall not develop this method of treating the example here.) The example *does* involve things which are of fundamental importance to the theory of reference and also to the theory of necessary truth, which we shall now discuss.

There are two obvious ways of telling someone what one means by a natural-kind term such as 'water' or 'tiger' or 'lemon.' One can give him a so-called ostensive definition – 'this (liquid) is water'; 'this (animal) is a tiger'; 'this (fruit) is a lemon'; where the parentheses are meant to indicate that the 'markers' *liquid, animal, fruit*, may be either explicit or implicit. Or one can give him a *description*. In the latter case the description one gives typically consists of one or more markers together with a *stereotype*[7] – a standardized description of features of the kind that are typical, or 'normal,' or at any rate stereotypical. The central features of the stereotype generally are *criteria* – features which in normal situations constitute ways of recognizing if a thing belongs to the kind or, at least, necessary conditions (or probabilistic necessary conditions) for membership in the kind. Not all criteria used by the linguistic community as a collective body are included in the stereotype, and in some cases the stereotype may be quite weak. Thus (unless I am a very atypical speaker), the stereotype of an elm is just that of a common deciduous tree. These features are indeed necessary conditions for membership in the kind (I mean 'necessary' in a loose sense; I don't think 'elm trees are deciduous' is *analytic*), but they fall far short of constituting a way of recognizing elms. On the other hand, the stereotype of a tiger does enable one to recognize tigers (unless they are albino, or some other atypical circumstance is present), and the stereotype of a lemon generally enables one to recognize lemons. In the extreme case, the stereotype may be *just* the marker: the stereotype of molybdenum might be *just* that molybdenum is a *metal*. Let us consider both of these ways of introducing a term into someone's vocabulary.

Suppose I point to a glass of liquid and say '*this* is water,' in order to teach someone the word 'water.' We have already described some of the empirical presuppositions of this act, and the way in which this kind of meaning-explanation is defeasible. Let us now try to clarify further how it is supposed to be taken.

In what follows, we shall take the notion of 'possible world' as primitive. We do this because we feel that in several senses the notion makes sense and is scientifically important even if it needs to be made more precise. We shall assume further that in at least some cases it is possible to speak of the same individual as existing in more than one possible world.[8] Our discussion leans heavily on the work of Saul Kripke, although the conclusions were obtained independently.

Let W_1 and W_2 be two possible worlds in which I exist and in which this glass exists and in which I am giving a meaning explanation by pointing to this glass and saying 'this is water.' (We do *not* assume that the *liquid* in the glass is the same in both worlds.) Let us suppose that in W_1 the glass is full of H_2O and in W_2 the glass is full of XYZ. We shall also suppose that W_1 is the *actual* world and that XYZ is the stuff typically called 'water' in the world W_2 (so that the relation between English speakers in W_1 and English speakers in W_2 is exactly the same as the relation between English speakers on Earth and English speakers on Twin Earth). Then there are two theories one might have concerning the meaning of 'water.'

1. One might hold that 'water' was *world-relative* but *constant* in meaning (i.e., the word has a *constant relative meaning*). On this

theory, 'water' *means the same* in W_1 and W_2; it's just that water is H_2O in W_1 and water is XYZ in W_2.

2. One might hold that water is H_2O in all worlds (the stuff called 'water' in W_2 isn't water), but 'water' doesn't have the same meaning in W_1 and W_2.

If what was said before about the Twin Earth case was correct, then 2 is clearly the correct theory. When I say '*this* (liquid) is water,' the 'this' is, so to speak, a *de re* 'this' – i.e., the force of my explanation is that 'water' is whatever bears a certain equivalence relation (the relation we called '$same_L$' above) to the piece of liquid referred to as 'this' *in the actual world*.

We might symbolize the difference between the two theories as a 'scope' difference in the following way. On theory 1, the following is true:

(1′) (For every world *W*) (For every *x* in *W*) (*x* is water ≡ *x* bears $same_L$ to the entity referred to as 'this' in *W*)

while on theory 2:

(2′) (For every world *W*) (For every *x* in *W*) (*x* is water ≡ *x* bears $same_L$ to the entity referred to as 'this' *in the actual world* W_1).

(I call this a 'scope' difference because in (1′) 'the entity referred to as "this" ' is within the scope of 'For every world *W*' – as the qualifying phrase 'in *W*' makes explicit, whereas in (2′) 'the entity referred to as "this" ' means 'the entity referred to as "this" *in the actual world*,' and has thus a reference *independent* of the bound variable '*W*.')

Kripke calls a designator 'rigid' (in a given sentence) if (in that sentence) it refers to the same individual in every possible world in which the designator designates. If we extend the notion of rigidity to substance names, then we may express Kripke's theory and mine by saying that the term 'water' is *rigid*.

The rigidity of the term 'water' follows from the fact that when I give the ostensive definition '*this* (liquid) is water' I intend (2′) and not (1′).

We may also say, following Kripke, that when I give the ostensive definition '*this* (liquid) is water,' the demonstrative 'this' is *rigid*.

What Kripke was the first to observe is that this theory of the meaning (or 'use,' or whatever) of the word 'water' (and other natural-kind terms as well) has startling consequences for the theory of necessary truth.

To explain this, let me introduce the notion of a *cross-world relation*. A two-term relation *R* will be called *cross-world* when it is understood in such a way that its extension is a set of ordered pairs of individuals *not all in the same possible world*. For example, it is easy to understand the relation *same height as* as a cross-world relation: just understand it so that, e.g., if x is an individual in a world W_1 who is five feet tall (in W_1) and y is an individual in W_2 who is five feet tall (in W_2), then the ordered pair x,y belongs to the extension of *same height as*. (Since an individual may have different heights in different possible worlds in which that same individual exists, strictly speaking it is not the ordered pair x,y that constitutes an element of the extension of *same height as*, but rather the ordered pair *x-in-world-*W_1, *y-in-world-*W_2.)

Similarly, we can understand the relation $same_L$ (same liquid as) as a cross-world relation by understanding it so that a liquid in world W_1 which has the same important physical properties (in W_1) that a liquid in W_2 possesses (in W_2) bears $same_L$ to the latter liquid.

Then the theory we have been presenting may be summarized by saying that an entity x, in an arbitrary possible world, is *water* if and only if it bears the relation $same_L$ (construed as a cross-world relation) to the stuff *we* call 'water' in the *actual* world.

Suppose, now, that I have not yet discovered what the important physical properties of water are (in the actual world) – i.e., I don't yet know that water is H_2O. I may have ways of *recognizing* water that are successful (of course, I may make a small number of mistakes that I won't be able to detect until a later stage in our scientific development) but not know the microstructure of water. If I agree that a liquid with the superficial properties of 'water' but a different microstructure *isn't really water*, then my ways of recognizing water (my 'operational definition,' so to speak) cannot be regarded as an analytical specification of *what it is to be* water. Rather, the operational definition, like the ostensive one, is simply a way of pointing out a standard – pointing out the stuff *in the actual world* such that for x to be water, in *any* world, is for x to bear the relation $same_L$ to the *normal* members of the class of *local* entities that satisfy the operational definition. 'Water' on Twin Earth is not water, even if it satisfies the operational definition, because it doesn't bear $same_L$ to the *local* stuff that satisfies the operational definition, and local stuff that satisfies the operational definition but has a microstructure different from the rest of the local stuff that satisfies the operational definition isn't water either, because it doesn't bear $same_L$ to the *normal* examples of the local 'water.'

Suppose, now, that I discover the microstructure of water – that water is H_2O. At this point I will be able to say that the stuff on Twin Earth that I earlier *mistook* for water isn't really water. In the same way, if you describe not another planet in the actual universe, but another possible universe in which there is stuff with the chemical formula XYZ which passes the 'operational test' for *water*, we shall have to say that that stuff isn't water but merely XYZ. You will not have described a possible world in which 'water is XYZ,' but merely a possible world in which there are lakes of XYZ, people drink XYZ (and not water), or whatever. In fact, once we have discovered the nature of water, nothing counts as a possible world in which water doesn't have that nature. Once we have discovered that water (in the actual world) is H_2O, *nothing counts as a possible world in which water isn't* H_2O. In particular, if a 'logically possible' statement is one that holds in some 'logically possible world,' *it isn't logically possible that water isn't* H_2O.

On the other hand, we can perfectly well imagine having experiences that would convince us (and that would make it rational to believe that) water *isn't* H_2O. In that sense, it is conceivable that water isn't H_2O. It is conceivable but it isn't logically possible! Conceivability is no proof of logical possibility.

Kripke refers to statements which are rationally unrevisable (assuming there are such) as *epistemically necessary*. Statements which are true in all possible worlds he refers to simply as necessary (or sometimes as 'metaphysically necessary'). In this terminology, the point just made can be restated as: a statement can be (metaphysically) necessary and epistemically contingent. Human intuition has no privileged access to metaphysical necessity.

Since Kant there has been a big split between philosophers who thought that all necessary truths were analytic and philosophers who thought that some necessary truths were synthetic a priori. But none of these philosophers thought that a (metaphysically) necessary truth could fail to be a priori: the Kantian tradition was as guilty as the empiricist tradition of equating metaphysical and epistemic necessity. In this sense Kripke's challenge to received doctrine goes far beyond the usual empiricism/Kantianism oscillation.

In this paper our interest is in theory of meaning, however, and not in theory of necessary truth. Points closely related to Kripke's have been made in terms of the notion of *indexicality*.[9] Words like 'now,' 'this,' 'here,' have long been recognized to be *indexical*, or *token-reflexive* – i.e., to have an extension which varied from context to context or token to token. For these words no one has ever suggested the traditional theory that 'intension determines extension.' To take our Twin Earth example: if I have a *Doppelgänger* on Twin Earth, then when I think 'I have a headache,' *he* thinks 'I have a headache.' But the extension of the particular token of 'I' in his verbalized thought is himself (or his unit class, to be precise), while the extension of the token of 'I' in *my* verbalized thought is *me* (or my unit class, to be precise). So the same word, 'I,' has two different extensions in two different idiolects; but it does not follow that the concept I have of myself is in any way different from the concept my *Doppelgänger* has of himself.

Now then, we have maintained that indexicality extends beyond the *obviously* indexical words and morphemes (e.g., the tenses of verbs). Our theory can be summarized as saying that words like 'water' have an unnoticed indexical component: 'water' is stuff that bears a certain similarity relation to the water *around here*. Water at another time or in another place or even in another possible world has to bear the relation same_L to *our* 'water' *in order to be water*. Thus the theory that (1) words have 'intensions,' which are something like concepts associated with the words by speakers; and (2) intension determines extension – this theory cannot be true of natural-kind words like 'water' for the same reason it cannot be true of obviously indexical words like 'I.'

The theory that natural-kind words like 'water' are indexical leaves it open, however, whether to say that 'water' in the Twin Earth dialect of English has the same *meaning* as 'water' in the Earth dialect and a different extension (which is what we normally say about 'I' in different idiolects), thereby giving up the doctrine that 'meaning (intension) determines extension'; or to say, as we have chosen to do, that difference in extension is *ipso facto* a difference in meaning for natural-kind words, thereby giving up the doctrine that meanings are concepts, or, indeed, mental entities of *any* kind.

It should be clear, however, that Kripke's doctrine that natural-kind words are rigid designators and our doctrine that they are indexical are but two ways of making the same point.

We heartily endorse what Kripke says when he writes:

> Let us suppose that we do fix the reference of a name by a description. Even if we do so, we do not then make the name synonymous with the description, but instead we use the name rigidly to refer to the object so named, even in talking about counterfactual situations where the thing named would not satisfy the description in question. Now, this is what I think is in fact true for those cases of naming where the reference is fixed by description. But, in fact, I also think, contrary to most recent theorists, that the reference of names is rarely or almost never fixed by means of description. And by this I do not just mean what Searle says: 'It's not a single description, but rather a cluster, a family of properties that fixes the reference.' I mean that properties in this sense are not used at all.[10]

Let's be realistic

I wish now to contrast my view with one which is popular, at least among students (it appears to arise spontaneously). For this discussion, let us take as our example of a natural-kind word the word *gold*. We will not distinguish between 'gold' and the cognate words in Greek, Latin, etc. And we will focus on 'gold' in the sense of gold in the solid state. With this understood, we maintain: 'gold' has not changed its *extension* (or not changed it significantly) in two thousand years. Our methods of *identifying* gold have grown incredibly sophisticated. But the extension of χρυσὸς in Archimedes' dialect of Greek is the same as the extension of *gold* in my dialect of English.

It is possible (and let us suppose it to be the case) that just as there were pieces of metal which could not have been determined *not* to be gold prior to Archimedes, so there were or are pieces of metal which could not have been determined *not* to be gold in Archimedes' day, but which we can distinguish from gold quite easily with modern techniques. Let *X* be such a piece of metal. Clearly *X* does not lie in the extension of 'gold' in standard English; my view is that it did not lie in the extension of χρυσὸς in Attic Greek, either, although an ancient Greek would have *mistaken X* for gold (or, rather, χρυσὸς).

The alternative view is that 'gold' *means* whatever satisfies the *contemporary* 'operational definition' of *gold*. 'Gold' a hundred years ago meant whatever satisfied the 'operational definition' of *gold* in use a hundred years ago; 'gold' now means whatever satisfies the operational definition of *gold* in use in 1973; and χρυσὸς meant whatever satisfied the operational definition of χρυσὸς in use *then*.

One common motive for adopting this point of view is a certain skepticism about *truth*. On the view I am advocating, when Archimedes asserted that something was gold (χρυσὸς) he was not just saying that it had the superficial characteristics of gold (in exceptional cases, something may belong to a natural kind and *not* have the superficial characteristics of a member of that natural kind, in fact); he was saying that it had the same general *hidden structure* (the same 'essence,' so to speak) as any normal piece of local gold. Archimedes would have said that our hypothetical piece of metal *X* was gold, but he would have been *wrong*. But *who's to say* he would have been wrong?

The obvious answer is: *we are* (using the best theory available today). For most people either the question (*who's to say?*) has bite, and our answer has no bite, or our answer has bite and the question has no bite. Why is this?

The reason, I believe, is that people tend either to be strongly anti-realistic or strongly realistic in their intuitions. To a strongly antirealistic intuition it makes little sense to say that what is in the extension of Archimedes' term χρυσὸς is to be determined using our theory. For the antirealist does not see our theory and Archimedes' theory as two approximately correct descriptions of some fixed realm of theory-independent entities, and he tends to be skeptical about the idea of 'convergence' in science – he does not think our theory is a *better* description of the *same* entities that Archimedes was describing. But if our theory is *just* our theory, then to use *it* in deciding whether or not *X* lies in the extension of χρυσὸς is just as arbitrary as using Neanderthal theory to decide whether or not *X* lies in the extension of χρυσὸς. The only theory that it is *not* arbitrary to use is the one the speaker himself subscribes to.

The trouble is that for a strong antirealist *truth* makes no sense except as an intra-theoretic notion.[11] The antirealist can use truth intra-theoretically in the sense of a 'redundancy theory'; but he does not have the notions of truth and reference available *extra-theoretically*. But *extension is tied to the notion of truth*. The extension of a term is just what the term is *true of*. Rather than try to retain the notion of extension via an awkward operationalism, the antirealist should reject the notion of extension as he does the notion of truth (in any extra-theoretic sense). Like Dewey, for example, he can fall back on a notion of 'warranted assertibility' instead of truth (relativized to the scientific method, if he thinks there is a *fixed* scientific method, or to the best methods available at the time, if he agrees with Dewey that the scientific method itself evolves). Then he can say that '*X* is gold (χρυσὸς)' was warrantedly assertible in Archimedes' time and is not warrantedly assertible today (indeed, this is a *minimal* claim, in the sense that it represents the minimum that the realist and the antirealist can agree on); but the assertion that *X* was in the extension of χρυσὸς will be rejected as meaningless, like the assertion that '*X* is gold (χρυσὸς)' was *true*.

It is well known that narrow operationalism cannot successfully account for the actual use of scientific or common-sense terms. Loosened versions of operationalism, like Carnap's version of Ramsey's theory, agree with if they do not account for actual scientific use (mainly because the loosened versions agree with any possible use!), but at the expense of making the communicability of scientific results a *miracle*. It is beyond question that scientists use terms as if the associated criteria were not *necessary and sufficient conditions*, but rather *approximately* correct characterizations of some world of theory-independent entities, and that they talk as if later theories in a mature science were, in general, *better* descriptions of the *same* entities that earlier theories referred to. In my opinion the hypothesis that this is *right* is the only hypothesis that can account for the communicability of scientific results, the closure of acceptable scientific theories under first-order logic, and many other features of the scientific method.[12] But it is not my task to argue this here. My point is that if we are to use the notions of truth and extension in an extra-theoretic way (i.e., to regard those notions as defined for statements couched in the languages of theories other than our own), then we should accept the realist perspective to which those notions belong. The doubt about whether *we* can say that *X* does not lie in the extension of 'gold' as *Jones* used it is the *same* doubt as the doubt whether it makes sense to think of Jones's statement that '*X* is gold' as *true or false* (and not just 'warrantedly assertible for Jones and not warrantedly assertible for us'). To square the notion of truth, which is essentially a realist notion, with one's antirealist prejudices by adopting an untenable theory of meaning is no progress.

A second motive for adopting an extreme operationalist account is a dislike of unverifiable hypotheses. At first blush it may seem as if we are saying that '*X* is gold (χρυσὸς)' was false in Archimedes' time although Archimedes could not *in principle* have known that it was false. But this is not exactly the situation. The fact is that there are a host of situations that *we* can describe (using the very theory that tells us that *X* isn't gold) in which *X* would have behaved quite unlike the rest of the stuff Archimedes classified as gold. Perhaps *X* would have separated into two different metals when melted, or would have had different conductivity properties, or would have vaporized at a different temperature, or whatever. If we had performed the experiments with Archimedes watching, he might not have known the theory, but he would have been able to check the empirical regularity that '*X* behaves differently from the rest of the stuff I classify as χρυσὸς in several respects.' Eventually he would have concluded that '*X* may not be gold.'

The point is that even if something satisfies the criteria used at a given time to identify gold (i.e., to recognize if something is gold), it may behave differently in one or more situations from the rest of the stuff that satisfies the criteria. This may not *prove* that it isn't gold, but it puts the hypothesis that it may not be gold in the running, even in the absence of theory. If, now, we had gone on to inform Archimedes that gold has such and such a molecular structure (except for *X*), and that *X* behaved differently because it had a different molecular structure, is there any doubt that he would have agreed with us that *X* isn't gold? In any case, to worry because things may be *true* (at a given time) that can't be *verified* (at that time) seems to me ridiculous. On any reasonable view there are surely things that are true and can't be verified at *any* time. For example, suppose there are infinitely many binary stars. *Must* we be able to verify this, even in *principle*?[13]

So far we have dealt with *metaphysical* reasons for rejecting our account. But someone might disagree with us about the empirical facts concerning the intentions of speakers. This would be the case if, for instance, someone thought that Archimedes (in the *Gedankenexperiment* described above) would have said: 'it doesn't matter if *X does* act differently from other pieces of gold; *X* is a piece of gold, because *X* has such-and-such properties and that's all it takes to be gold.' While, indeed, we cannot be certain that natural-kind words in ancient Greek had the properties of the corresponding words in present-day English, there cannot be any serious doubt concerning the properties of the latter. If we put philosophical prejudices aside, then I believe that we know perfectly well that no operational definition does provide a necessary and sufficient condition for the application of any such word. We may give an 'operational definition,' or a cluster of properties, or whatever, but the intention is never to 'make the name *synonymous* with the description.' Rather 'we use the name *rigidly*' to refer to whatever things share the *nature* that things satisfying the description normally possess.

Other Senses

What we have analyzed so far is the predominant sense of natural-kind words (or, rather, the predominant *extension*). But natural-kind words typically possess a number of senses. (Ziff has even suggested that they possess a *continuum* of senses.)

Part of this can be explained on the basis of our theory. To be water, for example, is to bear the relation $same_L$ to certain things. But what is the relation $same_L$?

x bears the relation $same_L$ to y just in case (1) x and y are both liquids, and (2) x and y agree in important *physical* properties. The term 'liquid' is itself a natural-kind term that I shall not try to analyze here. The term 'property' is a broad-spectrum term that we have analyzed in previous papers. What I want to focus on now is the notion of *importance*. Importance is an interest-relative notion. Normally the 'important' properties of a liquid or solid, etc., are the ones that are *structurally* important: the ones that specify what the liquid or solid, etc., is ultimately made out of – elementary particles, or hydrogen and oxygen, or earth, air, fire, water, or whatever – and how they are arranged or combined to produce the superficial characteristics. From this point of view the important characteristic of a typical bit of water is consisting of H_2O. But it may or may not be important that there are impurities; thus, in one context 'water' may mean *chemically pure water*, while in another it may mean the stuff in Lake Michigan. And structure may sometimes be unimportant; thus one may sometimes refer to XYZ as water if one is *using* it as water. Again, normally it is important that water is in the liquid state; but sometimes it is unimportant, and one may refer to a single H_2O molecule as water, or to water vapor as water ('water in the air').

Even senses that are so far out that they have to be regarded as a bit 'deviant' may bear a definite relation to the core sense. For example, I might say 'did you see the lemon,' meaning the *plastic* lemon. A less deviant case is this: we discover 'tigers' on Mars. That is, they look just like tigers, but they have a silicon-based chemistry instead of a carbon-based chemistry. (A remarkable example of parallel evolution!) Are Martian 'tigers' tigers? It depends on the context.

In the case of this theory, as in the case of any theory that is orthogonal to the way people have thought about something previously, misunderstandings are certain to arise. One which has already arisen is the following: a critic has maintained that the *predominant* sense of, say, 'lemon' is the one in which anything with (a sufficient number of) the superficial characteristics of a lemon is a lemon. The same critic has suggested that having the hidden structure – the genetic code – of a lemon is necessary to being a lemon only when 'lemon' is used as a term of *science.* Both of these contentions seem to me to rest on a misunderstanding, or, perhaps, a pair of complementary misunderstandings.

The sense in which literally *anything* with the superficial characteristics of a lemon is necessarily a lemon, far from being the dominant one, is extremely deviant. In that sense something would be a lemon if it looked and tasted like a lemon, even if it had a silicon-based chemistry, for example, or even if an electron-microscope revealed it to be a *machine.* (Even if we include growing 'like a lemon' in the superficial characteristics, this does not exclude the silicon lemon, if there are 'lemon' trees on Mars. It doesn't even exclude the machine-lemon; maybe the tree is a machine too!)

At the same time the sense in which to be a lemon something has to have the genetic code of a lemon is *not* the same as the technical sense (if there is one, which I doubt). The technical sense, I take it, would be one in which 'lemon' was *synonymous* with a description which *specified* the genetic code. But when we said (to change the example) that to be *water* something has to be H_2O we did not mean, as we made clear, that the *speaker* has to *know* this. It is only by confusing *metaphysical* necessity with *epistemological* necessity that one can conclude that, if the (metaphysically necessary) truth-condition for being water is being H_2O, then 'water' must be synonymous with H_2O – in which case it is certainly a term of science. And similarly, even though the predominant sense of 'lemon' is one in which to be a lemon something has to have the genetic code of a lemon (I believe), it does not follow that 'lemon' is synonymous with a description which specifies the genetic code explicitly or otherwise.

The mistake of thinking that there is an important sense of 'lemon' (perhaps the predominant one) in which to have the superficial characteristics of a lemon is at least *sufficient* for being a lemon is more plausible if among the superficial characteristics one includes *being cross-fertile with lemons.* But the characteristic of being cross-fertile with lemons presupposes the notion of being a lemon. Thus, even if one can obtain a sufficient condition in *this* way, to take this as inconsistent with the characterization offered here is question-begging. Moreover, the characterization in terms of *lemon*-presupposing 'superficial characteristics' (like being cross-fertile with *lemons*) gives no truth-condition which would enable us to decide which objects in other possible worlds (or which objects a million years ago, or which objects a million light years from here) are lemons. (In addition, I don't think this characterization, question-begging as it is, is correct, even as a sufficient condition. I think one could invent cases in which something which was not a lemon was cross-fertile with lemons and looked like a lemon, etc.)

Again, one might try to rule out the case of the machine-lemon (lemon-machine?) which 'grows' on a machine-tree (tree-machine?) by saying that 'growing' is not really *growing.* That is right; but it's right because *grow* is a natural-kind *verb*, and precisely the sort of account we have been presenting applies to *it*.

Another misunderstanding that should be avoided is the following: to take the account we have developed as implying that the members of the extension of a natural-kind word necessarily *have* a common hidden structure. It could have turned out that the bits of liquid we call 'water' had *no* important common physical characteristics *except* the superficial ones. In that case the necessary and sufficient condition for being 'water' would have been possession of sufficiently many of the superficial characteristics.

Incidentally, the last statement does not imply that water could have failed to have a hidden structure (or that water could have been anything but H_2O). When we say that it could have *turned out* that water had no hidden structure, what we mean is that a liquid with no hidden structure (i.e., many bits of different liquids, with nothing in common *except* superficial characteristics) could have looked like water, tasted like water, and have filled the lakes, etc., that are actually full of water. In short, we could have been in the same epistemological situation with respect to a liquid with no hidden structure as we were actually with respect to water at one time. Compare Kripke on the 'lectern made of ice.'[14]

There are, in fact, almost continuously many cases. Some diseases, for example, have turned out to have no hidden structure (the only thing the paradigm cases have in common is a cluster of symptoms), while others have turned out to have a common hidden structure in the sense of an etiology (e.g., tuberculosis). Sometimes we still don't know; there is a controversy still raging about the case of multiple sclerosis.

An interesting case is the case of *jade*. Although the Chinese do not recognize a difference, the term 'jade' applies to two minerals: jadeite and nephrite. Chemically, there is a marked difference. Jadeite is a combination of sodium and aluminum. Nephrite is made of calcium, magnesium, and iron. These two quite different microstructures produce the same unique textural qualities!

Coming back to the Twin Earth example, for a moment, if H_2O and XYZ had both been plentiful on Earth, then we would have had a case similar to the jadeite/nephrite case: it would have been correct to say that there were *two kinds of 'water*.' And instead of saying that 'the stuff on Twin Earth turned out not to really be water,' we would have to say 'it turned out to be the XYZ *kind of water*.'

To sum up: if there is a hidden structure, then generally it determines what it is to be a member of the natural kind, not only in the actual world, but in all possible worlds. Put another way, it determines what we can and cannot counterfactually suppose about the natural kind ('water could have all been vapor?' yes/'water could have been XYZ?' no). But the local water, or whatever, may have two or more hidden structures – or so many that 'hidden structure' becomes irrelevant, and superficial characteristics become the decisive ones.

Other Words

So far we have only used natural-kind words as examples, but the points we have made apply to many other kinds of words as well. They apply to the great majority of all nouns, and to other parts of speech as well.

Let us consider for a moment the names of artifacts – words like 'pencil,' 'chair,' 'bottle,' etc. The traditional view is that these words are certainly defined by conjunctions, or possibly clusters, of properties. Anything with all of the properties in the conjunction (or sufficiently many of the properties in the cluster, on the cluster model) is necessarily a *pencil, chair, bottle*, or whatever. In addition, some of the properties in the cluster (on the cluster model) are usually held to be *necessary* (on the conjunction-of-properties model, *all* of the properties in the conjunction are necessary). *Being an artifact* is supposedly necessary, and belonging to a kind with a certain standard purpose – e.g., 'pencils are artifacts,' and 'pencils are standardly intended to be written with' are supposed to be necessary. Finally, this sort of necessity is held to be *epistemic* necessity – in fact, analyticity.

Let us once again engage in science fiction. This time we use an example devised by Rogers Albritton. Imagine that we someday discover that *pencils are organisms*. We cut them open and examine them under the electron microscope, and we see the almost invisible tracery of nerves and other organs. We spy upon them, and we see them spawn, and we see the offspring grow into full-grown pencils. We discover that these organisms are not imitating other (artifactual) pencils – there are not and never were any pencils except these organisms. It is strange, to be sure, that there is *lettering* on many of these organisms – e.g., BONDED *Grants* DELUXE made in U.S.A. No. 2 – perhaps they are intelligent organisms, and this is their form of camouflage. (We also have to explain why no one ever attempted to manufacture pencils, etc., but this is clearly a possible world, in some sense).

If this is conceivable, and I agree with Albritton that it is, then it is epistemically possible that *pencils could turn out to be organisms*. It follows that *pencils are artifacts* is not epistemically necessary in the strongest sense and, a fortiori, not analytic.

Let us be careful, however. Have we shown that there is a possible world in which pencils are organisms? I think not. What we have shown is that there is a possible world in which certain organisms are the *epistemic counterparts* of pencils (the phrase is Kripke's). To return to the device of Twin Earth: imagine this time that pencils on Earth are just what we think they are, artifacts manufactured to be written with, while 'pencils' on Twin Earth are organisms a la Albritton. Imagine, further, that this is totally unsuspected by the Twin Earthians – they have exactly the beliefs about 'pencils' that we have about pencils. When we discovered this, we would not say: 'some pencils are organisms.' We would be far more likely to say: 'the things on Twin Earth that pass for pencils aren't really pencils. They're really a species of organism.'

Suppose now the situation to be as in Albritton's example both on Earth and on Twin Earth. Then we would say 'pencils are organisms.' Thus, whether the 'pencil-organisms' on Twin Earth (or in another possible universe) are really *pencils* or not is a function of whether or not the *local* pencils are organisms or not. If the local pencils are just what we think they are, then a possible world in which there are pencil-organisms is *not* a possible world in which *pencils are organisms*; there are *no* possible worlds in which pencils are organisms in this case (which is, of course, the actual one). That pencils are artifacts *is* necessary in the sense of true in all possible worlds – metaphysically necessary. But it doesn't follow that it's epistemically necessary.

It follows that 'pencil' is not *synonymous* with any description – not even loosely synonymous with a *loose* description. When we use the word 'pencil,' we intend to refer to whatever has the same *nature* as the normal examples of the local pencils in the actual world. 'Pencil' is just as *indexical* as 'water' or 'gold.'

In a way, the case of pencils turning out to be organisms is complementary to the case we discussed some years ago[15] of cats turning out to be robots (remotely controlled from Mars). In his contribution to the present volume [see Gunderson (1975)], Katz argues that we misdescribed this case: that the case should rather be described as its *turning out that there are no cats in this world*. Katz admits that we might *say* 'Cats have turned out not to be animals, but robots'; but he argues that this is a semantically deviant sentence which is glossed as 'the things I am referring to as "cats" have turned out not to be animals, but robots.' Katz's theory is bad linguistics, however. First of all, the explanation of how it is we can say 'Cats are robots' is simply an all-purpose explanation of how we can say *anything*. More important, Katz's theory predicts that 'Cats are robots' is *deviant*, while 'There are no cats in the world' is non-deviant, in fact standard, in the case described. Now then, I don't deny that there *is* a case in which 'There are not (and never were) any cats in the world' would be standard: we might (speaking epistemically) discover that we have been suffering from a collective hallucination. ('Cats' are like pink elephants.) But in the case I described, 'Cats have turned out to be robots remotely controlled from Mars' is surely nondeviant, and 'There are no cats in the world' is highly deviant.

Incidentally, Katz's account is not only bad linguistics; it is also bad as a rational reconstruction. The reason we *don't* use 'cat' as synonymous with a description is surely that we know enough about cats to know that they do have a hidden structure, and it is good scientific methodology to use the name to refer rigidly to the things that possess that hidden structure, and not to whatever happens to satisfy some description. Of course, if we *knew* the hidden structure we could frame a description in terms of *it*; but we don't at this point. In this sense the use of natural-kind words reflects an important fact about our relation to the world: we know that there are kinds of things with common hidden structure, but we don't yet have the knowledge to describe all those hidden structures.

Katz's view has more plausibility in the 'pencil' case than in the 'cat' case, however. We think we *know* a necessary and sufficient condition for being a *pencil*, albeit a vague one. So it is possible to make 'pencil' synonymous with a loose description. We *might say*, in the case that 'pencils turned out to be organisms' *either* 'Pencils have turned out to be organisms' or 'There are no pencils in the world' – i.e., we might use 'pencil' either as a natural-kind word or as a 'one-criterion' word.[16]

On the other hand, we might doubt that there *are* any true one-criterion words in natural language, apart from stipulative contexts. Couldn't it turn out that pediatricians aren't doctors but Martian spies? Answer 'yes,' and you have abandoned the synonymy of 'pediatrician' and 'doctor specializing in the care of children.' It seems that there is a strong tendency for words which are introduced as 'one-criterion' words to develop a 'natural kind' sense, with all the concomitant rigidity and indexicality. In the case of artifact-names, this natural-kind sense seems to be the predominant one.

(There is a joke about a patient who is on the verge of being discharged from an insane asylum. The doctors have been questioning him for some time, and he has been giving perfectly sane responses. They decide to let him leave, and at the end of the interview one of the doctors inquires casually, 'What do you want to be when you get out?' 'A teakettle.' The joke would not be intelligible if it were literally inconceivable that a person could be a teakettle.)

There are, however, words which retain an almost pure one-criterion character. These are words whose meaning derives from a transformation: *hunter = one who hunts*.

Not only does the account given here apply to most nouns, but it also applies to other parts of speech. Verbs like 'grow,' adjectives like 'red,' etc., all have indexical features. On the other hand, some syncategorematic words seem to have more of a one-criterion character. 'Whole,' for example, can be explained thus: *The army surrounded the town* could be true even if the A division did not take part. *The whole army surrounded the town* means every part of the army (of the relevant kind, e.g., the A Division) took part in the action signified by the verb.[17]

Meaning

Let us now see where we are with respect to the notion of meaning. We have now seen that the extension of a term is not fixed by a concept that the individual speaker has in his head, and this is true both because extension is, in general, determined *socially* – there is division of linguistic labor as much as of 'real' labor – and because extension is, in part, determined *indexically*.

The extension of our terms depends upon the actual nature of the particular things that serve as paradigms,[18] and this actual nature is not, in general, fully known to the speaker. Traditional semantic theory leaves out only two contributions to the determination of extension – the contribution of society and the contribution of the real world!

We saw at the outset that meaning cannot be identified with extension. Yet it cannot be identified with 'intension' either, if intension is something like an individual speaker's *concept*. What are we to do?

There are two plausible routes that we might take. One route would be to retain the identification of meaning with concept and pay the price of giving up the idea that meaning determines extension. If we followed this route, we might say that 'water' has the same *meaning* on Earth and on Twin Earth, but a different *extension*. (Not just a different *local* extension but a different *global* extension. The XYZ on Twin Earth isn't in the extension of the tokens of 'water' that I utter, but it is in the extension of the tokens of 'water' that my *Doppelgänger* utters, and this isn't just because Twin Earth is far away from me, since molecules of H_2O are in the extension of the tokens of 'water' that I utter no matter how far away from me they are in space and time. Also, what I can counterfactually suppose water to be is different from what my *Doppelgänger* can counterfactually suppose 'water' to be.) While this is the correct route to take for an *absolutely* indexical word like 'I,' it seems incorrect for the words we have been discussing. Consider 'elm' and 'beech,' for example. If these are 'switched' on Twin Earth, then surely we would *not* say that 'elm' has the same meaning on Earth and Twin Earth, even if my *Doppelgänger's* stereotype of a beech (or an 'elm,' as he calls it) is identical with my stereotype of an elm. Rather, we would say that 'elm' in my *Doppelgänger's* idiolect means *beech*. For this reason, it seems preferable to take a different route and identify 'meaning' with an ordered pair (or possibly an ordered *n-tuple*) of entities, *one of which is the extension*. (The other components of the, so to speak, 'meaning vector' will be specified later.) Doing this makes it trivially true that *meaning determines extension* (i.e., difference in extension is ipso facto difference in meaning), but totally abandons the idea that if there is a difference in the meaning my *Doppelgänger* and I assign to a word, then there *must* be some difference in our concepts (or in our psychological state). Following this route, we can say that my *Doppelgänger* and I *mean something different* when we say 'elm,' but this will not be an assertion about our psychological states. All this means is that the tokens of the word he utters have a different extension than the tokens of the word I utter; but this difference in extension is not a reflection of any difference in our individual linguistic competence considered in isolation.

If this is correct, and I think it is, then the traditional problem of meaning splits into two problems. The first problem is to account for the *determination of extension*. Since, in many cases, extension is determined socially and not individually, owing to the division of linguistic labor, I believe that this problem is properly a problem for sociolinguistics. Solving it would involve spelling out in detail exactly how the division of linguistic labor works. The so-called 'causal theory of reference,' introduced by Kripke for proper names and extended by us to natural-kind words and physical-magnitude terms,[19] falls into this province. For the fact that, in many contexts, we assign to the tokens of a name that I utter whatever referent we assign to the tokens of the same name uttered by the person from whom I acquired the name (so that the reference is transmitted from speaker to speaker, starting from the speakers who were present at the 'naming ceremony,' even though no fixed *description* is transmitted) is simply a special case of social cooperation in the determination of reference.

The other problem is to describe *individual competence.* Extension may be determined socially, in many cases, but we don't assign the standard extension to the tokens of a word *W* uttered by Jones *no matter how* Jones uses *W*. Jones has to have some particular ideas and skills in connection with *W* in order to play his part in the linguistic division of labor. Once we give up the idea that individual competence has to be so strong as to actually determine extension, we can begin to study it in a fresh frame of mind.

In this connection it is instructive to observe that nouns like 'tiger' or 'water' are very different from proper names. One can use the proper name 'Sanders' correctly without knowing anything about the referent except that he is called 'Sanders' – and even that may not be correct. ('Once upon a time, a very long time ago now, about last Friday, Winnie-the-Pooh lived in a forest all by himself under the name of Sanders.') But one cannot use the word tiger correctly, save *per accidens*, without knowing a good deal about tigers, or at least about a certain conception of tigers. In this sense concepts *do* have a lot to do with meaning.

Just as the study of the first problem is properly a topic in sociolinguistics, so the study of the second problem is properly a topic in psycholinguistics. To this topic we now turn.

Stereotypes and Communication

Suppose a speaker knows that 'tiger' has a set of physical objects as its extension, but no more. If he possesses normal linguistic competence in other respects, then he could use 'tiger' in *some* sentences: for example, 'tigers have mass,' 'tigers take up space,' 'give me a tiger,' 'is that a tiger?' etc. Moreover, the *socially determined* extension of 'tiger' in these sentences would be the standard one, i.e., the set of tigers. Yet we would not count such a speaker as 'knowing the meaning' of the word *tiger*. Why not?

Before attempting to answer this question, let us reformulate it a bit. We shall speak of someone as having *acquired* the word 'tiger' if he is able to use it in such a way that (1) his use passes muster (i.e., people don't say of him such things as 'he doesn't know what a tiger *is*,' 'he doesn't know the meaning of the word "tiger," ' etc.); and (2) his total way of being situated in the world and in his linguistic community is such that the socially determined extension of the word 'tiger' in his idiolect is the set of tigers. Clause (1) means, roughly, that speakers like the one hypothesized in the preceding paragraph don't count as having acquired the word 'tiger' (or whichever). We might speak of them, in some cases, as having *partially acquired* the word; but let us defer this for the moment. Clause (2) means that speakers on Twin Earth who have the same linguistic habits as we do, count as having acquired the word 'tiger' only if the extension of 'tiger' in their idiolect is the set of tigers. The burden of the preceding sections of this paper is that it does *not* follow that the extension of 'tiger' in Twin Earth dialect (or idiolects) is the set of tigers merely because their linguistic habits are the same as ours; the nature of Twin Earth 'tigers' is also relevant. (If Twin Earth organisms have a silicon chemistry, for example, then their 'tigers' aren't really tigers, even if they look like tigers, although the linguistic habits of the lay Twin Earth speaker exactly correspond to those of Earth speakers.) Thus clause (2) means that in this case we have decided to say that Twin Earth speakers have not acquired our word 'tiger' (although they have acquired another word with the same spelling and pronunciation).

Our reason for introducing this way of speaking is that the question 'does he know the meaning of the word "tiger"?' is biased in favor of the theory that acquiring a word is coming to possess a thing called its 'meaning.' Identify this thing with a concept, and we are back at the theory that a sufficient condition for acquiring a word is associating it with the right concept (or, more generally, being in the right psychological state with respect to it) – the very theory we have spent all this time refuting. So, henceforth, we will 'acquire' words, rather than 'learn their meaning.'

We can now reformulate the question with which this section began. The use of the speaker we described does not pass muster, although it is not such as to cause us to assign a nonstandard extension to the word 'tiger' in his idiolect. Why doesn't it pass muster?

Suppose our hypothetical speaker points to a snowball and asks, 'is that a tiger?' Clearly there isn't much point in talking tigers with *him*. Significant communication requires that people know something of what they are talking about. To be sure, we hear people 'communicating' every day who clearly know nothing of what they are talking about; but the sense in which the man who points to a snowball and asks 'is that a tiger' doesn't know anything about tigers is so far beyond the sense in which the man who thinks that Vancouver is going to win the Stanley Cup, or that the Vietnam War was fought to help the South Vietnamese, doesn't know what he is talking about as to boggle the mind. The problem of people who think that Vancouver is going to win the Stanley Cup, or that the Vietnam War was fought to help the South Vietnamese, is one that obviously cannot be remedied by the adoption of linguistic conventions; but not knowing what one is talking about in the second, mind-boggling sense can be and is prevented, near enough, by our conventions of language. What I contend is that speakers are *required* to know something about (stereotypical) tigers in order to count as having acquired the word 'tiger'; something about elm trees (or, anyway, about the stereotype thereof) to count as having acquired the word 'elm'; etc.

This idea should not seem too surprising. After all, we do not permit people to drive on the highways without first passing some tests to determine that they have a *minimum* level of competence; and we do not dine with people who have not learned to use a knife and fork. The linguistic community too has its minimum standards, with respect both to syntax and to 'semantics.'

The nature of the required minimum level of competence depends heavily upon both the culture and the topic, however. In our culture speakers are required to know what tigers look like (if they acquire the word 'tiger,' and this is virtually obligatory); they are not required to know the fine details (such as leaf shape) of what an elm tree looks like. English speakers are *required by their linguistic community* to be able to tell tigers from leopards; they are not required to be able to tell elm trees from beech trees.

This could easily have been different. Imagine an Indian tribe, call it the Cheroquoi, who have words, say *uhaba'* and *wa'arabi* for elm trees and beech trees respectively, and who make it *obligatory* to know the difference. A Cheroquoi who could not recognize an elm would be said not to know what an uhaba' is, not to know the meaning of the word 'uhaba' ' (perhaps, not to know the word, or not to *have* the word), just as an English speaker who had no idea that tigers are striped would be said not to know what a tiger is, not to know the meaning of the word 'tiger' (of course, if he at least knows that tigers are large felines we might say he knows part of the meaning, or partially knows the meaning), etc. Then the translation of 'uhaba' ' as 'elm' and 'wa'-arabi' as 'beech' would, on our view, be only *approximately* correct. In this sense there is a real difficulty with radical translation,[20] but this is not the abstract difficulty that Quine is talking about.[21]

What Stereotypes Are

I introduced the notion of a 'stereotype' in my lectures at the University of Washington and at the Minnesota Center for the Philosophy of Science in 1968. I will not review all the argumentation from the subsequently published 'Is Semantics Possible' in the present essay, but I do want to introduce the notion again and to answer some questions that have been asked about it.

In ordinary parlance a 'stereotype' is a conventional (frequently malicious) idea (which may be wildly inaccurate) of what an *X* looks like or acts like or is. Obviously I am trading on some features of the ordinary parlance. I am not concerned with malicious stereotypes (save where the language itself is malicious); but I am concerned with conventional ideas, which may be inaccurate. I am suggesting that just such a conventional idea is associated with 'tiger,' with 'gold,' etc., and, moreover, that this is the sole element of truth in the 'concept' theory.

On this view someone who knows what 'tiger' means (or, as we have decided to say instead, has acquired the word 'tiger') is *required* to know that *stereotypical* tigers are striped. More precisely, there is *one* stereotype of tigers (he may have others) which is required by the linguistic community as such; he is required to have this stereotype, and to know (implicitly) that it is obligatory. This stereotype must include the feature of stripes if his acquisition is to count as successful.

The fact that a feature (e.g. stripes) is included in the stereotype associated with a word *X* does not mean that it is an analytic truth that all *X*s have that feature, nor that most *X*s have that feature, nor that all normal *X*s have that feature, nor that some *X*s have that feature.[22] Three-legged tigers and albino tigers are not logically contradictory entities. Discovering that our stereotype has been based on nonnormal or unrepresentative members of a natural kind is not discovering a logical contradiction. If tigers lost their stripes they would not thereby cease to be tigers, nor would butterflies necessarily cease to be butterflies if they lost their wings.

(Strictly speaking, the situation is more complicated than this. It is possible to give a word like 'butterfly' a sense in which butterflies would cease to be butterflies if they lost their wings – through mutation, say. Thus one can find a sense of 'butterfly' in which it is analytic that 'butterflies have wings.' But the most important sense of the term, I believe, is the one in which the wingless butterflies would still be butterflies.)

At this point the reader may wonder what the value to the linguistic community of having stereotypes is, if the 'information' contained in the stereotype is not necessarily correct. But this is not really such a mystery. Most stereotypes do in fact capture features possessed by paradigmatic members of the class in question. Even where stereotypes go wrong, the way in which they go wrong sheds light on the contribution normally made by stereotypes to communication. The stereotype of gold, for example, contains the feature *yellow* even though chemically pure gold is nearly white. But the gold we see in jewelry is typically yellow (due to the presence of copper), so the presence of this feature in the stereotype is even useful in lay contexts. The stereotype associated with *witch* is more seriously wrong, at least if taken with existential import. Believing (with existential import) that witches enter into pacts with Satan, that they cause sickness and death, etc., facilitates communication only in the sense of facilitating communication internal to witch-theory. It does not facilitate communication in any situation in which what is needed is more agreement with the world than agreement with the theory of other speakers. (Strictly speaking, I am speaking of the stereotype as it existed in New England three hundred years ago; today that witches aren't *real* is itself part of the stereotype, and the baneful effects of witch-theory are thereby neutralized.) But the fact that our language has *some* stereotypes which impede rather than facilitate our dealings with the world and each other only points to the fact that we aren't infallible beings, and how could we be? The fact is that we could hardly communicate successfully if most of our stereotypes weren't pretty accurate as far as they go.

The 'Operational Meaning' of Stereotypes

A trickier question is this: how far is the notion of stereotype 'operationally definable'? Here it is necessary to be extremely careful. Attempts in the physical sciences to *literally* specify operational definitions for terms have notoriously failed; and there is no reason the attempt should succeed in linguistics when it failed in physics. Sometimes Quine's arguments against the possibility of a theory of meaning seem to reduce to the demand for operational definitions in linguistics; when this is the case the arguments should be ignored. But it frequently happens that terms do have operational definitions not in the actual world but in idealized circumstances. Giving these 'operational definitions' has heuristic value, as idealization frequently does. It is only when we mistake operational definition for more than convenient idealization that it becomes harmful. Thus we may ask what is the 'operational meaning' of the statement that a word has such and such a stereotype, without supposing that the answer to this question counts as a theoretical account of what it is to be a stereotype.

The theoretical account of what it is to be a stereotype proceeds in terms of the notion of *linguistic obligation*; a notion which we believe to be fundamental to linguistics and which we shall not attempt to explicate here. What it means to say that being striped is part of the (linguistic) stereotype of 'tiger' is that it is '*obligatory*' to acquire the information that stereotypical tigers are striped if one acquires the word 'tiger', in the same sense of 'obligatory' as that it is obligatory to indicate whether one is speaking of lions in the singular or lions in the plural when one speaks of lions in English. To describe an idealized experimental test of this hypothesis is not difficult. Let us introduce a person whom we may call the linguist's *confederate*. The confederate will be (or pretend to be) an adult whose command of English is generally excellent, but who for some reason (raised in an alien culture? brought up in a monastery?) has totally failed to acquire the word 'tiger.' The confederate will say the word 'tiger' or, better yet, point to it (as if he wasn't sure how to pronounce it), and ask 'what does this word mean?' or 'what is this?' or some such question. Ignoring all the things that go wrong with experiments in practice, what our hypothesis implies is that informants should typically tell the confederate that tigers are, inter alia, striped.

Instead of relying on confederates, one might expect the linguist to study children learning English. But children learning their native language aren't taught it nearly as much as philosophers suppose; they learn it but they aren't taught it, as Chomsky has emphasized. Still, children do sometimes ask such questions as 'what is a tiger?' and our hypothesis implies that in these cases too informants should tell them, inter alia, that tigers are striped. But one problem is that the informants are likely to be parents, and there are the vagaries of parental time, temper, and attention to be allowed for.

It would be easy to specify a large number of additional 'operational' implications of our hypothesis, but to do so would have no particular value. The fact is that we are fully competent speakers of English ourselves, with a devil of a good sense of what our linguistic obligations are. Pretending that we are in the position of Martians with respect to English is not the route to methodological clarity; it was, after all, only when the operational approach was abandoned that transformational linguistics blossomed into a handsome science.

Thus if anyone were to ask me for the meaning of 'tiger,' I know perfectly well what I would tell him. I would tell him that tigers were feline, something about their size, that they are yellow with black stripes, that they (sometimes) live in the jungle, and are fierce. Other things I might tell him too, depending on the context and his reason for asking; but the above items, save possibly for the bit about the jungle, I would regard it as *obligatory* to convey. I don't have to experiment to know that this is what I regard it as obligatory to convey, and I am sure that approximately this is what other speakers regard it as obligatory to convey too. Of course, there is some variation from idiolect to idiolect; the feature of having stripes (apart from figure-ground relations, e.g., are they black stripes on a yellow ground, which is the way I see them, or yellow stripes on a black ground?) would be found in all normal idiolects, but some speakers might regard the information that tigers (stereotypically) inhabit jungles as obligatory, while others might not. Alternatively, some features of the stereotype (big-cat-hood, stripes) might be regarded as obligatory, and others as *optional*, on the model of certain syntactical features. But we shall not pursue this possibility here.

Quine's 'Two Dogmas' Revisited

In 'Two Dogmas of Empiricism' Quine launched a powerful and salutory attack on the currently fashionable analytic-synthetic distinction. The distinction had grown to be a veritable philosophical man-eater: analytic *equaling* necessary *equaling* unrevisable in principle *equaling* whatever truth the individual philosopher wished to explain away. But Quine's attack itself went too far in certain respects; some limited class of analytic sentences can be saved, we feel.[23] More importantly, the attack was later construed, both by Quine himself and by others, as implicating the whole notion of meaning in the downfall of the analytic-synthetic distinction. While we have made it clear that we agree that the traditional notion of meaning has serious troubles, our project in this paper is constructive, not destructive. We come to revise the notion of meaning, not to bury it. So it will be useful to see how Quine's arguments fare against our revision.

Quine's arguments against the notion of analyticity can basically be reduced to the following: that no behavioral significance can be attached to the notion. His argument (again simplifying somewhat) was that there are, basically, only two candidates for a behavioral index of analyticity, and both are totally unsatisfactory, although for different reasons. The first behavioral index is *centrality*: many contemporary philosophers call a sentence analytic if, in effect, some community (say, Oxford dons) holds it immune from revision. But, Quine persuasively argues, maximum immunity from revision is no exclusive prerogative of analytic sentences. Sentences expressing fundamental laws of physics (e.g. the conservation of energy) may well enjoy maximum behavioral immunity from revision, although it would hardly be customary or plausible to classify them as analytic. Quine does not, however, rely on the mere implausibility of classifying all statements that we are highly reluctant to give up as analytic; he points out that 'immunity from revision' is, in the actual history of science, a *matter of degree*. There is no such thing, in the actual practice of rational science, as *absolute* immunity from revision. Thus to identify analyticity with immunity from revision would alter the notion in two fundamental ways: analyticity would become a matter of degree, and there would be no such thing as an absolutely analytic sentence. This would be such a departure from the classical Carnap-Ayer-et al. notion of analyticity that Quine feels that if *this* is what we mean to talk about, then it would be less misleading to introduce a different term altogether, say, *centrality*.

The second behavioral index is *being called 'analytic.'* In effect, some philosophers take the hallmark of analyticity to be that trained informants (say, Oxford dons) *call* the sentence analytic. Variants of this index are: that the sentence be deducible from the sentences in a finite list at the top of which someone who bears the ancestral of the graduate-student relation to Carnap has printed the words 'Meaning Postulate'; that the sentence be obtainable from a theorem of logic by substituting synonyms for synonyms. The last of these variants looks promising, but Quine launches against it the question, 'what is the criterion of synonymy?' One possible criterion might be that words W_1 and W_2 are synonymous if and only if the biconditional (x) (x is in the extension of $W_1 \equiv x$ is in the extension of W_2) is *analytic*; but this leads us right back in a circle. Another might be that words W_1 and W_2 are synonymous if and only if trained informants *call* them synonymous; but this is just our second index in a slightly revised form. A promising line is that words W_1 and W_2 are synonymous if and only if W_1 and W_2 are interchangeable (i.e., the words can be switched) *salva veritate* in all contexts of a suitable class. But Quine convincingly shows that this proposal too leads us around in a circle. Thus the second index reduces to this: a sentence is analytic if either it or some expression, or sequence of ordered pairs of expressions, or set of expressions, related to the sentence in certain specified ways, lies in a class to all the members of which trained informants apply a certain *noise*: either the *noise* ANALYTIC, or the *noise* MEANING POSTULATE, or the *noise* SYNONYMOUS. Ultimately, this proposal leaves 'analytic,' etc., *unexplicated noises*.

Although Quine does not discuss this explicitly, it is clear that taking the intersection of the two unsatisfactory behavioral indexes would be no more satisfactory; explicating the analyticity of a sentence as consisting in centrality *plus* being called ANALYTIC is just saying that the analytic sentences are a subclass of the central sentences without in any way telling us wherein the exceptionality of the subclass consists. In effect, Quine's conclusion is that analyticity is either centrality misconceived or it is nothing.

In spite of Quine's forceful argument, many philosophers have gone on abusing the notion of analyticity, often confusing it with a supposed highest degree of centrality. Confronted with Quine's alternatives, they have elected to identify analyticity with centrality, and to pay the price – the price of classifying such obviously synthetic-looking sentences as 'space has three dimensions' as analytic, and the price of undertaking to maintain the view that there is, after all, such a thing as absolute unrevisability in science in spite of the impressive evidence to the contrary. But this line can be blasted by coupling Quine's argument with an important argument of Reichenbach's.

In his book *The Theory of Relativity and A Priori Knowledge*, Reichenbach showed that there exists a *set* of principles (see p. 31) each of which Kant would have regarded as synthetic a priori, but whose conjunction is incompatible with the principles of special relativity and general covariance. (These include normal induction, the continuity of space, and the euclidean character of space.) A Kantian can consistently hold on to euclidean geometry come what may; but then experience may force him to give up normal induction or the continuity of space. Or he may hold on to normal induction and the continuity of space come what may; but then experience may force him to give up euclidean geometry (this happens in the case that physical space is not even homeomorphic to any euclidean space). In his article in *Albert Einstein, Philosopher-Scientist*, Reichenbach gives essentially the same argument in a slightly different form.

Applied to our present context, what this shows is that there are principles such that philosophers fond of the overblown notion of analyticity, and in particular philosophers who identify analyticity with (maximum) unrevisability, would classify them as analytic, but whose conjunction has testable empirical consequences. Thus either the identification of analyticity with centrality must be given up once and for all, or one must give up the idea that analyticity is closed under conjunction, or one must swallow the unhappy consequence that an analytic sentence can have testable empirical consequences (and hence that an *analytic* sentence might turn out to be *empirically false*).

It is no accident, by the way, that the sentences that Kant would have classified as synthetic a priori would be classified by these latter-day empiricists as analytic; their purpose in bloating the notion of analyticity was precisely to dissolve Kant's problem by identifying a prioricity with analyticity and then identifying analyticity in turn with truth by convention. (This last step has also been devastatingly criticized by Quine, but discussion of it would take us away from our topic.)

Other philosophers have tried to answer Quine by distinguishing between *sentences* and *statements*: all *sentences* are revisable, they agree, but some *statements* are not. Revising a sentence is not changing our mind about the statement formerly expressed by that sentence just in case the sentence (meaning the syntactical object together with its meaning) after the revision is, in fact, not synonymous with the sentence prior to the revision, i.e., just in case the revision is a case of meaning change and not change of theory. But (1) this reduces at once to the proposal to explicate analyticity in terms of synonymy; and (2) if there is one thing that Quine has decisively contributed to philosophy, it is the realization that meaning change and theory change cannot be sharply separated. We do not agree with Quine that meaning change cannot be defined at all, but it does not follow that the dichotomy 'meaning change *or* theory change' is tenable. Discovering that we live in a non-euclidean world *might* change the meaning of 'straight line' (this would happen in the – somewhat unlikely – event that something like the parallels postulate was part of the stereotype of straightness); but it would not be a *mere* change of meaning. In particular it would not be a change of *extension*: thus it would not be right to say that the parallels postulate was 'true in the former sense of the words.' From the fact that giving up a sentence *S* would involve meaning change, it does not follow that *S* is *true*. Meanings may not fit the world; and meaning change can be forced by empirical discoveries.

Although we are not, in this paper, trying to explicate a notion of analyticity, we are trying to explicate a notion that might seem closely related, the notion of meaning. Thus it might seem that Quine's arguments would also go against our attempt. Let us check this out.

On our view there is a perfectly good sense in which being striped is part of the meaning of 'tiger.' But it does not follow, on our view, that 'tigers are striped' is analytic. If a mutation occurred, all tigers might be albinos. Communication presupposes that I have a stereotype of tigers which includes stripes, and that you have a stereotype of tigers which includes stripes, and that I know that your stereotype includes stripes, and that you know that my stereotype includes stripes, and that you know that I know . . . (and so on, a la Grice, forever). But it does not presuppose that any particular stereotype be *correct*, or that the majority of our stereotypes remain correct forever. Linguistic obligatoriness is not supposed to be an index of unrevisability or even of truth; thus we can hold that 'tigers are striped' is part of the meaning of 'tiger' without being trapped in the problems of analyticity.

Thus Quine's arguments against identifying analyticity with centrality are not arguments against identifying a feature's being 'part of the meaning' of *X* with its being obligatorily included in the stereotype of *X*. What of Quine's 'noise' argument?

Of course, evidence concerning what people *say*, including explicit metalinguistic remarks, is important in 'semantics' as it is in syntax. Thus, if a speaker points to a *clam* and asks 'is that a tiger?' people are likely to guffaw. (When they stop laughing) they might say 'he doesn't know the meaning of "tiger,"' or 'he doesn't know what tigers are.' Such comments can be helpful to the linguist. But we are not *defining* the stereotype in terms of such comments. To say that being 'big-cat-like' is part of the meaning of tiger is not merely to say that application of 'tiger' to something which is not big-cat-like (and also not a tiger) would provoke certain *noises*. It is to say that speakers acquire the information that 'tigers are (stereotypically) big-cat-like' as they acquire the word 'tiger' and that they feel an obligation to guarantee that those to whom they teach the use of the word do likewise. Information about the minimum skills required for entry into the linguistic community is significant information; no circularity of the kind Quine criticized appears here.

Radical Translation

What our theory does not do, by itself at any rate, is solve Quine's problem of 'radical translation' (i.e., translation from an alien language/culture). We cannot translate our hypothetical Cheroquoi into English by matching stereotypes, just because finding out what the stereotype of, say, *wa'arabi* is involves translating Cheroquoi utterances. On the other hand, the constraint that each word in Cheroquoi should match its image in English under the translation-function as far as stereotype is concerned (or approximately match, since in many cases exact matching may not be attainable), places a severe *constraint* on the translation-function. Once we have succeeded in translating the basic vocabulary of Cheroquoi, we can start to elicit stereotypes, and these will serve both to constrain future translations and to check the internal correctness of the piece of the translation-function already constructed.

Even where we can determine stereotypes (relative, say, to a tentative translation of 'basic vocabulary'), these do not suffice, in general, to determine a unique translation. Thus the German words *Ulme* and *Buche* have the same stereotype as *elm*; but *Ulme* means 'elm' while *Buche* means 'beech.' In the case of German, the fact that *Ulme* and *elm* are cognates could point to the correct translation (although this is far from foolproof – in general, cognate words are not synonymous); but in the case of Greek we have no such clue as to which of the two words 'οξύα, πτελέα means *elm* and which *beech*; we would just have to find a Greek who could tell elms from beeches (or *oxya* from *ptelea*). What this illustrates is that it may not be the *typical* speakers' dispositions to assent and dissent that the linguist must seek to discover; because of the division of linguistic labor, it is frequently necessary for the linguist to assess who are the experts with respect to *oxya*, or *wa'arabi*, or *gavagai*, or whatever, before he can make a guess at the socially determined extension of a word. Then this socially determined extension *and* the stereotype of the *typical* speaker, inexpert though he is, will *both* function as constraints upon the translation-function. Discovery that the stereotype of *oxya* is wildly different from the stereotype of *elm* would disqualify the translation of *oxya* by *elm* in all save the most extensional contexts; but the discovery that the *extension* of *oxya* is not even approximately the class of elms would wipe out the translation altogether, in all contexts.

It will be noted that we have already enlarged the totality of facts counted as evidence for a translation-function beyond the ascetic base that Quine allows in *Word and Object*. For example, the fact that speakers say such-and-such when the linguist's 'confederate' points to the word *oxya* and asks 'what does this mean?' or 'what is this?' or whatever is not allowed by Quine (as something the linguist can 'know') on the ground that this sort of 'knowledge' presupposes already having translated the query 'what does this word mean?'. However, if Quine is willing to assume that one can *somehow* guess at the words which signify *assent* and *dissent* in the alien language, it does not seem at all unreasonable to suppose that one can somehow convey to a native speaker that one does not understand a word. It is not necessary that one discover a locution in the alien language which literally means 'what does this word *mean*?' (as opposed to: 'I don't understand this word,' or 'this word is unfamiliar to me' or 'I am puzzled by this word,' etc.). Perhaps just saying the word *oxya*, or whatever, with a tone of puzzlement would suffice. Why should *puzzlement* be less accessible to the linguist than *assent*?

Also, we are taking advantage of the fact that segmentation into *words* has turned out to be linguistically universal (and there even exist tests for word and morpheme segmentation which are independent of meaning). Clearly, there is no motivated reason for allowing the linguist to utter whole sentences and look for assent and dissent, while refusing to allow him to utter words and morphemes in a tone of puzzlement.

I repeat, the claim is not being advanced that enlarging the evidence base in this way solves the problem of radical translation. What it does is add further constraints on the class of admissible candidates for a correct translation. What I believe is that enlarging the class of constraints can determine a unique translation, or as unique a translation as we are able to get in practice. But constraints that go beyond linguistic theory proper will have to be used, in my opinion; there will also have to be constraints on what sorts of beliefs (and connections between beliefs, and connections of beliefs to the culture and the world) we can reasonably impute to people. Discussion of these matters will be deferred to another paper.

A Critique of Davidsonian Semantic Theory

In a series of publications, Donald Davidson has put forward the interesting suggestion that a semantic theory of a natural language might be modeled on what mathematical logicians call a *truth definition* for a formalized language. Stripped of technicalities, what this suggestion comes down to is that one might have a set of rules specifying (1) for each word, under what conditions that word is true of something (for words for which the concept of an extension makes sense; all other words are to be treated as syncategorematic); (2) for sentences longer than a single word, a rule is given specifying the conditions under which the sentence is true as a function of the way it is built up out of shorter sentences (counting words as if they were one-word sentences, e.g., 'snow' as 'that's snow'). The choice of one-word sentences as the starting point is my interpretation of what Davidson intends; in any case, he means one to start with a *finite* stock of *short* sentences for which truth conditions are to be laid down *directly*. The intention of (2) is not that there should be a rule for each sentence not handled under (1), since this would require an infinite number of rules, but that there should be a rule for each sentence *type*. For example, in a formalized language one of the rules of kind (2) might be: if S is (S_1 & S_2) for some sentences S_1,S_2, *then* S is true if and only if S_1,S_2, are both true.

It will be noticed that, in the example just given, the truth condition specified for sentences of the sentence type (S_1 & S_2) performs the job of specifying the meaning of '&.' More precisely, it specifies the meaning of the structure (—— & ——). This is the sense in which a truth definition can be a theory of meaning. Davidson's contention is that the *entire* theory of meaning for a natural language can be given in this form.

There is no doubt that rules of the type illustrated can give the meaning of some words and structures. The question is, what reason is there to think that the meaning of most words can be given in this way, let alone all?

The obvious difficulty is this: for many words, an extensionally correct truth definition can be given which is in no sense a theory of the meaning of the word. For example, consider *'Water' is true of x if and only if x is* H_2O. This is an extensionally correct truth definition for 'water' (strictly speaking, it is not a truth definition but a 'truth of' definition – i.e., a *satisfaction*-in-the-sense-of-Tarski definition, but we will not bother with such niceties here). At least it is extensionally correct if we ignore the problem that water with impurities is also called 'water,' etc. Now, suppose most speakers don't *know* that water is H_2O. Then this formula in no way tells us anything about the *meaning* of 'water.' It might be of interest to a chemist, but it doesn't count as a theory of the meaning of the term 'water.' Or, it counts as a theory of the *extension* of the term 'water,' but Davidson is promising us more than just that.

Davidson is quite well aware of this difficulty. His answer (in conversation, anyway) is that we need to develop a theory of *translation*. This he, like Quine, considers to be the real problem. Relativized to such a theory (relativized to what we admittedly don't yet have), the theory comes down to this: we want a system of truth definitions which is simultaneously a system of translations (or approximate translations, if perfect translation is unobtainable). If we had a theory which specified what it is to be a good translation, then we could rule out the above truth definition for 'water' as uninteresting on the grounds that *x* is H_2O is not an acceptable translation or even near-translation of *x is water* (in a prescientific community), even if water = H_2O happens to be true.

This comes perilously close to saying that a theory of meaning is a truth definition plus a theory of meaning. (If we had ham and eggs we'd have ham and eggs – *if* we had ham and *if* we had eggs.) But this story suffers from worse than promissoriness, as we shall see.

A second contention of Davidson's is that the theory of translation that we don't yet have is necessarily a theory whose basic units are *sentences* and not *words* on the grounds that our *evidence* in linguistics necessarily consists of assent and dissent from sentences. Words can be handled, Davidson contends, by treating them as sentences ('water' as 'that's water,' etc.).

How does this ambitious project of constructing a theory of meaning in the form of a truth definition constrained by a theory of translation tested by 'the only evidence we have,' speakers' dispositions to use sentences, fare according to the view we are putting forward here?

Our answer is that the theory cannot succeed in principle. In special cases, such as the word 'and' in its truth-functional sense, a truth definition (strictly speaking, a clause in what logicians call a 'truth definition' – the sum total of all the clauses is the inductive definition of 'truth' for the particular language) can give the meaning of the word or structure because the stereotype associated with the word (if one wants to speak of a stereotype in the case of a word like 'and') is so strong as to actually constitute a necessary and sufficient condition. If all words were like 'and' and 'bachelor' the program could succeed. And Davidson certainly made an important contribution in pointing out that linguistics has to deal with inductively specified truth conditions. But for the great majority of words, the requirements of a theory of truth and the requirements of a theory of meaning are mutually incompatible, at least in the English-English case. But the English-English case – the case in which we try to provide a significant theory of the meaning of English words which is itself couched in English – is surely the basic one.

The problem is that in general the only expressions which are both coextensive with *X* and have roughly the same stereotype as *X* are expressions containing *X* itself. If we rule out such truth definitions (strictly speaking, clauses, but I shall continue using 'truth definition' both for individual clauses and for the whole system of clauses, for simplicity) as

'X is water' is true if and only if X is water

on the grounds that they don't say anything about the meaning of the word 'water,' and we rule out such truth definitions as

'X is water' is true if and only if X is H_2O

on the grounds that what they say is wrong as a description of the *meaning* of the word 'water,' then we shall be left with nothing.

The problem is that we want

W is true of x if and only if ——

to satisfy the conditions that (1) the clause be extensionally correct (where —— is to be thought of as a condition containing '*x*,' e.g. '*x* is H_2O'); (2) that —— be a *translation* of *W* – on our theory, this would mean that the stereotype associated with *W* is approximately the same as the stereotype associated with ——; (3) that —— not contain *W* itself, or syntactic variants of *W*. If we take *W* to be, for example, the word 'elm,' then there is absolutely no way to fulfill all three conditions simultaneously. Any condition of the above form that does not contain 'elm' and that is extensionally correct will contain a —— that is absolutely terrible as a *translation* of 'elm.'

Even where the language contains two exact synonyms, the situation is little better. Thus

'Heather' is true of x if and only if x is gorse

is true, and so is

'Gorse' is true of x if and only if x is heather

—— *this* is a *theory* of the *meaning* of 'gorse' and 'heather'?

Notice that the condition (3) is precisely what logicians do *not* impose on *their* truth definitions.

'Snow is white' is true if and only if snow is white

is the paradigm of a truth definition in the logician's sense. But logicians are trying to give the extension of 'true' with respect to a particular language, not the meaning of 'snow is white.' Tarski would have gone so far as to claim he was giving the *meaning* (and not just the extension) of 'true'; but he would never have claimed he was saying *anything* about the meaning of 'snow is white.'

It may be that what Davidson really thinks is that theory of meaning, in any serious sense of the term, is impossible, and that all that is possible is to construct translation-functions. If so, he might well think that the only 'theory of meaning' possible for English is one that says ' "elm" is true of x if and only if x is an elm,' ' "water" is true of x if and only if x is water,' etc., and only rarely something enlightening like 'S_1 & S_2 is true if and only if S_1, S_2 are both true.' But if Davidson's 'theory' is just Quinine skepticism under the disguise of a positive contribution to the study of meaning, then it is a bitter pill to swallow.

The contention that the only evidence available to the linguist is speakers' dispositions with respect to whole sentences is, furthermore, vacuous on one interpretation, and plainly false on the interpretation on which it is not vacuous. If dispositions to say certain things *when queried about individual words or morphemes or syntactic structures* are included in the notion of dispositions to use sentences, then the restriction to dispositions to use sentences seems to rule out nothing whatsoever. On the non-vacuous interpretation, what Davidson is saying is that the linguist cannot have access to such data as what informants (including the linguist himself) say when asked the meaning of a word or morpheme or syntactic structure. No reason has ever been given why the linguist cannot have access to such data, and it is plain that actual linguists place heavy reliance on informants' testimony about such matters, in the case of an alien language, and upon their own intuitions as native speakers, when they are studying their native languages. In particular, when we are trying to translate a whole sentence, there is no reason why we should not be guided by our knowledge of the syntactic and semantic properties of the constituents of that sentence, including the deep structure. As we have seen, there are procedures for gaining information about individual constituents. It is noteworthy that the procedure that Quine and Davidson claim is the only *possible* one – going from whole sentences to individual words – is the *opposite* of the procedure upon which every success ever attained in the study of natural language has been based.

Critique of California Semantics

I wish now to consider an approach to semantic theory pioneered by the late Rudolf Carnap. Since I do not wish to be embroiled in textual questions, I will not attribute the particular form of the view I am going to describe to any particular philosopher but will simply refer to it as 'California semantics.'

We assume the notion of a *possible world*. Let f be a function defined on the 'space' of all possible worlds whose value $f(x)$ at any possible world x is always a subset of the set of entities in x. Then f is called an *intension*. A term

T has meaning for a speaker X if X associates T with an intension f_T. The term T is *true of* an entity e in a possible world x if and only if e belongs to the set $f(x)$. Instead of using the term 'associate,' Carnap himself tended to speak of 'grasping' intensions; but, clearly, what was intended was not just that X 'grasp' the intension f, but that he grasp *that* f is the intension *of* T – i.e., that he *associate* f with T in some way.

Clearly this picture of what it is to understand a term disagrees with the story we tell in this paper. The reply of a California semanticist would be that California semantics is a description of an *ideal* language; that actual language is *vague*. In other words, a term T in actual language does not have a single precise intension; it has a set – possibly a fuzzy set – of intensions. Nevertheless, the first step in the direction of describing natural language is surely to study the idealization in which each term T has exactly one intension.

(In his book *Meaning and Necessity*, Carnap employs a superficially different formulation: an intension is simply a *property*. An entity e belongs to the extension of a term T just in case e has whichever property is the intension of T. The later formulation in terms of functions f as described above avoids taking the notion of *property* as primitive.)

The first difficulty with this position is the use of the totally unexplained notion of *grasping* an intension (or, in our reformulation of the position, *associating* an intension with a term). Identifying intensions with set-theoretic entities f provides a 'concrete' realization of the notion of intension in the current mathematical style (relative to the notions of possible world and set), but at the cost of making it very difficult to see how anyone could have an intension in his mind, or what it is to think about one or 'grasp' one or 'associate' one with anything. It will not do to say that thinking of an intension is using a word or functional substitute for a word (i.e., the analogue of a word in 'brain code,' if, as seems likely, the brain 'computes' in a 'code' that has analogies to and possibly borrowings from language; or a thought form such as a picture or a private symbol, in cases where such are employed in thinking) which *refers* to the intension in question, since *reference* (i.e., being in the extension of a term) has just been defined in terms of *intension*. Although the characterization of what it is to think of an abstract entity such as a function or a property is certainly correct, in the present context it is patently circular. But no non-circular characterization of this fundamental notion of the theory has ever been provided.

This difficulty, is related to a general difficulty in the philosophy of mathematics pointed out by Paul Benacerraf.[24] Benacerraf has remarked that philosophies of mathematics tend to fall between two stools: either they account for what mathematical objects are and for the necessity of mathematical truth and fail to account for the fact that people can *learn* mathematics, can *refer* to mathematical objects, etc., or else they account for the latter facts and fail to account for the former. California semantics accounts for what intensions *are*, but provides no account that is not completely circular of how it is that we can 'grasp' them, associate them with terms, think about them, *refer to* them, etc.

Carnap may not have noticed this difficulty because of his Verificationism. In his early years Carnap thought of understanding a term as possessing the *ability to verify* whether or not any given entity falls in the extension of the term. In terms of intensions: 'grasping' an intension would amount, then, to possessing the ability to verify if an entity e in any possible world x belongs to $f(x)$ or not. Later Carnap modified this view, recognizing that, as Quine puts it, sentences face the tribunal of experience collectively and not individually. There is no such thing as the way of verifying that a term T is true of an entity, in general, independent of the context of a particular set of theories, auxiliary hypotheses, etc. Perhaps Carnap would have maintained that something like the earlier theory was correct for a limited class of terms, the so-called 'observation terms.' Our own view is that the verifiability theory of meaning is false both in its central idea and for observation terms, but we shall not try to discuss this here. At any rate, if one is *not* a verificationist, then it is hard to see Califiornia semantics as a theory at all, since the notion of *grasping* an intension has been left totally unexplained.

Second, if we assume that 'grasping an intension' (associating an intension with a term T) is supposed to be a *psychological state* (in the narrow sense), then California semantics is committed to both principles (1) and (2) that we criticized in the first part of this paper. It must hold that the psychological state of the speaker determines the intension of his terms which in turn determines the extension of his terms. It would follow that if two human beings are in the same total psychological state, then they necessarily assign the same extension to every term they employ. As we have seen, this is totally wrong for natural language. The reason this is wrong, as we saw above, is in part that extension is determined socially, not by individual competence alone. Thus California semantics is committed to treating language as something private – to totally ignoring the linguistic division of labor. The extension of each term is viewed by this school as totally determined by something in the head of the individual speaker all by himself. A second reason this is wrong, as we also saw, is that most terms are *rigid*. In California semantics every term is treated as, in effect, a *description*.The *indexical* component in meaning – the fact that our terms refer to things which are similar, in certain ways, to things that we designate *rigidly*, to *these* things, to the stuff we call 'water,' or whatever, *here* – is ignored.

But what of the defense that it is not actual language that the California semanticist is concerned with, but an idealization in which we 'ignore vagueness,' and that terms in natural language may be thought of as associated with a set of intensions rather than with a single well-defined intension?

The answer is that an *indexical* word cannot be represented as a vague family of non-indexical words. The word 'I,' to take the extreme case, is *indexical* but not *vague*. 'I' is not synonymous with a *description*; neither is it synonymous with a fuzzy set of descriptions. Similarly, if we are right, 'water' is synonymous neither with a description nor with a fuzzy set of descriptions (intensions).

Similarly, a word whose extension is fixed socially and not individually is not the same thing as a word whose extension is *vaguely* fixed individually. The reason my individual 'grasp' of 'elm tree' does not fix the extension of elm is not that the word is vague – if the problem were simple vagueness, then the fact that my concepts do not distinguish elms from beeches would imply that elms are beeches, as I use the term, or, anyway, borderline cases of beeches, and that beeches are elms, or borderline cases of elms. The reason is rather that the extension of 'elm tree' in my dialect is not fixed by what the average speaker 'grasps' or doesn't 'grasp' at all; it is fixed by the community, including the experts, through a complex cooperative process. A language which exemplifies the division of linguistic labor cannot be approximated successfully by a language which has vague terms and no linguistic division of labor. Cooperation isn't vagueness.

But one might reply, couldn't one replace our actual language by a language in which (1) terms were replaced by coextensive terms which were *not* indexical (e.g., 'water' by 'H_2O,' assuming 'H_2O' is not indexical); and (2) we eliminated the division of linguistic labor by making every speaker an expert on every topic?

We shall answer this question in the negative; but suppose, for a moment, the answer were 'yes.' What significance would this have? The 'ideal' language would in no sense be similar to our actual language; nor would the difference be a matter of 'the vagueness of natural language.'

In fact, however, one can't carry out the replacement, for the very good reason that *all* natural-kind words and physical-magnitude words are indexical in the way we have described, 'hydrogen,' and hence 'H_2O,' just as much as 'water.' Perhaps 'sense data' terms are not indexical (apart from terms for the self), if such there be; but 'yellow' as a *thing* predicate is indexical for the same reason as 'tiger'; even if something *looks* yellow it may not *be* yellow. And it doesn't help to say that things that look yellow in normal circumstances (to normal perceivers) are yellow; 'normal' here has precisely the feature we called indexicality. There is simply no reason to believe that the project of reducing our language to non-indexical language could be carried out in principle.

The elimination of the division of linguistic labor might, I suppose, be carried out 'in principle.' But, if the division of linguistic labor is, as I conjectured, a linguistic universal, what interest is there in the possible existence of a language which lacks a constitutive feature of *human* language? A world in which every one is an expert on every topic is a world in which social laws are almost unimaginably different from what they now are. What is the *motivation* for taking such a world and such a language as the model for the analysis of *human* language?

Incidentally, philosophers who work in the tradition of California semantics have recently begun to modify the scheme to overcome just these defects. Thus it has been suggested that an intension might be a function whose arguments are not just possible worlds but, perhaps, a possible world, a speaker, and a non-linguistic context of utterance. This would permit the representation of some kinds of indexicality and some kinds of division of linguistic labor in the model. As David Lewis develops these ideas, 'water,' for example, would have the same *intension* (same function) on Earth and on Twin Earth, but a different extension. (In effect, Lewis retains assumption (1) from the discussion in the first part of this paper and gives up (2); we chose to give up (1) and retain (2).) There is no reason why the formal models developed by Carnap and his followers should not prove valuable when so modified. Our interest here has been not in the utility of the mathematical formalism but in the philosophy of language underlying the earlier versions of the view.

Semantic Markers

If the approach suggested here is correct, then there is a great deal of scientific work to be done in (1) finding out what sorts of items can appear in stereotypes; (2) working out a convenient system for representing stereotypes; etc. This work is not work that can be done by philosophical discussion, however. It is rather the province of linguistics and psycholinguistics. One idea that can, I believe, be of value is the idea of a *semantic marker*. The idea comes from the work of J. J. Katz and J. A. Fodor; we shall modify it somewhat here.

Consider the stereotype of 'tiger' for a moment. This includes such features as being an animal; being big-cat-like; having black stripes on a yellow ground (yellow stripes on a black ground?); etc. Now, there is something very special about the feature *animal*. In terms of Quine's notion of *centrality* or *unrevisability*, it is qualitatively different from the others listed. It is not impossible to imagine that tigers might not be animals (they might be robots). But spelling this out, they must always have been robots; we don't want to tell a story about the tigers being *replaced* by robots, because then the robots wouldn't be tigers. Or, if they weren't always robots, they must have *become* robots, which is even harder to imagine. If tigers are and always were robots, these robots mustn't be too 'intelligent,' or else we may not have a case in which tigers aren't animals – we may, rather, have described a case in which some robots are animals. Best make them 'other directed' robots – say, have an operator on Mars controlling each motion remotely. Spelling this out, I repeat, is difficult, and it is curiously hard to think of the case to begin with, which is why it is easy to make the mistake of thinking that it is 'logically impossible' for a tiger *not* to be an animal. On the other hand, there is no difficulty in imagining an individual tiger that is not striped; it might be an albino. Nor is it difficult to imagine an individual tiger that doesn't look like a big cat: it might be horribly deformed. We can even imagine the whole species losing its stripes or becoming horribly deformed. But tigers ceasing to be animals? Great difficulty again!

Notice that we are not making the mistake that Quine rightly criticized, of attributing an absolute unrevisability to such statements as 'tigers are animals,' 'tigers couldn't change from animals into something else and still be tigers.' Indeed, we can describe farfetched cases in which these statements would be given up. But we maintain that it is *qualitatively* harder to revise 'all tigers are animals' than 'all tigers have stripes' – indeed, the latter statement is not even true.

Not only do such features as 'animal,' 'living thing,' 'artifact,' 'day of the week,' 'period of time,' attach with enormous centrality to the words 'tiger,' 'clam,' 'chair,' 'Tuesday,' 'hour'; but they also form part of a widely used and important *system of classification*. The centrality guarantees that items classified under these headings virtually never have to be reclassified; thus these headings are the natural ones to use as category-indicators in a host of contexts. It seems to me reasonable that, just as in syntax we use such markers as 'noun,' 'adjective,' and, more narrowly, 'concrete noun,' 'verb taking a person as subject and an abstract object,' etc., to classify words, so in semantics these category-indicators should be used as markers.

It is interesting that when Katz and Fodor originally introduced the idea of a semantic marker, they did not propose to exhaust the meaning – what we call the stereotype – by a list of such markers. Rather, the markers were restricted to just the category-indicators of high centrality, which is what we propose. The remaining features were simply listed as a 'distinguisher.' Their scheme is not easily comparable with ours, because they wanted the semantic markers *plus* the distinguisher to always give a necessary and sufficient condition for membership in the extension of the term. Since the whole thing – markers and distinguisher – were supposed to represent what every speaker implicitly knows, they were committed to the idea that every speaker implicitly knows of a necessary and sufficient condition for membership in the extension of 'gold,' 'aluminum,' 'elm' – which, as we have pointed out, is not the case. Later Katz went further and demanded that *all* the features constitute an *analytically* necessary and sufficient condition for membership in the extension. At this point he dropped the distinction between marker and distinguishers; if all the features have, so to speak, the infinite degree of centrality, why call some 'markers' and some 'distinguishers'? From our point of view, their original distinction between 'markers' and 'distingishers' was sound – provided one drop the idea that the distinguisher provides (together with the markers) a necessary and sufficient condition, and the idea that any of this is a theory of *analyticity*. We sugggest that the idea of a semantic marker is an important contribution, when taken as suggested here.

The Meaning of 'Meaning'

We may now summarize what has been said in the form of a proposal concerning how one might reconstruct the notion of 'meaning.' Our proposal is not the only one that might be advanced on the basis of these ideas, but it may serve to encapsulate some of the major points. In addition, I feel that it recovers as much of ordinary usage in common sense talk and in linguistics as one is likely to be able to conveniently preserve. Since on my view something like the assumptions 1 and 2 listed in the first part of this paper are deeply embedded in ordinary meaning talk, and these assumptions are jointly inconsistent with the facts, no reconstruction is going to be without some counter-intuitive consequences.

Briefly, my proposal is to define 'meaning' not by picking out an object which will be identified with the meaning (although that might be done in the usual set-theoretic style if one insists), but by specifying a normal form (or, rather, a *type* of normal form) for the description of meaning. If we know what a 'normal form description' of the meaning of a word should be, then, as far as I am concerned, we know what meaning *is* in any scientifically interesting sense.

My proposal is that the normal form description of the meaning of a word should be a finite sequence, or 'vector,' whose components should certainly include the following (it might be desirable to have other types of components as well): (1) the syntactic markers that apply to the word, e.g., 'noun'; (2) the semantic markers that apply to the word, e.g., 'animal,' 'period of time'; (3) a description of the additional features of the stereotype, if any; (4) a description of the extension.

The following convention is a part of this proposal: the components of the vector all represent a hypothesis about the individual speaker's competence, *except the extension*. Thus the normal form description for 'water' might be, in part:

Syntactic Markers	*Semantic Markers*	*Stereotype*	*Extension*
mass noun, concrete	natural kind, liquid	colorless, transparent, tasteless, thirst-quenching, etc.	H_2O (give or take impurities)

– this does *not* mean that knowledge of the fact that water is H_2O is being imputed to the individual speaker or even to the society. It means that (*we* say) the extension of the term 'water' as *they* (the speakers in question) use it is *in fact* H_2O. The objection 'who are *we* to say what the extension of *their* term is in fact' has been discussed above. Note that this is fundamentally an objection to the notion of *truth*, and that extension is a relative of truth and inherits the family problems.

Let us call two descriptions *equivalent* if they are the same except for the description of the extension, and the two descriptions are co-extensive. Then, if the set variously described in the two descriptions is, *in fact*, the extension of the word in question, and the other components in the description are correct characterizations of the various aspects of competence they represent, *both* descriptions count as correct. Equivalent descriptions are both correct or both incorrect. This is another way of making the point that, although we have to use a *description* of the extension to *give* the extension, we think of the component in question as being the *extension* (the set), not the description of the extension.

In particular the representations of the words 'water' in Earth dialect and 'water' in Twin Earth dialect would be the same except that in the last column the normal form description of the Twin Earth word 'water' would have XYZ and not H_2O. This means, in view of what has just been said, that we are ascribing the *same* linguistic competence to the typical Earthian/Twin Earthian speaker, but a different extension to the word, nonetheless.

This proposal means that we keep assumption 2 of our early discussion. Meaning determines extension – by construction, so to speak. But 1 is given up; the psychological state of the individual speaker does not determine 'what he means.'

In most contexts this will agree with the way we speak, I believe. But one paradox: suppose Oscar is a German-English bilingual. On our view, in his total collection of dialects, the words *beech* and *Buche* are *exact synonyms*. The normal form descriptions of their meanings would be identical. But he might very well not know that they are synonyms! A speaker can have two synonyms in his vocabulary and not know that they are synonyms!

It is instructive to see how the failure of the apparently obvious 'if S_1 and S_2 are synonyms and Oscar understands both S_1 and S_2 then Oscar knows that S_1 and S_2 are synonyms' is related to the falsity of 1, on our analysis. Notice that if we had chosen to omit the extension as a component of the 'meaning-vector,' which is David Lewis's proposal as I understand it, then we would have the paradox that 'elm' and 'beech' have the *same meaning* but different extensions!

On just about any materialist theory, believing a proposition is likely to involve processing some *representation* of that proposition, be it a sentence in a language, a piece of 'brain code,' a thought form, or whatever. Materialists, and not only materialists, are reluctant to think that one can believe propositions *neat*. But even materialists tend to believe that, if one believes a proposition, *which* representation one employs is (pardon the pun) immaterial. If S_1 and S_2 are both representations that are *available* to me, then if I believe the proposition expressed by S_1 under the representation S_1, I must also believe it under the representation S_2 – at least, I must do this if I have any claim to rationality. But, as we have just seen, this isn't right. Oscar may well believe that *this* is a 'beech' (it has a sign on it that says 'beech'), but not believe or disbelieve that this is a '*Buche*.' It is not just that belief is a process involving representations; he believes the proposition (if one wants to introduce 'propositions' at all) under one representation and not under another.

The amazing thing about the theory of meaning is how long the subject has been in the grip of philosophical misconceptions, and how strong these misconceptions are. Meaning has been identified with a necessary and sufficient condition by philosopher after philosopher. In the empiricist tradition, it has been identified with method of verification, again by philosopher after philosopher. Nor have these misconceptions had the virtue of exclusiveness; not a few philosophers have held that meaning = method of verification = necessary and sufficient condition.

On the other side, it is amazing how weak the grip of the facts has been. After all, what have been pointed out in this essay are little more than home truths about the way we use words and how much (or rather, how little) we actually know when we use them. My own reflection on these matters began after I published a paper in which I confidently maintained that the meaning of a word was 'a battery of semantical rules,'[25] and then began to wonder how the meaning of the common word 'gold' could be accounted for in this way. And it is not that philosophers had never considered such examples: Locke, for example, uses this word as an example and is not troubled by the idea that its meaning is a necessary and sufficient condition!

If there is a reason for both learned and lay opinion having gone so far astray with respect to a topic which deals, after all, with matters which are in everyone's experience, matters concerning which we all have more data than we know what to do with, matters concerning which we have, if we shed preconceptions, pretty clear intuitions, it must be connected to the fact that the grotesquely mistaken views of language which are and always have been current reflect two specific and very central philosophical tendencies: the tendency to treat cognition as a purely *individual* matter and the tendency to ignore the *world*, insofar as it consists of more than the individual's 'observations'. Ignoring the division of linguistic labor is ignoring the social dimension of cognition; ignoring what we have called the *indexicality* of most words is ignoring the contribution of the environment. Traditional philosophy of language, like much traditional philosophy, leaves out other people and the world; a better philosophy and a better science of language must encompass both.

Notes

1 The contributors to this area are now too numerous to be listed; the pioneers were, of course, Zellig Harris and Noam Chomsky.
2 For a discussion of this question, see my 'The "Innateness Hypothesis" and Explanatory Models in Linguistics,' *Synthese*, 17 (1967): 12–22.
3 This is discussed by Ziff if *Understanding Understanding* (Ithaca: Cornell University Press, 1972), especially chap. 1.
4 This tradition grew up because *the* term whose analysis provoked all the discussion in medieval philosophy was the term 'God,' and the term 'God' was thought to be defined through the conjunction of the terms 'Good,' 'Powerful,' 'Omniscient,' etc. – the so-called 'Perfections.' There was a problem, however, because God was supposed to be a Unity, and Unity was thought to exclude His essence's being complex in *any* way – i.e., 'God' was defined through a conjunction of terms, but God (without quotes) could not be the logical product of properties, nor could He be the unique thing exemplifying the logical product of two or more *distinct* properties, because even this highly abstract kind of 'complexity' was held to be incompatible with His perfection of Unity. This is a theological paradox with which Jewish, Arabic, and Christian theologians wrestled for centuries (e.g., the doctrine of the Negation of Privation in Maimonides and Aquinas). It is amusing that theories of contemporary interest, such as conceptualism and nominalism, were first proposed as solutions to the problem of predication in the case of God. It is also amusing that the favorite model of definition in all of this theology – the conjunction-of-properties model – should survive, at least through its consequences, in philosophy of language until the present day.
5 Or rather, they will report: 'On Twin Earth (*the Twin Earthian name for Terra* – H.P.) the word 'water' means H_2O.'
6 The substance of this section was presented at a series of lectures I gave at the University of Washington (Summer Institute in Philosophy) in 1968, and at a lecture at the University of Minnesota (at the conference out of which this volume originated).
7 See my 'Is Semantics Possible,' *Metaphilosophy*, 1, no. 3 (July 1970).
8 This assumption is not actually needed in what follows. What *is* needed is that the same *natural kind* can exist in more than one possible world.
9 These points were made in my 1968 lectures at the University of Washington and the University of Minnesota.
10 See Kripke's 'Identity and Necessity,' in M. Munitz, ed., *Identity and Individuation* (New York: New York University Press, 1972), p. 157.
11 For a discussion of this point, see my 'Explanation and Reference,' in G. Pearce and P. Maynard, eds., *Conceptual Change* (Dordrecht: Reidel, 1973).
12 For an illuminating discussion of just these points, see R. Boyd's 'Realism and Scientific Epistemology' (unpublished; draft circulated by the author, Cornell University Department of Philosophy).
13 See my 'Logical Positivism and the Philosophy of Mind,' in P. Achinstein, *The Legacy of Logical Positivism* (Baltimore: Johns Hopkins Press, 1969); and also my 'Degree of Confirmation and Inductive Logic,' in P. A. Schilpp, ed., *The Philosophy of Rudolf Carnap* (La Salle, Ill.: Open Court, 1962), and my

'Probability and Confirmation' (broadcast for the Voice of America Philosophy of Science Series, Spring 1963; reprinted in A. Danto and S. Morgenbesser, eds., *Philosophy of Science Today* (New York: Basic Books, 1967).

14 See Kripke's 'Identity and Necessity.'

15 See my 'It Ain't Necessarily So,' *Journal of Philosophy*, 59 (1962): 658–671.

16 The idea of a 'one-criterion' word, and a theory of analyticity based on this notion, appears in my 'The Analytic and the Synthetic,' in H. Feigl and G. Maxwell, eds., *Minnesota Studies in the Philosophy of science*, vol. 3 (Minneapolis: University of Minnesota Press, 1962).

17 This example comes from an analysis by Anthony Kroch, in his doctoral dissertation, M.I.T. Department of Linguistics, 1974.

18 I *don't* have in mind the Flewish notion of 'paradigm' in which any paradigm of a *K* is necessarily a *K* (in reality).

19 In my 'Explanation and Reference,' in Pearce and Maynard, eds., *Conceptual Change*.

20 The term is due to Quine (in *Word and Object*); it signifies translation without clues from either shared culture or cognates.

21 For a discussion of the supposed impossibility of uniquely correct radical translation, see my 'The Refutation of Conventionalism' (forthcoming in *Noûs* and also, in a longer version, in a collection edited by M. Munitz to be published by New York University Press under the title *Semantics and Philosophy*).

22 This is argued in 'Is Semantics Possible?'

23 See 'The Analytic and the Synthetic.'

24 See his 'Mathematical Truth,' *Journal of Philosophy*, 70 (1973): 661–678 661–678.

25 'How Not to Talk About Meaning,' in R. Cohen and M. Wartofsky, eds., *Boston Studies in the Philosophy of Science*, vol. 2 (New York: Humanities Press, 1965).

Chapter 12

Demonstratives

An essay on the semantics, logic, metaphysics, and epistemology of demonstratives and other indexicals

D. Kaplan

Preface

In about 1966 I wrote a paper about quantification into epistemological contexts. There are very difficult metaphysical, logical, and epistemological problems involved in providing a treatment of such idioms which does not distort our intuitions about their proper use and which is up to contemporary logical standards. I did not then, and do not now, regard the treatment I provided as fully adequate. And I became more and more intrigued with problems centering on what I would like to call the *semantics of direct reference*. By this I mean theories of meaning according to which certain singular terms refer directly without the mediation of a Fregean *Sinn* as meaning. If there are such terms, then the proposition expressed by a sentence containing such a term would involve individuals directly rather than by way of the 'individual concepts' or 'manners of presentation' I had been taught to expect. Let us call such putative singular terms (if there are any) *directly referential terms* and such putative propositions (if there are any) *singular propositions*. Even if English contained no singular terms whose proper semantics was one of direct reference, could we determine to introduce such terms? And even if we had no directly referential terms and introduced none, is there a need or use for singular propositions?

[· · ·]

The most important hold-out against semantical theories that required singular propositions is Alonzo Church, the great modern champion of Frege's semantical theories. Church also advocates a version of quantified intensional logic, but with a subtle difference that finesses the need for singular propositions. (In Church's logic, given a sentential formula containing free variables and given an assignment of values to the variables, no proposition is yet determined. An additional assignment of 'senses' to the free variables must be made before a proposition can be associated with the formula.) It is no accident that Church rejects *direct reference* semantical theories. For if there were singular terms which referred directly, it seems likely that Frege's problem: how can $\ulcorner \alpha = \beta \urcorner$, if true, differ in meaning from $\ulcorner \alpha = \alpha] \urcorner$, could be reinstated, while Frege's solution: that α and β, though referring to the same thing, do so by way of different senses, would be blocked. Also: because of the fact that the component of the proposition is being determined by the individual rather than vice versa, we have something like a violation of the famous Fregean dictum that *there is no road back* from denotation to sense [propositional component]. (Recently, I have come to think that if we countenance singular propositions, a collapse of Frege's intensional ontology into Russell's takes place.)

I can draw some little pictures to give you an idea of the two kinds of semantical theories I want to contrast [Figures 1 and 2].

(These pictures are not entirely accurate for several reasons, among them, that the contrasting pictures are meant to account for more than just singular terms and that the relation marked 'refers' may already involve a kind of Fregean sense used to fix the referent.)

[. . .]

I. Introduction

I believe my theory of demonstratives to be uncontrovertable and largely uncontroversial. This is not a tribute to the power of my theory but a concession of its obviousness. In the past, no one seems to have followed these obvious facts out to their obvious consequences. I do that. What is original with me is some terminology to help fix ideas when things get complicated. It has been fascinating to see how interesting the obvious consequences of obvious principles can be.[7]

II. Demonstratives, Indexicals, and Pure Indexicals

I tend to describe my theory as 'a theory of demonstratives', but that is poor usage. It stems from the fact that I began my investigations by asking what is said when a speaker points at someone and says, 'He is suspicious.'[8] The word 'he', so used, is a demonstrative, and the accompanying pointing is the requisite associated demonstration. I hypothesized a certain semantical theory for such demonstratives, and then I invented a new demonstrative, 'dthat', and

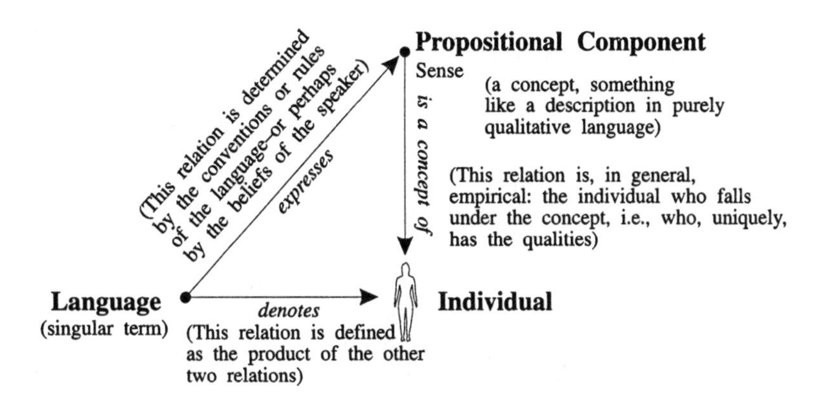

Figure 1 Fregean Picture

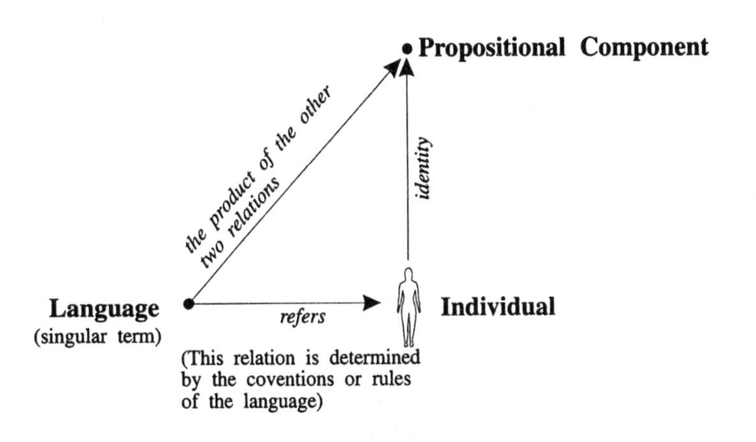

Figure 2 Direct Reference Picture

stipulated that its semantics be in accord with my theory. I was so delighted with this methodological sleight of hand for my demonstrative 'dthat', that when I generalized the theory to apply to words like 'I', 'now', 'here', etc. – words which do *not* require an associated demonstration – I continued to call my theory a 'theory of demonstratives' and I referred to these words as 'demonstratives'.

That terminological practice conflicts with what I preach, and I will try to correct it. (But I tend to backslide.)

The group of words for which I propose a semantical theory includes the pronouns 'I', 'my', 'you', 'he', 'his', 'she', 'it', the demonstrative pronouns 'that', 'this', the adverbs 'here', 'now', 'tomorrow', 'yesterday', the adjectives 'actual', 'present', and others. These words have uses other than those in which I am interested (or, perhaps, depending on how you individuate words, we should say that they have homonyms in which I am not interested). For example, the pronouns 'he' and 'his' are used not as demonstratives but as bound variables in

> For what is a man profited, if he shall gain
> the whole world, and lose his own soul?

What is common to the words or usages in which I am interested is that the referent is dependent on the context of use and that the meaning of the word provides a rule which determines the referent in terms of certain aspects of the context. The term I now favor for these words is 'indexical'. Other authors have used other terms; Russell used 'egocentric particular' and Reichenbach used 'token reflexive'. I prefer 'indexical' (which, I believe, is due to Pierce) because it seems less theory laden than the others, and because I regard Russell's and Reichenbach's theories as defective.

Some of the indexicals require, in order to determine their referents, an associated demonstration: typically, though not invariably, a (visual) presentation of a local object discriminated by a pointing.[9] These indexicals are the true demonstratives, and 'that' is their paradigm. The demonstra*tive* (an expression) refers to that which the demon*stration* demonstrates. I call that which is demonstrated the 'demonstratum'.

A demonstrative without an associated demonstration is incomplete. The linguistic rules which govern the use of the true demonstratives 'that', 'he', etc., are not sufficient to determine their referent in all contexts of use. Something else – an associated demonstration – must be provided. The linguistic rules assume that such a demonstration accompanies each (demonstrative) use of a demonstrative. An incomplete demonstrative is not *vacuous* like an improper definite description. A demonstrative *can* be vacuous in various cases. For example, when its associated demonstration has no demonstratum (a hallucination) – or the wrong kind of demonstratum (pointing to a flower and saying 'he' in the belief that one is pointing to a man disguised as a flower[10]) – or too many demonstrata (pointing to two intertwined vines and saying 'that vine'). But it is clear that one can distinguish a demonstrative with a vacuous demonstration: no referent; from a demonstrative with no associated demonstration: incomplete.

All this is by way of contrasting true demonstratives with pure indexicals. For the latter, *no associated demonstration is require, and any demonstration supplied is either for emphasis or is irrelevant.*[11] Among the pure indexicals are 'I', 'now', 'here' (in one sense), 'tomorrow', and others. The linguistic rules which govern *their* use fully determine the referent for each context.[12] No supplementary actions or intentions are needed. The speaker refers to himself when he uses 'I', and no pointing to another or believing that he is another or intending to refer to another can defeat this reference.[13]

Michael Bennett has noted that some indexicals have both a pure *and* a demonstrative use. 'Here' is a pure indexical in

I am in here

and is a demonstrative in

In two weeks, I will be here [pointing at a city on a map].

III. Two Obvious Principles

So much for preliminaries. My theory is based on two obvious principles. The first has been noted in every discussion of the subject.

Principle 1 *The referent of a pure indexical depends on the context, and the referent of a demonstrative depends on the associated demonstration.*

If you and I both say 'I' we refer to different persons. The demonstratives 'that' and 'he' can be correctly used to refer to any one of a wide variety of objects simply by adjusting the accompanying demonstration.

The second obvious principle has less often been formulated explicitly.

Principle 2 *Indexicals, pure and demonstrative alike, are directly referential.*

IV. Remarks on Rigid Designators

In an earlier draft I adopted the terminology of Kripke, called indexicals 'rigid designators', and tried to explain that my usage differed from his. I am now shying away from that terminology. But because it is so well known, I will make some comments on the notion or notions involved.

The term 'rigid designator' was coined by Saul Kripke to characterize those expressions which designate the same thing in every possible world in which that thing exists and which designate nothing elsewhere. He uses it in connection with his controversial, though, I believe, correct claim that proper names, as well as many common nouns, are rigid designators. There is an unfortunate confusion in the idea that a proper name would designate nothing if the bearer of the name were not to exist.[14] Kripke himself adopts positions which seem inconsistent with this feature of rigid designators. In arguing that the object designated by a rigid designator need not exist in every possible world, he seems to assert that under certain circumstances what is expressed by 'Hitler does not exist' would have been true, and not because 'Hitler' would have designated nothing (in *that* case we might have given the sentence *no* truth-value) but because what 'Hitler' would have designated – namely Hitler – would not have existed.[15] Furthermore, it is a striking and important feature of the possible world semantics for quantified intensional logics, which Kripke did so much to create and popularize, that variables, those paradigms of rigid designation, designate the same individual in *all* possible worlds whether the individual 'exists' or not.[16]

Whatever Kripke's intentions (did he, as I suspect, misdescribe his own concept?) and whatever associations or even meaning the phrase 'rigid designator' may have, I intend to use '*directly referential*' for an expression whose referent, once determined, is taken as fixed for all possible circumstances, i.e., is taken as *being* the propositional component.

For me, the intuitive idea is not that of an expression which *turns out* to designate the same object in all possible circumstances, but an expression whose semantical *rules* provide *directly* that the referent in all possible circumstances is fixed to be the actual referent. In typical cases the semantical rules will do this only implicitly, by providing a way of determining the *actual* referent and no way of determining any other propositional component.[17]

We should beware of a certain confusion in interpreting the phrase 'designates the same object in all circumstances'. We do not mean that the expression *could not have been used* to designate a different object. We mean rather that given a *use* of the expression, we may ask of *what has been said* whether *it* would have been true or false in various counterfactual circumstances, and in such counterfactual circumstances, which are the individuals relevant to determining truth-value. Thus we must distinguish possible occasions of *use* – which I call *contexts* – from possible circumstances of *evaluation* of what was said on a given occasion of use. Possible circumstances of evaluation I call circumstances or, sometimes, just *counterfactual situations*. A directly referential term *may* designate different objects when used in different *contexts*. But when evaluating what was said in a given context, only a single object will be relevant to the evaluation in all circumstances. This sharp distinction between *contexts of use* and *circumstances of evaluation* must be kept in mind if we are to avoid a seeming conflict between Principles 1 and 2.[18] To look at the matter from another point of view, once we recognize the obviousness of both principles (I have not yet argued for Principle 2) the distinction between contexts of use and circumstances of evaluation is forced upon us.

If I may wax metaphysical in order to fix an image, let us think of the vehicles of evaluation – the what-is-said in a given context – as proposition. Don't think of propositions as sets of possible worlds, but rather as structured entities looking something like the sentences which express them. For each occurrence of a singular term in a sentence there will be a corresponding constituent in the proposition expressed. The constituent of the proposition determines, for each circumstance of evaluation, the object relevant to evaluating the proposition in that circumstance. In general, the constituent of the proposition will be some sort of complex, constructed from various attributes by logical composition. But in the case of a singular term which is directly referential, the constituent of the proposition is just the object itself. Thus it is that it does not just *turn out* that the constituent determines the same object in every circumstance, the constituent (corresponding to a rigid designator) just *is* the object. *There is no determining to do at all.* On this picture – and this is *really* a picture and not a theory – the definite description

(1) The $n[(\text{Snow is slight} \wedge n^2 = 9) \vee (\sim\text{Snow is slight} \wedge 2^2 = n + 1)]$[19]

would yield a constituent which is complex although it would determine the same object in all circumstances. Thus, (1), though a rigid designator, is not directly referential from this (metaphysical) point of view. Note, however, that every proposition which contains the complex expressed by (1) is *equivalent* to some singular proposition which contains just the number three itself as constituent.[20]

The semantical feature that *I* wish to highlight in calling an expression *directly referential* is not the *fact* that it designates the same object in every circumstance, but the *way* in which it designates an object in any circumstance. Such an expression is a *device of direct reference*. This does not imply that it has no conventionally fixed semantical rules which determine its referent in each context of use; quite the opposite. There are semantical rules which determine the referent in each context of use – but that is all. *The rules do not provide a complex which together with a circumstance of evaluation yields an object. They just provide an object.*

If we keep in mind our sharp distinction between contexts of use and circumstances of evaluation, we will not be tempted to confuse a rule which assigns an object to each *context* with a 'complex' which assigns an object to each *circumstance*. For example, each context has an *agent* (loosely, a speaker). Thus an appropriate designation rule for a directly referential term would be:

(2) In each possible context of use the given term refers to the agent of the context.

But this rule could not be used to assign a relevant object to each circumstance of evaluation. Circumstances of evaluation do not, in general, have agents. Suppose I say,

(3) I do not exist.

Under what circumstances would *what I said* be true? It would be true in circumstances in which I did not exist. Among such circumstances are those in which no one, and thus, no speakers, no agents exist. To search a circumstance of evaluation for a speaker in order to (mis)apply rule (2) would be to go off on an irrelevant chase.

Three paragraphs ago I sketched a metaphysical picture of the structure of a proposition. The picture is taken from the semantical parts of Russell's *Principles of Mathematics*.[21] Two years later, in 'On Denoting,'[22] even Russell rejected that picture. But I still like it. It is not a part of my theory, but it well conveys my conception of a directly referential expression and of the semantics of direct reference. (The picture needs *some* modification in order to avoid difficulties which Russell later noted – though he attributed them to Frege's theory rather than his own earlier theory.)[23]

If we adopt a possible worlds semantics, all directly referential terms will be regarded as rigid designators in the *modified* sense of an expression which designates the same thing in *all* possible worlds (irrespective of whether the thing exists in the possible world or not).[24] However, as already noted, I do not regard all rigid designators – not even all strongly rigid designators (those that designate something that exists in all possible worlds) or all rigid designators in the modified sense – as directly referential. I believe that proper names, like variables, are directly referential. They are not, in general, strongly rigid designators nor are they rigid designators in the original sense.[25] What is characteristic of directly referential terms is that the designatum (referent) determines the propositional component rather than the propositional component, along with a circumstance, determining the designatum. It is for this reason that a directly referential term that designates a contingently existing object will still be a rigid designator in the modified sense. The propositional component need not choose its designatum from those offered by a passing circumstance; it has already secured its designatum before the encounter with the circumstance.

When we think in terms of possible world semantics this fundamental distinction becomes subliminal. This is because the style of the semantical rules obscures the distinction and makes it appear that directly referential terms differ from ordinary definite descriptions only in that the propositional component in the former case must be a *constant* function of circumstances. In actual fact, the referent, in a circumstance, of a directly referential term is simply *independent* of the circumstance and is no more a function (constant or otherwise) of circumstance, than my action is a function of your desires when I decide to do it whether you like it or not. The distinction that is obscured by the style of possible world semantics is dramatized by the structured propositions picture. That is part of the reason why I like it.

Some directly referential terms, like proper names, may have no semantically relevant descriptive meaning, or at least none that is specific: that distinguishes one such term from another. Others, like the indexicals, may have a limited kind of specific descriptive meaning relevant to the features of a context of use. Still others, like 'dthat' terms (see below), may be associated with full-blown

Fregean senses used to fix the referent. But in any case, the descriptive meaning of a directly referential term is no part of the propositional content.

V. Argument for Principle 2: Pure Indexicals

As stated earlier, I believe this principle is uncontroversial. But I had best distinguish it from similar principles which are false. I am *not* claiming, as has been claimed for proper names, that indexicals lack anything that might be called 'descriptive meaning'. Indexicals, in general, have a rather easily statable descriptive meaning. But it is clear that this meaning is relevant only to determining a referent in a context of use and *not* to determining a relevant individual in a circumstance of evaluation. Let us return to the example in connection with the sentence (3) and the indexical 'I'. The bizarre result of taking the descriptive meaning of the indexical to be the propositional constituent is that what I said in uttering (3) would be true in a circumstance of evaluation if and only if the speaker (assuming there is one) of the circumstance does not exist in the circumstance. Nonsense! If *that* were the correct analysis, what I said could not be true. From which it follows that

It is impossible that I do not exist.

Here is another example to show that the descriptive meaning of an indexical may be entirely *inapplicable* in the circumstance of evaluation. When I say,

I wish I were not speaking now.

The circumstances desired do not involve contexts of *use* and *agents* who are not speaking. The *actual* context of use is used to determine the relevant individual: *me* – and time: *now* – and then we query the various circumstances of evaluation with respect to *that* individual and *that* time.

Here is another example, not of the inapplicability of the descriptive meaning to circumstances but of its irrelevance. Suppose I say at t_0, 'It will soon be the case that all that is now beautiful is faded.' Consider what was said in the subsentence,

All that is now beautiful is faded.

I wish to evaluate that content at some near future time t_1. What is the relevant time associated with the indexical 'now'? Is it the future time t_1? No, it is t_0, of course: the time of the context of use.

See how rigidly the indexicals cling to the referent determined in the context of use:

> (4) It is possible that in Pakistan, in five years, only those who are actually here now are envied.

The point of (4) is that the circumstance, place, and time referred to by the indexicals 'actually', 'here', and 'now' are the circumstance, place, and time of the *context* not a circumstance, place, and time determined by the modal, locational, and temporal operators within whose scope the indexicals lie.

It may be objected that this only shows that indexicals always take *primary* scope (in the sense of Russell's scope of a definite description). This objection attempts to relegate all direct reference to implicit use of the paradigm of the semantics of direct reference, the variable. Thus (4) is transformed into,

> The actual circumstances, here, and now are such that it is possible that in Pakistan in five years only those who, in the first, are located at the second, during the third, are envied.

[. . .]

Perhaps enough has been said to establish the following.

(T1) *The descriptive meaning of a pure indexical determines the referent of the indexical with respect to a context of use but is either inapplicable or irrelevant to determining a referent with respect to a circumstance of evaluation.*

I hope that your intuition will agree with mine that it is for this reason that:

(T2) *When what was said in using a pure indexical in a context c is to be evaluated with respect to an arbitrary circumstance, the relevant object is always the referent of the indexical with respect to the context c.*

This is just a slightly elaborated version of Principle 2.

Before turning to true demonstratives, we will adopt some terminology.

Terminological Remarks

Principle 1 and Principle 2 taken together imply that sentences containing pure indexicals have two kinds of meaning.

VI.(i) Content and circumstance

What is said in using a given indexical in different contexts may be different. Thus if I say, today,

I was insulted yesterday

and you utter the same words tomorrow, what is said is different. If what we say differs in truth-value, that is enough to show that we say different things. But even if the truth-values were the same, it is clear that there are possible circumstances in which what I said would be true but what you said would be false. Thus we say different things.

Let us call this first kind of meaning – what is said – *content*. The content of a sentence in a given context is what has traditionally been called a proposition. Strawson, in noting that the sentence

The present king of France is bald

could be used on different occasions to make different statements, used 'statement' in a way similar to our use of *content of a sentence*. If we wish to express the same content in different contexts, we may have to change indexicals. Frege, here using 'thought' for content of a sentence, expresses the point well.

> If someone wants to say the same today as he expressed yesterday using the word 'today', he must replace this word with 'yesterday'. Although the thought is the same its verbal expression must be different so that the sense, which would otherwise be affected by the differing times of utterance, is readjusted.[26]

I take *content* as a notion applying not only to sentences taken in a context but to any meaningful part of speech taken in a context. Thus we can speak of the content of a definite description, an indexical, a predicate, etc. It is *contents* that are evaluated in circumstances of evaluation. If the content is a proposition (i.e., the content of a sentence taken in some context), the result of the evaluation will be a truth-value. The result of evaluating the content of a singular term at a circumstance will be an object (what I earlier called 'the relevant object'). In general, the result of evaluating the content of a well-formed expression α at a circumstance will be an appropriate extension for α (i.e., for a sentence, a truth-value; for a term, an individual; for an n-place predicate, a set of n-tuples of individuals, etc.). This suggests that we can represent a content by a function from circumstances of evaluation to an appropriate extension. Carnap called such functions *intensions*.

The representation is a handy one and I will often speak of contents in terms of it, but one should note that contents which are distinct but equivalent (i.e., share a value in all circumstances) are represented by the same intension. Among other things, this results in the loss of my distinction between terms which are devices of direct reference and descriptions which *turn out* to be rigid designators. (Recall the metaphysical paragraph of section IV.) I wanted the content of an indexical to be just the referent itself, but the intension of such a content will be a constant function. Use of representing intensions does not mean I am abandoning that idea – just ignoring it temporarily.

A *fixed content* is one represented by a constant function. All directly referential expressions (as well as all rigid designators) have a fixed content. [What I elsewhere call a *stable* content.]

Let us settle on *circumstances* for possible circumstances of evaluation. By this I mean both actual and counterfactual situations with respect to which it is appropriate to ask for the extensions of a given well-formed expression. A circumstance will usually include a possible state or history of the world, a time, and perhaps other features as well. The amount of information we require from a circumstance is linked to the degree of specificity of contents, and thus to the kinds of operators in the language.

Operators of the familiar kind treated in intensional logic (modal, temporal, etc.) operate on contents. (Since we represent contents by intensions, it is not surprising that intensional operators operate on contents.) Thus an appropriate extension for an intensional operator is a function from intensions to extensions.[27] A modal operator when applied to an intension will look at the behavior of the intension with respect to the possible state of the world feature of the circumstances of evaluation. A temporal operator will, similarly, be concerned with the time of the circumstance. If we built the time of evaluation into the contents (thus removing time from the circumstances leaving only, say, a possible world history, and making contents *specific* as to time), it would make no sense to have temporal operators. To put the point another way, if *what is said* is thought of as incorporating reference to a specific time, or state of the world, or whatever, it is otiose to ask whether what is said would have been true at another time, in another state of the world, or whatever. Temporal operators applied to eternal sentences (those whose contents incorporate a specific time of evaluation) are redundant. Any intensional operators applied to *perfect* sentences (those whose contents incorporate specific values for all features of circumstances) are redundant.[28]

What sorts of intensional operators to admit seems to me largely a matter of language engineering. It is a question of which features of what we intuitively think of as possible circumstances can be sufficiently well defined and isolated. If we wish to isolate location and regard it as a feature of possible circumstances we can introduce locational operators: 'Two miles north it is the case that', etc. Such operators can be iterated and can be mixed with modal and temporal operators. However, to make such operators interesting we must have contents which are locationally neutral. That is, it must be appropriate to ask if *what is said* would be true in Pakistan. (For example, 'It is raining' seems to be locationally as well as temporally and modally neutral.)

This functional notion of the content of a sentence in a context may not, because of the neutrality of content with respect to time and place, say, exactly correspond to the classical conception of a proposition. But the classical conception can be introduced by adding the demonstratives 'now' and 'here' to the sentence and taking the content of the result. I will continue to refer to the content of a sentence as a proposition, ignoring the classical use.

Before leaving the subject of circumstances of evaluation I should, perhaps, note that the mere attempt to show that an expression is directly referential requires that it be meaningful to ask of an individual in one circumstance whether and with what properties it exists in another circumstance. If such questions cannot be raised because they are regarded as metaphysically meaningless, the question of whether a particular expression is directly referential (or even, a rigid designator) cannot be raised. I have elsewhere referred to the view that such questions are meaningful as *haecceitism*, and I have described other metaphysical manifestations of this view.[29] I advocate this position, although I am uncomfortable with some of its seeming consequences (for example, that the world might be in a state qualitatively exactly as it is, but with a permutation of individuals).

It is hard to see how one could think about the semantics of indexicals and modality without adopting such a view.

VI.(ii) Character

The second kind of meaning, most prominent in the case of indexicals, is that which determines the content in varying contexts. The rule,

> 'I' refers to the speaker or writer

is a meaning rule of the second kind. The phrase 'the speaker or writer' is not supposed to be a complete description, nor is it supposed to refer to the speaker or writer of the *word* 'I'. (There are many such.) It refers to the speaker or writer of the relevant *occurrence* of the word 'I', that is, the agent of the context.

Unfortunately, as usually stated, these meaning rules are incomplete in that they do not explicitly specify that the indexical is directly referential, and thus do not completely determine the content in each context. I will return to this later.

Let us call the second kind of meaning, *character*. The character of an expression is set by linguistic conventions and, in turn, determines the content of the expression in every context.[30] Because character is what is set by linguistic conventions, it is natural to think of it as *meaning* in the sense of what is known by the competent language user.

Just as it was convenient to represent contents by functions from possible circumstances to extensions (Carnap's intentions), so it is convenient to represent characters by functions from possible contexts to contents. (As before we have the drawback that equivalent characters are identified.[31]) This gives us the following picture:

Character: Contexts ⇛ Contents

Content: Circumstances ⇛ Extensions

or, in more familiar language,

Meaning + Context ⇛ Intension ⇛

Intension + Possible World ⇛ Extension

Indexicals have a *context-sensitive* character. It is characteristic of an indexical that its content varies with context. Nonindexicals have a *fixed* character. The same content is invoked in all contexts. This content will typically be sensitive to circumstances, that is, the non-indexicals are typically not rigid designators but will vary in extension from circumstance to circumstance. Eternal sentences are generally good examples of expressions with a fixed character.

All persons alive in 1977 will have died by 2077

expresses the same proposition no matter when said, by whom, or under what circumstances. The truth-value of that proposition may, of course, vary with possible circumstances, but the character is fixed. Sentences with fixed character are very useful to those wishing to leave historical records.

Now that we have two kinds of meaning in addition to extension, Frege's principle of intensional interchange[32] becomes two principles:

(F1) The character of the whole is a function of the character of the parts. That is, if two compound well-formed expressions differ only with respect to components which have the same Character, then the Character of the compounds is the same.

(F2) The Content of the whole is a function of the Content of the parts. That is, if two compound well-formed expressions, each set in (possibly different) contexts differ only with respect to components which *when taken in their respective contexts* have the same content, then the content of the two compounds *each taken in its own context* is the same.

It is the second principle that accounts for the often noted fact that speakers in different contexts can say the same thing by switching indexicals. (And indeed they often *must* switch indexicals to do so.) Frege illustrated this point with respect to 'today' and 'yesterday' in 'The Thought.' (But note that his treatment of 'I' suggests that he does not believe that utterances of 'I' and 'you' could be similarly related!)

Earlier, in my metaphysical phase, I suggested that we should think of the content of an indexical as being just the referent itself, and I resented the fact that the representation of contents as intensions forced us to regard such contents as constant functions. A similar remark applies here. If we are not overly concerned with standardized representations (which certainly have their value for model-theoretic investigations) we might be inclined to say that the character of an indexical-free word or phrase just *is* its (constant) content.

[· · ·]

IX. Argument for Principle 2: True Demonstratives

I return now to the argument that all indexicals are directly referential. Suppose I point at Paul and say,

> He now lives in Princeton, New Jersey.

Call *what I said* – i.e., the content of my utterance, the proposition expressed – 'Pat'. Is Pat true or false? True! Suppose that unbeknownst to me, Paul had moved to Santa Monica last week. Would Pat have then been true or false? False! Now, the tricky case: Suppose that Paul and Charles had each disguised themselves as the other and had switched places. If that had happened, *and* I had uttered as I did, then the proposition I *would have* expressed would have been false. But in that possible context the proposition I *would have* expressed is not Pat. That is easy to see because the proposition I *would have* expressed, had I pointed to Charles instead of Paul – call this proposition 'Mike' – not only *would have* been false but actually is false. Pat, I would claim, would still be true in the circumstances of the envisaged possible context provided that Paul – in whatever costume he appeared – were still residing in Princeton.

IX.(i) The arguments

I am arguing that in order to determine what the truth-value of a proposition expressed by a sentence containing a demonstrative *would be* under other possible circumstances, the relevant individual is not the individual that *would have* been demonstrated had those circumstances obtained and the demonstration been set in a context of those circumstances, but rather the individual demonstrated in the context which *did* generate the proposition being evaluated. As I have already noted, it is characteristic of sentences containing demonstratives – or, for that matter, any indexical – that they may express different propositions in different contexts. We must be wary of confusing the proposition that would have been expressed by a similar utterance in a slightly different context – say, one in which the demonstratum is changed – with the proposition that was actually expressed. If we keep this distinction in mind – i.e., we distinguish Pat and Mike – we are less likely to confuse what the truth-value of the proposition *actually* expressed would have been under some possible circumstances with what the truth-value of the proposition that *would have been* expressed would have been under those circumstances.

When we consider the vast array of possible circumstances with respect to which we might inquire into the truth of a proposition expressed in some context *c* by an utterance *u*, it quickly becomes apparent that only a small fraction of these circumstances will involve an utterance of the same sentence in a similar context, and that there must be a way of evaluating the truth-value of propositions expressed using demonstratives in counterfactual circumstances in which no demonstrations are taking place and no individual has the exact characteristics exploited in the demonstration. Surely, it is irrelevant to determining whether what I said would be true or not in some counterfactual circumstance, whether Paul, or anyone for that matter, *looked* as he does now. All that would be relevant is *where he lives*. Therefore,

(T3) *the relevant features of the demonstratum* qua demonstratum *(compare, the relevant features of the x Fx* qua the x Fx*) – namely, that the speaker is pointing at it, that it has a certain appearance, is presented in a certain way – cannot be the essential characteristics used to identify the relevant individual in counterfactual situations.*

These two arguments: the distinction between Pat and Mike, and consideration of counterfactual situations in which no demonstration occurs, are offered to support the view that demonstratives are devices of direct reference (rigid designators, if you will) and, by contrast, to reject a Fregean theory of demonstratives.

IX.(ii) The Fregean theory of demonstrations

In order to develop the latter theory, in contrast to my own, we turn first to a portion of the Fregean theory which I accept: the Fregean theory of demonstrations.

As you know, for a Fregean the paradigm of a meaningful expression is the definite description, which picks out or denotes an individual, a unique individual, satisfying a condition *s*. The individual is called the *denotation* of the definite description and the condition *s* we may identify with the *sense* of the definite description. Since a given individual may uniquely satisfy several distinct conditions, definite descriptions with distinct senses may have the same denotation. And since some conditions may be uniquely satisfied by no individual, a definite description may have a sense but no denotation. The condition by means of which a definite description picks out its denotation is *the manner of presentation* of the denotation by the definite description.

The Fregean theory of demonstratives claims, correctly I believe, that the analogy between descriptions (short for 'definite descriptions') and demonstrations is close enough to provide a sense and denotation analysis of the 'meaning' of a demonstration. The denotation is the demonstratum (that which is demonstrated), and it seems quite natural to regard each demonstration as presenting its demonstratum in a particular manner, which we may regard as the sense of the demonstration. The same individual could be demonstrated by demonstrations so different in manner of presentation that it would be informative to a competent auditor-observer to be told that the demonstrata were one. For example, it might be informative to you for me to tell you that

> That [pointing to Venus in the morning sky] is identical with
> that [pointing to Venus in the evening sky].

(I would, of course, have to speak very slowly.) The two demonstrations – call the first one 'Phos' and the second one 'Hes' – which accompanied the two occurrences of the demonstrative expression 'that' have the same demonstratum but distinct manners of presentation. It is this difference between the sense of Hes and the sense of Phos that accounts, the Fregean claims, for the informativeness of the assertion.

It is possible, to pursue the analogy, for a demonstration to have no demonstratum. This can arise in several ways: through hallucination, through carelessness (not noticing, in the darkened room, that the subject had jumped off the demonstration platform a few moments before the lecture began), through a sortal conflict (using the demonstrative phrase ⌜that *F*⌝, where *F* is a common noun phrase, while demonstrating something which is not an *F*), and in other ways.

Even Donnellans's important distinction between referential and attributive uses of definite descriptions seems to fit, equally comfortably, the case of demonstrations.[38]

The Fregean hypostatizes demonstrations in such a way that it is appropriate to ask of a given demonstration, say Phos, what *would* it have demonstrated under various counterfactual circumstances. Phos and Hes might have demonstrated distinct individuals.[39]

We should not allow our enthusiasm for analogy to overwhelm judgment in this case. There are some relevant respects in which descriptions and demonstrations are disanalogous. First, as David Lewis has pointed out, demonstrations do not have a syntax, a fixed formal structure in terms of whose elements we might try to define, either directly or recursively, the notion of sense.[40] Second, to different audiences (for example, the speaker, those sitting in front of the demonstration platform, and those sitting behind the demonstration platform) the same demonstration may have different senses. Or perhaps we should say that a single performance may involve distinct demonstrations from the perspective of distinct audiences. ('Exactly like proper names!' says the Fregean, 'as long as the demonstratum remains the same, these fluctuations in sense are tolerable. But they should be avoided in the system of a demonstrative science and should not appear in a perfect vehicle of communication.')

IX.(iii) The Fregean theory of demonstratives

Let us accept, tentatively and cautiously, the Fregean theory of demonstrations, and turn now to the Fregean theory of demonstratives.[41]

According to the Fregean theory of demonstratives, an occurrence of a demonstrative expression functions rather like a place-holder for the associated demonstration. The sense of a sentence containing demonstratives is to be the result of replacing each demonstrative by a constant whose sense is given as the sense of the associated demonstration. An important aim of the Fregean theory is, of course, to solve Frege's problem. And it does that quite neatly. You recall that the Fregean accounted for the informativeness of

> That [Hes] = that [Phos]

in terms of the distinct senses of Iles and Phos. Now we see that the senses of the two occurrences of 'that' are identified with these two distinct senses so that the ultimate solution is exactly like that given by Frege originally. The sense of the left 'that' differs from the sense of the right 'that'.

IX.(iv) Argument against the Fregean theory of demonstratives

Let us return now to our original example:

> He [Delta] now lives in Princeton, New Jersey

where 'Delta' is the name of the relevant demonstration. I assume that in the possible circumstances described earlier, Paul and Charles having disguised themselves as each other, Delta would have demonstrated Charles. Therefore, according to the Fregean theory, the proposition I just expressed, Pat, would have been false under the counterfactual circumstances of the switch. But this, as argued earlier, is wrong. Therefore, the Fregean theory of demonstratives though it nicely solves Frege's problem, is simply incorrect in associating propositions with utterances.

Let me recapitulate. We compared two theories as to the proposition expressed by a sentence containing a demonstrative along with an associated demonstration. Both theories allow that the demonstration can be regarded as having both a sense and a demonstratum. My theory, the direct reference theory, claims that in assessing the proposition in counterfactual circumstances it is the actual demonstratum – in the example, Paul – that is the relevant individual. The Fregean theory claims that the proposition is to be construed as if the sense of the demonstration were the sense of the demonstrative. Thus, in counterfactual situations it is the individual that *would* have been demonstrated that is the relevant individual. According to the direct reference theory, demonstratives are rigid designators. According to the Fregean theory, their denotation varies in different counterfactual circumstances as the demonstrata of the associated demonstration would vary in those circumstances.

The earlier distinction between Pat and Mike, and the discussion of counterfactual circumstances in which, as we would now put it, the demonstration would have demonstrated nothing, argue that with respect to the problem of associating propositions with utterances the direct reference theory is correct and the Fregean theory is wrong.

I have carefully avoided arguing for the direct reference theory by using modal or subjunctive sentences for fear the Fregean would claim that the peculiarity of demonstratives is not that they are rigid designators but that they always take primary scope. If I had argued only on the basis of our intuitions as to the truth-value of

> If Charles and Paul had changed chairs, then he (Delta) would not now be living in Princeton

such a scope interpretation could be claimed. But I didn't.

The perceptive Fregeans among you will have noted that I have said nothing about how Frege's problem fares under a direct reference theory of demonstratives. And indeed, if 'that' accompanied by a demonstration is a rigid designator for the demonstratum, then

> that (Hes) = that (Phos)

looks like two rigid designators designating the same thing. Uh Oh! I will return to this in my Epistemological Remarks (section XVII).

X. Fixing the Reference vs. Supplying a Synonym[42]

The Fregean is to be forgiven. He has made a most natural mistake. Perhaps he thought as follows: If I point at someone and say 'he', that occurrence of 'he' must refer to the male at whom I am now pointing. It does! So far, so good. Therefore, the Fregean reasons, since 'he' (in its demonstrative sense) means the same as 'the male at whom I am now pointing' and since the denotation of the latter varies with circumstances the denotation of the former must also. But this is wrong. Simply because it is a rule of the language that 'he' *refers* to the male at whom I am now pointing (or, whom I am now demonstrating, to be more general), it does not follow that any synonymy is thereby established. In fact, this is one of those cases in which – to use Kripke's excellent idiom – the rule simply tells us how to *fix the reference* but does not supply a synonym.

Consider the proposition I express with the utterance

> He [Delta] is the male at whom I am now pointing.

Call that proposition 'Sean'. Now Sean is certainly true. We know from the rules of the language that any utterance of that form must express a true proposition. In fact we would be justified in calling the *sentence*

> He is the male at whom I am now pointing.

almost analytic. ('Almost' because of the hypothesis that the demonstrative is *proper* – that I am pointing at a unique male – is needed.)

But is Sean necessary? Certainly not, I might have pointed at someone else.

This kind of mistake – to confuse a semantical rule which tells how to fix the reference to a directly referential term with a rule which supplies a synonym – is easy to make. Since semantics must supply a meaning, in the sense of content (as I call it), for expressions, one thinks naturally that whatever way the referent of an expression is given by the semantical rules, that *way* must stand for the content of the expression. (Church [or was it Carnap?] says as much, explicitly.) This hypothesis seems especially plausible, when, as is typical of indexicals,

> the semantical rule which fixes the reference seems to exhaust our knowledge of the meaning of the expression.

X.(i) Reichenbach on token reflexives

It was from such a perspective, I believe, that Reichenbach built his ingenious theory of indexicals. Reichenbach called such expressions 'token-reflexive words' in accordance with his theory. He writes as follows:

> We saw that most individual-descriptions are constructed by reference to other individuals. Among these there is a class of descriptions in which the individual referred to is the act of speaking. We have special words

> to indicate this reference; such words are 'I', 'you', 'here', 'now', 'this'. Of the same sort are the tenses of verbs, since they determine time by reference to the time when the words are uttered. To understand the function of these words we have to make use of the distinction between *token* and *symbol*, 'token' meaning the individual sign, and 'symbol' meaning the class of similar tokens (cf. §2). Words and sentences are symbols. The words under consideration are words which refer to the corresponding token used in an individual act of speech, or writing; they may therefore be called *token-reflexive* words.
>
> It is easily seen that all these words can be defined in terms of the phrase 'this token'. The word 'I', for instance, means the same as 'the person who utters this token'; 'now' means the same as 'the time at which this token was uttered'; 'this table' means the same as 'the table pointed to by a gesture accompanying this token'. We therefore need inquire only into the meaning of the phrase 'this token'.[43]

But is it true, for example, that

(10) 'I' means the same as 'the person who utters this token'?

It is certainly true that

I am the person who utters this token.

But if (10) correctly asserted a synonymy, then it would be true that

(11) If no one were to utter this token, I would not exist.

Beliefs such as (11) could make one a compulsive talker.

XI. The Meaning of Indexicals

In order to correctly and more explicitly state the semantical rule which the dictionary attempts to capture by the entry

I: the person who is speaking or writing

we would have to develop our semantical theory – the semantics of direct reference – and then state that

(D1) 'I' is an indexical, different utterances of which may have different contents
(D3) 'I' is, in each of its utterances, directly referential
(D2) In each of its utterances, 'I' refers to the person who utters it.

We have seen errors in the Fregean analysis of demonstratives and in Reichenbach's analysis of indexicals, all of which stemmed from failure to realize that these words are directly referential. When we say that a word is directly referential are we saying that its meaning *is* its reference (its only meaning is its reference, its meaning is nothing more than its reference)? Certainly not.[44] Insofar as meaning is given by the rules of a language and is what is known by competent speakers, I would be more inclined to say in the case of directly referential words and phrases that their reference is *no* part of their meaning. The meaning of the word 'I' does not change when different persons use it. The meaning of 'I' is given by the rules (D1) , (D2), and (D3) above.

Meanings tell us how the content of a word or phrase is determined by the context of use. Thus the meaning of a word or phrase is what I have called its *character*. (Words and phrases with no indexical element express the same content in every context; they have a fixed character.) To supply a synonym for a word or phrase is to find another with the same *character*; finding another with the same *content* in a particular context certainly won't do. The content of 'I' used by me may be identical with the content of 'you' used by you. This doesn't make 'I' and 'you' synonyms. Frege noticed that if one wishes to say again what one said yesterday using 'today', today one must use 'yesterday'. (Incidentally the relevant passage, quoted on page [323], propounds what I take to be a direct reference theory of the indexicals 'today' and 'yesterday'.) But 'today' and 'yesterday' are not synonyms. For two words or phrases to be synonyms, they must have the same content in every context. In general, for indexicals, it is not possible to find synonyms. This is because indexicals are directly referential, and the compound phrases which can be used to give their reference ('the person who is speaking', 'the individual being demonstrated', etc.) are not.

XII. Dthat[45]

It would be useful to have a way of converting an arbitrary singular term into one which is directly referential.

Recall that we earlier regarded demonstrations, which are required to 'complete' demonstratives, as a kind of description. The demonstrative was then treated as a directly referential term whose referent was the demonstratum of the associated demonstration.

Now why not regard descriptions as a kind of demonstration, and introduce a special demonstrative which requires completion by a description and which is treated as a directly referential term whose referent is the denotation of the associated description? Why not? Why not indeed! I have done so, and I write it thus:

dthat[α]

where α is any description, or, more generally, any singular term. 'Dthat' is simply the demonstrative 'that' with the following singular term functioning as its demonstration. (Unless you hold a Fregean theory of demonstratives, in which case its meaning is as stipulated above.)

Now we can come much closer to providing genuine synonyms.

> 'I' means the same as 'dthat' [the person who utters this token]'.

(The fact that this alleged synonymy is cast in the theory of utterances rather than occurrences introduces some subtle complications, which have been discussed by Reichenbach.)

XIII. Contexts, Truth, and Logical Truth

I wish, in this section, to contrast an *occurrence* of a well-formed expression (my *technical* term for the combination of an expression and a context) with an *utterance* of an expression.

There are several arguments for my notion, but the main one is from Remark 1 on the Logic of Demonstratives (section XIX below [not included]): I have sometimes said that the content of a sentence in a context is, roughly, the proposition the sentence would express if uttered in that context. This description is not quite accurate on two counts. First, it is important to distinguish an *utterance* from a *sentence-in-a-context*. The former notion is from the theory of speech acts, the latter from semantics. Utterances take time, and utterances of distinct sentences cannot be simultaneous (i.e., in the same context). But in order to develop a logic of demonstratives we must be able to evaluate several premises and a conclusion all in the same context. We do not want arguments involving indexicals to become valid simply because there is no possible context in which all the premises are uttered, and thus no possible context in which all are uttered truthfully.

Since the content of an occurrence of a sentence containing indexicals depends on the context, the notion of *truth* must be relativized to a context.

> If c is a context, then an occurrence of ϕ in c is true iff the content expressed by ϕ in this context is true when evaluated with respect to the circumstance of the context.

We see from the notion of truth that among other aspects of a context must be a possible circumstance. Every context occurs in a particular circumstance, and there are demonstratives such as 'actual' which refer to that circumstance.

If you try out the notion of truth on a few examples, you will see that it is correct. If I now utter a sentence, I will have uttered a truth just in case *what I said*, the content, is true in *these* circumstances.

As is now common for intensional logics, we provide for the notion of a *structure*, comprising a family of circumstances. Each such structure will determine a set of possible contexts. Truth in a structure, is truth in every possible context of the structure. Logical truth is truth in every structure.

XIV. Summary of Findings (so far): Pure Indexicals

Let me try now to summarize my findings regarding the semantics of demonstratives and other indexicals. First, let us consider the non-demonstrative indexicals such as 'I', 'here' (in its nondemonstrative sense), 'now', 'today', 'yesterday', etc. In the case of these words, the linguistic conventions which constitute *meaning* consist of rules specifying the referent of a given *occurrence* of the word (we might say, a given token, or even utterance, of the word, if we are willing to be somewhat less abstract) in terms of various features of the context of the occurrence. Although these rules fix the referent and, in a very special sense, might be said to define the indexical, the way in which the rules are given does not provide a synonym for the indexical. The rules tell us for any possible occurrence of the indexical what the referent would be, but they do *not* constitute the content of such an occurrence. Indexicals are directly referential. The rules tell us what it is that is referred to. Thus, they *determine* the content (the propositional constituent) for a particular occurrence of an indexical. But they are not a *part* of the content (they constitute no part of the propositional constituent). In order to keep clear on a topic where ambiguities constantly threaten, I have introduced two technical terms: *content* and *character* for the two kinds of meaning (in addition to extension) I associate with indexicals. Distinct occurrences of an indexical (in distinct contexts) may not only have distinct referents, they may have distinct meanings in the sense of *content*. If I say 'I am tired today' today and Montgomery Furth says 'I am tired today' tomorrow, our utterances have different contents in that the factors which are relevant to determining the truth-value of what Furth said in both actual and counterfactual circumstances are quite different from the factors which are relevant to determining the truth-value of what I said. Our two utterances are as different in content as are the sentences 'David Kaplan is tired on 26 March 1977' and 'Montgomery Furth is tired on 27 March 1977.' But there is another sense of meaning in which, absent lexical or syntactical ambiguities, two occurrences of the *same* word or phrase *must* mean the same. (Otherwise how could we learn and communicate with language?) This sense of meaning – which I call *character* – is what determines the content of an occurrence of a word or phrase in a given context. For indexicals, the rules of language constitute the meaning in the sense of *character*. As normally expressed, in dictionaries and the like, these rules are incomplete in that, by omitting to mention that indexicals are directly referential, they fail to specify the full content of an occurrence of an indexical.

Three important features to keep in mind about these two kinds of meaning are:

1. Character applies only to words and phrases as types, content to occurrences of words and phrases in contexts.
2. Occurrences of two phrases can agree in content although the phrases differ in character, and two phrases can agree in character but differ in content in distinct contexts.
3. The relationship of character to content is something like that traditionally regarded as the relationship of sense to denotation, character is a way of presenting content.

XV. Further Details: Demonstratives and Demonstrations

Let me turn now to the demonstratives proper, those expressions which must be associated with a demonstration in order to determine a referent. In addition to the pure demonstratives 'that' and 'this' there are a variety of demonstratives which contain built-in sortals: 'he' for 'that male', 'she' for 'that female',[46] etc., and there are demonstrative phrases built from a pure demonstrative and a common noun phrase: 'that man drinking a martini', etc. Words and phrases which have demonstrative use may have other uses as well, for example, as bound variable or pronouns of laziness (anaphoric use).

I accept, tentatively and cautiously, the Fregean theory of demonstrations according to which:

1. A demonstration is a way of presenting an individual.
2. A given demonstration in certain counterfactual circumstances would have demonstrated (i.e., presented) an individual other than the individual actually demonstrated.
3. A demonstration which fails to demonstrate any individual might have demonstrated one, and a demonstration which demonstrates an individual might have demonstrated no individual at all.

So far we have asserted that it is not an essential property of a given demonstration (according to the Fregean theory) that it demonstrate a given individual, or indeed, that it demonstrate any individual at all. It is this feature of demonstrations: that demonstrations which in fact demonstrate the same individual might have demonstrated distinct individuals, which provides a solution to the demonstrative version of Frege's problem (why is an utterance of 'that [Hes] = that [Phos]' informative?) analogous to Frege's own solution to the definite description version. There is some theoretical lattitude as to how we should regard such other features of a demonstration as its place, time, and agent. Just to fix ideas, let us regard all these features as accidental. (It may be helpful to think of demonstrations as *types* and particular performances of them as their *tokens*). Then,

4. A given demonstration might have been mounted by someone other than its actual agent, and might be repeated in the same or a different place.

Although we are not now regarding the actual place and time of a demonstration as essential to it, it does seem to me to be essential to a demonstration that it present its demonstrata from some perspective, that is, as the individual that looks thusly *from here now*. On the other hand, it does not seem to me to be essential to a demonstration that it be mounted by any agent at all.[47]

We now have a kind of standard form for demonstrations:

> The individual that has appearance *A* from here now

where an appearance is something like a picture with a little arrow pointing to the relevant subject. Trying to put it into words, a particular demonstration might come out like:

> The brightest heavenly body now visible from here.

In this example we see the importance of perspective. The same demonstration, differently located, may present a different demonstratum (a twin, for example).

If we set a demonstration, δ, in a context, *c*, we determine the relevant perspective (i.e., the values of 'here' and 'now'). We also determine the demonstratum, if there is one – if, that is, in the circumstances of the context there is an individual that appears that way from the place and time of the context.[48] In setting δ and *c* we determine more than just the demonstratum in the possible world of the context. By fixing the perspective, we determine for each possible circumstance what, if anything, would appear like that from that perspective. This is to say, we determine a *content*. This content will not, in general, be fixed (like that determined by a rigid designator). Although it was Venus that appeared a certain way from a certain location in ancient Greece, it might have been Mars. Under certain counterfactual conditions, it *would* have been Mars that appeared just that way from just that location. Set in a different context, δ, may determine a quite different content or no content at all. When I look at myself in the mirror each morning I know that I didn't look like that ten years ago – and I suspect that nobody did.

The preceding excursion into a more detailed Fregean theory of demonstrations was simply in order to establish the following structural features of demonstrations:

1. A demonstration, when set in a context (i.e., an *occurrence* of a demonstration), determines a content.
2. It is not required that an occurrence of a demonstration have a fixed content.

In view of these features, we can associate with each demonstration a *character* which represents the 'meaning' or manner of presentation of the demonstration. We have now brought the semantics of demonstrations and descriptions into isomorphism.[49] Thus, I regard my 'dthat' operator as representing the general case of a demonstrative. Demonstratives are incomplete expressions which must be completed by a demonstration (type). A complete sentence (type) will include an associated demonstration (type) for each of its demonstratives. Thus each demonstrative, d, will be accompanied by a demonstration, δ, thus:

$d[\delta]$

The character of a *complete* demonstrative is given by the semantical rule:

> In any context c, $d[\delta]$ is a directly referential term that designates the demonstratum, if any, of δ in c, and that otherwise designates nothing.

Obvious adjustments are to be made to take into account any common noun phrase which accompanies or is built-in to the demonstrative.

Since no immediately relevant structural differences have appeared between demonstrations and descriptions, I regard the treatment of the 'dthat' operator in the formal logic LD as accounting for the general case. It would be a simple matter to add to the syntax a category of 'nonlogical demonstration constants'. (Note that the indexicals of LD are all logical signs in the sense that their meaning [character] is not given by the structure but by the evaluation rules.)

XVI. Alternative Treatments of Demonstrations

The foregoing development of the Fregean theory of demonstration is not inevitable. Michael Bennett has proposed that only places be demonstrata and that we require an explicit or implicit common noun phrase to accompany the demonstrative, so that:

that [pointing at a person]

becomes

dthat [the person who is there [pointing at a place]].

My findings do not include the claim that the – or better, a – Fregean theory of demonstrations is correct. I can provide an alternative account for those who regard demonstrations as nonrepeatable nonseparable features of contexts. The conception now under consideration is that in certain contexts the agent is demonstrating something, or more than one thing, and in others not. Thus just as we can speak of agent, time, place, and possible world history as features of a context, we may also speak of first demonstratum, second demonstratum, . . . (some of which may be null) as features of a context. We then attach subscripts to our demonstratives and regard the n-th demonstrative, when set in a context, as rigid designator of the n-th demonstratum of the context. Such a rule associates a character with each demonstrative. In providing no role for demonstrations as separable 'manners of presentation' this theory eliminates the interesting distinction between demonstratives and other indexicals. We might call it the *Indexical theory of demonstratives*. (Of course every reasonable theory of demonstratives treats them as indexicals of some kind. I regard my own theory of indexicals in general, and the nondemonstrative indexicals in particular, as essentially uncontroversial. Therefore I reserve *Indexical theory of demonstratives* for the controversial alternative to the Fregean theory of demonstrations – the Fregean theory of demonstra*tives* having been refuted.)

Let us call my theory as based on the Fregean theory of demonstrations the *Corrected Fregean theory of demonstratives*. The Fregean theory of demonstrations may be extravagant, but compared with its riches, the indexical theory is a mean thing. From a logical point of view, the riches of the Corrected Fregean theory of demonstratives are already available in connection with the demonstrative 'dthat' and its descriptive pseudodemonstrations, so a decision to enlarge the language of LD with additional demonstratives whose semantics are in accord with the Indexical theory need not be too greatly lamented.

If we consider Frege's problem, we have the two formulations:

that [Hes] = that [Phos]

and

$\text{that}_1 = \text{that}_2$

Both provide their sentence with an informative character. But the Fregean idea that that very demonstration might have picked out a different demonstratum seems to me to capture more of the epistemological situation than the Indexicalist's idea that in some contexts the first and second demonstrata differ.

The Corrected Fregean theory, by incorporating demonstration types in its sentence types, accounts for more differences in informativeness and differences in meaning (character). It thereby provides a nice Frege-type solution to many Frege-type problems. Bt it can only forestall the resort to directly epistemological issues, it cannot hold them in abeyance indefinitely. Therefore I turn to epistemological remarks.

XVII. Epistemological Remarks[50]

How do content and character serve as objects of thought? Let us state, once again, Frege's problem

(FP) How can (an occurrence of $\ulcorner \alpha = \beta \urcorner$ (in a given context), if true, differ in cognitive significance from (an occurrence of) $\ulcorner \alpha = \alpha \urcorner$ (in the same context)?

In (FP) α, β are arbitrary singular terms. (In future formulatons, I will omit the parentheticals as understood.) When α and β are demonstrative free, Frege explained the difference in terms of his notion of sense. A notion which, his writings generally suggest, should be identified with our *content*. But it is clear that Frege's problem can be reinstituted in a form in which resort to contents will not explain differences in 'cognitive significance'. We need only ask,

(FPD) How can $\ulcorner$dthat[[α] = dthat[β]$\urcorner$ if true, differ in cognitive significance from $\ulcorner$dthat[α] = dthat[α]$\urcorner$?

Since, as we shall show, for any term γ,

$\ulcorner \gamma =$ dthat[γ]$\urcorner$ is analytic

the sentence pair in (FP) will differ in cognitive significance if and only if the sentence pair in (FPD) differ similarly. [There are a few assumptions built in here, but they are O.K.] Note, however, that the *content* of $\ulcorner$dthat[α]$\urcorner$ and the *content* of $\ulcorner$dthat[β]$\urcorner$ are the same whenever $\ulcorner \alpha = \beta \urcorner$ is true. Thus the difference in cognitive significance between the sentence pair in (FPD) cannot be accounted for in terms of content.

If Frege's solution to (FP) was correct, then α and β have different contents. From this it follows that $\ulcorner$dthat[α]$\urcorner$ and $\ulcorner$dthat[β]$\urcorner$ have different characters. [It doesn't really, because of the identification of contents with intensions, but let it pass.] Is character, then, the object of thought?

If you and I both say to ourselves,

(B) 'I am getting bored'

have we thought the same thing? We could not have, because what you thought was true while what I thought was false.

What we must do is disentangle two epistemological notions: *the objects of thought* (what Frege called 'Thoughts') and the *cognitive significance of an object of thought*. As has been noted above, a character may be likened to a manner of presentation of a content. This suggests that we identify objects of thought with contents and the cognitive significance of such objects with characters.

E. Principle 1 *Objects of thought (Thoughts) = Contents*

E. Principle 2 *Cognitive significance of a Thought = Character*

According to this view, the thoughts associated with ⌜dthat[α] = dthat[β]⌝ and ⌜dthat[α] = dthat[α]⌝ are the same, but the thought (not the denotation, mind you, but the *thought*) is *presented* differently.

It is important to see that we have not *simply* generalized Frege's theory, providing a higher order Fregean sense for each name of a regular Fregean sense.[51] In Frege's theory, a given manner of presentation presents the same object to all mankind.[52] But for us, a given manner of presentation – a character – what we both said to ourselves when we both said (B) – will, in general, present different objects (of thought) to different persons (and even different Thoughts to the same person at different times).

How then can we claim that we have captured the idea of cognitive significance? To break the link between cognitive significance and universal Fregean senses and at the same time forge the link between cognitive significance and character we must come to see the *context-sensitivity* (dare I call it ego-orientation?) of cognitive states.

Let us try a Putnam-like experiment. We raise two identical twins, Castor and Pollux, under qualitatively identical conditions, qualitatively identical stimuli, etc. If necessary, we may monitor their brain states and make small corrections in their brain structures if they begin drifting apart. They respond to all cognitive stimuli in identical fashion.[53] Have we not been successful in achieving the same cognitive (i.e., psychological) state? Of course we have, what more could one ask! But wait, they believe different things. Each sincerely says,

My brother was born before I was

and the beliefs they thereby express conflict. In this, Castor speaks the truth, while Pollux speaks falsely. This does not reflect on the identity of their cognitive states, for, as Putnam has emphasized, circumstances alone do not determine extension (here, the truth-value) from cognitive state. Insofar as distinct persons can be in the same cognitive state, Castor and Pollux are.

E. Corollary 1 *It is an almost inevitable consequence of the fact that two persons are in the* same *cognitive state, that they will* disagree *in their attitudes toward some object of thought.*

The corollary applies equally well to the same person at different times, and to the same person at the same time in different circumstances.[54] In general, the corollary applies to any individuals *x*, *y* in different contexts.

My aim was to argue that the cognitive significance of a word or phrase was to be identified with its character, the way the content is presented to us. In discussing the twins, I tried to show that persons could be in the same total cognitive state and still, as we would say, believe different things. This doesn't prove that the cognitive content of, say, a single sentence or even a word is to be identified with its character, but it strongly suggests it.

Let me try a different line of argument. We agree that a given content may be presented under various characters and that consequently we may hold a propositional attitude toward a given content under one character but not under another. (For example, on March 27 of this year, having lost track of the date, I may continue to hope to be finished by this March 26, without hoping to be finished by yesterday.) Now instead of arguing that character is what we would ordinarily call cognitive significance, let me just ask why we should be interested in the character under which we hold our various attitudes. Why should we be interested in that special kind of significance that is sensitive to the use of indexicals; 'I', 'here', 'now', 'that', and the like? John Perry, in his stimulating and insightful paper 'Frege on Demonstratives' asks and answers this question. [Perry uses 'thought' where I would use 'object of thought' or 'content', he uses 'apprehend' for 'believe' but *note that other psychological verbs would yield analogous cases.* I have taken a few liberties in substituting my own terminology for Perry's and have added the emphasis.']

> Why should we care under what character someone apprehends a thought, so long as he does? I can only sketch the barest suggestion of an answer here. *We use the manner of presentation, the character, to individuate psychological states, in explaining and predicting action.* It is the manner of presentation, the character and not the thought apprehended, that is tied to human action. When you and I have beliefs under the common character of 'A bear is about to attack me', we behave similarly. We both roll up in a ball and try to be as still as possible. Different thoughts apprehended, same character, same behavior. When you and I both apprehend that I am about to be attacked by a bear, we behave differently. I roll up in a ball, you run to get help. Same thought apprehended, different characters, different behaviors.[55]

Perry's examples can be easily multiplied. My hope to be finished by a certain time is sensitive to how the content corresponding to the time is presented, as 'yesterday' or as 'this March 26'. If I see, reflected in a window, the image of a man whose pants appear to be on fire, my behavior is sensitive to whether I think, 'His pants are on fire' or 'My pants are on fire', though the object of thought may be the same.

So long as Frege confined his attention to indexical free expressions, and given his theory of proper names, it is not surprising that he did not distinguish objects of thought (content) from cognitive significance (character), for that is the realm of *fixed* character and thus, as already remarked, there is a natural identification of character with content. Frege does, however, discuss indexicals in two places. The first passage, in which he discusses 'yesterday' and 'today' I have already discussed. Everything he says there is essentially correct. (He does not go far enough.) The second passage has provoked few endorsements and much skepticism. It too, I believe, is susceptible of an interpretation which makes it essentially correct. I quote it in full.

> Now everyone is presented to himself in a particular and primitive way, in which he is presented to no one else. So, when Dr. Lauben thinks that he has been wounded, he will probably take as a basis this primitive way in which he is presented to himself. And only Dr. Lauben himself can grasp thoughts determined in this way. But now he may want to communicate with others. He cannot communicate a thought which he alone can grasp. Therefore, if he now says 'I have been wounded', he must use the 'I' in a sense that can be grasped by others, perhaps in the sense of 'he who is speaking to you at this moment', by doing which he makes the associated conditions of his utterance serve for the expression of his thought.[56]

What is the particular and primitive way in which Dr. Lauben is presented to himself? What cognitive content presents Dr. Lauben to himself, but presents him to nobody else? Thoughts determined this way can be grasped by Dr. Lauben, but no one else can grasp *that* thought determined in *that* way. The answer, I believe, is, simply, that Dr. Lauben is presented to himself under the character of 'I'.

A sloppy thinker might succumb to the temptation to slide from an acknowledgement of the privileged *perspective* we each have on ourselves – only I can refer to me as 'I' – to the conclusions: first, that this perspective necessarily yields a privileged *picture* of what is seen (referred to), and second, that this picture is what is intended when one makes use of the privileged perspective (by saying 'I'). These conclusions, even if correct, are not forced upon us. The character of 'I' provides the acknowledged privileged perspective, whereas the analysis of the content of particular occurrences of 'I' provides for (and needs) no privileged pictures. There may be metaphysical, epistemological, or ethical reasons why I (so conceived) am especially *important* to myself. (Compare: why *now* is an especially important time to me. It too is presented in a particular and primitive way, and this moment cannot be presented at any other time in the same way.)[57] But the phenomenon noted by Frege – that everyone is presented to himself in a particular and primitive way – can be fully accounted for using only our semantical theory.

Furthermore, regarding the first conclusion, I sincerely doubt that there is, for each of us on each occasion of the use of 'I', a particular, primitive, and incommunicable Fregean self-concept which we tacitly express to ourselves. And regarding the second conclusion: even if Castor were sufficiently narcissistic to associate such self-concepts with his every use of 'I', his twin, Pollux, whose mental life is qualitatively identical with Castor's, would associate the *same* self-concept with *his* every (matching) use of 'I'.[58] The second conclusion would lead to the absurd result that when Castor and Pollux each say 'I', they do not thereby distinguish themselves from one another. (An even more astonishing result is possible. Suppose that due to a bit of self-deception the self-concept held in common by Castor and Pollux fits neither of them. The second conclusion then leads irresistibly to the possibility that when Castor and Pollux each say 'I' they each refer to a third party!)

The perceptive reader will have noticed that the conclusions of the sloppy thinker regarding the pure indexical 'I' are not unlike those of the Fregean regarding true demonstratives. The sloppy thinker has adopted a *demonstrative theory of indexicals:* 'I' is synonymous with 'this person' [along with an appropriate *subjective* demonstration], 'now' with 'this time', 'here' with 'this place' [each associated with some demonstration], etc. Like the Fregean, the sloppy thinker errs in believing that the sense of the demonstration is the sense of the indexical, but the sloppy thinker commits an additional error in believing that such senses are in any way necessarily associated with uses of pure indexicals. The slide from privileged perspective to privileged picture is the sloppy thinker's original sin. Only one who is located in the exact center of the Sahara Desert is entitled to refer to that place as 'here', but aside from that, the place may present no distinguishing features.[59]

The sloppy thinker's conclusions may have another source. Failure to distinguish between the cognitive significance of a thought and the thought itself seems to have led some to believe that the elements of an object of thought must each be directly accessible to the mind. From this it follows that if a singular proposition is an object of thought, the thinker must somehow be immediately acquainted with each of the individuals involved. But, as we have seen, the situation is rather different from this. Singular propositions may be presented to us under characters which neither imply nor presuppose any special form of acquaintance with the individuals of the singular propositions. The psychological states, perhaps even the epistemological situations, of Castor and Pollux are alike, yet they assert distinct singular propositions when they each say 'My brother was born before me'. Had they lived at different times they might still have been situated alike epistemologically while asserting distinct singular propositions in saying 'It is quiet here now'. A kidnapped heiress, locked in the trunk of a car, knowing neither the time nor where she is, may think 'It is quiet here now' and the indexicals will remain directly referential.[60]

E. Corollary 2 *Ignorance of the referent does not defeat the directly referential character of indexicals.*

From this it follows that a special form of knowledge of an object is neither required nor presupposed in order that a person may entertain as object of thought a singular proposition involving that object.

There is nothing inaccessible to the mind about the semantics of direct reference, even when the reference is to that which we know only by description. What allows us to take various propositional attitudes towards singular propositions is not the form of our acquaintance with the objects but is rather our ability to manipulate the conceptual apparatus of direct reference.[61]

The foregoing remarks are aimed at refuting *Direct Acquaintance Theories of direct reference.* According to such theories, the question whether an utterance expresses a singular proposition turns, in the first instance, on the speaker's *knowledge of the referent* rather than on the *form of the reference.* If the speaker lacks the appropriate form of acquaintance with the referent, the utterance cannot express a singular proposition, and any apparently directly referring expressions used must be abbreviations or disguises for something like Fregean descriptions. Perhaps the Direct Acquaintance theorist thought that only a theory like his could permit singular propositions while still providing a solution for Frege's problem. If we could *directly* refer to a given object in nonequivalent ways (e.g., as 'dthat[Hes]' and 'dthat[Phos]'), we could not – so he thought – explain the difference in cognitive significance between the appropriate instances of $\ulcorner \alpha = \alpha \urcorner$ and $\ulcorner \alpha = \beta \urcorner$. Hence, the objects susceptible to direct reference must not permit such reference in inequivalent ways. These objects must, in a certain sense, be wholly local and completely given so that for any two *directly* coreferential terms α and β, $\ulcorner \alpha = \beta \urcorner$ will be uninformative to anyone appropriately situated, epistemologically, to be able to use these terms.[62] I hope that my discussion of the two kinds of meaning – content and character – will have shown the Direct Acquaintance Theorist that his views are not the inevitable consequence of the admission of directly referential terms. From the point of view of a lover of direct reference this is good, since the Direct Acquaintance theorist admits direct reference in a portion of language so narrow that it is used only by philosophers.[63]

I have said nothing to dispute the epistemology of the Direct Acquaintance theorist, nothing to deny that there exists his special kind of object with which one can have his special kind of acquaintance. I have only denied the relevance of these epistemological claims to the semantics of direct reference. If we sweep aside metaphysical and epistemological pseudo-explanations of what are essentially semantical phenomena, the result can only be healthy for all three disciplines.

Before going on to further examples of the tendency to confuse metaphysical and epistemological matters with phenomena of the semantics of direct reference, I want to briefly raise the problem of *cognitive dynamics*. Suppose that yesterday you said, and believed it, 'It is a nice day today.' What does it mean to say, today, that you have retained *that* belief? It seems unsatisfactory to just believe the same content under any old character – where is the *retention*?[64] You *can't* believe that content under the same character. Is there some obvious standard adjustment to make to the character, for example, replacing *today* with *yesterday*? If so, then a person like Rip van Winkle, who loses track of time, can't retain any such beliefs. This seems strange, Can we only *retain* beliefs presented under a fixed character? This issue has obvious and important connections with Lauben's problem in trying to communicate the thought he expresses with 'I have been wounded'. Under what character must his auditor believe Lauben's thought in order for Lauben's communication to have been successful? It is important to note that if Lauben said 'I am wounded' in the usual meaning of 'I', there is no one else who can report what he said, using *indirect* discourse, and convey the cognitive significance (to Lauben) of what he said. This is connected with points made in section VIII, and has interesting consequences for the inevitability of so-called *de re* constructions in indirect discourse languages which contain indexicals. (I use 'indirect discourse' as a general term for the analogous form of all psychological verbs.)

A prime example of the confusion of direct reference phenomena with metaphysical and epistemological ideas was first vigorously called to our attention by Saul Kripke in *Naming and Necessity*. I wish to parallel his remarks disconnecting the *a priori* and the *necessary*.

The form of *a prioricity* that I will discuss is that of logical truth (in the logic of demonstratives). We saw very early that a truth of the logic of demonstratives, like 'I am here now' need not be necessary. There are many such cases of logical truths which are not necessary. If α is any singular term, then

$$\alpha = \text{dthat}[\alpha]$$

is a logical truth. But

$$\Box(\alpha = \text{dthat}[\alpha])$$

is generally false. We can, of course, also easily produce the opposite effect.

$$\Box(\text{dthat}[\alpha] = \text{dthat}[\beta])$$

may be true, although

$$\text{dthat}[\alpha] = \text{dthat}[\beta]$$

is not logically true, and is even logically equivalent to the contingency,

$$\alpha = \beta$$

(I call ϕ and ψ logically equivalent when $\ulcorner\phi \leftrightarrow \psi\urcorner$ is logically true.) These cases are reminiscent of Kripke's case of the terms, 'one meter' and 'the length of bar *x*'. But where Kripke focuses on the special epistemological situation of one who is present at the dubbing, the descriptive meaning associated with our directly referential term dthat[α] is carried in the semantics of the language.[65]

How can something be both logically true, and thus *certain*, and *contingent* at the same time? In the case of indexicals the answer is easy to see.

E. Corollary 3 *The bearers of logical truth and of contingency are different entities. It is the* character *(or, the sentence, if you prefer) that is logically true, producing a true content in every context. But it is the* content *(the proposition, if you will) that is contingent or necessary.*

As can readily be seen, the modal logic of demonstratives is a rich and interesting thing.

It is easy to be taken in by the effortless (but fallacious) move from certainty (logical truth) to necessity. In his important article 'Three Grades of Modal Involvement,'[66] Quine expresses his scepticism of the first grade of modal involvement: the sentence predicate and all it stands for, and his distaste for the second grade of modal involvement: disguising the predicate as an operator 'It is necessary that'. But he suggests that no new metaphysical undesirables are admitted until the third grade of modal involvement: quantification across the necessary operator into an open sentence.

I must protest. That first step let in some metaphysical undesirables, falsehoods. All logical truths are analytic, but they can go false when you back them up to '□'.

One other notorious example of a logical truth which is not necessary,

I exist.

One can quickly verify that in every context, this character yields a true proposition – but rarely a necessary one. It seems likely to me that it was a conflict between the feelings of contingency and of certainty associated with this sentence that has led to such painstaking examination of its 'proofs'. It is just a truth of logic!

Dana Scott has remedied one lacuna in this analysis. What of the premise

I think

and the connective

Therefore ?

His discovery was that the premise is incomplete, and that the last five words

up the logic of demonstratives

had been lost in an early manuscript version.[67]

Notes

[· · ·]

7. Not everything I assert is part of my theory. At places I make judgments about the correct use of certain words and I propose detailed analyses of certain notions. I recognize that these matters may be controversial. I do not regard them as part of the basic, obvious, theory.
8. See 'Dthat,' p. 320 in Martinich.
9. However, a demonstration may also be opportune and require no special action on the speaker's part, as when someone shouts 'Stop that man' while only one man is rushing toward the door. My notion of a demonstration is a theoretical concept. I do not, in the present work, undertake a detailed 'operational' analysis of this notion although there are scattered remarks relevant to the issue. I do consider, in XVI below, some alternative theoretical treatments of demonstrations.
10. I am aware (1) that in some languages the so-called masculine gender pronoun may be appropriate for flowers, but it is not so in English; (2) that a background story can be provided that will make pointing at the flower a contextually appropriate, though deviant, way of referring to a man; for example, if we are talking of great hybridizers; and (3) that it is possible to treat the example as a *referential use* of the demonstrative 'he' on the model of Donnellan's referential use of a definite description (see 'Reference and Definite Descriptions'). Under the referential use treatment we would assign as referent for 'he' whatever the speaker *intended* to demonstrate. I intended the example to exemplify a failed demonstration, thus, a case in which the speaker, falsely believing the flower to be some man or other in disguise, but having no particular man in mind, and certainly not intending to refer to anything other than that man, says, pointing at the flower, 'He has been following me around all day.'
11. I have in mind such cases as pointing at oneself while saying 'I' (emphasis) or pointing at someone else while saying 'I' (irrelevance or madness or what?)
12. There are certain uses of pure indexicals that might be called 'messages recorded for later broadcast', which exhibit a special uncertainty as to the referent of 'here' and 'now'. If the message: 'I am not here now' is recorded on a telephone

answering device, it is to be assumed that the time referred to by 'now' is the time of playback rather than the time of recording. Donnellan has suggested that if there were typically a significant lag between our production of speech and its audition (for example, if sound traveled very very slowly), our language might contain two forms of 'now': one for the time of production, another for the time of audition. The indexicals 'here' and 'now' also suffer from vagueness regarding the size of the spatial and temporal neighborhoods to which they refer. These facts do not seem to me to slur the difference between demonstratives and pure indexicals.

13. Of course it is certain intentions on the part of the speaker that make a particular vocable the first person singular pronoun rather a nickname for Irving. My semantical theory is a theory of word meaning, not speaker's meaning. It is based on linguistic rules known, explicitly or implicitly, by all competent users of the language.
14. I have discussed this and related issues in 'Bob and Carol and Ted and Alice,' in *Approaches to Natural Language*, ed. J. Hintikka et al. (Dordrecht: Reidel, 1973), especially appendix X.
15. Kripke, *Naming and Necessity,* p. 78.
16. The matter is even more complicated. There are two 'definitions' of 'rigid designator' in *Naming and Necessity*, pp. 48–49. The first conforms to what seems to me to have been the intended concept – same designation in *all* possible worlds – the second, scarcely a page later, conforms to the more widely held view that a rigid designator need not designate the object, or any object, at worlds in which the object does not exist. According to this conception a designator cannot, at a given world, designate something which does not exist in that world. The introduction of the notion of a *strongly* rigid designator – a rigid designator whose designatum exists in all possible worlds – suggests that the latter idea was uppermost in Kripke's mind. (The second definition is given, unequivocally, on page 146 of 'Identity and Necessity,' in *Identity and Individuation*, ed. M. K. Munitz (New York: New York University Press, 1971).) In spite of the textual evidence, systematic considerations, including the fact that variables cannot be accounted for otherwise, leave me with the conviction that the former notion was intended.
17. Here, and in the preceding paragraph, in attempting to convey my notion of a directly referential singular term, I slide back and forth between two metaphysical pictures: that of possible worlds and that of structured propositions. It seems to me that a truly semantical idea should presuppose neither picture, and be expressible in terms of either. Kripke's discussion of rigid designators is, I believe, distorted by an excessive dependence on the possible worlds picture and the associated semantical style. For more on the relationship between the two pictures, see pages 724–25 of my 'How to Russell a Frege-Church,' *The Journal of Philosophy* 72 (1975): 716–29.
18. I think it likely that it was just the failure to notice this distinction that led to a failure to recognize Principle 2. Some of the history and consequences of the conflation of Context and Circumstance is discussed in section VII.
19. I would have used 'snow is white', but I wanted a contingent clause, and so many people (possibly including me) nowadays seem to have views which allow that 'snow is white' may be necessary.

20. I am ignoring propositions expressed by sentences containing epistemic operators or others for which equivalence is not a sufficient condition for interchange of operand.
21. Bertrand Russell, *The Principles of Mathematics* (London: Allen & Unwin, 1903).
22. Bertrand Russell, 'On Denoting,' *Mind* 14 (1905): 479–93.
23. Here is a difficulty in Russell's 1903 picture that has some historical interest. Consider the proposition expressed by the sentence, 'The centre of mass of the Solar System is a point'. Call the proposition, '*P*'. *P* has in its subject place a certain complex, expressed by the definite description. Call the complex, 'Plexy'. We can describe Plexy as 'the complex expressed by "the center of mass of the solar system".' Can we produce a directly referential term which designates Plexy? Leaving aside for the moment the controversial question of whether 'Plexy' is such a term, let us imagine, as Russell believed, that we can directly refer to Plexy by affixing a kind of *meaning marks* (on the analogy of quotation marks) to the description itself. Now consider the sentence '^{m}the center of mass of the solar system^{m} is a point'. Because the subject of this sentence is directly referential and refers to Plexy, the proposition the sentence expresses will have its subject constituent Plexy itself. A moment's reflection will reveal that this proposition is simply *P* again. But this is absurd since the two sentences speak about radically different objects.

    (I believe the foregoing argument lies behind some of the largely incomprehensible arguments mounted by Russell against Frege in 'On Denoting,' though there are certainly other difficulties in that argument. It is not surprising that Russell there confused Frege's theory with his own of *Principle of Mathematics*. The first footnote of 'On Denoting' asserts that the two theories are 'very nearly the same.')

    The solution to the difficulty is simple. Regard the 'object' places of a singular proposition as marked by some operation which cannot mark a complex. (There always will be some such operation.) For example, suppose that no complex is (represented by) a set containing a single member. Then we need only add $\{\ldots\}$ to mark the places in a singular proposition which correspond to directly referential terms. We no longer need worry about confusing a complex with a propositional constituent corresponding to a directly referring term because no complex will have the form $\{x\}$. In particular, Plexy $\neq$ {Plexy}. This technique can also be used to resolve another confusion in Russell. He argued that a sentence containing a nondenoting directly referential term (he would have called it a nondenoting 'logically proper name') would be meaningless, presumably because the purported singular proposition would be incomplete. But the braces themselves can fill out the singular proposition, and if they contain nothing, no more anomalies need result than what the development of Free Logic has already inured us to.
24. This is the *first sense* of note 16.
25. This is the *second sense* of note 16.
26. From 'The Thought: A Logical Inquiry,' *Mind* 65 (1956): 289–311. If Frege had only supplemented these comments with the observation that indexicals are devices of direct reference, the whole theory of indexicals would have been his. But this theory of meaning blinded him to this obvious point. Frege, I believe,

mixed together the two kinds of meaning in what he called *Sinn*. A *thought* is, for him, the *Sinn* of a sentence, or perhaps we should say a *complete* sentence. *Sinn* is to contain both 'the manner and context of presentation [of the denotation],' according to 'Über Sinn and Bedeutung' (*Zeitschrift für Philosophie und philosophische Kritik* 100 (1892); trans. as 'On Sense and Nominatum,' in *Contemporary Readings in Logical Theory*, ed. Copi and Gould (Macmillan, 1967); mistrans. as 'On Sense and Meaning,' in Martinich, op. cit.). *Sinn* is first introduced to represent the cognitive significance of a sign, and thus to solve Frege's problem: how can $\ulcorner \alpha = \beta \urcorner$ if true differ in cognitive significance from $\ulcorner \alpha = \alpha \urcorner$. However, it also is taken to represent the truth-conditions or *content* (in our sense). Frege felt the pull of the two notions, which he reflects in some tortured passages about 'I' in 'The Thought' (quoted below in XVII). If one says 'Today is beautiful' on Tuesday and 'Yesterday was beautiful' on Wednesday, one expresses the same thought according to the passage quoted. Yet one can clearly lose track of the days and not realize one is expressing the same thought. It seems then that thoughts are not appropriate bearers of cognitive significance. I return to this topic in XVII. A detailed examination of Frege on demonstratives is contained in John Perry's 'Frege on Demonstratives,' *Philosophical Review* 86 (1977): 474–97.

27. As we shall see, indexical operators such as 'It is now the case that,' 'It is actually the case that,' and 'dthat' (the last takes a term rather than a sentence as argument) are also intensional operators. They differ from the familiar operators in only two ways: first, their extension (the function from intensions to extensions) depends on context, and second, they are directly referential (thus they have a fixed content). I shall argue below (in section VII: Monsters) that all operators that can be given an English reading are 'at most' intensional. Note that when discussing issues in terms of the formal representations of the model-theoretic semantics, I tend to speak in terms of intensions and intensional operators rather than contents and content operators.

28. The notion of redundancy involved could be made precise. When I speak of building the time of evaluation into contents, or making contents specific as to time, or taking what is said to incorporate reference to a specific time, what I have in mind is this. Given a sentence *S*: 'I am writing', in the present context *c*, which of the following should we take as the content: (i) the proposition that David Kaplan is writing at 10 A.M. on 3/26/77, or (ii) the 'proposition' that David Kaplan is writing? The proposition (i) is specific as to time, the 'proposition' (ii) [the scare quotes reflect my feeling that this is not the traditional notion of a proposition] is neutral with respect to time. If we taken the content of *S* in *c* to be (ii), we can ask whether it would be true at times other than the time of *c*. Thus we think of the temporally neutral 'proposition' as changing its truth-value over time. Note that it is not just the noneternal sentence *S* that changes its truth-value over time, but the 'proposition' itself. Since the sentence *S* contains an indexical 'I', it will express different 'propositions' in different contexts. But since *S* contains no *temporal* indexical, the time of the context will not influence the 'proposition' expressed. An alternative [and more traditional] view is to say that the verb tense in *S* involves an implicit temporal indexical, so that *S* is understood as synonymous with *S′*: 'I am writing now'. If we taken this point of view we will take the content of *S* in *c* to be (i). In this

case *what is said* is eternal; it does not change its truth-value over time, although S will express different propositions at different times.

There are both technical and philosophical issues involved in choosing between (i) and (ii). Philosophically, we may ask why the temporal indexical should be taken to be implicit (making the proposition eternal) when no modal indexical is taken to be implicit. After all, we *could* understand S as synonymous with S'': 'I am actually writing now'. The content of S'' in c is not only eternal, it is perfect. Its truth changes neither through time nor possibility. Is there some good philosophical reason for preferring contents which are neutral with respect to possibility but draw fixed values from the context for all other features of a possible circumstance whether or not the sentence contains an explicit indexical? (It may be that the traditional view was abetted by one of the delightful anomalies of the logic of indexicals, namely that S, S', and S'' are all logically equivalent! See Remark 3, p. 547 [not included].) Technically, we must note that intensional operators must, if they are not to be vacuous, operate on contents which are neutral with respect to the feature of circumstance the operator is interested in. Thus, for example, if we take the content of S to be (i), the application of a temporal operator to such a content would have no effect; the operator would be vacuous. Furthermore, if we do not wish the iteration of such operators to be vacuous, the content of the compound sentence containing the operator must again be neutral with respect to the relevant feature of circumstance. This is not to say that no such operator can have the effect of *fixing* the relevant feature and thus, in effect, rendering subsequent operations vacuous; indexical operators do just this. It is just that this must not be the general situation. A content must be the *kind* of entity that is subject to modification in the feature relevant to the operator. [The textual material to which this note is appended is too cryptic and should be rewritten.]

29. 'How to Russell a Frege-Church.' The pronunciation is: 'Hex́-ee-i-tis-m.' The epithet was suggested by Robert Adams. It is not an accident that it is derived from a demonstrative.
30. This does not imply that if you know the character and are in first one and then another context, you can *decide* whether the contents are the same. I may twice use 'here' on separate occasions and not recognize that the place is the same, or twice hear 'I' and not know if the content is the same. What I do know is this: if it was the same person speaking, then the content was the same. [More on this epistemological stuff later.]
31. I am, at this stage, deliberately ignoring Kripke's theory of proper names in order to see whether the revision in Fregean semantical theory, which seem plainly required to accommodate indexicals (this is the 'obviousness' of my theory), can throw any light on it. Here we assume that aside from indexicals, Frege's theory is correct, roughly, that words and phrases have a kind of descriptive meaning or sense which at one and the same time constitutes their cognitive significance and their conditions of applicability.

    Kripke says repeatedly in *Naming and Necessity* that he is only providing a picture of how proper names refer and that he does not have an exact theory. His picture yields some startling results. In the case of indexicals we do have a rather precise theory, which avoids the difficulty of specifying a chain of communication and which yields many analogous results. In facing the vastly more difficult problems associated with a theory of reference for proper names, the theory of indexicals may prove useful; if only to show – as I believe – that proper names are not indexicals and have no meaning in the sense in which indexicals have meaning (namely a 'cognitive content' which fixes the references in all contexts). [The issues that arise, involving token reflexives, homonymous words with distinct character, and homonymous token reflexives with the same character are best saved for later – much later.]

32. See §28 of Rudolf Carnap's *Meaning and Necessity* (Chicago: University of Chicago Press, 1947).

[. . .]

38. I have written elsewhere, in appendices VII and VIII of 'Bob and Carol and Ted and Alice,' of these matters and won't pursue the topic now.
39. It could then be proposed that demonstrations be individuated by the principle: $d_1 = d_2$ if and only if, for all appropriate circumstances c, the demonstratum of d_1 in c = the demonstratum of d_2 in c. An alternative principle of individuation is that the same demonstration is being performed in two different contexts if the standard audience can't determine, from the demonstration alone, whether the contexts are distinct or identical. This makes the individuation of demonstrations more epistemological than the metaphysical proposal above.
40. Although recent work on computer perception has attempted to identify a syntax of pictures. See P. Suppes and Rottmayer, 'Automata,' in *Handbook of Perception*, vol. 1 (New York: Academic Press, 1974).
41. The Fregean theory of demonstrations is not a part of my obvious and uncontroversial theory of indexicals. On the contrary, it has the fascination of the speculative.
42. I use Kripke's terminology to expound the important distinction he introduces in *Naming and Necessity* for descriptive meaning that may be associated with a proper name. As in several other cases of such parallels between proper names and indexicals, the distinction, and its associated argument, seems more obvious when applied to indexicals.
43. H. Reichenbach, *Elements of Symbolic Logic* (New York: Macmillan, 1947), p. 284.
44. We see here a drawback to the terminology 'direct reference'. It suggests falsely that the reference is not mediated by a meaning, which it is. The meaning (character) is directly associated, by convention, with the word. The meaning determines the referent; and the referent determines the content. It is this to which I alluded in the parenthetical remark [on page 314 (referring to Figures 1 and 2)]. Note, however, that the kind of descriptive meaning involved in giving the character of indexicals like 'I', 'now', etc., is, because of the focus on context rather than circumstance, unlike that traditionally thought of as Fregean sense. It is the idea that the referent determines the content – that, contra Frege, there *is* a road back – that I wish to capture. This is the importance of Principle 2.
45. Pronunciation note on 'dthat'. The word is not pronounced dee-that or duh-that. It has only one syllable. Although articulated differently from 'that' (the tongue begins behind the teeth), the sounds are virtually indistinguishable to all but native speakers.

46. 'Male' and 'female' are here used in the grammatical sense of gender, not the biological sense.
47. If the current speculations are accepted, then in the original discussion of Pat and Mike the emphasis on the counterfactual situation in which the same agent was doing the pointing was misguided and that feature of counterfactual situations is irrelevant. It is the agent of course who focuses your attention on the relevant local individual. But that needn't be done *by* anyone; we might have a convention that whoever is appearing on the demonstration platform is the demonstratum, or the speaker might take advantage of a natural demonstration of opportunity: an explosion or a shooting star.
48. Since, as remarked earlier, the speaker and different members of the audience generally have different perspectives on the demonstration, it may appear slightly different to each of them. Thus each may take a slightly different demonstration to have been performed. Insofar as the agent and audience of a given context can differ in location, the location of a context is the location of the agent. Therefore the demonstratum of a given demonstration set in a given context will be the individual, if any, thereby demonstrated from the speaker's point of view.
49. We should not, of course, forget the many disanalogies noted earlier nor fail to note that though a description is associated with a particular character by linguistic *convention*, a demonstration is associated with *its* character by *nature*.
50. This section has benefited from the opportunity to read, and discuss with him, John Perry's paper 'Frege on Demonstratives.'
51. According to Church, such higher order Fregean senses are already called for by Frege's theory.
52. See his remarks in 'On Sense and Nominatum' regarding the 'common treasure of thoughts which is transmitted from generation to generation' and remarks there and in 'The Thought' in connection with tensed sentences, that 'Only a sentence supplemented by a time-indication and complete in every respect expresses a thought.'
53. Perhaps it should be mentioned here, to forestall an objection, that neither uses a proper name for the other or for himself – only 'my brother' and 'I' – and that raising them required a lot of environmental work to maintain the necessary symmetries, or, alternatively, a lot of work with the brain state machine. If proper names are present, and each uses a different name for himself (or, for the other), they will never achieve the same *total* cognitive state since one will sincerely say, 'I am Castor' and the other will not. They may still achieve the same cognitive state in its relevant part.
54. The corollary would also apply to the same person at the same time in the same circumstances but in different places, if such could be.
55. John Perry, 'Frege on Demonstratives,' p. 494.
56. Gottlob Frege, 'The Thought: A Logical Inquiry,' p. 298.
57. At other times, earlier and later, we can know it only externally, by description as it were. But now we are directly acquainted with it. (I believe I owe this point to John Perry.)
58. Unless, of course, the self-concept involved a bit of direct reference. In which case (when direct reference is admitted) there seems no need for the whole theory of Fregean self-concepts. Unless, of course, direct reference is limited to items of direct acquaintance, of which more below.

59. So far, we have limited our attention to the first three sentences of the quotation from Frege. How are we to account for the second part of Frege's remarks?

    Suppose Dr. Lauben wants to communicate his thought without disturbing its cognitive content. (Think of trying to tell a color-blind person that the green light should be replaced. You would have to find another way of communicating what you wanted to get across.) He can't communicate *that* thought with *that* significance, so, he himself would have to attach a nonstandard significance to 'I'. Here is a suggestion. He points at his auditor and uses the demonstrative 'you'. If we neglect fine differences in perspective, the demonstration will have the same character for all present and it certainly will have the same demonstratum for all present, therefore the demonstrative will have the same *character and content* for all present. The indexical 'now' will certainly have the same character and content for all present. Thus 'the person who is speaking to you [points] now' will have a common character and content for all those present. Unfortunately the content is not that of 'I' as Dr. Lauben standardly uses it. He needs a demonstrative like 'dthat' to convert the description to a term with a fixed content. He chooses the demonstrative 'he', with a relative clause construction to make clear his intention. Now, if Dr. Lauben uses 'I' with the nonstandard meaning usually attached to 'he who is speaking to you [points] now' he will have found a way to communicate his original thought in a form whose cognitive significance is common to all. Very clever, Dr. Lauben.

    [Perhaps it is a poor pedagogy to join this fanciful interpretation of the second part of the passage with the serious interpretation of the first part.]
60. Can the heiress plead that she could not have had believed a singular proposition involving the place p since when thinking 'here' she didn't *know* she was at p, that she was, in fact, unacquainted with the place p? No! Ignorance of the referent is no excuse.
61. This makes it sound as if an exact and conscious mastery of semantics is prerequisite to having a singular proposition as object of thought. I will try to find a better way to express the point in a succeeding draft.
62. For some consequences of this view with regard to the interpretation of demonstratives see 'Bob and Carol and Ted and Alice,' appendix VII.
63. There is an obvious connection between the fix in which the Direct Acquaintance Theorist finds himself, and *Kripke's problem*: how can $\ulcorner \alpha = \beta \urcorner$ be informative if α and β differ in neither denotation nor sense (nor, as I shall suggest is the case for proper names, character)?
64. The sort of case I have in mind is this. I first think, 'His pants are on fire.' I later realize, 'I am he' and thus come to think 'My pants are on fire.' Still later, I decide that I was wrong in thinking 'I am he' and conclude 'His pants were on fire.' If, in fact, I *am* he, have I *retained* my belief that my pants are on fire simply because I believe the same content, though under a different character? (I also deny that content under the former, but for change of tense, character.) When I first thought 'My pants are on fire,' a certain singular proposition, call it 'Eek', was the object of thought. At the later stage, both Eek and its negation are believed by me. In this sense, I still believe what I believed before, namely Eek. But this does not capture my sense of *retaining a belief*: a sense that I associate with saying that some people have a very rigid cognitive structure whereas others

are very flexible. It is tempting to say that cognitive dynamics is concerned not with retention and change in what is believed, but with retention and change in the characters under which our beliefs are held. I think that this is basically correct. But it is not obvious to me what relation between a character under which a belief is held at one time and the set of characters under which beliefs are held at a later time would constitute retaining the original belief. Where indexicals are involved, for the reasons given below, we cannot simply require that the very same character still appear at the later time. Thus the problem of cognitive dynamics can be put like this: what does it mean to say of an individual who at one time sincerely asserted a sentence containing indexicals that at some later time he has (or has not) *changed his mind* with respect to his assertion? What sentence or sentences must he be willing to assert at the later time?

65. A case of a seemingly different kind is that of the logical equivalence between an arbitrary sentence ϕ and the result of prefixing either or both of the indexical operators, 'it is actually the case that' (symbolized 'A') and 'it is now the case that' (symbolized 'N'). The biconditional $\ulcorner(\phi \leftrightarrow AN\phi)\urcorner$ is logically true, but prefixing either '$\Box$' or its temporal counterpart can lead to falsehood. (This case was adverted to in note 28.) It is interesting to note, in this case, that the parallel between modal and temporal modifications of sentences carries over to indexicals. The foregoing claims are verified by the formal system (sections XVIII and XIX, see especially Remark 3 [not included]). Note that the formal system is constructed in accordance with Carnap's proposal that the intension of an expression be that function which assigns to each circumstance, the extension of the expression with respect to that circumstance. This has commonly been thought to insure that logically equivalent expressions have the same intension (Church's Alternative 2 among principles of individuation for the notion of sense) and that logically true sentences express the (unique) necessary proposition. Homework Problem: What went wrong here?
66. *Proceedings of the XI International Congress of Philosophy* 14, 65–81; reprinted in W. V. Quine, *The Ways of Paradox* (New York: Random House, 1966).
67. Again, it is probably a pedagogical mistake to mix this playful paragraph with the preceding serious one.

Part III

Opacity and Attributions of Attitude

Introduction

Graeme Forbes

One venerable principle of metaphysics, known variously as Leibniz's Law or the Indiscernibility of Identicals, states the following:

> LL: if *x* and *y* are the same objects, then *x* and *y* have the same properties.

For example, if Constantinople and Istanbul are the same city (as in fact they are) then if Constantinople has a population in excess of one million, so does Istanbul. If Superman and Clark Kent are the same person, then if Superman is an extraterrestrial, so is Clark Kent. And if Jocasta is Oedipus's mother, then if Jocasta is taller than Oedipus, Oedipus's mother is taller than Oedipus.

Leibniz's Law is implemented in formal systems of deduction by an inference rule which permits substitution of one expression for an object by another expression for that object. This inference rule has many names; here we will call it *The Substitutivity of Identity*, or 'Sub Id' for short. We can describe the rule in a schema, which exhibits the essential pattern to which any application of the rule conforms

$$\frac{t_1 = t_2 \qquad\qquad S(t_1)}{S(t_2/t_1)} \quad \text{Sub Id}$$

t_1 and t_2 are called *singular terms*, a singular term being an expression which is used to pick out a single particular thing, such as a person, a place or a time. Thus 'Clark Kent' and 'Oedipus's mother' are singular terms (assuming, as we will, that both stories are factual) the former being a proper name, the

1. I thank Kent Bach for helpful comments on the first version of this essay.

latter, a definite description ('the mother of Oedipus'). In words, therefore, a schema for Sub Id says that if we have already established an identity sentence $t_1 = t_2$ (the *major* premise of the inference) and also some other sentence S which contains occurrences of the singular term t_1 (the *minor* premise), then we may infer a sentence $S(t_2/t_1)$, where $S(t_2/t_1)$ is obtained from S by replacing at least one occurrence of t_1 in S by t_2. The following is a simple example of an inference that uses Sub Id

(A) (1) Superman = Clark Kent
(2) Superman can fly
(3) ∴ Clark Kent can fly.

We have used the identity sentence (1) to replace the occurrence of 'Superman' in (2) with 'Clark Kent', resulting in (3). The other illustrations of Leibniz's Law in our opening paragraph could also be rewritten as inferences using Sub Id. As these examples indicate, there is great intuitive plausibility in this rule of inference. If one can use a sentence to say something true about an object specified in it, then surely, if we specify the object in a different way but say the same thing about it, what we say will again be true? This principle about the truth-value of what we say does not seem so very far removed from the underlying metaphysical doctrine of Leibniz's Law.

Nevertheless, there are examples which appear to show that Sub Id is an unsound rule of inference (an *unsound* rule is one which can carry us from true premises to false conclusion). One of the enduring problems in philosophy of language is to give a satisfactory account of these cases, of which two follow

(B): (1) Superman is Clark Kent
(2) Lois Lane believes that Superman can fly
(3) ∴ Lois Lane believes that Clark Kent can fly.

(C): (1) Jocasta is Oedipus's mother
(2) Oedipus wants to marry Jocasta
(3) ∴ Oedipus wants to marry Oedipus's mother.

On the face of it, (B) and (C) demonstrate that Sub Id is an unsound rule, since the premises of both inferences are true but the conclusions appear to be false. On the other hand, it seems that the inferences are warranted by Leibniz's Law, and it is hard to see how *that* could be mistaken. So there is at least a puzzle, perhaps a paradox, to be addressed.

In each of (B) and (C), the second premise and the conclusion is what is known as a *propositional attitude* attribution (or 'ascription'). The reason for this terminology is that it seems natural to parse, say, (B2), as involving a two-place relation of *believing* in which the first place is occupied by a *subject*, and the second place by an *object* of the relation. In the case of (B2), we get the parsing

(4) Bel(Lois, that Superman can fly).

This says that Lois stands in the believing relation to a certain object of belief, *that Superman can fly*. Traditionally, the things which are the objects of belief are called *propositions* and psychological relations like belief are construed as *attitudes towards* propositions. Thus (4), and hence (B2), says that Lois has the attitude of belief towards the proposition that Superman can fly.

The same parsing can be applied to (C2), though it is a little less natural. On the analogy of (4), (C2) can be construed as saying that Oedipus stands in the wanting relation towards the proposition that he himself marries Jocasta. The wanting relation here is actually the wanting-to-be-true relation, which holds between a subject and a proposition when the subject wants the proposition to be or become true. Analysing wanting as wanting a certain proposition to be true might be regarded as forced, but it keeps the treatment of (B) and (C) uniform.

If the entire semantic function of the name 'Superman' in (B2) consisted in its referring to a certain individual then it is at least initially plausible that, if there is another expression which would have precisely the same semantic function in (B2) were it to replace 'Superman' there, the truth-value of the sentence resulting from substituting that other expression would be the same as the truth-value of (B2). This leads Quine to conclude that in cases like (B2), the semantic function of the name following 'believes' cannot be, or cannot simply be, to refer to a certain item. On the other hand, in (A2), 'Superman can fly', there is no problem with substitution, so it seems that the occurrence of 'Superman' there does have the semantic function simply of referring to Superman. When an occurrence of a name has the semantic function simply of referring to a certain object, Quine calls that occurrence *purely referential*, and the position of the occurrence *purely referential position*; and when an occurrence's function is not, or not simply, to refer to an object, the occurrence and the position are said to be *referentially opaque* (1960, p. 142). This terminology is widespread even among those who do not use it to mark a change in semantic function. We can say that when an occurrence of a name resists substitution by a co-referential term, *whatever* the reason, the name occurs opaquely, or in opaque position, and when substitution is unproblematic, the occurrence and position are transparent.

Whether an occurrence of a name is opaque or transparent depends on the context in which it occurs. In the move from (A2) to (B2) the crucial change is the prefixing of a *propositional attitude context*, 'Lois believes that'. Propositional attitude contexts may be said to be *opacity-inducing*, by contrast with such *transparent* contexts as 'It is true that', which permits substitution – clearly, if it is true that Superman can fly, it is true that

Clark Kent can fly. A context itself may be said to be opaque, or transparent, according to whether or not it induces opacity in occurrences of terms within it. Quine's definition is: a context ϕ is referentially transparent 'if, whenever an occurrence of a singular term t is purely referential in a term or sentence $\psi(t)$, it is purely referential also in the containing term or sentence $\phi(\psi(t))$' (1960, p. 144). Otherwise, we call ϕ *referentially opaque*; thus 'Lois believes that' is referentially opaque, since 'Superman' occurs transparently in (A2) but not (B2).

There is one further, at least *partly* terminological issue to be resolved. While there certainly seems to be a reading of the conclusions of (B) and (C) where we are inclined to say that they are false, there is also undeniably a reading on which they are true. Since Jocasta *is* Oedipus's mother, anyone who wants to marry Jocasta thereby *does* want to marry Oedipus's mother, whether or not they are aware of it. And if you believe that Superman can fly, well, you simply *do* believe that Clark Kent can fly, even though you might refuse to put it that way. To grant the truth of (B3), 'Lois believes that Clark can fly', and (C3), 'Oedipus wants to marry Oedipus's mother', on this kind of ground, is to treat the positions of 'Superman' and 'Jocasta' in (B2) and (C2) as referentially transparent, ie. as open to substitution.

However, one is not treating the positions, or name-occurrences, as transparent just by decree. Rather, the transparency is a consequence of resolving a *scope-ambiguity* in (B2) and (C2) in a particular way. For example, though (B2), 'Lois believes Superman can fly', is one way of ascribing a belief to Lois, another way is

(5) Superman is someone whom Lois believes can fly.

(5) contrasts with (B2) with respect to the scope of 'Lois believes', for in (B2) the name 'Superman' is explicitly within the scope of 'Lois believes', while in (5) it is explicitly outside the scope of the opacity-inducing context. This means that 'Superman' in (5) does not occur opaquely, and so can be substituted, resulting in

(6) Clark Kent is someone whom Lois believes can fly.

This time the substitution seems proper. Hence, if someone maintains that (B3) is true because believing that Superman can fly just is believing that Clark Kent can fly, a reasonable explanation of this judgment is that it results from interpreting (B2) *as* (5) and (B3) *as* (6), readings in which the name is moved from opaque to transparent position. No doubt such a reading is legitimate, even if not preferred. The important moral which emerges is that we must be careful not to endorse any thesis about the mechanics of the inferences (B) and (C) that depends on a slide from one scope disambiguation of an attitude ascription to another. So whenever we intend an ascription to be read in the style of (5) and (6) we will explicitly formulate it that way. Other ascriptions are to be read as (B2) and (B3) are when the inference seems incorrect.

The contrast between (5) and (B2), and between (6) and (B3), is sometimes marked by the terminology *de re/de dicto*. Attitude ascriptions such as (5) and (6) are said to be *de re*, the others *de dicto*; or it can be said that the attitudes ascribed by (5) and (6) are *de re*, the others *de dicto*. However, since '*de re*' means 'about the object', the nomenclature is unfortunate, suggesting as it does that (B2), 'Lois believes that Superman can fly' and (B3), 'Lois believes Clark can fly', are *not* ascriptions about, or not about, an object. There are indeed beliefs which are in a good sense not about any particular object. For example, suppose Ralph believes that spies exist, that there are only finitely many of them, and that no two have the same height. Then Ralph may reason purely logically to the conclusion that the shortest spy is a spy. So we have

(7) Ralph believes that the shortest spy is a spy

which seems to ascribe a belief that is not about an object. By contrast, if

(8) The shortest spy is someone whom Ralph believes to be a spy

is true, then Ralph has a true belief about a particular person, the one picked out by the description 'the shortest spy'. However, whether or not the ascribed belief is about a particular object (is *de re*) does not turn on whether or not the singular term is within or outside the scope of the attitude context, for (5) and (B2) *both* appear to ascribe beliefs about particular objects. By '*de re*' we should mean just that, 'about a particular object', and leave open the question of whether the *de re/de dicto* distinction, as illustrated by the contrast between (8) and (7), is the same distinction as the scope distinction which (8) and (7) also illustrate. It may be that what prevents (7) from ascribing a belief about a particular object is that it contains a definite description, as opposed to a proper name, in opaque position, not merely that it contains a term of one sort or another in opaque position. Note that in these remarks we have not distinguished between '*de re* ascription of a belief' and 'ascription of a *de re* belief': a *de re* ascription just is, for us, an ascription of a *de re* belief.

A last preliminary. We have now distinguished two questions about an occurrence of a singular term in an attitude ascription. One is whether it is purely referential, and the other is whether its occurrence makes the ascribed attitude about an object. Quine's criterion for purely referential occurrence is substitutability of the term used in specifying that content of the attitude. The criterion which we might consider for settling whether or not an attitude is about an object is *exportability* of the term used in specifying that content of the attitude. Exportation takes place in the step from (B2) to (5) and in the step from (7) to (8). It is impermissible in the latter case, and hence (7) does not ascribe a belief about the person who is in fact the shortest spy. But if (B2) does ascribe a belief about Superman, exportation to (5) ought to be legitimate.

An objection to exportation in the case of (5) is that it introduces existential commitment where none existed before. (5) says that Superman is *someone* whom Lois has such-and-such a belief about, and this could not be true if there is no such person as Superman. But (B2) *could* be true in this case, it might be said. Another example: an atheist might be happy to assert

(9) Mary trusts God to forgive her

but would presumably balk at

(10) God is someone whom Mary trusts to forgive her.

If (9) does not imply (10), or (B2) imply (5), perhaps there is after all no sense in which (9) and (B2) ascribe attitudes about particular objects.

But matters are not so simple. Undeniably, (5), (8) and (10) are all untrue if their initial singular terms fail to refer. However, it is arguable that (B2) and (9) are also untrue in this case. It would be *natural* for an atheist to assert (9), but in so doing she may not be using 'God' in the existentially committing manner of (10). Perhaps her use is arch, or perhaps she used it to pick out not a putative concrete, spiritual, being, but an abstract entity, a creature of myth (or obsessional wish-fulfillment, if Freud is right). More generally, there is a good argument that the ordinary use of names in opaque position is as existentially committing as their use outside such contexts. One of the central intuitions about the occurrence of words in opaque contexts is that they continue to refer to the things to which they refer in transparent contexts. If we say that Ralph believes that Marilyn Monroe was murdered, then *even if* we do not allow substitution of 'Norma Jean Baker', it still seems that we refer to Marilyn Monroe in ascribing this belief to Ralph. This point embodies an objection to any theory which tries to account for substitution-failure by ascribing special meanings to names in opaque contexts (as many historically prominent theories have done), an objection we will call the objection from *semantic innocence*, after its best-known expression:

> If we could recover our pre-Fregean semantic innocence, I think it would seem to us plainly incredible that . . . words [in opaque contexts] mean anything different, or refer to anything else, than is their wont when they come in other environments. (Davidson 1969, p. 172).

If Davidson's remark is right, names will be as existentially committing in opaque contexts as anywhere else. Thus if (10) is untrue because 'God' fails to refer, (9), construed literally, will be untrue for the same reason, at least in the absence of a much more complicated parsing than is afforded by the style of (4), *Bel(B, that p)*. Consequently, exportation of names will not lead from truths to falsehoods by altering existential commitments and so exportability can be used a criterion for a belief's being *de re*. Among other things, this points up the importance of Quine's qualifier 'purely' in the definition of opaque occurrence as not *purely* referential occurrence. For by semantic innocence, an opaque occurrence of a name is *at least* referential, unless it is being used non-standardly, for instance in the arch way an atheist might use 'God' in (9).

Theories of Opacity

We can classify theories of opacity by considering the range of possible reactions to our supposed counter-examples (B) and (C) to the Substitutivity of Identity. One reaction, of course, would be to take the examples at face value as counter-examples, not just to Sub Id, but to Leibniz's Law. But it is unprofitable to pursue this line of thought, since satisfaction of Leibniz's Law is exactly what distinguishes identity from other relations which are structurally similar. A second reaction, the most common one, is that the inferences (B) and (C) are not correct applications of Sub Id. The Sub Id schema is set up to be applicable to sentences of a formal language, and so to apply it to a natural language argument, we need some formal regimentation of the natural language argument. Most of the better-known theories of opacity embody some semantic account of attitude ascriptions which parses (B2), 'Lois believes that Superman can fly', and (C2), 'Oedipus wants to marry Jocasta', in a way that makes it clear that the arguments (B) and (C) do not fit the Sub Id schema. In fact, (B) and (C) may be treated separately. In (C) the definite description 'Oedipus's mother' replaces the proper name 'Jocasta', yet in first-order regimentations, definite descriptions are often not even treated as terms (Russell 1918, Smullyan 1948); on such regimentations, (C) manifestly fails to fit the Sub Id schema. Alternatively, even if definite descriptions are treated as terms syntactically, we may distinguish sharply between a term which specifies an object by referring to it and a term which specifies an object by describing it. If we then restrict the applicability of Sub Id to inferences which involve only terms that refer, (C) is again not an instance of the schema. The extent to which this seems *ad hoc* will vary inversely with the strength of the grounds for semantically distinguishing reference and description (Evans 1982).

But this still leaves the truly hard cases, like (B), where a proper name is replaced by a proper name. And many theories which parse the likes of (B) so that they fail to fit the schema are problematic because they run foul of the objection from semantic innocence. In part because of this, a third reaction to apparent substitution-failure has recently found a number of proponents.

According to this proposal, (B) is a legitimate application of Sub Id, but there is no counterexample to the rule, because the conclusions of these inferences are in fact *true*. This reaction is also problematic, in view of the strength of the intuition that, on at least one reading, it is not true that Lois believes that Clark can fly: it seems to be the whole point of much of the Superman saga that Lois never acquires beliefs which she could express or which anyone else could ascribe to her in the actual cognitive circumstances with 'Clark can fly', 'Clark is an extraterrestrial', 'Clark is Superman' and so on. But of course, defenders of substitution have a way of deflecting the thrust of this intuition.

The idea that (B) and (C) do not really exemplify Sub Id has initial plausibility. To reflect the intuitive idea of Leibniz's Law, the minor premise of an application of Sub Id should be construable as a subject-predicate sentence, containing a subject-term which picks out a subject of discourse, and also some other material, the predicate, which says something about the subject of discourse. (5) fits this description very nicely, 'Superman is someone Lois believes can fly' having the subject term 'Superman' and the complex predicate 'is someone Lois believes can fly'. But it is harder to impose the subject-predicate structure on (B2), 'Lois believes Superman can fly', taking 'Superman' as subject term. The point is not just that (B2) has more than one subject term, as in 'Superman is the same height as Clark Kent', for in such a case we can construe the sentence as subject-predicate taking either term as the subject. Rather, in (B2) it is difficult to hear 'Superman' as a subject term at all, except if (B2) is read as (5), which is beside the point, since we want the interpretation of (B2) on which it means something different from (5).

The first systematic account of attitude ascriptions, due to Frege, respects this point. According to Frege, every expression, or at least every expression in an ideal language, has both a reference and a sense. In the case of a name, the reference is the person or thing for which the name stands, and in the case of a sentence, the reference is the truth-value which the sentence has. The sense of a name is a way of thinking of its reference, and for Lois, 'Superman' and 'Clark Kent' have different senses, since Lois expresses two very different ways of thinking of the same individual with those names. The sense of a sentence is the thought or proposition which it expresses, and this thought, or proposition, is *composed out of* the senses of the constituent words of the sentence. Thus for Lois, (A2), 'Superman can fly', and (A3), 'Clark Kent can fly', express different thoughts, since the thought expressed by (A2) has the sense of 'Superman' as a constituent, while the thought expressed by (A3) has the sense of 'Clark Kent' as a constituent. However, when we put (A2) or (A3) into the context 'Lois believes that' to obtain (B2) and (B3), and parse the result in the style of (4), (A2) and (A3) function as parts of terms for propositions, in each case the very proposition (A2) or (A3) expresses when asserted by itself. This proposition has constituents, and it seems reasonable that in the term 'that Superman can fly', the constituent words should stand for the corresponding constituent of the proposition. So we arrive at the conclusion that while 'Superman' stands for Superman in (A2), it stands for a way of thinking of Superman in (B2), the way of thinking it *expresses* in (A2). Correspondingly, (A2) is a sentence which refers to a truth-value and expresses a proposition, but when (A2) is embedded to produce (B2), (A2) in *that* context refers to the proposition that it formerly expressed. Consequently, (B) is not an application of Sub Id, since in the major premise, the names 'Superman' and 'Clark Kent' refer to a certain person, but in the minor premise the name 'Superman' refers to a way of thinking of that person. Thus the name's reference shifts in the two premises, which means that it is ambiguous. In a disambiguated notation, the major premise would have 'Superman_0' in it and the minor premise 'Superman_1', similarly for 'Clark Kent', and so (B) would manifestly fail to fit the Sub Id schema.

This is an ingenious account of the mechanics of opacity and substitution-failure, and fits elegantly into a systematic semantics for natural language. But in addition to the many questions of detail which could be raised about it, there are two rather substantial difficulties in its way. First, there are questions about the viability of the semantic system itself, as briefly sketched by Kripke in 'A puzzle about belief' in this volume and at greater length elsewhere (Kripke 1980). Second, even if we grant, *contra* Kripke and his followers, that the Fregean notion of sense has a role to play in a systematic semantics for natural language, the particular use to which Frege puts it here runs foul of the objection from semantic innocence. Surely it is clear that in making the ascriptions (B2) and (C2) we are referring to Superman and to Jocasta? Indeed, Fregean views violate semantic innocence in a particularly radical way. The Fregean account proposes the following two principles: (a) in a sentence C(E) consisting in an opacity-inducing context C governing a sentence E, E refers to the sense it would express, taken as a complete sentence by itself (eg. (A2) as it occurs in (B2) refers to the thought it expresses as it stands by itself); and (b) there can be no difference between the references of two sentences E and E′ without a corresponding difference between their senses (ie. if one sentence is true and another is false they cannot express the same thought). The result is that as we increase the depth of the embedding of E by prefixing more and more opacity-inducing contexts, the reference of E, which starts out as its customary sense when E is embedded to depth 1, changes with each additional prefix to a new sense unique to the new depth of embedding (Forbes 1987, pp. 27–9). But this is quite implausible; we have no grasp of the ever more abstruse senses that this account postulates, yet we are able to understand iteration of opacity-inducing contexts, as in 'I wonder if Lois knows that Ralph is spreading the rumor that the police suspect that Superman is a spy', without difficulty.

Many other accounts of the mechanics of opacity conflict with semantic innocence. For example, one might try to formulate some kind of quotational account, according to which belief ascriptions are really mentioning rather than using the words which are not open to substitution. For when mention replaces use, substitution of co-referential *mentioned* words is illegitimate. Thus, even though Constantinople is Istanbul, we cannot infer from

(11) 'Constantinople' has 14 letters

that

(12) 'Istanbul' has 14 letters.

So here is a familiar mechanism which, if present in the case of attitude ascriptions, would explain opacity.

A crude version of a quotational theory of opacity might propose that

(13) Ralph believes that snow is white

means

(14) Ralph believes that 'snow is white' is true as a sentence of English.

The qualification 'as a sentence of . . .' is necessary, since it is conceivable that the same sequence of letters and spaces might occur in two languages but with different meanings. However, (14) is neither necessary nor sufficient for (13). It is not necessary because Ralph may be a monolingual German who believes that snow is white but has no beliefs about the English sentence 'snow is white', and it is not sufficient because Ralph may be a monolingual German who has no beliefs about snow but who believes that 'snow is white' is a true sentence of English because a bilingual friend has so-informed him. The proposal also appears to be unstable. If (14) is the real meaning of (13) then since (14) contains 'believes that', the analysis also applies to it. Thus the real meaning of (14) is

(15) Ralph believes that ' "snow is white" is true as a sentence of English' is true as a sentence of English.

And so on.

The quotational approach can be complicated to deal with these difficulties (though with what success is another matter) but the core idea, that words in opaque position are being mentioned rather than used, must survive the complications if a *quotational* explanation of substitution-failure is to be preserved. So on a quotational approach, semantic innocence is violated, since the opaquely occurring name is represented as not referring to the thing to which it normally refers, just as, in (11), the occurrence of the sequence of letters comprising 'Constantinople' is not referring to Constantinople (it is an interesting question in the theory of quotation just *what* semantic function, if any, should be assigned to terms displayed within quotes).

At this point, two thoughts suggest themselves. The first is a question: is there any *other* familiar mechanism which, like quotation, will explain substitution-failure, but which, unlike quotation, will *also* allow semantic innocence to be preserved? The second thought is motivated by the difficulties which theories that seek to explain substitution-failure have been seen to face: one begins to wonder if it is not a mistake to look for a *semantic* explanation of substitution-failure at all. Something peculiar is going on in (B) and (C), but it may not be fallacious inference.

Though this is not the place to pursue the matter, there is a type of theory, dubbed by Schiffer 'hidden indexical theory' (Schiffer 1979), according to which some element in an attitude ascription contains a hidden indexical whose reference is disturbed when substitution is made. On theories of this type, the answer to the question about the existence of another mechanism to explain substitution-failure is in the affirmative. A simple version of such a theory is inspired by the following example of failure of substitutivity given by Quine (1960, p. 153)

(D) (1) Giorgione = Barbarelli
(2) Giorgione is so-called because of his size
(3) ∴ Barbarelli is so-called because of his size.

Substitution fails because in the move from (2) to (3) the reference of 'so' changes, and in an adequate regimentation, (D) would be exhibited as manifestly failing to fit the Sub Id schema. Nevertheless, there is no violation of semantic innocence, since the meaning of 'Giorgione' in (2) is its normal meaning; its *only* semantic function is to refer to Giorgione, while it is the semantic function of another expression to refer to *it* (this shows that Quine's terminology 'not wholly referential position' for the position of 'Giorgione' in (2) is infelicitous). (D) is suggestive of a semantics for attitude ascriptions which, broadly speaking, uncovers an implicit reference in an attitude ascription to specific words used in specifying the content of the attitude, or to items associated with such words. (This idea is worked out in (Forbes 1990); for other hidden indexical theories, see (Crimmins 1992, Loar 1972, Richard 1990)).

An alternative line of thought which has been much discussed in the recent literature proposes that the use of Sub Id in (B) is not, or may not be, objectionable. Why do we think the conclusion of (B), 'Lois believes Clark is an extraterrestrial', is false? One reason is that Lois would refuse to assent to the sentence 'Clark Kent is an extraterrestrial' though there is nothing deficient in her understanding of it, and would assent to the sentence 'Clark Kent is not an extraterrestrial' though she is not so unperceptive as to have obviously contradictory beliefs in the forefront of her mind. That is, if we take linguistic behavior at face value, we are likely to think that Sub Id in (B) leads from true premises to false conclusion. But with the aid of his now famous 'Paderewski' example, Kripke argues that Sub Id may not be at fault. In this example (Kripke 1979), Kripke presents us with the character of Peter, about whom he tells a story along the following lines. Peter attends a concert at which the Polish pianist Paderewski performs with verve and flair, so that Peter, who has taste in these matters, firmly asserts 'Paderewski has musical talent'. Later, Peter meets the Polish Prime Minister Paderewski at a reception, and failing to recognize the pianist, deduces from his general belief 'every politician is musically talentless' that Paderewski has no musical talent, and says so in just these words. This story motivates all three of the following

(16) Peter believes Paderewski has musical talent
(17) Peter believes Paderewski does not have musical talent
(18) Peter does not believe Paderewski has musical talent.

But (16) and (17) ascribe explicitly contradictory beliefs to Peter, a contradiction he should be able to spot *a priori*, simply by running the beliefs he would express using 'Paderewski' through his internal consistency checker. Yet it is clear that Peter is in no position to diagnose error in his beliefs using such a method. Worse, despite the inclination to assert both (16) and (18), it seems that no self-respecting reporter should do so, since (16) and (18) are themselves explicitly contradictory.

Kripke's point is that our ordinary principles of belief ascription, which lead to (16)–(18), are producing paradoxical results. These principles are ones that everyone subscribes to – they are of the very nature of belief – so it may be that the paradox which (16)–(18) represent is a consequence of, as Kripke puts it, 'the nature of the realm being entered' (1979, p. 206). In that case, the trouble with (B3), 'Lois believes Clark can fly', may also be traced to the problematic nature of this realm, and not to any particular principle such as Sub Id used in deriving it. Hence a semantics of attitude ascriptions which predicts that Sub Id is correctly applicable need not be rejected simply because of its strange consequences – strange consequences come with the territory, so to speak.

If substitution of co-designating names is to be allowed, the conclusion of (B) is in fact true. That we think it false is indicative, according to Salmon, of a deficiency in language that compels speakers to violate its rules in order to convey what they intend (Salmon 1986, p. 84). Salmon distinguishes between what a belief ascription literally says (the information it semantically encodes) and what it pragmatically imparts. He provides a semantic account of attitude ascriptions which uses the three-place notion of a subject believing a proposition in a particular way. The propositions of his account are non-Fregean: for example, the proposition that Clark Kent is an extraterrestrial is the same proposition as the proposition that Superman is an extraterrestrial. But this proposition may be believed in different ways, one way being invoked by the words 'Clark Kent is an extraterrestrial' and another by 'Superman is an extraterrestrial'. When we ascribe belief there is a pragmatic implication that the believer believes the proposition in the way invoked by the words the ascriber uses to specify the content of the belief. What is wrong with the conclusion of (B) is not that it is false, but that it involves a pragmatically misleading specification of the attitude-content, since Lois does not believe that Superman is an extraterrestrial in the Clark-Kent-is-an-extraterrestrial way of believing it.

The qualification of two paragraphs back, that linguistic behavior is only to be taken at face value in belief-attribution if the subject does not misunderstand the relevant words, leads to some interesting complications. A natural picture is that a subject who does not misunderstand his or her language and who wishes to express a belief chooses appropriate words, the ones whose meanings are constituents of the beliefs, and expresses the belief by asserting the words. Such a picture is suggestive of a certain primacy of individual thought over language: words get their meanings by being used to express antecedently grasped concepts. But Burge has argued that at least in some cases, this puts the cart before the horse (1979, p. 109). Consider Bertrand, who misunderstands what arthritis is, in that he thinks it can afflict muscles as well as joints. It seems that such a misunderstanding would not prevent us from ascribing beliefs about arthritis to Bertrand, using 'arthritis' opaquely. Thus we might say, for example, that Bertrand believes that the older you get, the bigger the threat of arthritis is. Now imagine counterfactual circumstances in which the word 'arthritis' *is* used to include rheumatic inflammation of the muscles, that is, circumstances in which the word is correctly used in exactly the way that Bertrand actually misuses it. In such circumstances, Bertrand would *not* believe that the risk of arthritis increases with age. The reason is that, in speculating about the beliefs subjects would and would not have in counterfactual circumstances, the words we use to specify the beliefs retain their actual references, as in 'Lois would believe that Clark can fly were she to discover that he is Superman'. So if we say 'in such-and-such possible circumstances Bertrand would believe that the risk of arthritis increases with age' we are using 'arthritis' to pick out the disease to which it actually refers. But in the imagined circumstances, Bertrand belongs to a community in which 'arthritis' is used for a different disease, and there is no reason to suppose that in *those* circumstances, the way of thinking Bertrand expresses with 'arthritis' is a way of thinking of the word's *actual* reference; it would instead be a way of thinking of the reference it has in those circumstances. The strange thing is that though Bertrand would not have beliefs about arthritis in the counterfactual circumstances, this fact is not underpinned by any difference in *Bertrand*, only a difference in the sociolinguistic context in which he is situated – thus the anti-individualistic moral of the case on which Burge dwells.

The relatively uncontroversial part of Burge's example concerns the claim that in the counterfactual circumstances, Bertrand would not believe eg. that arthritis is painful. Suppose there is a distant planet on which the history of the Earth is exactly duplicated. Then it is clearly false that if I had been born there, I would (still) have believed that I was born in Glasgow. If I had been born *there*, how could I have had any beliefs about Glasgow? Of course, I would have had beliefs about a city which on that planet is called 'Glasgow', but that is not sufficient for the truth of the just-stated counterfactual about what I would have believed. If I had been born on that other planet, I would have no more believed that I was born in Glasgow than I would have *been* born in Glasgow.

The more controversial part of Burge's example concerns the claim that despite the misunderstanding about arthritis, it is still correct to say, eg. that Bertrand believes the risk of arthritis increases with age. By treating 'arthritis' as a name (of a disease), we can make this palatable, since there is no general puzzle about how it can be correct to use a name is ascribing a belief when the subject has misconceptions about the bearer of the name: having misconceptions about the bearer is consistent with using the name for that bearer. For Burge's own purposes, this is as much as he needs to make his points against individualism. But to relate the case to the topic of this essay, there are interesting ramifications for substitution problems which involve synonymous predicates rather than co-referential names (Mates 1952). However, the reader will have to pursue this area of the study of opacity independently.

References

Burge, T. (1979), 'Individualism and the mental', in *Midwest Studies in Philosophy Volume IV: Studies in Metaphysics*, edited by P. French, T. Vehling and M. Weltstein, Minneapolis: University of Minnesota Press.

Crimmins, M. (1992), *Talk About Belief*, Cambridge, Mass: The MIT Press.

Davidson, D. (1969), 'On saying that', in *Words and Objections: Essays on the Work of W. V. Quine*, edited by D. Davidson and J. Hintikka, Dordrecht: D. Reidel.

Evans, G. (1982), *The Varieties of Reference*, Oxford and New York: Oxford University Press.

Forbes, G. (1987), 'Indexicals and intentionality', *The Philosophical Review*, 96: 3–31.

Forbes, G. (1990), 'The indispensability of *Sinn*', *The Philosophical Review*, 99: 535–63.

Kripke, S. (1979), 'A puzzle About belief', in *Meaning and Use*, edited by A. Margalit, Dordrecht: D. Reidel.

Kripke, S. (1980), *Naming and Necessity*, Cambridge, Mass.: Harvard University Press.
Loar, B. (1972), 'Reference and propositional attitudes', *Philosophical Review*, 81: 43–62.
Mates, B. (1952), 'Synonymity', in *Semantics and the Philosophy of Language*, edited by L. Linsky, Chicago: University of Illinois Press.
Quine, W. V. (1960), *Word and Object*, Cambridge, Mass.: The MIT Press.
Richard, M. (1990), *Propositional Attitudes*, Cambridge, United Kingdom: Cambridge University Press.
Russell, B. (1918), '*The Philosophy of Logical Atomism*', in *Russell's Logical Atomism* edited by D. Pears, 1972, London: Fontana.
Salmon, N. (1986), *Frege's Puzzle*, Cambridge, Mass.: The MIT Press.
Schiffer, S. (1979), 'Naming and knowing', in *Contemporary Perspectives in the Philosophy of Language* edited by P. French *et al.*, Minneapolis: University of Minnesota Press, pp. 61–74.
Smullyan, A. (1948), 'Modality and description', *The Journal of Symbolic Logic*, 13: 31–7.

Chapter 13

Referential Opacity

W. Quine

§30. Referential Opacity

Definite singular terms may shift in reference with occasions of use, either through ambiguity or through the peculiar functions of 'the', 'this', and 'that'. Under some circumstances the term may simply fail of reference, through there being no object of the required sort. And there is a further kind of variation: in sentences there are positions where the term is used as a means simply of specifying its object, or purporting to, for the rest of the sentence to say something about, and there are positions where it is not. An example of the latter sort is the position of 'Tully' in:

(1) 'Tully was a Roman' is trochaic.

When a singular term is used in a sentence purely to specify its object, and the sentence is true of the object, then certainly the sentence will stay true when any other singular term is substituted that designates the same object. Here we have a criterion for what may be called *purely referential position*: the position must be subject to the *substitutivity of identity*.[1] That the position of 'Tully' in (1) is not purely referential is reflected in the falsity of what we get by supplanting 'Tully' in (1) by 'Cicero'.

If we understand the sentence:

(2) The commissioner is looking for the chairman of the hospital board

in such a way as to be prepared to affirm it and yet to deny:

(3) The commissioner is looking for the dean

From W. Quine (1960), *Word and Objects*, Boston, Mass.: MIT Press.

even though, by recent appointment and unknown to the commissioner,

(4) The dean = the chairman of the hospital board,

then we are treating the position to the right of 'looking for' as not purely referential. On the other hand if, aware of the commissioner's persistent avoidance of the dean, we are still constrained by (2) and (4) to treat (3) as true, then we are indeed treating the position as purely referential.

Example (2), even if taken in the not purely referential way, differs from (1) in that it still seems to have far more bearing on the chairman of the hospital board, dean though he be, than (1) has on Tully. Hence my cautious phrase 'not purely referential', designed to apply to all such cases and to affirm no distinction among them. If I omit the adverb, the motive will be brevity.

An illustration of purely referential position is the position of singular terms under predication. For, the predication is true so long merely as the predicated general term is true of the object named by the singular term (§20); hence the substitution of a new singular term that names the same object leaves the predication true. In particular the question whether to take the main singular-term positions in (2) as purely referential is the question whether to treat (2) as a predication of a relative term 'looking for'.

The positions that we have been classifying into purely referential and other are positions of singular terms relative to sentences that contain them. Now it is convenient to extend the concept to apply also to positions of singular terms relative to singular terms that contain them. Thus, take quotation marks: applied to any sort of expression, what they produce is a singular term (naming, as it happens, the expression inside). It is convenient to be able to speak of the personal name in (1) as having non-referential position not only in the sentence (1), but equally in the singular tern, of quotational form, that is the grammatical subject of (1). Indeed, it is rather the quotation than (1) as a whole that is primarily in point here; the personal name has non-referential position in (1) simply because of the quotation.

As a criterion of referential position, substitutivity of identity works as well for positions within singular terms as for positions within sentences. For positions in sentences, what it says is that the containing sentence keeps its truth value when the contained singular term is supplanted by any other having the same reference. For positions in singular terms, what it says is that the containing singular term keeps its reference when the contained singular term is so supplanted. Thus what shows the position of the personal name in the quotation:

(5) 'Tully was a Roman'

to be non-referential is that, though Tully = Cicero, yet

'Tully was a Roman' ≠ 'Cicero was a Roman'.

Quotation, we see, gives rise to non-referential positions. Now this is not true of an alternative device to the same purpose as quotation, viz. *spelling*. Instead of (5) we can as well say:

> tee⁀yu⁀ell⁀ell⁀wye⁀space⁀doubleyu⁀ay⁀ess
> ⁀space⁀ay⁀space⁀ar⁀oh⁀em⁀ay⁀en,

thus using explicit names of the letters and an arch (following Tarski) to indicate concatenation. The shift from quotation to spelling has an independent advantage (cf. §39), but incidentally it is instructive as stressing that any non-referential occurrences caused by quotation are surface appearances, dispelled by an easy change in notation.

Also apart from quotation there are frequent cases where a not purely referential occurrence of a singular term can be banished by paraphrase. But there is no compulsion upon us to banish all non-referential occurrences of singular terms, nor to reduce them to quotation. We are not unaccustomed to passing over occurrences that somehow 'do not count' – 'mary' in 'summary', 'can' in 'canary'; and we can allow similarly for all non-referential occurrences of terms, once we know what to look out for.

One and the same occurrence of a term may have purely referential position with respect to its immediate surroundings and not with respect to a broader context. For example, the personal name has purely referential position in the sentence:

> (6) Tully was a Roman

and yet in neither of the more extended expressions (1) and (5). Quotation, which thus interrupts the referential force of a term, many be said to fail of referential *transparency*.[2]

Referential transparency has to do with constructions (§11); modes of containment, more specifically, of singular terms or sentences in singular terms or sentences. I call a mode of containment ϕ referentially transparent if, whenever an occurrence of a singular term t is purely referential in a term or sentence $\psi(t)$, it is purely referential also in the containing term or sentence $\phi(\psi(t))$. Take $\phi(\psi(t))$ as (5), $\psi(t)$ as (6), and t as the personal name, and you have the referential opacity of quotation.

Alternation, in contrast, is referentially transparent. That is, if a sentence is compounded of component sentences by means of 'or', all purely referential positions in the component sentences qualify still as purely referential positions in the compound. Clearly any truth function (§13) is referentially transparent.

General terms predicatively used may be looked on as constructions: modes of containment of the subject singular terms in sentences. As constructions they are referentially transparent; for this is simply to say, what was remarked above, that the subject position in a predication is purely referential.

Again the construction 'looking for' counts as transparent if adjacent term positions are treated as referential, and not otherwise. In the one case 'look for' is a genuine relative term; in the other not. What it is in the other case will become clearer in §32.

A construction that may be transparent or opaque is the belief construction, '*a* believes that *p*'. Thus suppose that though

(7) Tom believes that Cicero denounced Catiline,

he is ill-informed enough to think that the Cicero of the orations and the Tully of *De Senectute* were two. Faced with his unequivocal denial of 'Tully denounced Catiline', we are perhaps prepared both to affirm (7) and to deny that Tom believes that Tully denounced Catiline. If so, the position of 'Cicero' in (7) is not purely referential. But the position of 'Cicero' in the part 'Cicero denounced Catiline', considered apart, is purely referential. So 'believes that' (so conceived) is opaque.

At the same time there is an alternative way of construing belief that is referentially transparent.[3] The difference is as follows. In the opaque sense of belief considered above, Tom's earnest 'Tully never denounced Catiline' counts as showing that he does not believe that Tully denounced Catiline, even while he believes that Cicero did. In the transparent sense of belief, on the other hand, Tom's earnest 'Cicero denounced Catiline' counts as showing that he does believe that Tully denounced Catiline, despite his own misguided verbal disclaimer.

'Cicero' has purely referential occurrence in (7) or not according as 'believes' is taken transparently or not. If belief is taken transparently, then (7) expresses an outright relation between the men Tom and Cicero, viz. the relation of deeming denouncer of Catiline; if belief is taken opaquely, then (7) expressly relates Tom to no man.

There will be more to say of the distinction between transparent and opaque belief. But note meanwhile that the distinction is unrelated to the familiar quirk of English usage whereby '*x* does not believe that *p*' is equated to '*x* believes that not *p*' rather than to 'It is not the case that *x* believes that *p*'. I have been avoiding the concatenation 'does not believe', lest this incidental idiomatic complication seem to figure in the reasoning.

It would be wrong to suppose that an occurrence of a term within an opaque construction is barred from referential position in every broader context. Examples to the contrary are provided by the occurrences of the personal name in:

(8) 'Tully was a Roman' is true,
(9) 'Tully' refers to a Roman.

Despite the opacity of quotation, these occurrences of the personal name are clearly subject to substitutivity of identity *salva veritate*, thanks to the peculiarities of the main verbs involved. On this account 'non-transparent' would be more suggestive than 'opaque'; but the term would be cumbersome, and it is rather a fine point.

§31. Opacity and Indefinite Terms

Since indefinite singular terms do not designate objects (§23), we have had only definite singular terms in mind in our considerations of referential position. The terms that we replace by others of like designation, in testing for substitutivity of identity, are definite singular terms. Still, what we are testing are positions, and indefinite singular terms can be put into them. Let us see with what effect.

We saw that the position after 'The commissioner is looking for' might or might not be taken as purely referential, with unlike effects. But if we put an indefinite singular term in it, say 'someone', we cease to be free to choose between two interpretations. To make proper sense of 'The commissioner is looking for someone' we have to think of the position as purely referential. For, who is this person the commissioner is looking for? The chairman of the hospital board, i.e., the dean. In the sense of 'looking for' in which the commissioner can be said to be looking for someone, (3) in the previous section has to be reckoned true along with (2). The treatment that would count (2) as true and (3) as false makes the truth value of such statements depend on what epithet is used in designating the sought person; and such a distinction is inapplicable in 'The commissioner is looking for someone', where the sought person is not designated at all. To put the point paradoxically, indefinite singular terms need referential position because they do not refer.

The same consideration would seem to suggest that for purposes of 'Tom believes that someone denounced Catiline' we must take 'believes' transparently; i.e., take the position of 'someone' as referential. But this case is complicated by a second, intersecting ambiguity: a question of the scope of the indefinite singular term. According as that scope is taken as narrow or wide, the sentence is explained by one or the other of:

(1) Tom believes that someone (is such that he) denounced Catiline.
(2) Someone is such that Tom believes that he denounced Catiline.

Surely (1) is likelier than (2) to do justice to 'Tom believes that someone denounced Catiline'; the words 'is such that he' in (1) are indeed immediately felt as superfluous. But in (1), unlike 'The commissioner is looking for someone', we remain quite free to take the position of 'someone' as referential or not as we please. This is because 'someone' obviously and unequivocally occupies referential position in the subsidiary sentence 'someone denounced

Catiline' considered alone. And just because the subsidiary sentence makes sense in any event, (1) does too. In short, therefore, the denouncing position in (1) can freely be taken as referential or non-referential in (1) as a whole. In other words, belief can be construed transparently or opaquely; (1) makes sense either way.

Not so (2), which may be put more idiomatically as 'There is (or was) someone whom Tom believes to have denounced Catiline'. Here it is that those reflections apply that applied to 'The commissioner is looking for someone'. For, who is this person whom Tom believes to have denounced Catiline? Cicero, i.e., Tully. In the sense of 'believes' in which there can be said to be someone whom Tom believes to have denounced Catiline, 'Tom believes that Tully denounced Catiline' has to be reckoned true along with 'Tom believes that Cicero denounced Catiline'. In short, belief must be taken transparently to make proper sense of (2), though it can be taken either way for (1).

The two interpretations of 'I believe he saw a letter of mine' (§29) are on this score quite like (1) and (2). Where transparency matters in relation to indefinite singular terms is that there must not be a pronominal cross-reference from inside an opaque construction to an indefinite singular term outside the construction. Such is the lesson of (2). Parallel considerations show also that there must not be a pronominal cross-reference from inside an opaque construction to a 'such that' outside the construction. Adapted to variables (§28) the maxim is this: an indefinite singular term outside an opaque construction does not bind a variable inside the construction.

The need of cross-reference from inside a belief construction to an indefinite singular term outside is not to be doubted. Thus see what urgent information the sentence 'There is someone whom I believe to be a spy' imparts, in contrast to 'I believe that someone is a spy' (in the weak sense of 'I believe there are spies'). The one corresponds to (2), the other to (1). Surely, therefore, the transparent sense of belief is not to be lightly dismissed. Yet let its urgency not blind us to its oddity. 'Tully,' Tom insists, 'did not denounce Catiline. Cicero did.' Surely Tom must be acknowledged to believe, in every sense, that Tully did not denounce Catiline and that Cicero did. But still he must be said also to believe, in the referentially transparent sense, that Tully *did* denounce Catiline. The oddity of the transparent sense of belief is that it has Tom believing that Tully did and that he did not denounce Catiline. This is not yet a self-contradiction on our part or even on Tom's, for a distinction can be reserved between (*a*) Tom's believing that Tully did and that Tully did not denounce Catiline, and (*b*) Tom's believing that Tully did and did not denounce Catiline. But the oddity is there, and we have to accept it as the price of saying such things as (2) or that there is someone whom one believes to be a spy.

Certainly we are not to blame the oddity on Tom's mere misunderstanding of a proper name, for there are parallel examples without names. Thus instead of having Tom say, 'Tully did not denounce Catiline; Cicero did,' have him say, 'The dean is not married, but the chairman of the hospital board is,' not appreciating that they are one.

Now if this much oddity on the part of the transparent sense of belief is tolerable, more remains that is not. Where '*p*' represents a sentence, let us write 'δp' (following Kronecker) as short for the description:

$$\text{the number } x \text{ such that } ((x = 1) \text{ and } p), \text{ or } ((x = 0) \text{ and not } p.$$

We may suppose that poor Tom, whatever his limitations regarding Latin literature and local philanthropies, is enough of a logician to believe a sentence of the form '$\delta p = 1$' when and only when he believes the sentence represented by '*p*'. But then we can argue from the transparency of belief that he believes everything. For, by the hypotheses already before us,

(3) Tom believes that δ(Cicero denounced Catiline) $= 1$.

But, whenever '*p*' represents a true sentence,

$\delta p = \delta$(Cicero denounced Catiline).

But then, by (3) and the transparency of belief,

Tom believes that $\delta p = 1$,

from which it follows, by the hypothesis about Tom's logical acumen, that

(4) Tom believes that *p*.

But '*p*' represented any true sentence. Repeating the argument using the falsehood 'Tully did not denounce Catiline' instead of the truth 'Cicero denounced Catiline', we establish (4) also where '*p*' represents any falsehood. Tom ends up believing everything.[4]

Thus in declaring belief invariably transparent for the sake of (2) and 'There is someone whom I believe to be a spy', we would let in too much. It can sometimes best suit us to affirm 'Tom believes that Cicero denounced Catiline' and still deny 'Tom believes that Tully denounced Catiline', at the cost – on *that* occasion – of (2). In general what is wanted is not a doctrine of transparency or opacity of belief, but a way of indicating, selectively and changeably, just what positions in the contained sentence are to shine through as referential on any particular occasion.

A way of doing that is to agree to localize the failure of transparency regularly in the 'that' of 'believes that' and the 'to' of 'believes to' and not in the 'believes'. Thus we may continue to write 'Tom believes that Cicero denounced Catiline' when we are content to leave the occurrences of 'Cicero' and 'Catiline' non-referential, but write rather:

(5) Tom believes Cicero to have denounced Catiline

if we want to bring 'Cicero' into referential position.[5] Similarly we can get 'Catiline' into referential position thus:

(6) Tom believes Catiline to have been denounced by Cicero.

If we want to get both into referential position, we are driven to something like:

(7) Tom believes Cicero and Catiline to be related as denouncer and denounced.

On this convention 'believes that' is unequivocally opaque and (2) therefore simply goes by the board as a bad formulation involving cross-reference from inside an opaque construction to an indefinite singular term outside. What was offered before as an idiomatic equivalent of (2) remains legitimate, however: 'There is (or was) someone whom Tom believes to have denounced Catiline'. Similarly (13) of §29 goes by the board, but the originally intended sense of it survives in the legitimate version 'There is (or was) a letter of mine which I believe to have been seen by him'.

Here as usual we can revise the relative clauses at will into 'such that' clauses (§23); thus '. . . whom Tom believes to . . .' and '. . . which I believe to . . .' become '. . . such that Tom believes him to . . .' and '. . . such that I believe it to. . .', without ever disturbing the insides of the opaque 'to' construction. Note that the 'that' of 'such that' is referentially transparent; it is only the 'that' of 'believes that', and the 'to' of 'believes to', that our convention counts opaque.

The constructions 'believes that', 'says that', 'wishes that', 'endeavors that', 'urges that', 'fears that', 'is surprised that', etc., are what Russell calls expressions of *propositional attitude*.[6] What has been observed of the first of them in recent pages applies equally to the lot. The contortions of (5)–(7) strain ordinary language in varying degrees when applied to the rest of the verbs of propositional attitude. 'Wishes', 'urges', and 'fears' fit (5)–(7) as naturally as 'believes' (except that 'urges' is inappropriate to our particular example on account of the past tense). 'Says' falls into place with no great violence. 'Endeavors' and 'is surprised' have to be reworded in some such fashion as 'endeavors-to-cause' and 'is surprised-to-learn' when fitted to those positions.

An opaque construction is one in which you cannot in general supplant a singular term by a *codesignative* term (one referring to the same object) without disturbing the truth value of the containing sentence. In an opaque construction you also cannot in general supplant a general term by a *coextensive* term (one true of the same objects), nor a component sentence by a sentence of the same truth value, without disturbing the truth value of the containing sentence. All three failures are called failures of *extensionality*. A reason for stressing the first is that one rightly expects substitutivity of identity in discourse about the identical object, whereas no such presumption is evident for full extensionality. A related reason is that the first failure is what disallows cross-reference from inside opaque constructions. Frege was bound to stress all three failures, for he treated general terms and sentences as naming classes and truth values; all failures and extensionality became failures of substitutivity of identity.[7] Failures of substitutivity of identity, moreover, were in Frege's view unallowable; so he nominally rectified them by decreeing that when a sentence or term occurs within a construction of propositional attitude or the like it ceases to name a truth value, class, or individual and comes to name a proposition, attribute, or 'individual concept.' (In some ways this account better fits Church, who has sharpened and elaborated the doctrine.[8]) I make none of these moves. I do not disallow failure of substitutivity, but only take it as evidence of non-referential position; nor do I envisage shifts of reference under opaque constructions.

§32. Opacity in Certain Verbs

We have hit upon a convenient trick of so phrasing our statements of propositional attitude as to keep selected positions referential and others not. The device does not yet apply to our earlier example:

> (1) The commissioner is looking for the chairman of the hospital board,

since this example contains no expression of propositional attitude. But it can be made to do so by expanding 'look for' into 'endeavor to find':

> (2) The commissioner is endeavoring that the commissioner finds the chairman of the hospital board.

The point of the bad English is to stress the parallel of 'Tom believes that Cicero denounced Catiline'. Now if we carry over the convention of [p. 345], the term 'the chairman of the hospital board' has non-referential position in (2). Sentence (2) expands (1) in a way that counts 'looking for . . .' opaque. To get an expansion of (1) in a transparent sense, we must operate on (2) to bring 'the chairman of the hospital board' out from under the opaque 'endeavoring that'. The desired operation on (2) is precisely the operation which, applied to 'Tom believes that Cicero denounced Catiline', gave 'Tom believes Cicero to have denounced Catiline'. Applied to (2), the operation delivers:

> (3) The commissioner is endeavoring (-to-cause) the chairman of the hospital board to be found by the commissioner.

Note that the opaque 'to' of (3) is the one after 'board' and not the one in parentheses; the parenthetical expression is for our purposes merely part of the inflection of 'endeavor'. (See end of §31.)

So (2) construes (1) with opaque 'looking for . . .', and (3) construes (1) with transparent 'looking for . . .' Thus (2) construes (1) in such a way that substituting 'someone' for 'the chairman of the hospital board' produces nonsense; (3) construes (1) in such a way that substituting 'someone' makes sense. Again (2) construes (1) in such a way that substitution of 'the dean' produces falsity; (3) construes (1) in such a way that substitution of 'the dean' preserves truth.

In both (2) and (3), the first occurrence of 'the commissioner' has referential position and the second has not. Thus (1), no matter whether we take its 'looking for . . .' in the opaque manner of (2) or in the transparent manner of (3), is a sentence whose single grammatical subject implicitly plays two roles, a referential one and a non-referential one. An example in which this same phenomenon of two-role subject comes out more vividly is:

> (4) Giorgione was so-called because of his size,

which anyone is ready enough to paraphrase into:

> Giorgione was called 'Giorgione' because of his size.

Taking (4) as it stands, we have of course to reckon the position of the subject as not (purely) referential, because of the non-referential character of one of its two implicit roles. And the same conclusion emerges by the direct substitutivity criterion: substitution in (4) according to the identity 'Giorgione = Barbarelli' yields a falsehood.

'The commissioner' in (1) is likewise found to resist substitutivity, if (1) is construed as (2) or (3). Thus suppose the commissioner, for all his self-importance, is the least competent of the county officials. Substitution in (1) according to this identity would give 'The least competent official is endeavoring that the least competent official finds etc.', if we construe (1) as (2); and this, with opaque 'endeavoring that', is doubtless to be adjudged false. The case is similar when we construe (1) as (3).

Now the account of (4) was unexceptionable, but this parallel account of (1) is certainly a distortion.[9] Surely, on a fair account, 'the commissioner' should have referential position in (1), and be replaceable by 'the least competent official' *salva veritate*.

The non-referential status of the subject position in (4) excludes 'someone' from that position, and rightly; 'Someone was so-called because of his size' is nonsense. But the non-referential status of the subject position in (1) would likewise exclude 'someone' from that position; whereas we must surely insist on saying 'Someone is looking for the chairman of the hospital board'.

The upshot of these reflections is that (1) is wrongly construed in both (2) and (3). We must bring the second occurrence of 'the commissioner' into referential position by an additional twist, analogous to the one used on 'Cicero' in (5) or (7) of §31. The proper account of (1) with opaque 'looking for . . .' is not (2) above, but rather this analogue of (5) of §31:

> (5) The commissioner is endeavoring (-to-cause) himself to find the chairman of the hospital board.

The proper account of (1) with transparent 'looking for . . .' is not (3) above, but rather this analogue of (7) of §31:

> (6) The commissioner is endeavoring (-to-cause) himself and the chairman of the hospital board to be related as finder and found.

Sentences (2) and (3) remain all right in themselves, but not as versions of (1).

If (1) were construed as (2) or (3), which would be indefensible, and again if (1) is construed as (5), which is one of two admissible interpretations, the verb 'is looking for' does not count as a relative term; not as a term at all, but an opaque verb whose function is explained by the overall paraphrase. If (1) is construed as (6), on the other hand, 'is looking for' qualifies as a relative term. Subject and object in (1) have referential position when (1) is construed as (6). This does not make (6) preferable to (5). Sentence (5) explains (1) with 'looking for' taken as opaque and hence not as a term, and (6) explains (1) with 'looking for' taken as transparent and hence as a term; and both uses of 'looking for' have their place.

The contrast between the two uses of 'looking for' is the same as the contrast between hunting lions in the abstract and hunting or stalking known ones (§28). For, observe how lion-hunting turns out. Just as looking for is endeavoring to find, so hunting is endeavoring to shoot or capture. The difference between the two cases of 'Ernest is hunting lions' is *prima facie* a difference in scope:

> (7) Ernest is endeavoring that some lion is such that Ernest shoots it,
> (8) Some lion is such that Ernest is endeavoring that Ernest shoots it.

(cf. (12) and (13) of §29, also (1) and (2) of §31). This symmetrical pair of formulations brings the contrast of scopes instructively to the fore, but we shall not want to leave them thus. Sentence (7), to begin with, can as well be put more concisely:

> (9) Ernest is endeavoring that Ernest shoots a lion.

And (8) is simply wrong under the convention of §31, for that convention counts 'is endeavoring that' unequivocally as opaque. Sentence (8) is like (2) of §31 in involving a cross-reference from inside an opaque construction to an indefinite singular term outside. Correcting (8) as we did (2) of §31, we have:

> There is a lion which Ernest is endeavoring (-to-cause) to be shot by Ernest.

or, if we feel we can keep the intended scope of the indefinite singular term in mind with less extravagant aids,

> (10) Ernest is endeavoring (-to-cause) a (certain) lion to be shot by Ernest.

Now note that (9) and (10) have the same forms as (2) and (3) of the present section, except that they use an indefinite singular term instead of a definite one. Consequently the objection to (2) and (3) as versions of (1) applies equally to (9) and (10) as versions of 'Ernest is hunting lions': they fail to give 'Ernest' purely referential position at its second occurrences. Rather, just as we dropped (2) and (3) (as versions of (1)) in favor of (5) and (6), so we must drop (9) and (10) (as versions of 'Ernest is hunting lions') in favor of:

> (11) Ernest is endeavoring (-to-cause) himself to shoot a lion,
> (12) Ernest is endeavoring (-to-cause) himself and a (certain) lion to be related as shooter and shot.

When 'Ernest is hunting lions' is construed as (12), 'hunt' qualifies as a straightforward relative term. 'Hunt' is so used in 'man-hunting', as applied to the police; not as applied to man-hunting lions. 'Hunt' in the latter use, and in 'unicorn-hunting' and in the commonest use of 'lion-hunting', is not a term; it is an opaque verb whose use is clarified by the paraphrase (11).

What we have been remarking of 'hunt' or 'look for' and 'endeavor' applies *mutatis mutandis* to 'want' and 'wish'; for to want is to wish to have. 'I want a sloop' in the opaque sense is parallel to (11): 'I wish myself to have a sloop (to be a sloop owner)'; 'I want a sloop' in the transparent sense, 'There is a sloop I want', comes out parallel to (12). Only in the latter sense is 'want' a relative term, relating people to sloops. In the other or opaque sense it is not a relative term relating people to anything at all, concrete or abstract, real or ideal. It is a shortcut verb whose use is set forth by 'I wish myself to have a sloop', wherein 'have' and 'sloop' continue to rate as general terms as usual but merely happen to have an opaque construction 'wish to' overlying them. This point needs to be noticed by philosophers worried over the nature of objects of desire.

Whenever sentences capable of containing 'want' or 'hunt' or 'look for' in an opaque sense are up for consideration in an at all analytic vein, it behooves us forthwith to paraphrase them into the more explicit idiom of propositional attitude. The question of transparency thereupon stands forth and can be settled, now as in (5) and (11) and now as in (6) and (12), in clear view of the alternative commitments and consequences. In general it is a good rule thus to try by paraphrase to account for non-referential positions by explicitly opaque constructions. And in the present instances there is also another benefit from the paraphrase: it exposes a structure startlingly unlike what one usually associates with the grammatical form of 'Ernest is hunting lions' and 'I want a sloop' (cf. 'I hear lions').

When 'hunt lions' and the like are meant rather in the transparent way, there is seldom call to paraphrase them into the idiom of propositional attitudes; for here the verb is a well-behaved relative term as it stands. Usually we are well enough off with 'There is a lion that Ernest is hunting', 'There is a sloop I want'; nothing is gained by expanding it in the grotesque manner of (12), except for purposes of comparisons of the sort in which we have just now been engaged. Our paraphrases, aimed at bringing out the distinction between referential and non-referential positions, have been cumbersome at best; but the most cumbersome ones are the ones least needed.

Notes

1. The concept and its criterion are due essentially to Frege, 'On sense and reference.' But there is much in his associated theory that I do not adopt; see end of §31.
2. The term is from Whitehead and Russell, 2d ed., vol. 1, p. 665.
3. This is apparent from an example of Goodman cited by Scheffler, 'On synonymy and indirect discourse,' p. 42.
4. See Church's review of Carnap for a related argument in another connection.
5. Davidson points out to me that the rearrangement 'By Tom, Cicero is believed to have denounced Catiline' has, along with the drawback of unnaturalness, the virtue of being more graphic than (5) in two respects: it unifies the opaque 'believe to', and it displays the referential positions before mentioning belief. Similar rearrangements work for (6) and (7).
6. *Inquiry into Meaning and Truth*, p. 210. See also Reichenbach, pp. 277 ff.
7. Even apart from this special doctrine, the following connection between referential transparency and extensionality can be established: if a construction is transparent

and allows substitutivity of concretion (§48), it is extensional. The argument is obvious, but see Church's review of 'On Frege's way out' for exposure of a fallacy in my adaptation of it to Whitehead and Russell's theory.

8. Church, 'A formulation of the logic of sense and denotation.'
9. I am indebted here to a remark of Davidson's.

Chapter 14

A Puzzle about Belief

S. Kripke

In this paper I will present a puzzle about names and belief. A moral or two will be drawn about some other arguments that have occasionally been advanced in this area, but my main thesis is a simple one: that the puzzle *is* a puzzle. And, as a corollary, that any account of belief must ultimately come to grips with it. Any speculation as to solutions can be deferred.

The first section of the paper gives the theoretical background in previous discussion, and in my own earlier work, that led me to consider the puzzle. The background is by no means necessary to *state* the puzzle: As a philosophical puzzle, it stands on its own, and I think its fundamental interest for the problem of belief goes beyond the background that engendered it. As I indicate in the third section, the problem really goes beyond beliefs expressed using names, to a far wider class of beliefs. Nevertheless, I think that the background illuminates the genesis of the puzzle, and it will enable me to draw one moral in the concluding section.

The second section states some general principles which underlie our general practice of reporting beliefs. These principles are stated in much more detail than is needed to comprehend the puzzle; and there are variant formulations of the principles that would do as well. Neither this section nor the first is necessary for an intuitive grasp of the central problem, discussed in the third section, though they may help with fine points of the discussion. The reader who wishes rapid access to the central problem could skim the first two sections lightly on a first reading.

In one sense the problem may strike some as no puzzle at all. For, in the situation to be envisaged, all the relevant facts can be described in *one* terminology without difficulty. But, in *another* terminology, the situation seems to be impossible to describe in a consistent way. This will become clearer later.

From Margalit, A. (ed.) (1979) *Meaning and Use*, Dordrecht: D. Reidel.

I. Preliminaries: Substitutivity

In other writings,[1] developed a view of proper names closer in many ways to the old Millian paradigm of naming than to the Fregean tradition which probably was dominant until recently. According to Mill, a proper name is, so to speak, *simply* a name. It *simply* refers to its bearer, and has no other linguistic function. In particular, unlike a definite description, a name does not describe its bearer as possessing any special identifying properties.

The opposing Fregean view holds that to each proper name, a speaker of the language associates some property (or conjunction of properties) which determines its referent as the unique thing fulfilling the associated property (or properties). This property(ies) constitutes the 'sense' of the name. Presumably, if '. . .' is a proper name, the associated properties are those that the speaker would supply, if asked, 'Who is ". . ."?' If he would answer '. . . is the man who ———,' the properties filling the second blank are those that determine the reference of the name for the given speaker and constitute its 'sense.' Of course, given the name of a famous historical figure, individuals may give different, and equally correct, answers to the 'Who is . . .?' question. Some may identify Aristotle as the philosopher who taught Alexander the Great, others as the Stagirite philosopher who studied with Plato. For these two speakers, the sense of 'Aristotle' will differ: in particular, speakers of the second kind, but not of the first kind, will regard 'Aristotle, if he existed, was born in Stagira' as an analytic.[2] Frege (and Russell)[3] concluded that, strictly speaking, different speakers of English (or German!) ordinarily use a name such as 'Aristotle' in different senses (though with the same reference). Differences in properties associated with such names, strictly speaking, yield different idiolects.[4]

Some later theorists in the Frege-Russellian tradition have found this consequence unattractive So they have tried to modify the view by 'clustering' the sense of the name (e.g., Aristotle is the thing having the following long list of properties, or at any rate most of them), or, better for the present purpose, socializing it (what determines the reference of 'Aristotle' is some roughly specified set of *community-wide* beliefs about Aristotle).

One way to point up the contrast between the strict Millian view and Fregean views involves – if we permit ourselves this jargon – the notion of propositional content. If a strict Millian view is correct, and the linguistic function of a proper name is completely exhausted by the fact that it names its bearer, it would appear that proper names of the same thing are everywhere interchangeable not only *salva veritate* but even *salva significatione*: the proposition expressed by a sentence should remain the same no matter what name of the object it uses. Of course this will not be true if the names are 'mentioned' rather than 'used': ' "Cicero" has six letters' differs from ' "Tully" has six letters' in truth value, let alone in content. (The example, of course, is Quine's.) Let us confine ourselves at this stage to *simple* sentences involving no connectives or other sources of intensionality. If Mill is completely right, not only should 'Cicero was lazy' have the same *truth value* as 'Tully was lazy,' but the two sentences should express the same *proposition*, have the same content. Similarly 'Cicero admired Tully,' 'Tully admired Cicero,' 'Cicero admired Cicero,' and 'Tully admired Tully,' should be four ways of saying the same thing.[5]

If such a consequence of Mill's view is accepted, it would seem to have further consequences regarding 'intensional' contexts. Whether a sentence expresses a necessary truth or a contingent one depends only on the proposition expressed and not on the words used to express it. So any simple sentence should retain its 'modal value' (necessary, impossible, contingently true, or contingently false) when 'Cicero' is replaced by 'Tully' in one or more places, since such a replacement leaves the content of the sentence unaltered. Of course this implies that coreferential names are substitutable in modal contexts *salva veritate*: 'It is necessary (possible) that Cicero . . .' and 'It is necessary (possible) that Tully . . .' must have the same truth value no matter how the dots are filled by a simple sentence.

The situation would seem to be similar with respect to contexts involving knowledge, belief, and epistemic modalities. Whether a given subject believes something is presumably true or false of such a subject no matter how that belief is expressed; so if proper name substitution does not change the content of a sentence expressing a belief, coreferential proper names should be interchangeable *salva veritate* in belief contexts. Similar reasoning would hold for epistemic contexts ('Jones knows that . . .') and contexts of epistemic necessity ('Jones knows *a priori* that . . .') and the like.

All this, of course, would contrast strongly with the case of definite descriptions. It is well known that substitution of coreferential descriptions in simple sentences (without operators), on any reasonable conception of 'content,' *can* alter the content of such a sentence. In particular, the modal value of a sentence is not invariant under changes of coreferential descriptions: 'The smallest prime is even' expresses a necessary truth, but 'Jones's favorite number is even' expresses a contingent one, even if Jones's favorite number happens to be the smallest prime. It follows that coreferential descriptions are *not* interchangeable *salva veritate* in modal contexts: 'It is necessary that the smallest prime is even' is true while 'It is necessary that Jones's favorite number is even' is false.

Of course there is a '*de re*' or 'large scope' reading under which the second sentence is true. Such a reading would be expressed more accurately by 'Jones's favorite number is such that it is necessarily even' or, in rough Russellian transcription, as 'One and only one number is admired by Jones above all others, and any such number is necessarily even (has the property of necessary evenness).' Such a *de re* reading, if it makes sense at all, by definition must be subject to a principle of substitution *salva veritate*, since necessary evenness is a property of the *number*, independently of how it is designated; in this respect there can be no contrast between names and descriptions. The contrast, according to the Millian view, must come in the *de dicto* or 'small scope' reading, which is the *only* reading, for belief contexts as well as modal contexts, that will concern us in this paper. If we wish, we can emphasize that this is our reading in various ways. Say, 'It is necessary that: Cicero was bald', or more explicitly, 'The following proposition is necessarily true: Cicero was bald,' or even, in Carnap's 'formal' mode of speech,[6] ' "Cicero was bald" expresses a necessary truth.' Now the Millian asserts that all these formulations retain their truth value when 'Cicero' is replaced by 'Tully,' even though 'Jones's favorite Latin author' and 'the man who denounced Catiline' would *not* similarly be interchangeable in these contexts even if they are codesignative.

Similarly for belief contexts. Here too *de re* beliefs – as in 'Jones believes, *of* Cicero (or: *of* his favorite Latin author) that he was bald' do *not* concern us in this paper. Such contexts, if they make sense, are by definition subject to a substitutivity principle for both names and descriptions. Rather we are concerned with the *de dicto* locution expressed explicitly in such formulations as, 'Jones believes that: Cicero was bald' (or: 'Jones believes that: the man who denounced Catiline was bald'). The material after the colon expresses the *content* of Jones's belief. Other, more explicit, formulations are: 'Jones believes that the proposition – that – Cicero – was – bald,' or even in the 'formal' mode, 'The sentence "Cicero was bald" gives the content of a belief of Jones.' In all such contexts, the strict Millian seems to be committed to saying that codesignative names, but not codesignative descriptions, are interchangeable *salva veritate*.[7]

Now it has been widely assumed that these apparent consequences of the Millian view are plainly false. First, it seemed that sentences can alter their *modal* values by replacing a name by a codesignative one. 'Hesperus is Hesperus' (or, more cautiously: 'If Hesperus exists, Hesperus is Hesperus') expresses a necessary truth, while 'Hesperus is Phosphorus' (or: 'If Hesperus exists, Hesperus is Phosphorus'), expresses an empirical discovery, and hence, it has been widely assumed, a contingent truth. (It might have turned out, and hence might have been, otherwise).

It has seemed even more obvious that codesignative proper names are not interchangeable in belief contexts and epistemic contexts. Tom, a normal speaker of the language, may sincerely assent to 'Tully denounced Catiline,' but not 'Cicero denounced Catiline.' He may even deny the latter. And his denial is compatible with his status as a normal English speaker who satisfies normal criteria for using both 'Cicero' and 'Tully' as the names for the famed Roman (without knowing that 'Cicero' and 'Tully' name the same person). Given this, it seems obvious that Tom believes that: Tully denounced Catiline, but that he does not believe (lacks the belief) that: Cicero denounced Catiline.[8] So it seems clear that codesignative proper names are not interchangeable in belief contexts. It also seems clear that there must be two distinct propositions or contents expressed by 'Cicero denounced Catiline' and 'Tully denounced

Catiline.' How else can Tom believe one and deny the other? And the difference in propositions thus expressed can only come from a difference in *sense* between 'Tully' and 'Cicero.' Such a conclusion agrees with a Fregean theory and seems to be incompatible with a purely Millian view.[9]

In the previous work mentioned above, I rejected one of these arguments against Mill, the modal argument. 'Hesperus is Phosphorus,' I maintained, expresses just as necessary a truth as 'Hesperus is Hesperus'; there are no counterfactual situations in which Hesperus and Phosphorus would have been different. Admittedly, the truth of 'Hesperus is Phosphorus' was not known *a priori*, and may even have been widely disbelieved before appropriate empirical evidence came in. But these epistemic questions should be separated, I have argued, from the metaphysical question of the necessity of 'Hesperus is Phosphorus.' And it is a consequence of my conception of names as 'rigid designators' that codesignative proper names are interchangeable *salva veritate* in all contexts of (metaphysical) necessity and possibility; further, that replacement of a proper name by a codesignative name leaves the modal value of any sentence unchanged.

But although my position confirmed the Millian account of names in modal contexts, it equally appears at first blush to imply a *nonMillian* account of epistemic and belief contexts (and other contexts of propositional attitude). For I presupposed a sharp contrast between epistemic and metaphysical possibility: Before appropriate empirical discoveries were made, men might well have failed to know that Hesperus was Phosphorus, or even to believe it, even though they of course knew and believed that Hesperus was Hesperus. Does not this support a Fregean position that 'Hesperus' and 'Phosphorus' have different 'modes of presentation' that determine their references? What else can account for the fact that, before astronomers identified the two heavenly bodies, a sentence using 'Hesperus' could express a common belief, while the same context involving 'Phosphorus' did not? In the case of 'Hesperus' and 'Phosphorus,' it is pretty clear what the different 'modes of presentation' would be: one mode determines a heavenly body by its typical position and appearance, in the appropriate season, in the evening; the other determines the same body by its position and appearance, in the appropriate season, in the morning. So it appears that even though, according to my view, proper names would be *modally* rigid – would have the same reference when we use them to speak of counterfactual situations as they do when used to describe the actual world – they would have a kind of Fregean 'sense' according to how that rigid reference is fixed. And the divergences of 'sense' (in this sense of 'sense') would lead to failures of interchangeability of codesignative names in contexts of propositional attitude, though not in modal contexts. Such a theory would agree with Mill regarding modal contexts but with Frege regarding belief contexts. The theory would not be *purely* Millian.[10]

After further thought, however, the Fregean conclusion appears less obvious. Just as people are said to have been unaware at one time of the fact that

Hesperus is Phosphorus, so a normal speaker of English apparently may not know that Cicero is Tully, or that Holland is the Netherlands. For he may sincerely assent to 'Cicero was lazy,' while dissenting from 'Tully was lazy,' or he may sincerely assent to 'Holland is a beautiful country,' while dissenting from 'The Netherlands is a beautiful country.' In the case of 'Hesperus' and 'Phosphorus,' it seemed plausible to account for the parallel situation by supposing that 'Hesperus' and 'Phosphorus' fixed their (rigid) references to a single object in two conventionally different ways, one as the 'evening star' and one as the 'morning star'. But what corresponding *conventional* 'senses,' even taking 'senses' to be 'modes of fixing the reference rigidly,' can plausibly be supposed to exist for 'Cicero' and 'Tully' (or 'Holland' and 'the Netherlands')? Are not these just two names (in English) for the same man? Is there any special *conventional, community-wide* 'connotation' in the one lacking in the other?[11] I am unaware of any.[12]

Such considerations might seem to push us toward the extreme Frege-Russellian view that the senses of proper names vary, strictly speaking, from speaker to speaker, and that there is no community-wide sense but only a community-wide reference.[13] According to such a view, the sense a given speaker attributes to such a name as 'Cicero' depends on which assertions beginning with 'Cicero' he accepts and which of these he regards as *defining*, for him, the name (as opposed to those he regards as mere factual beliefs 'about Cicero'). Similarly, for 'Tully.' For example, someone may define 'Cicero' as 'the Roman orator whose speech was Greek to Cassius,' and 'Tully' as 'the Roman orator who denounced Catiline.' Then such a speaker may well fail to accept 'Cicero is Tully' if he is unaware that a single orator satisfied both descriptions (if Shakespeare and history are both to be believed). He may well, in his ignorance, affirm 'Cicero was bald' while rejecting 'Tully was bald,' and the like. Is this not what actually occurs whenever someone's expressed beliefs fail to be indifferent to interchange of 'Tully' and 'Cicero'? Must not the source of such a failure lie in two distinct associated descriptions, or modes of determining the reference, of the two names? If a speaker does, as luck would have it, attach the same identifying properties both to 'Cicero' and to 'Tully,' he *will*, it would seem, use 'Cicero' and 'Tully' interchangeably. All this appears at first blush to be powerful support for the view of Frege and Russell that in general names are peculiar to idiolects, with 'senses' depending on the associated 'identifying descriptions.'

Note that, according to the view we are now entertaining, one *cannot* say, 'Some people are unaware that Cicero is Tully.' For, according to this view, there is no single proposition denoted by the 'that' clause, that the community of normal English speakers expresses by 'Cicero is Tully.' Some – for example, those who define both 'Cicero' and 'Tully' as 'the author of *De Fato*' – use it to express a trivial self-identity. Others use it to express the proposition that the man who satisfied one description (say, that he denounced Catiline) is one and the same as the man who satisfied another (say, that his speech was Greek to Cassius). There is no single fact, 'that Cicero is Tully', known by some but not all members of the community.

If I were to assert, 'Many are unaware that Cicero is Tully,' *I* would use 'that Cicero is Tully' to denote the proposition that *I* understand by these words. If this, for example, is a trivial self-identity, I would assert falsely, and irrelevantly, that there is widespread ignorance in the community of a certain self-identity.[14] I *can*, of course, say, 'Some English speakers use both "Cicero" and "Tully" with the usual referent (the famed Roman) yet do not assent to "Cicero is Tully." '

This aspect of the Frege-Russellian view can, as before, be combined with a concession that names are rigid designators and that hence the description used to fix the reference of a name is not synonymous with it. But there are considerable difficulties. There is the obvious intuitive unpalatability of the notion that we use such proper names as 'Cicero,' 'Venice,' 'Venus' (the planet) with differing 'senses' and for this reason do not 'strictly speaking' speak a single language. There are the many well-known and weighty objections to any description or cluster-of-descriptions theory of names. And is it definitely so clear that failure of interchangeability of belief contexts implies some difference of sense? After all, there is a considerable philosophical literature arguing that even word pairs that are straightforward synonyms if any pairs – 'doctor' and 'physician,' to give one example – are not interchangeable *salva veritate* in belief contexts, at least if the belief operators are iterated.[15]

A minor problem with this presentation of the argument for Frege and Russell will emerge in the next section: if Frege and Russell are right, it is not easy to state the very argument from belief contexts that appears to support them.

But the clearest objection, which shows that the others should be given their proper weight, is this: the view under consideration does not in fact account for the phenomena it seeks to explain. As I have said elsewhere,[16] individuals who 'define "Cicero" by such phrases as 'the Catiline denouncer,' 'the author of *De Fato*, etc., are relatively rare: their prevalence in the philosophical literature is the product of the excessive classical learning of some philosophers. Common men who clearly use 'Cicero' as a name for Cicero may be able to give no better answer to 'Who was Cicero?' than 'a famous Roman orator,' and they probably would say the same (if anything!) for 'Tully.' (Actually, most people probably have never heard the name 'Tully.') Similarly, many people who have heard of both Feynman and Gell-Mann, would identify each as 'a leading contemporary theoretical physicist.' Such people do not assign 'senses' of the usual type to the names that uniquely identify the referent (even though they use the names with a determinate reference). But to the extent that the *indefinite* descriptions attached or associated can be called 'senses,' the 'senses' assigned to 'Cicero' and 'Tully,' or to 'Feynman' and 'Gell-Mann,' are *identical*.[17] Yet clearly speakers of this type can ask, 'Were Cicero and Tully one Roman orator, or two different ones?' or 'Are Feynman and Gell-Mann two different physicists, or one?' without knowing the answer to either question by inspecting 'senses' alone. Some such speaker might even conjecture, or be under the vague false impression, that, as he would say, 'Cicero was bald but Tully was not.' The premise of the argument we are considering for the classic position of Frege and Russell – that whenever two codesignative names fail to be interchangeable in the expression of a speaker's beliefs, failure of interchangeability arises from a difference in the 'defining' descriptions the speaker associated with these names – is, therefore, false. The case illustrated by 'Cicero' and 'Tully' is, in fact, quite usual and ordinary. So the apparent failure of codesignative names to be everywhere interchangeable in belief contexts, is not to be explained by differences in the 'senses' of these names.

Since the extreme view of Frege and Russell does not in fact explain the apparent failure of the interchangeability of names in belief contexts, there seems to be no further reason – for present purposes – not to give the other overwhelming *prima facie* considerations against the Frege-Russell view their full weight. Names of famous cities, countries, persons, and planets are the common currency of our common language, not terms used homonymously in our separate idiolects.[18] The apparent failure of codesignative names to be interchangeable in belief contexts remains a mystery, but the mystery no longer seems so clearly to argue for a Fregean view as against a Millian one. Neither differing public senses nor differing private senses peculiar to each speaker account for the phenomena to be explained. So the apparent existence of such phenomena no longer gives a *prima facie* argument for such differing senses.

One final remark to close this section. I have referred before to my own earlier views in 'Naming and Necessity.' I said above that these views, inasmuch as they make proper names rigid and transparent[19] in modal contexts, favor Mill, but that the concession that proper names are not transparent in belief contexts appears to favor Frege. On a closer examination, however, the extent to which these opacity phenomena really support Frege against Mill becomes much more doubtful. And there are important theoretical reasons for viewing the 'Naming and Necessity' approach in a Millian light. In that work I argued that ordinarily the real determinant of the reference of names of a former historical figure is a chain of communication, in which the reference of the name is passed from link to link. Now the legitimacy of such a chain accords much more with Millian views than with alternatives. For the view supposes that a learner acquires a name from the community by determining to use it with the same reference as does the community. We regard such a learner as using 'Cicero is bald' to express the same thing the community expresses, regardless of variations in the properties different learners associate with 'Cicero,' as long as he determines that he will use the name with the referent current in the community. That a name can be transmitted in this way accords nicely with a Millian picture, according to which only the reference, not more specific properties associated with the name, is relevant to the semantics of sentences containing it. It has been suggested that the chain of communication, which on the present picture determines the reference, might thereby itself be called a 'sense.' Perhaps so – if we wish[20] – but we should not thereby forget that the legitimacy of such a chain suggests that it is just preservation of reference, as Mill thought, that we regard as necessary for correct language learning.[21] (This contrasts with such terms as 'renate' and 'cordate,' where more than learning the correct extension is needed.) Also, as suggested above, the doctrine of rigidity in modal contexts is dissonant, though not necessarily inconsistent, with a view that invokes antiMillian considerations to explain propositional attitude contexts.

The spirit of my earlier views, then, suggests that a Millian line should be maintained as far as is feasible.

II. Preliminaries: Some General Principles

Where are we now? We seem to be in something of a quandary. On the one hand, we concluded that the failure of 'Cicero' and 'Tully' to be interchangeable *salva veritate* in contexts of propositional attitude was by no means explicable in terms of different 'senses' of the two names. On the other hand, let us not forget the initial argument against Mill: If reference is *all there is* to naming, what semantic difference can there be between 'Cicero' and 'Tully'? And if there is no semantic difference, do not 'Cicero was bald' and 'Tully was bald' express exactly the same proposition? How, then, can anyone believe that Cicero was bald, yet doubt or disbelieve that Tully was?

Let us take stock. Why do we think that anyone can believe that Cicero was bald, but fail to believe that Tully was? Or believe, without any logical inconsistency, that Yale is a fine university, but that Old Eli is an inferior one? Well, a normal English speaker, Jones, can sincerely assent to 'Cicero was bald' but not to 'Tully was bald.' And this even though Jones uses 'Cicero' and 'Tully' in standard ways – he uses 'Cicero' in this assertion as a name for the Roman, not, say, for his dog, or for a German spy.

Let us make explicit the *disquotational principle* presupposed here, connecting sincere assent and belief. It can be stated as follows, where '*p*' is to be replaced, inside and outside all quotation marks, by any appropriate standard English sentence: '*If a normal English speaker, on reflection, sincerely assents to "p," then he believes that p.*' The sentence replacing '*p*' is to lack indexical or pronominal devices or ambiguities, that would ruin the intuitive sense of the principle (e.g., if he assents to 'You are wonderful,' he need not believe that *you* – the reader – are wonderful).[22] When we suppose that we are dealing with a normal speaker of English, we mean that he uses all words in the sentence in a standard way, combines them according to the appropriate syntax, etc.: in short, he uses the sentence to mean what a normal speaker should mean by it. The 'words' of the sentence may include proper names, where these are part of the common discourse of the community, so that we can speak of using them in a standard way. For example, if the sentence is 'London is pretty,' then the speaker should satisfy normal criteria for using 'London' as a name of London, and for using 'is pretty' to attribute an appropriate degree of pulchritude. The qualification 'on reflection' guards against the possibility that a speaker may, through careless inattention to the meaning of his words or other momentary conceptual or linguistic confusion, assert something he does not really mean, or assent to a sentence in linguistic error. 'Sincerely' is meant to exclude mendacity, acting, irony, and the like. I fear that even with all this it is possible that some astute reader – such, after all, is the way of philosophy – may discover a qualification I have overlooked, without which the asserted principle is subject to counterexample. I doubt, however, that any such modification will affect any of the uses of the principle to be considered below. Taken in its obvious intent, after all, the principle appears to be a self-evident truth. (A similar principle holds for sincere affirmation or assertion in place of assent.)

There is also a strengthened 'biconditional' form of the disquotational principle, where once again any appropriate English sentence may replace '*p*' throughout: *A normal English speaker who is not reticent will be disposed to sincere reflective assent to 'p' if and only if he believes that p.*[23] The biconditional form strengthens the simple one by adding that failure to assent indicates lack of belief, as assent indicates belief. The qualification about reticence is meant to take account of the fact that a speaker may fail to avow his beliefs because of shyness, a desire for secrecy, to avoid offense, etc. (An alternative formulation would give the speaker a sign to indicate lack of belief – not necessarily disbelief – in the assertion propounded, in addition to his sign of assent.) Maybe again the formulation needs further tightening, but the intent is clear.

Usually below the simple disquotational principle will be sufficient for our purposes, but once we will also invoke the strengthened form. The simple form can often be used as a test for disbelief, provided the subject is a speaker with the modicum of logicality needed so that, at least after appropriate reflection, he does not hold simultaneously beliefs that are straightforward contradictions of each other – of the forms '*p*' and '~*p*.'[24] (Nothing in such a requirement prevents him from holding simultaneous beliefs that jointly *entail* a contradiction.) In this case (where '*p*' may be replaced by any appropriate English sentence), the speaker's assent to the negation of '*p*' indicates not only his disbelief that *p* but also his failure to believe that *p*, using only the simple (unstrengthened) disquotational principle.

So far our principle applies only to speakers of English. It allows us to infer, from Peter's sincere reflective assent to 'God exists,' that he believes that God exists. But of course we ordinarily allow ourselves to draw conclusions, stated in English, about the beliefs of speakers of any language: we infer that Pierre believes that God exists from his sincere reflective assent to '*Dieu existe.*' There are several ways to do this, given conventional translations of French into English. We choose the following route. We have stated the disquotational principle in English, for English sentences; an analogous principle, stated in French (German, etc.) will be assumed to hold for French (German, etc.) sentences. Finally, we assume the *principle of translation: If a sentence of one language expresses a truth in that language, then any translation of it into any other language also expresses a truth (in that other language).* Some of our ordinary practice of translation may violate this principle; this happens when the translator's aim is not to preserve the content of the sentence, but to serve – in some other sense – the same purposes in the home language as the original utterance served in the foreign language.[25] But if the translation of a sentence is to mean the same as the sentence translated, preservation of truth value is a minimal condition that must be observed.

Granted the disquotational principle expressed in each language, reasoning starting from Pierre's assent to '*Dieu existe*' continues thus. First, on the basis of his utterance and the French disquotational principle we infer (in French):

> *Pierre croit que Dieu existe.*

From this we deduce,[26] using the principle of translation:

> Pierre believes that God exists.

In this way we can apply the disquotational technique to all languages.

Even if I apply the disquotational technique to English alone, there is a sense in which I can be regarded as tacitly invoking a principle of translation. For presumably I apply it to speakers of the language other than myself. As Quine has pointed out, to regard others as speaking the same language as I is in sense tacitly to assume a *homophonic* translation of their language into my own. So when I infer from Peter's sincere assent to or affirmation of 'God exists' that he believes that God exists, it is arguable that, strictly speaking, I combine the disquotational principle (for Peter's idiolect) with the principle of (homophonic) translation (of Peter's idiolect into mine). But for most purposes, we can formulate the disquotational principle for a single language, English, tacitly supposed to be the common language of English speakers. Only when the possibility of individual differences of dialect is relevant need we view the matter more elaborately.

Let us return from these abstractions to our main theme. Since a normal speaker – normal even in his use of 'Cicero' and 'Tully' as names – can give sincere and reflective assent to 'Cicero was bald' and simultaneously to 'Tully was not bald,' the disquotational principle implies that he believes that Cicero was bald and believes that Tully was not bald. Since it seems that he need not have contradictory beliefs (even if he is a brilliant logician, he need not be able to deduce that at least one of his beliefs must be in error), and since a substitutivity principle for coreferential proper names in belief contexts would imply that he does have contradictory beliefs, it would seem that such a substitutivity principle must be incorrect. Indeed, the argument appears to be a *reductio ad absurdum* of the substitutivity principle in question.

The relation of this argument against substitutivity to the classical position of Russell and Frege is a curious one. As we have seen, the argument can be used to give *prima facie* support for the Frege-Russell view, and I think many philosophers have regarded it as such support. But in fact this very argument, which has been used to support Frege and Russell, cannot be stated in a straightforward fashion if Frege and Russell are right. For suppose Jones asserts, 'Cicero was bald, but Tully was not.' If Frege and Russell are right, I cannot deduce, using the disquotational principle:

(1) Jones believes that Cicero was bald but Tully was not,

since, in general, Jones and I will not, strictly speaking, share a common idiolect unless we assign the same 'senses' to all names. Nor can I combine disquotation and translation to the appropriate effect, since homophonic translation of Jones's sentence into mine will in general be incorrect for the same reason. Since in fact I make no special distinction in sense between 'Cicero' and 'Tully' – to me, and probably to you as well, these are interchangeable names for the same man – and since according to Frege and Russell, Jones's very affirmation of (1) shows that for him there *is* some distinction of sense, Jones must therefore, on Frege-Russellian views, use one of these names differently from me, and homophonic translation is illegitimate. Hence, if Frege and Russell are right, we *cannot* use this example in the usual straightforward way to conclude that proper names are not substitutable in belief contexts – even though the example, and the ensuing negative verdict on substitutivity, has often been thought to support Frege and Russell!

Even according to the Frege-Russellian view, however, *Jones* can conclude, using the disquotational principle, and expressing his conclusion in his own idiolect:

(2) I believe that Cicero was bald but Tully was not.

I cannot endorse this conclusion in Jones's own words, since I do not share Jones's idiolect. I *can* of course conclude, '(2) expresses a truth in Jones's idiolect.' I can also, if I find out the two 'senses' Jones assigns to 'Cicero' and 'Tully,' introduce two names 'X' and 'Y' into my own language with these same two senses ('Cicero' and 'Tully' have already been preempted) and conclude:

(3) Jones believes that X was bald and Y was not.

All this is enough so that we can still conclude, on the Frege-Russellian view, that codesignative names are not interchangeable in belief contexts. Indeed this can be shown more simply on this view, since codesignative descriptions plainly are not interchangeable in these contexts and for Frege and Russell names, being essentially abbreviated descriptions, cannot differ in this respect. Nevertheless, the simple argument, apparently free of such special Frege-Russellian doctrinal premises (and often used to support these premises), in fact cannot go through if Frege and Russell are right.

However, if, *pace* Frege and Russell, widely used names are common currency of our language, then there no longer is any problem for the simple argument, using the disquotational principle, to (2). So, it appears, on pain of convicting Jones of inconsistent beliefs – surely an unjust verdict – we must not hold a substitutivity principle for names in belief contexts. If we used the *strengthened* disquotational principle, we would invoke Jones's presumed lack of any tendency to assent to 'Tully was bald' to conclude that he does not believe (lacks the belief) that Tully was bald. Now the refutation of the substitutivity principle is even stronger, for when applied to the conclusion that Jones believes that Cicero was bald but does not believe that Tully was bald, it would lead to a straightout contradiction. The contradiction would no longer be in Jones's beliefs but in our own.

This reasoning, I think, had been widely accepted as proof that codesignative proper names are not interchangeable in belief contexts. Usually the reasoning is left tacit, and it may well be thought that I have made heavy weather of an obvious conclusion. I wish, however, to question the reasoning. I shall do so without challenging any particular step of the argument. Rather I shall present – and this will form the core of the present paper – an argument for a paradox about names in belief contexts that invokes *no* principle of substitutivity. Instead it will be based on the principles – apparently so obvious that their use in these arguments is ordinarily tacit – of disquotation and translation.

Usually the argument will involve more than one language, so that the principle of translation and our conventional manual of translation must be invoked. We will also give an example, however, to show that a form of the paradox may result within English alone, so that the only principle invoked is that of disquotation (or, perhaps, disquotation plus *homophonic* translation). It will intuitively be fairly clear, in these cases, that the situation of the subject is 'essentially the same' as that of Jones with respect to 'Cicero' and 'Tully.' Moreover, the paradoxical conclusions about the subject will parallel those drawn about Jones on the basis of the substitutivity principle, and the arguments will parallel those regarding Jones. Only in these cases, no special substitutivity principle is invoked.

The usual use of Jones's case as a counterexample to the substitutivity principle is thus, I think, somewhat analogous to the following sort of procedure. Someone wishes to give a *reductio ad absurdum* argument against a hypothesis in topology. He does succeed in refuting this hypothesis, but his derivation of an absurdity from the hypothesis makes essential use of the unrestricted comprehension schema in set theory, which he regards as self-evident. (In particular, the class of all classes not members of themselves plays a key role in his argument.) Once we know that the unrestricted comprehension schema and the Russell class lead to contradiction by themselves, it is clear that it was an error to blame the earlier contradiction on the topological hypothesis.

The situation would have been the same if, after deducing a contradiction from the topological hypothesis plus the 'obvious' unrestricted comprehension schema, it was found that a similar contradiction followed if we replaced the topological hypothesis by an apparently 'obvious' premise. In both cases it would be clear that, even though we may still not be confident of any specific flaw in the argument against the topological hypothesis, blaming the contradiction on that hypothesis is illegitimate: rather we are in a 'paradoxical' area where it is unclear *what* has gone wrong.[27]

It is my suggestion, then, that the situation with respect to the interchangeability of codesignative names is similar. True, such a principle, when combined with our normal disquotational judgments of belief, leads to straightforward absurdities. But we will see that the 'same' absurdities can be derived by replacing the interchangeability principle by our normal practices of translation and disquotation, or even by disquotation alone.

The particular principle stated here gives just one particular way of 'formalizing' our normal inferences from explicit affirmation or assent to belief; other ways of doing it are possible. It is undeniable that we *do* infer, from a normal Englishman's sincere affirmation of 'God exists' or 'London is pretty,' that he believes, respectively, that God exists or that London is pretty; and that we would make the same inferences from a Frenchman's affirmation of '*Dieu existe*' or '*Londres est jolie*.' Any principles that would justify such inferences are sufficient for the next section. It will be clear that the particular principles stated in the present section are sufficient, but in the next section the problem will be presented informally in terms of our inferences from foreign or domestic assertion to belief.

III. The Puzzle

Here, finally(!), is the puzzle. Suppose Pierre is a normal French speaker who lives in France and speaks not a word of English or of any other language except French. Of course he has heard of that famous distant city, London (which he of course calls '*Londres*') though he himself has never left France. On the basis of what he has heard of London, he is inclined to think that it is pretty. So he says, in French, '*Londres est jolie*.'

On the basis of his sincere French utterance, we will conclude:

(4) Pierre believes that London is pretty.

I am supposing that Pierre satisfies all criteria for being a normal French speaker, in particular, that he satisfies whatever criteria we usually use to judge that a Frenchman (correctly) uses '*est jolie*' to attribute pulchritude and uses '*Londres*' – standardly – as a name of London.

Later, Pierre, through fortunate or unfortunate vicissitudes, moves to England, in fact to London itself, though to an unattractive part of the city with fairly uneducated inhabitants. He, like most of his neighbors, rarely ever leaves this part of the city. None of his neighbors know any French, so he must learn English by 'direct method,' without using any translation of English into French: by talking and mixing with the people he eventually begins to pick up English. In particular, everyone speaks of the city, 'London,' where they all live. Let us suppose for the moment – though we will see below that this is not crucial – that the local population are so uneducated that they know few of the facts that Pierre heard about London in France. Pierre learns from them everything they know about London, but there is little overlap with what he heard before. He learns, of course – speaking English – to call the city he lives in 'London.' Pierre's surroundings are, as I said, unattractive, and he is unimpressed with most of the rest of what he happens to see. So he is inclined to assent to the English sentence:

(5) London is not pretty.

He has *no* inclination to assent to:

(6) London is pretty.

Of course he does not for a moment withdraw his assent from the French sentence, '*Londres est jolie*'; he merely takes it for granted that the ugly city in which he is now stuck is distinct from the enchanting city he heard about in France. But he has no inclination to change his mind for a moment about the city he still calls '*Londres*.'

This, then, is the puzzle. If we consider Pierre's past background as a French speaker, his entire linguistic behavior, on the same basis as we would draw such a conclusion about many of his countrymen, supports the conclusion ((4) above) that he believes that London is pretty. On the other hand, after Pierre lived in London for some time, he did not differ from his neighbors – his French background aside – either in his knowledge of English or in his command of the relevant facts of local geography. His English vocabulary differs little from that of his neighbors. He, like them, rarely ventures from the dismal quarter of the city in which they all live. He, like them, knows that the city he lives in is called 'London' and knows a few other facts. Now Pierre's neighbors would surely be said to use 'London' as a name for London and to speak English. Since, as an English speaker, he does not differ at all from them, we should say the same of him. But then, on the basis of his sincere assent to (5), we should conclude:

(7) Pierre believes that London is not pretty.

How can we describe this situation? It seems undeniable that Pierre *once* believed that London is pretty – at least before he learned English. For at that time, he differed not at all from countless numbers of his countrymen, and we would have exactly the same grounds to say of him as of any of them that he believes that London is pretty: if any Frenchman who was both ignorant of English and never visited London believed that London is pretty, Pierre did. Nor does it have any plausibility to suppose, because of his later situation *after* he learns English, that Pierre should *retroactively* be judged *never* to have believed that London is pretty. To allow such *ex post facto* legislation would, as long as the future is uncertain, endanger our attributions of belief to *all* monolingual Frenchmen. We would be forced to say that Marie, a monolingual who firmly and sincerely asserts, '*Londres est jolie*,' may or may not believe that London is pretty depending on the *later* vicissitudes of her career (if later she learns English and . . ., . . .) No: Pierre, like Marie, believed that London is pretty when he was monolingual.

Should we say that Pierre, now that he lives in London and speaks English, no longer believes that London is pretty? Well, unquestionably Pierre *once* believed that London is pretty. So we would be forced to say that Pierre has *changed his mind, has given up his previous belief*. But has he really done so? Pierre is very set in his ways. He reiterates, with vigor, every assertion he has ever made in French. He says he has not changed his mind about anything, has *not* given up any belief. Can we say he is wrong about this? If we did not have the story of his living in London and his English utterances, on the basis of his normal command of French we would be *forced* to conclude that he *still* believes that London is pretty. And it does seem that this is correct. Pierre has neither changed his mind nor given up any belief he had in France.

Similar difficulties beset any attempt to deny him his new belief. His French past aside, he is just like his friends in London. Anyone else, growing up in London with the same knowledge and beliefs that he expresses in England, we would undoubtedly judge to believe that London is not pretty. Can Pierre's French past nullify such a judgment? Can we say that Pierre, because of his French past, does not believe that (5)? Suppose an electric shock wiped out all his memories of the French language, what he learned in France, and his French past. He would then be *exactly* like his neighbors in London. He would have the *same* knowledge, beliefs, and linguistic capacities. We then presumably would be forced to say that Pierre believes that London is ugly if we say it of his neighbors. But surely no shock that *destroys* part of Pierre's memories and knowledge can *give* him a new belief. If Pierre believes (5) *after* the shock, he believed it before, despite his French language and background.

If we would deny Pierre, in his bilingual stage, his belief that London is pretty *and* his belief that London is not pretty, we combine the difficulties of both previous options. We still would be forced to judge that Pierre once believed that London is pretty but does no longer, in spite of Pierre's own sincere denial that he has lost any belief. We also must worry whether Pierre would *gain* the belief that London is not pretty if he totally forgot his French past. The option does not seem very satisfactory.

So now it seems that we must respect both Pierre's French utterances and their English counterparts. So we must say that Pierre has contradictory beliefs, that he believes that London is pretty *and* he believes that London is not pretty. But there seem to be insuperable difficulties with this alternative as well. We may suppose that Pierre, in spite of the unfortunate situation in which he now finds himself, is a leading philosopher and logician. He would *never* let contradictory beliefs pass. And surely anyone, leading logician or no, is in principle in a position to notice and correct contradictory beliefs if he has them. Precisely for this reason, we regard individuals who contradict themselves as subject to greater censure than those who merely have false beliefs. But it is clear that Pierre, as long as he is unaware that the cities he calls 'London' and '*Londres*' are one and the same, is in no position to see, by logic alone, that at least one of his beliefs must be false. He lacks information, not logical acumen. He cannot be convicted of inconsistency: to do so is incorrect.

We can shed more light on this if we change the case. Suppose that, in France, Pierre, instead of affirming '*Londres est jolie*,' had affirmed, more cautiously, '*Si New York est jolie, Londres est jolie aussi*,' so that he believed that *if* New York is pretty, so is London. Later Pierre moves to London, learns English as before, and says (in English) 'London is not pretty.' So he now believes, further, that London is *not* pretty. Now from the two premises, both of which appears to be among his beliefs (a) If New York is pretty, London is, and (b) London is not pretty. Pierre should be able to deduce by *modus tollens* that New York is not pretty. But no matter how great Pierre's logical acumen may be, *he cannot in fact make any such deduction, as long as he supposes that 'Londres' and 'London' may name two different cities*. If he *did* draw such a conclusion, he would be guilty of a fallacy.

Intuitively, he may well suspect that New York is pretty, and just this suspicion may lead him to suppose that '*Londres*' and 'London' probably name distinct cities. Yet, if we follow our normal practice of reporting the beliefs of French and English speakers, *Pierre has available to him (among his beliefs) both the premises of a modus tollens argument that New York is not pretty.*

Again, we may emphasize Pierre's *lack* of belief instead of his belief. Pierre, as I said, has no disposition to assent to (6). Let us concentrate on this, ignoring his disposition to assent to (5). In fact, if we wish we may change the case: Suppose Pierre's neighbors think that since they rarely venture outside their own ugly section, they have no right to any opinion as to the pulchritude of the whole city. Suppose Pierre shares their attitude. Then, judging by his failure to respond affirmatively to 'London is pretty,' we may judge, from Pierre's behavior as an *English* speaker, that he lacks the belief that London is pretty: never mind whether he disbelieves it, as before, or whether, as in the modified story, he insists that he has no firm opinion on the matter.

Now (using the *strengthened* disquotational principle), we can derive a contradiction, not merely in Pierre's judgments, but in our own. For on the basis of his behavior as an English speaker, we concluded that he does *not* believe that London is pretty (that is, that it is not the case that he believes that London is pretty). But on the basis of his behavior as a *French* speaker, we must conclude that he *does* believe that London is pretty. This is a contradiction.[28]

We have examined four possibilities for characterizing Pierre while he is in London: (a) that at that time we no longer respect his French utterance ('*Londres est jolie*'), that is that we no longer ascribe to him the corresponding belief; (b) that we do not respect his English utterance (or lack of utterance); (c) that we respect neither; (d) that we respect both. Each possibility seems to lead us to say something either plainly false or even downright contradictory. Yet the possibilities appear to be logically exhaustive. This, then, is the paradox.

I have no firm belief as to how to solve it. But beware of one source of confusion. It is no solution in itself to observe that some *other* terminology, which evades the question whether Pierre believes that London is pretty, may be sufficient to state all the relevant facts. I am fully aware that complete and straightforward descriptions of the situation are possible and that in this sense there is no paradox. Pierre is disposed to sincere assent to '*Londres est jolie*' but not to 'London is pretty.' He uses French normally, English normally. Both with '*Londres*' and 'London' he associates properties sufficient to determine that famous city, but he does not realize that they determine a single city. (And his uses of '*Londres*' and 'London' are historically (causally) connected with the same single city, though he is unaware of that.) We may even give a rough statement of his beliefs. He believes that the city he calls '*Londres*' is pretty, that the city he calls 'London' is not. No doubt other straightforward descriptions are possible. No doubt some of these are, in a certain sense, *complete* descriptions of the situation.

But none of this answers the original question. Does Pierre, or does he not, believe that London is pretty? I know of no answer to *this* question that seems satisfactory. It is no answer to protest that, in some *other* terminology, one can state 'all the relevant facts.'

To reiterate, this is the puzzle: Does Pierre, or does he not, believe that London is pretty? It is clear that our normal criteria for the attribution of belief lead, when applied to *this* question, to paradoxes and contradictions.

One set of principles adequate to many ordinary attributions of belief, but which leads to paradox in the present case, was stated in Section 2; and other formulations are possible. As in the case of the logical paradoxes, the present puzzle presents us with a problem for customarily accepted principles and a challenge to formulate an acceptable set of principles that does not lead to paradox, is intuitively sound, and supports the inferences we usually make. Such a challenge cannot be met simply by a description of Pierre's situation that evades the question whether he believes that London is pretty.

One aspect of the presentation may misleadingly suggest the applicability of Frege-Russellian ideas that each speaker associates his own description or properties to each name. For as I just set up the case Pierre learned one set of facts about the so-called '*Londres*' when he was in France and *another* set of facts about 'London' in England. Thus it may appear that 'what's really going on' is that Pierre believes that *the city* satisfying *one* set of properties *is* pretty, while he believes that *the city* satisfying *another* set of properties *is not* pretty.

As we just emphasized, the phrase 'what's really going on' is a danger signal in discussions of the present paradox. The conditions stated may – let us concede for the moment – describe 'what's really going on.' But they do not resolve the problem with which we began, that of the behavior of names in belief contexts: Does Pierre, or does he not, believe that London (not the city satisfying such-and-such descriptions, but *London*) is pretty? No answer has yet been given.

Nevertheless, these considerations may appear to indicate that descriptions, or associated properties, are highly relevant somehow to an ultimate solution, since at this stage it appears that the entire puzzle arises from the fact that Pierre originally associated different identifying properties with 'London' and '*Londres*.' Such a reaction may have some force even in the face of the now fairly well-known arguments against 'identifying descriptions' as in any way 'defining,' or even 'fixing the reference' of names. But in fact the special features of the case, as I set it out, are misleading. The puzzle can arise even if Pierre associates exactly the same identifying properties with both names.

First, the considerations mentioned above in connection with 'Cicero' and 'Tully' establish this fact. For example, Pierre may well learn, in France, '*Platon*' as the name of a major Greek philosopher, and later, in England, learns 'Plato' with the same identification. Then the same puzzle can arise: Pierre may have believed, when he was in France and was monolingual in French, that Plato was bald (he would have said, '*Platon était chauve*'), and later conjecture, in English, 'Plato was not bald,' thus indicating that he believes or suspects that Plato was *not* bald. He need only suppose that, in spite of the similarity of their names, the man he calls '*Platon*' and the man he calls 'Plato' were two distinct major Greek philosophers. In principle, the same thing could happen with 'London' and '*Londres*.'

Of course, most of us learn a *definite* description about London, say 'the largest city in England.' Can the puzzle still arise? It is noteworthy that the puzzle can still arise even if Pierre associates to '*Londres*' and to 'London' *exactly* the same *uniquely identifying* properties. How can this be? Well, suppose that Pierre believes that London is the largest city in (and capital of) England, that it contains Buckingham Palace, the residence of the Queen of England, and he believes (correctly) that these properties, conjointly, uniquely identify the city. (In this case, it is best to suppose that he has never seen London, or even England, so that he uses *only* these properties to identify the city. Nevertheless, he has learned English by 'direct method.') These uniquely identifying properties he comes to associate with 'London' after he learned English, and he expresses the appropriate beliefs about 'London' in English. Earlier, when he spoke nothing but French, however, he associated *exactly* the same uniquely identifying properties with '*Londres*.' He believed that '*Londres*,' as he called it, could be uniquely identified as the capital of England, that it contained Buckingham Palace, that the Queen of England lived there, etc. Of course he expressed these beliefs, like most monolingual Frenchmen, in French. In particular, he used '*Angleterre*' for England, '*le Palais de Buckingham*' (pronounced '*Bookeengam*'!) for Buckingham Palace, and '*la Reine d'Angleterre*' for the Queen of England. But if any Frenchman who speaks no English can ever be said to associate *exactly* the properties of being the capital of England etc., with the name '*Londres*,' Pierre in his monolingual period did so.

When Pierre becomes a bilingual, *must* he conclude that 'London' and '*Londres*' name the same city, because he defined each by the same uniquely identifying properties?

Surprisingly, no! Suppose Pierre had affirmed, '*Londres est jolie*.' If Pierre has any reason – even just a 'feeling in his bones,' or perhaps exposure to a photograph of a miserable area which he was told (in English) was part of 'London' – to maintain 'London is not pretty,' he need not contradict himself. He need only conclude that 'England' and '*Angleterre*' name two different countries, that 'Buckingham Palace' and '*le Palais de Buckingham*' (recall the pronunciation!), name two different palaces, and so on. Then he can maintain *both* views without contradiction, and regard *both* properties as uniquely identifying.

The fact is that the paradox reproduced itself on the level of the 'uniquely identifying properties' that description theorists have regarded as 'defining' proper names (and *a fortiori*, as fixing their references). Nothing is more reasonable than to suppose that if two names, *A* and *B*, and a single set of properties, *S*, are such that a certain speaker believes that the referent of *A* uniquely satisfies all of *S* and that the referent of *B* also uniquely satisfies all of *S*, then that speaker is committed to the beliefs that *A* and *B* have the same reference. In fact, the identity of the referents of *A* and *B* is an easy *logical consequence* of the speaker's beliefs.

From this fact description theorists concluded that names can be regarded as synonymous, and hence interchangeable *salva veritate* even in belief contexts, provided that they are 'defined' by the same uniquely identifying properties.

We have already seen that there is a difficulty in that the set *S* of properties need not in fact be uniquely identifying. But in the present paradoxical situation there is a surprising difficulty even if the supposition of the description theorist (that the speaker believes that *S* is uniquely fulfilled) in fact holds. For, as we have seen above, Pierre is in no position to draw ordinary logical consequences from the conjoint set of what, when we consider him separately as a speaker of English and as a speaker of French, we would call his beliefs. He cannot infer a contradiction from his separate beliefs that London is pretty and that London is not pretty. Nor, in the modified situation above, would Pierre make a normal *modus tollens* inference from his beliefs that London is not pretty and that London is pretty if New York is. Similarly here, if we pay attention only to Pierre's behavior as a French speaker (and at least in his monolingual days he was no different from any other Frenchmen), Pierre satisfies all the normal criteria for believing that '*Londres*' has a referent uniquely satisfying the properties of being the largest city in England, containing Buckingham Palace, and the like. (If Pierre did not hold such beliefs, no Frenchman *ever* did.) Similarly, on the basis of his (later) beliefs expressed in English, Pierre also believes that the referent of 'London' uniquely satisfies these same properties. But Pierre cannot combine the two beliefs into a single set of beliefs from which he can draw the normal conclusion that 'London' and '*Londres*' must have the same referent. (Here the trouble comes not from 'London' and '*Londres*' but from 'England' and '*Angleterre*' and the rest.) Indeed, if he *did* draw what would appear to be the normal conclusion in this case and any of the other cases, Pierre would in fact be guilty of a logical fallacy.

Of course the description theorist could hope to eliminate the problem by 'defining' '*Angleterre*,' 'England,' and so on by appropriate descriptions also. Since in principle the problem may rear its head at the next 'level' and at each subsequent level, the description theorist would have to believe that an 'ultimate' level can eventually be reached where the defining properties are 'pure' properties not involving proper names (nor natural kind terms or related terms, see below!). I know of no convincing reason to suppose that such a level can be reached in any plausible way, or that the properties can continue to be uniquely identifying if one attempts to eliminate all names and related devices.[29] Such speculation aside, the fact remains that Pierre, judged by the *ordinary* criteria for such judgments, *did* learn both '*Londres*' and 'London' by *exactly* the same set of identifying properties; yet the puzzle remains even in this case.

Well, then, is there any way out of the puzzle? Aside from the principles of disquotation and translation, only our normal practice of translation of French into English has been used. Since the principles of disquotation and translation seem self-evident, we may be tempted to blame the trouble on the translation of '*Londres est jolie*' as 'London is pretty,' and ultimately, then, on the translation of '*Londres*' as 'London.'[30] Should we, perhaps, permit ourselves to conclude that '*Londres*' should not, 'strictly speaking' be translated as 'London'? Such an expedient is, of course, desperate: the translation in question is a standard one, learned by students together with other standard translations of French into English. Indeed, '*Londres*' is, in effect, introduced into French as the French version of 'London.'

Since our backs, however, are against the wall, let us consider this desperate and implausible expedient a bit further. If '*Londres*' is *not* a correct French version of the English 'London,' under what circumstances can proper names be translated from one language to another?

Classical description theories suggest the answer: Translation, strictly speaking, is between idiolects; a name in one idiolect can be translated into another when (and only when) the speakers of the two idiolects associate the same uniquely identifying properties with the two names. We have seen that any such proposed restriction, not only fails blatantly to fit our normal practices of translation and indirect discourse reportage, but does not even appear to block the paradox.[31]

So we still want a suitable restriction. Let us drop the references to idiolects and return to '*Londres*' and 'London' as names in French and English, respectively – the languages of two communities. If '*Londres*' is not a correct French translation of 'London,' could any other version do better? Suppose I introduced another word into French, with the stipulation that *it* should always be used to translate 'London.' Would not the same problem arise for this word as well? The only feasible solution in this direction is the most drastic: decree that no sentence containing a name can be translated except by a sentence containing the phonetically identical name. Thus when Pierre asserts '*Londres est jolie*,' we English speakers can at best conclude, if anything: Pierre believes that *Londres* is pretty. Such a conclusion is, of course, not expressed in English, but in a word salad of English and French; on the view now being entertained, we cannot state Pierre's belief in *English* at all.[32] Similarly, we would have to say: Pierre believes that *Angleterre* is a monarchy, Pierre believes that *Platon* wrote dialogues, and the like.[33]

This 'solution' appears at first to be effective against the paradox, but it is drastic. What is it about sentences containing names that makes them – a substantial class – intrinsically untranslatable, express beliefs that cannot be reported in any other language? At best, to report them in the other language, one is forced to use a word salad in which names from the one language are imported into the other. Such a supposition is both contrary to our normal practice of translation and very implausible on its face.

Implausible though it is, there is at least this much excuse for the 'solution' at this point. Our normal practice with respect to some famous people and especially for geographical localities is to have different names for them in different languages, so that in translating sentences we translate the names. But for a large number of names, especially names of people, this is not so: the person's name is used in the sentences of all languages. At least the restriction in question merely urges us to mend our ways by doing *always* what we presently do *sometimes*.

But the really drastic character of the proposed restriction comes out when we see how far it may have to extend. In 'Naming and Necessity' I suggested that there are important analogies between proper names and natural kind terms, and it seems to me that the present puzzle is one instance where the analogy will hold. Putnam, who has proposed views on natural kinds similar to my own in many respects, stressed this extension of the puzzle in his comments at the Conference. Not that the puzzle extends to all translations from English to French. At the moment, at least, it seems to me that Pierre, if he learns English and French separately, without learning any translation manual between them, *must* conclude, if he reflects enough, that 'doctor' and *médecin*,' and '*heureux*' and 'happy,' are synonymous, or at any rate, coextensive;[34] any potential paradox of the present kind for these word pairs is thus blocked. But what about '*lapin*' and 'rabbit,' or 'beech' and '*hêtre*'? We may suppose that Pierre is himself neither a zoologist nor a botanist. He has learned each language in its own country and the examples he has been shown to illustrate '*les lapins*' and 'rabbits'; 'beeches' and '*les hêtres*' are distinct. It thus seems to be possible for him to suppose that '*lapin*' and 'rabbit, or 'beech' and '*hêtre*,' denote distinct but superficially similar kinds or species, even though the differences may be indiscernible to the untrained eye. (This is especially plausible if, as Putman supposes, an English speaker – for example, Putnam himself – who is not a botanist may use 'beech' and 'elm' with their normal (distinct) meanings, even though he cannot himself distinguish the two trees.[35] Pierre may quite plausibly be supposed to wonder whether the trees which in France he called '*les hêtres*' were beeches or elms, even though as a speaker of French he satisfies all usual criteria for using '*les hêtres*' normally. If beeches and elms will not serve, better pairs of ringers exist that cannot be told apart except by an expert.) Once Pierre is in such a situation, paradoxes analogous to the one about London obviously can arise for rabbits and beeches. Pierre could affirm a French statement with '*lapin*,' but deny its English translation with 'rabbit.' As above, we are hard-pressed to say what Pierre *believes*. We were considering a 'strict and philosophical' reform of translation procedures which proposed that foreign proper names should always be appropriate rather than translated. Now it seems that we will be forced to do the same with all words for natural kinds. (For example, on price of paradox, one must not translate '*lapin*' as 'rabbit'!) No longer can the extended proposal be defended, even weakly, as 'merely' universalizing what we already do sometimes. It is surely too drastic a change to retain any credibility.[36]

There is yet another consideration that makes the proposed restriction more implausible: Even this restriction does not really block the paradox. Even if we confine ourselves to a single language, say English, and to phonetically identical tokens of a single name, we can still generate the puzzle. Peter (as we may as well say now) may learn the name 'Paderewski' with an identification of the person named as a famous pianist. Naturally, having learned this, Peter will assent to 'Paderewski had musical talent,' and *we* can infer – using 'Paderewski,' as we usually do, to name the Polish musician and statesman:

(8) Peter believes that Paderewski had musical talent.

Only the disquotational principle is necessary for our inference; no translation is required. Later, in a different circle, Peter learns of someone called 'Paderewski' who was a Polish nationalist leader and Prime Minister. Peter is skeptical of the musical abilities of politicians. He concludes that probably two people, approximate contemporaries no doubt, were both named 'Paderewski.' Using 'Paderewski' as a name for the *statesman*, Peter assents to, 'Paderewski has no musical talent.' Should we infer, by the disquotational principle,

(9) Peter believes that Paderewski had no musical talent

or should we not? If Peter had not had the past history of learning the name 'Paderewski' in another way, we certainly would judge him to be using 'Paderewski' in a normal way, with the normal reference, and we would infer (9) by the disquotational principle. The situation is parallel to the problem with Pierre and London. Here, however, no restriction that names should not be translated, but should be phonetically repeated in the translation, can help us. Only a single language and a single name are involved. If any notion of translation is involved in this example, it is homophonic translation. Only the disquotational principle is used explicitly.[37] (On the other hand, the original 'two languages' case had the advantage that it would apply even if we spoke languages in which all names must denote uniquely and unambiguously.) The restriction that names must not be translated is thus ineffective, as well as implausible and drastic.

I close this section with some remarks on the relation of the present puzzle to Quine's doctrine of the 'indeterminacy of translation,' with its attendant repudiation of intensional idioms of 'propositional attitude' such as belief and even indirect quotation. To a sympathizer with these doctrines the present puzzle may well seem to be just more grist for a familiar mill. The situation of the puzzle seems to lead to a breakdown of our normal practices of attributing belief and even of indirect quotation. No obvious paradox arises if we describe the same situation in terms of Pierre's sincere assent to various sentences, together with the conditions under which he has learned the name in question. Such a description, although it does not yet conform to Quine's strict behavioristic standards, fits in well with his view that in some sense direct quotation is a more 'objective' idiom than the propositional attitudes. Even those who, like the present writer, do not find Quine's negative attitude to the attitudes completely attractive must surely acknowledge this.

But although sympathizers with Quine's view can use the present examples to support it, the differences between these examples and the considerations Quine adduces for his own skepticism about belief and translation should not escape us. Here we make no use of hypothetical exotic systems of translation differing radically from the usual one, translating '*lapin*,' say, as 'rabbit stage' or 'undetached part of a rabbit.' The problem arises entirely within our usual and customary system of translation of French into English; in one case, the puzzle arose even within English alone, using at most 'homophonic' translation. Nor is the problem that many different interpretations or translations fit our usual criteria, that, in Davidson's phrase,[38] there is more than one 'way of getting it right.' The trouble here is not that many views as to Pierre's beliefs get it right, but that they all definitely get it *wrong*. A straightforward application of the principles of translation and disquotation to all Pierre's utterances, French and English, yields the result that Pierre holds inconsistent beliefs, that logic alone should teach him that one of his beliefs is false. Intuitively, this is plainly incorrect. If we refuse to apply the principles to his French utterances at all, we would conclude that Pierre never believed that London is pretty, even though, before his unpredictable move, he was like any other monolingual Frenchman. This is absurd. If we refuse to ascribe the belief in London's pulchritude only after Pierre's move to England, we get the counterintuitive result that Pierre has changed his mind, and so on. But we have surveyed the possibilities above: the point was not that they are 'equally good,' but that all are *obviously wrong*. If the puzzle is to be used as an argument for a Quinean position it is an argument of a fundamentally different kind from those given before. And even Quine, if he wishes to incorporate the notion of belief even into a 'second level' of canonical notation,[39] must regard the puzzle as a real problem.

The alleged indeterminacy of translation and indirect quotation causes relatively little trouble for such a scheme for belief; the embarrassment it presents to such a scheme is, after all, one of riches. But the present puzzle indicates that the usual principles we use to ascribe beliefs are apt, in certain cases, to lead to contradiction, or at least, patent falsehoods. So it presents a problem for any project, Quinean or other, that wishes to deal with the 'logic' of belief on any level.[40]

IV. Conclusion

What morals can be drawn? The primary moral – quite independent of any of the discussion of the first two sections – is that the puzzle *is* a puzzle. As any theory of truth must deal with the Liar Paradox, so any theory of belief and names must deal with this puzzle.

But our theoretical starting point in the first two sections concerned proper names and belief. Let us return to Jones, who assents to 'Cicero was bald' and 'Tully was not bald.' Philosophers, using the disquotational principle, have concluded that Jones believes that Cicero was bald but that Tully was not. Hence, they have concluded, since Jones does not have contradictory beliefs, belief contexts are not 'Shakespearean' in Geach's sense: codesignative proper names are not interchangeable in these contexts *salva veritate*.[41]

I think the puzzle about Pierre shows that the simple conclusion was unwarranted. Jones' situation strikingly resembles Pierre's. A proposal that 'Cicero' and 'Tully' *are* interchangeable amounts roughly to a homophonic 'translation' of English into itself in which 'Cicero' is mapped into 'Tully' and *vice versa*, while the rest is left fixed. Such a 'translation' can, indeed, be used to obtain a paradox. But should the problem be blamed on this step? Ordinarily we would suppose without question that sentences in French with '*Londres*' should be translated into English with 'London.' Yet the same paradox results when we apply this translation too. We have seen that the problem can even arise with a single name in a single language, and that it arises with natural kind terms in two languages (or one: see below).

Intuitively, Jones' assent to both 'Cicero was bald' and 'Tully was not bald' arises from sources of just the same kind as Pierre's assent to both '*Londres est jolie*' and 'London is not pretty.'

It is wrong to blame unpalatable conclusions about Jones on substitutivity. The reason does not lie in any specific fallacy in the argument but rather in the nature of the realm being entered. Jones's case is just like Pierre's: both are in an area where our normal practices of attributing belief, based on the principles of disquotation and translation or on similar principles, are questionable.

It should be noted in this connection that the principles of disquotation and translation can lead to 'proofs' as well as 'disproofs' of substitutivity in belief contexts. In Hebrew there are two names for Germany, transliteratable roughly as '*Ashkenaz*' and '*Germaniah*' – the first of these may be somewhat archaic. When Hebrew sentences are translated into English, both become 'Germany.' Plainly a normal Hebrew speaker analogous to Jones might assent to a Hebrew sentence involving '*Ashkenaz*' while dissenting from its counterpart with '*Germaniah*.' So far there is an argument *against* substitutivity. But there is also an argument *for* substitutivity, based on the principle of translation. Translate a Hebrew sentence involving '*Ashkenaz*' into English, so that 'Ashkenaz' goes into 'Germany.' Then retranslate the result into Hebrew, this time translating 'Germany' as '*Germaniah*.' By the principle of translation, both translations preserve truth value. So: the truth value of any sentence of Hebrew involving '*Ashkenaz*' remains the same when '*Ashkenaz*' is replaced by '*Germaniah*' – a 'proof' of substitutivity! A similar 'proof' can be provided wherever there are two names in one language, and a normal practice of translating both indifferently into a single name of another language.[42] (If we combine the 'proof' and 'disproof' of substitutivity in this paragraph, we could get yet another paradox analogous to Pierre's: our Hebrew speaker both believes, and disbelieves, that Germany is pretty. Yet no amount of pure logic or semantic introspection suffices for him to discover his error.)

Another consideration, regarding natural kinds: Previously we pointed out that a bilingual may learn '*lapin*' and 'rabbit' normally in each respective language yet wonder whether they are one species or two, and that this fact can be used to generate a paradox analogous to Pierre's. Similarly, a speaker of *English* alone may learn 'furze' and 'gorse normally (separately), yet wonder whether these are the same, or resembling kinds. (What about 'rabbit' and 'hare'?) It would be easy for such a speaker to assent to an assertion formulated with 'furze' but withhold assent from the corresponding assertion involving 'gorse.' The situation is quite analogous to that of Jones with respect to 'Cicero' and 'Tully.' Yet 'furze' and 'gorse,' and other pairs of terms for the same natural kind, are normally thought of as *synonyms*.

The point is *not*, of course, that codesignative proper names *are* interchangeable in belief contexts *salva veritate*, or that they *are* interchangeable in simple contexts even *salva significatione*. The point is that the absurdities that disquotation plus substitutivity would generate are exactly paralleled by absurdities generated by disquotation plus translation, or even 'disquotation alone' (or: disquotation plus homophonic translation). Also, though our naive practice may lead to 'disproofs' of substitutivity in certain cases, it can also lead to 'proofs' of substitutivity in some of these same cases, as we saw two paragraphs back. When we enter into the area exemplified by Jones and Pierre, we enter into an area where our normal practices of interpretation and attribution of belief are subjected to the greatest possible strain, perhaps to the point of breakdown. So is the notion of the *content* of someone's assertion, the *proposition* it expresses. In the present state of our knowledge, I think it would be foolish to draw any conclusion, positive or negative, about substitutivity.[43]

Of course nothing in these considerations prevents us from observing that Jones can sincerely assert both 'Cicero is bald' and 'Tully is not bald,' even though he is a normal speaker of English and uses 'Cicero' and 'Tully' in normal ways, and with the normal referent. Pierre and the other paradoxical cases can be described similarly. (For those interested in one of my own doctrines, we can still say that there was a time when men were in no epistemic position to assent to 'Hesperus is Phosphorus' for want of empirical information, but it nevertheless expressed a necessary truth.)[44] But it is no surprise that quoted contexts fail to satisfy a substitutivity principle within the quotation marks. And, in our *present* state of clarity about the problem, we are in no position to apply a disquotation principle to these cases, nor to judge when two such sentences do or do not, express the same 'proposition.'

Nothing in the discussion impugns the conventional judgment that belief contexts are 'referentially opaque,' if 'referential opacity' is construed so that failure of coreferential *definite descriptions* to be interchangeable *salva veritate* is sufficient for referential opacity. No doubt Jones can believe that the number of planets is even, without believing that the square of three is even, if he is under a misapprehension about the astronomical, but not the arithmetical facts. The question at hand was whether belief contexts were 'Shakespearean,' not whether they were 'referentially transparent.' (Modal contexts, in my opinion, are 'Shakespearean' but 'referentially opaque.')[45]

Even were we inclined to rule that belief contexts are not Shakespearean, it would be implausible at present to use the phenomenon to support a Frege-Russellian theory that names have descriptive 'senses' through 'uniquely identifying properties.' There are the well-known arguments against description theories, independent of the present discussion; there is the implausibility of the view that difference in names is difference in idiolect; and finally, there are the arguments of the present paper that differences of associated properties do not explain the problems in any case. Given these considerations, and the cloud our paradox places over the notion of 'content' in this area, the relation of substitutivity to the dispute between Millian and Fregean conclusions is not very clear.

We repeat our conclusions: Philosophers have often, basing themselves on Jones' and similar cases, supposed that it goes virtually without saying that belief contexts are not 'Shakespearean.' I think that, at present, such a definite conclusion is unwarranted. Rather Jones' case, like Pierre's, lies in an area where our normal apparatus for the ascription of belief is placed under the greatest strain and may even break down. There is even less warrant at the present time, in the absence of a better understanding of the paradoxes of this paper, for the use of alleged failures of substitutivity in belief contexts to draw any significant theoretical conclusion about proper names. Hard cases make bad law.[46]

Notes

1. 'Naming and Necessity,' in: *The Semantics of Natural Languages*, D. Davidson and G. Harman (eds.), Dordrecht, Reidel, 1971, pp. 253–355 and 763–769. (Also forthcoming as a separate monograph, pub. Basil Blackwell.) 'Identity and Necessity' in: *Identity and Individuation*, M. Munitz (ed.), New York University Press, 1971, pp. 135–164. Acquaintance with these papers is not a prerequisite for understanding the central puzzle of the present paper, but is helpful for understanding the theoretical background.
2. Frege gives essentially this example as the second footnote of 'On Sense and Reference.' For the 'Who is . . .?' to be applicable one must be careful to elicit from one's informant properties that he regards as defining the name and determining the referent, not mere well-known facts about the referent. (Of

course this distinction may well seem fictitious, but it is central to the original Frege-Russell theory.)

3. For convenience Russell's terminology is assimilated to Frege's. Actually, regarding genuine or 'logically proper' names, Russell is a strict Millian: 'logically proper names' *simply* refer (to immediate objects of acquaintance). But, according to Russell, what are ordinarily called 'names' are not genuine, logically proper names, but disguised definite descriptions. Since Russell also regards definite descriptions as in turn disguised notation, he does not associate any 'senses' with descriptions, since they are not genuine singular terms. When all disguised notation is eliminated, the only singular terms remaining are logically proper names, for which no notion of 'sense' is required. When we speak of Russell as assigning 'senses' to names, we mean ordinary names and for convenience we ignore his view that the descriptions abbreviating them ultimately disappear on analysis.

   On the other hand, the explicit doctrine that names are abbreviated definite descriptions is due to Russell, Michael Dummett, in his recent *Frege* (Duckworth and Harper and Row, 1973, pp. 110–111) denies that Frege held a description theory of senses. Although as far as I know Frege indeed makes no explicit statement to that effect, his examples of names conform to the doctrine, as Dummet acknowledges. Especially his 'Aristotle' example is revealing. He defines 'Aristotle' just as Russell would; it seems clear that in the case of a famous historical figure, the 'name' is indeed to be given by answering, in a uniquely specifying way, the 'who is' question. Dummett himself characterizes a sense as a 'criterion . . . such that the referent of the name, if any, is whatever object satisfies that criterion.' Since presumably the satisfaction of the criterion must be unique (so a unique referent is determined), doesn't this amount to defining names by unique satisfaction of properties, *i.e.*, by descriptions? *Perhaps* the point is that the property in question need not be expressible by a usual predicate of English, as might be plausible if the referent is one of the speaker's acquaintances rather than a historical figure. But I doubt that even Russell, father of the explicitly formulated description theory, ever meant to require that the description must always be expressible in (unsupplemented) English.

   In any event, the philosophical community has generally understood Fregean senses in terms of descriptions, and we deal with it under this usual understanding. For present purposes this is more important than detailed historical issues. Dummett acknowledges (p. 111) that few substantive points are affected by his (allegedly) broader interpretation of Frege; and it would not seem to be relevant to the problems of the present paper.

4. See Frege's footnote in 'On Sense and Reference' mentioned in note 2 above and especially his discussion of 'Dr. Gustav Lauben' in '*Der Gedanke*.' (In the recent Geach-Stoothoff translation, 'Thoughts,' *Logical Investigations,* Oxford, Blackwell, 1977, pp. 11–12).

5. Russell, as a Millian with respect to genuine names, accepts this argument with respect to 'logically proper names.' For example – taking for the moment 'Cicero' and 'Tully' as 'logically proper names,' Russell would hold that if I judge that Cicero admired Tully, I am related to Cicero, Tully, and the admiration relation in a certain way: Since Cicero *is* Tully, I am related in exactly the same way to Tully, Cicero, and admiration; therefore I judge that Tully admired Cicero. Again, if Cicero *did* admire Tully, then according to Russell a single

fact corresponds to all of 'Cicero admired Tully,' 'Cicero admired Cicero,' etc. Its constituent (in addition to admiration) is the man Cicero, taken, so to speak, twice.

Russell thought that 'Cicero admired Tully' and 'Tully admired Cicero' are in fact obviously not interchangeable. For him, this was one argument that 'Cicero' and 'Tully' are *not* genuine names, and that the Roman orator is no constituent of propositions (or 'facts,' or 'judgments') corresponding to sentences containing the name.

6. Given the arguments of Church and others, I do not believe that the formal mode of speech is synonymous with other formulations. But it can be used as a rough way to convey the idea of scope.

7. It may well be argued that the Millian view implies that proper names are *scopeless* and that for them the *de dicto-de re* distinction vanishes. This view has considerable plausibility (my own views on rigidity will imply something like this for *modal* contexts), but it need not be argued here either way: *de re* uses are simply not treated in the present paper.

   Christopher Peacocke ('Proper Names, Reference, and Rigid Designation,' in: *Meaning, Reference, and Necessity*, S. Blackburn (ed.), Cambridge, 1975; see Section I), uses what amounts to the equivalence of the *de dicto-de re* constructions in *all* contexts (or, put alternatively, the lack of such a distinction) to characterize the notion of rigid designation. I agree that for *modal* contexts, this is (roughly) equivalent to my own notion, also that for proper names Peacocke's equivalence holds for temporal contexts. (This is roughly equivalent to the 'temporal rigidity' of names.) I also agree that it is very plausible to extend the principle to all contexts. But, as Peacocke recognizes, this appears to imply a substitutivity principle for codesignative proper names in belief contexts, which is widely assumed to be false. Peacocke proposes to use Davidson's theory of intensional contexts to block this conclusion (the material in the 'that' clause is a separate sentence). I myself cannot accept Davidson's theory; but even if it were true, Peacocke in effect acknowledges that it does not really dispose of the difficulty (p. 127, first paragraph). (Incidentally, if Davidson's theory does block any reference to the transparency of belief contexts with respect to names, why does Peacocke assume without argument that it does not do so for modal contexts, which have a similar grammatical structure?) The problems are thus those of the present paper; until they are resolved I prefer at present to keep to my earlier more cautious formulation.

   Incidentally, Peacocke hints a recognition that the received platitude – that codesignative names are not interchangeable in belief contexts – may not be so clear as is generally supposed.

8. The example comes from Quine, *Word and Object*, M.I.T. Press, 1960, p. 145. Quine's conclusion that 'believes that' construed *de dicto* is opaque has widely been taken for granted. In the formulation in the text I have used the colon to emphasize that I am speaking of belief *de dicto*. Since, as I have said, belief *de dicto* will be our *only* concern in this paper, in the future the colon will usually be suppressed, and all 'believes that' contexts should be read *de dicto* unless the contrary is indicated explicitly.

9. In many writings Peter Geach has advocated a view that is nonMillian (he would say 'nonLockean') in that to each name a sortal predicate is attached by definition

('Geach,' for example, by *definition* names a man). On the other hand, the theory is not completely Fregean either, since Geach denies that any definite description that would identify the referent of the name among things of the same sort is analytically tied to the name. (See, for example, his *Reference and Generality*, Cornell, 1962, pp. 43–45.) As far as the present issues are concerned, Geach's view can fairly be assimilated to *Mill*'s rather than Frege's. For such ordinary names as 'Cicero' and 'Tully' will have both the same reference and the same (Geachian) sense (namely, that they are names of a man). It would thus seem that they ought to be interchangeable everywhere. (In *Reference and Generality*, Geach appears not to accept this conclusion, but the *prima facie* argument for the conclusion will be the same as on a purely Millian view.)

10. In an unpublished paper, Diana Ackerman urges the problem of substitutivity failures against the Millian view and, hence, against my own views. I believe that others may have done so as well. (I have the impression that the paper has undergone considerable revision, and I have not seen recent versions.) I agree that this problem is a considerable difficulty for the Millian view, and for the Millian *spirit* of my own views in 'Naming and Necessity.' (See the discussion of this in the text of the present paper.) On the other hand I would emphasize that there need be no *contradiction* in maintaining that names are *modally* rigid, and satisfy a substitutivity principle for modal contexts, while denying the substitutivity principle for belief contexts. The entire apparatus elaborated in 'Naming and Necessity' of the distinction between epistemic and metaphysical necessity, and of giving a meaning and fixing a reference, was meant to show, among other things, that a Millian substitutivity doctrine for modal contexts can be maintained even if such a doctrine for epistemic contexts is rejected. 'Naming and Necessity' never asserted a substitutivity principle for epistemic contexts.

    It is even consistent to suppose that differing modes of (rigidly) fixing the reference is responsible for the substitutivity failures, thus adopting a position intermediate between Frege and Mill, on the lines indicated in the text of the present paper. 'Naming and Necessity' may even perhaps be taken as suggesting, for some contexts where a conventional description rigidly fixes the reference ('Hesperus-Phosphorus'), that the mode of reference fixing is relevant to epistemic questions. I knew when I wrote 'Naming and Necessity' that substitutivity issues in epistemic contexts were really very delicate, due to the problems of the present paper, but I thought it best not to muddy the waters further. (See notes 43–44).

    After this paper was completed, I saw Alvin Plantinga's paper 'The Boethian Compromise,' *The American Philosophical Quarterly* 15 (April, 1978): 129–138. Plantinga adopts a view intermediate between Mill and Frege, and cites substitutivity failures as a principal argument for his position. He also refers to a forthcoming paper by Ackerman. I have not seen this paper, but it probably is a descendant of the paper referred to above.

11. Here I use 'connotation' so as to imply that the associated properties have in *a priori* tie to the name, at least as rigid reference fixers, and therefore must be true of the referent (if it exists). There is another sense of 'connotation,' as in 'The Holy Roman Empire,' where the connotation need not be assumed or even believed to be true of the referent. In some sense akin to this, classicists and others with some classical learning may attach certain distinct 'connotations' to 'Cicero'

and 'Tully.' Similarly, 'The Netherlands' may suggest low altitude to a thoughtful ear. Such 'connotations' can hardly be thought of as community-wide; many use the names unaware of such suggestions. Even a speaker aware of the suggestion of the name may not regard the suggested properties as true of the object; *cf.* 'The Holy Roman Empire.' A 'connotation' of this type neither gives a meaning nor fixes a reference.

12. Some might attempt to find a difference in 'sense' between 'Cicero' and 'Tully' on the grounds that 'Cicero is called "Cicero"' is trivial, but 'Tully is called "Cicero"' may not be. Kneale, and in one place (probably at least implicitly) Church, have argued in this vein. (For Kneale, see 'Naming and Necessity,' p. 283.) So, it may be argued, being called 'Cicero,' is part of the sense of the name 'Cicero,' but not part of that of 'Tully.'

    I have discussed some issues related to this in 'Naming and Necessity,' pp. 283–286. (See also the discussions of circularity conditions elsewhere in 'Naming and Necessity.') Much more could be said about and against this kind of argument; perhaps I will sometime do so elsewhere. Let me mention very briefly the following parallel situation (which may be best understood by reference to the discussion in 'Naming and Necessity'). Anyone who understands the meaning of 'is called' and of quotation in English (and that 'alienists' is meaningful and grammatically appropriate), knows that 'alienists are called "alienists"' expresses a truth in English, even if he has no idea what 'alienists' means. He need *not* know that 'psychiatrists are called "alienists"' expresses a truth. None of this goes to show that 'alienists' and 'psychiatrists' are not synonymous, or that 'alienists' has *being called 'alienists'* as part of its meaning when 'psychiatrists' does not. Similarly for 'Cicero' and 'Tully.' There is no more reason to suppose that being so-called is part of the meaning of a name than of any other word.
13. A view follows Frege and Russell on this issue even if it allows each speaker to associate a cluster of descriptions with each name, provided that it holds that the cluster varies from speaker to speaker and that variations in the cluster are variations in idiolect. Searle's view thus is Frege-Russellian when he writes in the concluding paragraph of 'Proper Names' (*Mind* 67 (1958): 166–173), 'Tully = Cicero' would, I suggest, be analytic for most people; the same descriptive presuppositions are associated with each name. But of course if the descriptive presuppositions were different it might be used to make a synthetic statement.'
14. Though here I use the jargon of propositions, the point is fairly insensitive to differences in theoretical standpoints. For example, on Davidson's analysis, I would be asserting (roughly) that many are unaware-of-the-content-of the following *utterance* of mine: Cicero is Tully. This would be subject to the same problem.
15. Benson Mates, 'Synonymity,' *University of California Publications in Philosophy* 25 (1950): 201–226; reprinted in: *Semantics and the Philosophy of Language*, L. Linsky (ed.), University of Illinois Press, 1952. (There was a good deal of subsequent discussion. In Mates's original paper the point is made almost parenthetically.) Actually, I think that Mates's problem has relatively little force against the argument we are considering for the Fregean position. Mates's puzzle in no way militates against some such principle as: If one word is synonymous with another, then a sufficiently reflective speaker subject to no linguistic inadequacies or conceptual confusions who sincerely assents to a simple sentence containing

the one will also (sincerely) assent to the corresponding sentence with the other in its place.

It is surely a crucial part of the present 'Fregean' argument that codesignative names may have distinct 'senses,' that a speaker may assent to a simple sentence containing one and deny the corresponding sentence containing the other, even though he is *guilty of no conceptual or linguistic confusion, and of no lapse in logical consistency*. In the case of two straightforward synonyms, this is not so.

I myself think that Mates's argument is of considerable interest, but that the issues are confusing and delicate and that, if the argument works, it probably leads to a paradox or puzzle rather than to a definite conclusion. (See also notes 23, 28, and 46.)

16. 'Naming and Necessity,' pp. 291 (bottom)–293.
17. Recall also note 12.
18. Some philosophers stress that names are not *words* of a language, or that names are not *translated* from one language to another. (The phrase 'common currency of our common language' was meant to be neutral with respect to any such alleged issue.) Someone may use 'Mao Tse-Tung,' for example, in English, though he knows not one word of Chinese. It seems hard to deny, however, that '*Deutschland*,' '*Allemagne*,' and 'Germany,' are the German, French, and English names of a single country, and that one translates a French sentence using '*Londres*' by an English sentence using 'London.' Learning these facts *is* part of learning, German, French, and English.

It would appear that *some* names, especially names of countries, other famous localities, and some famous people *are* thought of as part of a language (whether they are called 'words' or not is of little importance). Many other names are not thought of as part of a language, especially if the referent is not famous (so the notation used is confined to a limited circle), or if the same name is used by speakers of all languages. As far as I can see, it makes little or no *semantic* difference whether a particular name is thought of as part of a language or not. Mathematical notation such as '<' is also ordinarily not thought of as part of English, or any other language, though it is used in combination with English words in sentences of mathematical treatises written in English. (A French mathematician can use the notation though he knows not one word of English.) 'Is less than,' on the other hand, *is* English. Does this difference have any semantic significance?

I will speak in most of the text as if the names I deal with are part of English, French, etc. But it matters little for what I say whether they are thought of as parts of the language or as adjuncts to it. And one need not say that a name such as '*Londres*' is 'translated' (if such a terminology suggested that names have 'senses,' I too would find it objectionable), as long as one acknowledges that *sentences* containing it are properly translated into English using 'London.'

19. By saying that names are transparent in a context, I mean that codesignative names are interchangeable there. This is a deviation for brevity from the usual terminology, according to which the *context* is transparent. (I use the usual terminology in the paper also.)
20. But we must use the term 'sense' here in the sense of 'that which fixes the reference,' not 'that which gives the meaning,' otherwise we shall run afoul of the rigidity of proper names. If the source of a chain for a certain name is in

fact a given object, we use the name to designate that object even when speaking of counterfactual situations in which some *other* object originated the chain.

21. The point is that, according to the doctrine of 'Naming and Necessity,' when proper names are transmitted from link to link, even though the beliefs about the referent associated with the name change radically, the change is not to be considered a linguistic change, in the way it *was* a linguistic change when 'villain' changed its meaning from 'rustic' to 'wicked man.' As long as the reference of a name remains the same, the associated beliefs about the object may undergo a large number of changes without these changes constituting a change in the language.

    If Geach is right, an appropriate sortal must be passed on also. But see footnote 58 of 'Naming and Necessity.'

22. Similar appropriate restrictions are assumed below for the strengthened disquotational principle and for the principle of translation. Ambiguities need not be excluded if it is tacitly assumed that the sentence is to be understood in one way in all its occurrences. (For the principle of translation it is similarly assumed that the translator matches the *intended* interpretation of the sentence.) I do not work out the restrictions on indexicals in detail, since the intent is clear.

    Clearly, the disquotational principle applies only to *de dicto*, not *de re*, attributions of belief. If someone sincerely assents to the near triviality 'The tallest foreign spy is a spy,' it follows that he believes that: the tallest foreign spy is a spy. It is well known that it does *not* follow that he believes, *of* the tallest foreign spy, that he is a spy. In the latter case, but not in the former, it would be his patriotic duty to make contact with the authorities.

23. What if the speaker assents to a sentence, but fails to assent to a synonymous assertion? Say, he assents to 'Jones is a doctor,' but not to 'Jones is a physician.' Such a speaker either does not understand one of the sentences normally, or he should be able to correct himself 'on reflection.' As long as he confusedly assents to 'Jones is a doctor' but not to 'Jones is a physician,' we *cannot* straightforwardly apply disquotational principles to conclude that he does or does not believe that Jones is a doctor, because his assent is not 'reflective.'

    Similarly, if someone asserts, 'Jones is a doctor but not a physician,' he should be able to recognize his inconsistency without further information. We have formulated the disquotational principles so they need not lead us to attribute belief as long as we have grounds to suspect conceptual or linguistic confusion, as in the case just mentioned.

    Note that if someone says, 'Cicero was bald but Tully was not,' there need be *no* grounds to suppose that he is under *any* linguistic or conceptual confusion.

24. This should not be confused with the question whether the speaker simultaneously believes *of* a given object, both that it has a certain property and that it does not have it. Our discussion concerns *de dicto* (notional) belief, not *de re* belief.

    I have been shown a passage in Aristotle that appears to suggest that *no one* can really believe both of two explicit contradictories. If we wish to use the *simple* disquotational principle as a test for disbelief, it suffices that this be true of *some* individuals, after reflection, who are simultaneously aware of both beliefs, and have sufficient logical acumen and respect for logic. Such individuals, if they have contradictory beliefs, will be shaken in one or both beliefs after they note the contradiction. For such individuals, sincere reflective assent to the negation of a sentence implies disbelief in the proposition it expresses, so the test in the text applies.

25. For example, in translating a historical report into another language, such as, 'Patrick Henry said, "Give me liberty or give me death!" ' the translator may well translate the quoted material attributed to Henry. He translates a presumed truth into a falsehood, since Henry spoke English; but probably his reader is aware of this and is more interested in the content of Henry's utterance than in its exact words. Especially in translating fiction, where truth is irrelevant, this procedure is appropriate. But some objectors to Church's 'translation argument' have allowed themselves to be misled by the practice.
26. To state the argument precisely, we need in addition a form of the Tarskian disquotation principle for truth: For each (French or English) replacement for '*p*,' infer ' "*p*" is true' from '*p*,' and conversely. (Note that ' "p" is true' becomes an English sentence even if '*p*' is replaced by a French sentence.) In the text we leave the application of the Tarskian disquotational principle tacit.
27. I gather that Burali-Forti originally thought he had 'proved' that the ordinals are not linearly ordered, reasoning in a manner similar to our topologist. Someone who heard the present paper delivered told me that König made a similar error.
28. It is not possible, in this case, as it is in the case of the man who assents to 'Jones is a doctor' but not to 'Jones is a physician,' to refuse to apply the disquotational principle on the grounds that the subject must lack proper command of the language or be subject to some linguistic or conceptual confusion. As long as Pierre is unaware that 'London' and '*Londres*' are codesignative, he need not lack appropriate linguistic knowledge, nor need he be subject to any linguistic or conceptual confusion, when he affirms, '*Londres est jolie*' but denies 'London is pretty.'
29. The 'elimination' would be most plausible if we believed, according to Russellian epistemology, that all my language, when written in unabbreviated notation, refers to constituents with which I am 'acquainted' in Russell's sense. Then no one speaks a language intelligible to anyone else; indeed, no one speaks the same language twice. Few today will accept this.

    A basic consideration should be stressed here. Moderate Fregeans attempt to combine a roughly Fregean view with the view that names are part of our common language, and that our conventional practices of interlinguistic translation and interpretation are correct. The problems of the present paper indicate that it is very difficult to obtain a requisite socialized notion of sense that will enable such a program to succeed. Extreme Fregeans (such as Frege and Russell) believe that in general names are peculiar to idiolects. They therefore would accept no general rule translating '*Londres*' as 'London,' nor even translating one person's use of 'London' into another's. However, if they follow Frege in regarding senses as 'objective,' they must believe that in principle it makes sense to speak of two people using two names in their respective idiolects with the same sense, and that there must be (necessary and) sufficient conditions for this to be the case. If these conditions for sameness of sense are satisfied, translation of one name into the other is legitimate, otherwise not. The present considerations (and the extension of these below to natural kind and related terms), however, indicate that the notion of sameness of sense, if it is to be explicated in terms of sameness of identifying properties and if these properties are themselves expressed in the languages of the two respective idiolects, presents interpretation problems of the same type presented by the names themselves. Unless the Fregean can give a method for identifying sameness of sense that is free of such problems, he *has no sufficient conditions for sameness of sense, nor for translation to be legitimate.* He would therefore be forced to maintain, contrary to Frege's intent, that not only in practice do few people use proper names with the same sense but that *it is in principle meaningless to compare senses.* A view that the identifying properties used to define senses should always be expressible in a Russellian language of 'logically proper names' would be one solution to this difficulty but involves a doubtful philosophy of language and epistemology.

30. If any reader finds the term 'translation' objectionable with respect to names, let him be reminded that all I mean is that French sentences containing '*Londres*' are uniformly translated into English with 'London.'
31. The paradox would be blocked if we required that they define the names by the same properties expressed in the same words. There is nothing in the motivation of the classical description theories that would justify this extra clause. In the present case of French and English, such a restriction would amount to a decree that neither '*Londres*,' nor any other conceivable French name, could be translated as 'London.' I deal with this view immediately below.
32. Word salads of two languages (like ungrammatical 'semisentences' of a single language) need not be unintelligible, though they are makeshifts with no fixed syntax. 'If God did not exist, Voltaire said, *il faudrait l'inventer.*' The meaning is clear.
33. Had we said, 'Pierre believes that the country he calls "*Angleterre*" is a monarchy,' the sentence would be English, since the French word would be mentioned but not used. But for this very reason we would not have captured the sense of the French original.
34. Under the influence of Quine's *Word and Object*, some may argue that such conclusions are not inevitable: perhaps he will translate '*médecin*' as 'doctor stage,' or 'undetached part of a doctor'! If a Quinean skeptic makes an empirical prediction that such reactions from bilinguals as a matter of fact can occur, I doubt that he will be proved correct. (I don't know what Quine would think. But see *Word and Object*, p. 74, first paragraph.) On the other hand, if the translation of 'médecin' as 'doctor' rather than 'doctor part' in this situation *is*, empirically speaking, inevitable, then even the advocate of Quine's thesis will have to admit that there is something special about one particular translation. The issue is not crucial to our present concerns, so I leave it with these sketchy remarks. But see also note 36.
35. Putnam gives the example of elms and beeches in 'The Meaning of "Meaning" ' (in: *Language, Mind, and Knowledge*, Minnesota Studies in the Philosophy of Science 7; also reprinted in Putnam's *Collected Papers*). See also Putnam's discussion of other examples on pp. 139–143; also my own remarks on 'fool's gold,' tigers, etc, in 'Naming and Necessity,' pp. 316–323.
36. It is unclear to me how far this can go. Suppose Pierre hears English spoken only in England, French in France, and learns both by direct method. (Suppose also that no one else in each country speaks the language of the other.) Must he be sure that 'hot' and '*chaud*' are coextensive? In practice he certainly would. But suppose somehow his experience is consistent with the following bizarre –

and of course, false! – hypothesis: England and France differ atmospherically so that human bodies are affected very differently by their interaction with the surrounding atmosphere. (This would be more plausible if France were on another planet.) In particular, within reasonable limits, things that feel cold in one of the countries feel hot in the other, and *vice versa*. Things don't change their *temperature* when moved from England to France, they just *feel* different because of their effects on human physiology. Then '*chaud*,' in French, would be true of the things that are called 'cold' in English! (Of course the present discussion is, for space, terribly compressed. See also the discussion of 'heat' in 'Naming and Necessity.' We are simply creating, for the physical property 'heat,' a situation analogous to the situation for natural kinds in the text.)

If Pierre's experiences were arranged somehow so as to be consistent with the bizarre hypothesis, and he somehow came to believe it, he might simultaneously assent to '*C'est chaud*' and 'This is cold' without contradiction, even though he speaks French and English normally in each country separately.

This case needs much more development to see if it can be set up in detail, but I cannot consider it further here. Was I right in assuming in the text that the difficulty could not arise for '*médecin*' and 'doctor'?

37. One might argue that Peter and we do speak different dialects, since in Peter's idiolect 'Paderewski' is used ambiguously as a name for a musician and a statesman (even though these are in fact the same), while in our language it is used unambiguously for a musician-statesman. The problem then would be whether Peter's dialect can be translated homophonically into our own. Before he hears of 'Paderewski-the-statesman,' it would appear that the answer is affirmative for his (then unambiguous) use of 'Paderewski,' since he did not differ from anyone who happens to have heard of Paderewski's musical achievements but not of his statesmanship. Similarly for his later use of 'Paderewski,' if we ignore his earlier use. The problem is like Pierre's, and is essentially the same whether we describe it in terms of whether Peter satisfies the condition for the disquotational principle to be applicable, or whether homophonic translation of his dialect into our own is legitimate.
38. D. Davidson, 'On Saying That,' in: *Words and Objections*, D. Davidson and J. Hintikka (eds.), Dordrecht, Reidel, 1969, p. 166.
39. In *Word and Object*, p. 221, Quine advocates a second level of canonical notation, 'to dissolve verbal perplexities or facilitate logical deductions,' admitting the propositional attitudes, even though he thinks them 'baseless' idioms that should be excluded from a notation 'limning the true and ultimate structure of reality.'
40. In one respect the considerations mentioned above on natural kinds show that Quine's translation apparatus is insufficiently skeptical. Quine is sure that the native's *sentence* 'Gavagai!' should be translated 'Lo, a rabbit!', provided that its affirmative and negative stimulus meanings for the native match those of the English sentence for the Englishman; skepticism sets in only when the linguist proposes to translate the *general term* 'gavagai' as 'rabbit' rather than 'rabbit stage,' 'rabbit part,' and the like. But there is another possibility that is independent of (and less bizarre than) such skeptical alternatives. In the geographical area inhabited by the natives, there may be a species indistinguishable to the nonzoologist from rabbits but forming a distinct species. Then the 'stimulus meanings,' in Quine's sense, of 'Lo, a rabbit!' and 'Gavagai!'

may well be identical (to nonzoologists), especially if the ocular irradiations in question do not include a specification of the geographical locality. ('Gavagais' produce the same ocular irradiation patterns as rabbits.) Yet 'Gavagai!' and 'Lo, a rabbit!' are hardly synonymous; on typical occasions they will have opposite truth values.

I believe that the considerations about names, let alone natural kinds, emphasized in 'Naming and Necessity' go against any simple attempt to base interpretation solely on maximizing agreement with the affirmations attributed to the native, matching of stimulus meanings, etc. The 'Principle of Charity' on which such methodologies are based was first enunciated by Neil Wilson in the special case of proper names as a formulation of the cluster-of-descriptions theory. The argument of 'Naming and Necessity' is thus directed against the simple 'Principle of Charity' for that case.

41. Geach introduced the term 'Shakespearean' after the line, 'a rose/By any other name, would smell as sweet.'

Quine seems to define 'referentially transparent' contexts so as to imply that coreferential names and definite descriptions must be interchangeable *salva veritate*. Geach stresses that a context may be 'Shakespearean' but not 'referentially transparent' in this sense.

42. Generally such cases may be slightly less watertight than the 'London'-'*Londres*' case. '*Londres*' just is the French version of 'London,' while one cannot quite say that the same relation holds between '*Ashkenaz*' and '*Germaniah*.' Nevertheless:

(a) Our standard practice in such cases is to translate both names of the first language into the single name of the second.

(b) Often no naunces of 'meaning' are discernible differentiating such names as '*Ashkenaz*' and '*Germaniah*,' such that we would not say either that Hebrew would have been impoverished had it lacked one of them (or that English is impoverished because it has only one name for Germany), any more than a language is impoverished if it has only one word corresponding to 'doctor' and 'physician.' Given this, it seems hard to condemn our practice of translating both names as 'Germany' as 'loose'; in fact, it would seem that Hebrew just has two names for the same country where English gets by with one.

(c) Any inclinations to avoid problems by declaring, say, the translation of '*Ashkenaz*' as 'Germany' to be loose should be considerably tempered by the discussion of analogous problems in the text.

43. In spite of this official view, perhaps I will be more assertive elsewhere.

In the case of 'Hesperus' and 'Phosophorus' (in contrast to 'Cicero' and 'Tully'), where there is a case for the existence of conventional community-wide 'senses' differentiating the two – at least, two distinct modes of 'fixing the reference of two rigid designators' – it is more plausible to suppose that the two names are definitely not interchangeable in belief contexts. According to such a supposition, a belief that Hesperus is a planet is a belief that a certain heavenly body, rigidly picked out as seen in the evening in the appropriate season, is a planet; and similarly for Phosphorus. One may argue that translation problems like Pierre's will be blocked in this case, that '*Vesper*' must be translated as 'Hesperus,' not as 'Phosphorus.' As against this, however, two things:

(a) We should remember that sameness of properties used to fix the reference does *not* appear to guarantee in general that paradoxes will not arise. So one may be reluctant to adopt a solution in terms of reference-fixing properties for this case if it does not get to the heart of the general problem.

(b) The main issue seems to me here to be – how essential is a particular mode of fixing the reference to a correct learning of the name? If a parent, aware of the familiar identity, takes a child into the fields in the morning and says (pointing to the morning star) 'That is called "Hesperus,"' has the parent mistaught the language? (A parent who says, 'Creatures with kidneys are called "cordates,"' definitely has mistaught the language, even though the statement is extensionally correct.) To the extent that it is *not* crucial for correct language learning that a particular mode of fixing the reference be used, to that extent there is no 'mode of presentation' differentiating the 'content' of a belief about 'Hesperus' from one about 'Phosphorus.' I am doubtful that the original method of fixing the reference *must* be preserved in transmission of the name.

If the mode of reference fixing *is* crucial, it can be maintained that otherwise identical beliefs expressed with 'Hesperus' and with 'Phosphorus' have definite differences of 'content,' at least in an epistemic sense. The conventional ruling against substitutivity could thus be maintained without qualms for some cases, though not as obviously for others, such as 'Cicero' and 'Tully.' But it is unclear to me whether even 'Hesperus' and 'Phosphorus' do have such conventional 'modes of presentation.' I need not take a definite stand, and the verdict may be different for different particular pairs of names. For a brief related discussion, see 'Naming and Necessity,' p. 331, first paragraph.

44. However, some earlier formulations expressed disquotationally such as 'It was once unknown that Hesperus is Phosphorus' are questionable in the light of the present paper (but see the previous note for this case). I was aware of this question by the time 'Naming and Necessity' was written, but I did not wish to muddy the waters further than necessary at that time. I regarded the distinction between epistemic and metaphysical necessity as valid in any case and adequate for the distinctions I wished to make. The considerations in this paper are relevant to the earlier discussion of the 'contingent *a priori*' as well; perhaps I will discuss this elsewhere.

45. According to Russell, definite descriptions are not genuine singular terms. He thus would have regarded any concept of 'referential opacity' that includes definite descriptions as profoundly misleading. He also maintained a substitutivity principle for 'logically proper names' in belief and other attitudinal contexts, so that for him belief contexts were as 'transparent,' in any philosophically decent sense, as truth-functional contexts.

Independently of Russell's views, there is much to be said for the opinion that the question whether a context is 'Shakespearean' is more important philosophically – even for many purposes for which Quine invokes his own concept – than whether it is 'referentially opaque.'

46. I will make some brief remarks about the relations of Benson Mates's problem (see note 15) to the present one. Mates argued that such a sentence as (*) 'Some doubt that all who believe that doctors are happy believe that physicians are happy,' may be true, even though 'doctors' and 'physicians' are synonymous, and even though it would have been false had 'physicians' been replaced in it by a second occurrence of 'doctors.' Church countered that (*) could not be true, since its translation into a language with only one word for doctors

(which would translate both 'doctors' and 'physicians') would be false. If *both* Mates's and Church's intuitions were correct, we might get a paradox analogous to Pierre's.

Applying the principles of translation and disquotation to Mates's puzzle, however, involves many more complications than our present problem. First, if someone assents to 'Doctors are happy,' but refuse assent to 'Physicians are happy,' *prima facie* disquotation does not apply to him since he is under a linguistic or conceptual confusion. (See note 23.) So there are as yet no grounds, merely because this happened, to doubt that all who believe that doctors are happy believe that physicians are happy.

Now suppose someone assents to 'Not all who believe that doctors are happy believe that physicians are happy.' What is the source of his assent? If it is failure to realize that 'doctors' and 'physicians' are synonymous (this was the situation Mates originally envisaged), then he is under a linguistic or conceptual confusion, so disquotation does not clearly apply. Hence we have no reason to conclude from this case that (*) is true. Alternatively, he may realize that 'doctors' and 'physicians' are synonymous; but he applies disquotation to a man who assents to 'Doctors are happy' but not to 'Physicians are happy,' ignoring the caution of the previous paragraph. Here he is not under a simple linguistic confusion (such as failure to realize that 'doctors' and 'physicians' are synonymous), but he appears to be under a deep conceptual confusion (misapplication of the disquotational principle). Perhaps, it may be argued, he misunderstands the 'logic of belief.' Does his conceptual confusion mean that we cannot straightforwardly apply disquotation to his utterance, and that therefore we cannot conclude from his behavior that (*) is true? I think that, although the issues are delicate, and I am not at present completely sure what answers to give, there is a case for an affirmative answer. (Compare the more extreme case of someone who is so confused that he thinks that someone's *dissent* from 'Doctors are happy' implies that he believes that doctors are happy. If someone's utterance, 'Many believe that doctors are happy,' is based on such a misapplication of disquotation, surely we in turn should not apply disquotation to it. The utterer, at least in this context, does not really know what 'belief' means.)

I do *not* believe the discussion above ends the matter. Perhaps I can discuss Mates's problem at greater length elsewhere. Mates's problem is perplexing, and its relation to the present puzzle is interesting. But it should be clear from the preceding that Mates's argument involves issues even more delicate than those that arises with respect to Pierre. First, Mates's problem involves delicate issues regarding iteration of belief contexts, whereas the puzzle about Pierre involves the application of disquotation only to affirmations of (or assents to) *simple* sentences. More important, Mates's problem would not arise in a world where no one ever was under a linguistic or a conceptual confusion, no one ever thought anyone else was under such a confusion, no one ever thought anyone ever thought anyone was under such a confusion, and so on. It is important, both for the puzzle about Pierre and for the Fregean argument that 'Cicero' and 'Tully' differ in 'sense,' that they would still arise in such a world. They are entirely free of the delicate problem of applying disquotation to utterances directly or indirectly based on the existence of linguistic confusion. See notes 15 and 28, and the discussion in the text of Pierre's logical consistency.

Another problem discussed in the literature to which the present considerations may be relevant is that of 'self-consciousness,' or the peculiarity of 'I.' Discussions of this problem have emphasized that 'I,' even when Mary Smith uses it, is not interchangeable with 'Mary Smith,' nor with any other conventional singular term designating Mary Smith. If she is 'not aware that she is Mary Smith,' she may assent to a sentence with 'I,' but dissent from the corresponding sentence with 'Mary Smith.' It is quite possible that any attempt to clear up the logic of all this will involve itself in the problem of the present paper. (For this purpose, the present discussion might be extended to demonstratives and indexicals.)

The writing of this paper had partial support from a grant from the National Science Foundation, a John Simon Guggenheim Foundation Fellowship, a Visiting Fellowship at All Souls College, Oxford, and a sabbatical leave from Princeton University. Various people at the Jerusalem Encounter and elsewhere, who will not be enumerated, influenced the paper through discussion.

Chapter 15

Individualism and the Mental

T. Burge

Since Hegel's *Phenomenology of Spirit*, a broad, inarticulate division of emphasis between the individual and his social environment has marked philosophical discussions of mind. On one hand, there is the traditional concern with the individual subject of mental states and events. In the elderly Cartesian tradition, the spotlight is on what exists or transpires 'in' the individual – his secret cogitations, his innate cognitive structures, his private perceptions and introspections, his grasping of ideas, concepts, or forms. More evidentially oriented movements, such as behaviorism and its liberalized progeny, have highlighted the individual's publicly observable behavior – his input-output relations and the dispositions, states, or events that mediate them. But both Cartesian and behaviorist viewpoints tend to feature the individual subject. On the other hand, there is the Hegelian preoccupation with the role of social institutions in shaping the individual and the content of his thought. This tradition has dominated the continent since Hegel. But it has found echoes in English-speaking philosophy during this century in the form of a concentration on language. Much philosophical work on language and mind has been in the interests of Cartesian or behaviorist viewpoints that I shall term 'individualistic.' But many of Wittgenstein's remarks about mental representation point up a social orientation that is discernible from his flirtations with behaviorism. And more recent work on the theory of reference has provided glimpses of the role of social cooperation in determining what an individual thinks.

In many respects, of course, these emphases within philosophy – individualistic and social – are compatible. To an extent, they may be regarded simply as different currents in the turbulent stream of ideas that has washed the

From P. French *et al.* (eds) (1979), *Midwest Studies in Philosophy* Vol IV, Minneapolis, MN: University of Minnesota Press.

intellectual landscape during the last hundred and some odd years. But the role of the social environment has received considerably less clear-headed philosophical attention (though perhaps not less philosophical attention) than the role of the states, occurrences, or acts in, on, or by the individual. Philosophical discussions of social factors have tended to be obscure, evocative, metaphorical, or platitudinous, or to be bent on establishing some large thesis about the course of history and the destiny of man. There remains much room for sharp delineation. I shall offer some considerations that stress social factors in descriptions of an individual's mental phenomena. These considerations call into question individualistic presuppositions of several traditional and modern treatments of mind. I shall conclude with some remarks about mental models.

I. Terminological Matters

Our ordinary mentalistic discourse divides broadly into two sorts of idiom. One typically makes reference to mental states or events in terms of sentential expressions. The other does not. A clear case of the first kind of idiom is 'Alfred thinks that his friends' sofa is ugly'. A clear case of the second sort is 'Alfred is in pain'. Thoughts, beliefs, intentions, and so forth are typically specified in terms of subordinate sentential clauses, that-clauses, which may be judged as true or false. Pains, feels, tickles, and so forth have no special semantical relation to sentences or to truth or falsity. There are intentional idioms that fall in the second category on this characterization, but that share important semantical features with expressions in the first – idioms like 'Al worships Buicks'. But I shall not sort these out here. I shall discuss only the former kind of mentalistic idiom. The extension of the discussion to other intentional idioms will not be difficult.

In an ordinary sense, the noun phrases that embed sentential expressions in mentalistic idioms provide the *content* of the mental state or event. We shall call that-clauses and their grammatical variants '*content clauses*.' Thus the expression 'that sofas are more comfortable than pews' provides the content of Alfred's belief that sofas are more comfortable than pews. My phrase 'provides the content' represents an attempt at remaining neutral, at least for present purposes, among various semantical and metaphysical accounts of precisely how that-clauses function and precisely what, if anything, contents are.

Although the notion of content is, for present purposes, ontologically neutral, I do think of it as holding a place in a systematic *theory* of mentalistic language. The question of when to count contents different, and when the same, is answerable to theoretical restrictions. It is often remarked that in a given context we may ascribe to a person two that-clauses that are only loosely equivalent and count them as attributions of the 'same attitude.' We may say that Al's intention to climb Mt. McKinley and his intention to climb the highest mountain in the United States are the 'same intention.' (I intend the terms for the mountain to occur obliquely here. See later discussion.) This sort of point extends even to content clauses with extensionally non-equivalent counterpart notions. For contextually relevant purposes, we might count a thought that the glass contains some water as 'the same thought' as a thought that the glass contains some thirst-quenching liquid, particularly if we have no reason to attribute either content as opposed to the other, and distinctions between them are contextually irrelevant. Nevertheless, in both these examples, every systematic theory I know of would want to represent the semantical contribution of the content-clauses in distinguishable ways – as 'providing different contents.'

One reason for doing so is that the person himself is capable of having different attitudes described by the different content-clauses, even if these differences are irrelevant in a particular context. (Al might have developed the intention to climb the highest mountain before developing the intention to climb Mt. McKinley – regardless of whether he, in fact, did so.) A second reason is that the counterpart components of the that-clauses allude to distinguishable elements in people's cognitive lives. 'Mt. McKinley' and 'the highest mountain in the U.S.' serve, or might serve, to indicate cognitively different notions. This is a vague, informal way of generalizing Frege's point: the thought that Mt. McKinley is the highest mountain in the U.S. is potentially interesting or informative. The thought that Mt. McKinley is Mt. McKinley is not. Thus when we say in a given context that attribution of different contents is attribution of the 'same attitude,' we use 'same attitude' in a way similar to the way we use 'same car' when we say that people who drive Fords (or green 1970 Ford Mavericks) drive the 'same car.' For contextual purposes different cars are counted as 'amounting to the same.'

Although this use of 'content' is theoretical, it is not I think theoretically controversial. In cases where we shall be counting contents different, the cases will be uncontentious: On any systematic theory, differences in the *extension* – the actual denotation, referent, or application – of counterpart expressions in that-clauses will be semantically represented, and will, in our terms, make for differences in content. I shall be avoiding the more controversial, but interesting, questions about the general conditions under which sentences in that-clauses can be expected to provide the same content.

I should also warn of some subsidiary terms. I shall be (and have been) using the term '*notion*' to apply to components or elements of contents. Just as whole that-clauses provide the content of a person's attitude, semantically relevant components of that-clauses will be taken to indicate notions that enter into the attitude (or the attitude's content). This term is supposed to be just as ontologically neutral as its fellow. When I talk of understanding or mastering the notion of contract, I am not relying on any special epistemic or ontological theory, except insofar as the earlier-mentioned theoretical restrictions on the notion of content are inherited by the notion of notion. The expression, '*understanding (mastering) a notion*' is to be construed more or less intuitively. Understanding the notion of contract comes roughly to knowing what a contract is. One can master the notion of contract without mastering the term 'contract' – at the very least if one speaks some language other than English that has a term roughly synonymous with 'contract'. (An analogous point holds for my use of 'mastering a content'.) Talk of notions is roughly similar to talk of concepts in an informal sense. 'Notion' has the advantage of being easier to separate from traditional theoretical commitments.

I speak of *attributing* an attitude, content, or notion, and of *ascribing* a that-clause or other piece of language. Ascriptions are the linguistic analogs of attributions. This use of 'ascribe' is nonstandard, but convenient and easily assimilated.

There are semantical complexities involving the behavior of expressions in content clauses, most of which we can skirt. But some must be touched on. Basic to the subject is the observation that expressions in content clauses are often not intersubstitutable with extensionally equivalent expressions in such a way as to maintain the truth value of the containing sentence. Thus from the facts that water is H_2O and that Bertrand thought that water is not fit to drink, it does not follow that Bertrand thought that H_2O is not fit to drink. When an expression like 'water' functions in a content clause so that it is not freely exchangeable with all extensionally equivalent expressions, we shall say that it has *oblique occurrence*. Roughly speaking, the reason why 'water' and 'H_2O' are not interchangeable in our report of Bertrand's thought is that 'water' plays a role in characterizing a different mental act or state from that which 'H_2O' would play a role in characterizing. In this context at least, thinking that water is not fit to drink is different from thinking that H_2O is not fit to drink.

By contrast, there are non-oblique occurrences of expressions in content clauses. One might say that some water – say, the water in the glass over there – is thought by Bertrand to be impure; or that Bertrand thought that *that* water is impure. And one might intend to make no distinction that would be lost by replacing 'water' with 'H_2O' – or 'that water' with 'that H_2O' or 'that common liquid', or any other expression extensionally equivalent with 'that water'. We might allow these exchanges even though Bertrand had never heard of, say, H_2O. In such purely non-oblique occurrences, 'water' plays *no role* in providing the *content* of Bertrand's thought, *on our use of 'content'*, or (in any narrow sense) in characterizing Bertrand or his mental state. Nor is the water part of Bertrand's thought content. We speak of Bertrand *thinking his content of* the water. At its nonoblique occurrence, the term 'that water' simply isolates, in one of many equally good ways, a portion of wet stuff to which Bertrand or his thought is related or applied. In certain cases, it may also mark a context in which Bertrand's thought is applied. But it is expressions at oblique occurrences within content clauses that primarily do the job of providing the content of mental states or events, and in characterizing the person.

Mentalistic discourse containing obliquely occurring expressions has traditionally been called *intentional discourse.* The historical reasons for this nomenclature are complex and partly confused. But roughly speaking, grammatical contexts involving oblique occurrences have been fixed upon as specially relevant to the representational character (sometimes called 'intentionality') of mental states and events. Clearly oblique occurrences in mentalistic discourse have something to do with characterizing a person's epistemic perspective – how things seem to him, or in an informal sense, how they are represented to him. So without endorsing all the commitments of this tradition, I shall take over its terminology.

The crucial point in the preceding discussion is the assumption that obliquely occurring expressions in content clauses are a primary means of identifying a person's intentional mental states or events. A further point is worth remarking here. It is normal to suppose that those content clauses correctly ascribable to a person that are not in general intersubstitutable *salva veritate* – and certainly those that involve extensionally non-equivalent counterpart expressions – identify different mental states or events.

I have cited contextual exceptions to this normal supposition, at least in a manner of speaking. We sometimes count distinctions in content irrelevant for purposes of a given attribution, particularly where our evidence for the precise content of a person or animal's attitude is skimpy. Different contents may contextually identify (what amount to) the 'same attitude.' I have indicated that even in these contexts, I think it best, strictly speaking, to construe distinct contents as describing different mental states or events that are merely equivalent for the purposes at hand. I believe that this view is widely accepted. But nothing I say will depend on it. For any distinct contents, there will be imaginable contexts of attribution in which, even in the loosest, most informal ways of speaking, those contents would be said to describe different mental states or events. This is virtually a consequence of the theoretical role of contents, discussed earlier. Since our discussion will have an 'in principle' character, I shall take these contexts to be the relevant ones. Most of the cases we discuss will involve *extensional* differences between obliquely occurring counterpart expressions in that-clauses. In such cases, it is particularly natural and normal to take different contents as identifying different mental states or events.

II. A Thought Experiment

IIa First case

We now turn to a three-step thought experiment. Suppose first that:

> A given person has a large number of attitudes commonly attributed with content clauses containing 'arthritis' in oblique occurrence. For example, he thinks (correctly) that he has had arthritis for years, that his arthritis in his wrists and fingers is more painful than his arthritis in his ankles, that it is better to have arthritis than cancer of the liver, that stiffening joints is a symptom of arthritis, that certain sorts of aches are characteristic of arthritis, that there are various kinds of arthritis, and so forth. In short, he has a wide range of such attitudes. In addition to these unsurprising attitudes, he thinks falsely that he has developed arthritis in the thigh.

Generally competent in English, rational and intelligent, the patient reports to his doctor his fear that his arthritis has now lodged in his thigh. The doctor replies by telling him that this cannot be so, since arthritis is specifically an inflammation of joints. Any dictionary could have told him the same. The patient is surprised, but relinquishes his view and goes on to ask what might be wrong with his thigh.

The second step of the thought experiment consists of a counterfactual supposition. We are to conceive of a situation in which the patient proceeds from birth through the same course of physical events that he actually does, right to and including the time at which he first reports his fear to his doctor. Precisely the same things (non-intentionally described) happen to him. He has the same physiological history, the same diseases, the same internal physical occurrences. He goes through the same motions, engages in the same behavior, has the same sensory intake (physiologically described). His dispositions to respond to stimuli are explained in physical theory as the effects of the same proximate causes. All of this extends to his interaction with linguistic expressions. He says and hears the same words (word forms) at the same times he actually does. He develops the disposition to assent to 'Arthritis can occur in the thigh' and 'I have arthritis in the thigh' as a result of the same physically described proximate causes. Such dispositions might have arisen in a number of ways. But we can suppose that in both actual and counterfactual situations, he acquires the word 'arthritis' from casual conversation or reading, and never hearing anything to prejudice him for or against applying it in the way that he does, he applies the word to an ailment in his thigh (or to ailments in the limbs of others) which seems to produce pains or other symptoms roughly similar to the disease in his hands and ankles. In both actual and counterfactual cases, the disposition is never reinforced or extinguished up until the time when he expresses himself to his doctor. We further imagine that the patient's non-intentional, phenomenal experience is the same. He has the same pains, visual fields, images, and internal verbal rehearsals. The *counterfactuality* in the supposition touches only the patient's social environment. In actual fact, 'arthritis', as used in his community, does not apply to ailments outside joints. Indeed, it fails to do so by a standard, non-technical dictionary definition. But in our imagined case, physicians, lexicographers, and informed laymen apply 'arthritis' not only to arthritis but to various other rheumatoid ailments. The standard use of the term is to be conceived to encompass the patient's actual misuse. We could imagine either that arthritis had not been singled out as a family of diseases, or that some other term besides 'arthritis' were applied, though not commonly by laymen, specifically to arthritis. We may also suppose that this difference and those necessarily associated with it are the only differences between the counterfactual situation and the actual one. (Other people besides the patient will, of course, behave differently.) To summarize the second step:

> The person might have had the same physical history and non-intentional mental phenomena while the word 'arthritis' was conventionally applied, and defined to apply, to various rheumatoid ailments, including the one in the person's thigh, as well as to arthritis.

The final step is an interpretation of the counterfactual case, or an addition to it as so far described. It is reasonable to suppose that:

> In the counterfactual situation, the patient lacks some – probably *all* – of the attitudes commonly attributed with content clauses containing 'arthritis' in oblique occurrence. He lacks the occurrent thoughts or beliefs that he has arthritis in the thigh, that he has had arthritis for years, that stiffening joints and various sorts of aches are symptoms of arthritis, that his father had arthritis, and so on.

We suppose that in the counterfactual case we cannot correctly ascribe any content clause containing an oblique occurrence of the term 'arthritis'. It is hard to see how the patient could have picked up the notion of arthritis. The word 'arthritis' in the counterfactual community does not mean *arthritis*. It does not apply only to inflammations of joints. We suppose that no other word in the patient's repertoire means *arthritis*. 'Arthritis', in the counterfactual situation, differs both in dictionary definition and in extension from 'arthritis' as we use it. Our ascriptions of content clauses to the patient (and ascriptions within his community) would not constitute attributions of the same contents we actually attribute. For counterpart expressions in the content clauses that are actually and counterfactually ascribable are not even extensionally equivalent. However we describe the patient's attitudes in the counterfactual situation, it will not be with a term or phrase extensionally equivalent with 'arthritis'. So the patient's counterfactual attitude contents differ from his actual ones.

The upshot of these reflections is that the patient's mental contents differ while his entire physical and non-intentional mental histories, considered in isolation from their social context, remain the same. (We could have supposed that he dropped dead at the time he first expressed his fear to the doctor.) The differences seem to stem from differences 'outside' the patient considered as an isolated physical organism, causal mechanism, or seat of consciousness. The difference in his mental contents is attributable to differences in his social environment. In sum, the patient's internal qualitative experiences, his physiological states and events, his behaviorally described stimuli and responses, his dispositions to behave, and whatever sequences of states (non-intentionally described) mediated his input and output – all these remain constant, while his attitude contents differ, even in the extensions of counterpart notions. As we observed at the outset, such differences are ordinarily taken to spell differences in mental states and events.

IIb Further exemplifications

The argument has an extremely wide application. It does not depend, for example, on the kind of word 'arthritis' is. We could have used an artifact term, an ordinary natural kind word, a color adjective, a social role term, a term for a historical style, an abstract noun, an action verb, a physical movement verb, or any of various other sorts of words. I prefer to leave open precisely how far one can generalize the argument. But I think it has a very wide scope. The argument can get under way in any case where it is intuitively possible to attribute a mental state or event whose content involves a notion that the subject incompletely understands. As will become clear, this possibility is the key to the thought experiment. I want to give a more concrete sense of the possibility before going further.

It is useful to reflect on the number and variety of intuitively clear cases in which it is normal to attribute a content that the subject incompletely understands. One need only thumb through a dictionary for an hour or so to develop a sense of the extent to which one's beliefs are infected by incomplete understanding.[1] The phenomenon is rampant in our pluralistic age.

a. Most cases of incomplete understanding that support the thought experiment will be fairly idiosyncratic. There is a reason for this. Common linguistic errors, if entrenched, tend to become common usage. But a generally competent speaker is bound to have numerous words in his repertoire, possibly even common words, that he somewhat misconstrues. Many of these misconstruals will not be such as to deflect ordinary ascriptions of that-clauses involving the incompletely mastered term in oblique occurrence. For example, one can imagine a generally competent, rational adult having a large number of attitudes involving the notion of sofa – including beliefs that *those* (some sofas) are sofas, that some sofas are beige, that his neighbors have a new sofa, that he would rather sit in a sofa for an hour than on a church pew. In addition, he might think that sufficiently broad (but single-seat) overstuffed armchairs are sofas. With care, one can develop a thought experiment parallel to the one in section IIa, in which at least some of the person's attitude contents (particularly, in this case, contents of occurrent mental events) differ, while his physical history, dispositions to behavior, and phenomenal experience – non-intentionally and asocially – remain the same.

b. Although most relevant misconstruals are fairly idiosyncratic, there do seem to be certain types of error which are relatively common – but not so common and uniform as to suggest that the relevant terms take on new sense. Much of our vocabulary is taken over from others who, being specialists, understand our terms better than we do.[2] The use of scientific terms by laymen is a rich source of cases. As the arthritis example illustrates, the thought experiment does not depend on specially technical terms. I shall leave it to the imagination of the reader to spin out further examples of this sort.

c. One need not look to the laymen's acquisitions from science for examples. People used to buying beef brisket in stores or ordering it in restaurants (and conversant with it in a general way) probably often develop mistaken beliefs (or uncertainties) about just what brisket is. For example, one might think that brisket is a cut from the flank or rump, or that it includes not only the lower part of the chest but also the upper part, or that it is specifically a cut of beef and not of, say, pork. No one hesitates as ascribe to such people content-clauses with 'brisket' in oblique occurrence. For example, a person may believe that he is eating brisket under these circumstances (where 'brisket' occurs in oblique position); or he may think that brisket tends to be tougher than loin. Some of these attitudes may be false; many will be true. We can imagine a counterfactual case in which the person's physical history, his dispositions, and his non-intentional mental life, are all the same, but in which 'brisket' is commonly applied in a different way – perhaps in precisely the way the person thinks it applies. For example, it might apply only to beef and to the upper and lower parts of the chest. In such a case, as in the sofa and arthritis cases, it would seem that the person would (or might) lack some or all of the propositional attitudes that are actually attributed with content clauses involving 'brisket' in oblique position.

d. Someone only generally versed in music history, or superficially acquainted with a few drawings of musical instruments, might naturally but mistakenly come to think that clavichords included harpsichords without legs. He may have many other beliefs involving the notion of clavichord, and many of these may be true. Again, with some care, a relevant thought experiment can be generated.

e. A fairly common mistake among lawyers' clients is to think that one cannot have a contract with someone unless there has been a written agreement. The client might be clear in intending 'contract' (in the relevant sense) to apply to agreements, not to pieces of paper. Yet he may take it as part of the meaning of the word, or the essence of law, that a piece of formal writing is a necessary condition for establishing a contract. His only experiences with contracts might have involved formal documents, and he undergeneralizes. It is not terribly important here whether one says that the client misunderstands the term's meaning, or alternatively that the client makes a mistake about the essence of contracts. In either case, he misconceives what a contract is; yet ascriptions involving the term in oblique position are made anyway.

It is worth emphasizing here that I intend the misconception to involve the subject's attaching counterfactual consequences to his mistaken belief about contracts. Let me elaborate this a bit. A common dictionary definition of 'contract' is 'legally binding agreement'. As I am imagining the case, the client does not explicitly define 'contract' to himself in this way (though he might use this phrase in explicating the term). And he is not merely making a mistake about what the law happens to enforce. If asked why unwritten agreements are not contracts, he is likely to say something like, 'They just aren't' or 'It is part of the nature of the law and legal practice that they have no force'. He is not disposed without prodding to answer, 'It would be possible but impractical to give unwritten agreements legal force'. He might concede this. But he would add that such agreements would not be contracts. He regards a document as inseparable from contractual obligation, regardless of whether he takes this to be a matter of meaning or a metaphysical essentialist truth about contracts.

Needless to say, these niceties are philosopher's distinctions. They are not something an ordinary man is likely to have strong opinions about. My point is that the thought experiment is independent of these distinctions. It does not depend on misunderstandings of dictionary meaning. One might say that the client understood the term's dictionary meaning, but misunderstood its essential application in the law – misconceived the nature of contracts. The thought experiment still flies. In a counterfactual case in which the law enforces both written and unwritten agreements and in which the subject's behavior and so forth are the same, but in which 'contract' *means* 'legally binding agreement based on written document', we would not attribute to him a mistaken belief that a contract requires written agreement, although the lawyer might have to point out that there are other legally binding agreements that do not require documents. Similarly, the client's other propositional attitudes would no longer involve the notion of contract, but another more restricted notion.

f. People sometimes make mistakes about color ranges. They may correctly apply a color term to a certain color, but also mistakenly apply it to shades of a neighboring color. When asked to explain the color term, they cite the standard cases (for 'red', the color of blood, fire engines, and so forth). But they apply the term somewhat beyond its conventionally established range – beyond the reach of its vague borders. They think that fire engines, including *that* one, are red. They observe that red roses are covering the trellis. But they also think that *those* things are a shade of red (whereas they are not). Second looks do not change their opinion. But they give in when other speakers confidently correct them in unison.

This case extends the point of the contract example. The error is linguistic or conceptual in something like the way that the shopper's mistake involving the notion of brisket is. It is not an ordinary empirical error. But one may reasonably doubt that the subjects misunderstand the dictionary meaning of the color term. Holding their non-intentional phenomenal experience, physical history, and behavioral dispositions constant, we can imagine that 'red' were applied as they mistakenly apply it. In such cases, we would no longer ascribe content-clauses involving the term 'red' in oblique position. The attribution of the correct beliefs about fire engines and roses would be no less affected than the attribution of the beliefs that, in the actual case, display the misapplication. Cases bearing out the latter point are common in anthropological reports on communities whose color terms do not match ours. Attributions of content typically allow for the differences in conventionally established color ranges.

Here is not the place to refine our rough distinctions among the various kinds of misconceptions that serve the thought experiment. Our philosophical purposes do not depend on how these distinctions are drawn. Still, it is important to see what an array of conceptual errors is common among us. And it is important to note that such errors do not always or automatically prevent attribution of mental content provided by the very terms that are incompletely understood or misapplied. The thought experiment is nourished by this aspect of common practice.

IIc Expansion and delineation of the thought experiment

As I have tried to suggest in the preceding examples, the relevant attributions in the first step of the thought experiment need not display the subject's error. They may be attributions of a true content. We can begin with a propositional attitude that involved the misconceived notion, but in a true, unproblematic application of it: for example, the patient's belief that he, like his father, developed arthritis in the ankles and wrists at age 58 (where 'arthritis' occurs obliquely).

One need not even rely on an underlying *mis*conception in the thought experiment. One may pick a case in which the subject only partially understands an expression. He may apply it firmly and correctly in a range of cases, but be unclear or agnostic about certain of its applications or implications which, in fact, are fully established in common practice. Most of the examples we gave previously can be reinterpreted in this way. To take a new one, imagine that our protagonist is unsure whether his father has mortgages on the car and house, or just one on the house. He is a little uncertain about exactly how the loan and collateral must be arranged in order for there to be a mortgage, and he is not clear about whether one may have mortgages on anything other than houses. He is sure, however, that Uncle Harry paid off his mortgage. Imagine our man constant in the ways previously indicated and that 'mortgage' commonly applied only to mortgages on houses. But imagine banking practices themselves to be the same. Then the subject's uncertainty would plausibly not involve the notion of mortgage. Nor would his other propositional attitudes be correctly attributed with the term 'mortgage' in oblique position. Partial understanding is as good as misunderstanding for our purposes.

On the other hand, the thought experiment does appear to depend on the possibility of someone's having a propositional attitude despite an incomplete mastery of some notion in its content. To see why this appears to be so, let us try to run through a thought experiment, attempting to avoid any imputation of incomplete understanding. Suppose the subject thinks falsely that all swans are white. One can certainly hold the features of swans and the subject's non-intentional phenomenal experience, physical history, and non-intentional dispositions constant, and imagine that 'swan' meant 'white swan' (and perhaps some other term unfamiliar to the subject, meant what 'swan' means). Could one reasonably interpret the subject as having different attitude contents without at some point invoking a misconception? The questions to be asked here are about the subject's dispositions. For example, in the actual case, if he were shown a black swan and told that he was wrong, would he fairly naturally concede his mistake? Or would he respond, 'I'm doubtful that that's a swan,' until we brought in dictionaries, encyclopedias, and other native speakers to correct his usage? In the latter case, his understanding of 'swan' would be deviant. Suppose then that in the actual situation he would respond normally to the counterexample. Then there is reason to say that he understands the notion of swan correctly; and his error is not conceptual or linguistic, but empirical in an ordinary and narrow sense. (Of course, the line we are drawing here is pretty fuzzy.) When one comes to the counterfactual stage of the thought experiment, the subject has the same dispositions to respond pliably to the presentation of a black specimen. But such a response would suggest a misunderstanding of the term 'swan' as counterfactually used. For in the counterfactual community, what they call 'swans' could not fail to be white. The mere presentation of a black swan would be irrelevant to the definitional truth 'All swans are white'. I have not set this case up as an example of the thought experiment's going through. Rather I have used it to support the conjecture that *if* the thought experiment is to work, one must at some stage find the subject believing (or having some attitude characterized by) a content, despite an incomplete understanding or misapplication. An ordinary empirical error appears not to be sufficient.

It would be a mistake, however, to think that incomplete understanding, in the sense that the argument requires, is in general an unusual or even deviant phenomenon. *What I have called 'partial understanding' is common or even normal in the case of a large number of expressions in our vocabularies.*

'Arthritis' is a case in point. Even if by the grace of circumstance a person does not fall into views that run counter to the term's meaning or application, it would not be in the least deviant or 'socially unacceptable ' to have no clear attitude that would block such views. 'Brisket', 'contract', 'recession', 'sonata', 'deer', 'elm' (to borrow a well-known example), 'pre-amplifier', 'carburetor', 'gothic', 'fermentation', probably provide analogous cases. Continuing the list is largely a matter of patience. The sort of 'incomplete understanding' required by the thought experiment includes quite ordinary, nondeviant phenomena.

It is worth remarking that the thought experiment as originally presented might be run in reverse. The idea would be to start with an ordinary belief or thought involving no incomplete understanding. Then we find the incomplete understanding in the second step. For example, properly understanding 'arthritis', a patient may think (correctly) that he has arthritis. He happens to have heard of arthritis only occurring in joints, and he correctly believes that that is where arthritis always occurs. Holding his physical history, dispositions, and pain constant, we imagine that 'arthritis' commonly applies to rheumatoid ailments of all sorts. Arthritis has not been singled out for special mention. If the patient were told by a doctor 'You also have arthritis in the thigh', the patient would be disposed (as he is in the actual case) to respond, 'Really? I didn't know that one could have arthritis except in joints'. The doctor would answer, 'No, arthritis occurs in muscles, tendons, bursas, and elsewhere'. The patient would stand corrected. The notion that the doctor and patient would be operating with in such a case would not be that of arthritis.

My reasons for not having originally set out the thought experiment in this way are largely heuristic. As will be seen, discussion of the thought experiment will tend to center on the step involving incomplete understanding. And I wanted to encourage you, dear reader, to imagine actual cases of incomplete understanding in your own linguistic community. Ordinary intuitions in the domestic case are perhaps less subject to premature warping in the interests of theory. Cases involving not only mental content attribution, but also translation of a foreign tongue are more vulnerable to intrusion of side issues.

A secondary reason for not beginning with this 'reversed' version of the thought experiment is that I find it doubtful whether the thought experiment always works in symmetric fashion. There may be special intuitive problems in certain cases – perhaps, for example, cases involving perceptual natural kinds. We may give special interpretations to individuals' misconceptions in imagined foreign communities, when those misconceptions seem to match our conceptions. In other words, there may be some systematic intuitive bias in favor of at least certain of our notions for purposes of interpreting the misconceptions of imagined foreigners. I do not want to explore the point here. I think that any such bias is not always crucial, and that the thought experiment frequently works 'symmetrically.' We have to take account of a person's community in interpreting his words and describing his attitudes – and this holds in the foreign case as well as in the domestic case.

The reversal of the thought experiment brings home the important point that *even those propositional attitudes not infected by incomplete understanding* depend for their content on social factors that are independent of the individual, asocially and non-intentionally described. For if the social environment had been appropriately different, the contents of those attitudes would have been different.

Even *apart* from reversals of the thought experiment, it is plausible (in the light of its original versions) that our well-understood propositional attitudes depend partly for their content on social factors independent of the individual, asocially and non-intentionally construed. For each of us can reason as follows. Take a set of attitudes that involve a given notion and whose contents are well-understood by me. It is only contingent that I understand that notion as well as I do. Now holding my community's practices constant, imagine that I understand the given notion incompletely, but that the deficient understanding is such that it does not prevent my having attitude contents involving that notion. In fact, imagine that I am in the situation envisaged in the first step of one of the original thought experiments. In such a case, a proper subset of the original set of my actual attitude contents would, or might, remain the same – intuitively, at least those of my actual attitudes whose justification or point is untouched by my imagined deficient understanding. (In the arthritis case, an example would be a true belief that many old people have arthritis.) These attitude contents remain constant despite the fact that my understanding, inference patterns, behavior, dispositions, and so on would in important ways be different and partly inappropriate to applications of the given notion. What is it that enables these unaffected contents to remain applications of the relevant notion? It is not *just* that my understanding, inference patterns, behavior, and so forth are enough like my actual understanding, inference patterns, behavior, and so forth. For if communal practice had *also* varied so as to apply the relevant notion as I am imagining I misapply it, then my attitude contents would not involve the relevant notion at all. This argument suggests that communal practice is a factor (in addition to my understanding, inference patterns, and perhaps behavior, physical activity, and other features) in fixing the contents of my attitudes, even in cases where I fully understand the content.

IId Independence from factive-verb and indexical-reference paradigms

The thought experiment does not play on psychological 'success' verbs or 'factive' verbs – verbs like 'know', 'regret', 'realize', 'remember', 'foresee', 'perceive'. This point is important for our purposes because such verbs suggest an easy and clearcut distinction between the contribution of the individual subject and the objective, 'veridical' contribution of the environment to making the verbs applicable. (Actually the matter becomes more complicated on reflection, but we shall stay with the simplest cases.) When a person knows that snow is common in Greenland, his knowledge obviously depends on more that the way the person is. It depends on there actually being a lot of snow in Greenland. His mental state (belief that snow is common in Greenland) must be successful in a certain way (true). By changing the environment, one could change the truth value of the content, so that the subject could no longer be said to know the content. It is part of the burden of our argument that even intentional mental states of the individual like beliefs, which carry no implication of veridicality or success, cannot be understood by focusing purely on the individual's acts, dispositions, and 'inner' goings on.

The thought experiment also does not rest on the phenomenon of indexicality, or on *de re* attitudes, in any direct way. When Alfred refers to an apple, saying to himself 'That is wholesome,' what he refers to depends not just on the content of what he says or thinks, but on what apple is before him. Without altering the meaning of Alfred's utterance, the nature of his perceptual experiences, or his physical acts or dispositions, we could conceive an exchange of the actual apple for another one that is indistinguishable to Alfred. We would thereby conceive him as referring to something different and even as saying something with a different truth value.

This rather obvious point about indexicality has come to be seen as providing a model for understanding a certain range of mental states or events – *de re* attitudes. The precise characterization of this range is no simple philosophical task. But the clearest cases involve non-obliquely occurring terms in content clauses. When we say that Bertrand thinks of some water that it would not slake his thirst (where 'water' occurs in purely non-oblique position), we attribute a *de re* belief to Bertrand. We assume that Bertrand has something like an indexical relation to the water. The fact that Bertrand believes something of some water, rather than of a portion of some other liquid that is indistinguishable to him, depends partly on the fact that it is water to which Bertrand is contextually, 'indexically' related. For intuitively we could have exchanged the liquids without changing Bertrand and thereby changed what Bertrand believed his belief content *of* – and even whether his belief was true of it.[3] It is easy to interpret such cases by holding that the subject's mental states and contents (with allowances for brute differences in the contexts in which he applies those contents) remain the same. The differences in the situations do not pertain in any fundamental way to the subject's mind or the nature of his mental content, but to how his mind or content is related to the world.

I think this interpretation of standard indexical and *de re* cases is broadly correct, although it involves oversimplifications and demands refinements. But what I want to emphasize here is that it is inapplicable to the cases our thought experiment fixes upon.

It seems to me clear that the thought experiment need not rely on *de re* attitudes at all. The subject need not have entered into special *en rapport* or quasi-indexical relations with objects that the misunderstood term applies to in order for the argument to work. We can appeal to attitudes that would usually be regarded as paradigmatic cases of *de dicto*, non-indexical, *non-de-re*, mental attitudes or events. The primary mistake in the contract example is one such, but we could choose others to suit the reader's taste. To insist that such attitudes must all be indexically infected or *de re* would, I think, be to trivialize and emasculate these notions, making nearly all attitudes *de re*. All *de dicto* attitudes presuppose *de re* attitudes. But it does not follow that indexical or *de re* elements in every attitude. (Cf. notes 2 and 3.)

I shall not, however, argue this point here. The claim that is crucial is not that our argument does not fix on *de re* attitudes. It is, rather, that the social differences between the actual and counterfactual situations affect the *content* of the subject's attitudes. That is, the difference affects standard cases of obliquely occurring, cognitive-content-conveying expressions in content clauses. For example, still with his misunderstanding, the subject might think that this (referring to his disease in his hands) is arthritis. Or he might think *de re* of the disease in his ankle (or of the disease in his thigh) that his arthritis is painful. It does not really matter whether the relevant attitude is *de re* or purely *de dicto*. What is crucial to our argument is that the occurrence of 'arthritis' is oblique and contributes to a characterization of the subject's mental content. One might even hold, implausibly I think, that all the subject's attitudes involving the notion of arthritis are *de re*, that 'arthritis' in that-clauses *indexically* picks out the property of being arthritis, or something like that. The fact remains that the term occurs obliquely in the relevant cases and serves in characterizing the *dicta* or contents of the subject's attitudes. The thought experiment exploits this fact.

Approaches to the mental that I shall later criticize as excessively individualistic tend to assimilate environmental aspects of mental phenomena to either the factive-verb or indexical-reference paradigm. (Cf. note 2.) This sort of assimilation suggests that one might maintain a relatively clearcut distinction between extramental and mental aspects of mentalistic attributions. And it may encourage the idea that the distinctively mental aspects can be understood fundamentally in terms of the individual's abilities, dispositions, states, and so forth, considered in isolation from his social surroundings. Our argument undermines this latter suggestion. Social context infects even the distinctively mental features of mentalistic attributions. No man's intentional mental phenomena are insular. Every man is a piece of the social continent, a part of the social main.

III. Reinterpretations

IIIa Methodology

I find that most people unspoiled by conventional philosophical training regard the three steps of the thought experiment as painfully obvious. Such folk tend to chafe over my filling in details or elaborating on strategy. I think this naivete appropriate. But for sophisticates the three steps require defense.

Before launching a defense, I want to make a few remarks about its methodology. My objective is to better understand our common mentalistic notions. Although such notions are subject to revision and refinement, I take it as evident that there is philosophical interest in theorizing about them as they now are. I assume that a primary way of achieving theoretical understanding is to concentrate on our *discourse* about mentalistic notions. Now it is, of course, never obvious at the outset how much idealization, regimentation, or special interpretation is necessary in order to adequately understand ordinary discourse. Phenomena such as ambiguity, ellipsis, indexicality, idioms, and a host of others certainly demand some regimentation or special interpretation for purposes of linguistic theory. Moreover, more global considerations – such as simplicity in accounting for structural relations – often have effects on the cast of one's theory. For all that, there is a methodological bias in favor of taking natural discourse literally, other things being equal. For example, unless there are clear reasons for construing discourse as ambiguous, elliptical or involving special idioms, we should not so construe it. Literal interpretation is *ceteris paribus* preferred. My defense of the thought experiment, as I have interpreted it, partly rests on this principle.

This relatively non-theoretical interpretation of the thought experiment should be extended to the gloss on it that I provided in Section IIc. The notions of misconception, incomplete understanding, conceptual or linguistic error, and ordinary empirical error are to be taken as carrying little theoretical weight. I assume that these notions mark defensible, common-sense distinctions. But I need not take a position on available philosophical interpretations of these distinctions. In fact, I do not believe that understanding, in our examples, can be explicated as independent of empirical knowledge, or that the conceptual errors of our subjects are best seen as 'purely' mistakes about concepts and as involving no 'admixture' of error about 'the world.' With Quine, I find such talk about purity and mixture devoid of illumination or explanatory power. But my views on this matter neither entail nor are entailed by the premises of the arguments I give (cf. e.g., IIId). Those arguments seem to me to remain plausible under any of the relevant philosophical interpretations of the conceptual-ordinary-empirical distinction.

I have presented the experiment as appealing to ordinary intuition. I believe that common practice in the attribution of propositional attitudes is fairly represented by the various steps. This point is not really open to dispute. Usage may be divided in a few of the cases in which I have seen it as united. But broadly speaking, it seems to me undeniable that the individual steps of the thought experiment are acceptable to ordinary speakers in a wide variety of examples. The issue open to possible dispute is whether the steps should be taken in the literal way in which I have taken them, and thus whether the conclusion I have drawn from those steps is justified. In the remainder of

Section III, I shall try to vindicate the literal interpretation of our examples. I do this by criticizing, in order of increasing generality or abstractness, a series of attempts to reinterpret the thought experiment's first step. Ultimately, I suggest (IIId and IV) that these attempts derive from characteristically philosophical models that have little or no independent justification. A thoroughgoing review of these models would be out of bounds, but the present paper is intended to show that they are deficient as accounts of our actual practice of mentalistic attribution.

I shall have little further to say in defense of the second and third steps of the thought experiment. Both rest on their intuitive plausibility, not on some particular theory. The third step, for example, certainly does not depend on a view that contents are merely sentences the subject is disposed to utter, interpreted as his community interprets them. It is compatible with several philosophical accounts of mental contents, including those that appeal to more abstract entities such as Fregean thoughts or Russellian propositions, and those that seek to deny that content-clauses indicate any *thing* that might be called a content. I also do not claim that the fact that our subject lacks the relevant beliefs in the third step follows from the facts I have described. The point is that it is plausible, and certainly possible, that he would lack those beliefs.

The exact interpretation of the second step is relevant to a number of causal or functional theories of mental phenomena that I shall discuss in Section IV. The intuitive idea of the step is that none of the different physical, non-intentionally described causal chains set going by the differences in communal practice need affect our subjects in any way that would be relevant to an account of their mental contents. Differences in the behavior of other members of the community will, to be sure, affect the gravitational forces exerted on the subject. But I assume that these differences are irrelevant to macro-explanations of our subjects' physical movements and inner processes. They do not relevantly affect ordinary non-intentional physical explanations of how the subject acquires or is disposed to use the symbols in his repertoire. Of course, the social origins of a person's symbols do differ between actual and counterfactual cases. I shall return to this point in Sections IV and V. The remainder of Section III will be devoted to the first step of the thought experiment.

IIIb Incomplete understanding and standard cases of reinterpretation

The first step, as I have interpreted it, is the most likely to encounter opposition. In fact, there is a line of resistance that is second nature to linguistically oriented philosophers. According to this line, we should deny that, say, the patient really believed or thought that arthritis can occur outside of joints because he misunderstood the word 'arthritis'. More generally, we should deny that a subject could have any attitudes whose contents he incompletely understands.

What a person understands is indeed one of the chief factors that bear on what thoughts he can express in using words. If there were not deep and important connections between propositional attitudes and understanding, one could hardly expect one's attributions of mental content to facilitate reliable predictions of what a person will do, say, or think. But our examples provide reason to believe that these connections are not simple entailments to the effect that having a propositional attitude strictly implies full understanding of its content.

There are, of course, numerous situations in which we normally reinterpret or discount a person's words in deciding what he thinks. Philosophers often invoke such cases to bolster their animus against such attributions as the ones we made to our subjects: 'If a foreigner were to mouth the words "arthritis may occur in the thigh" or "my father had arthritis", not understanding what he uttered in the slightest, we would not say that he believed that arthritis may occur in the thigh, or that his father had arthritis. So why should we impute the belief to the patient?' Why, indeed? Or rather, why do we?

The question is a good one. We do want a general account of these cases. But the implied argument against our attribution is anemic. We tacitly and routinely distinguish between the cases I described and those in which a foreigner (or anyone) utters something without any comprehension. The best way to understand mentalistic notions is to recognize such differences in standard practice and try to account for them. One can hardly justify the assumption that full understanding of a content is in general a necessary condition for believing the content by appealing to some cases that tend to support the assumption in order to reject others that conflict with it.

It is a good method of discovery, I think, to note the sorts of cases philosophers tend to gravitate toward when they defend the view that the first step in the thought experiment should receive special interpretation. By reflecting on the difference between these cases and the cases we have cited, one should learn something about principles controlling mentalistic attribution.

I have already mentioned foreigners without command of the language. A child's imitation of our words and early attempts to use them provide similar examples. In these cases, mastery of the language and responsibility to its precepts have not been developed; and mental content attribution based on the meaning of words uttered tends to be precluded.

There are cases involving regional dialects. A person's deviance or ignorance judged by the standards of the larger community may count as normality or full mastery when evaluated from the regional perspective. Clearly, the regional standards tend to be the relevant ones for attributing content when the speaker's training or intentions are regionally oriented. The conditions for such orientation are complex, and I shall touch on them again in Section V. But there is no warrant in actual practice for treating each person's idiolect as always analogous to dialects whose words we automatically reinterpret – for purposes of mental content attribution – when usage is different. People are frequently held, and hold themselves, to the standards of their community when misuse or misunderstanding are at issue. One should distinguish these cases, which seem to depend on a certain *responsibility* to communal practice, from cases of automatic reinterpretation.

Tongue slips and Spoonerisms form another class of example where reinterpretation of a person's words is common and appropriate in arriving at an attribution of mental content. In these cases, we tend to exempt the speaker even from commitment to a homophonically formulated assertion content, as well as to the relevant mental content. The speaker's own behavior usually follows this line, often correcting himself when what he uttered is repeated back to him.

Malapropisms form a more complex class of examples. I shall not try to map it in detail. But in a fairly broad range of cases, we reinterpret a person's words at least in attributing mental content. If Archie says, 'Lead the way and we will precede', we routinely reinterpret the words in describing his expectations. Many of these cases seem to depend on the presumption that there are simple, superficial (for example, phonological) interference or exchange mechanisms that account for the linguistic deviance.

There are also examples of quite radical misunderstandings that sometimes generate reinterpretation. If a generally competent and reasonable speaker thinks that 'orangutan' applies to a fruit drink, we would be reluctant, and it would unquestionably be misleading, to take his words as revealing that he thinks he has been drinking orangutans for breakfast for the last few weeks. Such total misunderstanding often *seems* to block literalistic mental content attribution, at least in cases where we are not directly characterizing his mistake. (Contrary to philosophical lore, I am not convinced that such a man cannot correctly and literally be attributed a belief that an orangutan is a kind of fruit drink. But I shall not deal with the point here.)

There are also some cases that do not seem generally to prevent mental content attribution on the basis of literal interpretation of the subject's words in quite the same way as the others, but which deserve some mention. For almost any content except for those that directly display the subject's incomplete understanding, there will be many contexts in which it would be misleading to attribute that content to the subject without further comment. Suppose I am advising you about your legal liabilities in a situation where you have entered into what may be an unwritten contract. You ask me what Al would think. It would be misleading for me to reply that Al would think that you do not have a contract (or even do not have any legal problems), if I know that Al thinks a contract must be based on a formal document. Your evaluation of Al's thought would be crucially affected by his inadequate understanding. In such cases, it is incumbent on us to cite the subject's eccentricity: '(He would think that you do not have a contract, but then) he thinks that there is no such thing as a verbally based contract.'

Incidentally, the same sort of example can be constructed using attitudes that are abnormal, but that do not hinge on misunderstanding of any one notion. If Al had thought that only traffic laws and laws against violent crimes are ever prosecuted, it would be misleading for me to tell you that Al would think that you have no legal problems.

Both sorts of cases illustrate that in reporting a single attitude content, we typically suggest (implicate, perhaps) that the subject has a range of other attitudes that are normally associated with it. Some of these may provide reasons for it. In both sorts of cases, it is usually important to keep track of, and often to make explicit, the nature and extent of the subject's deviance. Otherwise, predictions and evaluations of his thought and action, based on normal background assumptions, will go awry. When the deviance is huge, attributions demand reinterpretation of the subject's words. Radical misunderstanding and mental instability are cases in point. But frequently, common practice seems to allow us to cancel the misleading suggestions by making explicit the subject's deviance, retaining literal interpretation of his words in our mentalistic attributions all the while.

All of the foregoing phenomena are relevant to accounting for standard practice. But they are no more salient than cases of straightforward belief attribution where the subject incompletely understands some notion in the attributed belief content. I think any impulse to say that common practice is *simply* inconsistent should be resisted (indeed, scorned). We cannot expect such practice to follow general principles rigorously. But even our brief discussion of the matter should have suggested the beginnings of generalizations about differences between cases where reinterpretation is standard and cases where it is not. A person's overall linguistic competence, his allegiance and responsibility to communal standards, the degree, source, and type of misunderstanding, the purposes of the report – all affect the issue. From a theoretical point of view, it would be a mistake to try to assimilate the cases in one direction or another. We do not want to credit a two-year-old who memorizes '$e = mc^2$' with belief in relativity theory. But the patient's attitudes involving the notion of arthritis should not be assimilated to the foreigner's uncomprehending pronunciations.

For purposes of defending the thought experiment and the arguments I draw from it, I can afford to be flexible about exactly how to generalize about these various phenomena. The thought experiment depends only on there being some cases in which a person's incomplete understanding does not force reinterpretation of his expressions in describing his mental contents. Such cases appear to be legion.

IIIc Four methods of reinterpreting the thought experiment

I now want to criticize attempts to argue that even in cases where we ordinarily do ascribe content clauses despite the subject's incomplete understanding of expressions in those clauses, such ascriptions should not be taken literally. In order to overturn our interpretation of the thought experiment's first step, one must argue that none of the cases I have cited is appropriately taken in the literal manner. One must handle (apparent) attributions of unproblematically true contents involving incompletely mastered notions, as well as attributions of contents that display the misconceptions or partial understandings. I do not doubt that one can erect logically coherent and metaphysically traditional reinterpretations of all these cases. What I doubt is that such reinterpretations taken *in toto* can present a plausible view, and that taken individually they have any claim to superiority over the literal interpretations – either as accounts of the language of ordinary mentalistic ascription, or as accounts of the evidence on which mental attributions are commonly based.

Four types of reinterpretation have some currency. I shall be rather short with the first two, the first of which I have already warned against in Section IId. Sometimes relevant mentalistic ascriptions are reinterpreted as attributions of *de re* attitudes *of* entities not denoted by the misconstrued expressions. For example, the subject's belief that he has arthritis in the thigh might be interpreted as a belief *of* the non-arthritic rheumatoid ailment that it is in the thigh. The subject will probably have such a belief in this case. But it hardly accounts for the relevant attributions. In particular, it ignores the oblique occurrence of 'arthritis' in the original ascription. Such occurrences bear on the characterization of the subject's viewpoint. The subject thinks of the disease in his thigh (and of his arthritis) in a certain way. He thinks of each disease that it is arthritis. Other terms for arthritis (or for the actual trouble in his thigh) may not enable us to describe his attitude content nearly as well. The appeal to *de re* attitudes in this way is not adequate to the task of reinterpreting these ascriptions so as to explain away the difference between actual and counterfactual situations. It simply overlooks what needs explication.

A second method of reinterpretation, which Descartes proposed (cf. Section IV) and which crops up occasionally, is to claim that in cases of incomplete understanding, the subject's attitude or content is indefinite. It is surely true that in cases where a person is extremely confused, we are sometimes at a loss in describing his attitudes. Perhaps in such cases, the subject's mental content *is* indefinite. But in the cases I have cited, common practice lends virtually no support to the contention that the subject's mental contents are indefinite. The subject and his fellows typically know and agree on precisely *how to confirm or infirm* his beliefs – both in the cases where they are unproblematically true (or just empirically false) and in the cases where they display the misconception. Ordinary attributions typically specify the mental content without qualifications or hesitations.

In cases of partial understanding – say, in the mortgage example – it may indeed be unclear, short of extensive questioning, just how much mastery the subject has. But even this sort of unclarity does not appear to prevent, under ordinary circumstances, straightforward attributions utilizing 'mortgage' in oblique position. The subject is uncertain whether his father has two mortgages; he knows that his uncle has paid off the mortgage on his house. The contents are unhesitatingly attributed and admit of unproblematic testing for truth value, despite the subject's partial understanding. There is thus little *prima facie* ground for the appeal to indefiniteness. The appeal appears to derive from a prior assumption that attribution of a content entails attribution of full understanding. Lacking an easy means of attributing something other than the misunderstood content, one is tempted to say that there *is* no definite content. But this is unnecessarily mysterious. It reflects on the prior assumption, which so far has no independent support.

The other two methods of reinterpretation are often invoked in tandem. One is to attribute a notion that just captures the misconception, thus replacing contents that are apparently false on account of the misconception, by true contents. For example, the subject's belief (true or false) that that is a sofa would be replaced by, or reinterpreted as, a (true) belief that that is a *chofa*, where 'chofa' is introduced to apply not only to sofas, but also to the armchairs the subject thinks are sofas. The other method is to count the error of the subject as purely metalinguistic. Thus the patient's apparent belief that he had arthritis in the thigh would be reinterpreted as a belief that 'arthritis' applied to something (or some disease) in his thigh. The two methods can be applied simultaneously, attempting to account for an ordinary content attribution in terms of a reinterpreted object-level content together with a metalinguistic error. It is important to remember that in order to overturn the thought experiment, these methods must not only establish that the subject held the particular attitudes that they advocate attributing; they must also justify a *denial* of the ordinary attributions literally interpreted.

The method of invoking object-level notions that precisely capture (and that replace) the subject's apparent misconception has little to be said for it as a natural and generally applicable account of the language of mentalistic ascriptions. We do not ordinarily seek out true object-level attitude contents to attribute to victims of errors based on incomplete understanding. For example, when we find that a person has been involved in a misconception in examples like ours, we do not regularly reinterpret those ascriptions that involved the misunderstood term, but were untuitively unaffected by the error. An attribution to someone of a true belief that he is eating brisket, or that he has just signed a contract, or that Uncle Harry has paid off his mortgage, is not typically reformulated when it is learned that the subject had not fully understood what brisket (or a contract, or a mortgage) is. A similar point applies when we know about the error at the time of the attribution – at least if we avoid misleading the audience in cases where the error is crucial to the issue at hand. Moreover, we shall frequently see the subject as sharing beliefs with others who understand the relevant notions better. In counting beliefs as shared, we do not require, in every case, that the subjects 'fully understand' the notions in those belief contents, or understand them in just the same way. Differences in understanding are frequently located as differences over other belief contents. We agree that you have signed a contract, but disagree over whether someone else could have made a contract by means of a verbal agreement.

There are reasons why ordinary practice does not follow the method of object-level reinterpretation. In many cases, particularly those involving partial understanding, finding a reinterpretation in accord with the method would be entirely nontrivial. It is not even clear that we have agreed upon means of pursuing such inquiries in all cases. Consider the arthritic patient. Suppose we are to reinterpret the attribution of his erroneous belief that he has arthritis in the thigh. We make up a term 'tharthritis' that covers arthritis and whatever it is he has in his thigh. The appropriate restrictions on the application of this term and of the patient's supposed notion are unclear. Is just any problem in the thigh that the patient wants to call 'arthritis' to count as tharthritis? Are other ailments covered? What would decide? The problem is that there are no recognized standards governing the application of the new term. In such cases, the method is patently *ad hoc*.

The method's willingness to invoke new terminology whenever conceptual error or partial understanding occurs is *ad hoc* in another sense. It proliferates terminology without evident theoretical reward. We do not engender better understanding of the patient by inventing a new word and saying that he thought (correctly) that tharthritis can occur outside joints. It is simpler and equally informative to construe him as thinking that arthritis may occur outside joints. When we are making other attributions that do not directly display the error, we must simply bear the deviant belief in mind, so as not to assume that all of the patient's inferences involving the notion would be normal.

The method of object-level reinterpretation often fails to give a plausible account of the evidence on which we base mental attributions. When caught in the sorts of errors we have been discussing, the subject does not normally respond by saying that his views had been misunderstood. The patient does not say (or think)that he had thought he had some-category-of-disease-like-arthritis-and-including-arthritis-but-also-capable-of-occurring-outside-of-joints in the thigh *instead* of the error commonly attributed. This sort of response would be disingenuous. Whatever other beliefs he had, the subject thought that he had arthritis in the thigh. In such cases, the subject will ordinarily give no evidence of having maintained a true object-level belief. In examples like ours, he typically admits his mistake, changes his views, and leaves it at that. Thus the subject's own behavioral dispositions and inferences often fail to support the method.

The method may be seen to be implausible as an account of the relevant evidence in another way. The patient knows that he has had arthritis in the ankle and wrists for some time. Now with his new pains in the thigh, he fears and believes that he has got arthritis in the thigh, that his arthritis is spreading. Suppose we reinterpret all of these attitude attributions in accord with the method. We use our recently coined term 'tharthritis' to cover (somehow) arthritis and whatever it is he has in the thigh. On this new interpretation, the patient is right in thinking that he has tharthritis in the ankle and wrists. His belief that it has lodged in the thigh is true. His fear is realized. But these attributions are out of keeping with the way we do and should view his actual beliefs and fears. His belief is not true, and his fear is not realized. He will be relieved when he is told that one cannot have arthritis in the thigh. His relief is bound up with a network of assumptions that he makes about his arthritis: that it is a kind of disease, that there are debilitating consequences of its occurring in multiple locations, and so on. When told that arthritis cannot occur in the thigh, the patient does not decide that his fears were realized, but that perhaps he should not have had those fears. He does not think: Well, my tharthritis *has* lodged in the thigh; but judging from the fact that what the doctor called 'arthritis' cannot occur in the thigh, tharthritis may not be a single kind of disease; and I suppose I need not worry about the effects of its occurring in various locations, since evidently the tharthritis in my thigh is physiologically unrelated to the tharthritis in my joints. There will rarely if ever be an empirical basis for such a description of the subject's inferences. The patient's behavior (including his reports, or thinkings-out-loud) in this sort of case will normally not indicate any such pattern of inferences at all. But this is the description that the object-level reinterpretation method appears to recommend.

On the standard attributions, the patient retains his assumptions about the relation between arthritis, kinds of disease, spreading, and so on. And he concludes that his arthritis is not appearing in new locations – at any rate, not in his thigh. These attributions will typically be supported by the subject's behavior. The object-level reinterpretation method postulates inferences that are more complicated and different in focus from the inferences that the evidence supports. The method's presentation in such a case would seem to be an *ad hoc* fiction, not a description with objective validity.

None of the foregoing is meant to deny that frequently when a person incompletely understands an attitude content he has some other attitude content that more or less captures his understanding. For example, in the contract example, the client will probably have the belief that if one breaks *a legally binding agreement based on formal documents*, then one may get into trouble. There are also cases in which it is reasonable to say that, at least in a sense, a person has a notion that is expressed by his dispositions to classify things in a certain way – even if there is no conventional term in the person's repertoire that neatly corresponds to that 'way.' The sofa case may be one such. Certain animals as well as people may have non-verbal notions of this sort. On the other hand, the fact that such attributions are justifiable *per se* yields no reason to deny that the subject (also) has object-level attitudes whose contents involve the relevant incompletely understood notion.

Whereas the third method purports to account for the subject's thinking at the object level, the fourth aims at accounting for his error. The error is construed as purely a metalinguistic mistake. The relevant false content is seen to involve notions that denote or apply to linguistic expressions. In examples relevant to our thought experiment, we ordinarily attribute a metalinguistic as well as an object-level attitude to the subject, at least in the case of non-occurrent propositional attitudes. For example, the patient probably believes that 'arthritis' applies in English to the ailment in his thigh. He believes that his father had a disease called 'arthritis.' And so on. Accepting these metalinguistic attributions, of course, does nothing *per se* toward making plausible a denial that the subjects in our examples have the counterpart object-level attitudes.

Like the third method, the metalinguistic reinterpretation method has no *prima facie* support as an account of the language of mentalistic ascriptions. When we encounter the subject's incomplete understanding in examples like ours, we do not decide that all the mental contents which we had been attributing to him with the misunderstood notion must have been purely metalinguistic in form. We also count people who incompletely understand terms in ascribed content clauses as sharing true and unproblematic object-level attitudes with others who understand the relevant terms better. For example, the lawyer and his client may share a wish that the client had not signed the contract to buy the house without reading the small print. A claim that these people share *only* attitudes with metalinguistic contents would have no support in linguistic practice.

The point about shared attitudes goes further. If the metalinguistic reinterpretation account is to be believed, we cannot say that a relevant English speaker shares a view (for example) that many old people have arthritis, with *anyone* who does not use the English word 'arthritis'. For the foreigner does not have the word 'arthritis' to hold beliefs about, thought he does have attitudes involving the notion arthritis. And the attribution to the English speaker is to be interpreted metalinguistically, making reference to the word, so as not to involve attritution of the notion arthritis. This result is highly implausible. Ascriptions of such that-clauses as the above, regardless of the subject's language, serve to provide single descriptions and explanations of similar patterns of behavior, inference, and communication. To hold that we cannot accurately ascribe single content-clauses to English speakers and foreigners in such cases would not only accord badly with linguistic practice. It would substantially weaken the descriptive and explanatory power of our common attributions. In countless cases, unifying accounts of linguistically disparate but cognitively and behaviorally similar phenomena would be sacrificed.

The method is implausible in other cases as an account of standard evidence on which mental attributions are based. Take the patient who fears that his arthritis is spreading. According to the metalinguistic reinterpretation method, the patient's reasoning should be described as follows. He thinks that the word 'arthritis' applies to a single disease in him, that the disease in him called 'arthritis' is debilitating if it spreads, that 'arthritis' applies to the disease in his wrists and ankles. He fears that the disease called 'arthritis' has lodged in his thigh, and so on. Of course, it is often difficult to find evidential grounds for attributing an object-level attitude *as opposed* to its metalinguistic counterpart. As I noted, when a person holds one attitude, he often holds the other. But there are types of evidence, in certain contexts, for making such discriminations, particularly contexts in which *occurrent* mental events are at issue. The subject may maintain that his reasoning did not fix upon words. He may be brought up short by a metalinguistic formulation of his just-completed ruminations, and may insist that he was not interested in labels. In such cases, especially if the reasoning is not concerned with linguistic issues in any informal or antecedently plausible sense, attribution of an object-level thought content is supported by the relevant evidence, and metalinguistic attribution is not. To insist that the occurrent mental event really involved a metalinguistic content would be a piece of *ad hoc* special pleading, undermined by the evidence we actually use for deciding whether a thought was metalinguistic.

In fact, there appears to be a general presumption that a person is reasoning at the object level, other things being equal. The basis for this presumption is that metalinguistic reasoning requires a certain self-consciousness about one's words and social institutions. This sort of sophistication emerged rather late in human history. (Cf. any history of linguistics.) Semantical notions were a product of this sophistication.

Occurrent propositional attitudes prevent the overall reinterpretation strategy from providing a plausible total account which would block our thought experiment. For such occurrent mental events as the patient's thought that his arthritis is especially painful in the knee this morning are, or can be imagined to be, clear cases of object-level attitudes. And such thoughts may enter into or connect up with pieces of reasoning – say the reasoning leading to relief that the arthritis had not lodged in the thigh – which cannot be plausibly accounted for in terms of object-level reinterpretation. The other reinterpretation methods (those that appeal to *de re* contents and to indefiniteness) are non-starters. In such examples, the literally interpreted ascriptions appear to be straightforwardly superior accounts of the evidence that is normally construed to be relevant. Here one need not appeal to the principle that literal interpretation is, other things equal, preferable to reinterpretation. Other things are not equal.

At this point, certain philosophers may be disposed to point out what a person says and how he behaves do not infallibly determine what his attitude contents are. Despite the apparent evidence, the subject's attitude contents may in all cases I cited be metalinguistic, and may fail to involve the incompletely understood notion. It is certainly true that how a person acts and what he says, even sincerely, do not determine his mental contents. I myself have mentioned a number of cases that support the point. (CF. IIIb.) But the point is often used in a sloppy and irresponsible manner. It is incumbent on someone making it (and applying it to cases like ours) to indicate considerations that override the linguistic and behavioral evidence. In Section IIId, I shall consider intuitive or *a priori* philosophical arguments to this end. But first I wish to complete our evaluation of the metalinguistic reinterpretation method as an account of the language of mentalistic ascription in our examples.

In this century philosophers have developed the habit of insisting on metalinguistic reinterpretation for any content attribution that directly *displays* the subject's incomplete understanding. These cases constitute but a small number of the attributions that serve the thought experiment. One could grant these reinterpretations and still maintain our overall viewpoint. But even as applied to these cases, the method seems dubious. I doubt that any evidentially supported account of the language of these attributions will show them in general to be attributions of metalinguistic contents – contents that involve denotative reference to linguistic expressions.

The ascription 'He believes that broad overstuffed armchairs are sofas', as ordinarily used, does not in general *mean* 'He believes that broad, overstuffed armchairs are covered by the expression "sofas"' (or something like that). There are clear grammatical and semantical differences between

(i) broad, overstuffed armchairs are covered by the expression 'sofas'

and

(ii) broad, overstuffed armchairs are sofas.

When the two are embedded in belief contexts, they produce grammatically and semantically distinct sentences.

As noted, ordinary usage approves ascriptions like

(iii) He believes that broad, overstuffed armchairs are sofas.

It would be wildly *ad hoc* and incredible from the point of view of linguistic theory to claim that there is *no* reading of (iii) that embeds (ii). But there is no evidence from speaker behavior that *true* ascriptions of (iii) always (or perhaps even *ever*) derive from embedding (i) rather than (ii). In fact, I know of no clear evidence that (iii) is ambiguous between embedding (i) and (ii), or that (ii) is ambiguous, with one reading identical to that of (i). People do not in general seem to regard ascriptions like (iii) as elliptical. More important, in most cases no amount of nonphilosophical badgering will lead them to withdraw (iii), under some interpretation, *in favor of* an ascription that clearly embeds (i). At least in the cases of *non-occurrent* propositional attitudes, they will tend to agree to a clearly metalinguistic ascription – a belief sentence explicitly embedding something like (i) – in cases where they make an ascription like (iii). But this is evidence that they regard ascriptions that embed (i) and (ii) as both true. It hardly tells against counting belief ascriptions that embed (ii) as true, or against taking (iii) in the obvious, literal manner. In sum, there appears to be no ordinary empirical pressure on a theory of natural language to represent true ascriptions like (iii) as *not* embedding sentences like (ii). And other things being equal, literal readings are correct readings. Thus it is strongly plausible to assume that ordinary usage routinely accepts as true and justified even ascriptions like (iii), literally interpreted as embedding sentences like (ii).

There are various contexts in which we may be indifferent over whether to attribute a metalinguistic attitude or the corresponding object-level attitude. I have emphasized that frequently, though not always, we may attribute both. Or we might count the different contents as describing what contextually 'amount to the same attitude.' (Cf. Section I.) Even this latter locution remains compatible with the thought experiment, as long as both contents are *equally attributable* in describing 'the attitude.' In the counterfactual step of the thought experiment, the metalinguistic content (say, that broad, overstuffed armchairs are called 'sofas') will still be attributable. But in these circumstances it contextually 'amounts to the same attitude' as an object-level attitude whose content is in no sense equivalent to, or 'the same as,' the original object-level content. For they have different truth values. Thus, assuming that the object-level and metalinguistic contents are equally attributable, it remains informally plausible that the person's attitudes are different between actual and counterfactual steps in the thought experiment. This contextual conflation of object-level and metalinguistic contents is not, however, generally acceptable even in describing non-occurrent attitudes, much less occurrent ones. There are contexts in which the subject himself may give evidence of making the distinction.

IIId Philosophical arguments for reinterpretation

I have so far argued that the reinterpretation strategies that I have cited do not provide a plausible account of evidence relevant to a theory of the language of mentalistic ascriptions or to descriptions of mental phenomena themselves. I now want to consider characteristically philosophical arguments for revising ordinary discourse or for giving it a nonliteral reading, arguments that rely purely on intuitive or *a priori* considerations. I have encountered three such arguments, or argument sketches.[4]

One holds that the content clauses we ascribed must be reinterpreted so as to make reference to words because they clearly concern linguistic matters – or are about language. Even if this argument were sound, it would not affect the thought experiment decisively. For most of the mental contents that vary between actual and counterfactual situations are not in any intuitive sense 'linguistic.' The belief that certain armchairs are sofas is intuitively linguistic. But beliefs that some sofas are beige, that Kirkpatrick is playing a clavichord, and that Milton had severe arthritis in his hands are not.

But the argument is unpersuasive even as applied to the contents that, in an intuitive sense, do concern linguistic matters. A belief that broad, overstuffed armchairs are sofas is linguistic (or 'about' language) in the same senses as an 'analytically' true belief that no armchairs are sofas. But the linguistic nature of the latter belief does not make its logical form metalinguistic. So citing the linguistic nature of the former belief does not suffice to show it metalinguistic. No semantically relevant component of either content applies to or denotes linguistic expressions.

Both the 'analytically' true and the 'analytically' false attitudes are linguistic in the sense that they are tested by consulting a dictionary or native linguistic intuitions, rather than by ordinary empirical investigation. We do not scrutinize pieces of furniture to test these beliefs. The pragmatic focus of expressions of these attitudes will be on usage, concepts, or meaning. But it is simply a mistake to think that these facts entail, or even suggest, that the relevant contents are metalinguistic in form. Many contents with object-level logical forms have primarily linguistic or conceptual implications.

A second argument holds that charitable interpretation requires that we not attribute to rational people beliefs like the belief that one may have arthritis in the thigh. Here again, the argument obviously does not touch most of the attitudes that may launch the thought experiment; for many are straightforwardly true, or false on ordinary empirical grounds. Even so, it is not a good argument. There is nothing irrational or stupid about the linguistic or conceptual errors we attribute to our subjects. The errors are perfectly understandable as results of linguistic misinformation.

In fact, the argument makes sense only against the background of the very assumption that I have been questioning. A belief that arthritis may occur in the thigh appears to be inexplicable or uncharitably attributed only if it is assumed that the subject must fully understand the notions in his attitude contents.

A third intuitive or *a priori* argument is perhaps the most interesting. Sometimes it is insisted that we should not attribute contents involving incompletely understood notions because *the individual must mean something different by the misunderstood word than what we non-deviant speakers mean by it*. Note again that it would not be enough to use this argument from deviant speaker meaning to show that the subject has notions that are not properly expressed in the way he thinks they are. In some sense of 'expressed', this is surely often the case. To be relevant, the argument must arrive at a negative conclusion: that the subject cannot have the attitudes that seem commonly to be attributed.

The expression 'the individual meant something different by his words' can be interpreted in more than one way. On one group of interpretations, the expression says little more than that the speaker incompletely understood his words: The patient thought 'arthritis' meant something that included diseases that occur outside of joints. The client would have misexplained the meaning, use, or application of 'contract'. The subject applied 'sofa' to things that, unknown to him, are not sofas. A second group of interpretations emphasizes that not only does the speaker misconstrue or misapply his words, but he had *in mind* something that the words do not denote or express. The subject sometimes had in mind certain armchairs when he used 'sofa.' The client regarded the notion of legal agreement based on written documents as approximately interchangeable with what is expressed by 'contract', and thus had such a notion in mind when he used 'contract'. A person with a problem about the range of red might sometimes have in mind a mental image of a non-red color when he used 'red'.

The italicized premise of the argument is, of course, always true in our examples under the first group of interpretations, and often true under the second. But interpreted in these ways, the argument is a *non sequitur*. It does not follow from the assumption that the subject thought that a word means something that it does not (or misapplies the word, or is disposed to misexplain its meaning) that the word cannot be used in literally describing his mental contents. It does not follow from the assumption that a person has in mind something that a word does not denote or express that the word cannot occur obliquely (and be interpreted literally) in that-clauses that provide some of his mental contents. As I have pointed out in Section IIIb, there is a range of cases in which we commonly reinterpret a person's incompletely understood words for purposes of mental-content attribution. But the present argument needs to show that deviant speaker-meaning always forces such reinterpretation.

In many of our examples, the idea that the subject has some deviant notion *in mind* has no intuitively clear application. (Consider the arthritis and mortgage examples.) But even where this expression does seem to apply, the argument does not support the relevant conclusion. At best it shows that a notion deviantly associated with a word plays a role in the subject's attitudes. For example, someone who has in mind the notion of an agreement based on written documents when he says, 'I have just entered into a contract,' may be correctly said to believe that he has just entered into an agreement based on written documents. It does not follow from this that he *lacks* a belief or thought that he has just entered into a contract. In fact, in our view, the client's having the deviant notion in mind is a *likely consequence* of the fact that he believes that contracts are impossible without a written document.

Of course, given the first, more liberal set of interpretations of 'means something different', the fact that in our examples the subject means something different by his words (or at least applies them differently) is *implied* by certain of his beliefs. It is implied by a belief that he has arthritis in the thigh. A qualified version of the converse implication also holds. Given appropriate background assumptions, the fact that the subject has certain deviant (object-level) beliefs is implied by his meaning something different by his words. So far, no argument has show that we cannot accept these implications and retain the literal interpretation of common mentalistic ascriptions.

The argument from deviant speaker-meaning downplays an intuitive feature that can be expected to be present in many of our examples. The subject's willingness to submit his statement and belief to the arbitration of an authority suggests a willingness to have his words taken in the normal way – regardless of mistaken associations with the word. Typically, the subject will regard recourse to a dictionary, and to the rest of us, as at once a check on his usage and his belief. When the verdict goes against him, he will not usually plead that we have simply misunderstood his views. This sort of behavior suggests that (given the sorts of background assumptions that common practice uses to distinguish our examples from those of foreigners, radical misunderstandings, and so forth) we can say that in a sense our man meant by 'arthritis' *arthritis* – where '*arthritis*' occurs, of course, obliquely. We can say this despite the fact that his incomplete understanding leads us, in one of the senses explicated earlier, to say that he meant something different by 'arthritis'.

If one tries to turn the argument from deviant speaker-meaning into a valid argument, one arrives at an assumption that seems to guide all three of the philosophical arguments I have discussed. The assumption is that what a person thinks his words mean, how he takes them, fully determines what attitudes he can express in using them: the contents of his mental states and events are strictly limited to notions, however idiosyncratic, that he understands; a person cannot think with notions he incompletely understands. But supplemented with this assumption, the argument begs the question at issue.

The least controversial justification of the assumption would be an appeal to standard practice in mentalistic attributions. But standard practice is what brought the assumption into question in the first place. Of course, usage is not sacred if good reasons for revising it can be given. But none have been.

The assumption is loosely derived, I think, from the old model according to which a person must be directly acquainted with, or must immediately apprehend, the contents of his thoughts. None of the objections explicitly invoke this model – and many of their proponents would reject it. But I think that all the objections derive some of their appeal from philosophical habits that have been molded by it. I shall discuss this model further in Section IV.

One may, of course, quite self-consciously neglect certain aspects of common mentalistic notions in the interests of a revised or idealized version of them. One such idealization could limit itself to just those attitudes involving 'full understanding' (for some suitably specified notion of understanding). This limitation is less clearcut than one might suppose, since the notion of understanding itself tends to be used according to misleading stereotypes. Still, oversimplified models, idealizations, of mentalistic notions are defensible, as long as the character and purpose of the oversimplifications are clear. In my opinion, limiting oneself to 'fully understood' attitudes provides no significant advantage in finding elegant and illuminating formal semantical theories of natural language. Such a strategy has perhaps a better claim in psychology, though even there its propriety is controversial. (CF. Section IV.) More to the point, I think that models that neglect the relevant social factors in mentalistic attributions are not likely to provide long-run philosophical illumination of our actual mentalistic notions. But this view hardly admits of detailed support here and now.

Our argument in the preceding pages may, at a minimum, be seen as inveighing against a long-standing philosophical habit of denying that it *is* an oversimplification to make 'full understanding' of a content a necessary condition for having a propositional attitude with that content. The oversimplification does not constitute neglect of some quirk of ordinary usage. Misunderstanding and partial understanding are pervasive and inevitable phenomena, and attributions of content despite them are an integral part of common practice.

I shall not here elaborate a philosophical theory of the social aspects of mentalistic phenomena, thought in Section V I shall suggest lines such a theory might take. One of the most surprising and exciting aspects of the thought experiment is that its most literal interpretation provides a perspective on the mental that has received little serious development in the philosophical tradition. The perspective surely invites exploration.

IV. Applications

I want to turn now to a discussion of how our argument bears on philosophical approaches to the mental that may be termed *individualistic*. I mean this term to be somewhat vague. But roughly, I intend to apply it to philosophical treatments that seek to see a person's intentional mental phenomena ultimately and purely in terms of what happens to the person, what occurs within him, and how he responds to his physical environment, without any essential reference to the social context in which he or the interpreter of his mental phenomena are situated. How I apply the term 'individualistic' will perhaps become clearer by reference to the particular cases that I shall discuss.

a. As I have already intimated, the argument of the preceding sections affects the traditional intro- (or extro-)spectionist treatments of the mind, those of Plato, Descartes, Russell, and numerous others. These treatments are based on a model that likens the relation between a person and the contents of his thought to seeing, where seeing is taken to be a kind of direct, immediate experience. On the most radical and unqualified versions of the model, a person's inspection of the contents of his thought is infallible: the notion of incompletely understanding them has no application at all.

The model tends to encourage individualistic treatments of the mental. For it suggests that what a person thinks depends on what occurs of 'appears' within his mind. Demythologized, what a person thinks depends on the power and extent of his comprehension and on his internal dispositions toward the comprehended contents. The model is expressed in perhaps its crudest and least qualified form in a well-known passage by Russell:

> Whenever a relation of supposing or judging occurs, the terms to which the supposing or judging mind is related by the relation of supposing or judging must be terms with which the mind in question is acquainted. . . . It seems to me that the truth of this principle is evident as soon as the principle is understood.[5]

Acquaintance is (for Russell) direct, infallible, non-propositional, non-perspectival knowledge. 'Terms' like concepts, ideas, attributes, forms, meanings, or senses are entities that occur in judgments more or less immediately before the mind on a close analogy to the way sensations are supposed to.

The model is more qualified and complicated in the writings of Descartes. In particular, he emphasizes the possibility that one might perceive the contents of one's mind unclearly or indistinctly. He is even high-handed enough to write, 'Some people throughout their lives perceive nothing so correctly as to be capable of judging it properly.'[6] This sort of remark appears to be a concession to the points made in Sections I and II about the possibility of a subject's badly understanding his mental contents. But the concession is distorted by the underlying introspection model. On Descartes' view, the person's faculty of understanding, properly so-called, makes no errors. Failure to grasp one's mental contents results from either blind prejudice or interference by 'mere' bodily sensations and corporeal imagery. The implication is that with sufficiently careful reflection on the part of the individual subject, these obstacles to perfect understanding can be cleared. That is, one need only be careful or properly guided in one's introspections to achieve full understanding of the content of one's intentional mental phenomena. Much that Descartes says suggests that where the subject fails to achieve such understanding, no definite content can be attributed to him. In such cases, his 'thinking' consists of unspecifiable or indeterminate imagery; attribution of definite conceptual content is precluded. These implications are reinforced in Descartes' appeal to self-evident, indubitable truths:

> There are some so evident and at the same time so simple that we cannot think of them without believing them to be true. . . . For we cannot doubt them unless we think of them; and we cannot think of them without at the same time believing them to be true, i.e. we can never doubt them.[7]

The self-evidence derives from the mere understanding of the truths, and fully understanding them is a precondition for thinking them at all. It is this last requirement that we have been questioning.

In the Empiricist tradition Descartes' qualifications on the direct experience model – particularly those involving the interfering effects of sensations and imagery – tend to fall away. What one thinks comes to be taken as a sort of impression (whether more imagistic or more intellectual) on or directly grasped by the individual's mind. The tendency to make full comprehension on the part of the subject a necessary condition for attributing a mental content to him appears both in philosophers who take the content to be a Platonic abstraction and in those who place it, in some sense, inside the individual's mind. This is certainly the direction in which the model pulls, with its picture of immediate accessibility to the individual. Thus Descartes' original concessions to cases of incomplete understanding became lost as his model became entrenched. What Wölfflin said of painters is true of philosophers: they learn more from studying each other than from reflecting on anything else.

The history of the model makes an intricate subject. My remarks are meant merely to provide a suggestive caricature of it. It should be clear, however, that in broad outline the model mixes poorly with the thought experiment of Section II, particularly its first step. The thought experiment indicates that certain 'linguistic truths' that have often been held to be indubitable can be thought yet doubted. And it shows that a person's thought *content* is not fixed by what goes on in him, or by what is accessible to him simply by careful reflection. The reason for this last point about 'accessibility' need not be that the content lies too deep in the unconscious recesses of the subject's psyche. Contents are sometimes 'inaccessible' to introspection simply because much mentalistic attribution does not presuppose that the subject has fully mastered the content of his thought.

In a certain sense, the metaphysical model has fixed on some features of our use of mentalistic notions to the exclusion of others. For example, the model fastens on the facts that we are pretty good at identifying our own beliefs and thoughts, and we have at least a *prima facie* authority in reporting a wide range of them. It also underlines the point that for certain contents we tend to count understanding as a sufficient condition for acknowledging their truth. (It is debatable, of course, how well it explains or illumines these observations.) The model also highlights the truism that a certain measure of understanding is required of a subject if we are to attribute intentional phenomena on the basis of what he utters. As we have noted, chance or purely rote utterances provide no ground for mental content attributions; certain verbal pathologies are discounted. The model extrapolates from these observations to the claim that a person can never fail to understand the content of his beliefs or thoughts, or that the remedy for such failure lies within his own resources of reflection (whether autonomous and conscious, or unconscious and guided). It is this extrapolation that requires one to pass over the equally patent practice of attributing attitudes where the subject incompletely understands expressions that provide the content of those attitudes. Insistence on metalinguistic reinterpretation and talk about the indefiniteness of attitude contents in cases of incomplete understanding seem to be rearguard defenses of a vastly overextended model.

The Cartesian-Russellian model has few strict adherents among prominent linguistic philosophers. But although it has been widely rejected or politely talked around, claims that it bore and nurtured are commonplace, even among its opponents. As we have seen in the objections to the first step of the argument of Section II, these claims purport to restrict the contents we can attribute to a person on the basis of his use of language. The restrictions simply mimic those of Descartes. Freed of the picturesque but vulnerable model that formed them, the claims have assumed the power of dogma. Their strictures, however, misrepresent ordinary mentalistic notions.

b. This century's most conspicuous attempt to replace the traditional Cartesian model has been the behaviorist movement and its heirs. I take it as obvious that the argument of Section II provides yet another reason to reject the most radical version of behaviorism – 'philosophical,' 'logical' or 'analytical' behaviorism. This is the view that mentalistic attributions can be 'analytically' defined, or given strict meaning equivalences, purely in non-mental, behavioral terms. No analysis resting purely on the individual's dispositions to behavior can give an 'analytic' definition of a mental content attribution because we can conceive of the behavioral definiens applying while the mentalistic definiendum does not. But a new argument for this conclusion is hardly needed since 'philosophical' behaviorists are, in effect, extinct.

There is, however, an heir of behaviorism that I want to discuss at somewhat greater length. The approach sometimes goes by the name 'functionalism,' although that term is applied to numerous slogans and projects, often vaguely formulated. Even views that seem to me to be affected by our argument are frequently stated so sketchily that one may be in considerable doubt about what is being proposed. So my remarks should be taken less as an attempt to refute the theses of particular authors than as an attack on a way of thinking that seems to inform a cluster of viewpoints. The quotations I give in footnotes are meant to be suggestive, if not always definitive, of the way of thinking the argument tells against.[8]

The views affected by the argument of Section II attempts to give something like a philosophical 'account' of the mental. The details and strategy – even the notion of 'account' – vary from author to author. But a recurrent theme is that mental notions are to be seen ultimately in terms of the individual subject's input, output, and inner dispositions and states, where these latter are characterized purely in terms of how they lead to or from output, input, or other inner states similarly characterized. Mental notions are to be explicated or identified in functional, non-mentalistic, non-intentional terminology. Proponents of this sort of idea are rarely very specific about what terms may be used in describing input and output, or even what sorts of terms count as 'functional' expressions. But the impression usually given is that input and output are to be specified in terms (acceptable to a behaviorist) of irritations of the subject's surfaces and movements of his body. On some versions, neurophysiological terms are allowed. More recently, there have been liberalized appeals to causal input and output relations with particular, specified physical objects, stuffs, or magnitudes. Functional terms include terms like 'causes', 'leads to with probability n', and the like. For our purposes, the details do not matter much, as long as an approach allows no mentalistic or other intentional terms (such as 'means' or that-clauses) into its vocabulary, and as long as it applies to individuals taken one by one.

A difference between this approach and that of philosophical behaviorism is that a whole array of dispositional or functional states – causally or probabilistically interrelated – may enter into the 'account' of a single mental attribution. The array must be ultimately secured to input and output, but the internal states need not be so secured one by one. The view is thus not immediately vulnerable to claims against simplistic behaviorisms, that a *given* stimulus-response pattern may have different contents in different social contexts. Such claims, which hardly need a defender, have been tranquilly accepted on this view. The view's hope is that differences in content depend on functional differences in the individual's larger functional structure. From this viewpoint, analytical behaviorism erred primarily in its failure to recognize the interlocking or wholistic character of mental attributions and in its oversimplification of theoretical explanation.

As I said, the notion of an account of the mental varies from author to author. Some authors take over the old-fashioned ideal of an 'analysis' from philosophical behaviorism and aim at a definition of the meaning of mentalistic vocabulary, or a definitional elimination of it. Others see their account as indicating a series of scientific hypotheses that identify mental states with causal or functional states, or roles, in the individual. These authors reject behaviorism's goal of providing meaning equivalences, as well as its restrictive methods. The hypotheses are supposed to be type or property identities and are nowadays often thought to hold necessarily, even if they do not give meaning relations. Moreover, these hypotheses are offered not merely as speculation about the future of psychology, but as providing a philosophically illuminating account of our ordinary notion of the mental. Thus if the view systematically failed to make plausible type identities between functional states and mental states, ordinarily construed, then by its own lights it would have failed to give a philosophical 'account' of the mental. I have crudely over-schematized the methodological differences among the authors in this tradition. But the differences fall roughly within the polar notions of *account* that I have described. I think our discussion will survive the oversimplifications.[9]

Any attempt to give an account of specific beliefs and thoughts along the lines I have indicated will come up short. For we may fix the input, output, and total array of dispositional or functional states of our subject, as long as these are non-intentionally described and are limited to what is relevant to accounting for his activity taken in isolation from that of his fellows. But we can still conceive of his mental contents as varying. Functionally equivalent people – on any plausible notion of functional equivalence that has been sketched – may have non-equivalent mental-state and event contents, indicated by obliquely non-equivalent content clauses. Our argument indicates a systematic inadequacy in attempts of the sort I described.

Proponents of functionalist accounts have seen them as revealing the true nature of characteristic marks of the mental and as resolving traditional philosophical issues about such marks. In the case of beliefs, desires, and thoughts, the most salient mark is intentionality – the ill-specified information-bearing, representational feature that seems to invest these mental states and events.[10] In our terminology, accounting for intentionality largely amounts to accounting for the content of mental states and events. (There is also, of course, the application of content in *de re* cases. But we put this aside here.) Such content is clearly part of what the functional roles of our subjects' states fail to determine.

It is worth re-emphasizing here that the problem is unaffected by suggestions that we specify input and output in terms of causal relations to particular objects or stuffs in the subject's physical environment. Such specifications may be thought to help with some examples based on indexicality or psychological success verbs, and perhaps in certain arguments concerning natural kind terms (though even in these cases I think that one will be forced to appeal to intentional language). (Cf. note 2.) But this sort of suggestion has no easy application to our argument. For the relevant causal relations between the subject and the physical environment to which his terms apply – where such relations are non-intentionally specified – were among the elements held constant while the subject's beliefs and thoughts varied.

The functionalist approaches I have cited seem to provide yet another case in which mental contents are not plausibly accounted for in non-intentional terms. They are certainly not explicable in terms of causally or functionally specified states and events of the *individual* subject. The intentional or semantical role of mental states and events is not a function merely of their functionally specified roles in the individual. The failure of these accounts of intentional mental states and events derives from an underestimation of socially dependent features of cognitive phenomena.

Before extending the application of our argument, I want to briefly canvass some ways of being influenced by it, ways that might appeal to someone fixed on the functionalist ideal. One response might be to draw a strict distinction between mental states, ordinarily so-called, and psychological states. One could then claim that the latter are the true subject matter of the science of psychology and may be identified with functional states functionally specified, after all. Thus one might claim that the subject was in the same psychological (functional) states in both the actual and the imagined situations, although he had different beliefs and thoughts ordinarily so-called.

There are two observations that need to be entered about this position. The first is that it frankly jettisons much of the philosophical interest of functionalist accounts. The failure to cope with mental contents is a case in point. The second observation is that it is far from clear that such a distinction between the psychological and the mental is or will be sanctioned by psychology itself. Functionalist accounts arose as philosophical interpretations of developments in psychology influenced by computer theory. The interpretations have been guided by philosophical interests, such as throwing light on the mind-body problem and accounting for mentalistic features in non-mentalistic terms. But the theories of cognitive psychologists, including those who place great weight on the computer analogy, are not ordinarily purified of mentalistic or intentional terminology. Indeed, intentional terminology plays a central role in much contemporary theorizing. (This is also true of theories that appeal to 'sub-personal' states or processes. The 'sub-personal' states themselves are often characterized intentionally.) Purifying a theory of mentalistic and intentional features in favor of functional or causal features is more clearly demanded by the goals of philosophers than by the needs of psychology. Thus it is at least an open question whether functional approaches of the sort we have discussed give a satisfactory account of *psychological* states and events. It is not evident that psychology will ever be methodologically 'pure' (or theoretically purifiable by some definitional device) in the way these approaches demand. *This* goal of functionalists may be simply a meta-psychological mistake.

To put the point another way, it is not clear that functional states, characterized purely in functional, non-intentional terms (and non-intentional descriptions of input and output) are the natural subject matter of psychology. Psychology would, I think, be an unusual theory if it restricted itself (or could be definitionally restricted) to specifying abstract causal or functional structures in purely causal or functional terms, together with vocabulary from other disciplines. Of course, it *may* be that functional states, functionally specified, form a psychological natural kind. And it is certainly not to be assumed that psychology will respect ordinary terminology in its individuation of types of psychological states and events. Psychology must run its own course. But the assumption that psychological terminology will be ultimately non-intentional and purely functional seems without strong support. More important from our viewpoint, if psychology did take the individualistic route suggested by the approaches we have cited, then its power to illumine the everyday phenomena alluded to in mentalistic discourse would be correspondingly limited.

These remarks suggest a second sort of functionalist response to the argument of Section II, one that attempts to take the community rather than the individual as the object of functional analysis. One might, for example, seek to explain an individual's responsibility to communal standards in terms of his having the right kind of interaction with other individuals who collectively had functional structures appropriate to those standards. Spelling out the relevant notions of interaction and appropriateness is, of course, anything but trivial. (Cf. Section V.) Doing so in purely functional, non-intentional terms would be yet a further step. Until such a treatment is developed and illustrated in some detail, there is little point in discussing it. I shall only conjecture that, if it is to remain non-intentional, such a treatment is likely to be so abstract – at least in our present state of psychological and sociological ignorance – that it will be unilluminating from a philosophical point of view. Some of the approaches we have been discussing already more than flirt with this difficulty.

c. Individualistic assumptions about the mental have infected theorizing about the relation between mind and meaning. An example is the Gricean project of accounting for conventional or linguistic meaning in terms of certain complex intentions and beliefs of individuals.[11] The Gricean program analyzes conventional meaning in terms of subtle 'mutual knowledge,' or beliefs and intentions about each other's beliefs and intentions, on the part of most or all members of a community. Seen as a quasi-definitional enterprise, the program presupposes that the notion of an individual's believing or intending something is always 'conceptually' independent of the conventional meaning of symbols used to express that something. Insofar as 'conceptually' has any intuitive content, this seems not to be the case. Our subject's belief or intention contents can be conceived to vary simply by varying conventions in the community around him. The content of individuals' beliefs seems sometimes to depend partly on social conventions in their environment. It is true that our subjects are actually rather abnormal members of their community, at least with respect to their use and understanding of a given word. But normality here is judged against the standards set by communal conventions. So stipulating that the individuals whose mental states are used in defining conventional meaning be relevantly normal will not avoid the circularity that I have indicated. I see no way to do so. This charge of circularity has frequently been raised on intuitive grounds. Our argument gives the intuitions substance. Explicating convention in terms of belief and intention may provide various sorts of insight. But it is not defining a communal notion in terms of individualistic notions. Nor is it reducing, in any deep sense, the semantical, or the intentional generally, to the psychological.

d. Individualistic assumptions have also set the tone for much discussion of the ontology of the mental. This subject is too large to receive detailed consideration here. It is complicated by a variety of crosscurrents among different projects, methodologies, and theses. I shall only explore how our argument affects a certain line of thinking closely allied to the functionalist approaches already discussed. These approaches have frequently been seen as resuscitating an old argument for the materialist identity theory. The argument is three-staged. First, one gives a philosophical 'account' of each mentalistic locution, an account that is *prima facie* neutral as regards ontology. For example, a belief or a thought that sofas are comfortable is supposed to be accounted for as one functionally specified state or event within an array of others – all of which are secured to input and output. Second, the relevant functionally specified states or events are expected to be empirically correlated or correlatable with physiological states or events in a person (states or events that have those functions). The empirical basis for believing in these correlations is claimed to be provided by present or future physical science. The nature of the supposed correlations is differently described in different theories. But the most prevalent views expect only that the correlations will hold for each organism and person (perhaps at a given time) taken one by one. For example, the functionally specified event type that is identified with a thought that sofas are comfortable may be realized in one person by an instance (or 'token') of one physiological event type, and in another person by an instance of another physiological event type. Third, the ('token') mental state or event in the person is held to be identical with the relevant ('token') physiological state or event, on general grounds of explanatory simplicity and scientific method. Sometimes, this third stage is submerged by building uniqueness of occupancy of functional role into the first stage.[12]

I am skeptical about this sort of argument at every stage. But I shall doubt only the first stage here. The argument we gave in Section II directly undermines the attempt to carry out the first stage by recourse to the sort of functionalist approaches that we discussed earlier. Sameness of functional role, individualistically specified, is compatible with difference of content. I know of no better non-intentional account of mentalistic locutions. If a materialist argument of this genre is to arrive, it will require a longer first step.

I shall not try to say whether there is a philosophically interesting sense in which intentional mental phenomena are physical or material. But I do want to note some considerations against materialist *identity* theories.

State-like phenomena (say, beliefs) raise different problems from event-like phenomena (say, occurrent thoughts). Even among identity theorists, it is sometimes questioned whether an identity theory is the appropriate goal for materialism in the case of states. Since I shall confine myself to identity theories, I shall concentrate on event-like phenomena. But our considerations will also bear on views that hope to establish some sort of token identity theory for mental states like beliefs.

One other preliminary. I want to remain neutral about how best to describe the relation between the apparent event-like feature of occurrent thoughts and the apparent relational feature (their relation to a content). One might think of there being an event, the token thought event, that is in a certain relation to a content (indicated by the that-clause). One might think of the event as consisting – as not being anything 'over and above' – the relevant relation's holding at a certain time between a person and content. Or one might prefer some other account. From the viewpoint of an identity theory, the first way of seeing the matter is most advantageous. So I shall fit my expositon to that point of view.

Our ordinary method of identifying occurrent thought events and differentiating between them is to make reference to the person or organism to whom the thought occurs, the time of its occurrence, and the content of the thought. If person, time, and content are the same, we would normally count the thought event the same. If any one of these parameters differs in descriptions of thought events (subject to qualifications about duration), then the events or occurrences described are different. Of course, we can differentiate between events using descriptions that do not home in on these particular parameters. But these parameters are dominant. (It is worth noting that differentiations in terms of causes and effects usually tend to rely on the content of mental events or states at some point, since mental states or events are often among the causes or effects of a given mental event, and these causes or effects will usually be identified partly in terms of their content.) The important point for our purposes is that in ordinary practice, sameness of thought content (or at least some sort of strong equivalence of content) is taken as a necessary condition for sameness of thought occurrence.

Now one might codify and generalize this point by holding that no occurrence of a thought (that is, no token thought event) could have a different (or extensionally non-equivalent) content and be the very same token event. If this premise is accepted, then our argument of Section II can be deployed to show that a person's thought event is not *identical* with any event in him that is described by physiology, biology, chemistry, or physics. For let *b* be any given event described in terms of one of the physical sciences that occurs in the subject while he thinks the relevant thought. Let '*b*' be such that it denotes the same physical event occurring in the subject in our counterfactual situation. (If you want, let '*b*' be rigid in Kripke's sense, though so strong a stipulation is not needed.) The second step of our argument in Section II makes it plausible that *b* need not be affected by counterfactual differences in the communal use of the word 'arthritis'. Actually, the subject thinks that his ankles are stiff from arthritis, while *b* occurs. But we can conceive of the subject's *lacking* a thought event that his ankles are stiff from arthritis, while *b* occurs. Thus in view of our initial premise, *b* is not identical with the subject's occurrent thought.[13]

Identity theorists will want to reject the first premise – the premise that no event with a different content could be identical with a given thought event. On such a view, the given thought event that his ankles are stiff from arthritis might well have been a thought that his ankles are stiff from tharthritis, yet be precisely the same token thought event. Such a view is intuitively very implausible. I know of only one reasonably spelled-out basis of support for this view. Such a basis would be provided by showing that mentalistic phenomena are causal or functional states, in one of the strong senses discussed earlier, and that mental events are physical tokens or realizations of those states.

If 'that thought that his ankles are stiff from arthritis' could be accounted for in terms like 'that event with such and such a causal or functional role' (where 'such and such' does not itself involve intentional terminology), and if independently identified physical events systematically filled these roles (or realized these states), we could perhaps see a given thought event as having a different role – and hence content – in different possible situations. Given such a view, the functional specification could perhaps be seen as revealing the contingency of the intentional specification as applied to mental event tokens. Just as we can imagine a given physiological event that actually plays the role of causing the little finger to move two inches, as playing the role of causing the little finger to move three inches (assuming compensatory differences in its physiological environment), so we could perhaps imagine a given thought as having a different functional role from its actual one – and hence, assuming the functionalist account, as having a different content. But the relevant sort of functionalist account of intentional phenomena has not been made good.[14]

The recent prosperity of materialist-functionalist ways of thinking has been so great that it is often taken for granted that a given thought event might have been a thought with a different, obliquely non-equivalent content. Any old event, on this view, could have a different content, a different significance, if its surrounding context were changed. But in the case of occurrent thoughts – and intentional mental events generally – it is hardly obvious, or even initially plausible, that anything is more essential to the identity of the event than the content itself. Materialist identity theories have schooled the imagination to picture the content of a mental event as varying while the event remains fixed. But whether such imaginings are possible fact or just philosophical fancy is a separate question.[15]

At any rate, functionalist accounts have not provided adequate specification of what it is to be a thought that ___, for particular fillings of the blank. So a specification of a given thought event in functionalist terms does not reveal the contingency of the usual, undisputed intentional specifications.

Well, *is* it possible for a thought event to have had a different content from the one it has and be the very same event? It seems to me natural and certainly traditional to assume that this is not possible. Rarely, however, have materialists seen the identity theory as natural or intuitive. Materialists are generally revisionist about intuitions. What is clear is that we currently do identify and distinguish thought events primarily in terms of the person who has them, the rough times of their occurrence, and their contents. And we do assume that a thought event with a different content is a different thought event (insofar as we distinguish at all between the thinking event and the person's being related to a thought content at a time). I think these facts give the premise *prima facie* support and the argument against the identity theory some interest. I do not claim that we have '*a priori*' certainty that no account of intentional phenomena will reveal intentional language to be only contingently applicable to belief states or thought events. I am only dubious.

One might nurture faith or hope that some more socially oriented functionalist specification could be found. But no such specification is ready to hand. And I see no good reason to think that one must be found. Even if such a specification were found, it is far from clear that it would deflect the argument against the identity theory just considered. The 'functional' states envisaged would depend not merely on what the individual does and what inner causal states lead to his activity – non-intentionally specified – but also on what his fellows do. The analogy between functional states and physiological states in causing the individual's internal and external activity was the chief support for the view that a given token mental event might have been a token of a different content. But the envisaged socially defined 'functional states' bear no intuitive analogy to physiological states or other physical causal states within the individual's body. Their function is not simply that of responding to environmental influences and causing the individual's activity. It is therefore not clear (short of *assuming* an identity theory) that any event that is a token of one of the envisaged socially defined 'functional states' could have been a token of a different one. The event might be essentially identified in terms of its social role. There is as yet no reason to identify it in terms of physically described events in the individual's body. Thus it is not clear that such a socially oriented functional account of thought contents would yield grounds to believe that the usual intentional specifications of mental events are merely contingent. It is, I think, even less clear that an appropriate socially oriented functional account is viable.

Identity theories, of course, do not exhaust the resources of materialism. To take one example, our argument does not speak directly to a materialism based on composition rather than identity. On such a view, the same physical material might compose different thoughts in different circumstances. I shall say nothing evaluative about this sort of view. I have also been silent about other arguments for a token identity theory – such as those based on philosophical accounts of the notions of causality or explanation. Indeed, my primary interest has not been ontology at all. It has been to identify and question individualistic assumptions in materialist as well as Cartesian approaches to the mental.

V. Models of the Mental

Traditional philosophical accounts of mind have offered metaphors that produce doctrine and carry conviction where argument and unaided intuition flag. Of course, any such broad reconstructions can be accused of missing the pied beauties of the natural article. But the problem with traditional philosophy of mind is more serious. The two overwhelmingly dominant metaphors of the mental – the infallible eye and the automatic mechanism – have encouraged systematic neglect of prominent features of a wide range of mental phenomena, broadly speaking, social features. Each metaphor has its attractions. Either can be elaborated or doctored to fit the facts that I have emphasized. But neither illumines those facts. And both have played some part in inducing philosophers to ignore them.

I think it optimistic indeed to hope that any one picture, comparable to the traditional ones, will provide insight into all major aspects of mental phenomena. Even so, a function of philosophy is to sketch such pictures. The question arises whether one can make good the social debts of earlier accounts while retaining at least some of their conceptual integrity and pictorial charm. This is no place to start sketching. But some summary remarks may convey a sense of the direction in which our discussion has been tending.

The key feature of the examples of Section II was the fact that we attribute beliefs and thoughts to people even where they incompletely understand contents of those very beliefs and thoughts. This point about intentional mental phenomena is not everywhere applicable: non-linguistic animals do not seem to be candidates for misunderstanding the contents of their beliefs. But the point is certainly salient and must be encompassed in any picture of intentional mental phenomena. Crudely put, wherever the subject has attained a certain competence in large relevant parts of his language and has (implicitly) assumed a certain general commitment or responsibility to the communal conventions governing the language's symbols, the expressions the subject uses take on a certain inertia in determining attributions of mental content to him. In particular, the expressions the subject uses sometimes provide the content of his mental states or events even though he only partially understands, or even misunderstands, some of them. Global coherence and responsibility seem sometimes to override localized incompetence.

The detailed conditions under which this 'inertial force' is exerted are complicated and doubtless more than a little vague. Clearly, the subject must maintain a minimal internal linguistic and rational coherence and a broad similarity to others' use of the language. But meeting this condition is hardly sufficient to establish the relevant responsibility. For the condition is met in the case of a person who speaks a regional dialect (where the same words are sometimes given different applications). The person's aberrations relative to the larger community may be normalities relative to the regional one. In such cases, of course, the regional conventions are dominant in determining what contents should be attributed. At this point, it is natural to appeal to etiological considerations. The speaker of the dialect developed his linguistic habits from interaction with others who were a party to distinctively regional conventions. The person is committed to using the words according to the conventions maintained by those from whom he learned the words. But the situation is more complicated than this observation suggests. A person born and bred in the parent community might simply decide (unilaterally) to follow the usage of the regional dialect or even to fashion his own usage with regard to particular words, self-consciously opting out of the parent community's conventions in these particulars. In such a case, members of the parent community would not, and should not, attribute mental contents to him on the basis of homophonic construal of his words. Here the individual's intentions or attitudes toward communal conventions and communal conceptions seem more important than the causal antecedents of his transactions with a word – unless those intentions are simply included in the etiological story.

I shall not pursue these issues here. The problem of specifying the conditions under which a person has the relevant general competence in a language and a responsibility to its conventions is obviously complicated. The mixture of 'causal' and intentional considerations relevant to dealing with it has obvious near analogs in other philosophical domains (etiological accounts of perception, knowledge, reference). I have no confidence that all of the details of the story would be philosophically interesting. What I want to stress is that to a fair degree, mentalistic attribution rests not on the subject's having mastered the contents of the attribution, and not on his having behavioral dispositions peculiarly relevant to those contents, but on his having a certain responsibility to communal conventions governing, and conceptions associated with, symbols that he is disposed to use. It is this feature that must be incorporated into an improved model of the mental.

I think it profitable to see the language of content attribution as constituting a complex *standard* by reference to which the subject's mental states and events are estimated, or an abstract grid on which they are plotted. Different people may vary widely in the degree to which they master the elements and relations within the standard, even as it applies to them all. This metaphor may be developed in several directions and with different models: applied geometry, measurement of magnitudes, evaluation by a monetary standard, and so forth. A model I shall illustrate briefly here borrows from musical analysis.

Given that a composer has fulfilled certain general conditions for establishing a musical key, his chordal structures are plotted by reference to the harmonic system of relations appropriate to the tonic key. There is vast scope for variation and novelty within the harmonic framework. The chords may depart widely from traditional 'rules' or practices governing what count as interesting or 'reasonable' chordal structures and progressions. And the composer may or may not grasp the harmonic implications and departures present in his composition. The composer may sometimes exhibit harmonic incompetence (and occasionally harmonic genius) by radically departing from those traditional rules. But the harmonic system of relations applies to the composition in any case. Once established, the tonic key and its associated harmonic framework are applied unless the composer takes pains to set up another tonic key or some atonal arrangement (thereby intentionally opting out of the original tonal framework), or writes down notes by something like a slip of the pen (suffering mechanical interference in his compositional intentions), or unintentionally breaks the harmonic rules in a massive and unprincipled manner (thereby indicating chaos or complete incompetence). The tonic key provides a standard for describing the composition. The application of the standard depends on the composer's maintaining a certain overall coherence and minimal competence in conforming to the standard's conventions. And there are conditions under which the standard would be replaced by another. But once applied, the harmonic framework – its formal interrelations, its applicability even to deviant, pointless progressions – is partly independent of the composer's degree of harmonic mastery.

One attractive aspect of the metaphor is that it has some application to the case of animals. In making sounds, animals do sometimes behave in such a way that a harmonic standard can be roughly applied to them, even though the standard, at least in any detail, is no part of what they have mastered. Since they do not master the standard (though they may master some of its elements), they are not candidates for partial understanding or misunderstanding. (Of course, this may be said of many people as regards the musical standard.) The standard applies to both animals and people. But the conditions for its application are sensitive in various ways to whether the subject himself has mastered it. Where the subject does use the standard (whether the language, or a system of key relationships), his uses take on special weight in applications of the standard to him.

One of the metaphor's chief virtues is that it encourages one to seek social explications for this special weight. The key to our attribution of mental contents in the face of incomplete mastery or misunderstanding lies largely in social functions associated with maintaining and applying the standard. In broad outline, the social advantages of the 'special weight' are apparent. Symbolic expressions are the overwhelmingly dominant source of detailed information about what people think, intend, and so forth. Such detail is essential not only to much explanation and prediction, but also to fulfilling many of our cooperative enterprises and to relying on one another for second-hand information. Words interpreted in conventionally established ways are familiar, palpable, and public. They are common coin, a relatively stable currency. These features are crucial to achieving the ends of mentalistic attribution just cited. They are also critical in maximizing interpersonal comparability. And they yield a bias toward taking others at their word and avoiding *ad hoc* reinterpretation, once overall agreement in usage and commitment to communal standards can be assumed.

This bias issues in the practice of expressing even many differences in understanding without reinterpreting the subject's words. Rather than reinterpret the subject's word 'arthritis' and give him a trivally true object-level belief and merely a false metalinguistic belief about how 'arthritis' is used by others, it is common practice, and correct, simply to take him at his word.

I hardly need re-emphasize that the situation is vastly more complicated than I have suggested in the foregoing paragraphs. Insincerity, tongue slips, certain malapropisms, subconscious blocks, mental instability all make the picture more complex. There are differences in our handling of different sorts of expressions, depending, for example, on how clear and fixed social conventions regarding the expressions are. There are differences in our practices with different subject matters. There are differences in our handling of different degrees of linguistic error. There are differences in the way meaning-, assertion-, and mental-contents are attributed. (Cf. note 4.) I do not propose ignoring these points. They are all parameters affecting the inertial force of 'face value' construal. But I want to keep steadily in mind the philosophically neglected fact about social practice: Our attributions do not require that the subject always correctly or fully understand the content of his attitudes.

The point suggests fundamental misorientations in the two traditional pictures of the mental. The authority of a person's reports about his thoughts and beliefs (*modulo* sincerity, lack of subconscious interference, and so forth) does not issue from a special intellectual vision of the contents of those thoughts and beliefs. It extends even to some cases in which the subject incompletely understands those contents. And it depends partly on the social advantages of maintaining communally established standards of communication and mentalistic attribution. Likewise, the descriptive and explanatory role of mental discourse is not adequately modeled by complex non-intentional mechanisms or programs for the production of an individual's physical movement and behavior. Attributing intentional mentalistic phenomena to individuals serves not only to explain their behavior viewed in isolation but also to chart their activity (intentional, verbal, behavioral, physical) by complex comparison to others – and against socially established standards.[16] Both traditional metaphors make the mistake, among others, of treating intentional mental phenomena individualistically. New approaches must do better. The sense in which man is a social animal runs deeper than much mainstream philosophy of mind has acknowledged.[17]

Notes

1. Our examples suggest points about learning that need exploration. It would seem naive to think that we first attain a mastery of expressions or notions we use and then tackle the subject matters we speak and think about in using those expressions or notions. In most cases, the processes overlap. But while the subject's understanding is still partial, we sometimes attribute mental contents by the very terms the subject has yet to master. Traditional views take mastering a word to consist in matching it with an already mastered (or innate) concept. But it would seem, rather, that many concepts (or mental content components) are like words in that they may be employed before they are mastered. In both cases, employment appears to be an integral part of the process of mastery.
2. A development of a similar theme may be found in Hilary Putnam's notion of a division of linguistic labour. Cf. 'The Meaning of "Meaning",' *Philosophical Papers* 2 (London, 1975) pp. 227 ff. Putnam's imaginative work is in other ways

congenial with points I have developed. Some of his examples can be adapted in fairly obvious ways so as to give an argument with different premises, but a conclusion complementary to the one I arrive at in Section IIa:

Consider Alfred's belief contents involving the notion of water. Without changing Alfred's (or his fellows') non-intentional phenomenal experiences, internal physical occurrences, or dispositions to respond to stimuli on sensory surfaces, we can imagine that not water (H_2O), but a different liquid with different structure but similar macro-properties (and identical phenomenal properties) played the role in his environment that water does in ours. In such a case, we could ascribe no content clauses to Alfred with 'water' in oblique position. His belief contents would differ. The conclusion (with which I am in sympathy) is that mental contents are affected not only by the physical and qualitatively mental way the person is, but by the nature of his *physical environment*.

Putnam himself does not give quite this argument. He nowhere states the first and third steps, though he gives analogs of them for the meaning of 'water'. This is partly just a result of his concentration on meaning instead of propositional attitudes. But some of what he says even seems to oppose the argument's conclusion. He remarks in effect that the subject's *thoughts* remain constant between his actual and counterfactual cases (p. 224). In his own argument he explicates the difference between actual and counterfactual cases in terms of a difference in the extension of terms, not a difference in those aspects of their meaning that play a role in the cognitive life of the subject. And he tries to explicate his examples in terms of indexicality – a mistake, I think, and one that tends to divert attention from major implications of the examples he gives. (Cf. Section IId.) In my view, the examples do illustrate the fact that all attitudes involving natural kind notions, including *de dicto* attitudes, presuppose *de re* attitudes. But the examples do not show that natural kind linguistic expressions are in any ordinary sense indexical. Nor do they show that beliefs involving natural kind notions are always *de re*. Even if they did, the change from actual to counterfactual cases would affect oblique occurrences of natural kind terms in that-clauses – occurrences that are the key to attributions of cognitive content (Cf. above and note 3.) In the cited paper and earlier ones, much of what Putnam says about psychological states (and implies about mental states) has a distinctly individualistic ring. Below in Section IV, I criticize viewpoints about mental phenomena influenced by and at least strongly suggested in his earlier work on functionalism. (Cf. note 9.)

On the other hand, Putnam's articulation of social and environmental aspects of the meaning of natural kind terms complements and supplements our viewpoint. For me, it has been a rich rewarder of reflection. More recent work of his seems to involve shifts in his viewpoint on psychological states. It may have somewhat more in common with our approach than the earlier work, but there is much that I do not understand about it.

The argument regarding the notion of water that I extracted from Putnam's paper is narrower in scope than our argument. The Putnam-derived argument seems to work only for natural kind terms and close relatives. And it may seem not to provide as direct a threat to certain versions of functionalism that I discuss in Section IV: At least a few philosophers would claim that one could accommodate the Putnamian argument in terms of *non*-intentional formulations of input-output relations (formulations that make reference to the specific nature of the physical environment). Our argument does not submit to this maneuver. In our thought experiment, the physical environment (sofas, arthritis, and so forth in our examples) and the subject's causal relations with it (at least as these are usually conceived) were held constant. The Putnamian argument, however, has fascinatingly different implications from our argument. I have not developed these comparisons and contrasts here because doing justice to Putnam's viewpoint would demand a distracting amount of space, as the ample girth of this footnote may suggest.

3. I have discussed *de re* mental phenomena in 'Belief *De Re*,' *The Journal of Philosophy* 74 (1977): 338–62. There I argue that all attitudes with content presuppose *de re* attitudes. Our discussion here may be seen as bearing on the details of this presupposition. But for reasons I merely sketch in the next paragraph, I think it would be a superficial viewpoint that tried to utilize our present argument to support the view that nearly all intentional mental phenomena are covertly indexical or *de re*.
4. Cf. my 'Belief and Synonymy,' *The Journal of Philosophy* 75 (1978): 119–38, Section III, where I concentrate on attribution of belief contents containing 'one criterion' terms like 'vixen' or 'fortnight' which the subject misunderstands. The next several pages interweave some of the points in that paper. I think that a parallel thought experiment involving even these words is constructible, at least for a narrowly restricted set of beliefs. We can imagine that the subject believes that some female foxes – say, those that are virgins – are not vixens. Or he could believe that a fortnight is a period of ten days. (I believed this for many years.) Holding his physical history, qualitive experience, and dispositions constant, we can conceive of his linguistic community defining these terms as he actually misunderstands them. In such a case, his belief contents would differ from his actual ones.
5. Bertrand Russell, *Mysticism and Logic* (London, 1959), p. 221. Although Russell's statement is unusually unqualified, its kinship to Descartes' and Plato's model is unmistakable. Cf. Plato, *Phaedrus*, 249b–c, *Phaedo*, 47b6–c4; Descartes, *Philosophical Works*, eds. Haldane and Ross 2 vols. (New York, 1955), *Rules for the Direction of the Mind*, section XII, Vol. 1, pp. 41–42, 45; *Principles of Philosophy*, Part I, XXXII–XXXV. Vol. I, pp. 232–33; *Replies*, Vol. II, 52; Hume, *A Treatise of Human Nature*, I, 3, 5; II, 2, 6; Kant, *A Critique of Pure Reason*, A7–B11; Frege, *The Foundations of Arithmetic*, section 105; G. F. Moore, *Principia Ethica*, 86.
6. Descartes, *Principles of Philosophy*, XLV–XLI.
7. Descartes, *Philosophical Works*, Vol II., *Replies*, p. 42.
8. Certain movements sometimes called 'functionalist' are definitely not my present concern. Nothing I say is meant to oppose the claim that hypotheses in psychology do and should make reference to 'sub-personal' states and processes in explaining human action and ordinary mental states and processes. My remarks may bear on precisely how such hypotheses are construed philosophically. But the hypotheses themselves must be judged primarily by their fruits. Similarly, I am not concerned with the claim that computers provide an illuminating perspective for viewing the mind. Again, our view may bear on the interpretation of the computer analogy, but I have no intention of questioning its general fruitfulness. On the other hand,

insofar as functionalism is merely a slogan to the effect that 'once you see how computers might be made to work, you realize such and such about the mind,' I am inclined to let the cloud condense a little before weighing its contents.

9. A representative of the more nearly 'analytical' form of functionalism is David Lewis, 'Psychophysical and Theoretical Identifications,' *Australasian Journal of Philosophy* 50 (1972): 249–58: 'Applied to common-sense psychology – folk science rather than professional science, but a theory nonetheless – we get the hypothesis . . . that a mental state M . . . is definable as the occupant of a certain causal role R – that is, as the state, of whatever sort, that is causally connected in specified ways to sensory stimuli, motor responses, and other mental states' (249–50). Actually, it should be noted that the argument of Section I applies to Lewis's position less directly than one might suppose. For reasons unconnected with matters at hand, Lewis intends his *definition* to apply to relational mentalistic predicates like 'thinks' but not to complex predicates that identify actual mental states or events, like 'thinks that snow is white'. Cf. *Ibid.*, p. 256, n13. This seems to me a puzzling halfway house for some of Lewis's philosophical purposes. But our argument appears to apply anyway, since Lewis is explicit in holding that physical facts about a person take in isolation from his fellows 'determine' all his specific intentional events and states. Cf. 'Radical Interpretation', *Synthese* 27 (1974): 331ff. I cite Lewis's definitional approach because it has been the most influential recent piece of its genre, and many of those influenced by it have not excluded its application to specific intentional mental states and events. Other representatives of the definitional approach are J. J. C. Smart, 'Further Thoughts on the Identity Theory,' *Monist* 56 (1972): 149–62; D. W. Armsstrong, *A Materialist Theory of Mind* (London, 1968), pp. 90–91 and *passim*; Sidney Shoemaker, 'Functionalism and Qualia,' *Philosophical Studies* 27 (1975): 306–7. A representative of the more frequently held 'hypothesis' version of functionalism is Hilary Putnam, 'The Mental Life of Some Machines,' *Philosophical Papers* 2 (Cambridge, 1975), and 'The Nature of Mental States,' *Ibid.*, cf. p. 437: '. . . if the program of finding psychological laws that are not species specific . . . ever succeeds, then it will bring in its wake a delineation of the kind of functional organization that is necessary and sufficient for a given psychological state, as well as a precise definition of the notion 'psychological state'.' In more recent work, Putnam's views on the relation between functional organization and psychological (and also mental) states and events have become more complicated. I make no claims about how the argument of Section II bears on them. Other representatives of the 'hypothesis' approach are Gilbert Harman, 'Three Levels of Meaning,' *The Journal of Philosophy* 65 (1968); 'An Introduction to 'Translation and Meaning,' *Words and Objections*, eds. D. Davidson and J. Hintikka (Reidel, 1969), p. 21; and *Thought* (Princeton, 1973), pp. 43–46, 56–65, for example, p. 45: '. . . mental states and processes are to be functionally defined (by a psychological theory). They are constituted by their function or role in the relevant programme'; Jerry Fodor, *The Language of Thought* (New York, 1975), Chapter I; Armstrong, *A Materialist Theory of Mind*, p. 84. An attempt to articulate the common core of the different types of functionalist 'account' occurs in Ned Block and Jerry Fodor's 'What Psychological States are Not,' *Philosophical Review* 81 (1972), p. 173: '. . . functionalism in the broad sense of that doctrine which holds that type identity conditions for

psychological states refer only to their relations to inputs, outputs and one another.'

10. Often functionalists give mental contents only cursory discussion, if any at all. But claims that a functional account explains intentionality by accounting for all specific intentional states and events in non-intentional, functional language occur in the following: Daniel Dennett, *Content and Consciousness* (London, 1969), Chapter II and *passim*; Harman, *Thought*, for example, p. 60:'To specify the meaning of a sentence used in communication is partly to specify the belief or other mental state expressed; and the representative character of that state is determined by its functional role'; Fodor, *The Language of Thought*, Chapters I and II, for example, p. 75: 'The way that information is stored, computed . . . or otherwise processed by the organism explains its cognitive states and in particular, its propositional attitudes'; Smart, 'Further Thoughts on the Identity Theory'; Hartry Field, 'Mental Representation,' *Erkenntnis* 13 (1978): 9–61. I shall confine discussion to the issue of intentionality. But it seems to me that the individualistic cast of functionalist accounts renders them inadequate in their handling of another major traditional issue about intentional mental states and events – first-person authority.
11. H. P. Grice, 'Meaning,' *Philosophical Review* 66 (1957): 377–88; 'Utterer's Meaning, Sentence-Meaning, and Word-Meaning,' *Foundations of Language* 4 (1968): 225–42; Stephen Schiffer, *Meaning* (Oxford, 1972), cf. especially pp. 13, 50, 63ff; Jonathan Bennett, 'The Meaning-Nominalist Strategy,' *Foundations of Language* 10 (1974): 141–68. Another example of an individualistic theory of meaning is the claim to explicate all kinds of meaning ultimately in psychological terms, and these latter in functionalist terms. See, for example Harman, 'Three Levels of Meaning,' note 9. This project seems to rest on the functionalist approaches just criticized.
12. Perhaps the first reasonably clear modern statement of the strategy occurs in J. J. C. Smart, 'Sensations and Brain Processes,' *Philosophical Review* 68 (1959): 141–56. This article treats qualitative experiences; but Smart is explicit in applying it to specific intentional states and events in 'Further Thoughts on the Identity Theory.' Cf. also David Lewis, 'An Argument for the Identity Theory,' *The Journal of Philosophy* 63 (1966): 17–25; 'Psychophysical and Theoretical Identifications'; Armstrong, *A Materialist Theory of Mind, passim*; Harman, *Thought*, pp. 42–43; Fodor, *The Language of Thought*, Introduction.
13. The argument is basically Cartesian in style, (cf. *Meditations* II), though the criticism of functionalism, which is essential to its success, is not in any obvious sense Cartesian. (Cf. note 14.) Also the conclusion gives no special support to Cartesian ontology. The terminology of rigidity is derived from Saul Kripke, 'Naming and Necessity,' *Semantics of Natural Language*, eds., Davidson and Harman (Dordrecht, 1972), though as mentioned above, a notion of rigidity is not essential for the argument. Kripke has done much to clarify the force of the Cartesian sort of argument. He gives such an argument aimed at showing the non-identity of sensations with brain processes. The argument as presented seems to suffer from a failure to criticize materialistic accounts of sensation language and from not indicating clearly how token physical events and token sensation events that are *prima facie* candidates for identification could have occurred independently. For criticism of Kripke's argument, see Fred Feldman,

'Kripke on the Identity Theory,' *The Journal of Philosophy* 71 (1974): 665–76; William G. Lycan, 'Kripke and the Materialists,' *Ibid.*, pp. 677–89; Richard Boyd, 'What Physicalism Does Not Entail,' *Readings in the Philosophy of Psychology*, ed. N. Block (forthcoming); Colin McGinn, 'Anomalous Monism and Kripke's Cartesian Intuitions,' *Analysis* 37 (1977): 78–80. It seems to me, however, that these issues are not closed.

14 It is important to note that our argument against functionalist specifications of mentalistic phenomena did not depend on the assumption that no occurrent thought could have a different content from the one it has and be the very same occurrence or event. If it did, the subsequent argument against the identity theory would, in effect, beg the question. The strategy of the latter argument is rather to presuppose an independent argument that undermines non-intentional functionalist specifications of what it is to be *a* thought that (say) sofas are comfortable; then to take as plausible and undefeated the assumption that no occurrent thought could have a different (obliquely non-equivalent) content and be the same occurrence or event; and, finally, to use this assumption with the modal considerations appealed to earlier, to arrive at the non-identity of an occurrent thought event with any event specified by physical theory (the natural sciences) that occurs within the individual.

Perhaps it is worth saying that the metaphorical claim that mental events are identified by their *role* in some 'inference-action language game' (to use a phrase of Sellars's) does not provide a plausible ground for rejecting the initial premise of the argument against the identity theory. For even if one did not reject the 'role-game' idea as unsupported metaphor, one could agree with the claim on the understanding that the roles are largely the intentional contents themselves and the same event in *this* sort of 'game' could not have a different role. A possible view in the philosophy of mathematics is that numbers are identified by their role in a progression and such roles are essential to their identity. The point of this comparison is just that appeal to the role metaphor, even if accepted, does not settle the question of whether an intentional mental event or state could have had a different content.

15. There are *prima facie* viable philosophical accounts that take sentences (whether tokens or types) as truth bearers. One might hope to extend such accounts to mental contents. On such treatments, contents are not things over and above sentences. They simply *are* sentences interpreted in a certain context, treated in a certain way. Given a different context of linguistic interpretation, the content of the same sentence might be different. One could imagine mental events to be analogous to the sentences on this account. Indeed, some philosophers have thought of intentional mental events as being inner, physical sentence (or symbol) tokens – a sort of brain writing. Here again, there is a picture according to which the same thought event might have had a different content. But here again the question is whether there is any reason to think it is a true picture. There is the prior question of whether sentences can reasonably be treated as contents. (I think sentence types probably can be; but the view has hardly been established, and defending it against sophisticated objections is treacherous.) Even if this question is answered affirmatively, it is far from obvious that the analogy between sentences and contents, on the one hand, and thought events and contents, on the other, is a good one. Sentences (types or tokens) are

commonly identified independently of their associated contents (as evidenced by inter- and intra-linguistic ambiguity). It is *relatively* uncontroversial that sentences can be identified by syntactical, morphemic, or perceptual criteria that are in principle specifiable independently of what particular content the sentence has. The philosophical question about sentences and contents is whether discourse about contents can be reasonably interpreted as having an ontology of nothing more than sentences (and intentional agents). The philosophical question about mental events and contents is 'What is the nature of the events?' 'Regardless of what contents are, could the very same thought event have a different content?' The analogous question for sentences – instead of thought events – has an uncontroversial affirmative answer. Of course, we know that when and where non-intentionally identifiable physical events have contents, the same physical event could have had a different content. But it can hardly be *assumed* for purposes of arguing a position on the mind-body problem that mental events are non-intentionally identifiable physical events.

16. In emphasizing social and pragmatic features in mentalistic attributions, I do not intend to suggest that mental attributions are any the less objective, descriptive, or on the ontological up and up. There are substantial arguments in the literature that might lead one to make such inferences. But my present remarks are free of such implications. Someone might want to insist that from a 'purely objective viewpoint' one can describe 'the phenomena' equally well in accord with common practice, literally interpreted, or in accord with various reinterpretation strategies. Then our arguments would, perhaps, show only that it is 'objectively indeterminate' whether functionalism and the identity theory are true. I would be inclined to question the application of the expressions that are scare-quoted.

17. I am grateful to participants at a pair of talks given at the University of London in the spring of 1978, and to Richard Rorty for discussions earlier. I am also indebted to Robert Adams and Rogers Albritton whose criticisms forced numerous improvements. I appreciatively acknowledge support of the John Simon Guggenheim Foundation.

Chapter 16

Frege's Puzzle

N. Salmon

Chapter 1

Frege's Puzzle and the Naive Theory

1.1 Frege's puzzle and information content

> Identity challenges reflection through questions which are connected with it and are not altogether easy to answer. . . . $\ulcorner a = a \urcorner$ $\ulcorner a = b \urcorner$ are obviously sentences of a different cognitive value [Erkenntniswerte]: $\ulcorner a = a \urcorner$ holds a priori and is according to Kant to be called analytic, whereas sentences of the form $\ulcorner a = b \urcorner$ often contain very valuable extensions of our knowledge and are not always to be grounded a priori. . . . If we then wanted to view identity as a relation between that which the names a and b signify, then $\ulcorner a = b \urcorner$ and $\ulcorner a = a \urcorner$ would seem to be potentially not different, in case, that is, $\ulcorner a = b \urcorner$ is true. There would be thereby expressed a relation of a thing to itself, one in which each thing stands to itself, but no thing stands to another.

With the German equivalent of these words, Frege tortuously poses the problem that gave rise to his celebrated theory of sense: How can $\ulcorner a = b \urcorner$, if true, differ in 'cognitive value' – that is, in cognitive information content – from $\ulcorner a = a \urcorner$? Clearly they differ, since the first is informative and a posteriori where the latter is uninformative and a priori. But, assuming that $\ulcorner a = b \urcorner$ predicates the relation of identity between the referent of the name a and the referent of the name b, and that $\ulcorner a = a \urcorner$ predicates the relation of

From N. Salmon (1986/91), *Frege's Puzzle*, MIT, Ridgeview

identity between the referent of *a* and the referent of *a*, then if $\ulcorner a = b \urcorner$ is true, it predicates the same relation between the same pair of objects as does $\ulcorner a = a \urcorner$. It would seem, then, that $\ulcorner a = b \urcorner$ and $\ulcorner a = a \urcorner$ ought to convey the same piece of information. But clearly they do not. So what gives here?

A number of philosophers have found the identity relation, taken as the relation that 'each thing stands in to itself but no thing stands to another,' curious, mysterious, or bogus. In the *Tractatus* (sections 5.53–5.535), Wittgenstein denies that there is any such relation.[1] Earlier, in *Begriffsschrift* (section 8), Frege took a similar tack, proposing an analysis of identity sentences according to which singular terms 'display their own selves [appear in propria persona] when they are combined by means of the sign ['='] for identity of content [referent], for this expresses the circumstance of two names [singular terms] having the same content [referent].' Thus the early Frege and Wittgenstein attempted to rid themselves of the puzzle. More recent philosophy has followed Frege's later characterization of the origins of the puzzle as one arising from reflection on the concept of the identity by the use of such epithets as 'Frege's puzzle about identity' or 'Frege's identity problem'. The first point I wish to emphasize about 'Frege's puzzle about identity' is that, pace Frege, it is not a puzzle about identity. It has virtually nothing to do with identity. Different versions of the very same puzzle, or formally analogous puzzles that pose the very same set of questions and philosophical issues in the very same way, arise with certain constructions not involving the identity predicate or the identity relation. For example, the sentence 'Shakespeare wrote *Timon of Athens*' is informative, whereas 'The author of *Timon of Athens* wrote *Timon of Athens*' is not. The same question arises: How can that be? Given that the first sentence is true, it would seem that both sentences contain the same piece of information; they both attribute the same property (authorship of *Timon of Athens*) to the same individual (Shakespeare). This kind of example is unlike Frege's version of the puzzle in that it involves a definite description, whereas Frege's can involve two proper names and consequently applies pressure against a wider range of semantic theories. It is not difficult, however, to construct further puzzling examples involving two names without using the identity predicate; the sentence 'Hesperus is a planet if Phosphorus is' is informative and apparently a posteriori, whereas the sentence 'Phosphorus is a planet if Phosphorus is' is uninformative and a priori. However, both sentences attribute the same property, *being a planet if Phosphorus is*, to the same entity, the planet Venus. Looked at another way, both sentences attribute the same relation, *x is a planet if y is*, to the same (reflexive) pair of objects. In either case, the two sentences seem to contain the very same information.

It is easy to see from these examples that versions of Frege's Puzzle can be constructed in connection with any predicate whatsoever, not just with the identity predicate. What, then, is the general puzzle about if it is not a puzzle about identity? These same examples provide the answer. The general problem is a problem concerning pieces of information (in a nontechnical sense), such as the information that Socrates is wise or the information that Socrates is wise if Plato is. The various versions of Frege's Puzzle are stated in terms of declarative sentences rather than in terms of information. This is because there is an obvious and intimate relation between pieces of information (such as the information that Socrates is wise) and declarative sentences (such as 'Socrates is wise'). Declarative sentences have various semantic attributes: they are true, or false, or neither; they have semantic intentions (i.e., correlated functions from possible worlds to truth values); they involve reference to individuals, such as Socrates; and so on. But the fundamental semantic role of a declarative sentence is to encode information.[2] I mean the term 'information' in a broad sense to include misinformation (that is, inaccurate or incorrect pieces of information), and even pieces of information that are neither true nor false. Pragmatically, we use declarative sentences to communicate or convey information to others (generally, not just the information encoded by the sentence), but we may also use declarative sentences simply to record information for possible future use, and perhaps even to record information with no anticipation of any future use. If for some reason I need to make a record of the date of my marriage, say to recall that piece of information on a later occasion, I can simply write the words 'I was married on August 28, 1980', or memorize them, or repeat them to myself. Declarative sentences are primarily a means of encoding information, and they are a remarkably efficient means at that. Many of their other semantic and pragmatic functions follow from or depend upon their fundamental semantic role of encoding information.

This statement of the semantic relation between declarative sentences and information is somewhat vague, but it is clear enough to convey one of the fundamental presuppositions of Frege's Puzzle. Vague though it may be, it is also obviously correct. Any reasonable semantic theory for declarative sentences ought to allow for some account of declarative sentences as information encoders, at least to the extent of not contradicting it. A conception of sentences as information encoders will be assumed throughout this book. A declarative sentence will be said to *contain* the information it encodes, and that piece of information will be described as the *information content* of the sentence.

Pieces of information are, like the sentences that encode them, abstract entities. Many of their properties can be 'read off' from the encoding sentences. Thus, for instance, it is evident that pieces of information are not ontologically simple, but complex. The information that Socrates is wise and the information that Socrates is snub-nosed are both, in the same way, pieces of information directly about Socrates; hence, they must have some component in common. Likewise, the information that Socrates is wise has some component in common with the information that Plato is wise, and that component is different from what it has in common with the information that Socrates is snub-nosed. Correspondingly, the declarative sentence 'Socrates is wise' shares certain syntactic components with the sentences 'Socrates is snub-nosed' and 'Plato is wise'. These syntactic components – the name 'Socrates' and the predicate 'is wise' – are separately semantically correlated with the corresponding component of the piece of information encoded by the sentence. Let us call the information component semantically correlated with an expression the *information value* of the expression. The information value of the name 'Socrates' is that which the name contributes to the information encoded by such sentences as 'Socrates is wise' and 'Socrates is snub-nosed'; similarly, the information value of the predicate 'is wise' is that entity which the predicate contributes to the information encoded by such sentences as 'Socrates is wise' and 'Plato is wise'. As a limiting case, the information value of a declarative sentence is the piece of information it encodes, its information content.

[. . .]

4. The Structure of Frege's Puzzle

4.1 Compositionality

I have claimed that Frege's Puzzle concerns the nature and structure of pieces of information (the sort of information semantically contained in a declarative sentence), and that an adequate solution must address this issue directly. It is important for this purpose to focus on the principles and assumptions involved in the derivation of Frege's Puzzle.

Preliminary investigation into the nature and structure of pieces of information uncovered that a piece of information is a complex abstract entity whose components are the information values of the components of a sentence that contains the information (modulo the qualifications mentioned in note 4 to chapter 1 [not included]). There are two components of the information that Socrates is wise: what is had in common between the information that Socrates is wise and the information that Socrates is snub-nosed, and what it had in common between the information that Socrates is wise and the information that Plato is wise. It is natural to suppose that the first component is precisely the individual whom that information is about, i.e., the man Socrates. Frege's Puzzle challenges this natural idea by proposing two purportedly distinct pieces of information that have the very same predicative component and are about the very same individual. The implicit assumption is a principle of compositionality for pieces of information: If pieces of information are complex abstract entities, and two pieces of information p and q having the same structure and mode of composition are numerically distinct, then there must be some component of one that is not a component of the other;

otherwise p and q would be one and the very same piece of information. (Compare the principle of extensionality for classes or sets.)

This compositionality principle for pieces of information might be challenged. Complex entities having the very same components and mode of composition cannot always be identified with one another. The clipboard on which I am now writing has the very same component molecules as the matter that now constitutes it, but, for familiar philosophical reasons, the clipboard is not identical with its present matter. The clipboard came into existence long after its present matter did, and it will cease to exist long before its present matter does (if the matter ever ceases to exist). Moreover, strictly speaking, the clipboard is constituted by different (albeit largely overlapping) matter at different times, and is only briefly constituted by its present molecules, though the present matter is forever constituted by these very molecules. Similarly, to use an example due to Richard Sharvy, the Supreme Court of the United States has the very same membership as the set of its present justices, but the Court and the set of its present justices are distinct complex entities, since the Court changes its membership over time whereas no set can change its membership.[3] Even complex entities of the very same kind having the same constituents and mode of composition cannot always be identified. Different ad hoc committees within a university department can coincide exactly in membership though they remain different committees with different functions and responsibilities.

In contrast with these examples, it would seem that pieces of information do obey the principle of compositionality implicit in Frege's Puzzle. For each of the complex entities mentioned above as violators of a corresponding compositionality principle, there is some significant aspect of the entity, some crucial feature of it, that differentiates it from any distinct entity composed of the very same constituents in the very same way. The Supreme Court and the set of its present justices differ in their flexibility with respect to change in membership. Any two distinct ad hoc committees differ in at least some of their functions or purposes. But pieces of information having the very same structure and components, combined in the very same way, cannot change in constitution, and they fulfill the same purposes and perform the same functions. In any event, if two pieces of information, p and q, are composed of the very same components in the very same way but are distinct, it would seem that there must also be some important aspect in which they differ, some significant property had by p and not by q or vice versa. This, however, raises the same challenging question posed by Frege, or at least a philosophically important question similar to Frege's original question: What in the world is this mysterious feature or aspect of pieces of information in which two pieces of information composed of the same components in the same way can yet differ? Even if the principle of compositionality for pieces of information fails, some variant of Frege's Puzzle remains a pressing philosophical problem for semantic theory.

4.2 Frege's law

In order to produce two distinct pieces of information that are about the same individuals and that have the same predicative component, Frege offers a pair of declarative sentences involving the same predicate but different singular terms for the same object and argues that these sentences must be seen as containing different pieces of information. To this end, Frege's Puzzle, in its original form, tacitly invokes the following principle concerning information content:

> If a declarative sentence *S* has the very same cognitive information content (Erkenntniswerte) as a declarative sentence *S′*, then *S* is informative ('contains an extension of our knowledge') if and only if *S′* is (does).

I shall call this principle *Frege's Law*. It is an exceedingly plausible principle connecting the concepts of *information content* and *informativeness*. Still, it might be thought that it is precisely the unquestioning acceptance of this principle that is the source of the puzzle. It might even be argued that the puzzle should be recast as a reductio ad absurdum of the principle. 'What independent reason can there be,' one might ask, 'for holding this principle to be true? In fact, isn't it clear that the informativeness or uninformativeness of a sentence depends on more factors than just the information content of the sentence, so that two sentences having the same content may yet differ in their informativeness?'[4]

This line of attack against Frege's Puzzle is sorely mistaken. Given the sense of 'informative' that is relevant to the puzzle, Frege's Law is unassailable. Properly understood, Frege's Law should be seen as a special instance of Leibniz's Law, the Indiscernibility of Identicals. This is because, on a proper understanding of 'informative', the informativeness or uninformativeness (a posteriority or a priority, etc.) of a sentence is a *derivative* semantic property of the sentence, one that the sentence has only by virtue of encoding the information that it does encode. That is, to say that a sentence, on a particular occasion of use, is (as the term is used in the context of Frege's Puzzle) *informative* (or that it is *a posteriori*) is to say something about the *information content* of the sentence: It is to say that the information content is not somehow already given, or that the content is nontrivial, or that it is knowable only by recourse to experience and not merely by reflection on the concepts involved, or that it is an 'extension of our knowledge,' or something along these lines. There is some such property *P* of pieces of information such that a sentence is informative, in the sense relevant to Frege's Puzzle, if and only if its information content has the property *P*.

Of course, there are other senses of 'informative' on which even a trivial identity statement may be described as 'informative'. For example, if you do not speak a word of French but you have it on good authority that Jean-Paul's next inscription will be of a true French sentence, and you observe Jean-Paul then write the words 'Cicéron est identique à Cicéron', the sentence in question, on this occasion of use, may be said to be 'informative' on several counts. By way of its inscription, you are given a great deal of nontrivial information; you are thereby given that a certain sequence of marks is a meaningful and grammatical expression of French, that it is in fact a French sentence, and that it is a true sentence. If you also know even a minimum about the grammar of Romance or Indo-European languages, and you know that 'Cicéron' is a name, you are also thereby given the information that the words 'est identique à' probably signify some relation in French, a relation that the relevant person called 'Cicéron' in French bears to himself. However, all this is quite irrelevant to Frege's Puzzle.

It is extremely important in dealing with Frege's Puzzle and related philosophical problems to distinguish the notion of the *information content* of a sentence on a particular occasion of its use from the notion of the *information imparted* by the particular utterance of the sentence. The first is a semantic notion, the second a pragmatic notion. Failure to make this distinction has led many a well-meaning philosopher astray. I have already discussed the notion of semantically encoded information at some length in the previous chapter. In claiming that it is a basic function of sentences to encode information, I invoke the notion of semantically encoded information. To illustrate the quite different notion of pragmatically imparted information, it is best to begin with a nonlinguistic and uncontroversial example. Consider some of the ways in which one might receive or learn the information that Smith has a cold. One way, of course, is for someone (perhaps Smith) to produce with assertive intent a conventional symbol that semantically encodes that information; for example, Smith may utter the sentence 'I have a cold' in conversation. Under certain circumstances, another way to learn that Smith has a cold – one not involving language – is simply to observe Smith sneeze and then blow his nose. In this sense, Smith's blowing his nose imparts, or can impart, the information that he has a cold. Though the blowing of a nose may thus impart certain information, it would be utterly ridiculous to suppose that nose blowing has any semantic content. One can imagine a society in which blowing one's nose is a linguistic gesture – a move in the language game – much like shaking one's head 'no' is in our society; fortunately, however, we do not live in such a society. In our society, nose blowing has no semantic significance whatsoever. It is an entirely nonlinguistic act.

Now, just as Smith's nose blowing may impart the information that Smith has a cold, without itself having any semantic attributes and hence without semantically encoding any information, so any observable event typically imparts some information to the astute observer – hence the saying 'Actions speak louder than words.' Utterances are no exception. In uttering a sentence, one produces a symbol that semantically encodes a piece of information, and in so doing one performs an action (indeed, several actions) that, like any other action, may impart information in the nonsemantic way that even nose blowing may impart information. Of course, typically the information semantically encoded by a sentence will be pragmatically imparted by utterances of the sentence. But the two notions may diverge and often do. In addition to (sometimes instead of) the information semantically encoded by a sentence, an utterance of the sentence may impart further information concerning the speaker's beliefs, intentions, and attitudes, information concerning the very form of words chosen, or other extraneous information. The further information thus imparted can often be of greater significance than the information actually encoded by the sentence itself. Such is the case with Jean-Paul's inscription of 'Cicéron est identique à Cicéron'. In this sense, even utterances can 'speak louder than words.' In particular, one piece of information typically imparted by the utterance of a sentence *S* is the information that *S* is true with respect to the context of the utterance. It is rarely the case, however, that a sentence semantically encodes the information about itself that it is true (or, for that matter, that it is not true – such is the stuff of which paradoxes are made).

Frege himself was aware of the distinction between semantically encoded and pragmatically imparted information. Using his word 'thought' (Gedanke) for what I am calling 'information', Frege explicitly drew the distinction, or something very similar to it, in a section entitled 'Separating a Thought from its Trappings' of an essay entitled 'Logic,' estimated to have been composed in 1897:

> . . . we have to make a distinction between the thoughts that are expressed and those which the speaker leads others to take as true although he does not express them. If a commander conceals his weakness from the enemy by making his troops keep changing their uniforms, he is not telling a lie; for he is not expressing any thoughts, although his actions are calculated to induce thoughts in others. And we find the same thing in the case of speech itself, as when one gives a special tone to the voice or chooses special words. (in *Posthumous Writings*, ed. Hermes et al., at p. 140)

Frege's Puzzle concerns only the information content of Jean-Paul's sentence – the nature and structure of the information semantically contained in or encoded by the sentence with respect to the particular context of use – and not the information pragmatically imparted by the particular utterance. When Frege claims that sentences of the form $\ulcorner a = a \urcorner$ are a priori and do not 'contain very valuable extensions of our knowledge,' and are in this respect different from sentences of the form $\ulcorner a = b \urcorner$, there is no question but that he is concerned only with the 'thought expressed' by this form of sentence, i.e. its information content and not with the unexpressed 'thoughts' that the utterance 'leads us to take as true.' The information content of Jean-Paul's sentence is utterly trivial. It is in this essentially semantic sense of 'informative', having to do with the character of the information encoded by a sentence, that this French sentence is quite definitely uninformative. Its information content is a *given*, and does not 'extend our knowledge.'

To take another example due to Carnap, consider the numerical equation '5 = V', using both the Arabic and the Roman numeral for five.[5] To someone familiar with one but not both of these numeral systems, an inscription of this equation pragmatically imparts nontrivial information, e.g. the information concerning one of the numerals that it is a numeral for the number five. But the information semantically encoded by the equation is precisely the same as that encoded by '5 = 5'. This is an instance of the trivial law of reflexivity of equality. The encoded information is not a 'valuable extension of knowledge,' or anything of the sort. In the relevant sense, the equation is utterly uninformative. A similar situation obtains with respect to sentences like 'Opthalmologists are oculists' and Alienists are psychiatrists'. To someone unfamiliar with the grammatical subject term but familiar with the grammatical predicate term, an utterance or inscription of one of these sentences pragmatically imparts nontrivial linguistic information concerning the meaning of the grammatical subject term, though the semantically encoded information is utterly trivial. Indeed, it is just this feature of these sentences – the fact that their semantic information content is trivial – that suits them to the task of conveying the meanings of 'ophthalmologist' and 'alienist'. This is unlike the examples that give rise to Frege's Puzzle (e.g. 'Hesperus is Phosphorus'), in which we are to suppose that the audience has complete mastery of both terms and finds the utterance or inscription informative nevertheless.

Properly understood, then, Frege's Law is not merely a plausible principle connecting the concepts of information content and informativeness, or even a fundamental law of semantics. It is a truth of logic. Hence, it is no solution to the puzzle to challenge Frege's Law.

[· · ·]

6. The Crux of Frege's Puzzle

6.1 The minor premise

There are three main elements in Frege's Puzzle, and in the corresponding strategy: Frege's Law, the compositionality principle, and the further premise that $\ulcorner a = b \urcorner$ is informative and a posteriori whereas $\ulcorner a = a \urcorner$ is not. I have argued that there is nothing to be gained by challenging the compositionality principle, and that Frege's Law is beyond challenge, since properly understood it is simply a special instance of Leibniz's Law. Still to be considered is the minor premise that $\ulcorner a = b \urcorner$ is informative whereas $\ulcorner a = a \urcorner$ is not.

Historically, philosophers who have had some inclination toward something like the naive theory, including Frege, Mill, and Russell, have allowed that $\ulcorner a = b \urcorner$ is informative and a posteriori whereas $\ulcorner a = a \urcorner$ is not. This was thought too obvious to be denied, and other means for coming to grips with Frege's Puzzle were sought and devised. In contemporary philosophy, direct-reference theorists – who should find the naive theory particularly congenial – have typically conceded this point, or something tantamount to it, and have therefore abstained from outright, unequivocal endorsement of the naive theory or any modification of the naive theory. Consider the following remarks:

> [You] see a star in the evening and it's called 'Hesperus'. . . . We see a star in the morning and call it 'Phosphorus'. Well, then we find . . . that Hesperus and Phosphorus are in fact the same. So we express this by 'Hesperus is Phosphorus'. Here we're certainly not just saying of an object that it's identical with itself. This is something that we discovered. (Saul Kripke, *Naming and Necessity*, pp. 28–29)

> [We] do not know *a priori* that Hesperus is Phosphorus, and are in no position to find out . . . except empirically. (ibid., p. 104; see also the disclaimer on pp. 20–21)

> Before appropriate empirical discoveries were made, men might have failed to know that Hesperus was Phosphorus, or even to believe it, even though they of course knew and believed that Hesperus was Hesperus. (Kripke, 'A Puzzle About Belief,' p. 243 – but see p. 281, note 44; see also the disclaimer at p. 273, note 10)

> Certainly Frege's argument shows meaning cannot just *be* reference. . . . (Hilary Putnam, 'Comments,' p. 285)

> If we distinguish a sentence from the proposition it expresses then the terms 'truth' and 'necessity' apply to the proposition expressed by a sentence, while the terms '*a priori*' and '*a posteriori*' are sentence relative. Given that it is true that Cicero is Tully (and whatever we need about what the relevant sentences express) 'Cicero is Cicero' and 'Cicero is Tully' express the same *proposition*. And the proposition is necessarily true. But looking at the proposition through the lens of the *sentence* 'Cicero is Cicero' the proposition can be seen *a priori* to be true, but through 'Cicero is Tully' one may need an *a posteriori* investigation. (Keith Donnellan, 'Kripke and Putnam on Natural Kind Terms,' note 2 on p. 88)

> Faced with Frege's identity puzzle, it is difficult indeed to maintain that the names 'Hesperus' and 'Phosphorus' make precisely the same contribution to

the information content of sentences that contain either one. Such a claim would be extremist. (Nathan Salmon, *Reference and Essence*, p. 13)

Here is where well-intentioned philosophers have been led astray. It is precisely the seemingly trivial premise that $\ulcorner a = b \urcorner$ is informative whereas $\ulcorner a = a \urcorner$ is not informative that should be challenged, and a proper appreciation for the distinction between semantically encoded and pragmatically imparted information points the way. Recall that Frege's Law is erected into a truth of logic by understanding the word 'informative' in such a way that to say that a sentence is informative is to say something about its information content. By the same token, however, with 'informative' so understood, and with a sharp distinction between semantically encoded information and pragmatically imparted information kept in mind, it is not in the least bit obvious, as Frege's Puzzle maintains, that $\ulcorner a = b \urcorner$ is, whereas $\ulcorner a = a \urcorner$ is not, informative *in the relevant sense*. To be sure, $\ulcorner a = b \urcorner$ *sounds* informative, whereas $\ulcorner a = a \urcorner$ does not. Indeed, an utterance of $\ulcorner a = b \urcorner$ genuinely imparts information that is more valuable than that imparted by an utterance of $\ulcorner a = a \urcorner$. for example, it imparts the nontrivial linguistic information about the sentence $\ulcorner a = b \urcorner$ that is true, and hence that the names *a* and *b* are co-referential. But that is pragmatically imparted information, and presumably not semantically encoded information. (See the discussion in section 3.2 of the 'Begriffsschrift' solution to Frege's Puzzle.) It is by no means clear that the sentence $\ulcorner a = b \urcorner$, stripped naked of its pragmatic impartations and with only its properly semantic information content left, is any more informative in the relevant sense than $\ulcorner a = a \urcorner$. Abstracting from their markedly different pragmatic impartations, one can see that these two sentences may well semantically encode the very same piece of information. I believe that they do. At the very least, it is by no means certain, as Frege's Puzzle pretends, that the difference in 'cognitive significance' we seem to hear is not due entirely to a difference in pragmatically imparted information. Yet, until we can be certain of this, Frege's Law cannot be applied and Frege's Puzzle does not get off the ground. In effect, then, Frege's Strategy begs the question against the modified naive theory. Of course, if one fails to draw the distinction between semantically encoded and pragmatically imparted information, as so many philosophers have, it is small wonder that information pragmatically imparted by (utterances of) $\ulcorner a = b \urcorner$ may be mistaken for semantically encoded information.[6] If Frege's Strategy is ultimately to succeed, a further argument must be made to show that the information imparted by $\ulcorner a = b \urcorner$ that makes it sound informative is, in fact, semantically encoded. In the meantime, Frege's Puzzle by itself is certainly not the final and conclusive refutation of the modified naive theory that the orthodox theorists have taken it to be. For all that Frege's Strategy achieves, the modified naive theory remains the best and most plausible theory available concerning the nature and structure of the information encoded by declarative sentences.

Ironically, as was noted in section 4.2, Frege was not unaware of the distinction between semantically encoded and merely pragmatically imparted information. He did not fully appreciate the significance of this distinction for his theory of information content. In particular, he failed to notice that the distinction undermines his main argument against the naive theory.

6.2 Substitutivity

The general puzzle, however, is not so easily put to rest. Although the premise that $\ulcorner a = b \urcorner$ is informative whereas $\ulcorner a = a \urcorner$ is not facilitates the derivation of Frege's Puzzle, this premise is not an essential element in the general puzzle. The premise is invoked in conjunction with Frege's Law to establish the result that there are pairs of sentences of the form ϕ_a and ϕ_b that differ in information content from one another – i.e., that encode different pieces of information – even though a and b are co-referential (genuine) proper names, demonstratives, single-word indexical singular terms, or any combination thereof. This is the crux of Frege's Puzzle. One might attempt to establish this result in some more general way, without invoking the suspect premise that $\ulcorner a = b \urcorner$ is informative. As Michael Dummett has stressed, and as Frege's formulation of the puzzle clearly indicates, the notion of *information content* relevant to Frege's Puzzle is closely tied to the ordinary, everyday notions of *knowledge* and *belief*. One intuitively appealing picture that is entrenched in philosophical tradition depicts belief as a type of inward assent, or a disposition toward inward assent, to a piece of information. To believe that p is to concur covertly with, to endorse mentally, to nod approval to, the information that p when p occurs to you. At the very least, to believe that p one must adopt some sort of favorable disposition or attitude toward the information that p. In fact, the adoption of some such favorable attitude toward a piece of information is both necessary and sufficient for belief. That is just what belief is.[7] To believe that p is, so to speak, to include that piece of information in one's personal inner 'data bank.' It is to have that information at one's disposal to rely upon, to act upon, to draw inferences from, or to do nothing with. Belief is thus a relation to pieces of information.

These observations suggest the following principal schema, where the substituends for S and S' are declarative English sentences:

> If the information that S = the information that S', then someone believes that S if and only if he or she believes that S'.

Analogous schemata may be written for assertion and the other so called propositional attitudes of knowledge, hope, and so forth. Like Frege's Law, each of these schemata may be regarded as (formal mode renderings of) so many instances of Leibniz's Law. In fact, Frege's Law can be viewed as a minor variation of one such schema:

> If the information that S = the information that S', then it is informative (knowable only a posteriori, a valuable extension of our

knowledge, etc.) that S if and only if it is informative (a posteriori, etc.) that S'.

The *thesis of the substitutivity of co-informational sentences in propositional attitude contexts* is the thesis that every proper instance of any of these schemata is true. This may be separated into the *thesis of the substitutivity of co-informational sentences in assertion contexts* and so on for each of the attitudes. The thesis, or theses, is virtually a logical consequence of the idea that the object or content of a given belief, piece of knowledge, etc., is a piece of information, or a 'proposition', and that a sentence encoding that information thereby gives the content of the belief. This idea, or something like it, is a commonplace in the philosophy of language; it is usually taken for granted without challenge by both sides in philosophical disputes over related issues (such as the question of the logical form of belief attributions). Some philosophers, in an effort to rescue a favored theory of propositions from the pitfalls of propositional attitude contexts, have rejected the thesis of substitutivity of co-informational (or co-propositional) sentences in propositional attitude contexts. But doing so seems both extreme and ad hoc. If the favored theory of propositions conflicts with the thesis, it would be more plausible to reject the theory.[8]

Insofar as some of the substitutivity theses are accepted as plausible principles concerning the relation between the pieces of information contained in a sentence and the content of an attitude (belief, knowledge, etc.) thereby expressed, they yield an important procedure for establishing that two given pieces of information are distinct. One may simply rely on our ordinary, everyday criteria, whatever they happen to be, for correctly saying that someone believes or knows something or does not believe or know it. We do not have to be able to specify these criteria; we need only to be able to apply them correctly in certain paradigm cases.

Now, there is no denying that, given the proper circumstances, we say things like 'Lois Lane does not realize (know, believe) that Clark Kent is Superman' and 'There was a time when it was not known that Hesperus is Phosphorus'. Such pronouncements are in clear violation of the modified naive theory taken together with the thesis of substitutivity of co-informational sentences in doxastic and epistemic contexts. When we make these utterances, we typically do not intend to be speaking elliptically or figuratively; we take ourselves to be speaking literally and truthfully. Of course, one could intentionally utter such sentences in a metaphorical vein, or as an ellipsis for something else, but such circumstances are quite different from the usual circumstances in which such utterances are made, which are so familiar to teachers and students of contemporary analytic philosophy. The crucial question, however, is whether when we say such things we are correctly applying the criteria that govern the correct use of propositional-attitude locutions.

Recently a number of philosophers, mostly under the influence of the direct reference theory, have expressed doubt about the literal truth of such utterances in ordinary usage. If someone believes that Hesperus is a planet, they claim, then, strictly speaking, he or she also believes that Phosphorus is a planet, regardless of what the philosophically untutored or unenlightened say about his or her belief state. Whatever fact such speakers are attempting to convey by denying the belief ascription, the fact is not the lack of the ascribed belief but something else – perhaps the lack of a corresponding metalinguistic belief to the effect that a certain sentence is true. It is my view that this general approach to these problems is essentially correct, as far as it has been developed. The major problem with this approach is that it has not been developed far enough. I shall say more about this in due course. First, however, it is important to note a glaring philosophical difficulty inherent in this approach.

It is easy nowadays to get caught up in direct-reference mania, but one should never be blinded to possible departures from standard and generally reliable philosophical method and practice. What is ordinarily said in everyday language about a certain set of circumstances – where we take ourselves to be speaking literally and truthfully, and where the circumstances are judged to constitute a paradigm case of what we are saying, etc. – is often regarded as an important datum, sometimes the only possible datum, relevant to a certain philosophical or conceptual question about the facts in the matter. Of course, what we ordinarily say in everyday language is sometimes misleading, sometimes irrelevant, sometimes just plain wrong, but in cases where the issue concerns the applicability or inapplicability of a certain concept or term ordinary usage is often the best available guide to the facts. Consider, for example, the sorts of considerations invoked by epistemologists in deciding that Edmund Gettier's celebrated examples constitute genuine counterexamples to the traditional analysis of knowledge as justified true belief, or the sorts of considerations invoked by philosophers of perception in deciding that the state of experiencing a visual impression that is in fact caused by and resembles a certain external object is not the same thing as *seeing* the object. In the familiar problem cases, we simply do not say that the subject *knows* the relevant piece of information, or that he or she *sees* the relevant object. That is not the way we speak. Our forbearance in attributing knowledge or visual perception in these cases is rightly taken as conclusive evidence that such attributions are strictly false, given the actual and ordinary meanings of 'know' and 'see'. Philosophical programs such as that of analyzing knowledge or that of analyzing perception are, in a significant sense, at least partly an attempt to specify and articulate the implicit criteria or principles that govern the correct application of such terms as 'know' and 'see'. It is precisely for this reason that philosophers so often consult linguistic intuition in doing epistemology or metaphysics. Ordinary language is relevant because it is, at least to some extent, ordinary language that is under investigation.

And ordinary usage is a reliable guide to the principles governing the correct use of ordinary language. When the traditional analyses of knowledge or perception are challenged through thought experiments concerning what we would say in certain problem cases, philosophers are rightly skeptical of the reply that ordinary usage is incorrect and that the subject does indeed know the proposition in question, or see the object in question, even thought we typically say that he or she does not. Anyone maintaining this position may well be suspected of protecting an invested interest in the theory being challenged, rather than pursuing in good faith the philosopher's primary purpose of seeking truth no matter where the facts may lead. This is not to disparage such concepts as *justified true belief* and *experiencing a visual impression caused by and resembling an external object*. Such concepts may be epistemologically important. However, they demonstrably do not correspond – at least, they do not correspond exactly – to the everyday criteria that are implicit in ordinary usage for knowing or seeing. These criteria are, in a significant sense, *what are in question*.

Similarly, the claim that Lois Lane does, strictly speaking, believe and even know that Clark Kent is Superman (since she knows that he is Clark Kent) must not be made lightly, lest he or she who makes it be placed under the same suspicion. For here the question concerns, at least partly, the tacit principles governing the correct use of ordinary-language words such as 'believe', and the ordinary-usage evidence against the claim is strong indeed. The plain fact is that we simply do not speak that way. Perhaps we should learn to use a language in which propositional-attitude idioms function in strict accordance with the modified naive theory across the board, including the troublesome 'Hesperus'-'Phosphorus' and 'Cicero'-'Tully' cases, since ordinary language already agrees with the modified naive theory in the other, more commonplace sorts of cases. But that is a question for prescriptive philosophy of language, not one for descriptive philosophy of language. The more immediate and pressing philosophical question concerns the actual criteria that are implicitly at work in the everyday notion of belief, and the other attitudes, in their crude form, as they arise in real life without theoretical or aesthetic alteration.

I maintain that, according to these very criteria (in the standard sort of circumstance), it is, strictly speaking, correct to say that Lois Lane does know that Clark Kent is Superman, and what when ordinary speakers deny this they are typically operating under a linguistic confusion, systematically misapplying the criteria that govern the applicability or inapplicability of their own doxastic and epistemic terms and concepts. Similarly, anyone who knows that Hesperus is Hesperus knows that Hesperus is Phosphorus, no matter how strongly he or she may deny the latter. Moreover, anyone who knows that he or she knows that Hesperus is Hesperus also knows that he or she knows that Hesperus is Phosphorus, no matter how self-consciously he or she may disbelieve that Hesperus is Phosphorus.[4]

These claims clash sharply with ordinary usage. Whereas it is (as I have argued) extremely important not to lose sight of the tried and true philosophical tool of looking to ordinary usage in such matters, it is equally important to recognize the limitations of that test. Ordinary usage is a reliable guide to correct usage, but it is only a guide. Ordinary usage can sometimes be incorrect usage. Even when the ordinary usage of a certain locution is systematic, it can be systematically incorrect – if, for example, the language is deficient in ways that compel speakers to violate its rules in order to convey what they intend, or if the principles and social conventions governing the appropriateness of certain utterances require certain systematic violations of the principles and rules governing correct and incorrect applications of the terms used. My claim is that ordinary usage with regard to such predicates as 'is aware that Clark Kent is Superman' and 'believes that Hesperus is Phosphorus' conflicts with the criteria governing their correct application in just this way. However inappropriate it may be in most contexts to say so, Lois Lane is (according to the myth) fully aware that Clark Kent is Superman, and anyone who believes that Hesperus is Hesperus does in fact believe that Hesperus is Phosphorus. We do not speak this way; in fact, it is customary to say just the opposite. But if we wish to utter what is true, and if we care nothing about social convention, we should speak this way. The customary way of speaking involves us in uttering falsehoods.

Of course, it is no defense of the modified naive theory simply to make these bold claims. It is incumbent on the philosopher who makes these claims (i.e., me) to offer some reason for supposing that ordinary speakers, in the normal course of things, would be led to distort the rules of language systematically, so that ordinary usage cannot be relied upon in these cases as a guide to the correct-applicability conditions of the relevant terms and concepts. The account I shall offer is complex. The main part of this account will be given in section 8.4. For now, a tentative account is provided by repeating the distinction between semantically encoded and pragmatically imparted information. If one is not careful to keep this distinction in mind, it is altogether too easy to confuse information pragmatically imparted by (utterances of) 'Hesperus is Phosphorus' for semantically encoded information. In saying that *A* believes that Hesperus is Phosphorus, taken literally, we are merely attributing to *A* a relation (belief) to a certain piece of information (the information semantically encoded by 'Hesperus is Phosphorus'). The 'that'-clause 'that Hesperus is Phosphorus' functions here as a means for referring to that piece of information. Since the form of words 'Hesperus is Phosphorus' is considerably richer in pragmatic impartations than other expressions having the same semantic information content (e.g. 'Hesperus is Hesperus'), if one is not careful one cannot help but mistake the 'that'-clause as referring to this somewhat richer information – information which *A* may not believe. (See note 1.) Utterances of the locution ⌜*a* believes that *S*⌝ may even typically involve a Gricean implicature to the effect that the person referred to by *a* believes the information that is typically pragmatically imparted by utterances of *S*. Even so, that is not part of the literal content of the belief attribution. The general masses, and most philosophers, are not sufficiently aware of the effect that an implicature of this kind would have on ordinary usage. It is no embarrassment to the modified naive theory that ordinary speakers typically deny literally true belief attributions (and other propositional-attitude attributions) when these attributions involve a 'that'-clause whose utterance typically pragmatically imparts information which the speaker recognizes not to be among the beliefs (or other propositional attitudes) of the subject of the attribution. In fact, it would be an embarrassment to the modified naive theory if speakers did not do this. With widespread ignorance of the significance of the distinction between semantically encoded and pragmatically imparted information, such violation of the rules of the language is entirely to be expected.

7. More Puzzles

7.1 The new Frege Puzzle

The distinction between semantically encoded and pragmatically imparted information goes a long way toward solving the problems posed by Frege's Puzzle and the apparent failure of substitutivity of proper names and other single-word singular terms in propositional-attitude contexts. There can be little doubt that failure to appreciate the distinction is largely responsible for the relative unpopularity of the modified naive theory in favor of its rivals throughout the history of the theory of meaning. Unfortunately, the distinction does not yield the final word on the general problem. A version of this general problem arises again, this time in a particularly strengthened form, when one takes note of the following fact: Even a speaker who has been fully apprised of the distinction between semantically encoded and pragmatically imparted information, and who has learned to be scrupulously careful about separating out pragmatic impartations when dealing with matters of semantics, may give assent to some sentence *S* which encodes a certain piece of information and which the speaker fully understands, while the same speaker may fail to give assent, and may even give dissent, to some sentence *S′* which the speaker also fully understands and which, according to the modified naive theory, encodes the very same information. This can easily happen even if the speaker is perfectly rational, mentally acute (in fact, an ideally perfect thinker), eager to indicate his or her beliefs through verbal assent and dissent, and a firm and dogmatic believer in the modified naive theory!

In saying that someone fully understands a sentence, I mean only that he or she associates the right proposition with the sentence in the right way (that is, unconsciously 'computes' the semantically encoded content of the sentence from the recursion rules of semantic composition, or something along these lines – however it is that we get things right when we understand a sentence), and that he or she has a complete grasp of this proposition. In particular, knowing the truth value of the proposition is not required for complete understanding.

For example, suppose that Lois Lane is forced to endure a full academic year of intensive training in the theory of meaning through the writings of a famous Kryptonian philosopher of language. On Krypton (Superman's native planet, according to the myth), the distinction between semantically encoded and pragmatically imparted information was duly appreciated, and the modified naive theory was held in the highest esteem by all but a very small minority of semanticists. The modified naive theory is drilled into her head. She is instructed in the distinction between semantically encoded and pragmatically imparted information, and she is taught to assent to all and only those sentences whose semantically encoded information content she believes and to dissent from all and only those sentences whose negation commands her assent. Now consider the following two sentences:

(5) Superman fights a never-ending battle for truth, justice, and the American way.

(6) Clark Kent fights a never-ending battle for truth, justice and the American way.

If anyone understands these sentences, Lois does. She fully grasps the proposition encoded by these sentences, and she associates the right proposition with each sentence. One might wonder whether she fully understands sentence 6, but a moment's reflection confirms that she does. For example, she certainly does not misunderstand sentence 6 to mean that Perry White is a tyrant. She correctly understands sentence 6 to mean that Clark Kent fights a never-ending battle for truth, justice, and the American way. Lois grasps this information as well as anyone does. Of course, she wrongly believes it to be misinformation, but getting clearer about its truth value would not enable her to grasp it any deeper. So Lois correctly understands both sentences. Yet she verbally assents to sentence 5 and verbally dissents from sentence 6. The fact that she fails to assent to, and in fact dissents from, sentence 6 when she correctly understands it to mean that Clark Kent fights a never-ending battle for truth, justice, and the American way, is very strong evidence that she does not believe this information. This is especially true if one takes seriously the analysis of belief suggested in the preceding section, whereby belief is identified with inward assent or agreement to a piece of information or with a disposition toward inward assent. Given that Lois sincerely wishes to reveal her opinions through verbal assent and dissent, that she correctly understands what is meant by sentence 6, and that she is a perfectly rational and competent thinker, her verbal dissent from sentence 6 would seem to be as good an indication as one could possibly have that she inwardly dissents from the proposition. If she inwardly assented to the proposition, it would seem, she would outwardly assent to the sentence. Her failure to assent to sentence 6, therefore, provides an extremely compelling reason to suppose that she does not believe what she correctly understands it to mean. Similarly, Lois's assent to sentence 5 provides extremely compelling evidence, evidence as good as one could ever have, that she believes this piece of information. Her combined verbal behavior, then, provides an extremely compelling reason to conclude that she believes that Superman fights a never-ending battle for truth, justice, and the American way, but does not believe that Clark Kent does. No doubt, this is also part of the original justification for saying just this about Lois's beliefs. This characterization of Lois's beliefs flatly contradicts the modified naive theory.

It is no help to appeal here to ignorance of the distinction between semantically encoded and pragmatically imparted information, for both Lois (whose beliefs we are talking about) and we (who are talking about those beliefs) are by now well aware of the distinction. Awareness of the distinction does nothing to obviate the compelling force of the evidence provided by Lois's verbal behavior. In particular, it does nothing to dissipate the extremely compelling grounds, provided by Lois's failure to assent to sentence 6, for concluding that she does not believe that Clark Kent fights a never-ending battle.

These considerations generate another puzzle for the modified naive theory. It was argued that Lois correctly, completely, and fully understands both sentence 5 and sentence 6. In particular, she correctly understands sentence 6 to mean that Clark Kent fights a never-ending battle for truth, justice, and the American way. Which proposition does she take sentence 6 to encode? Given her working knowledge of English, her acquaintance with Clark Kent, and her recent training in the philosophy of language, it can only be the singular proposition about Clark Kent that he fights a never-ending battle for truth, justice, and the American way. Now, according to the modified naive theory, Lois believes this singular proposition, for she believes of Superman that he fights a never-ending battle for truth, justice, and the American way. If anyone is ever in a position to have de re beliefs about Superman, Lois has this particular de re belief about him. On the modified naive theory, the content of this de re belief simply is the very proposition that she correctly takes sentence 6 to encode. Hence, on the modified naive theory, Lois – whom we may suppose to be an ideally rational and competent speaker and who sincerely wishes to reveal her opinions through verbal assent and dissent – correctly identifies which proposition is encoded by sentence 6, and she firmly believes this very proposition. Yet, even on reflection, she fails to assent to sentence 6, and in fact dissents from it. What, on the modified naive theory, can account for her behavior? How can the theory explain away her failure to assent to sentence 6 as grounds for concluding that she does not believe that Clark Kent fights a never-ending battle for truth, justice and the American way?

Let us take a more familiar example. An ancient astronomer-philosopher, well versed in the modified naive theory and the distinction between semantically encoded and pragmatically imparted information, verbally assents to (his sentence for) the sentence 'Hesperus is Hesperus' without assenting to the sentence 'Hesperus is Phosphorus'. It is not enough to explain this phenomenon by pointing out that the astronomer-philosopher does not realize that the second sentence encodes information that he believes, or that the two sentences encode the same information, or that one sentence is true and commands his assent if and only if the other one is and does. The question is: How can he fail to realize any of this? We may suppose (1) that he fully grasps the proposition about the planet Venus and the planet Venus that the former is the latter, (2) that, being an adherent of the modified naive theory, he takes the first sentence to encode this very proposition and no other, and (3) that it is this very same proposition and no other that he also takes the second sentence to encode (since this is also the proposition about Hesperus and Phosphorus that they are identical). How then can he fail to see that the sentences are informationally equivalent? Moreover, he fully endorses this proposition, so how, upon reflection, can he fail to be moved to assent to the second sentence when it is this very proposition – one he fully grasps and believes – that he takes the second sentence to encode? The situation becomes especially puzzling for the adherent of the modified naive theory if we suppose that, in believing the proposition that Hesperus is Hesperus, the ancient astronomer-philosopher inwardly assents to it, or is so disposed. If he assents inwardly to the proposition, or is so disposed, why, if he is reflective and eager to reveal his beliefs through verbal assent, is he not similarly disposed to assent outwardly to a sentence which he takes to encode that very proposition? The distinction between semantically encoded and pragmatically imparted information sheds no light on this new problem, for we are supposing that the ancient astronomer-philosopher is well aware of the distinction and never allows himself to be misled by pragmatic impartations in matters concerning semantic content. Moreover, we may also suppose that there is nothing whatsoever wrong or imperfect about the astronomer-philosopher's reasoning or thought processes. We may even suppose him to have superhuman intelligence (or as much intelligence as is compatible with his not knowing the truth of 'Hesperus is Phosphorus'). What, then, is preventing him from making the connection between what he takes the sentence to encode and his belief of that very information?

It appears that the modified naive theory turns against itself in discourse involving propositions about singular propositions, for, on the modified naive theory, these too are singular propositions. (See note 8.) If the ancient astronomer-philosopher believes that 'Hesperus is Phosphorus' encodes the information that Hesperus is Phosphorus, then, on the modified naive theory, he also believes that 'Hesperus is Phosphorus' encodes the information that Hesperus is Hesperus – information which he fully grasps and firmly believes on logical grounds alone. It seems to follow that the mere understanding of the sentence should suffice to elicit his unhesitating and unequivocal assent, even if he is not so intelligent. But, as Frege rightly noted, there was a time when the mere understanding of this sentence was not sufficient to elicit the assent of astronomers who understood it, and may even have elicited emphatic dissent. This is not a particularly bizarre state of affairs: it is perfectly reasonable that this would be their reaction given the state of ignorance at the time. Yet the modified naive theory seems to lack the means to give a coherent account of this state of affairs without making it appear quite paradoxical.

What we have here is a new and stronger version of Frege's Puzzle, one that does not rely on the question-begging premise that 'Hesperus is Phosphorus' is (semantically) informative, or that someone may believe that Hesperus is Hesperus without believing that Hesperus is Phosphorus, or indeed any premise involving notions such as informativeness or a priority. The new version of the puzzle makes do instead with a weaker, less philosophical-theory-laden, and clearly undeniable premise. The new premise is this:

> Someone who is reflective, without mental defect, and eager to reveal his or her beliefs through verbal assent may correctly identify the information encoded by 'Hesperus is Hesperus', fully grasp that information, indicate concurrence with that information by readily assenting to the sentence, correctly identify the information encoded by 'Hesperus is Phosphorus', fully grasp that information, and yet not feel the slightest impulse to assent to the latter sentence.

In addition, Frege's Law is replaced by the following analogue:

> If a declarative sentence S has the very same cognitive information content (Erkenntniswerte) as a declarative sentence S', then an ideally competent speaker who fully understands both sentences perfectly, reflects on the matter, is without mental defect, is eager to indicate his or her beliefs through sincere verbal assent and dissent, and has no countervailing motives or desires that might prevent him or her from being disposed to assent verbally to a sentence while recognizing its information content as something believed, is disposed to assent verbally to S if and only if he or she is disposed to assent verbally to S'.

Given, further, the compositionality principle for pieces of information, we have all of the makings of a new and more powerful refutation of the modified naive theory. The distinction between semantically encoded and pragmatically imparted information simply has no bearing on this new argument.

7.2 Elmer's befuddlement

7.2.1 The example

The new version of Frege's Puzzle derives its additional strength by invoking dispositions to verbal assent in place of informativeness. We can construct a variant of this stronger version of the puzzle directly in terms of belief without invoking dispositions to verbal assent to sentences. One such variant of the new Frege Puzzle is, in some respects, even stronger than the new Frege Puzzle itself, though ironically it also helps to bring out the modified naive theory's means for solving the general problem. This is best demonstrated by means of a paradox generated by an elaborate example, which I shall call *Elmer's Befuddlement.* Rather than present the entire example all at once, it is more instructive to consider a major part of the example first, in order to test our intuitions about this aspect of the example before considering the example in its entirety.

Elmer's befuddlement (excerpts)

> Elmer, a bounty hunter, is determined to apprehend Bugsy Wabbit, a notorious jewel thief who has so far eluded the long arm of the law. Before setting out after Bugsy, Elmer spends several months scrutinizing the FBI's files on Bugsy, studying numerous photographs, movies, and slides, listening carefully to tape recordings of Bugsy's voice, interviewing people who know him intimately, and so on. After learning as much about Bugsy as he can, on January 1 Elmer forms the opinion that Bugsy is (is now, has always been, and will always be throughout his lifetime) dangerous. . . .
>
> On June 1, Elmer receives further information from the FBI that Bugsy was last seen in a club in uptown Manhattan, walking away from a poker game after a gangster type had accused him of cheating. This further information gives Elmer pause. He thinks to himself: 'Maybe Bugsy . . . is harmless after all. I used to believe that he is a dangerous man, but now . . . I don't know what to think. Maybe he's dangerous, maybe not. I'll just have to wait and see.'

Here now is a little two-part quiz: (A) Before June 1, did Elmer believe that Bugsy Wabbit is dangerous? (B) If so, does he continue to believe this even after taking into account the further information he received from the FBI on June 1?

Clearly, question A must be answered affirmatively; Elmer believed for a full five months, from January 1 to June 1, that Bugsy is dangerous, right up until he received the further information concerning Bugsy. This must be so on any reasonable theory of the nature of belief, and it is so on the modified naive theory in particular. On the modified naive theory, to believe that Bugsy is dangerous is to believe the singular proposition about Bugsy that he is dangerous, which is the same thing as believing of Bugsy that he is dangerous. Surely, Elmer had this belief about Bugsy before June 1. If anyone can ever be in a position to have beliefs about Bugsy Wabbit without actually meeting him face to face, then surely Elmer was in such a position when he first decided on January 1 that Bugsy is dangerous. He knew as much about Bugsy as anyone did, save perhaps Bugsy himself, and he may even have known a few things about Bugsy that Bugsy himself did not know.

It would appear equally obvious that question B should be answered negatively. Once he takes the new information into account, Elmer suspends judgment about whether Bugsy is dangerous. Hence, he no longer believes that Bugsy is dangerous. If anyone can ever give up a formerly held belief about someone, Elmer's situation on June 1 would appear to be a typical and central case of such an occurrence. This is not to say, of course, that Elmer now believes that Bugsy is not dangerous, for he does not. Elmer has reconsidered the question of whether Bugsy is dangerous, and he now withholds belief as well as disbelief. Having reconsidered the question, he now believes neither that Bugsy is dangerous nor that he is not. That is what it means to say that Elmer now suspends judgment.

But things are not as clear as they seem. Let us turn now to the example in its entirety.

Elmer's befuddlement (unabridged)

> As already recounted, Elmer the bounty hunter forms the opinion on January 1 that Bugsy is (is now, has always been, and will always be throughout his lifetime) dangerous.
>
> Shortly thereafter, having learned that there is a bounty hunter after him, Bugsy undergoes extensive plastic surgery, so that he looks nothing like his former photographs. He also has his voice surgically altered, adopts an entirely new set of personality traits and mannerisms, and so on. He retains his name, however, since it is such a common name.
>
> Hot on Bugsy's tail, Elmer eventually meets up with the new Bugsy Wabbit. Noting that this man is nothing like the Bugsy Wabbit he is pursuing, Elmer falls for Bugsy's ruse and concludes that this Bugsy Wabbit is simply another person with the same name. Elmer befriends Bugsy, but never learns his true identity.
>
> On April 1, Elmer happens to overhear a dispute (apparently over 24 carrots) between Bugsy and someone, and notices that the other party in the dispute is extremely deferential, almost as if he were positively frightened of Bugsy. Elmer decides then and there that this Bugsy Wabbit is also a dangerous man. He says to himself: 'I'd better watch my step with my new friend, for Bugsy is a dangerous fellow. In this one respect, the two Bugsy Wabbits are alike.'
>
> On June 1, as already recounted, Elmer receives from the FBI further information that gives him pause. He thinks to himself: 'Maybe Bugsy the criminal is harmless after all. I used to believe that he is a dangerous man, but now I'm not so sure. In every other respect he is nothing like my friend Bugsy Wabbit, so perhaps I was a bit hasty in deciding that the two Bugsies are like each other in this one respect. My friend Bugsy is definitely dangerous, I haven't changed my mind about that. But as for the jewel thief, I don't know what to think. Maybe he's dangerous, maybe not. I'll just have to wait and see.'

Elmer waits, but he never sees. Even today, Elmer feels certain that his friend Bugsy is dangerous, but still wonders whether Bugsy the criminal is dangerous or not.

The saga of Elmer's pursuit of Bugsy Wabbit presents many of the familiar problems. It is reminiscent of Quine's famous example about Ralph and Bernard J. Ortcutt, as well as Kripke's example about Pierre and London, and it has significant points in common with a number of other examples, including Castañeda's examples concerning belief about oneself. There are special aspects of Elmer's Befuddlement that are not present in these other examples and I shall focus on these special features to construct a paradox.[9]

7.2.2 The puzzle

Consider again question B: Once Elmer takes account of the further information obtained from the FBI on June 1, how does he stand with respect to the information (or misinformation, as the case may be) that Bugsy Wabbit is dangerous? Does he or does he not believe this piece of information concerning Bugsy?

Let us first consider a simpler question. Roll back the time to April, before Elmer came to have second thoughts about the criminal. Did he believe, at that time, that Bugsy Wabbit is dangerous?

The answer must be that he did. The reasoning that this must be the answer goes as follows: In considering question A, we had already decided that Elmer believed on January 1 that Bugsy is dangerous. We did not yet have the whole story concerning Elmer and Bugsy, but all of the additional information that we have been given concerns events that take place some time after January 1. Hence, the original grounds for claiming that Elmer believes on January 1 that Bugsy is dangerous still obtain. On the modified naive theory in particular, it is still true that Elmer's having familiarized himself with Bugsy's history and appearance in the way he did places him in a position on January 1 to be able to believe at that time of Bugsy that he is dangerous. Now, on April 1 Elmer formed the opinion that his friend Bugsy is dangerous. In doing so Elmer was ignorant of certain critical information concerning Bugsy, but that does not alter the fact that he also steadfastly maintained his view, which he had held since January 1, that Bugsy is dangerous. He did not yet change his mind about Bugsy, first believing him to be dangerous and then giving up that belief. If he believed it before, he believes it still.

There is, it must be admitted, something quite peculiar about Elmer's doxastic state on April 1. There is some sense in which Elmer *comes to* believe on April 1 that Bugsy Wabbit is dangerous (comes to believe of Bugsy that he is dangerous), but there is also some sense in which Elmer believed this about Bugsy since January and never stopped believing it. To give some account of how it is that someone can come to believe something that he or she already believes without ever having ceased to believe it is already a problem for the modified naive theory. I shall not pause here to discuss this. The problem I shall discuss is a sharpened version of this problem, and its solution entails a solution to the present problem. What matters so far is that, however peculiar his doxastic state on April 1, Elmer believed at that time that Bugsy is dangerous.

Now, what about the following summer? Does Elmer continue to believe that Bugsy Wabbit is dangerous even after taking account of the further information from the FBI?

Here no simple 'yes' or 'no' answer by itself is entirely satisfactory. In particular, no simple 'yes' or 'no' answer is satisfactory even if we presuppose the correctness of the modified naive theory. On the one hand, it is critical to the story that in some sense Elmer came to believe on January 1 that Bugsy is dangerous but that Elmer now suspends judgment. Hence, there is an important sense, critical to the story, in which Elmer now believes neither that Bugsy is dangerous nor that he is not dangerous. But it is surely not enough to say that Elmer believes neither that Bugsy is dangerous nor that he is not, and to leave the matter at that, for there is also a very compelling reason to say that Elmer still believes that Bugsy is dangerous: Something exactly analogous to the grounds for holding that Elmer continues to believe on April 1 that Bugsy is dangerous also obtains on June 1. Elmer has not relinquished his opinion that his friend Bugsy is dangerous. If he believed it on April 1, it would seem, he believes it still.

If Elmer had decided on January 1 that Bugsy is dangerous, and had come to have second thoughts on June 1 as he actually did, but had never met Bugsy in the interim and had never formed any further opinion about him, then we would not hesitate to say that Elmer believed on January 1 that Bugsy is dangerous but believes it no longer. Indeed, that is precisely what we did say when we first considered question B, before we knew about Elmer's encounters with Bugsy after January 1. All the information we had given seemed enough to determine that the answer to question B is that Elmer no longer believes that Bugsy is dangerous. Our being given further information concerning Elmer and Bugsy cannot alter what is already determined by the information on hand. If part of the story of Elmer's befuddlement entails that Elmer no longer believes that Bugsy is dangerous, then so does the whole story. (If S entails T, then so does $\ulcorner S$ and $S'\urcorner$.)

In fact, if Elmer had decided on January 1 that Bugsy is dangerous, and had come to have second thoughts on June 1 just as he actually did, but had never met Bugsy in the interim and had never formed any further opinion about him, then it would be true that Elmer no longer believes that Bugsy is dangerous. If anyone can ever give up a formerly held belief about someone, then this would be a typical and central case of such an occurrence. But Elmer is actually in exactly the same state as this, save for the fact that he had met Bugsy in the interim and had formed an opinion about him at that time. Why should Elmer's former beliefs make any difference here? It is just his present doxastic state that we want to capture in specifying his disposition with respect to the information that Bugsy is dangerous. Elmer's present attitude toward this information involves something that ordinarily *constitutes* relinquishing a former opinion. Unless we find some appropriate way to specify Elmer's withholding belief, we leave out of our account a very important element of Elmer's cognitive or doxastic state.

This seems to require us to say that Elmer does not believe that Bugsy is dangerous (or that Bugsy is not dangerous). But that contradicts something which we have also said, and which it appears we are required to say, concerning Elmer's befuddlement. Even during his soliloquy on June 1, Elmer steadfastly remained convinced of his friend's dangerousness. Thus, the facts of the matter in the story of Elmer's befuddlement seems to require us to say that Elmer still believes, at least since April 1, that Bugsy is dangerous, and they also seem to require us to say that Elmer no longer believes, as of June 1, that Bugsy is dangerous. Now, it sometimes happens that a story involves certain inconsistencies. For example, if the author of a series of mystery novels decides to alter some of the biographical facts concerning the detective who is the main character in all the novels (say, his birthdate), then stringing these novels together yields an inconsistent story. But nothing like this is the case with the story of Elmer's befuddlement. Clearly, the story is consistent. There is no logical reason why it could not be a true story. Perhaps some structurally similar befuddlement has actually occurred at some time in the history of intelligent life in the universe, or may yet occur at some time in the future.

Here, then, is the puzzle. Either Elmer believes that Bugsy is dangerous or he does not. Which is it? We seem to be required to say that Elmer does indeed believe that Bugsy is dangerous, for he remains convinced of his friend Bugsy's dangerousness. We also seem to be required to say Elmer does not believe that Bugsy is dangerous, for he now actively suspends judgment concerning the criminal's dangerousness. Yet we are logically prohibited from saying both together. How, then, are we to describe coherently Elmer's doxastic disposition with respect to the information that Bugsy Wabbit is dangerous? How can it be consistent for Elmer to believe that Bugsy is dangerous, on the one hand, and to withhold that belief, on the other?

The same puzzle can be stated with a different emphasis by focusing on the fact that on June 1 Elmer, in some obvious (but so far unclear) sense, changes his mind about whether Bugsy is dangerous. The change of mind is evident in Elmer's soliloquy. He suspends judgment where he used to have an opinion. Before that, at least since January, Elmer believed that Bugsy is dangerous. But there is also some obvious sense in which Elmer does not change his mind on June 1 concerning Bugsy, since he remains convinced of his friend's dangerousness. If we say, then, that Elmer continues to believe even on June 1 that Bugsy is dangerous, we fail to depict his change of mind. We represent him as believing on January 1 that Bugsy is dangerous, believing it still on April 1, and believing it still even on June 1 after taking into account the further information from the FBI. There is nothing in all this about any change of mind. In order to express the fact that Elmer has changed his mind concerning Bugsy's dangerousness, we would like to say that Elmer believed on January 1 that Bugsy is dangerous but by the following summer believes it no longer (and also does not believe that Bugsy is not dangerous). However, we seem to be prevented from saying this; else we lie about Elmer's continued and unwavering conviction concerning his friend's dangerousness. How, then, do we express the important fact about Elmer that he has changed his mind concerning the question of Bugsy Wabbit's dangerousness and has withdrawn his former opinion?

[. . .]

8. Resolution of the Puzzles

8.3 Resolution

8.3.1 Elmer's befuddlement

Now, whatever the necessary and sufficient conditions are for being in a position to entertain a singular proposition, it is clear that Elmer was in such a position on January 1, before he actually met Bugsy, when he first formed the opinion about Bugsy that he is dangerous. Elmer was an expert on Bugsy, well acquainted with his appearance and deeds through reports, photographs, tape recordings, and the rest; all these form a part of the means by which Elmer apprehends the proposition about Bugsy on January 1 that Bugsy is dangerous. Later, when Elmer meets up with Bugsy and forms for a second time the opinion that he is dangerous, Elmer apprehends this same proposition by entirely different means. His new mode of acquaintance with Bugsy, and thereby with the proposition that he is dangerous, involves perceptions of a wholly new appearance. The proposition takes on a new guise for Elmer. In failing to recognize Bugsy, Elmer also fails to recognize the very proposition that he is dangerous. It is precisely for this reason that Elmer is able to form for the second time the opinion that Bugsy is dangerous without having ceased believing this very same piece of information. Elmer took his friend Bugsy to be someone other than the notorious jewel thief. Consequently, he took the information that he is dangerous, when it occurred to him on April 1, to be a different piece of information from the proposition about the jewel thief that he is dangerous (information that Elmer already believed). Elmer's problem stems from the fact that he takes the information that Bugsy Wabbit is dangerous to be two distinct and utterly independent pieces of information. He grasps it by means of two distinct appearances or guises; he takes it in two different ways. When he takes it in one way, Elmer does not recognize this piece of information as the same information that he also takes the other way. On June 1, Elmer adopts conflicting doxastic dispositions with respect to what he takes to be two different pieces of information but what is in fact a single proposition. On the one hand, Elmer has the appropriate favorable attitude toward this information; he is disposed to assent. On the other hand, he does not have an appropriate favorable attitude toward this information. It all depends on how Elmer takes the information.

How do we avoid this apparent contradiction? Does Elmer believe the relevant information, or doesn't he?

I have said that belief is a favorable attitude toward a piece of information, perhaps a disposition to inward assent or agreement. I have not said, however, that there must be a disposition to inward assent or agreement no matter how the information is taken. Elmer assents to the proposition that Bugsy is dangerous; he agrees with this information when he takes it as information concerning his friend. Hence, Elmer does not believe this information. The fact that Elmer is no longer so disposed when he takes it as information concerning the notorious jewel thief does not entail that he has no disposition to assent to the proposition whatsoever. Indeed, he *has* such a disposition when he takes the proposition another way. This resolves the contradiction: Strictly speaking, Elmer does believe that Bugsy is dangerous, and it is strictly incorrect to say that he does not believe this, even after his change of mind on June 1.

We can still account for Elmer's change of mind with respect to the proposition that Bugsy is dangerous. When Elmer takes the information that Bugsy is dangerous as the information concerning his friend, he is continuously disposed to inward agreement since April 1. It is for this reason that we say that Elmer continues to believe that Bugsy is dangerous. However, when Elmer takes the proposition to be one about the notorious jewel thief, he agrees with it on January 1 but by the following summer he is no longer so disposed. There is a certain way of taking the proposition that Bugsy is dangerous such that Elmer grasps the proposition by means of it but is no longer disposed to assent to the proposition when taking it that way. In this special sense, Elmer now *withholds belief*. Strictly speaking, this is not to say that he *fails* to believe. Nonetheless, Elmer manifests the central and most significant characteristic of giving up this belief so long as he takes the proposition to be one about the criminal, for then he is disposed to neither inward assent nor inward dissent, neither agreement nor disagreement, with respect to the relevant proposition. The only thing that prevents Elmer from failing to believe altogether is the fact that he happens to harbor a disposition to inward assent when he takes the proposition another way. This, at any rate, is how the modified naive theory can explain the sense in which Elmer may be said to 'withhold belief'. The fact one attempts to convey is just the fact that Elmer now lacks the appropriate favorable attitude or disposition when he takes the proposition in a certain contextually significant way.

I have argued so far as if belief may be analyzed in terms of a notion of *disposition to inward assent or agreement when taken in such-and-such a way*. It does not matter much whether this is the relevant notion, only that the modified naive theory is compelled to acknowledge some such ternary relation whose existential generalization coincides with the binary relation of belief. The matter can be put more formally as follows: Let us call the relevant ternary relation, whatever it is, '*BEL*'. It is a relation among believers, propositions, and something else (e.g. the relation of disposition to inward agreement when taken in a certain way), such that

(i) ⌜*A* believes *p*⌝ may be analyzed as $(\exists x)[A$ grasps p by means of x & $BEL(A, p, x)]$,

(ii) *A* may stand in *BEL* to *p* and some *x* by means of which *A* grasps *p*, without standing in *BEL* to *p* and all *x* by means of which *A* grasps *p*,

and

(iii) ⌜*A* withholds belief from *p*⌝, in the sense relevant to Elmer's befuddlement, may be analyzed as $(\exists x)[A$ grasps p by means of x & $\sim BEL(A, p, x)]$.[1]

In the special case of Elmer's Befuddlement, we initially seemed compelled to say both that Elmer believes that Bugsy is dangerous and that Elmer does not believe that Bugsy is dangerous. The grounds for saying that Elmer does believe that Bugsy is dangerous are straightforward. Elmer formed this opinion on April 1 and has remained steadfastly convinced ever since. It is strictly incorrect, therefore, to say that Elmer does not believe that Bugsy is dangerous. How, them, do we express the other side of Elmer's doxastic state resulting from his recent change of mind? The specifics of the story do not allow us to say that Elmer believes that Bugsy is not dangerous, and so we are prevented from transferring the inconsistency from us to Elmer by saying that Elmer believes both that Bugsy is dangerous and that he is not dangerous. What, then, do we say to capture Elmer's apparent withheld belief, which we initially tried to capture by saying that he no longer believes that Bugsy is dangerous? The analysis in terms of *BEL* uncovers that there is yet a third position in which the negation sign may occur. What we are trying to say when we say, erroneously, that 'Elmer does not believe that Bugsy is dangerous' is not

$\sim(\exists x)$[Elmer grasps *that Bugsy is dangerous* by means of x & *BEL*(Elmer, *that Bugsy is dangerous*, x)]

(that is, it is not the case that Elmer believes that Bugsy is dangerous). This would saddle us with a contradiction. Nor is it

> $(\exists x)$[Elmer grasps *that Bugsy is not dangerous* by means of x & *BEL*(Elmer, *that Bugsy is not dangerous*, x)]

(That is, Elmer believes that Bugsy is not dangerous). This is straightforwardly false. Rather, it is

> $(\exists x)$[Elmer grasps *that Bugsy is dangerous* by means of x & ~*BEL* (Elmer, *that Bugsy is dangerous*, x)]

(that is, Elmer withholds belief about Bugsy's being dangerous). This is at once true, compatible with Elmer's believing that Bugsy is dangerous, and *constitutive* of Elmer's change of mind. There is some relevant third relatum x such that on January 1 Elmer stands in *BEL* to the proposition that Bugsy is dangerous and x but by the following summer Elmer no longer stands in *BEL* to this proposition and x. As in the case of Mrs. Jones's complex emotional attitude with respect to her husband, alias Jones the Ripper-Offer, no attempt to describe Elmer's complex doxastic state with respect to the singular proposition about Bugsy Wabbit that he is dangerous can succeed using only the two-place notion of belief as a binary relation between believers and propositions. Without some relativized, ternary notion, and the resulting distinction between withholding belief and failure to believe, the attempt to describe Elmer's complex doxastic state with respect to the relevant singular proposition breaks down. The only thing one can say using the binary notion of belief – to wit, that Elmer does believe the proposition that Bugsy is dangerous – is highly misleading at best. Thus, by casting singular propositions as objects of belief, the modified naive theory is compelled to acknowledge an analysis of belief as the existential generalization of some three-place relation *BEL* in order to uncover the appropriate position for the negation required by Elmer's change of mind in the face of his continued belief.

8.3.2 The new Frege puzzle

This modified naive theoretical scheme for solving the problems posed by Elmer's Befuddlement points the way to a similar and related treatment of some of the other problems encountered earlier. Consider again the new and stronger version of Frege's Puzzle: An ancient astronomer-philosopher, who is an ideally competent speaker and thinker and a firm believer in the modified naive theory, unhesitatingly assents to 'Hesperus is Hesperus', but is not in the least disposed to assent to the sentence 'Hesperus is Phosphorus', even though he understands both sentences perfectly and, in fact, associates the very same proposition with each sentence. The explanation now available on the modified naive theory begins with the observation that the astronomer-philosopher does not recognize the proposition he attaches to the second sentence as the very same proposition he attaches to the first sentence, and firmly believes on logical grounds alone. When he reads and understands the sentence 'Hesperus is

Phosphorus', he takes the proposition thereby encoded in a way different from the way in which he takes this same proposition when he reads and understands the sentence 'Hesperus is Hesperus'. He grasps the very same proposition in two different ways, by means of two different guises, and he takes this single proposition to be two different propositions. When he takes it as a singular proposition of self-identity between the first heavenly body sometimes visible in such-and-such location at dusk and itself, he unhesitatingly assents inwardly to it. When he takes it as a singular proposition identifying the first heavenly body sometimes visible in such-and-such location at dusk with the last heavenly body sometimes visible in so-and-so location at dawn, he has no inclination to assent inwardly to it, and may even inwardly dissent from it. His verbal assent and his refraining from verbal assent with respect to the two sentences are merely the outward manifestations of his inward dispositions relative to the ways he takes the proposition encoded by the two sentences. In the context of the new Frege Puzzle, this entails a rejection of the analogue of Frege's Law stated in terms of the verbal dispositions of ideally competent speakers. Unlike Frege's Law, this analogue is not a truth of logic but an empirically false hypothesis.

The account of belief as the existential generalization of a ternary relation *BEL* was constructed around the modified naive theory's account of de re belief as a binary relation between believers and singular propositions (see the introduction), so that the modified naive theory could accommodate Elmer's complex cognitive state. The analysis makes room for the modified naive theory's claim that whoever believes that Hesperus is Hesperus also believes that Hesperus is Phosphorus, for whoever agrees inwardly with the singular proposition about the planet Venus that it is it, taking the proposition as an affirmation of self-identity about the first heavenly body sometimes visible at dusk in such-and-such location, stands in *BEL* to the proposition that Hesperus is Phosphorus and some x or other, and hence believes this singular proposition, even if he or she is not so disposed when this same proposition is taken some other way (e.g. as information concerning the last heavenly body sometimes visible at dawn in so-and-so location). It is part of the account that one who stands in the *BEL* relation to the information about Venus that it is it, together with some third relatum x by means of which he or she grasps this information, need not also stand in the *BEL* relation to this same information together with some further relatum y distinct from x and by means of which he or she also grasps the information.

Why we speak the way we do

This aspect of the account yields another part (promised in section 6.2) of the explanation for the prevailing inclination to say – erroneously, according to the modified naive theory – that the ancient astronomer-philosopher does not believe that Hesperus is Phosphorus, and that Lois Lane is not aware that Superman is Clark Kent. The first part of the explanation was that most speakers, being insufficiently aware of the distinction between semantically encoded and pragmatically imparted information, will inevitably mistake information only pragmatically imparted by utterances of 'Hesperus is Phosphorus' (such as the information that the sentence is true) for part of the information content of the sentence, and hence will mistake the sentence 'The astronomer-philosopher believes that Hesperus is Phosphorus' for an assertion that the astronomer-philosopher believes this imparted information – information we know he does not believe. It was seen, however, that this explanation by itself cannot be the complete story, for, even when one takes care to distinguish semantically encoded and pragmatically imparted information, the astronomer-philosopher's failure to assent to the sentence 'Hesperus is Phosphorus', when he fully understands it and completely grasps the information thereby encoded, provides a compelling reason to suppose that he does not believe this information, and this reason is part of the original justification for denying that he believes that Hesperus is Phosphorus. The existential analysis of belief in terms of the ternary relation *BEL* reveals that this sort of evidence, compelling though it may be, is *defeasible*. When the astronomer-philosopher fails to assent verbally to 'Hesperus is Phosphorus', having fully understood the sentence, he also fails to assent mentally to the information thereby encoded, taking it in the way he does when it is presented to him through that particular sentence. He 'withholds belief,' in the sense defined earlier. This does not entail that he does not mentally agree with this information however he takes it. In the usual kind of case, one uniformly assents or fails to assent to a single piece of information, however it is taken, by whatever guise one is familiar with it. It is for this reason that failure to assent to a proposition when taking it one way – i.e., withholding belief – is very good evidence for failure to believe. But in this particular case it happens that the astronomer-philosopher is also familiar with the information that Hesperus is Phosphorus under its guise as a trivial truism, the way he takes it when it is presented to him through the sentence 'Hesperus is Hesperus'. Taking it this way, he unhesitatingly assents to it. Hence, he believes that Hesperus is Phosphorus, and his sincere denials constitute defeated, misleading evidence to the contrary. He 'withholds belief,' in the sense used here, but he also believes, in the sense used everywhere. To say that he does not is to say something false.

The true sentence 'The ancient astronomer believes that Hesperus is Phosphorus' may even typically involve the Gricean implicature, or suggestion, or presumption, that, assuming the ancient astronomer understands (his version of) the sentence 'Hesperus is Phosphorus', under normal circumstances, he would verbally assent to it if queried. Since he does not and would not, the implicatures of the sentence would also lead speakers to deny it, even thought its literal truth conditions are fulfilled.

The reasons just given why we speak the way we do in cases of propositional recognition failure may still fail to get to the bottom of the problem. In attributing beliefs, we are stating whether the believer is favorably disposed to a certain piece of information or proposition. In the 'Hesperus'-'Phosphorus' and 'Superman'-'Clark Kent' cases, however, the believer in question is favorably disposed toward a certain singular proposition when taking it one way, but fails to recognize this proposition and is not favorably disposed toward it when it is encountered again. Since our purpose in attributing belief is to specify how the believer stands with respect to a proposition, we should, in these cases where the believer's disposition depends upon and varies with the way the proposition is taken, want to specify not only the proposition agreed to but also something about the way the believer takes the proposition when agreeing to it. The dyadic predicate 'believes' is semantically inadequate for this purpose; we need a triadic predicate for the full *BEL* relation, which the belief relation existentially generalizes. But there may be no such predicate available in the language. Even if such a predicate is available, it may be inordinately long, or cumbersome, or inconvenient. We are accustomed to speaking with the dyadic predicate, 'believes', and we mean to continue doing so even in these problem cases. How, then, do we convey the third relatum of the *BEL* relation?

In the case of Elmer's believing that Bugsy Wabbit is dangerous, the sentence used to specify the information content of Elmer's belief, 'Bugsy Wabbit is dangerous', is itself understood by Elmer, though Elmer understands the sentence in two different ways. He mistakes the sentence to be semantically ambiguous. As one might say, he takes the single sentence to be two different sentences. This is unlike the 'Hesperus'-'Phosphorus' and 'Superman'-'Clark Kent' cases. In these cases, the two ways in which the believer takes the relevant proposition are associated, respectively, with two different sentences, either of which may be used in specifying the content of the belief in question. The ancient astronomer agrees to the proposition about the planet Venus that it is it when he takes it in the way it is presented to him through the logically valid sentence 'Hesperus is Hesperus', but he does not agree to this same proposition when he takes it in the way it is presented to him through the logically contingent sentence 'Hesperus is Phosphorus'. The fact that he agrees to it at all is, strictly speaking, sufficient for the truth of both the sentence 'The astronomer believes that Hesperus is Hesperus' and the sentence 'The astronomer believes that Hesperus is Phosphorus'. Though the sentences are materially equivalent, and even modally equivalent (true with respect to exactly the same possible worlds), there is a sense in which the first is better than the second, given our normal purpose in attributing belief. Both sentences state the same fact (that the astronomer agrees to the singular proposition in question), but the first sentence also manages to convey *how* the astronomer agrees to the proposition. Indeed, the second sentence, though true, is in some sense inappropriate; it is positively misleading in the way it (correctly) specifies the content of the astronomer's belief. It specifies the content by means of a 'that'-clause that presents the proposition in the

'the wrong way,' a way of taking the proposition with respect to which the astronomer does not assent to it. This does not affect the truth value of the second sentence, for it is no part of the semantic content of the sentence to specify the way the astronomer takes the proposition when he agrees to it. The 'that'-clause is there only to specify the proposition believed. It happens in the 'Hesperus'-'Phosphorus' type of case that the clause used to specify the believed proposition also carries with it a particular way in which the believer takes the proposition, a particular x by means of which he or she is familiar with the proposition. In these cases, the guise or appearance by means of which the believer would be familiar with a proposition at a particular time t were it presented to him or her through a particular sentence is a function of the believer and the sentence. Let us call this function f_t. For example, $f_t(x,S)$ might be the way x would take the information content of S, at t, were it presented to him or her through the very sentence S. In the case of the ancient astronomer, we have

(7) *BEL*[the astronomer, that Hesperus is Hesperus, f_t (the astronomer, 'Hesperus is Hesperus')]

and

(8) *BEL*[the astronomer, that Hesperus is Phosphorus, f_t(the astronomer, 'Hesperus is Hesperus')],

but not

(9) *BEL*[the astronomer, that Hesperus is Hesperus, f_t(the astronomer, 'Hesperus is Phosphorus')]

and not

(10) *BEL*[the astronomer, that Hesperus is Phosphorus, f_t(the astronomer, 'Hesperus is Phosphorus')].

The quasi-symbolizations 7 and 10 reveal that, though one cannot be explicit about the particular third relatum involved in the *BEL* relation using only the dyadic predicate 'believes', one can, so to speak, 'fake it' by using as a 'that'-clause a sentence that determines the third relatum in question. If one existentially generalizes on the third argument place in all of sentences 7–10, the first and the fourth, unlike the second and the third, typographically retain all that is obliterated by the variable of generalization – all, that is, but the functor 'f_t' and the quotation marks around and recurrence of its second argument. One can exploit this feature of the sentence 'The astronomer believes that Hesperus is Hesperus' to convey the third relatum of *BEL*. The 'that'-clause, whose semantic function is simply to specify the content of the astronomer's belief, is also used here to perform a pragmatic function involving an autonomous mention-use of the clause. This is the closest one can come to saying by means of the dyadic predicate what can, strictly speaking, be said only by means of the triadic predicate. To borrow Wittgenstein's terminology, one *shows* using 'believes' what one cannot *say* by its means alone.

Since it is our purpose in this case to convey not only what the astronomer agrees to but also how he takes what he agrees to when agreeing to it, the belief attribution 'The astronomer believes that Hesperus is Phosphorus' may typically involve the false (further) implicature (or suggestion, or presumption) that the astronomer agrees to the proposition that Hesperus is Phosphorus when he takes it in the way it is presented to him through the very sentence 'Hesperus is Phosphorus'. If we allowed ourselves the full triadic predicate, we could cancel the implicature without explicitly specifying the third relatum by uttering something like the following:

> The astronomer believes that Hesperus is Phosphorus, although he does not agree that Hesperus is Phosphorus when he takes this information the way he does when it is presented to him through the very sentence 'Hesperus is Phosphorus'.

The second conjunct here – the cancellation clause – is meant to take the sting out of the first conjunct, and the conjunction taken as a whole remains perfectly consistent. However, since the sentence that determines (via the function f_t) the way the astronomer takes the information when agreeing to it is readily available, it is easier and equally efficacious simply to retain the dyadic predicate 'believes' and to deny the literally true but misleading belief attribution 'The astronomer believes that Hesperus is Phosphorus' while asserting an equally true but not misleading attribution. Denying the misleading attribution is the closest one can come, using only the dyadic predicate, to denying proposition 9 (= proposition 10). Hence we are naturally led to say things like 'The astronomer believes that Hesperus is Hesperus, but he does not believe that Hesperus is Phosphorus'. We speak falsely, but the point is taken, and that is what matters. So it is that the modified naive theory, properly extended to acknowledge that believers may fail to recognize the singular propositions they embrace, predicts the sort of usage in propositional attitude discourse that we actually find where propositional recognition failure is involved.[11]

Notes

1. See also Wittgenstein, *Philosophical Grammar* (Berkeley: University of California Press, 1974), at pp. 315–318; *Philosophical Investigations* (New York: Macmillan), at p. 216. For a more recent endorsement of the general strategy see

Ian Hacking, 'Comment on Wiggins,' in *Philosophy of Logic*, ed. S. Körner (Berkeley: University of California Press, 1976).

2. A word of clarification is needed concerning my use of the semantic predicates 'encode' and 'information'. Throughout this book I am concerned with discrete units of information that are specifiable by means of a 'that'-clause, e.g. the information that Socrates was wise. These discrete units are *pieces of information.* I shall generally use the mass noun 'information' as if it were shorthand for the count noun phrase 'piece of information', i.e., as a general term whose extension is the class of pieces of information. Thus, I write 'information that is such-and-such' to mean 'pieces of information that are such-and-such,' 'the same information' to mean 'the same pieces of information,' 'different information' to mean 'different pieces of information,' and so on. I use the verb 'encode' in such a way that an unambiguous declarative sentence encodes (with respect to a given possible context *c*) a *single* piece of information, which is referred to (with respect to *c*) by the result of prefixing 'the information that' to the sentence and which is to be called 'the information content' of the sentence (with respect to *c*). A declarative sentence may encode (with respect to a given context) two or more pieces of information, but if it does so it is ambiguous. Pieces of information encoded by the logical consequences of an unambiguous sentence are not themselves encoded, in this sense, by the sentence. The (piece of) information that snow is white and grass is green is different information (a different piece of information) from the (piece of) information that snow is white, though intuitively the latter is included as part of the former. The sentence 'Snow is white and grass is green' encodes only the former, not the latter. This constitutes a departure from at least one standard usage, according to which the information content of a sentence is perhaps something like a class of pieces of information, closed under logical consequence.

   I am not concerned in this book with a notion of an *amount* of information, which arises in the mathematical theory of communication or information. The information *that snow is white and grass is green and Socrates is Socrates* may be no more or less information than the information *that both snow is white if and only if grass is green and either snow is white or grass is green.* Nevertheless, general considerations involving Leibniz's Law strongly suggest that they are numerically distinct pieces of information. For instance, the first concerns Socrates whereas the second does not.

3. R. Sharvy, 'Why a Class Can't Change Its Members,' *Noûs* 2, no. 4 (1968): 303–314.
4. One pair of sentences proposed to me as a counterinstance to Frege's Law in correspondence by a prominent philosopher of logic and semantics is '"Hesperus" refers to Hesperus' (uninformative) and '"Hesperus" refers to Phosphorus' (informative). I shall criticize the claim that Frege's Law *could be* (let alone that it *is*) subject to counterexample, but perhaps a special caveat is called for in connection with this particular example. These two sentences are equally informative, in the sense of the term 'informative' that is relevant to Frege's Puzzle. In particular, even the first sentence is informative – and not simply because it entails the nontrivial fact that 'Hesperus' is not nonreferring. The sentence 'If "Hesperus" refers to anything, it refers to Hesperus' is equally informative in the relevant sense. (In this connection, see Kripke, *Naming and Necessity*,

pp. 68–70.) These sentences are not only informative, they (or, more accurate, their information contents) are the subject of serious dispute among semanticists. Richard Montague denied that 'Hesperus' refers to Hesperus, as did Russell. (See note 2 to chapter 3, above.) If a semantic oracle were to have pronounced the truth that 'Hesperus' does indeed refer to Hesperus, these philosophers should have found the pronouncement only too painfully informative. (More probably, they might have denounced the oracle as a fraud.) The sentence '"Hesperus" refers to Hesperus' is, by itself and in abstraction from context, incomplete. Reference is a relation among expressions, objects, and linguistic systems; names refer to things (or fail to refer to things) in this or that language, or in this or that idiolect. There are (possible) languages in which 'Hesperus' refers to nothing, and still others in which it refers to the Milky Way. The information that 'Hesperus' refers to Hesperus in English is a nontrivial piece of information about English. Things might have been otherwise, and it is not 'given' or known a priori what the expression 'Hesperus' refers to in English.

One sentence that might be correctly regarded as uninformative, in the relevant sense, and is easily confused with '"Hesperus" refers to Hesperus', is the following: 'The sentence "'Hesperus' refers to Hesperus in English" is true in English**', where 'English**' refers to the extension of English into a metalanguage for English. The apparent triviality of this meta-metatheoretic sentence is no doubt the source of the erroneous claim that '"Hesperus" refers to Hesperus' is uninformative. But, as we shall see, it is crucial in discussing Frege's Puzzle to maintain a sharp distinction between the information content of a sentence *S* and the further and separate metalinguistic information that *S* is true. Frege's Puzzle concerns the former, and not generally the latter. The reasons behind the apparent triviality of the meta-metatheoretic sentence mentioned above are complex (see Kripke, *Naming and Necessity*, pp. 68–70), but in no way does this sentence present a problem for Frege's Law. That the two original sentences are equally informative does not entail that they semantically encode the same piece of information. It does entail that the modified-naive-theorist, in claiming that they encode the same information, has nothing to fear from Frege's Law.

5. R. Carnap, 'Reply to Leonard Linsky,' *Philosophy of Science* 16, no. 4 (1949): 347–350, at pp. 347–348.
6. In claiming that Frege and Russell and their followers have mistaken pragmatically imparted information for semantically encoded information, I do not mean that they would assent to such things as 'The sentence "Hesperus is Phosphorus" expresses in English the information about itself that it is true'. Clearly they would not; in any case, they need not. Nor would someone who mistakes a particular celebrity impersonator for the president of the United States assent to 'The president is the celebrity impersonator'. Philosophers mistake pragmatically imparted information for semantically encoded information in failing to keep the two sharply distinct and consequently judging whether a sentence *S* is informative partly on the basis of information pragmatically imparted by utterances of *S*.

   Other writers have drawn distinctions similar to the one drawn here between semantically encoded and pragmatically imparted information as part of a defense of something like the original or the modified naive theory, though I came upon the idea independently. See Michael Tye, 'The Puzzle of Hesperus and

Phosphorus,' *Australasian Journal of Philosophy* 56, no. 3 (1978): 219–224, at p. 224; Raymond Bradley and Norman Swartz, *Possible Worlds: An Introduction to Logic and Its Philosophy* (Indianapolis: Hackett, 1979), at pp. 191–192; Tom McKay, 'On Proper Names in Belief Ascriptions,' *Philosophical Studies* 39 (1981): 287–303, at pp. 294–295; R. M. Sainsbury, 'On a Fregean Argument for the Distinctness of Sense and Reference,' *Analysis* 43 (January 1983): 12–14; Takashi Yagisawa, Meaning and Belief, Ph.D. diss., Princeton University, 1981; J. Paul Reddam, Pragmatics and the Language of Belief, Ph.D. diss., University of Southern California, 1982. However, there are subtleties involved in Frege's Puzzle that these writers do not discuss. These subtleties will be developed in chapter 7 of this book with a new and stronger version of the puzzle, for which the solution presented here is simply irrelevant. (McKay comes very close to recognizing some of the finer aspects of the puzzle in his note 17, wherein he discusses an example (due to David Kaplan) involving a case of change of mind to suspension of judgement similar to the example to be presented in section 7.2 of this book. McKay's brief discussion of the example does not bring out the moral of my chapter 8.)

I am not talking here about overt verbal assent to a *sentence*, but about *mental* assent to a proposition.

The conception of belief as inward assent is apparently advanced by Saint Augustine in chapter 5 of *Predestination of the Saints*, where belief is analyzed as 'to think with assent.' For an illuminating contemporary discussion of the analysis of belief as assent to an entertained proposition, see H. H. Price, *Belief* (London: Allen and Unwin, 1969), especially series I, lectures 8 and 9, and series II, lectures 1–3.

In suggesting that belief might be understood in terms of inward assent, concurrence, or approval, I am not suggesting a reduction of belief to a phenomenological episode (in the style of Hume). By 'inward assent', etc., I do not mean merely a private, subjective experience directed toward or involving the relevant piece of information (such as the experience one typically has when reading or saying the words 'yes, I agree' to oneself, together with a 'feeling of understanding' of these words, etc.). Such an analysis would be unacceptable for familiar philosophical reasons: In unusual circumstances someone could have these experiences without believing, and without even grasping, the proposition. By 'inward assent', etc., I mean a state of *cognition*, with everything that this entails.

Furthermore, in speaking of a *disposition* to inward assent, or other favorable *dispositions*, I do not mean merely an inclination, tendency, or propensity to assent, etc. (the usual philosophical use of 'disposition' as in, e.g., 'dispositional property'). Here again, it is possible for someone to have such inclinations without believing the proposition, and vice versa. In saying that someone is favorably 'disposed' toward something, I mean that the person harbors a positive, favorable attitude (e.g. agreement, as opposed to disagreement or indifference) toward the thing. Typically, the harboring of this attitude will result in certain inclinations or propensities, but that is not part of the analysis of the attitude, and in extraordinary circumstances the harboring of the favorable attitude may not result in the typical inclinations. Conversely, the inclinations may be present in the absence of the favorable attitude. It is probably best to speak of 'attitudes' rather than 'dispositions'. So understood, the suggested analysis may appear unilluminating, but then at least it is not controversial.

I use the term 'believe', and its cognates, in such a way that one believes that *S* if one is convinced that *S*, of the opinion that *S*, confident that *S*, persuaded that *S*, etc., but it is not sufficient that one merely thinks it likely that *S*, guesses that *S*, suspects that *S*, theorizes that *S*, assumes that *S*, or supposes that *S*.

7. I have in mind theories like that given by Robert Stalnaker in 'Assertion,' in *Syntax and Semantics 9: Pragmatics*, ed. P. Cole (New York: Academic, 1978). See also Stalnaker, 'Indexical Belief,' *Synthèse* 49, no. 1 (1981): 129–151; David Lewis, 'What Puzzling Pierre Believes,' *Australasian Journal of Philosophy* 59, no. 3 (1981): 283–289. The favored theory of propositions here is one that identifies propositions with sets of possible worlds – a theory on which propositions are even more coarse-grained than on the modified naive theory – though that is largely irrelevant to the main idea behind Stalnaker's account. Stalnaker claims that, in at least some propositional-attitude contexts, a 'that'-clause, ⌜that *S*⌝, will sometimes refer not to the proposition expressed by the sentence *S* but instead to a related proposition, which Stalnaker calls 'the diagonal proposition of the propositional concept for *S*'. This so-called diagonal proposition, if it is a proposition at all, is best identified as the singular proposition about *S* that it is true – or, more accurate, as the proposition *that the proposition semantically encoded by S, as uttered in a context, is true.* (Stalnaker shows reluctance to so identify the diagonal proposition. The coarse-grainedness of his favored theory of propositions enables him to avoid specifying the relevant proposition in this way; however, from the point of view of a more fine-grained theory (such as the modified naive theory or the Fregean theory), the metatheoretic proposition that *S* is true is the most plausible candidate for being the diagonal proposition.) I shall not argue the point fully here. For present purposes, it is sufficient that this be one way of understanding what Stalnaker means by 'the diagonal proposition'. In effect, then, on Stalnaker's theory a 'that'-clause ⌜that *S*⌝ may be ambiguous. It sometimes refers to the proposition encoded by *S*, and it sometimes refers to a different, metatheoretic proposition about *S* itself. Rather than postulate this sort of complexity or ambiguity in connection with 'that'-clauses, it would be more plausible to claim that, in some cases, the speaker reporting a propositional attitude strictly speaking misspoke and, for complete accuracy, should have used a more complicated formal-mode 'that'-clause in place of the material-mode 'that'-clause used.
8. This consequence of the modified naive theory concerning nesting of propositional-attitude operators often goes unnoticed. In an attempt to soften the blow of the modified naive theory, it is sometimes argued that, for example, though the ancients strictly speaking did believe the proposition that Hesperus is Phosphorus, since this is just the trivial proposition that Hesperus is Hesperus, they did not realize that the proposition that Hesperus is Phosphorus is really the very same proposition as the trivial proposition that Hesperus is Hesperus, and hence they did not realize that they believed that Hesperus is Phosphorus. Similarly, it is sometimes argued that, since the name 'Hamlet' from Shakespeare's fiction actually refers to no one, there is no such thing as a proposition that Hamlet does not exist, and hence the sentence 'Hamlet does not exist' strictly speaking has no information content, but still there is a proposition that there exists no

proposition that Hamlet does not exist, and it is true. All of this is inconsistent with the modified naive theory. On the modified naive theory, if a is a single-word singular term (individual constant), then for any sentence ϕ_a containing a, barring quotation marks and other such aberrant devices, the 'that'-clause $\ulcorner$that $\phi_a\urcorner$ refers to the singular proposition that is the information content of the sentence. It is tempting to think of the 'that'-term as a sort of description of the proposition by specifying its components, like $\ulcorner$the proposition made up of a and the property of being $\phi\urcorner$, analogous to a set-theoretic abstraction term $\ulcorner<a_1$ the property of being $\phi>\urcorner$. But this in incorrect. A set-abstraction term $\ulcorner(\hat{x})\phi_x\urcorner$ may be regarded as a special sort of definite description, since it is equivalent to $\ulcorner(\iota y)[Set(y)$ & $(x)(x \in y \Xi \phi_x)]\urcorner$. Thus, a set-abstraction term is descriptional – specifically, descriptional in terms of the property of being a set with such-and-such membership. The 'that'-operator attaches to a sentence to form a singular term referring to the sentence's information content. Since 'that Plato is wise' refers to a different proposition from 'that the author of *The Republic* is wise', however, one cannot see the 'that'-term as referring to its referent proposition by mentioning the components of the referent proposition. Plato is not a component of the proposition that the author of *The Republic* is wise, though he is referred to by the component term 'the author of *The Republic*'. In a word, the 'that'-operator is nonextensional. One should think of the 'that'-operator as analogous to quotation marks, and of a 'that'-term $\ulcorner$that $S\urcorner$ as analogous to a quotation name, only referring to the information content of S rather than S itself. (See the introduction on the 'that'-operator.) A 'that'-clause, $\ulcorner$that $\phi_a\urcorner$, then, is a singular term whose information value is the ordered pair of the information value of the 'that'-operator and the information content of ϕ_a, the latter being a singular proposition p about the referent of a. A sentence involving this 'that'-clause, $\ulcorner\psi$[that ϕ_a]$\urcorner$, encodes a singular proposition about the proposition p, to wit, that (the proposition identical with) it is ψ, and the 'that'-clause formed from this sentence, $\ulcorner$that ψ[that ϕ_a]$\urcorner$, refers to this singular proposition about p. If b is any proper name or other single-word singular term co-referential with a, then $\ulcorner$that $\phi_b\urcorner$ refers to the very same proposition p, and $\ulcorner\psi$[that ϕ_b]$\urcorner$ encodes the same singular proposition about p that (the proposition identical with) it is ψ, so that $\ulcorner$that ψ[that ϕ_a]$\urcorner$ and $\ulcorner$that ψ[that ϕ_b]$\urcorner$ are co-referential. In particular, if the sentence 'Jones realizes that he believes that Hesperus is Hesperus' is true, then what Jones realizes is a certain singular proposition about the proposition that Hesperus is Hesperus, to the effect that he believes it. Since the proposition that Hesperus is Hesperus is, according to the modified naive theory, the same proposition as the proposition that Hesperus is Phosphorus, another way of specifying what Jones realizes, according to the modified naive theory, is 'that Jones believes that Hesperus is Phosphorus'. Hence, on the modified naive theory, if the original sentence is true, so is 'Jones realizes that he believes that Hesperus is Phosphorus'. The proposition that Jones believes that Hesperus is Hesperus is the same proposition as the proposition that Jones believes that Hesperus is Phosphorus, and thus if Jones realizes the former he realizes the latter. Similarly, if the nonexistence of Hamlet means that there is no such proposition as the proposition that Hamlet does not exist, then it also means that there is no such proposition as the proposition that the proposition that Hamlet does not exist does not itself exist. Few philosophers –

even direct-reference theorists who accede to the modified-naive-theoretical claim that the ancients strictly speaking believed that Hesperus is Phosphorus – have been willing to endorse these further consequences of the modified naive theory. Properly seen, however, they are no more unacceptable than the better-known controversial consequences of the modified naive theory.

These points concerning nested occurrences of 'that'-clauses are important in connection with the modified naive theory's account of Mates's problem concerning nested propositional attitude contexts. See appendix B [not included].

9. One special feature of Elmer's Befuddlement is that Elmer knows the relevant individual, Bugsy, by name, and by the same name in both of his guises, and Elmer comes to have his beliefs and his lack of belief concerning Bugsy (at least partly) by means of that name. This removes the wrongheaded temptation to identify the information value of a name with the name itself, for in this example Elmer's conflicting attitudes are directed toward a single sentence, 'Bugsy Wabbit is dangerous', involving a single name, 'Bugsy Wabbit'. Quine gives a name to his corresponding character, Ortcutt, but he frames the problem primarily in terms of definite descriptions – 'the man in the brown hat' and 'the man seen at the beach'. This introduces a host of further issues, some of which have tended to distract commentators from the primary philosophical issues involved in situations involving ignorance of an identity. Kripke framed his original example concerning Pierre in London using names instead of descriptions, but he used two different syntactic shapes, 'London' and 'Londres', which correspond in the example to two different guises of the city, and which are correct translations of one another. This also has the unfortunate tendency to digress the course of the discussion toward a host of issues concerning translation – issues which are, and which Kripke recognizes to be, entirely irrelevant to the primary philosophical problems raised by the example. In this respect, Elmer's Befuddlement is more like Kripke's more pointed example concerning Paderewski (discussed here in note 4 to chapter 4) [not included].

The most important aspect of Elmer's Befuddlement is the fact that Elmer has *changed his mind* about something and withholds belief where he once had an opinion. This aspect of the example – the change of mind from having an opinion to suspension of judgment – poses the most pressing and difficult philosophical problems, and is at the same time the most philosophically illuminating feature of the example. The importance of suspension of judgment to issues concerning propositional attitudes, especially de re propositional attitudes, was first noticed by Kaplan in an important and underappreciated argument in section XI of 'Quantifying In' [at pp. 139–142 of *Reference and Modality*, ed. L. Linsky (New York: Oxford University Press, 1971)]. See also Kripke, 'A Puzzle About Belief,' at p. 258. The similarity of my example involving Elmer and Bugsy, and the use to which I put it, to Kaplan's continuation of Quine's example should be apparent, though I do not argue for exactly the same conclusions as Kaplan. In particular, I do not argue, and I do not believe, that a de re or relational belief is reducible to a de dicto or notional one. (See note 7 to chapter 3.) [not included] Moreover, my proposal below to analyze belief as the existential generalization of a ternary relation among believers, propositions, and something else, unlike Kaplan's analysis in 'Quantifying In' of de re belief, allows the formulation of de re belief in the manner of '$(\exists x)[x$ is Elmer's friend & Elmer believes that x

is dangerous]', with ordinary unrestricted, objectual quantification into the same 'believes' predicate used in the formulation of de dicto belief.

10. Withheld belief, as defined here, is compatible with (in fact, perhaps entailed by) disbelief (belief of the negation). One can similarly define suspension of judgment so that its analysis is

$$(\exists x)[A \text{ grasps } p \text{ by means of } x \mathbin{\&} {\sim}BEL(A, p, x) \mathbin{\&} {\sim}BEL(A, {\sim}p, \mathrm{Neg}(x))],$$

e.g. under at least one relevant way of taking p, A is disposed neither to inward agreement nor to inward disagreement with respect to p. So understood, suspension of judgment entails withheld belief with respect to both the proposition in question and its negation, but not vice versa. The main idea is to see the various doxastic states of belief, disbelief, withheld belief, and suspension of judgment as existential generalizations of ternary relations relativized to guises, or some such items, so that it is consistent and reasonable for someone to be in conflicting doxastic states (e.g. belief and disbelief, or belief and suspension of judgment) with respect to the very same proposition.

11. There are important limitation to this device inherent in the complexities of natural language. Suppose that Jones believes that he is the best logician in the department, so that something like the following obtains:

⌜*BEL*[Jones, that he is the best logician in the department, *f*(Jones, 'I am the best logician in the department')],

where the function $f(x,S)$ is something like the way x takes the proposition encoded by S *with respect to a context in which x is agent* when it is presented to him through the very sentence S. That is, Jones assents to the proposition that he is the best logician in the department when he takes it in the way he does when he presents it to himself through the sentence 'I am the best logician in the department'. It will not do in this case to use for the 'that'-clause the sentence that determines via the function f the way Jones takes the relevant proposition when agreeing to it, since Jones does not believe that *I* am the best logician in the department. It is quite possible that belief attributions of the form ⌜a believes that he or she is ϕ⌝, understood on the reflexive reading of the pronoun, involve the analogous cancelable implicature, suggestion, or presumption, expressible using '*BEL*' by ⌜*BEL*[a, that he or she is ϕ, f (a, 'I am ϕ')]⌝, and similarly for other so-called first-person propositional-attitude attributions (i.e., propositional-attitude attributions concerning oneself) and for other indexical or tensed propositional-attitude attributions. Thus, for example, if Jones believed at time t that the meeting was over by *then*, he probably did so by agreeing to that information when taking it the way he would had it been presented to him at t through the present tensed sentence 'The meeting is over by now'. Where the relevant implicature, suggestion, or presumption is false, competent speakers may be inclined, erroneously from the point of view of truth, to deny the attribution, just as in the case of 'The ancient astronomer believes that Hesperus is Phosphorus' or 'The ancient astronomer believes that Hesperus appears at dawn'. This fact may help explain the widespread intuition, tapped by Hector-Neri Castañeda in support of his theory of so-called quasi-indicators and by others in support of equally or even more dramatically philosophical theses, that such attributions are literally false in such cases. See for example Castañeda, 'Indicators and Quasi-Indicators,' *American Philosophical Quarterly* 4, no. 2 (1967): 85–100; 'On the Logic of Attributions of Self-Knowledge to Others,' *Journal of Philosophy* 65, no. 15 (1968): 439–456; Roderick Chisholm, *The First Person* (Minneapolis: University of Minnesota Press, 1981); David Lewis, 'Attitudes *De Dicto* and *De Re*,' *Philosophical Review* 87 (1979): 513–443. For an account of first-person propositional-attitude attributions similar in broad outline and spirit to the one proposed here (although, as David Austin has pointed out, apparently lacking the full resources of the ternary account in terms of the *BEL* relation), see Steven Boër and William Lycan, 'Who Me?,' *Philosophical Review* 89, no. 3 (1980): 427–466.

Part IV

Meaning and Truth

Introduction

Scott Soames

The essays in this section are concerned with two related questions – What does it mean to say that something is true; and What is the connection between truth and meaning? Among the most basic facts that must be attended to in answering these questions are equivalences of the following sort.

(1a) Is it true that snow is white iff snow is white
(1b) The proposition that snow is white is true iff snow is white
(2a) 'Snow is white' is a true sentence of English iff snow is white
(2b) '*La nieve es blanca*' is a true sentence of Spanish iff snow is white

It has often been observed that equivalences like these are in some sense definitional of the notion of truth, and that understanding the word true involves knowing that which they state. In keeping with this observation it is widely believed that (at least some) such equivalences should be consequences of any adequate analysis of truth.

In addition, certain equivalences – those of the sort illustrated in (2) – have seemed important for another reason. These equivalences can be seen as providing substantial information about the meanings of the sentences they talk about. For example, it would seem that an important part of understanding the Spanish sentence, '*La nieve es blanca*', consists in knowing that it is true (in Spanish) iff snow is white. The underlying idea here is that since (standardly) sentences are used to make claims about the world, to understand a sentence is to understand the way it represents the world as being, ie. to know the conditions the world must satisfy if it is to conform to the representation. Since these are just the conditions under which the sentence is true, it follows that understanding a sentence involves knowing its truth conditions. Thus, it has been suggested, understanding the Spanish sentence '*La nieve es blanca*' involves knowing the fact stated by (2b), and understanding the Spanish language involves knowing a fact of this sort for each of its sentences. Since speakers presumably do not master these facts one by one, it is natural to suppose that what they do master can be represented by a finitely statable theory that entails all the relevant equivalences. On this view, a theory of meaning should allow one to derive an equivalence of the sort illustrated in (2) for each sentence of the language.

In short, equivalences involving truth predicates have been held to be central not only to our understanding of the notion of truth, but also to our understanding of the meanings of sentences to which the truth predicate may be applied. However, at this point a question should occur to you. Is there any single type of equivalence that is capable of playing both roles simultaneously? Think again about (2b). The reason it provides information about the meaning of the sentence, '*La nieve es blanca*', is that we already understand what it is for a sentence to be true. Without this prior understanding of the notion of truth no such information about the meaning of the Spanish sentence would be provided. In such a situation, the status of (2b) would be like that of (3), where *Eurt* is a new predicate that you do not understand.

(3) '*La nieve es blanca*' is an *EURT* sentence of Spanish iff snow is white.

If, prior to being given (3), you do not know the meaning of either the predicate *EURT* or the sentence '*La nieve es blanca*', then (3) itself will provide you with no further information about the meanings of either. Thus it seems that in order for an equivalence of the above sort to provide information about the meaning of a sentence, the notion of truth must already be taken for granted.

Suppose, on the other hand, that we do not take the notion of truth for granted, but instead seek to explain it. Can we use the equivalences for this purpose? This time imagine that we already understand both Spanish and English, and that a new predicate, *EURT*, is introduced using the following instructions:

> '*La nieve es blanca*' is an *EURT* sentence of Spanish iff snow is white, 'Snow is white' is a *EURT* sentence of English iff snow is white, and so on for every sentence of the form '. . .' ***is an EURT sentence of L iff* xxxxx**, where the dots are replaced by a sentence s of L and the x's are replaced by a sentence (of English) that means the same as s.

Given such instructions, plus our antecedent understanding of the meanings of the sentences of English and Spanish, we will come to understand *Eurt* as applying to precisely the truths. Thus it seems that in order for equivalences of this kind to provide information about the meaning of a truth predicate, the meanings of the sentences they talk about must already be understood.

One conclusion to be drawn from this is that no equivalence can be used to state information about the meaning of a sentence, while at the same time providing information about the meaning of the truth predicate. A closely related point is that if T is an equivalence that is part of the definition or analysis of the notion of truth, or if T is a logical consequence of such a definition or analysis, then T cannot express information about the meaning of any sentence in the way in which (2b) expresses something about the meaning of the Spanish sentence it mentions. For surely, that which is expressed by a definition or analysis is knowable a priori, without appeal to empirical evidence. Thus, if T follows from a correct definition or analysis of truth, then T will be a priori. But since one cannot know the meaning of any sentence without appealing to empirical evidence about how that sentence is used by speakers, T cannot make a substantial claim about the meaning of any sentence.

There are two lessons to be learned here. The first is that we need to clarify the differences between the kinds of equivalences illustrated by (1) and (2). It may be that certain of these follow directly from the analysis of truth, whereas others do not but instead provide information about the meanings of sentences. If that is so, then we need to sort out which is which. The second lesson is that we must be careful to spell out precisely what we mean when we speak of equivalences being definitional of the notion of truth, for there may be certain senses in which some of these equivalences are definitional and other senses in which they are not. With these lessons in mind we may return to our two questions, 'What does it mean to say that something is true?' and 'What is the connection between truth and meaning?', and to what the articles in this section say about them.

In the first article, Gottlob Frege makes an important distinction between sentences and the thoughts, or propositions, that sentences are used to express. For Frege, sentences are vehicles for the expression of information. The thought expressed by a sentence on a given occasion is the information content carried by the sentence on that occasion. Some sentences, like 'Two plus three equals five' are complete, and express the same thought on every occasion of use, whereas others, like, 'Today is sunny in Princeton', express different thoughts on different occasions.

When one assertively utters a sentence what one says or asserts is the thought expressed by the sentence on that occasion. An important reason for distinguishing sentences and thoughts, and for taking the latter to be the things that are asserted, comes from a pair of commonplace observations: (i) different sentences may be used to assert (or say) the same thing and (ii) the same sentence may be used on different occasions to assert (say) different things. As an illustration of (i) we may note that if x were to assertively utter the English sentence 'Two plus three equals five' and y were to assertively utter its Russian translation, or a synonymous English sentence, 'Five equals two plus three', then x and y would say the same thing; they would make the same assertion. Similarly, if x were to assertively utter 'Today is sunny in Princeton' on day d and y were to assertively utter the non-synonymous sentence 'Yesterday was sunny in Princeton' on day d plus 1, then x and y would assert the same proposition. In each case, x and y assert the same proposition (thought) even though they assertively utter different sentences. From this it follows that it cannot be the case that what each asserted was identical with the sentence he uttered. Nor do we want to say that what was asserted by one of them was identical with a sentence he didn't utter. Thus, we conclude that the proposition (thought) that both asserted is distinct from the sentence uttered by either (and, by parity of reasoning, from any other sentence). (Point (ii) is illustrated by utterances of 'Today is sunny in Princeton' on different days.)

Just as assertion is a relation between an agent and a thought (proposition), so, according to Frege, is belief, knowledge, and other attitudes. Whenever one asserts, believes, knows, proves, or verifies that p, what one asserts, believes, knows, proves, or verifies is the thought (proposition) that p. This is reflected in the analysis of sentences used to ascribe assertions, beliefs, and other attitudes, to agents. A sentence, 'α asserts (believes) that S' is true (on a particular occasion of use) iff the individual referred to by α (on that occasion) asserts (believes) the thought referred to by the phrase 'that S' – which is just the thought expressed by S (on that occasion). In general, when we want to refer to the thought expressed by a particular sentence, we use an expression of form 'that S', or 'the proposition that S'. The use of these expressions indicates that something is being said about a thought (proposition).

This brings us to the issue of the bearers of truth. Clearly, the sorts of things that may be asserted, believed, known, proved, or verified are the sorts of things that may be true. Thus, thoughts, or propositions, are bearers of truth (and falsity) for Frege. Although they are not the only things that may be true or false, they are the primary bearers of truth and falsity. We may speak of a sentence being true (on a particular occasion); but this just means that the thought expressed by the sentence (on that occasion) is true. Thus, for Frege, the proper focus for a theory or analysis of the notion of truth lies in its application to thoughts (propositions).

We are now in a position to appreciate the difference between equivalences of the kinds illustrated by (1) and (2). In (1) truth is predicated of thoughts (propositions); in (2) it is predicated of sentences. Because of this the equivalences in (1) are both necessary and a priori, whereas those in (2) are not. First consider necessity. The necessity of (1a) is indicated by the fact that for all the different possible states that the world might have been in, there is no such state in which snow is white but it is not true that snow is white; nor is there any possible state in which it is true that snow is white, but snow is not white. It is simply impossible for snow to be white without it being true that snow is white (or without the proposition that snow is white being true); and vice versa. What about the equivalences in (2)? Could the world have been such that 'Snow is white' was not a true sentence of English even though snow was white? Well, if 'Snow is white' had not been a sentence of English at all, or if it had meant something other than what it actually means (ie. if it had expressed some proposition other than the proposition that snow is white) then it could have failed to have been a true sentence of English despite the whiteness of snow. Thus, if it is possible that expressions could have meant something other than what they actually mean, or if they could have failed to exist or to belong to the language they actually belong to, the equivalences of the sort illustrated in (2) are not necessary.

Next consider a prioricity. The propositions, 'If snow is white, then it is true that snow is white' and 'if it is true that snow is white, then snow is white' can be known to be true simply by reflection. Since knowledge of them does not require empirical investigation, they are a priori, as are (1a) and (1b). This is not so for the equivalences in (2). For example, consider (2b). Someone who does not know Spanish might realize that snow is white without having the faintest idea whether '*La nieve es blanca*' is a true sentence of Spanish. For such a person there is no way to validly infer that the Spanish sentence is true simply from his knowledge that snow is white. To discover whether the proposition expressed by (2b) is true such a person must acquire additional empirical information about Spanish. The same point holds for (2a). Thus, these equivalences are not a priori.

These differences between (1) and (2) demonstrate that the propositions expressed by sentences of the form

(4a) It is true that S
(4b) The proposition that S is true

bear a much closer relationship to the proposition expressed by S, than do the propositions expressed by the corresponding sentences of the form

(5) 'S' is a true sentence of L.

Where p is the proposition expressed by a sentence s, the propositions expressed by (4a) and (4b) are true in precisely the same circumstances as p; in addition the former propositions are trivially inferable from p, and vice versa. Since p does not bear this relationship to the proposition expressed by (5), there should be no temptation to confuse the two propositions, or to identify them. To assert (or believe) the proposition expressed by (5) is to assert (or believe) a proposition that is very different from the proposition expressed by the sentence (5) talks about.

There is, however, a genuine question about the relationship between the proposition p expressed by a sentence s, and the proposition (or propositions) expressed by corresponding sentences of the form (4a) and (4b). Since they are true in precisely the same circumstances, as well as being trivially inferable from one another, it might seem that anyone who asserted, believed, or established one must have asserted, believed, or established the other. And if that is so, it might further seem that there is no real difference between them, ie. the proposition p expressed by s might seem to be the very same proposition as the proposition expressed by the corresponding sentences 'It is true that S' and 'The proposition that S is true'. Frege himself seems to endorse this view in the following passage:

> All the same it is something worth thinking about that we cannot recognize a property of a thing without at the same time finding the thought *this thing has this property* to be true. So with every property of a thing there is tied up a property of a thought, namely truth. It is also worth noticing that the sentence 'I smell the scent of violets' has just the same content as the sentence 'It is true that I smell the scent of violets.' So it seems that nothing is added to the thought by my ascribing to it the property of truth.

Although this view has clear appeal, it is also problematic. For if truth really is a property of thoughts, then surely it must be possible to refer to a thought and predicate the property truth of it. And how better to do this than to assert the thought expressed by an instance of (4a) or (4b)? For example, in asserting that the thought that the earth is round is true, one refers to a thought and predicates truth of it. Since one does not do this in asserting that the earth is round, it would seem that the two thoughts, though closely related, cannot be identical.

The view that truth is a genuine property of thoughts (propositions) gains further support from examples like those in (6)

(6a) Everything John says is true.
(6b) There are true propositions which are not supported by available evidence.
(6c) Every proposition is such that either it or its negation is true.

In cases like this, 'is true' functions as a genuine predicate, which cannot simply be eliminated in the way in which it might at first seem eliminable in cases like (4a) and (4b). For example, whereas there is at least some appeal in thinking that 'S' and 'The proposition that S is true' express the same proposition, there is no appeal in thinking that (6a) expresses the same proposition as the conjunction of all propositions John asserts. For one thing, one might believe the proposition expressed by (6a) (on the basis of one's assessment of John's character and intellect) without knowing everything he says, and hence without believing the conjunction of all propositions he asserts. In addition the proposition expressed by (6a) has different truth conditions from the proposition expressed by the conjunction of propositions that John asserts. Here one must not be misled by the fact that either both are actually true, or both are actually false. Despite this coincidence of actual truth values, either of these two propositions could have been true while the other was false. Suppose, for example, that John actually asserts p, q and r. Although the conjunction of these propositions would have been false if q had been false, the proposition expressed by (6a) might have been true in such a circumstance, provided that John had not asserted q in that circumstance. Consequently, the proposition expressed by (6a) is not identical with the conjunction of propositions John actually asserts.

Considerations like these suggest that truth is a genuine property which cannot be eliminated, or dispensed with, if we are to make sense of examples, like those in (6), in which the putative bearer of truth is not displayed in the manner of (4a) or (4b). Indeed it is just such examples that make truth an interesting and important notion. If we never wished to say of a proposition that it is true without at the same time displaying it, we could get along perfectly well without a truth predicate. If, however, we wish to state generalizations, including significant laws of truth (such as (6c)), such a predicate is indispensable.

This fact is compatible with the observation that propositions expressed by examples of the form (4a) and (4b) have a certain primacy in explaining what truth consists in, a primacy resulting from their role in equivalences of the sort illustrated by (1a) and (1b). In explaining what it is for the proposition that snow is white to be true, one can scarcely do better than to point out that it is true iff snow is white. In explaining what it is for an arbitrary proposition to be true it would seem to be enough to note that the same sort of explanation could be given in any individual case. Thus, in order to know what truth is, it seems to be enough to know that the proposition that snow is white is true iff snow is white, that the proposition that the earth is round is true iff the earth is round, and so on for any proposition whatsoever.[1]

In light of this one might speak of equivalences of the sort illustrated by (1a) and (1b) as definitional of our notion of a proposition (thought) being true, definitional in two senses. First, one might regard any explicit definition

(7) For all propositions p, p is true iff p is D

to be correct, or adequate, only if it entails all equivalences of the sort illustrated by (1a) and (1b).[2] Second, even if it proves to be impossible to formulate such a definition, one might maintain that there is nothing more to the notion of truth than what is given by the totality of such equivalences.

This last position bears important similarities to Frege's own. According to it, truth is, strictly speaking, indefinable, but its use in any particular case can be explained by the relevant equivalence. Frege's argument for taking truth to be indefinable comes in the form of an objection to any proposed definition (7). The problem, according to Frege, is that if such a definition were correct, then in order to decide in any particular case whether p was true, we would have to decide whether p was D; but in order to do this, says Frege, we would have to decide whether it was true that p was D. Frege clearly thinks that there is something amiss here in the reappearance of the notion of truth, which was supposed to have been defined away. However, it is not at all clear that anything is amiss.

Does the objection show that D itself is defined in terms of the conceptually prior notion of truth, thereby making the definition of truth in terms of D circular? No. The fact that the notion being defined can be applied to the claim that something is an instance of the defining concept establishes no such conceptual priority, or circularity. Does the objection indicate that in order to decide whether something is D one must ***first*** decide whether it is true that it is D, thereby generating a regress that would make the attribution of D to something dependent on infinitely many prior decisions? No. It may be that in doing whatever is necessary to decide whether something is D we have done everything necessary to decide whether the claim that it is D is true; however this does not mean that we must have explicitly raised and considered the latter question before having resolved the earlier one. Thus, Frege's argument does not show that truth is indefinable.

There is, however, a fundamental problem (not noted by Frege) with general definitions of truth of the sort that Frege had in mind. Such definitions attempt to define a notion of truth that can be applied to examples that already contain the notion of truth (or, equivalently, the defining concept). The problem is that notions of truth with this characteristic typically allow the construction of paradoxical examples which, together with apparently obvious assumptions, lead swiftly to contradiction. Following Alfred Tarski, we can illustrate this point using a predicate, 'is true,' applying to sentences, including sentences containing it.

One such sentence is (8), which is an instance of the liar paradox

(8) Sentence (8) is not true (in English).

The apparently undeniable assumptions (9–10) about this sentence lead to contradiction, (11)

(9) 'Sentence (8) is not true (in English)' is true in English iff sentence
(8) is not true (in English).
(10) Sentence (8) = 'Sentence (8) is not true in English'.
(11) Sentence (8) is true in English iff sentence (8) is not true in English.

Assumption (10) seems to be true simply as a matter of inspection. Assumption (9) is an instance of the schema 'S is true (in English) iff S'. To deny any such instance one would have to be prepared either to deny some sentence s while asserting that it is true, or to assert s while denying that it is true. Since neither alternative is acceptable, it appears that paradoxical sentences like (8) lead inevitably to paradox.

Such, at any rate, was Tarski's conclusion. His solution to the problem was to abandon as hopelessly paradoxical any general conception of truth that could be applied to arbitrary sentences, including sentences assessing their own truth or untruth. In place of this general conception, Tarski showed how, starting with a language L (the object language) containing no truth predicate or other semantic notions, one could introduce into a metalanguage M used to talk about L a restricted truth predicate T^* applying only to L. Since L doesn't contain a truth predicate, no liar paradoxical sentences are constructible in it. Since any sentence s of M containing the predicate T^* is not a sentence of L, the truth predicate contained in s is not one that applies to s itself, and thus the sentence cannot be seen as asserting or denying its own truth. (The process can be repeated by defining a truth predicate for M in a 'higher' meta-metalanguage M', and so on ad infinitum.) Thus liar paradoxical sentences like (8) are excluded by Tarski's construction.

With this problem taken care of, Tarski goes on to show how we can construct a definition of truth for the object language in a metalanguage that contains the object language as a part. Prior to presenting his definition, Tarski lays down certain conditions that it, and the truth predicate it introduces, should satisfy. His most important requirement involves the disquotational character of the truth predicate. Suppose, for example, that 'Snow is white' is a sentence of L, with the meaning that it has in English – namely that snow is white. If T^* is a truth predicate for L, then (12) should be assertable in M

(12) 'Snow is white' is T^* in L iff snow is white.

More generally, T^* will be a truth predicate for L iff all instances of schema T are assertable in M, where instances are obtained by replacing the letter 'X' in the schema with a name of a sentence of L and the letter 'P' either with that same sentence or with a paraphrase of it.

Schema T: X is T^* in L iff P

The importance of Schema T for Tarski is illustrated by his characterization of individual instances like (12) as 'partial definitions' of truth. If such instances are thought of as partial definitions, then the task of defining truth for an entire language may be seen as that of finding a way of generalizing the 'partial definitions' so as to cover every sentence. Tarski expressed this idea by requiring that a definition of truth for L must entail an instance of Schema T for each sentence of L. Any proposed definition of truth satisfying this condition is said to be **materially adequate.** If, in addition, it is **formally**

correct – ie. if it satisfies the usual formal rules for constructing definitions, – then Tarski would regard it as a satisfactory definition of truth. Finally, since other semantic terms, such as 'refers to', 'denotes', 'applies to' etc., raise problems similar to those involving truth, Tarski was interested in definitions that did not employ any undefined semantic terms.

Tarski's task, then, was to find a way to generalize the 'partial definitions of truth' provided by instances of Schema T, without appealing to undefined semantic primitives, in a way that would satisfy his conditions of material adequacy and formal correctness. In, 'Truth and proof,'[3] he points out that in the special case in which the object language has only finitely many sentences, the problem has a trivial solution. For example, let L be the fragment of English consisting of the following 100 sentences: '1 is an even number', '2 is an even number', . . . '100 is an even number'. A definition of truth for L satisfying Tarski's requirements can be constructed as follows

(13) For all sentences *s* of L, *s* is true in L iff either
s = '1 is an even number' and 1 is an even number, or
s = '2 is an even number' and 2 is an even number, or
.
.
.or
s = '100 is an even number' and 100 is an even number.

Although Tarski regards this sort of definition as perfectly satisfactory, he notes that it can be given only in the artificial case in which a definite, finite number of specifiable sentences exhausts an entire language. Since this condition is typically not met by the languages we are interested in, some other method of generalizing the 'partial definitions' provided by Schema T is needed.

Tarski's technique for solving this problem can be illustrated using the following simple language L. L contains two names 'a' (which refers to Alfred) and 'b' (which refers to Betty); it contains a single predicate, 'A' (which applies to a pair of individuals iff the first admires the second); in addition L contains the truth functional connectives '~' (meaning 'not') and 'v' (meaning 'or'); L also contains variables, 'x', 'y', etc. and the quantifiers '∀x' '∀y', etc. (meaning 'everyone'). An atomic formula of L consists of the predicate 'A' followed by a pair of terms. (A term is either a name or a variable.) Complex formulas are built up by the following rules: (i) the result, ~*F*, of prefixing '~' to any formula F is a formula; (ii) the result, (*F* v *G*), of placing 'v' between a pair of formulas F and G, and enclosing the whole in parentheses is a formula; (iii) where u is a variable and F is a formula the result, ∀*u F*, of prefixing the quantifier ∀*u* to F is a formula. Since there is no upper limit on the number of times these rules can be applied to form complex formulas, L contains infinitely many formulas.

A sentence is a formula that contains no free occurrences of variables. An occurrence of a variable in a formula is free iff it is not in the scope of any quantifier using that variable. The scope of a quantifier is the quantifier itself plus the smallest complete formula immediately following it. For example, consider the formulas in (14)

(14a) ∀x (Axa v Axb)
(14b) (∀x Axa v Axb)

In (14b) the smallest complete formula immediately following the quantifier *∀x* is *Axa*. Since an occurrence of *x* in (14b) is not within the scope of the quantifier, it is free and the formula is not a sentence. In (14a), on the other hand, the smallest compete formula immediately following the quantifier is *(Axa v Axb)*.[4] Since it contains no free occurrences of any variable, it is a sentence (which means that everyone either admires Alfred or admires Betty).

The idea behind Tarski's definition of truth for L can best be appreciated if we first make the simplifying assumption that the only individuals talked about in L are Alfred and Betty, so that the class of individuals covered by the quantifiers consists only of Alfred and Betty. Given this simplifying assumption, we can define truth for L in three steps. First, we say what it is for a name to denote (refer to) an individual and what it is for a predicate to apply to a pair of individuals; second, we use these notions to say what it is for an atomic sentence to be true; third, we characterize truth for complex sentences in terms of truth for simpler sentences. This is done in (15–16)

(15a) A name n of L denotes an object o iff either either n = the name 'a' and o = Alfred or n = the name 'b' and o = Betty.
(15b) A predicate P of L applies to a pair of individuals $<o_1, o_2>$ iff P = the predicate 'A' and o_1 admires o_2.
(16a) A sentence $A\ t_1\ t_2$, consisting of the predicate 'A' followed by a pair of names t_1 and t_2 is true in L iff 'A' applies to the pair of individuals $<o_1, o_2>$ denoted by t_1 and t_2 respectively.[5]
(16b) For any sentence S, the sentence, *~S*, is true in L iff S is not true in L.
(16c) For any sentences S and R, the sentence *(SvR)*, is true in L iff either S is true in L or R is true in L.
(16d) A sentence, *∀uF*, where u is a variable and F is a formula, is true in L iff for every name t, the result, *Ft/u*, of erasing the quantifier and replacing all free occurrences of u with the name t is a true sentence of L. (Remember, given the simplifying assumption, we know that everyone covered by the quantifier has a name in the language; also each name in the language is the name of someone covered by the quantifier.)

The material adequacy of this definition can be illustrated by the following (informal) derivation of an instance of Schema T.

(17a) The sentence ∀*x* (*Axa v Axb)* is true in L iff for every name t of L, (*Ata v Atb*) is a true sentence of L. (From 16d)
(17b) (*Ata v Atb*) is true in L iff either *Ata* is true in L or *Atb* is true in L. (From 16c)
(17c) *Ata* is true in L iff either t = 'a' and Alfred admires Alfred, or t = 'b' and Betty admires Alfred. (From 15 and 16a)
(17d) *Atb* is true in L iff either t = 'a' and Alfred admires Betty, or t = 'b' and Betty admires Betty. (From 15 and 16a)
(17e) (*Ata v Atb*) is true in L iff either t = 'a' and Alfred admires either Alfred or Betty, or t = 'b' and Betty admires either Alfred or Betty. (From 17b, c, d).
(17f) The sentence ∀*x* (*Axa v Axb*) is true in L iff for every name t of L, either t = 'a' and Alfred admires either Alfred or Betty, or t = 'b' and Betty admires either Alfred or Betty. This holds iff everyone under consideration (ie. Alfred and Betty) is such that either that person admires Alfred or that person admires Betty. (From 17a, e)
(17g) The sentence ∀*x* (*Axa v Axb*) is true in L iff everyone (ie. Alfred and Betty) is such that either that person admires Alfred or that person admires Betty.

Since the sentence on the right-hand side of 'iff' in (g) is a paraphrase of the sentence of L mentioned on the left, (g) is an instance of Schema T. Similar instances can be derived from the definition of truth for each sentence of L. Thus, the definition is materially adequate.

Now that we have illustrated Tarski's strategy we are in a position to relax the simplifying assumption and extend the truth definition to cases in which the language is used to make claims about objects for which there are no names in the language. In such cases we cannot characterize a sentence (∀*u F*) of L as true iff every sentence *F*(*t*) is true that results from erasing the quantifier and substituting a name t for free occurrences of *u*. The problem is this: The sentence (∀*u F*) 'says that' every object has the characteristics expressed by *F*. However, this may be false even if each object for which we happen to have a name in L has those characteristics (provided that some unnamed object lacks them). Thus, Tarski had to find some other way of characterizing what it means for a sentence (∀*u F*) to be true.

The natural solution is to allow variables to serve as temporary names of objects. Using this idea, one can say that (∀*u F*) is true iff for every object o, the formula *F*(*u*) that results from erasing the quantifier is true when *u* is treated as a name of o – ie. iff for every object o, *F*(*u*) is true relative to an assignment of o as the denotation of *u*. This was Tarski's strategy, though not his terminology. Instead of talking about 'an assignment of objects to variables,' Tarski spoke of ordered 'sequences of objects,' and instead of characterizing formulas as being 'true relative to a sequence,' he spoke of 'a sequence satisfying a formula.' However Tarski's sequences are designed solely to provide assignments of objects to variables, and the relation of satisfaction holding between sequences (assignments) and formulas is just the converse of the relation of truth-relative-to holding between a formula and a sequence (assignment) – ie., a sequence (assignment) satisfies a formula iff the formula is true relative to the sequence (assignment).[6]

With this means of providing variables with denotations relative to assignments we can define what it is for a formula to be true relative to an assignment using the same technique as before. Whereas before we defined truth for **atomic sentences,** and then extended the definition by characterizing the truth (or untruth) of **complex sentences** in terms of the truth (or untruth) of simpler **sentences,** this time we define truth relative to an assignment for **atomic formulas,** and extend the definition by characterizing the truth (or untruth) relative to assignments of **complex formulas** in terms of the truth (or untruth) of simpler **formulas** relative to assignments. In order to do this we begin by modifying (15) so that it provides us with a definition of the denotation of a term (ie. name or variable) relative to an assignment.

(15*) A term t of L denotes an object o relative to an assignment V of objects to variables iff either t is a variable and V assigns o to it, or t = the name 'a' and o = Alfred or, t = the name 'b' and o = Betty. (The denotation of a genuine name does not vary from one assignment to another.)

Inductive definition of truth relative to an assignment:

(15a) An atomic formula $A\ t_1\ t_2$, consisting of the predicate 'A' followed by a pair of terms (ie. names or variables) t_1 and t_2 is true relative to an assignment V iff 'A' applies to the pair of individuals $<o_1, o_2>$ denoted by t_1 and t_2 relative to V.

(15b) For any formula F, the formula, $\sim F$, is true relative to an assignment V iff F is not true relative to V.

(15c) For any formulas F and R, the formula, $(F v R)$, is true relative to an assignment V iff either F is true relative to V or R is true relative to V.

(15d) For any formula F and variable u, the formula, $\forall u\ F$, is true relative to an assignment V iff F is true relative to every assignment V* that differs from V at most in what it assigns the variable u. (This ensures that no matter what object is assigned as the denotation of u, the formula F will come out true relative to that assignment – in other words, every object 'is F'.)

Having defined what it is for a formula to be true relative to an assignment, it remains only to define what it is for a sentence to be true. Since sentences contain no free occurrences of variables (which require interpretation by assignments), it turns out that a sentence is true relative to one assignment iff it is true relative to all assignments. With this in mind we can define truth as follows

(18) A sentence S of L is true iff S is true relative to all assignments.

This definition can be shown to be materially adequate in precisely the manner illustrated above.

Finally, Tarski was interested in showing that his definition employed no undefined semantic notions, and that it could, in principle, be used to eliminate such notions entirely from the metalanguage (in favor of their defining concepts). In order to accomplish this, he used a technique for converting inductive definitions, like the definition of truth relative to an assignment given above, into explicit definitions. The relationship between inductive definitions and explicit definitions is straightforward. Inductive definitions employ the term being defined – in our case, 'truth relative to an assignment' – in clauses that specify its application to new cases in terms of its application to previously defined cases. To turn such a definition into an explicit definition, one trades such occurrences of the term being defined for occurrences of a set variable, and rewrites the clauses so that they specify set-membership conditions for new cases in terms of set-membership conditions for previously specified cases.[7]

Explicit definition of truth relative to an assignment:

A formula F of L is true relative to an assignment V iff there is a set T such that the pair <F, V> is a member of T, and for all formulas G and assignments Z, the pair <G, Z> is a member of T iff either (i)G = $A\ t_1\ t_2$,, for some terms t_1 and t_2, and 'A' applies to the pair of individuals $<o_1, o_2>$ denoted by t_1 and t_2 relative to Z; or (ii)G = the formula ~H, for some formula H, and <H, Z> is not a member of T; or (iii)G = the formula $(H\ v\ R)$, for some formulas H and R, and either <H, Z> is a member of T or <R, Z> is a member of T; or (iv)G = the formula $\forall u\ H$, for some variable u and formula H, and <H, Z^*> is a member of T for every assignment Z^* that differs from Z at most in what it assigns to u.

With this definition, together with (15*, 15b, and 18), Tarski could, in principle, eliminate semantic notions entirely from the metalanguage. Doing this would amount to systematically replacing claims of the form

(19a) Sentence s is true in L

with claims of the form

(19b) There is a set T such that for all assignments V of values to variables the pair <s,V> is a member of T, and for all formulas G and assignments Z, the pair <G,Z> is a member of T iff . . . (as above).

Given the extreme complexity of the formula replacing the truth predicate, no one would ever do this. Fortunately, however, actual replacement is not necessary. To take Tarski's construction as giving a genuine ***definition*** or ***analysis*** of truth is to take the content of claims of the form (19a) to be entirely given by corresponding claims of the form (19b).

Let us take Tarski's definition as introducing a notion of truth, restricted to a particular object language, with precisely the content specified by the definition. Many philosophers have thought that this definition provided a philosophically revealing analysis of truth as it has classically been understood. It is, of course, recognized that Tarski's truth predicate does not have precisely the same meaning as the English word 'true'. Whereas the former is restricted to a particular object language, the latter applies to sentences of arbitrary languages,[8] as well as to propositions expressed by sentences.

Given this difference, one might wonder how anyone could take Tarski's definition to be an analysis of our ordinary notion of truth. To understand this, one must remember that, according to Tarski and many others, our ordinary notion is defective precisely because its unrestrictedness gives rise to paradox. The sort of analysis of truth that Tarski attempted to provide is one that would eliminate this alleged defect while preserving the central and useful features of the notion. In effect, Tarski tried to specify not how 'true' is actually understood but how it ought to be understood if it is to function in our logical, mathematical, and scientific theories in the ways normally intended.

Analyses of this kind are often called 'explications'. In general, an explication of some pre-theoretically understood concept C consists in the definition of a related concept C′ which (i) applies to those things which are clear and central instances of the concept C; (ii) is precise and well-defined; (iii) is free of difficulties and obscurities present in the original concept C; and (iv) may play the role of C in all theoretical contexts in which that notion is legitimately required. The claim that Tarski's definition provides an analysis of truth can be understood as the claim that the definition satisfies these criteria.

If we restrict our attention to the sorts of object-languages for which Tarski provided truth definitions, then the material adequacy and formal correctness of the definitions will ensure that the first two of these criteria are satisfied. More interesting issues are raised by the third and fourth criteria, to which the selections by Hartry Field and Donald Davidson are directly relevant.

Field raises the question of whether Tarski's analysis is compatible with a general philosophical commitment to physicalism. Roughly put, physicalism is the doctrine that all genuine facts, all objects and all properties, are in principle reducible to physical facts, physical objects and physical properties. Physicalism requires that all biological differences between organisms, all psychological differences between individuals, and all cultural and institutional differences between societies be explicable ultimately in terms of differences of the sort described in theoretical physics. It also requires one to reject any concepts in the special sciences, including semantic concepts like truth, reference, and meaning, that are not replaceable in principle by a concept definable in physical theory.

At first glance it would certainly seem as if Tarski succeeded in reducing truth to physicalistically acceptable terms. What he showed is that for certain languages L, adequate for natural science and mathematics, one can define a truth predicate using only notions already expressible in L, plus certain syntactic and set-theoretic apparatus. Thus, if L is physicalistically pure, and if syntax and set theory are unproblematic, then defining an object language truth predicate in the metalanguage cannot introduce any difficulties.

Nevertheless Field challenges this conclusion. He does not, of course, dispute the fact that Tarski's truth predicate is extensionally correct, i.e. that it applies to precisely the set of true sentences of the language. He maintains, however, that extensional correctness is not enough. In addition, he requires that any genuine reduction must show semantic facts about expressions to be determined by physical facts about their users and the environments in which they are used. Tarski's definitions don't do this.

This can be seen by considering a simple example. Suppose that 'Aab' is a sentence of L and that the relevant semantic facts about it are given in (20).

(20a) 'a' denotes Alfred and 'b' denotes Betty (in L).
(20b) 'A' applies (in L) to a pair of individuals <o,o'>
iff o admires o'.
(20c) 'Aab' is true in L iff Alfred admires Betty.

If Tarski's definitions really specify the physicalistic content of semantic notions, then, in each case, we ought to be able to substitute the physicalistic defining expression for the semantic notion in the example without changing the physical fact thereby specified. Performing this substitution and simplifying results, we obtain

(21a) 'a' = 'a' and Alfred = Alfred, and 'b' = 'b' and Betty = Betty.
(21b) For all objects o, o′, 'A' = 'A' and o admires o′ iff o admires o′.
(21c) ('Aab' = 'Aab', and there are objects o, and o′ such that o = Alfred and o′ = Betty and o admires o′) iff Alfred admires Betty.

There is a problem in identifying these facts with those in (20). As Field points out, it is natural to suppose that the expressions of a language have semantic properties only in virtue of the ways they are used by speakers. Thus, he holds that the facts given in (20) wouldn't have obtained if speakers' linguistic behavior had been different.[9] Since the facts in (21) are not speaker-dependent in this way, Field concludes that they are not semantic facts and that Tarski's attempted reduction fails. Tarski's truth predicate is both physicalistic and coextensive with 'true in L'; but it is not, according to Field, a physicalistic conception of truth.

On Field's view, Tarski's truth definition inherits its inadequacy as a reduction from its dependence on the pseudo-reductions of denotation and application (15 and 15* above). Thus, Field's strategy for solving the problem is to provide genuine reductions for these notions. The picture that emerges from his discussion is one in which an adequate definition of truth is a two-stage affair. Stage 1 is Tarski's reduction of truth to denotation and application. Stage 2 is the imagined physicalistic reduction of the notions of terms denoting, and predicates applying to, objects. However, this picture is flawed and understates the nature of Field's objection to Tarski.

This can be seen by considering a pair of elementary examples. Imagine two languages, L_1 and L_2, which are identical except that in L_1 the predicate 'A' applies to pairs of individuals the first of which admires the second, whereas in L_2 it applies to pairs of individuals the first of which attacks the second. Owing to this difference, certain sentences will have different truth conditions in the two languages.

(22a) 'Aab' is true in L_1 iff Alfred admires Betty.
(22b) 'Aab' is true in L_2 iff Alfred attacks Betty.

Under Tarski's original definition, this difference will be traceable to the clauses where the applications of predicates are simply listed. Field's objection is that although Tarski's definitions correctly *report* that 'A' applies to different things in the two languages, they don't *explain* how this difference arises from the way in which speakers of the two languages use the predicate. What Field fails to point out is that exactly the same objection can be brought against Tarski's treatment of negation, disjunction, and quantification.

This time let L_1 and L_2 be identical except for their treatment of 'v'.

(23a) A formula (AvB) is true in L_1 (with respect to an assignment V) iff A is true in L_1 or B is true in L_1.

(23b) A formula (AvB) is true in L_2 (with respect to an assignment V) iff A is true in L_2 and B is true in L_2.

Owing to this difference, sentences containing 'v' will have different truth conditions in the two languages. In order to satisfy Field's requirements on reduction, it is not enough for a truth characterization to report such differences. Rather, such differences must be explained in terms of the manner in which speakers of the two languages treat 'v'. Since Tarski's truth definitions don't say anything about this, their inductive clauses should be just as objectionable to the physicalist as the base clauses. This means that the strategy of achieving a genuine reduction of truth by supplementing Tarski with non-trivial definitions of denotation and application cannot succeed. The reason it cannot is that, given Field's strictures on reduction, Tarski has not reduced truth to denotation and application.

It should be emphasized that this critique of Tarski is based on two contentious assumptions. The first is physicalism. The second is the contention that there is a genuine theoretical need for a truth predicate, tied to the behavior of speakers, of a kind not provided by Tarski. Presumably Field's idea is that there is some explanatory task involving the thought and action of speakers that requires a truth predicate that is physicalistic, but non-Tarskian. Whether or not this is so is a controversial issue.[10]

One area in which the notion of truth has been put to theoretical use is semantics, or the theory of meaning. In 'Truth and Meaning' Donald Davidson argues that the meaning of an expression consists in the contribution it makes to the meanings of sentences that contain it, and the meaning of a sentence is given by a statement of its truth conditions. For Davidson, truth conditions are expressed by instances of Schema T, and a theory of meaning for a language L is cast in the form of a Tarskian theory of truth in L. Such a theory is viewed as specifying the truth conditions of sentences on the basis of the semantically significant properties of their constituent parts. Since knowledge of that which is stated by the theory is held to be sufficient for understanding L, nothing essential to meaning is deemed to be lacking from the theory.

In addition to outlining this conception of a theory of meaning, Davidson indicates that he takes the notion of truth defined by Tarski to be capable of playing the central role in such a theory, thereby providing further vindication of Tarski's definition as an adequate explication, or analysis, of truth.[11] At this point two questions must clearly be distinguished. First, is Davidson's conception of a theory of meaning as a theory of truth acceptable? Second, could Tarski's notion of truth play the central role in such a theory? Although the answer to the first question is contentious and controversial, the answer to the second is not; Tarski's notion of truth cannot play the central role in a Davidsonian theory of meaning.

To see this, imagine that 'T^* in L' is a Tarskian truth predicate, and that (24) is an instance of Schema T derivable in the metalanguage from the definition of truth for L.

(24) 'Aab' is T^* in L iff Alfred admires Betty.

Since 'T^* in L' is the Tarskian truth predicate, nothing is lost by replacing it with its explicit definition, which results in something of the form (25).

(25) [There is a set T such that for all assignments V of values to variables the pair <'Aab',V> is a member of T, and for all formulas G and assignments Z, the pair <G, Z> is a member of T iff either (i) G = $A\ t_1\ t_2$, for some terms t_1 and t_2, and 'A' applies to the pair of individuals <o_1,o_2> denoted by t_1 and t_2 relative to Z; or (ii) . . . (as in the explicit definition of truth above)] iff Alfred admires Betty.

Since 'Aab' is a sentence consisting of the predicate 'A' followed by a pair of terms, we can simplify (25) by dropping the extraneous clauses '(ii) . . . '. We must also replace 'denotes (relative to an assignment)' and 'applies' with their Tarskian definitions, thereby producing something of the form (26).

(26) [There is a set T such that for all assignments V of values to variables the pair <'Aab',V> is a member of T, and for all formulas G and assignments Z such that G = $At_1\ t_2$, for some terms t_1 and t_2, <$At_1\ t_2$, Z> is a member of T iff there are objects o_1, and o_2, such that o_1 admires o_2 and (a) either t_1 = 'a' and o_1 = Alfred, or t_1 = 'b' and o_1 = Betty, or t_1 is a variable and Z assigns o_1 to it, and (b) either t_2 = 'a' and o_2 = Alfred, or t_2 = 'b' and o_2 = Betty, or t_2 is a variable and Z assigns o_2 to it] iff Alfred admires Betty.

The only information about 'Aab' that this provides is expressed by (27), which is equivalent to (28).

(27) [There is a set T such that for all assignments V of values to variables the pair <'Aab',V> is a member of T, and for any

assignment Z <'Aab',Z> will be a member of T iff 'Aab' = 'Aab' and there are objects o_1, and o_2, such that o_1 admires o_2, and 'a' = 'a' and o_1 = Alfred, and 'b' = 'b' and o_2 = Betty] iff Alfred admires Betty.

(28) [There are objects o_1 and o_2 such that o_1 admires o_2, and o_1 = Alfred and o_2 = Betty] iff Alfred admires Betty.

The crucial point to recognize is that none of these biconditionals (24–28) say anything that constrains the meaning of 'Aab'; one could know that which they express without knowing the first thing about what 'Aab' means, or doesn't mean. Suppose, for example, that one did not know that 'Aab' means in L that Alfred admires Betty, and was considering the hypothesis that it means in L that Alfred does not admire Betty. Given (24–28), plus an instance of Tarski's a priori constraint (29), one could conclude that either 'T^* in L' in (24) is not a truth predicate for L, or 'Aab' does not mean in L that Alfred does not admire Betty.

(29) If 'T^* in L' is a truth predicate for L (ie. if it applies to precisely the true sentences of L), and if moreover s means in L that P, then *s* is T^* in L iff P.

However, without knowing the meanings of the sentences of L, one could not determine whether 'T^* in L' is a truth predicate for L. Similarly, without knowing that 'T^* in L' is a truth predicate, one could determine nothing about the meaning of sentences of L.

The crucial point for theories of truth as theories of meaning is that instances of (30a), which contain our ordinary pre-theoretic notion of truth, are obvious and knowable a priori, whereas instances of (30b), which contain a Tarskian truth predicate for L, are anything but obvious, and are not knowable a priori.

(30a) If *s* means in L that P, then *s* is true in L iff P.
(30b) If *s* means in L that P, then *s* is T^* in L iff P.

It is precisely the obviousness and availability of (30a) that allows claims of the form '*s* is true in L iff P' to provide information about meaning. For example, if one knew that 'Aab' is true in L iff Alfred admires Betty, then one could immediately eliminate the hypothesis that 'Aab' means in L that Alfred does not admire Betty, since given that hypothesis, one could derive the contradictory result that Alfred admires Betty iff 'Aab' is true in L iff Alfred does not admire Betty. The unavailability of (30b) prevents similar conclusions from being drawn from claims of the form '*s* is T* in L iff P.' As a result, claims of this form provide no information about meaning.

The obviousness and a prioricity of instances of (30a) result from a conceptual connection between our ordinary notions of truth and meaning that does not hold between the notion of meaning and Tarski's concept of truth. The basis of this connection seems to be the primacy of propositions as bearers of truth in the ordinary sense. The bearers of truth are, in the first instance, what is said and believed, which in turn are the semantic contents of sentences. Sentences are true derivatively, just in case they express true propositions. Consequently, when we are told that a sentence is true in the ordinary sense, we are given information about the proposition it expresses, and thereby, about its meaning. Tarski's truth predicate 'T* in L', on the other hand, is defined independently of propositions. As a result, the claim that it applies to a sentence s gives us no information about the meaning of s. The predicates 'T* in L' and 'true in L' do, of course, apply to precisely the same sentences of L. However, they do not express the same concept, and, because of this, sentences containing them do not carry the same information.

This means that the notion of truth defined by Tarski cannot play the central role in a truth-conditional theory of meaning. Given an object-language L, one can use Tarskian techniques to construct a characterization of truth in L. However there are two diametrically opposed ways in which the characterization can be understood. Following Tarski, one may take it to be a definition which introduces and gives content to a truth predicate. If one takes this route, the resulting truth definition provides no information about meaning. Alternatively, one may take the truth characterization to contain our ordinary, antecedently understood notion of truth. If one takes this route, the resulting theory states the truth conditions of object-language sentences in a way that provides information constraining their meaning. This is the route one must take if one is to accept Davidson's conception of theories of truth as theories of meaning. Since these two construals of the significance of the truth characterization are mutually exclusive, we cannot have both.

This creates a potential problem for the view that Tarski's definition is a successful analysis, or explication, of truth. We already know that Tarski's notion of truth differs in certain respects from our ordinary notion. If there is an important theoretical role that truth is required to play, and if that role can be played by our ordinary notion but not by Tarski's, then the definition cannot be accepted as an adequate analysis – whatever its other merits, it does not tell us all we need to know about what truth is.

This does not mean that Davidson's view of theories of truth as theories of meaning must be accepted as the last word on the subject. One important problem with this view is taken up in a well-known passage from 'Truth and Meaning' in which Davidson discusses the true, but deviant, T-sentence (S)

(S) 'Snow is white' is true (in English) iff grass is green.

Davidson says that we ought *not* to think that a theory which entails the standard T-sentence 'Snow is white' is true (in English) iff snow is white is any more correct than a theory that entails (S)

> *provided the theory gives the correct results for every sentence (on the basis of its structure, there being no other way). It is not easy to see how (S) could be a party to such an enterprise,* [my emphasis] but if it were – if, that is, (S) followed from a characterization of the predicate 'is true' that led to the invariable pairing of truths with truths and falsehoods with falsehoods – then there would not, I think, be anything essential to the idea of meaning that remained to be captured.

The view here is that there is nothing more to be known about the meanings of the sentences of a language than is stated by a theory of truth that systematically derives a true T-sentence for each object-language sentence on the basis of its structurally significantly parts. It is suggested that the requirement that derivations be systematic, and based on structure, may eliminate grotesque theories that issue in non-translational T-sentences like (S). The idea, it seems, is that in order to derive (S) from a compositional account of the structure of the sentence 'Snow is white,' a theory would have to contain statements specifying grass as the reference of 'snow' and green things as the objects to which the predicate 'is white' applies. But with such statements one would end up deriving *false* T-sentences like '"Snow is grass" is true iff grass is grass' and '"The tree is green" is true iff the tree is white,' in addition to 'accidentally true' T-sentences like (S). Thus, it is thought, truth theories which are both *true* and appropriately *structural* will end up deriving instances of Schema T in which the metalanguage sentences on the right-hand side are close enough paraphrases of the object language sentences on the left that nothing essential to meaning would fail to be grasped by a speaker who knew the totality of that which is stated by the theory.

However, this view does not withstand scrutiny. It is now widely recognized that the requirement that a theory of truth derive its T-sentences on the basis of semantically significant structure does little to block the derivation of deviant T-sentences like (S).[12] To derive such sentences all one needs to do is replace the clauses in an otherwise acceptable truth theory that specify denotation and application with clauses of very different meanings that nevertheless specify the same denotation and application. If the theorems of the original truth theory were true, then the theorems of its replacement will also be true, despite the fact that knowledge of that which they state will not suffice for understanding the object language.

For example, one might replace a clause in the original truth theory stating that 'the predicate "*blanca*" applies in Spanish to an object iff it is white,' with a clause stating that 'the predicate "*blanca*" applies in Spanish to an object iff it is white and there is no largest prime number.' In such a case, the original theory would allow the derivation of the theorem (31a), in which the English sentence on the right-hand side is a meaning-preserving paraphrase of the Spanish sentence on the left, whereas the replacement truth theory would allow the derivation of (31b), in which no plausible relation of paraphrase holds.

(31a) '*La nieve es blanca*' is a true sentence of Spanish iff snow is white

(31b) '*La nieve es blanca*' is a true sentence of Spanish iff snow is white and there is no largest prime number.

Similar results might be derived for the other sentences of the language. Clearly, a truth theory that yielded only deviant T-sentences like (31b) could not be regarded as a theory of meaning (even if all its theorems were true).

One effect of this observation has been to stimulate the search for further constraints to impose on truth theories to ensure that the metalanguage sentences appearing on the right-hand sides of T-theorems are proper translations of the object language sentences on the left. However, there is a further difficulty. Even if we have such a theory, knowledge of that which it states is not sufficient for understanding the language. The problem is that one may know *that which is stated* by a properly translational truth theory without knowing that the theory is translational. Thus, one who knows a translational truth theory that issues in theorem (31a) may still believe that which is stated by (32), provided one believes that there is no largest prime.

(32) '*La nieve es blanca*' means in Spanish that snow is white and there is no largest prime number.

Such a person would combine true beliefs about truth conditions with false beliefs about meaning, and so would not understand the language. Consequently, knowledge of that which is stated by the most promising of truth theories does not suffice for understanding. But then one must ask, 'What justification is there for thinking that theories of truth are theories of meaning, after all?' Whether or not such a justification can be found is one of the hotly debated issues in contemporary philosophy of language.[13]

Notes

1. Problems involving the liar paradox require some modification of this point to deal with paradoxical propositions. We will not be concerned here with how they are treated. For more on the liar paradox see the afterword by McGee.
2. For every non-paradoxical proposition.
3. 'Truth and proof,' *Scientific American*, June 1969, 63–77.

4. The expression (*Axa*) is not a complete formula; the expression *Axa* is a complete formula, but it does not immediately follow the quantifier.
5. Note, in the presence of (15), (16a) is equivalent to the claim that an atomic sentence s is true in L iff either (i) s = 'Aaa' and Alfred admires Alfred, or (ii) s = 'Aab' and Alfred admires Betty, or (iii) s = 'Aba' and Betty admires Alfred, or (iv) s = 'Abb' and Betty admires Betty. Since there are only finitely many atomic sentences the clause for atomic sentences in the definition of truth can be reduced to what is in effect a list.
6. Tarski's notion of a sequence can be thought of as follows: Let D be the class of objects that sentences of L are used to talk about (the domain of L). A sequence is an infinite arrangement of objects from D. In effect, it amounts to a (totally defined) function that assigns each positive integer exactly one object from D. The ith member of a sequence is simply the object that is assigned to the integer i. There is no requirement that every element of D occur in every sequence and there is no limit on the number of times a single element of D can occur in a sequence – ie. if Q is an individual sequence and o is a particular object, Q may assign o to no integers, to every integer, or to any combination of integers. Since the variables of L can be arranged in a fixed, infinite list, each sequence can be seen as assigning each variable an object as value. The object a sequence assigns to the ith variable is just the object it assigns to the integer i – ie. the ith member of the sequence. In what follows I will speak of 'assignments' rather than 'sequences' and I will regard each assignment as assigning an object to each variable in the language.
7. This technique for converting an inductive to an explicit definition will work whenever the existence of the set required by the explicit definition is guaranteed. One will have this guarantee whenever the domain of the object-language is a set, and the metalanguage 'is essentially richer than the object language' – ie. contains quantifiers that range over arbitrary sequences of elements of the set that makes up the domain of the object language.
8. We can apply the English predicate 'is true' not only to sentences of English, but also to sentences of other languages, natural or artificial.
9. I use the phrase 'linguistic behavior' in a broad sense to include all facts about speakers relating to their use of language.
10. For further discussion of this and other issues raised by Field see, Scott Soames, (1984), 'What is a theory of truth?', *The Journal of Philosophy*, LXXXI, 8: 411–29.
11. See 'Truth and meaning', below.
12. See in particular J. A. Foster, (1976), 'Meaning and truth theory,' in *Truth and Meaning*, Gareth Evans and John McDowell (eds). Oxford: Oxford University Press.
13. See James Higginbotham, (1992), 'Truth and understanding,' *Philosophical Studies*, 65: 3–16, and Scott Soames, (1992), 'Truth, meaning, and understanding', *Philosophical Studies*, 65: 17–35.

Chapter 17

The Thought: A Logical Inquiry

G. Frege

The word 'true' indicates the aim of logic as does 'beautiful' that of aesthetics or 'good' that of ethics. All sciences have truth as their goal; but logic is also concerned with it in a quite different way from this. It has much the same relation to truth as physics has to weight or heat. To discover truths is the task of all sciences; it falls to logic to discern the laws of truth. The word 'law' is used in two senses. When we speak of laws of morals or the state we mean regulations which ought to be obeyed but with which actual happenings are not always in conformity. Laws of nature are the generalization of natural occurrences with which the occurrences are always in accordance. It is rather in this sense that I speak of laws of truth. This is, to be sure, not a matter of what happens so much as of what is. Rules for asserting, thinking, judging, inferring, follow from the laws of truth. And thus one can very well speak of laws of thought too. But there is an imminent danger here of mixing different things up. Perhaps the expression 'law of thought' is interpreted by analogy with 'law of nature' and the generalization of thinking as a mental occurrence is meant by it. A law of thought in this sense would be a psychological law. And so one might come to believe that logic deals with the mental process of thinking and the psychological laws in accordance with which it takes place. This would be a misunderstanding of the task of logic, for truth has not been given the place which is its due here. Error and superstition have causes just as much as genuine knowledge. The assertion both of what is false and of what is true takes place in accordance with psychological laws. A derivation from these and an explanation of a mental process that terminates in an assertion can never take the place of a proof of what is asserted. Could not logical laws also have played a part in this mental process? I do not want to dispute

From P. Strawson (ed.) (1967), *Philosophical Logic*, Oxford: Oxford University Press.
Translated by A. M. and Marcelle Quinton.

this, but when it is a question of truth possibility is not enough. For it is also possible that something not logical played a part in the process and deflected it from the truth. We can only decide this after we have discerned the laws of truth; but then we will probably be able to do without the derivation and explanation of the mental process if it is important to us to decide whether the assertion in which the process terminates is justified. In order to avoid this misunderstanding and to prevent the blurring of the boundary between psychology and logic, I assign to logic the task of discovering the laws of truth, not of assertion or thought. The meaning of the word 'true' is explained by the laws of truth.

But first I shall attempt to outline roughly what I want to call true in this connexion. In this way other uses of our word may be excluded. It is not to be used here in the sense of 'genuine' or 'veracious', nor, as it sometimes occurs in the treatment of questions of art, when, for example, truth in art is discussed, when truth is set up as the goal of art, when the truth of a work of art or true feeling is spoken of. The word 'true' is put in front of another word in order to show that this word is to be understood in its proper, unadulterated sense. This use too lies off the path followed here; that kind of truth is meant whose recognition is the goal of science.

Grammatically the word 'true' appears as an adjective. Hence the desire arises to delimit more closely the sphere in which truth can be affirmed, in which truth comes into the question at all. One finds truth affirmed of pictures, ideas, statements, and thoughts. It is striking that visible and audible things occur here alongside things which cannot be perceived with the senses. This hints that shifts of meaning have taken place. Indeed! Is a picture, then, as a mere visible and tangible thing, really true, and a stone, a leaf, not true? Obviously one would not call a picture true unless there were an intention behind it. A picture must represent something. Furthermore, an idea is not called true in itself but only with respect to an intention that it should correspond to something. It might be supposed from this that truth consists in the correspondence of a picture with what it depicts. Correspondence is a relation. This is contradicted, however, by the use of the word 'true', which is not a relation-word and contains no reference to anything else to which something must correspond. If I do not know that a picture is meant to represent Cologne Cathedral then I do not know with what to compare the picture to decide on its truth. A correspondence, moreover, can only be perfect if the corresponding things coincide and are, therefore, not distinct things at all. It is said to be possible to establish the authenticity of a banknote by comparing it stereoscopically with an authentic one. But it would be ridiculous to try to compare a gold piece with a twenty-mark note stereoscopically. It would only be possible to compare an idea with a thing if the thing were an idea too. And then, if the first did correspond perfectly with the second, they would coincide. But this is not at all what is wanted when truth is defined as the correspondence of an idea with something real.

For it is absolutely essential that the reality be distinct from the idea. But then there can be no complete correspondence, no complete truth. So nothing at all would be true; for what is only half true is untrue. Truth cannot tolerate a more or less. But yet? Can it not be laid down that truth exists when there is correspondence in a certain respect? But in which? For what would we then have to do to decide whether something were true? We should have to inquire whether it were true that an idea and a reality, perhaps, corresponded in the laid-down respect. And then we should be confronted by a question of the same kind and the game could begin again. So the attempt to explain truth as correspondence collapses. And every other attempt to define truth collapses too. For in a definition certain characteristics would have to be stated. And in application to any particular case the question would always arise whether it were true that the characteristics were present. So one goes round in a circle. Consequently, it is probable that the content of the word 'true' is unique and indefinable.

When one ascribes truth to a picture one does not really want to ascribe a property which belongs to this picture altogether independently of other things, but one always has something quite different in mind and one wants to say that that picture corresponds in some way to this thing. 'My idea corresponds to Cologne Cathedral' is a sentence and the question now arises of the truth of this sentence. So what is improperly called the truth of pictures and ideas is reduced to the truth of sentences. What does one call a sentence? A series of sounds; but only when it has a sense, by which is not meant that every series of sounds that has sense is a sentence. And when we call a sentence true we really mean its sense is. From which it follows that it is for the sense of a sentence that the question of truth arises in general. Now is the sense of a sentence an idea? In any case being true does not consist in the correspondence of this sense with something else, for otherwise the question of truth would reiterate itself to infinity.

Without wishing to give a definition, I call a thought something for which the question of truth arises. So I ascribe what is false to a thought just as much as what is true.[1] So I can say: the thought is the sense of the sentence without wishing to say as well that the sense of every sentence is a thought. The thought, in itself immaterial, clothes itself in the material garment of a sentence and thereby becomes comprehensible to us. We say a sentence expresses a thought.

A thought is something immaterial and everything material and perceptible is excluded from this sphere of that for which the question of truth arises. Truth is not a quality that corresponds with a particular kind of sense-impression. So it is sharply distinguished from the qualities which we denote by the words 'red', 'bitter', 'lilac-smelling'. But do we not see that the sun has risen and do we not then also see that this is true? That the sun has risen is not an object which emits rays that reach my eyes, it is not a visible thing like the sun itself. That the sun has risen is seen to be true on the basis of sense-impressions. But being true is not a material, perceptible property. For being magnetic is also recognized on the basis of sense-impressions of something, though this property corresponds as little as truth with a particular kind of sense-impressions. So far these properties agree. However, we need sense-impressions in order to recognize a body as magnetic. On the other hand, when I find that it is true that I do not smell anything at this moment, I do not do so on the basis of sense-impressions.

It may nevertheless be thought that we cannot recognize a property of a thing without at the same time realizing the thought that this thing has this property to be true. So with every property of a thing is joined a property of a thought, namely, that of truth. It is also worthy of notice that the sentence 'I smell the scent of violets' has just the same content as the sentence 'it is true that I smell the scent of violets'. So it seems, then, that nothing is added to the thought by my ascribing to it the property of truth. And yet is it not a great result when the scientist after much hesitation and careful inquiry, can finally say 'what I supposed is true'? The meaning of the word 'true' seems to be altogether unique. May we not be dealing here with something which cannot, in the ordinary sense, be called a quality at all? In spite of this doubt I want first to express myself in accordance with ordinary usage, as if truth were a quality, until something more to the point is found.

In order to work out more precisely what I want to call thought, I shall distinguish various kinds of sentences.[2] One does not want to deny sense to an imperative sentence, but this sense is not such that the question of truth could arise for it. Therefore I shall not call the sense of an imperative sentence a thought. Sentences expressing desires or requests are ruled out in the same way. Only those sentences in which we communicate or state something come into the question. But I do not count among these exclamations in which one vents one's feelings, groaning, sighing, laughing, unless it has been decided by some agreement that they are to communicate something. But how about interrogative sentences? In a word-question we utter an incomplete sentence which only obtains a true sense through the completion for which we ask. Word-questions are accordingly left out of consideration here. Sentence-questions are a different matter. We expect to hear 'yes' or 'no'. The answer 'yes' means the same as an indicative sentence, for in it the thought that was already completely contained in the interrogative sentence is laid down as true. So a sentence-question can be formed from every indicative sentence. An exclamation cannot be regarded as a communication on this account, since no corresponding sentence-question can be formed. An interrogative sentence and an indicative one contain the same thought; but the indicative contains something else as well, namely, the assertion. The interrogative sentence contains something more too, namely a request. Therefore two things must be distinguished in an indicative sentence: the content, which it has in common with the corresponding sentence-question, and the assertion. The former is the thought, or at least contains the thought.

So it is possible to express the thought without laying it down as true. Both are so closely joined in an indicative sentence that it is easy to overlook their separability. Consequently we may distinguish:

(1) the apprehension of a thought – thinking,
(2) the recognition of the truth of a thought – judgement,[3]
(3) the manifestation of this judgement – assertion.

We perform the first act when we form a sentence-question. An advance in science usually takes place in this way, first a thought is apprehended, such as can perhaps be expressed in a sentence-question, and, after appropriate investigations, this thought is finally recognized to be true. We declare the recognition of truth in the form of an indicative sentence. We do not have to use the word 'true' for this. And even when we do use it the real assertive force lies, not in it, but in the form of the indicative sentence and where this loses its assertive force the word 'true' cannot put it back again. This happens when we do not speak seriously. As stage thunder is only apparent thunder and a stage fight only an apparent fight, so stage assertion is only apparent assertion. It is only acting, only fancy. In his part the actor asserts nothing, nor does he lie, even if he says something of whose falsehood he is convinced. In poetry we have the case of thoughts being expressed without being actually put forward as true in spite of the form of the indicative sentence, although it may be suggested to the hearer to make an assenting judgement himself. Therefore it must still always be asked, about what is presented in the form of an indicative sentence, whether it really contains an assertion. And this question must be answered in the negative if the requisite seriousness is lacking. It is irrelevant whether the word 'true' is used here. This explains why it is that nothing seems to be added to a thought by attributing to it the property of truth.

An indicative sentence often contains, as well as a thought and the assertion, a third component over which the assertion does not extend. This is often said to act on the feelings, the mood of the hearer or to arouse his imagination. Words like 'alas' and 'thank God' belong here. Such constituents of sentences are more noticeably prominent in poetry, but are seldom wholly absent from prose. They occur more rarely in mathematical, physical, or chemical than in historical expositions. What are called the humanities are more closely connected with poetry and are therefore less scientific than the exact sciences which are drier the more exact they are, for exact science is directed toward truth and only the truth. Therefore all constituents of sentences to which the assertive force does not reach do not belong to scientific exposition but they are sometimes hard to avoid, even for one who sees the danger connected with them. Where the main thing is to approach what cannot be graspd in thought by means of guesswork these components have their justification. The more exactly scientific an exposition is the less will the nationality of its author be discernible and the easier will it be to translate. On the other hand, the constituents of language, to which I want to call attention here, make the translation of poetry very difficult, even make a complete translation almost always impossible, for it is in precisely that in which poetic value largely consists that languages differ most.

It makes no difference to the thought whether I use the word 'horse' or 'steed' or 'cart-horse' or 'mare'. The assertive force does not extend over that in which these words differ. What is called mood, fragrance, illumination in a poem, what is portrayed by cadence and rhythm, does not belong to the thought.

Much of language serves the purpose of aiding the hearer's understanding, for instance the stressing of part of a sentence by accentuation or word-order. One should remember words like 'still' and 'already' too. With the sentence 'Alfred has still not come' one really says 'Alfred has not come' and, at the same time, hints that his arrival is expected, but it is only hinted. It cannot be said that, since Alfred's arrival is not expected, the sense of the sentence is therefore false. The word 'but' differs from 'and' in that with it one intimates that what follows is in contrast with what would be expected from what preceded it. Such suggestions in speech make no difference to the thought. A sentence can be transformed by changing the verb from active to passive and making the object the subject at the same time. In the same way the dative may be changed into the nominative while 'give' is replaced by 'receive'. Naturally such transformations are not indifferent in every respect; but they do not touch the thought, they do not touch what is true or false. If the inadmissibility of such transformations were generally admitted then all deeper logical investigation would be hindered. It is just as important to neglect distinctions that do not touch the heart of the matter as to make distinctions which concern what is essential. But what is essential depends on one's purpose. To a mind concerned with what is beautiful in language what is indifferent to the logician can appear as just what is important.

Thus the contents of a sentence often go beyond the thoughts expressed by it. But the opposite often happens too, that the mere wording, which can be grasped by writing or the gramophone does not suffice for the expression of the thought. The present tense is used in two ways: first, in order to give a date, second, in order to eliminate any temporal restriction where timelessness or eternity is part of the thought. Think, for instance, of the laws of mathematics. Which of the two cases occurs is not expressed but must be guessed. If a time indication is needed by the present tense one must know when the sentence was uttered to apprehend the thought correctly. Therefore the time of utterance is part of the expression of the thought. If someone wants to say the same today as he expressed yesterday using the word 'today', he must replace this word with 'yesterday'. Although the thought is the same its verbal expression must be different so that the sense, which would otherwise be affected by the differing times of utterance, is readjusted. The case is the same with words like 'here' and 'there'. In all such cases the mere wording, as it is given in writing, is not the complete expression of the thought, but the knowledge of certain accompanying conditions of utterance, which are used as means of expressing the thought, are needed for its correct apprehension. The pointing of fingers, hand movements, glances may belong here too. The same utterance containing the word 'I' will express different thoughts in the mouths of different men, of which some may be true, others false.

The occurrence of the word 'I' in a sentence gives rise to some questions.

Consider the following case. Dr. Gustav Lauben says, 'I have been wounded'. Leo Peter hears this and remarks some days later, 'Dr. Gustav Lauben has been wounded'. Does this sentence express the same thought as the one Dr. Lauben uttered himself? Suppose that Rudolph Lingens were present when Dr. Lauben spoke and now hears what is related by Leo Peter. If the same thought is uttered by Dr. Lauben and Leo Peter then Rudolph Lingens, who is fully master of the language and remembers what Dr. Lauben has said in his presence, must now know at once from Leo Peter's report that the same thing is under discussion. But knowledge of the language is a separate thing when it is a matter of proper names. It may well be the case that only a few people associate a particular thought with the sentence 'Dr. Lauben has been wounded'. In this case one needs for complete understanding a knowledge of the expression 'Dr. Lauben'. Now if both Leo Peter and Rudolph Lingens understand by 'Dr. Lauben' the doctor who lives as the only doctor in a house known to both of them, then they both understand the sentence 'Dr. Gustav Lauben has been wounded' in the same way, they associate the same thought with it. But it is also possible that Rudolph Lingens does not know Dr. Lauben personally and does not know that he is the very Dr. Lauben who recently said, 'I have been wounded.' In this case Rudolph Lingens cannot know that the same thing is in question. I say, therefore, in this case: the thought which Leo Peter expresses is not the same as that which Dr. Lauben uttered.

Suppose further that Herbert Garner knows that Dr. Gustav Lauben was born on 13th September, 1875 in N.N. and this is not true of anyone else; against this, suppose that he does not know where Dr. Lauben now lives nor indeed anything about him. On the other hand, suppose Leo Peter does not know that Dr. Lauben was born on 13th September 1875, in N.N. Then as far as the proper name 'Dr. Gustav Lauben' is concerned, Herbert Garner and Leo Peter do not speak the same language, since, although they do in fact refer to the same man with this name, they do not know that they do so. Therefore Herbert Garner does not associate the same thought with the sentence 'Dr. Gustav Lauben has been wounded' as Leo Peter wants to express with it. To avoid the drawback of Herbert Garner's and Leo Peter's not speaking the same language, I am assuming that Leo Peter uses the proper name 'Dr. Lauben' and Herbert Garner, on the other hand, uses the proper name 'Gustav Lauben'. Now it is possible that Herbert Garner takes the sense of the sentence 'Dr. Lauben has been wounded' to be true while, misled by false information, taking the sense of the sentence 'Gustav Lauben has been wounded' to be false. Under the assumptions given these thoughts are therefore different.

Accordingly, with a proper name, it depends on how whatever it refers to is presented. This can happen in different ways and every such way corresponds with a particular sense of a sentence containing a proper name. The different thoughts which thus result from the same sentence correspond in their truth-value, of course; that is to say, if one is true then all are true, and if one is false then all are false. Nevertheless their distinctness must be recognized. So it must really be demanded that a single way in which whatever is referred to is presented be associated with every proper name. It is often unimportant that this demand should be fulfilled but not always.

Now everyone is presented to himself in a particular and primitive way, in which he is presented to no-one else. So, when Dr. Lauben thinks that he has been wounded, he will probably take as a basis this primitive way in which he is presented to himself. And only Dr. Lauben himself can grasp thoughts determined in this way. But now he may want to communicate with others. He cannot communicate a thought which he alone can grasp. Therefore, if he now says 'I have been wounded', he must use the 'I' in a sense which can be grasped by others, perhaps in the sense of 'he who is speaking to you at this moment', by doing which he makes the associated conditions of his utterance serve for the expression of his thought.[4]

Yet there is a doubt. Is it at all the same thought which first that man expresses and now this one?

A person who is still untouched by philosophy knows first of all things which he can see and touch, in short, perceive with the senses, such as trees, stones and houses, and he is convinced that another person equally can see and touch the same tree and the same stone which he himself sees and touches. Obviously a thought is not one of these things. Now can it, nevertheless, stand in the same relation to various persons, as does a tree?*

Even an unphilosophical person soon finds it necessary to recognize an inner world distinct from the outer world, a world of sense-impressions, of creations of his imagination, of sensations, of feelings and moods, a world of inclinations, wishes and decisions. For brevity I want to collect all these, with the exception of decisions, under the word 'idea'.

Now do thoughts belong to this inner world? Are they ideas? They are obviously not decisions. How are ideas distinct from the things of the outer world? First:

Ideas cannot be seen or touched, cannot be smelled, nor tasted, nor heard.

---

*Editor's note: The corrected translation of the last two sentences in this paragraph is the work of Albert E. Blumberg in 'A correction to the translation of Frege's "The Thought"', *Mind*, April 1971.

I go for a walk with a companion. I see a green field, I have a visual impression of the green as well. I have it but I do not see it.

Secondly: ideas are had. One has sensations, feelings, moods, inclinations, wishes. An idea which someone has belongs to the content of his consciousness.

The field and the frogs in it, the sun which shines on them are there no matter whether I look at them or not, but the sense-impression I have of green exists only because of me, I am its bearer. It seems absurd to us that a pain, a mood, a wish should rove about the world without a bearer, independently. An experience is impossible without an experient. The inner world presupposes the person whose inner world it is.

Thirdly: ideas need a bearer. Things of the outer world are however independent.

My companion and I are convinced that we both see the same field; but each of us has a particular sense-impression of green. I notice a strawberry among the green strawberry leaves. My companion does not notice it, he is colour-blind. The colour-impression, which he receives from the strawberry, is not noticeably different from the one he receives from the leaf. Now does my companion see the green leaf as red, or does he see the red berry as green, or does he see both as of one colour with which I am not acquainted at all? These are unanswerable, indeed really nonsensical, questions. For when the word 'red' does not state a property of things but is supposed to characterize sense-impressions belonging to my consciousness, it is only applicable within the sphere of my consciousness. For it is impossible to compare my sense-impression with that of someone else. For that it would be necessary to bring together in one consciousness a sense-impression, belonging to one consciousness with a sense-impression belonging to another consciousness. Now even if it were possible to make an idea disappear from one consciousness and, at the same time, to make an idea appear in another consciousness, the question whether it were the same idea in both would still remain unanswerable. It is so much of the essence of each of my ideas to be the content of my consciousness, that every idea of another person is, just as such, distinct from mine. But might it not be possible that my ideas, the entire content of my consciousness might be at the same time the content of a more embracing, perhaps divine, consciousness? Only if I were myself part of the divine consciousness. But then would they really be my ideas, would I be their bearer? This oversteps the limits of human understanding to such an extent that one must leave its possibility out of account. In any case it is impossible for us as men to compare another person's ideas with our own. I pick the strawberry, I hold it between my fingers. Now my companion sees it too, this very same strawberry; but each of us has his own idea. No other person has my idea but many people can see the same thing. No other person has my pain. Someone can have sympathy for me but still my pain always belongs to me and his sympathy to him. He does not have my pain and I do not have his sympathy.

Fourthly: every idea has only one bearer; no two men have the same idea. For otherwise it would exist independently of this person and independently of that one. Is that lime-tree my idea? By using the expression 'that lime-tree' in this question I have really already anticipated the answer, for with this expression I want to refer to what I see and to what other people can also look at and touch. There are now two possibilities. If my intention is realized when I refer to something with the expression 'that lime-tree' then the thought expressed in the sentence 'that lime-tree is my idea' must obviously be negated. But if my intention is not realized, if I only think I see without really seeing, if on that account the designation 'that lime-tree' is empty, then I have gone astray into the sphere of fiction without knowing it or wanting to. In that case neither the content of the sentence 'that lime-tree is my idea' nor the content of the sentence 'that lime-tree is not my idea' is true, for in both cases I have a statement which lacks an object. So then one can only refuse to answer the question for the reason that the content of the sentence 'that lime-tree is my idea' is a piece of fiction. I have, naturally, got an idea then, but I am not referring to this with the words 'that lime-tree'. Now someone may really want to refer to one of his ideas with the words 'that lime-tree'. He would then be the bearer of that to which he wants to refer with those words, but then he would not see that lime-tree and no-one else would see it or be its bearer.

I now return to the question: is a thought an idea? If the thought I express in the Pythagorean theorem can be recognized by others just as much as by me then it does not belong to the content of my consciousness, I am not its bearer; yet I can, nevertheless, recognize it to be true. However, if it is not the same thought at all which is taken to be the content of the Pythagorean theorem by me and by another person, one should not really say 'the Pythagorean theorem' but 'my Pythagorean theorem', 'his Pythagorean theorem' and these would be different; for the sense belongs necessarily to the sentence. Then my thought can be the content of my consciousness and his thought the content of his. Could the sense of my Pythagorean theorem be true while that of his was false? I said that the word 'red' was applicable only in the sphere of my consciousness if it did not state a property of things but was supposed to characterize one of my sense-impressions. Therefore the words 'true' and 'false', as I understand them, could also be applicable only in the sphere of my consciousness, if they were not supposed to be concerned with something of which I was not the bearer, but were somehow appointed to characterize the content of my consciousness. Then truth would be restricted to the content of my consciousness and it would remain doubtful whether anything at all comparable occurred in the consciousness of others.

If every thought requires a bearer, to the contents of whose consciousness it belongs, then it would be a thought of this bearer only and there would be no science common to many, on which many could work. But I, perhaps, have my science, namely, a whole of thought whose bearer I am and another person has his. Each of us occupies himself with the contents of his own consciousness. No contradiction between the two sciences would then be possible and it would really be idle to dispute about truth, as idle, indeed almost ludicrous, as it would be for two people to dispute whether a hundred-mark note were genuine, where each meant the one he himself had in his pocket and understood the word 'genuine' in his own particular sense. If someone takes thoughts to be ideas, what he then recognizes to be true is, on his own view, the content of his consciousness and does not properly concern other people at all. If he were to hear from me the opinion that a thought is not an idea he could not dispute it, for, indeed, it would not now concern him.

So the result seems to be: thoughts are neither things of the outer world nor ideas.

A third realm must be recognized. What belongs to this corresponds with ideas, in that it cannot be perceived by the senses, but with things, in that it needs no bearer to the contents of whose consciousness to belong. Thus the thought, for example, which we expressed in the Pythagorean theorem is timelessly true, true independently of whether anyone takes it to be true. It needs no bearer. It is not true for the first time when it is discovered, but is like a planet which, already before anyone has seen it, has been in interaction with other planets.[5]

But I think I hear an unusual objection. I have assumed several times that the same thing that I see can also be observed by other people. But how could this be the case, if everything were only a dream? If I only dreamed I was walking in the company of another person, if I only dreamed that my companion saw the green field as I did, if it were all only a play performed on the stage of my consciousness, it would be doubtful whether there were things of the outer world at all. Perhaps the realm of things is empty and I see no things and no men, but have only ideas of which I myself am the bearer. An idea, being something which can as little exist independently of me as my feeling of fatigue, cannot be a man, cannot look at the same field together with me, cannot see the strawberry I am holding. It is quite incredible that I should really have only my inner world instead of the whole environment, in which I am supposed to move and to act. And yet it is an inevitable consequence of the thesis that only what is my idea can be the object of my awareness. What would follow from this thesis if it were true? Would there then be other men? It would certainly be possible but I should know nothing of it. For a man cannot be my idea, consequently, if our thesis were true, he also cannot be an object of my awareness. And so the ground would be removed from under any process of thought in which I might assume that something was an object for another person as for myself, for even if this were to happen I should know nothing of it. It would be impossible for me to distinguish that of which I was the bearer from that of which I was not. In judging something not to be my idea I would make it the object of my thinking and, therefore, my idea. On this view, is there a green field? Perhaps, but it would not be visible to me. For if a field is not my idea, it cannot, according to our thesis, be an object of my awareness. But if it is my idea it is invisible, for ideas are not visible. I can indeed have the idea of a green field, but this is not green for there are no green ideas. Does a shell weighing a hundred kilogrammes exist, according to this view? Perhaps, but I could know nothing of it. If a shell is not my idea then, according to our thesis, it cannot be an object of my awareness, of my thinking. But if a shell were my idea, it would have no weight. I can have an idea of a heavy shell. This then contains the idea of weight as a part-idea. But this part-idea is not a property of the whole idea any more than Germany is a property of Europe. So it follows:

Either the thesis that only what is my idea can be the object of my awareness is false, or all my knowledge and perception is limited to the range of my ideas, to the stage of my consciousness. In this case I should have only an inner world and I should know nothing of other people.

It is strange how, upon such reflections, the opposites collapse into each other. There is, let us suppose, a physiologist of the senses. As is proper for a scholarly scientist, he is, first of all, far from supposing the things he is convinced he sees and touches to be his ideas. On the contrary, he believes that in sense-impressions he has the surest proof of things which are wholly independent of his feeling, imagining, thinking, which have no need of his consciousness. So little does he consider nerve-fibres and ganglion-cells to be the content of his consciousness that he is, on the contrary, rather inclined to regard his consciousness as dependent on nerve-fibres and ganglion-cells. He establishes that light-rays, refracted in the eye, strike the visual nerve-endings and bring about a change, a stimulus, there. Some of it is transmitted through nerve-fibres and ganglion-cells. Further processes in the nervous system are perhaps involved, colour-impressions arise and these perhaps join themselves to what we call the idea of a tree. Physical, chemical and physiological occurrences insert themselves between the tree and my idea. These are immediately connected with my consciousness but, so it seems, are only occurrences in my nervous system and every spectator of the tree has his particular occurrences in his particular nervous system. Now the light-rays, before they enter my eye, may be reflected by a mirror and be spread further as if they came from a place behind the mirror. The effects on the visual nerves and all that follows will now take place just as they would if the light-rays had come from a tree behind the mirror and had been transmitted undisturbed to the eye. So an idea of a tree will finally occur even though such a tree does not exist at all. An idea, to which nothing at all corresponds, can also arise through the bending of light, with the mediation of the eye and the nervous system. But the stimulation of the visual nerves need not even happen through light. If lightning strikes near us we believe we see flames, even though we cannot see the lightning itself. In this case the visual nerve is perhaps stimulated by electric currents which originate in our body in consequence of the flash of lightning. If the visual nerve is stimulated by this means, just as it would be stimulated by light-rays coming from flames, then we believe we see flames. It just depends on the stimulation of the visual nerve, it is indifferent how that itself comes about.

One can go a step further still. This stimulation of the visual nerve is not actually immediately given, but is only a hypothesis. We believe that a thing, independent of us, stimulates a nerve and by this means produces a sense-impression, but, strictly speaking, we experience only the end of this process which projects into our consciousness. Could not this sense-impression, this sensation, which we attribute to a nerve-stimulation, have other causes also, as the same nerve-stimulation can arise in different ways? If we call what happens in our consciousness idea, then we really experience only ideas but not their causes. And if the scientist wants to avoid all mere hypothesis, then only ideas are left for him, everything resolves into ideas, the light-rays, nerve-fibres and ganglion-cells from which he started. So he finally undermines the foundations of his own construction. Is everything an idea? Does everything need a bearer, without which it could have no stability? I have considered myself as the bearer of my ideas, but am I not an idea myself? It seems to me as if I were lying in a deck-chair, as if I could see the toes of a pair of waxed boots, the front part of a pair of trousers, a waistcoat, buttons, part of a jacket, in particular sleeves, two hands, the hair of a beard, the blurred outline of a nose. Am I myself this entire association of visual impressions, this total idea? It also seems to me as if I see a chair over there. It is an idea. I am not actually much different from this myself, for am I not myself just an association of sense-impressions, an idea? But where then is the bearer of these ideas? How do I come to single out one of these ideas and set it up as the bearer of the rest? Why must it be the idea which I choose to call 'I'? Could I not just as well choose the one that I am tempted to call a chair? Why, after all, have a bearer for ideas at all? But this would always be something essentially different from merely borne ideas, something independent, needing no extraneous bearer. If everything is idea, then there is no bearer of ideas. And so now, once again, I experience a change into the opposite. If there is no bearer of ideas then there are also no ideas, for ideas need a bearer without which they cannot exist. If there is no ruler, there are also no subjects. The dependence, which I found myself induced to confer on the experience as opposed to the experient, is abolished if there is no more bearer. What I called ideas are then independent objects. Every reason is wanting for granting an exceptional position to that object which I call 'I'.

But is that possible? Can there be an experience without someone to experience it? What would this whole play be without an onlooker? Can there be a pain without someone who has it? Being experienced is necessarily connected with pain, and someone experiencing is necessarily connected with being experienced. But there is something which is not my idea and yet which can be the object of my awareness, of my thinking, I am myself of this nature. Or can I be part of the content of my consciousness while another part is, perhaps, an idea of the moon? Does this perhaps take place when I judge that I am looking at the moon? Then this first part would have a consciousness and part of the content of this consciousness would be I myself once more. And so on. Yet it is surely inconceivable that I should be boxed into myself in this way to infinity, for then there would not be only one I but infinitely many. I am not my own idea and if I assert something about myself, e.g. that I do not feel any pain at this moment, then my judgement concerns something which is not a content of my consciousness, is not my idea, that is me myself. Therefore that about which I state something is not necessarily my idea. But, someone perhaps objects, if I think I have no pain at the moment, does not the word 'I' nevertheless correspond with something in the content of my consciousness and is that not an idea? That may be. A certain idea in my consciousness may be associated with the idea of the word 'I'. But then it is an idea among other ideas and I am its bearer as I am the bearer of the other ideas. I have an idea of myself but I am not identical with this idea. What is a content of my consciousness, my idea, should be sharply distinguished from what is an object of my thought. Therefore the thesis that only what belongs to the content of my consciousness can be the object of my awareness, of my thought, is false.

Now the way is clear for me to recognize another person as well as to be an independent bearer of ideas. I have an idea of him but I do not confuse it with him himself. And if I state something about my brother I do not state it about the idea that I have of my brother.

The invalid who has a pain is the bearer of this pain, but the doctor in attendance who reflects on the cause of this pain is not the bearer of the pain. He does not imagine he can relieve the pain by anaesthetizing himself. An idea in the doctor's mind may very well correspond to the pain of the invalid but that is not the pain and not what the doctor is trying to remove. The doctor might consult another doctor. Then one must distinguish: first, the pain whose bearer is the invalid, second, the first doctor's idea of this pain, third, the second doctor's idea of this pain. This idea does indeed belong to the content of the second doctor's consciousness, but it is not the object of his reflection, it is rather an aid to reflection, as a drawing can be such an aid perhaps. Both doctors have the invalid's pain, which they do not bear, as their common object of thought. It can be seen from this that not only a thing but also an idea can be the common object of thought of people who do not have the idea.

So, it seems to me, the matter becomes intelligible. If man could not think and could not take something of which he was not the bearer as the object of his thought he would have an inner world but no outer world. But may this not be based on a mistake? I am convinced that the idea I associate with the words 'my brother' corresponds to something that is not my idea and about which I can say something. But may I not be making a mistake about this? Such mistakes do happen. We then, against our will, lapse into fiction. Indeed! By the step with which I secure an environment for myself I expose myself to the risk of error. And here I come up against a further distinction between my inner and outer worlds. I cannot doubt that I have a visual impression of green but it is not so certain that I see a lime-leaf. So, contrary to widespread views, we find certainty in the inner world while doubt never altogether leaves us in our excursions into the outer world. It is difficult in many cases, nevertheless, to distinguish probability from certainty here, so we can presume to judge about things in the outer world. And we must presume this even at the risk of error if we do not want to succumb to far greater dangers.

In consequence of these last considerations I lay down the following: not everything that can be the object of my understanding is an idea. I, as a bearer of ideas, am not myself an idea. Nothing now stands in the way of recognizing other people to be bearers of ideas as I am myself. And, once given the possibility, the probability is very great, so great that it is in my opinion no longer distinguishable from certainty. Would there be a science of history otherwise? Would not every precept of duty, every law otherwise come to nothing? What would be left of religion? The natural sciences too could only be assessed as fables like astrology and alchemy. Thus the reflections I have carried on, assuming that there are other people besides myself who can take the same thing as the object of their consideration, of their thinking, remain essentially unimpaired in force.

Not everything is an idea. Thus I can also recognize the thought, which other people can grasp just as much as I, as being independent of me. I can recognize a science in which many people can be engaged in research. We are not bearers of thoughts as we are bearers of our ideas. We do not have a thought as we have, say, a sense-impression, but we also do not see a thought as we see, say, a star. So it is advisable to choose a special expression and the word 'apprehend' offers itself for the purpose. A particular mental capacity, the power of thought, must correspond to the apprehension[6] of thought. In thinking we do not produce thoughts but we apprehend them. For what I have called thought stands in the closest relation to truth. What I recognize as true I judge to be true quite independently of my recognition of its truth and of my thinking about it. That someone thinks it has nothing to do with the truth of a thought. 'Facts, facts, facts' cries the scientist if he wants to emphasize the necessity of a firm foundation for science. What is a fact? A fact is a thought that is true. But the scientist will surely not recognize something which depends on men's varying states of mind to be the firm foundation of science. The work of science does not consist of creation but of the discovery of true thoughts. The astronomer can apply a mathematical truth in the investigation of long past events which took place when on earth at least no one had yet recognized that truth. He can do this because the truth of a thought is timeless. Therefore that truth cannot have come into existence with its discovery.

Not everything is an idea. Otherwise psychology would contain all the sciences within it or at least it would be the highest judge over all the sciences. Otherwise psychology would rule over logic and mathematics. But nothing would be a greater misunderstanding of mathematics than its subordination to psychology. Neither logic nor mathematics has the task of investigating minds and the contents of consciousness whose bearer is a single person. Perhaps their task could be represented rather as the investigation of the mind, of the mind not of minds.

The apprehension of a thought presupposes someone who apprehends it, who thinks. He is the bearer of the thinking but not of the thought. Although the thought does not belong to the contents of the thinker's consciousness yet something in his consciousness must be aimed at the thought. But this should not be confused with the thought itself. Similarly Algol itself is different from the idea someone has of Algol.

The thought belongs neither to my inner world as an idea nor yet to the outer world of material, perceptible things.

This consequence, however cogently it may follow from the exposition, will nevertheless not perhaps be accepted without opposition. It will, I think, seem impossible to some people to obtain information about something not belonging to the inner world except by sense-perception. Sense-perception indeed is often thought to be the most certain, even to be the sole, source of knowledge about everything that does not belong to the inner world. But with what right? For sense-impressions are necessary constituents of sense-perceptions and are a part of the inner world. In any case two men do not have the same, though they may have similar, sense-impressions. These alone do not disclose the outer world to us. Perhaps there is a being that has only sense-impressions without seeing or touching things. To have visual impressions is not to see things. How does it happen that I see the tree just there where I do see it? Obviously it depends on the visual impressions I have and on the particular type which occur because I see with two eyes. A particular image arises, physically speaking, on each of the two retinas. Another person sees the tree in the same place. He also has two retinal images but they differ from mine. We must assume that these retinal images correspond to our impressions. Consequently we have visual impressions, not only not the same, but markedly different from each other. And yet we move about in the same outer world. Having visual impressions is certainly necessary for seeing things but not sufficient. What must still be added is non-sensible. And yet this is just what opens up the outer world for us; for without this non-sensible something everyone would remain shut up in his inner world. So since the answer lies in the non-sensible, perhaps something non-sensible could also lead us out of the inner world and enable us to grasp thoughts where no sense-impressions were involved. Outside one's inner world one would have to distinguish the proper outer world of sensible, perceptible things from the realm of the non-sensibly perceptible. We should need something non-sensible for the recognition of both realms but for the sensible perception of things we should need sense-impressions as well and these belong entirely to the inner world. So that in which the distinction between the way in which a thing and a thought is given mainly consists is something which is attributable, not to both realms, but to the inner world. Thus I cannot find this distinction to be so great that on its account it would be impossible for a thought to be given that did not belong to the inner world.

The thought, admittedly, is not something which it is usual to call real. The world of the real is a world in which this acts on that, changes it and again experiences reactions itself and is changed by them. All this is a process in time. We will hardly recognize what is timeless and unchangeable as real. Now is the thought changeable or is it timeless? The thought we express by the Pythagorean theorem is surely timeless, eternal, unchangeable. But are there not thoughts which are true today but false in six months time? The thought, for example, that the tree there is covered with green leaves, will surely be false in six months time. No, for it is not the same thought at all. The words 'this tree is covered with green leaves' are not sufficient by themselves for the utterance, the time of utterance is involved as well. Without the time-indication this gives we have no complete thought, i.e. no thought at all. Only a sentence supplemented by a time-indication and complete in every respect expresses a thought. But this, if it is true, is true not only today or tomorrow but timelessly. Thus the present tense in 'is true' does not refer to the speaker's present but is, if the expression be permitted, a tense of timelessness. If we use the mere form of the indicative sentence, avoiding the word 'true', two things must be distinguished, the expression of the thought and the assertion. The time-indication that may be contained in the sentence belongs only to the expression of the thought, while the truth, whose recognition lies in the form of the indicative sentence, is timeless. Yet the same words, on account of the variability of language with time, take on another sense, express another thought; this change, however, concerns only the linguistic aspect of the matter.

And yet! What value could there be for us in the eternally unchangeable which could neither undergo effects nor have effect on us? Something entirely and in every respect inactive would be unreal and non-existent for us. Even the timeless, if it is to be anything for us, must somehow be implicated with the temporal. What would a thought be for me that was never apprehended by me? But by apprehending a thought I come into a relation to it and it to me. It is possible that the same thought that is thought by me today was not thought by me yesterday. In this way the strict timelessness is of course annulled. But one is inclined to distinguish between essential and inessential properties and to regard something as timeless if the changes it undergoes involve only its inessential properties. A property of a thought will be called inessential which consists in, or follows from the fact that, it is apprehended by a thinker.

How does a thought act? By being apprehended and taken to be true. This is a process in the inner world of a thinker which can have further consequences in this inner world and which, encroaching on the sphere of the will, can also make itself noticeable in the outer world. If, for example, I grasp the thought which we express by the theorem of Pythagoras, the consequence may be that I recognize it to be true and, further, that I apply it, making a decision which brings about the acceleration of masses. Thus our actions are usually prepared by thinking and judgement. And so thought can have an indirect influence on the motion of masses. The influence of one person on another is brought about for the most part by thoughts. One communicates a thought. How does this happen? One brings about changes in the common outside world which, perceived by another person, are supposed to induce him to apprehend a thought and take it to be true. Could the great events of world history have come about without the communication of thoughts? And yet we are inclined to regard thoughts as unreal because they appear to be without influence on events, while thinking, judging, stating, understanding and the like are facts of human life. How much more real a hammer appears compared with a thought. How different the process of handing over a hammer is from the communication of a thought. The hammer passes from one control to another, it is gripped, it undergoes pressure and on account of this its density, the disposition of its parts, is changed in places. There is nothing of all this with a thought. It does not leave the control of the communicator by being communicated, for after all a person has no control over it. When a thought is apprehended, it at first only brings about changes in the inner world of the apprehender, yet it remains untouched in its true essence, since the changes it undergoes involve only inessential properties. There is lacking here something we observe throughout the order of nature: reciprocal action. Thoughts are by no means unreal but their reality is of quite a different kind from that of things. And their effect is brought about by an act of the thinker without which they would be ineffective, at least as far as we can see. And yet the thinker does not create them but must take them as they are. They can be true without being apprehended by a thinker and are not wholly unreal even then, at least if they could be apprehended and by this means be brought into operation.

Notes

1. In a similar way it has perhaps been said 'a judgement is something which is either true or false'. In fact I use the word 'thought' in approximately the sense which 'judgement' has in the writings of logicians. I hope it will become clear in what follows why I choose 'thought'. Such an explanation has been

objected to on the ground that in it a distinction is drawn between true and false judgements which of all possible distinctions among judgements has perhaps the least significance. I cannot see that it is a logical deficiency that a distinction is given with the explanation. As far as significance is concerned, it should not by any means be judged as trifling if, as I have said, the word 'true' indicates the aim of logic.

2. I am not using the word 'sentence' here in a purely grammatical sense where it also includes subordinate clauses. An isolated subordinate clause does not always have a sense about which the question of truth can arise, whereas the complex sentence to which it belongs has such a sense.
3. It seems to me that thought and judgement have not hitherto been adequately distinguished. Perhaps language is misleading. For we have no particular clause in the indicative sentence which corresponds to the assertion, that something is being asserted lies rather in the form of the indicative. We have the advantage in German that main and subordinate clauses are distinguished by the word-order. In this connexion it is noticeable that a subordinate clause can also contain an assertion and that often neither main nor subordinate clause express a complete thought by themselves but only the complex sentence does.
4. I am not in the happy position here of a mineralogist who shows his hearers a mountain crystal. I cannot put a thought in the hands of my readers with the request that they should minutely examine it from all sides. I have to content myself with presenting the reader with a thought, in itself immaterial, dressed in sensible linguistic form. The metaphorical aspect of language presents difficulties. The sensible always breaks in and makes expression metaphorical and so improper. So a battle with language takes place and I am compelled to occupy myself with language although it is not my proper concern here. I hope I have succeeded in making clear to my readers what I want to call a thought.
5. One sees a thing, one has an idea, one apprehends or thinks a thought. When one apprehends or thinks a thought one does not create it but only comes to stand in a certain relation, which is different from seeing a thing or having an idea, to what already existed beforehand.
6. The expression 'apprehend' is as metaphorical as 'content of consciousness'. The nature of language does not permit anything else. What I hold in my hand can certainly be regarded as the content of my hand but is all the same the content of my hand in quite a different way from the bones and muscles of which it is made and their tensions, and is much more extraneous to it than they are.

Chapter 18

The Semantic Conception of Truth and the Foundations of Semantics

A. Tarksi

This paper consists of two parts; the first has an expository character, and the second is rather polemical.

In the first part I want to summarize in an informed way the main results of my investigations concerning the definition of truth and the more general problem of the foundations of semantics. These results have been embodied in a work which appeared in print several years ago.[1] Although my investigations concern concepts dealt with in classical philosophy, they happen to be comparatively little known in philosophical circles, perhaps because of their strictly technical character. For this reason I hope I shall be excused for taking up the matter once again.[2]

Since my work was published, various objections, of unequal value, have been raised to my investigations; some of these appeared in print, and others were made in public and private discussions in which I took part.[3] In the second part of the paper I should like to express my views regarding these objections. I hope that the remarks which will be made in this context will not be considered as purely polemical in character, but will be found to contain some constructive contributions to the subject.

In the second part of the paper I have made extensive use of material graciously put at my disposal by Dr. Marja Kokoszyńska (University of Lwów). I am especially indebted and grateful to Professors Ernest Nagel (Columbia University) and David Rynin (University of California, Berkeley) for their help in preparing the final text and for various critical remarks.

Source: 'Symposium on meaning and truth' *Philosophy and Phenomenological Research*, Vol. IV, 1944.

I. Exposition

1. The main problem – a satisfactory definition of truth

Our discussion will be centered around the notion[4] of *truth*. The main problem is that of giving a *satisfactory definition* of this notion, i.e., a definition which is *materially adequate* and *formally correct*. But such a formulation of the problem, because of its generality, cannot be considered unequivocal, and requires some further comments.

In order to avoid any ambiguity, we must first specify the conditions under which the definition of truth will be considered adequate from the material point of view. The desired definition does not aim to specify the meaning of a familiar word used to denote a novel notion; on the contrary, it aims to catch hold of the actual meaning of an old notion. We must then characterize this notion precisely enough to enable anyone to determine whether the definition actually fulfills its task.

Secondly, we must determine on what the formal correctness of the definition depends. Thus, we must specify the words or concepts which we wish to use in defining the notion of truth; and we must also give the formal rules to which the definition should conform. Speaking more generally, we must describe the formal structure of the language in which the definition will be given.

The discussion of these points will occupy a considerable portion of the first part of the paper.

2. The extension of the term 'true'

We begin with some remarks regarding the extension of the concept of truth which we have in mind here.

The predicate '*true*' is sometimes used to refer to psychological phenomena such as judgments or beliefs, sometimes to certain physical objects, namely, linguistic expressions and specifically sentences, and sometimes to certain ideal entities called 'propositions.' By 'sentence' we understand here what is usually meant in grammar by 'declarative sentence'; as regards the term 'proposition,' its meaning is notoriously a subject of lengthy disputations by various philosophers and logicians, and it seems never to have been made quite clear and unambiguous. For several reasons it appears most convenient to *apply the term 'true' to sentences*, and we shall follow this course.[5]

Consequently, we must always relate the notion of truth, like that of a sentence, to a specific language; for it is obvious that the same expression which is a true sentence in one language can be false or meaningless in another.

Of course, the fact that we are interested here primarily in the notion of truth for sentences does not exclude the possibility of a subsequent extension of this notion to other kinds of objects.

3. The meaning of the term 'true'

Much more serious difficulties are connected with the problem of the meaning (or the intension) of the concept of truth.

The word '*true*,' like other words from our everyday language, is certainly not unambiguous. And it does not seem to me that the philosophers who have discussed this concept have helped to diminish its ambiguity. In works and discussions of philosophers we meet many different conceptions of truth and falsity, and we must indicate which conception will be the basis of our discussion.

We should like our definition to do justice to the intuitions which adhere to the *classical Aristotelian conception of truth* – intuitions which find their expression in the well-known words of Aristotle's *Metaphysics*:

> To say of what is that it is not, or of what is not that it is, is false, while to say of what is that it is, or of what is not that it is not, is true.

If we wished to adapt ourselves to modern philosophical terminology, we could perhaps express this conception by means of the familiar formula:

> The truth of a sentence consists in its agreement with (or correspondence to) reality.

(For a theory of truth which is to be based upon the latter formulation the term 'correspondence theory' has been suggested.)

If, on the other hand, we should decide to extend the popular usage of the term '*designate*' by applying it not only to names, but also to sentences, and if we agreed to speak of the designata of sentences as 'states of affairs,' we could possibly use for the same purpose the following phrase:

> A sentence is true if it designates an existing state of affairs.[6]

However, all these formulations can lead to various misunderstandings, for none of them is sufficiently precise and clear (though this applies much less to the original Aristotelian formulation than to either of the others); at any rate, none of them can be considered a satisfactory definition of truth. It is up to us to look for a more precise expression of our intuitions.

4. A criterion for the material adequacy of the definition[7]

Let us start with a concrete example. Consider the sentence '*snow is white*.' We ask the question under what conditions this sentence is true or false. It seems clear that if we base ourselves on the classical conception of truth, we shall say that the sentence is true if snow is white, and that it is false if snow is not white. Thus, if the definition of truth is to conform to our conception, it must imply the following equivalence:

The sentence 'snow is white' is true if, and only if, snow is white.

Let me point out that the phrase '*snow is white*' occurs on the left side of this equivalence in quotation marks, and on the right without quotation marks. On the right side we have the sentence itself, and on the left the name of the sentence. Employing the medieval logical terminology we could also say that on the right side the words '*snow is white*' occur in *suppositio formalis*, and on the left in *suppositio materialis*. It is hardly necessary to explain why we must have the name of the sentence, and not the sentence itself, on the left side of the equivalence. For, in the first place, from the point of view of the grammar of our language, an expression of the form 'X *is true*' will not become a meaningful sentence if we replace in it 'X' by a sentence or by anything other than a name – since the subject of a sentence may be only a noun or an expression functioning like a noun. And, in the second place, the fundamental conventions regarding the use of any language require that in any utterance we make about an object it is the name of the object which must be employed, and not the object itself. In consequence, if we wish to say something about a sentence, for example, that it is true, we must use the name of this sentence, and not the sentence itself.[8]

It may be added that enclosing a sentence in quotation marks is by no means the only way of forming its name. For instance, by assuming the usual order of letters in our alphabet, we can use the following expression as the name (the description) of the sentence '*snow is white*':

> the sentence constituted by three words, the first of which consists of the 19th, 14th, 15th, and 23rd letters, the second of the 9th and 19th letters, and the third of the 23rd, 8th, 9th, 20th, and 5th letters of the English alphabet.

We shall now generalize the procedure which we have applied above. Let us consider an arbitrary sentence; we shall replace it by the letter '*p*.' We form the name of this sentence and we replace it by another letter, say 'X.' We ask now what is the logical relation between the two sentences 'X *is true*' and '*p*.' It is clear that from the point of view of our basic conception of truth these sentences are equivalent. In other words, the following equivalence holds:

(T) X is true if, and only if, p.

We shall call any such equivalence (with '*p*' replaced by any sentence of the language to which the word '*true*' refers, and 'X' replaced by a name of this sentence) an '*equivalence of the form* (T).'

Now at last we are able to put into a precise form the conditions under which we will consider the usage and the definition of the term '*true*' as adequate from the material point of view: we wish to use the term '*true*' in such a way that all equivalences of the form (T) can be asserted, and *we shall call a definition of truth 'adequate' if all these equivalences follow from it.*

It should be emphasized that neither the expression (T) itself (which is not a sentence, but only a schema of a sentence) nor any particular instance of the form (T) can be regarded as a definition of truth. We can only say that every equivalence of the form (T) obtained by replacing '*p*' by a particular sentence, and '*X*' by a name of this sentence, may be considered a partial definition of truth, which explains wherein the truth of this one individual sentence consists. The general definition has to be, in a certain sense, a logical conjunction of all these partial definitions.

(The last remark calls for some comments. A language may admit the construction of infinitely many sentences; and thus the number of partial definitions of truth referring to sentences of such a language will also be infinite. Hence to give our remark a precise sense we should have to explain what is meant by a 'logical conjunction of infinitely many sentences'; but this would lead us too far into technical problems of modern logic.)

5. Truth as a semantic concept

I should like to propose the name '*the semantic conception of truth*' for the conception of truth which has just been discussed.

Semantics is a discipline which, speaking loosely, *deals with certain relations between expressions of a language and the objects* (or 'states of affairs') *'referred to' by those expressions.* As typical examples of semantic concepts we may mention the concepts of *designation, satisfaction*, and *definition* as these occur in the following examples:

> the expression 'the father of his country' designates (denotes) George Washington;
> snow satisfies the sentential function (the condition) 'x is white';
> the equation '2.x = 1' defines (uniquely determines) the number 1/2.

While the words '*designates*,' '*satisfies*,' and '*defines*' express relations (between certain expressions and the objects 'referred to' by these expressions), the word '*true*' is of a different logical nature: it expresses a property (or denotes a class) of certain expressions, viz., of sentences. However, it is easily seen that all the formulations which were given earlier and which aimed to explain the meaning of this word (cf. Sections 3 and 4) referred not only to sentences themselves, but also to objects 'talked about' by these sentences, or possibly to 'states of affairs' described by them. And, moreover, it turns out that the simplest and the most natural way of obtaining an exact definition of truth is one which involves the use of other semantic notions, e.g., the notion of satisfaction. It is for these reasons that we count the concept of truth which is discussed here among the concepts of semantics, and the problem of defining truth proves to be closely related to the more general problem of setting up the foundations of theoretical semantics.

It is perhaps worth while saying that semantics as it is conceived in this paper (and in former papers of the author) is a sober and modest discipline which has no pretentions of being a universal patent-medicine for all the ills and diseases of mankind, whether imaginary or real. You will not find in semantics any remedy for decayed teeth or illusions of grandeur or class conflicts. Nor is semantics a device for establishing that everyone except the speaker and his friends is speaking nonsense.

From antiquity to the present day the concepts of semantics have played an important rôle in the discussions of philosophers, logicians, and philologists. Nevertheless, these concepts have been treated for a long time with a certain amount of suspicion. From a historical standpoint, this suspicion is to be regarded as completely justified. For although the meaning of semantic concepts as they are used in everyday language seems to be rather clear and understandable, still all attempts to characterize this meaning in a general and exact way miscarried. And what is worse, various arguments in which these concepts were involved, and which seemed otherwise quite correct and based upon apparently obvious premises, led frequently to paradoxes and antinomies. It is sufficient to mention here the *antinomy of the liar*, Richard's *antinomy of definability* (by means of a finite number of words), and Grelling-Nelson's *antinomy of heterological terms*.[9]

I believe that the method which is outlined in this paper helps to overcome these difficulties and assures the possibility of a consistent use of semantic concepts.

6. Languages with a specified structure

Because of the possible occurrence of antinomies, the problem of specifying the formal structure and the vocabulary of a language in which definitions of semantic concepts are to be given becomes especially acute; and we turn now to this problem.

There are certain general conditions under which the structure of a language is regarded as *exactly specified*. Thus, to specify the structure of a language, we must characterize unambiguously the class of those words and expressions which are to be considered *meaningful*. In particular, we must indicate all words which we decide to use without defining them, and which are called '*undefined* (or *primitive*) *terms*'; and we must give the so-called *rules of definition* for introducing new or *defined terms*. Furthermore, we must set up criteria for distinguishing within the class of expressions those which we call '*sentences.*' Finally, we must formulate the conditions under which a sentence of the language can be *asserted.* In particular, we must indicate all *axioms* (or *primitive sentences*), i.e., those sentences which we decide to assert without proof; and we must give the so-called *rules of inference* (or *rules of proof*) by means of which we can deduce new asserted sentences from other sentences which have been previously asserted. Axioms, as well as sentences deduced from them by means of rules of inference, are referred to as '*theorems*' or '*provable sentences.*'

If in specifying the structure of a language we refer exclusively to the form of the expressions involved, the language is said to be *formalized.* In such a language theorems are the only sentences which can be asserted.

At the present time the only languages with a specified structure are the formalized languages of various systems of deductive logic, possibly enriched by the introduction of certain non-logical terms. However, the field of application of these languages is rather comprehensive; we are able, theoretically, to develop in them various branches of science, for instance, mathematics and theoretical physics.

(On the other hand, we can imagine the construction of languages which have an exactly specified structure without being formalized. In such a language the assertability of sentences, for instance, may depend not always on their form, but sometimes on other, non-linguistic factors. It would be interesting and important actually to construct a language of this type, and specifically one which would prove to be sufficient for the development of a comprehensive branch of empirical science; for this would justify the hope that languages with specified structure could finally replace everyday language in scientific discourse.)

The problem of the definition of truth obtains a precise meaning and can be solved in a rigorous way only for those languages whose structure has been exactly specified. For other languages – thus, for all natural, 'spoken' languages – the meaning of the problem is more or less vague, and its solution can have only an approximate character. Roughly speaking, the approximation consists in replacing a natural language (or a portion of it in which we are interested) by one whose structure is exactly specified, and which diverges from the given language 'as little as possible.'

7. The antinomy of the liar

In order to discover some of the more specific conditions which must be satisfied by languages in which (or for which) the definition of truth is to be given, it will be advisable to begin with a discussion of that antinomy which directly involves the notion of truth, namely, the antinomy of the liar.

To obtain this antinomy in a perspicuous form,[10] consider the following sentence:

The sentence printed in this paper on [p. 543, l. 1] is not true.

For brevity we shall replace the sentence just stated by the letter '*s*.'

According to our convention concerning the adequate usage of the term '*true*,' we assert the following equivalence of the form (T):

(1) 's' is true if, and only if, the sentence printed in this paper on [p. 543, l. 1], is not true.

On the other hand, keeping in mind the meaning of the symbol '*s*,' we establish empirically the following fact:

(2) 's' is identical with the sentence printed in this paper on [p. 543, l. 1].

Now, by a familiar law from the theory of identity (Leibniz's law), it follows from (2) that we may replace in (1) the expression '*the sentence printed in this paper on [p. 543, l. 1]*' by the symbol '"*s*."' We thus obtain what follows:

(3) 's' is true if, and only if, 's' is not true.

In this way we have arrived at an obvious contradiction.

In my judgment, it would be quite wrong and dangerous from the standpoint of scientific progress to depreciate the importance of this and other antinomies, and to treat them as jokes or sophistries. It is a fact that we are here in the presence of an absurdity, that we have been compelled to assert a false sentence (since (3), as an equivalence between two contradictory sentences, is necessarily false). If we take our work seriously, we cannot be reconciled with this fact. We must discover its cause, that is to say, we must analyze premises upon which the antinomy is based; we must then reject at least one of these premises, and we must investigate the consequences which this has for the whole domain of our research.

It should be emphasized that antinomies have played a preëminent rôle in establishing the foundations of modern deductive sciences. And just as class-theoretical antinomies, and in particular Russell's antinomy (of the class of all classes that are not members of themselves), were the starting point for the successful attempts at a consistent formalization of logic and mathematics, so the antinomy of the liar and other semantic antinomies give rise to the construction of theoretical semantics.

8. The inconsistency of semantically closed languages[7]

If we now analyze the assumptions which lead to the antinomy of the liar, we notice the following:

1. We have implicitly assumed that the language in which the antinomy is constructed contains, in addition to its expressions, also the names of these expressions, as well as semantic terms such as the term '*true*' referring to sentences of this language; we have also assumed that all sentences which determine the adequate usage of this term can be asserted in the language. A language with these properties will be called '*semantically closed*.'
2. We have assumed that in this language the ordinary laws of logic hold.
3. We have assumed that we can formulate and assert in our language an empirical premise such as the statement (2) which has occurred in our argument.

It turns out that the assumption (3) is not essential, for it is possible to reconstruct the antinomy of the liar without its help.[11] But the assumptions (1) and (2) prove essential. Since every language which satisfies both of these assumptions is inconsistent, we must reject at least one of them.

It would be superfluous to stress here the consequences of rejecting the assumption (2), that is, of changing our logic (supposing this were possible) even in its more elementary and fundamental parts. We thus consider only the possibility of rejecting the assumption (1). Accordingly, we decide *not to use any language which is semantically closed* in the sense given.

This restriction would of course be unacceptable for those who, for reasons which are not clear to me, believe that there is only one 'genuine' language (or, at least, that all 'genuine' languages are mutually translatable). However, this restriction does not affect the needs or interests of science in any essential way. The languages (either the formalized languages or – what is more frequently the case – the portions of everyday language) which are used in scientific discourse do not have to be semantically closed. This is obvious in case linguistic phenomena and, in particular, semantic notions do not enter in any way into the subject-matter of a science; for in such a case the language of this science does not have to be provided with any semantic terms at all. However, we shall see in the next section how semantically closed languages can be dispensed with even in those scientific discussions in which semantic notions are essentially involved.

The problem arises as to the position of everyday language with regard to this point. At first blush it would seem that this language satisfies both assumptions (1) and (2), and that therefore it must be inconsistent. But actually the case is not so simple. Our everyday language is certainly not one with an exactly specified structure. We do not know precisely which expressions are sentences, and we know even to a smaller degree which sentences are to be taken as assertible. Thus the problem of consistency has no exact meaning with respect to this language. We may at best only risk the guess that a language whose structure has been exactly specified and which resembles our everyday language as closely as possible would be inconsistent.

9. Object-language and meta-language

Since we have agreed not to employ semantically closed languages, we have to use two different languages in discussing the problem of the definition of truth and, more generally, any problems in the field of semantics. The first of these languages is the language which is 'talked about' and which is the subject-matter of the whole discussion; the definition of truth which we are seeking applies to the sentences of this language. The second is the language in which we 'talk about' the first language, and in terms of which we wish, in particular, to construct the definition of truth for the first language. We shall refer to the first language as '*the object-language*,' and to the second as '*the meta-language*.'

It should be noticed that these terms 'object-language' and 'meta-language' have only a relative sense. If, for instance, we become interested in the notion of truth applying to sentences, not of our original object-language, but of its meta-language, the latter becomes automatically the object-language of our discussion; and in order to define truth for this language, we have to go to a new meta-language – so to speak, to a meta-language of a higher level. In this way we arrive at a whole hierarchy of languages.

The vocabulary of the meta-language is to a large extent determined by previously stated conditions under which a definition of truth will be considered materially adequate. This definition, as we recall, has to imply all equivalences of the form (T):

(T) X is true if, and only if, p.

The definition itself and all the equivalences implied by it are to be formulated in the meta-language. On the other hand, the symbol '*p*' in (T) stands for an arbitrary sentence of our object-language. Hence it follows that every sentence which occurs in the object-language must also occur in the meta-language; in other words, the meta-language must contain the object-language as a part. This is at any rate necessary for the proof of the adequacy of the definition – even though the definition itself can sometimes be formulated in a less comprehensive meta-language which does not satisfy this requirement.

(The requirement in question can be somewhat modified, for it suffices to assume that the object-language can be translated into the meta-language; this necessitates a certain change in the interpretation of the symbol '*p*' in (T). In all that follows we shall ignore the possibility of this modification.)

Furthermore, the symbol '*X*' in (T) represents the name of the sentence which '*p*' stands for. We see therefore that the meta-language must be rich enough to provide possibilities of constructing a name for every sentence of the object-language.

In addition, the meta-language must obviously contain terms of a general logical character, such as the expression 'if, and only if.'[12]

It is desirable for the meta-language not to contain any undefined terms except such as are involved explicitly or implicitly in the remarks above, i.e.: terms of the object-language; terms referring to the form of the expressions of the object-language, and used in building names for these expressions; and terms of logic. In particular, we desire *semantic terms* (referring to the object-language) *to be introduced into the meta-language only by definition.* For, if this postulate is satisfied, the definition of truth, or of any other semantic concept, will fulfill what we intuitively expect from every definition; that is, it will explain the meaning of the term being defined in terms whose meaning appears to be completely clear and unequivocal. And, moreover, we have then a kind of guarantee that the use of semantic concepts will not involve us in any contradictions.

We have no further requirements as to the formal structure of the object-language and the meta-language; we assume that it is similar to that of other formalized languages known at the present time. In particular, we assume that the usual formal rules of definition are observed in the meta-language.

10. Conditions for a positive solution of the main problem

Now, we have already a clear idea both of the conditions of material adequacy to which the definition of truth is subjected, and of the formal structure of the language in which this definition is to be constructed. Under these circumstances the problem of the definition of truth acquires the character of a definite problem of a purely deductive nature.

The solution of the problem, however, is by no means obvious, and I would not attempt to give it in detail without using the whole machinery of contemporary logic. Here I shall confine myself to a rough outline of the solution and to the discussion of certain points of a more general interest which are involved in it.

The solution turns out to be sometimes positive, sometimes negative. This depends upon some formal relations between the object-language and its meta-language; or, more specifically, upon the fact whether the meta-language in its logical part is '*essentially richer*' than the object-language or not. It is not easy to give a general and precise definition of this notion of 'essential richness.' If we restrict ourselves to languages based on the logical theory of types, the condition for the meta-language to be 'essentially richer' than the object-language is that it contain variables of a higher logical type than those of the object-language.

If the condition of 'essential richness' is not satisfied, it can usually be shown that an interpretation of the meta-language in the object-language is possible; that is to say, with any given term of the meta-language a well-determined term of the object-language can be correlated in such a way that the assertible sentences of the one language turn out to be correlated with assertible sentences of the other. As a result of this interpretation, the hypothesis that a satisfactory definition of truth has been formulated in the meta-language turns out to imply the possibility of reconstructing in that language the antinomy of the liar; and this in turn forces us to reject the hypothesis in question.

(The fact that the meta-language, in its non-logical part, is ordinarily more comprehensive than the object-language does not affect the possibility of interpreting the former in the latter. For example, the names of expressions of the object-language occur in the meta-language, though for the most part they do not occur in the object-language itself; but, nevertheless, it may be possible to interpret these names in terms of the object-language.)

Thus we see that the condition of 'essential richness' is necessary for the possibility of a satisfactory definition of truth in the meta-language. If we want to develop the theory of truth in a meta-language which does not satisfy this condition, we must give up the idea of defining truth with the exclusive help of those terms which were indicated above (in Section 8). We have then to include the term '*true*,' or some other semantic term, in the list of undefined terms of the meta-language, and to express fundamental properties of the notion of truth in a series of axioms. There is nothing essentially wrong in such an axiomatic procedure, and it may prove useful for various purposes.[13]

It turns out, however, that this procedure can be avoided. For *the condition of the 'essential richness' of the meta-language proves to be, not only necessary, but also sufficient for the construction of a satisfactory definition of truth*; i.e., if the meta-language satisfies this condition, the notion of truth can be defined in it. We shall now indicate in general terms how this construction can be carried through.

11. The construction (in outline) of the definition.[14]

A definition of truth can be obtained in a very simple way from that of another semantic notion, namely, of the notion of *satisfaction*.

Satisfaction is a relation between arbitrary objects and certain expressions called '*sentential functions*.' These are expressions like '*x is white*,' '*x is greater than y*,' etc. Their formal structural is analogous to that of sentences; however, they may contain the so-called free variables (like '*x*' and '*y*' in '*x is greater than y*'), which cannot occur in sentences.

In defining the notion of a sentential function in formalized languages, we usually apply what is called a 'recursive procedure'; i.e., we first describe sentential functions of the simplest structure (which ordinarily presents no difficulty), and then we indicate the operations by means of which compound functions can be constructed from simpler ones. Such an operation may consist, for instance, in forming the logical disjunction or conjunction of two given functions, i.e. by combining them by the word '*or*' or '*and*.' A sentence can now be defined simply as a sentential function which contains no free variables.

As regards the notion of satisfaction, we might try to define it by saying that given objects satisfy a given function if the latter becomes a true sentence when we replace in it free variables by names of given objects. In this sense, for example, snow satisfies the sentential function '*x is white*' since the sentence '*snow is white*' is true. However, apart from other difficulties, this method is not available to us, for we want to use the notion of satisfaction in defining truth.

To obtain a definition of satisfaction we have rather to apply again a recursive procedure. We indicate which objects satisfy the simplest sentential functions; and then we state the conditions under which given objects satisfy a compound function – assuming that we know which objects satisfy the simpler functions from which the compound one has been constructed. Thus, for instance, we say that given numbers satisfy the logical disjunction '*x is greater than y or x is equal to y*' if they satisfy at least one of the functions '*x is greater than y*' or '*x is equal to y*.'

Once the general definition of satisfaction is obtained, we notice that it applies automatically also to those special sentential functions which contain no free variables, i.e., to sentences. It turns out that for a sentence only two cases are possible: a sentence is either satisfied by all objects, or by no objects. Hence we arrive at a definition of truth and falsehood simply by saying that a *sentence is true if it is satisfied by all objects, and false otherwise.*[15]

(It may seem strange that we have chosen a roundabout way of defining the truth of a sentence, instead of trying to apply, for instance, a direct recursive procedure. The reason is that compound sentences are constructed from simpler sentential functions, but not always from simpler sentences; hence no general recursive method is known which applies specifically to sentences.)

From this rough outline it is not clear where and how the assumption of the 'essential richness' of the meta-language is involved in the discussion; this becomes clear only when the construction is carried through in a detailed and formal way.[16]

12. Consequences of the definition

The definition of truth which was outlined above has many interesting consequences.

In the first place, the definition proves to be not only formally correct, but also materially adequate (in the sense established in Section 4); in other words, it implies all equivalences of the form (T). In this connection it is important to notice that the conditions for the material adequacy of the definition determine uniquely the extension of the term '*true*.' Therefore, every definition of truth which is materially adequate would necessarily be equivalent to that actually constructed. The semantic conception of truth gives us, so to speak, no possibility of choice between various non-equivalent definitions of this notion.

Moreover, we can deduce from our definition various laws of a general nature. In particular, we can prove with its help the *laws of contradiction and of excluded middle*, which are so characteristic of the Aristotelian conception of truth; i.e., we can show that one and only one of any two contradictory sentences is true. These semantic laws should not be identified with the related logical laws of contradiction and excluded middle; the latter belong to the sentential calculus, i.e., to the most elementary part of logic, and do not involve the term '*true*' at all.

Further important results can be obtained by applying the theory of truth to formalized languages of a certain very comprehensive class of mathematical disciplines; only disciplines of an elementary character and a very elementary logical structure are excluded from this class. It turns out that for a discipline of this class *the notion of truth never coincides with that of provability*; for all provable sentences are true, but there are true sentences which are not provable.[17] Hence it follows further that every such discipline is consistent, but incomplete; that is to say, of any two contradictory sentences at most one is provable, and – what is more – there exists a pair of contradictory sentences neither of which is provable.[18]

13. Extension of the results to other semantic notions

Most of the results at which we arrived in the preceding sections in discussing the notion of truth can be extended with appropriate changes to other semantic notions, for instance, to the notion of satisfaction (involved in our previous discussion), and to those of *designation* and *definition.*

Each of these notions can be analyzed along the lines followed in the analysis of truth. Thus, criteria for an adequate usage of these notions can be established; it can be shown that each of these notions, when used in a semantically closed language according to those criteria, leads necessarily to a contradiction;[19] a distinction between the object-language and the meta-language becomes again indispensable; and the 'essential richness' of the meta-language proves in each case to be a necessary and sufficient condition for a satisfactory definition of the notion involved. Hence the results obtained in discussing one particular semantic notion apply to the general problem of the foundations of theoretical semantics.

Within theoretical semantics we can define and study some further notions, whose intuitive content is more involved and whose semantic origin is less obvious; we have in mind, for instance, the important notions of *consequence, synonymity*, and *meaning*.[20]

We have concerned ourselves here with the theory of semantic notions related to an individual object-language (although no specific properties of this language have been involved in our arguments). However, we could also consider the problem of developing *general semantics* which applies to a comprehensive class of object-languages. A considerable part of our previous remarks can be extended to this general problem; however, certain new difficulties arise in this connection, which will not be discussed here. I shall merely observe that the axiomatic method (mentioned in Section 10) may prove the most appropriate for the treatment of the problem.[21]

II. Polemical Remarks

14. Is the semantic conception of truth the 'right' one?

I should like to begin the polemical part of the paper with some general remarks.

I hope nothing which is said here will be interpreted as a claim that the semantic conception of truth is the 'right' or indeed the 'only possible' one. I do not have the slightest intention to contribute in any way to those endless, often violent discussions on the subject 'What is the right conception of truth?'[22] I must confess I do not understand what is at stake in such disputes; for the problem itself is so vague that no definite solution is possible. In fact, it seems to me that the sense in which the phrase 'the right conception' is used has never been made clear. In most cases one gets the impression that the phrase is used in an almost mystical sense based upon the belief that every word has only one 'real' meaning (a kind of Platonic or Aristotelian idea), and that all the competing conceptions really attempt to catch hold of this one meaning; since, however, they contradict each other, only one attempt can be successful, and hence only one conception is the 'right' one.

Disputes of this type are by no means restricted to the notion of truth. They occur in all domains where – instead of an exact, scientific terminology – common language with its vagueness and ambiguity is used; and they are always meaningless, and therefore in vain.

It seems to me obvious that the only rational approach to such problems would be the following: We should reconcile ourselves with the fact that we are confronted, not with one concept, but with several different concepts which are denoted by one word; we should try to make these concepts as clear as possible (by means of definition, or of an axiomatic procedure, or in some other way); to avoid further confusions, we should agree to use different terms for different concepts; and then we may proceed to a quiet and systematic study of all concepts involved, which will exhibit their main properties and mutual relations.

Referring specifically to the notion of truth, it is undoubtedly the case that in philosophical discussions – and perhaps also in everyday usage – some incipient conceptions of this notion can be found that differ essentially from the classical one (of which the semantic conception is but a modernized form). In fact, various conceptions of this sort have been discussed in the literature, for instance, the pragmatic conception, the coherence theory, etc.[6]

It seems to me that none of these conceptions have been put so far in an intelligible and unequivocal form. This may change, however; a time may come when we find ourselves confronted with several incompatible, but equally clear and precise, conceptions of truth. It will then become necessary to abandon the ambiguous usage of the word '*true*,' and to introduce several terms instead, each to denote a different notion. Personally, I should not feel hurt if a future world congress of the 'theoreticians of truth' should decide – by a majority of votes – to reserve the word '*true*' for one of the non-classical conceptions, and should suggest another word, say, '*frue*,' for the conception considered here. But I cannot imagine that anybody could present cogent arguments to the effect that the semantic conception is 'wrong' and should be entirely abandoned.

15. Formal correctness of the suggested definition of truth

The specific objections which have been raised to my investigations can be divided into several groups; each of these will be discussed separately.

I think that practically all these objections apply, not to the special definition I have given, but to the semantic conception of truth in general. Even those which were leveled against the definition actually constructed could be related to any other definition which conforms to this conception.

This holds, in particular, for those objections which concern the formal correctness of the definition. I have heard a few objections of this kind; however, I doubt very much whether any one of them can be treated seriously.

As a typical example let me quote in substance such an objection.[23] In formulating the definition we use necessarily sentential connectives, i.e., expressions like '*if . . ., then*,' '*or*,' etc. They occur in the definiens; and one of them, namely, the phrase '*if, and only if*' is usually employed to combine the definiendum with the definiens. However, it is well known that the meaning of sentential connectives is explained in logic with the help of the words '*true*' and '*false*'; for instance, we say that an equivalence, i.e., a sentence of the form '*p if, and only if, q*,' is true if either both of its members, i.e., the sentences represented by '*p*' and '*q*,' are true or both are false. Hence the definition of truth involves a vicious circle.

If this objection were valid, no formally correct definition of truth would be possible; for we are unable to formulate any compound sentence without using sentential connectives, or other logical terms defined with their help. Fortunately, the situation is not so bad.

It is undoubtedly the case that a strictly deductive development of logic is often preceded by certain statements explaining the conditions under which sentences of the form '*if p, then q*,' etc., are considered true or false. (Such explanations are often given schematically, by means of the so-called truth-tables.) However, these statements are outside of the system of logic, and should not be regarded as definitions of the terms involved. They are not formulated in the language of the system, but constitute rather special consequences of the definition of truth given in the meta-language. Moreover, these statements do not influence the deductive development of logic in any way. For in such a development we do not discuss the question whether a given sentence is true, we are only interested in the problem whether it is provable.[24]

On the other hand, the moment we find ourselves within the deductive system of logic – or of any discipline based upon logic, e.g., of semantics – we either treat sentential connectives as undefined terms, or else we define them by means of other sentential connectives, but never by means of semantic terms like '*true*' or '*false*.' For instance, if we agree to regard the expressions '*not*' and '*if . . ., then*' (and possibly also '*if, and only if*') as undefined terms, we can define the term '*or*' by stating that a sentence of the form '*p or q*' is equivalent to the corresponding sentence of the form '*if not p, then q*.' The definition can be formulated, e.g., in the following way:

(p or q) if, and only if, (if not p, then q).

This definition obviously contains no semantic terms.

However, a vicious circle in definition arises only when the definiens contains either the term to be defined itself, or other terms defined with its help. Thus we clearly see that the use of sentential connectives in defining the semantic term '*true*' does not involve any circle.

I should like to mention a further objection which I have found in the literature and which seems also to concern the formal correctness, if not of the definition of truth itself, then at least of the arguments which lead to this definition.[25]

The author of this objection mistakenly regards scheme (T) (from Section 4) as a definition of truth. He charges this alleged definition with 'inadmissible brevity, i.e., incompleteness,' which 'does not give us the means of deciding whether by "equivalence" is meant a logical-formal, or a non-logical and also structurally non-describable relation.' To remove this 'defect' he suggests supplementing (T) in one of the two following ways:

(T′) X is true if, and only if, p is true.

or

(T″) X is true if, and only if, p is the case (i.e., if what p states is the case).

Then he discusses these two new 'definitions,' which are supposedly free from the old, formal 'defect,' but which turn out to be unsatisfactory for other, non-formal reasons.

This new objection seems to arise from a misunderstanding concerning the nature of sentential connectives (and thus to be somehow related to that previously discussed). The author of the objection does not seem to realize that the phrase '*if, and only if*' (in opposition to such phrases as '*are equivalent*' or '*is equivalent to*') expresses no relation between sentences at all since it does not combine names of sentences.

In general, the whole argument is based upon an obvious confusion between sentences and their names. It suffices to point out that – in contradistinction to (T) – schemata (T′) and (T″) do not give any meaningful expressions if we replace in them '*p*' by a sentence; for the phrases '*p is true*' and '*p is the case*' (i.e., '*what p states is the case*') become meaningful if '*p*' is replaced by a sentence, and not by the name of a sentence (cf. Section 4).[26]

While the author of the objection considers schema (T) 'inadmissibly brief,' I am inclined, on my part, to regard schemata (T′) and (T″) as 'inadmissibly long.' And I think even that I can rigorously prove this statement on the basis of the following definition: An expression is said to be 'inadmissibly long' if (i) it is meaningless, and (ii) it has been obtained from a meaningful expression by inserting superfluous words.

16. Redundancy of semantic terms – their possible elimination

The objection I am going to discuss now no longer concerns the formal correctness of the definition, but is still concerned with certain formal features of the semantic conception of truth.

We have seen that this conception essentially consists in regarding the sentence 'X *is true*' as equivalent to the sentence denoted by 'X' (where 'X' stands for a name of a sentence of the object-language). Consequently, the term '*true*' when occurring in a simple sentence of the form 'X *is true*' can easily be eliminated, and the sentence itself, which belongs to the meta-language, can be replaced by an equivalent sentence of the object-language; and the same applies to compound sentences provided the term '*true*' occurs in them exclusively as a part of the expressions of the form 'X *is true*.'

Some people have therefore urged that the term '*true*' in the semantic sense can always be eliminated, and that for this reason the semantic conception of truth is altogether sterile and useless. And since the same considerations apply to other semantic notions, the conclusion has been drawn that semantics as a whole is a purely verbal game and at best only a harmless hobby.

But the matter is not quite so simple.[27] The sort of elimination here discussed cannot always be made. It cannot be done in the case of universal statements which express the fact that all sentences of a certain type are true, or that all true sentences have a certain property. For instance, we can prove in the theory of truth the following statement:

All consequences of true sentences are true.

However, we cannot get rid here of the word '*true*' in the simple manner contemplated.

Again, even in the case of particular sentences having the form '*X is true*' such a simple elimination cannot always be made. In fact, the elimination is possible only in those cases in which the name of the sentence which is said to be true occurs in a form that enables us to reconstruct the sentence itself. For example, our present historical knowledge does not give us any possibility of eliminating the word '*true*' from the following sentence:

The first sentence written by Plato is true.

Of course, since we have a definition for truth and since every definition enables us to replace the definiendum by its definiens, an elimination of the term '*true*' in its semantic sense is always theoretically possible. But this would not be the kind of simple elimination discussed above, and it would not result in the replacement of a sentence in the meta-language by a sentence in the object-language.

If, however, anyone continues to urge that – because of the theoretical possibility of eliminating the word '*true*' on the basis of its definition – the concept of truth is sterile, he must accept the further conclusion that all defined notions are sterile. But this outcome is so absurd and so unsound historically that any comment on it is unnecessary. In fact, I am rather inclined to agree with those who maintain that the moments of greatest creative advancement in science frequently coincide with the introduction of new notions by means of definition.

17. Conformity of the semantic conception of truth with philosophical and common-sense usage

The question has been raised whether the semantic conception of truth can indeed be regarded as a precise form of the old, classical conception of this notion.

Various formulations of the classical conception were quoted in the early part of this paper (Section 3). I must repeat that in my judgment none of them is quite precise and clear. Accordingly, the only sure way of settling the question would be to confront the authors of those statements with our new formulation, and to ask them whether it agrees with their intentions. Unfortunately, this method is impractical since they died quite some time ago.

As far as my own opinion is concerned, I do not have any doubts that our formulation does conform to the intuitive content of that of Aristotle. I am less certain regarding the later formulations of the classical conception, for they are very vague indeed.[28]

Furthermore, some doubts have been expressed whether the semantic conception does reflect the notion of truth in its common-sense and everyday usage. I clearly realize (as I already indicated) that the common meaning of the word '*true*' – as that of any other word of everyday language – is to some extent vague, and that its usage more or less fluctuates. Hence the problem of assigning to this word a fixed and exact meaning is relatively unspecified, and every solution of this problem implies necessarily a certain deviation from the practice of everyday language.

In spite of all this, I happen to believe that the semantic conception does conform to a very considerable extent with the common-sense usage – although I readily admit I may be mistaken. What is more to the point, however, I believe that the issue raised can be settled scientifically, though of course not by a deductive procedure, but with the help of the statistical questionnaire method. As a matter of fact, such research has been carried on, and some of the results have been reported at congresses and in part published.[29]

I should like to emphasize that in my opinion such investigations must be conducted with the utmost care. Thus, if we ask a highschool boy, or even an adult intelligent man having no special philosophical training, whether he regards a sentence to be true if it agrees with reality, or if it designates an existing state of affairs, it may simply turn out that he does not understand the question; in consequence his response, whatever it may be, will be of no value for us. But his answer to the question whether he would admit that the sentence '*it is snowing*' could be true although it is not snowing, or could be false although it is snowing, would naturally be very significant for our problem.

Therefore, I was by no means surprised to learn (in a discussion devoted to these problems) that in a group of people who were questioned only 15% agreed that '*true*' means for them '*agreeing with reality*,' while 90% agreed that a sentence such as '*it is snowing*' is true if, and only if, it is snowing. Thus, a great majority of these people seemed to reject the classical conception of truth in its '*philosophical*' formulation, while accepting the same conception when formulated in plain words (waiving the question whether the use of the phrase 'the same conception' is here justified).

18. The definition in its relation to 'the philosophical problem of truth' and to various epistemological trends

I have heard it remarked that the formal definition of truth has nothing to do with 'the philosophical problem of truth.'[30] However, nobody has ever pointed out to me in an intelligible way just what this problem is. I have been informed in this connection that my definition, though it states necessary and sufficient conditions for a sentence to be true, does not really grasp the 'essence' of this concept. Since I have never been able to understand what the 'essence' of a concept is, I must be excused from discussing this point any longer.

In general, I do not believe that there is such a thing as 'the philosophical problem of truth.' I do believe that there are various intelligible and interesting (but not necessarily philosophical) problems concerning the notion of truth, but I also believe that they can be exactly formulated and possibly solved only on the basis of a precise conception of this notion.

While on the one hand the definition of truth has been blamed for not being philosophical enough, on the other a series of objections have been raised charging this definition with serious philosophical implications, always of a very undesirable nature. I shall discuss now one special objection of this type; another group of such objections will be dealt with in the next section.

It has been claimed that – due to the fact that a sentence like 'snow is white' is taken to be semantically true if snow is *in fact* white (italics by the critic) – logic finds itself involved in a most uncritical realism.[31]

If there were an opportunity to discuss the objection with its author, I should raise two points. First, I should ask him to drop the words '*in fact*,' which do not occur in the original formulation and which are misleading, even if they do not affect the content. For these words convey the impression that the semantic conception of truth is intended to establish the conditions under which we are warranted in asserting any given sentence, and in particular any empirical sentence. However, a moment's reflection shows that this impression is merely an illusion; and I think that the author of the objection falls victim to the illusion which he himself created.

In fact, the semantic definition of truth implies nothing regarding the conditions under which a sentence like (1):

(1) snow is white

can be asserted. It implies only that, whenever we assert or reject this sentence, we must be ready to assert or reject the correlated sentence (2):

(2) the sentence 'snow is white' is true.

Thus, we may accept the semantic conception of truth without giving up any epistemological attitude we may have had; we may remain naïve realists, critical realists or idealists, empiricists or metaphysicians – whatever we were before. The semantic conception is completely neutral toward all these issues.

In the second place, I should try to get some information regarding the conception of truth which (in the opinion of the author of the objection) does not involve logic in a most naïve realism. I would gather that this conception must be incompatible with the semantic one. Thus, there must be sentences which are true in one of these conceptions without being true in the other. Assume, e.g., the sentence (1) to be of this kind. The truth of this sentence in the semantic conception is determined by an equivalence of the form (T):

> The sentence 'snow is white' is true if, and only if, snow is white.

Hence in the new conception we must reject this equivalence, and consequently we must assume its denial:

> The sentence 'snow is white' is true if, and only if, snow is not white (*or perhaps*: snow, in fact, is not white).

This sounds somewhat paradoxical. I do not regard such a consequence of the new conception as absurd; but I am a little fearful that someone in the future may charge this conception with involving logic in a 'most sophisticated kind of irrealism.' At any rate, it seems to me important to realize that every conception of truth which is incompatible with the semantic one carries with it consequences of this type.

I have dwelt a little on this whole question, not because the objection discussed seems to me very significant, but because certain points which have arisen in the discussion should be taken into account by all those who for various epistemological reasons are inclined to reject the semantic conception of truth.

19. Alleged metaphysical elements in semantics

The semantic conception of truth has been charged several times with involving certain metaphysical elements. Objections of this sort have been made to apply not only to the theory of truth, but to the whole domain of theoretical semantics.[32]

I do not intend to discuss the general problem whether the introduction of a metaphysical element into a science is at all objectionable. The only point which will interest me here is whether and in what sense metaphysics is involved in the subject of our present discussion.

The whole question obviously depends upon what one understands by 'metaphysics.' Unfortunately, this notion is extremely vague and equivocal. When listening to discussions in this subject, sometimes one gets the impression that the term 'metaphysical' has lost any objective meaning, and is merely used as a kind of professional philosophical invective.

For some people metaphysics is a general theory of objects (ontology) – a discipline which is to be developed in a purely empirical way, and which differs from other empirical sciences only by its generality. I do not know whether such a discipline actually exists (some cynics claim that it is customary in philosophy to baptize unborn children); but I think that in any case metaphysics in this conception is not objectionable to anybody, and has hardly any connections with semantics.

For the most part, however, the term 'metaphysical' is used as directly opposed – in one sense or another – to the term 'empirical'; at any rate, it is used in this way by those people who are distressed by the thought that any metaphysical elements might have managed to creep into science. This general conception of metaphysics assumes several more specific forms.

Thus, some people take it to be symptomatic of a metaphysical element in a science when methods of inquiry are employed which are neither deductive nor empirical. However, no trace of this symptom can be found in the development of semantics (unless some metaphysical elements are involved in the object-language to which the semantic notions refer). In particular, the semantics of formalized languages is constructed in a purely deductive way.

Others maintain that the metaphysical character of a science depends mainly on its vocabulary and, more specifically, on its primitive terms. Thus, a term is said to be metaphysical if it is neither logical nor mathematical, and if it is not associated with an empirical procedure which enables us to decide whether a thing is denoted by this term or not. With respect to such a view of metaphysics it is sufficient to recall that a meta-language includes only three kinds of undefined terms: (i) terms taken from logic; (ii) terms of the corresponding object-language, and (iii) names of expressions in the object-language. It is thus obvious that no metaphysical undefined terms occur in the meta-language (again, unless such terms appear in the object-language itself).

There are, however, some who believe that, even if no metaphysical terms occur among the primitive terms of a language, they may be introduced by definitions; namely, by those definitions which fail to provide us with general criteria for deciding whether an object falls under the defined concept. It is argued that the term '*true*' is of this kind, since no universal criterion of truth follows immediately from the definition of this term, and since it is generally believed (and in a certain sense can even be proved) that such a criterion will never be found. This comment on the actual character of the notion of truth seems to be perfectly just. However, it should be noticed that the notion of truth does not differ in this respect from many notions in logic, mathematics, and theoretical parts of various empirical sciences, e.g., in theoretical physics.

In general, it must be said that if the term 'metaphysical' is employed in so wide a sense as to embrace certain notions (or methods) of logic, mathematics, or empirical sciences, it will apply *a fortiori* to those of semantics. In fact, as we know from Part I of the paper, in developing the semantics of a language we use all the notions of this language, and we apply even a stronger logical apparatus than that which is used in the language itself. On the other hand, however, I can summarize the arguments given above by stating that in no interpretation of the term 'metaphysical' which is familiar and more or less intelligible to me does semantics involve any metaphysical elements peculiar to itself.

I should like to make one final remark in connection with this group of objections. The history of science shows many instances of concepts which were judged metaphysical (in a loose, but in any case derogatory sense of this term) before their meaning was made precise; however, once they received a rigorous, formal definition, the distrust in them evaporated. As typical examples we may mention the concepts of negative and imaginary numbers in mathematics. I hope a similar fate awaits the concept of truth and other semantic concepts; and it seems to me, therefore, that those who have distrusted them because of their alleged metaphysical implications should welcome the fact that precise definitions of these concepts are now available. If in consequence semantic concepts lose philosophical interest, they will only share the fate of many other concepts of science, and this need give rise to no regret.

20. Applicability of semantics to special empirical sciences

We come to the last and perhaps the most important group of objections. Some strong doubts have been expressed whether semantic notions find or can find applications in various domains of intellectual activity. For the most part such doubts have concerned the applicability of semantics to the field of empirical science – either to special sciences or to the general methodology of this field; although similar skepticism has been expressed regarding possible applications of semantics to mathematical sciences and their methodology.

I believe that it is possible to allay these doubts to a certain extent, and that some optimism with respect to the potential value of semantics for various domains of thought is not without ground.

To justify this optimism, it suffices I think to stress two rather obvious points. First, the development of a theory which formulates a precise definition of a notion and establishes its general properties provides *eo ipso* a firmer basis for all discussions in which this notion is involved; and, therefore, it cannot be irrelevant for anyone who uses this notion, and desires to do so in a conscious and consistent way. Secondly, semantic notions are actually involved in various branches of science, and in particular of empirical science.

The fact that in empirical research we are concerned only with natural languages and that theoretical semantics applies to these languages only with certain approximation, does not affect the problem essentially. However, it has undoubtedly this effect that progress in semantics will have but a delayed and somewhat limited influence in this field. The situation with which we are confronted here does not differ essentially from that which arises when we apply laws of logic to arguments in everyday life – or, generally, when we attempt to apply a theoretical science to empirical problems.

Semantic notions are undoubtedly involved, to a larger or smaller degree, in psychology, sociology, and in practically all the humanities. Thus, a psychologist defines the so-called intelligence quotient in terms of the numbers of *true* (right) and *false* (wrong) answers given by a person to certain questions; for a historian of culture the range of objects for which a human race in successive stages of its development possesses adequate *designations* may be a topic of great significance; a student of literature may be strongly interested in the problem whether a given author always uses two given words with the same *meaning*. Examples of this kind can be multiplied indefinitely.

The most natural and promising domain for the applications of theoretical semantics is clearly linguistics – the empirical study of natural languages. Certain parts of this science are even referred to as 'semantics,' sometimes with an additional qualification. Thus, this name is occasionally given to that portion of grammar which attempts to classify all words of a language into parts of speech, according to what the words mean or designate. The study of the evolution of meanings in the historical development of a language is sometimes called 'historical semantics.' In general, the totality of investigations on semantic relations which occur in a natural language is referred to as 'descriptive semantics.' The relation between theoretical and descriptive semantics is analogous to that between pure and applied mathematics, or perhaps to that between theoretical and empirical physics; the rôle of formalized languages in semantics can be roughly compared to that of isolated systems in physics.

It is perhaps unnecessary to say that semantics cannot find any direct applications in natural sciences such as physics, biology, etc.; for in none of these sciences are we concerned with linguistic phenomena, and even less with semantic relations between linguistic expressions and objects to which these expressions refer. We shall see, however, in the next section that semantics may have a kind of indirect influence even on those sciences in which semantic notions are not directly involved.

21. Applicability of semantics to the methodology of empirical science

Besides linguistics, another important domain for possible applications of semantics is the methodology of science; this term is used here in a broad sense so as to embrace the theory of science in general. Independent of whether a science is conceived merely as a system of statements or as a totality of certain statements and human activities, the study of scientific language constitutes an essential part of the methodological discussion of a science. And it seems to me clear that any tendency to eliminate semantic notions (like those of truth and designation) from this discussion would make it fragmentary and inadequate.[33] Moreover, there is no reason for such a tendency today, once the main difficulties in using semantic terms have been overcome. The semantics of scientific language should be simply included as a part in the methodology of science.

I am by no means inclined to charge methodology and, in particular, semantics – whether theoretical or descriptive – with the task of clarifying the meanings of all scientific terms. This task is left to those sciences in which the terms are used, and is actually fulfilled by them (in the same way in which, e.g., the task of clarifying the meaning of the term '*true*' is left to, and fulfilled by, semantics). There may be, however, certain special problems of this sort in which a methodological approach is desirable or indeed necessary (perhaps, the problem of the notion of causality is a good example here); and in a methodological discussion of such problems semantic notions may play an essential rôle. Thus, semantics may have some bearing on any science whatsoever.

The question arises whether semantics can be helpful in solving general and, so to speak, classical problems of methodology. I should like to discuss here with some detail a special, though very important, aspect of this question.

One of the main problems of the methodology of empirical science consists in establishing conditions under which an empirical theory or hypothesis should be regarded as acceptable. This notion of acceptability must be relativized to a given stage of the development of a science (or to a given amount of presupposed knowledge). In other words, we may consider it as provided with a time coefficient; for a theory which is acceptable today may become untenable tomorrow as a result of new scientific discoveries.

It seems *a priori* very plausible that the acceptability of a theory somehow depends on the truth of its sentences, and that consequently a methodologist in his (so far rather unsuccessful) attempts at making the notion of acceptability precise, can expect some help from the semantic theory of truth. Hence we ask the question: Are there any postulates which can be reasonably imposed on acceptable theories and which involve the notion of truth? And, in particular, we ask whether the following postulate is a reasonable one:

An acceptable theory cannot contain (or imply) any false sentences.

The answer to the last question is clearly negative. For, first of all, we are practically sure, on the basis of our historical experience, that every empirical theory which is accepted today will sooner or later be rejected and replaced by another theory. It is also very probable that the new theory will be incompatible with the old one; i.e., will imply a sentence which is contradictory to one of the sentences contained in the old theory. Hence, at least one of the two theories must include false sentences, in spite of the fact that each of them is accepted at a certain time. Secondly, the postulate in question could hardly ever be satisfied in practice; for we do not know, and are very unlikely to find, any criteria of truth which enable us to show that no sentence of an empirical theory is false.

The postulate in question could be at most regarded as the expression of an ideal limit for successively more adequate theories in a given field of research; but this hardly can be given any precise meaning.

Nevertheless, it seems to me that there is an important postulate which can be reasonably imposed on acceptable empirical theories and which involves the notion of truth. It is closely related to the one just discussed, but is essentially weaker. Remembering that the notion of acceptability is provided with a time coefficient, we can give this postulate the following form:

> As soon as we succeed in showing that an empirical theory contains (or implies) false sentences, it cannot be any longer considered acceptable.

In support of this postulate, I should like to make the following remarks.

I believe everybody agrees that one of the reasons which may compel us to reject an empirical theory is the proof of its inconsistency: a theory becomes untenable if we succeed in deriving from it two contradictory sentences. Now we can ask what are the usual motives for rejecting a theory on such grounds. Persons who are acquainted with modern logic are inclined to answer this question in the following way: A well-known logical law shows that a theory which enables us to derive two contradictory sentences enables us also to derive every sentence; therefore, such a theory is trivial and deprived of any scientific interest.

I have some doubts whether this answer contains an adequate analysis of the situation. I think that people who do not know modern logic are as little inclined to accept an inconsistent theory as those who are thoroughly familiar with it; and probably this applies even to those who regard (as some still do) the logical law on which the argument is based as a highly controversial issue, and almost as a paradox. I do not think that our attitude toward an inconsistent theory would change even if we decided for some reasons to weaken our system of logic so as to deprive ourselves of the possibility of deriving every sentence from any two contradictory sentences.

It seems to me that the real reason of our attitude is a different one: We know (if only intuitively) that an inconsistent theory must contain false sentences; and we are not inclined to regard as acceptable any theory which has been shown to contain such sentences.

There are various methods of showing that a given theory includes false sentences. Some of them are based upon purely logical properties of the theory involved; the method just discussed (i.e., the proof of inconsistency) is not the sole method of this type, but is the simplest one, and the one which is most frequently applied in practice. With the help of certain assumptions regarding the truth of empirical sentences, we can obtain methods to the same effect which are no longer of a purely logical nature. If we decide to accept the general postulate suggested above, then a successful application of any such method will make the theory untenable.

22. Applications of semantics to deductive science

As regards the applicability of semantics to mathematical sciences and their methodology, i.e., to meta-mathematics, we are in a much more favorable position than in the case of empirical sciences. For, instead of advancing reasons which justify some hopes for the future (and thus making a kind of pro-semantics propaganda), we are able to point out concrete results already achieved.

Doubts continue to be expressed whether the notion of a true sentence – as distinct from that of a provable sentence – can have any significance for mathematical disciplines and play any part in a methodological discussion of mathematics. It seems to me, however, that just this notion of a true sentence constitutes a most valuable contribution to meta-mathematics by semantics. We already possess a series of interesting meta-mathematical results gained with the help of the theory of truth. These results concern the mutual relations between the notion of truth and that of provability; establish new properties of the latter notion (which, as well known, is one of the basic notions of meta-mathematics); and throw some light on the fundamental problems of consistency and completeness. The most significant among these results have been briefly discussed in Section 12.[34]

Furthermore, by applying the method of semantics we can adequately define several important meta-mathematical notions which have been used so far only in an intuitive way – such as, e.g., the notion of definability or that of a model of an axiom system; and thus we can undertake a systematic study of these notions. In particular, the investigations on definability have already brought some interesting results, and promise even more in the future.[35]

We have discussed the applications of semantics only to meta-mathematics, and not to mathematics proper. However, this distinction between mathematics and meta-mathematics is rather unimportant. For meta-mathematics is itself a deductive discipline and hence, from a certain point of view, a part of mathematics; and it is well known that – due to the formal character of deductive method – the results obtained in one deductive discipline can be automatically extended to any other discipline in which the given one finds an interpretation. Thus, for example, all meta-mathematical results can be interpreted as results of number theory. Also from a practical point of view there is no clear-cut line between meta-mathematics and mathematics proper; for instance, the investigations on definability could be included in either of these domains.

23. Final remarks

I should like to conclude this discussion with some general and rather loose remarks concerning the whole question of the evaluation of scientific achievements in terms of their applicability. I must confess I have various doubts in this connection.

Being a mathematician (as well as a logician, and perhaps a philosopher of a sort), I have had the opportunity to attend many discussions between specialists in mathematics, where the problem of applications is especially acute, and I have noticed on several occasions the following phenomenon: If a mathematician wishes to disparage the work of one of his colleagues, say, *A*, the most effective method he finds for doing this is to ask where the results can be applied. The hard-pressed man, with his back against the wall, finally unearths the researches of another mathematician *B* as the locus of the application of his own results. If next *B* is plagued with a similar question, he will refer to another mathematician *C*. After a few steps of this kind we find ourselves referred back to the researches of *A*, and in this way the chain closes.

Speaking more seriously, I do not wish to deny that the value of a man's work may be increased by its implications for the research of others and for practice. But I believe, nevertheless, that it is inimical to the progress of science to measure the importance of any research exclusively or chiefly in terms of its usefulness and applicability. We know from the history of science that many important results and discoveries have had to wait centuries before they were applied in any field. And, in my opinion, there are also other important factors which cannot be disregarded in determining the value of a scientific work. It seems to me that there is a special domain of very profound and strong human needs related to scientific research, which are similar in many ways to aesthetic and perhaps religious needs. And it also seems to me that the satisfaction of these needs should be considered an important task of research. Hence, I believe, the question of the value of any research cannot be adequately answered without taking into account the intellectual satisfaction which the results of that research bring to those who understand it and care for it. It may be unpopular and out-of-date to say – but I do not think that a scientific result which gives us a better understanding of the world and makes it more harmonious in our eyes should be held in lower esteem than, say, an invention which reduces the cost of paving roads, or improves household plumbing.

It is clear that the remarks just made become pointless if the word 'application' is used in a very wide and liberal sense. It is perhaps not less obvious that nothing follows from these general remarks concerning the specific topics which have been discussed in this paper; and I really do not know whether research in semantics stands to gain or lose by introducing the standard of value I have suggested.

Notes

1. Compare Tarski [2] (see bibliography at the end of the paper). This work may be consulted for a more detailed and formal presentation of the subject

of the paper, especially of the material included in Sections 6 and 9–13. It contains also references to my earlier publications on the problems of semantics (a communication in Polish, 1930; the article Tarski [1] in French, 1931; a communication in German, 1932; and a book in Polish, 1933). The expository part of the present paper is related in its character to Tarski [3]. My investigations on the notion of truth and on theoretical semantics have been reviewed or discussed in Hofstadter [1], Juhos [1], Kokoszyńska [1] and [2], Kotarbiński [2], Scholz [1], Weinberg [1], *et al.*

2. It may be hoped that the interest in theoretical semantics will now increase, as a result of the recent publication of the important work Carnap [2].
3. This applies, in particular, to public discussions during the I. International Congress for the Unity of Science (Paris, 1935) and the Conference of International Congresses for the Unity of Science (Paris, 1937); cf., e.g., Neurath [1] and Gonseth [1].
4. The words 'notion' and 'concept' are used in this paper with all of the vagueness and ambiguity with which they occur in philosophical literature. Thus, sometimes they refer simply to a term, sometimes to what is meant by a term, and in other cases to what is denoted by a term. Sometimes it is irrelevant which of these interpretations is meant; and in certain cases perhaps none of them applies adequately. While on principle I share the tendency to avoid these words in any exact discussion, I did not consider it necessary to do so in this informal presentation.
5. For our present purposes it is somewhat more convenient to understand by 'expressions,' 'sentences,' etc., not individual inscriptions, but classes of inscriptions of similar form (thus, not individual physical things, but classes of such things).
6. For the Aristotelian formulation see Article [1], Γ, 7, 27. The other two formulations are very common in the literature, but I do not know with whom they originate. A critical discussion of various conceptions of truth can be found, e.g., in Kotarbiński [1] (so far available only in Polish), pp. 123 ff., and Russell [1], pp. 362 ff.
7. For most of the remarks contained in Sections 4 and 8, I am indebted to the late S. Leśniewski who developed them in his unpublished lectures in the University of Warsaw (in 1919 and later). However, Leśniewski did not anticipate the possibility of a rigorous development of the theory of truth, and still less of a definition of this notion; hence, while indicating equivalences of the form (T) as premisses in the antinomy of the liar, he did not conceive them as any sufficient conditions for an adequate usage (or definition) of the notion of truth. Also the remarks in Section 8 regarding the occurrence of an empirical premiss in the antinomy of the liar, and the possibility of eliminating this premiss, do not originate with him.
8. In connection with various logical and methodological problems involved in this paper the reader may consult Tarski [6].
9. The antinomy of the liar (ascribed to Eubulides or Epimenides) is discussed here in Sections 7 and 8. For the antinomy of definability (due to J. Richard) see e.g., Hilbert-Bernays [1], Vol. 2, pp. 263 ff.; for the antinomy of heterological terms see Grelling-Nelson [1], p. 307.
10. Due to Professor J. Lukasiewicz (University of Warsaw).

11. This can roughly be done in the following way. Let *S* be any sentence beginning with the words '*Every sentence*.' We correlate with *S* a new sentence S^* by subjecting *S* to the following two modifications: we replace in *S* the first word, '*Every*,' by '*The*'; and we insert after the second word, '*sentence*,' the whole sentence *S* enclosed in quotation marks. Let us agree to call the sentence *S* '(self-)applicable' or 'non-(self-)applicable' dependent on whether the correlated sentence S^* is true or false. Now consider the following sentence:

    Every sentence is non-applicable.

    It can easily be shown that the sentence just stated must be both applicable and non-applicable; hence a contradiction. It may not be quite clear in what sense this formulation of the antinomy does not involve an empirical premiss; however, I shall not elaborate on this point.
12. The terms 'logic' and 'logical' are used in this paper in a broad sense, which has become almost traditional in the last decades; logic is assumed here to comprehend the whole theory of classes and relations (i.e., the mathematical theory of sets). For many different reasons I am personally inclined to use the term 'logic' in a much narrower sense, so as to apply it only to what is sometimes called 'elementary logic,' i.e., to the sentential calculus and the (restricted) predicate calculus.
13. Cf. here, however, Tarski [3], pp. 5 f.
14. The method of construction we are going to outline can be applied – with appropriate changes – to all formalized languages that are known at the present time; although it does not follow that a language could not be constructed to which this method would not apply.
15. In carrying through this idea a certain technical difficulty arises. A sentential function may contain an arbitrary number of free variables; and the logical nature of the notion of satisfaction varies with this number. Thus, the notion in question when applied to functions with one variable is a binary relation between these functions and single objects; when applied to functions with two variables it becomes a ternary relation between functions and couples of objects; and so on. Hence, strictly speaking, we are confronted, not with one notion of satisfaction, but with infinitely many notions; and it turns out that these notions cannot be defined independently of each other, but must all be introduced simultaneously.

    To overcome this difficulty, we employ the mathematical notion of an infinite sequence (or, possibly, of a finite sequence with an arbitrary number of terms). We agree to regard satisfaction, not as a many-termed relation between sentential functions and an indefinite number of objects, but as a binary relation between functions and sequences of objects. Under this assumption the formulation of a general and precise definition of satisfaction no longer presents any difficulty; and a true sentence can now be defined as one which is satisfied by every sequence.
16. To define recursively the notion of satisfaction, we have to apply a certain form of recursive definition which is not admitted in the object-language. Hence the 'essential richness' of the meta-language may simply consist in admitting this type of definition. On the other hand, a general method is known which makes it possible to eliminate all recursive definitions and to replace them by normal, explicit ones. If we try to apply this method to the definition of satisfaction, we see that we have either to introduce into the meta-language variables of

a higher logical type than those which occur in the object-language; or else to assume axiomatically in the meta-language the existence of classes that are more comprehensive than all those whose existence can be established in the object-language. See here Tarski [2], pp. 393 ff., and Tarski [5], p. 7.

17. Due to the development of modern logic, the notion of mathematical proof has undergone a far-reaching simplification. A sentence of a given formalized discipline is provable if it can be obtained from the axioms of this discipline by applying certain simple and purely formal rules of inference, such as those of detachment and substitution. Hence to show that all provable sentences are true, it suffices to prove that all the sentences accepted as axioms are true, and that the rules of inference when applied to true sentences yield new true sentences; and this usually presents no difficulty.

    On the other hand, in view of the elementary nature of the notion of provability, a precise definition of this notion requires only rather simple logical devices. In most cases, those logical devices which are available in the formalized discipline itself (to which the notion of provability is related) are more than sufficient for this purpose. We know, however, that as regards the definition of truth just the opposite holds. Hence, as a rule, the notions of truth and provability cannot coincide; and since every provable sentence is true, there must be true sentences which are not provable.

18. Thus the theory of truth provides us with a general method for consistency proofs for formalized mathematical disciplines. It can be easily realized, however, that a consistency proof obtained by this method may possess some intuitive value – i.e., may convince us, or strengthen our belief, that the discipline under consideration is actually consistent – only in case we succeed in defining truth in terms of a meta-language which does not contain the object-language as a part (cf. here a remark in Section 9). For only in this case the deductive assumptions of the meta-language may be intuitively simpler and more obvious than those of the object-language – even though the condition of 'essential richness' will be formally satisfied. Cf. here also Tarski [3], p. 7.

    The incompleteness of a comprehensive class of formalized disciplines constitutes the essential content of a fundamental theorem of K. Gödel; cf. Gödel [1], pp. 187 ff. The explanation of the fact that the theory of truth leads so directly to Gödel's theorem is rather simple. In deriving Gödel's result from the theory of truth we make an essential use of the fact that the definition of truth cannot be given in a meta-language which is only as 'rich' as the object-language (cf. note 17); however, in establishing this fact, a method of reasoning has been applied which is very closely related to that used (for the first time) by Gödel. It may be added that Gödel was clearly guided in his proof by certain intuitive considerations regarding the notion of truth, although this notion does not occur in the proof explicitly; cf. Gödel [1], pp. 174 f.

19. The notions of designation and definition lead respectively to the antinomies of Grelling-Nelson and Richard (cf. note 9). To obtain an antinomy for the notion of satisfaction, we construct the following expression:

    The sentential function X does not satisfy X.

    A contradiction arises when we consider the question whether this expression, which is clearly a sentential function, satisfies itself or not.

20. All notions mentioned in this section can be defined in terms of satisfaction. We can say, e.g., that a given term designates a given object if this object satisfies the sentential function '*x is identical with T*' where '*T*' stands for the given term. Similarly, a sentential function is said to define a given object if the latter is the only object which satisfies this function. For a definition of consequence see Tarski [4], and for that of synonymity – Carnap [2].
21. General semantics is the subject of Carnap [2]. Cf. here also remarks in Tarski [2], pp. 388 f.
22. Cf. various quotations in Ness [1], pp. 13 f.
23. The names of persons who have raised objections will not be quoted here, unless their objections have appeared in print.
24. It should be emphasized, however, that as regards the question of an alleged vicious circle the situation would not change even if we took a different point of view, represented, e.g., in Carnap [2]; i.e., if we regarded the specification of conditions under which sentences of a language are true as an essential part of the description of this language. On the other hand, it may be noticed that the point of view represented in the text does not exclude the possibility of using truth-tables in a deductive development of logic. However, these tables are to be regarded then merely as a formal instrument for checking the provability of certain sentences; and the symbols '*T*' and '*F*' which occur in them and which are usually considered abbreviations of '*true*' and '*false*' should not be interpreted in any intuitive way.
25. Cf. Juhos [1]. I must admit that I do not clearly understand von Juhos' objections and do not know how to classify them; therefore, I confine myself here to certain points of a formal character. Von Juhos does not seem to know my definition of truth; he refers only to an informal presentation in Tarski [3] where the definition has not been given at all. If he knew the actual definition, he would have to change his argument. However, I have to doubt that he would discover in this definition some 'defects' as well. For he believes he has proved that 'on ground of principle it is impossible to give such a definition at all.'
26. The phrases '*p is true*' and '*p is the case*' (or better '*it is true that p*' and '*it is the case that p*') are sometimes used in informal discussions, mainly for stylistic reasons; but they are considered then as synonymous with the sentence represented by '*p*'. On the other hand, as far as I understand the situation, the phrases in question cannot be used by von Juhos synonymously with '*p*'; for otherwise the replacement of (T) by (T′) or (T″) would not constitute any 'improvement.'
27. Cf. the discussion of this problem in Kokoszyńska [1], pp. 161 ff.
28. Most authors who have discussed my work on the notion of truth are of the opinion that my definition does conform with the classical conception of this notion; see, e.g. Kotarbiński [2] and Scholz [1].
29. Cf. Ness [1]. Unfortunately, the results of that part of Ness' research which is especially relevant for our problem are not discussed in his book; compare p. 148, footnote 1.
30. Though I have heard this opinion several times, I have seen it in print only once and, curiously enough, in a work which does not have a philosophical character – in fact, in Hilbert-Bernays [1], Vol. II, p. 269 (where, by the way, it is not expressed as any kind of objection). On the other hand, I have not found any

remark to this effect in discussions of my work by professional philosophers (cf. note 1).

31. Cf. Gonseth [1], pp. 187 f.
32. See Nagel [1], and Nagel [2], pp. 471 f. A remark which goes, perhaps, in the same direction is also to be found in Weinberg [1], p. 77; cf., however, his earlier remarks, pp. 75 f.
33. Such a tendency was evident in earlier works of Carnap (see, e.g., Carnap [1], especially Part V) and in writings of other members of The Vienna Circle. Cf. here Kokoszyńska [1] and Weinberg [1].
34. For other results obtained with the help of the theory of truth see Gödel [2]; Tarski [2], pp. 401 ff.; and Tarski [5], pp. 111 f.
35. An object – e.g., a number or a set of numbers – is said to be definable (in a given formalism) if there is a sentential function which defines it; cf. note 20. Thus, the term 'definable,' though of a meta-mathematical (semantic) origin, is purely mathematical as to its extension, for it expresses a property (denotes a class) of mathematical objects. In consequence, the notion of definability can be re-defined in purely mathematical terms, though not within the formalized discipline to which this notion refers; however, the fundamental idea of the definition remains unchanged. Cf. here – also for further bibliographic references – Tarski [1]; various other results concerning definability can also be found in the literature, e.g., in Hilbert-Bernays [1] Vol. 1, pp. 354 ff., 369 ff., 456 ff., etc., and in Lindenbaum-Tarski [1]. It may be noticed that the term 'definable' is sometimes used in another, meta-mathematical (but not semantic), sense; this occurs, for instance, when we say that a term is definable in other terms (on the basis of a given axiom system). For a definition of a model of an axiom system see Tarski [4].

Bibliography

Only the books and articles actually referred to in the paper will be listed here.

Aristotle [1]. *Metaphysica* (*Works*, Vol. VIII). English translation by W. D. Ross, Oxford, 1908.

Carnap, R. [1]. *Logical Syntax of Language*, London and New York, 1937.

Carnap, R. [2]. *Introduction to Semantics*, Cambridge, 1942.

Gödel, K. [1]. 'Über formal unentscheidbare Sätze der *Principia Mathematica* und verwandter Systeme, I', *Monatshefte für Mathematik und Physik*, Vol. XXXVIII, 1931, pp. 173–198.

Gödel, K. [2]. 'Über die Länge von Beweisen', *Ergebnisse eines mathematischen Kolloquiums*, Vol. VII, 1936, pp. 23–24.

Gonseth, F. [1], 'Le Congrès Descartes Questions de Philosophie scientifique', *Revue thomiste*, Vol. XLIV, 1938, pp. 183–193.

Grelling, K., and Nelson, L. [1]. 'Bemerkungen zu den Paradoxien von Russell und Burali-Forti', *Abhandlungen der Fries'schen Schule*, Vol. II (new series), 1908, pp. 301–334.

Hofstadter, A. [1]. 'On Semantic Problems', *The Journal of Philosophy*, Vol. XXXV, 1938, pp. 225–232.

Hilbert, D., and Bernays, P. [1]. *Grundlagen der Mathematik*, 2 vols., Berlin, 1934–1939.

Juhos, B. von. [1]. 'The Truth of Empirical Statements', *Analysis*, Vol. IV, 1937, pp. 65–70.

Kokoszyńska, M. [1]. 'Über den absoluten Wahrheitsbegriff und einige andere semantische Begriffe', *Erkenntnis*, 6, 1936, pp. 143–165.

Kokoszyńska, M. [2]. 'Syntax, Semantik und Wissenschaftslogik,' *Actes du Congrès International de Philosophie Scientifique*, Vol. III, Paris, 1936, pp. 9–14.

Kotarbiński, T. [1]. *Elementy teorji poznania, logiki formalnej i metodologji nauk* (*Elements of Epistemology, Formal Logic, and the Methodology of Sciences*, in Polish), Lwów, 1929.

Kotarbiński, T. [2]. 'W sprawie pojęcia prawdy' ('*Concerning the Concept of Truth*,' in Polish), *Przegląd filozoficzny*, Vol. XXXVII, pp. 85–91.

Lindenbaum, A., and Tarski, A. [1]. 'Über die Beschränktheit der Ausdrucksmittel deduktiver Theorien.' *Ergebnisse eines mathematischen Kolloquiums*, vol. VII, 1936, pp. 15–23.

Nagel, E. [1]. Review of Hofstadter [1]. *The Journal of Symbolic Logic*, vol. III, 1938, p. 90.

Nagel, E. [2]. Review of Carnap [2]. *The Journal of Philosophy*, vol. XXXIX, 1942, pp. 468–473.

Ness, A. [1]. '"Truth" As Conceived by Those Who Are Not Professional Philosophers.' *Skrifter utgitt av Det Norske Videnskaps-Akademi i Oslo, II. Hist.-Filos. Klasse*, vol. IV, Oslo, 1938.

Neurath, O. [1]. 'Erster Internationaler Kongress für Einheit der Wissenschaft in Paris 1935.' *Erkenntnis*, vol. V, 1935, pp. 377–406.

Russell, B. [1]. *An Inquiry Into Meaning and Truth*. New York, 1940.

Scholz, H. [1]. Review of *Studia philosophica*, vol. I. *Deutsche Literaturzeitung*, vol. LVIII, 1937, pp. 1914–1917.

Tarski, A. [1]. 'Sur les ensembles définissables de nombres réels. I.' *Fundamenta mathematicae*, vol. XVII, 1931, pp. 210–239.

Tarski, A. [2]. 'Der Wahrheitsbegriff in den formalisierten Sprachen.' (German translation of a book in Polish, 1933.) *Studia philosophica*, vol. I, 1935, pp. 261–405.

Tarski, A. [3]. 'Grundlegung der wissenschaftlichen Semantik.' *Actes du Congrès International de Philosophie Scientifique*, vol. III, Paris, 1936, pp. 1–8.

Tarski, A. [4]. 'Über den Begriff der logischen Folgerung.' *Actes du Congrès International de Philosophie Scientifique*, vol. VII, Paris, 1937, pp. 1–11.

Tarski, A. [5]. 'On Undecidable Statements in Enlarged Systems of Logic and the Concept of Truth.' *The Journal of Symbolic Logic*, vol. IV, 1939, pp. 105–112.

Tarski, A. [6]. *Introduction to Logic*. New York, 1941.

Weinberg, J. [1]. Review of *Studia philosophica*, vol. I. *The Philosophical Review*, vol. XLVII, pp. 70–77.

Chapter 19

Tarski's Theory of Truth*

H. Field

In the early 1930s there was prevalent, among scientifically minded philosophers, the view that semantic notions such as the notions of truth and denotation were illegitimate: that they could not or should not be incorporated into a scientific conception of the world. But when Tarski's work on truth became known, all this changed. Popper reports: 'As a result of Tarski's teaching, I no longer hesitate to speak of "truth" and "falsity"'[1]; and Popper's reaction was widely shared.[2]

A philosopher who shared Popper's reaction to Tarski's discoveries would presumably argue as follows. 'What Tarski did was to define the term 'true', using in his definitions only terms that are clearly acceptable. In particular, he did not employ any undefined semantic terms in his definitions. So Tarski's work should make the term 'true' acceptable even to someone who is initially suspicious of semantic terms.'

This contention has an initial plausibility, but I will argue that it is radically wrong. My contrary claim will be that Tarski succeeded in reducing the notion of truth *to certain other semantic notions*; but that he did not in any way explicate these other notions, so that his results ought to make the word 'true' acceptable only to someone who already regarded these other semantic notions as acceptable.

By claiming that Tarski merely reduced truth to other semantic notions, I don't mean to suggest that his results on truth are trivial. On the contrary, I think that they are extremely important, and have applications not only to mathematics but also to linguistics and to more directly philosophical problems about realism and objectivity. I think, however, that the real value of Tarski's discoveries for linguistics and philosophy is widely misunderstood, and I hope to eradicate the most central misunderstandings by clarifying and defending the claim that Tarski merely reduced truth to other semantic notions.

First published in *The Journal of Philosophy*, Vol. LXIX, No. 13, July 13, 1972.

I

I believe that Tarski presented his semantic theory in a very misleading way, one which has encouraged the misinterpretations just alluded to. In this section I will present Tarski's theory as I think he should have presented it. However, I do not expect instant agreement that this new way is better than the old, and so I will use the name 'Tarski*' for a logician who gave the sort of semantic theory I will now sketch. Later in the paper I will compare Tarski*s semantics to the semantics that the real Tarski actually gave; by doing this I will cast light on the issues raised in my introductory paragraphs.

In sketching Tarski*s theory, I will focus my attention on a particular object language L. The language L that I choose will be a quantificational language with names ('c_1', 'c_2', . . .), one-place function symbols ('f_1', 'f_2', . . .), and one-place predicates ('p_1', 'p_2', . . .). The language of course cannot be viewed as an 'uninterpreted' language, i.e., as just a bunch of strings of meaningless marks, for then there would be no truth to worry about. Instead, the language should be regarded as something that people actually speak or write; and it is because the speakers speak or write the way they do that the words of the language have the meaning they have.[3]

Initially I will follow Tarski in supposing that in L 'the sense of every expression is unambiguously determined by its form,'[4] i.e., that whenever two speakers use the same name (or one speaker uses it on two occasions) they are referring to the same thing, that whenever two speakers use the same sentence either both are saying something true or neither is, etc. In these circumstances it makes sense to speak of the names of the language denoting things (a name denotes whatever the users of the name refer to) and the sentences being true or false (true when speakers who use it say something true by so doing). The more general situation, in which there are expressions whose 'sense' is not determined wholly by their form, will be dealt with later. (We'll see that it is one of the advantages of Tarski*s semantics that it can easily handle this more general situation.)

The syntax of L can be given by two recursive definitions: first we define the *singular terms* by saying that all names and variables are singular terms, and a function symbol followed by a singular term is a singular term; then we define the *formulas* by saying that a predicate followed by a singular term is a formula, as is the negation of a formula, the conjunction of two formulas, and the universal quantification of a formula with any variable. The *sentences*, or *closed formulas*, are then singled out in the usual way.

Now we can proceed to Tarski*s semantics. Rather than characterize truth directly, we characterize it relative to some assignment of objects to the variables, say s_k to 'x_k'. The idea is going to be to treat the variables, or at least the free variables, as sort of 'temporary names' for the objects assigned to them. So we proceed by fixing a sequence $s = <s_1, s_2, \ldots>$ of objects, to be assigned to 'x_1', 'x_2', . . ., respectively; and we want to say what it is for a formula to be true$_s$, i.e., true relative to the assignment s. As a preliminary we say what it is for a term to denote$_s$ an object, i.e., to denote it relative to the assignment s. The denotation of 'x_k' relative to s is evidently s_k, for this is the object assigned to 'x_k'. But what is the denotation relative to s of 'c_k'? Evidently what objects are assigned to the variables here is irrelevant, and the denotation$_s$ of 'c_k' is some fixed object that users of the language refer to when they use the name 'c_k'. Just what this object is depends on facts we have not yet been given about the use of 'c_k'. Similarly there are facts we have not yet been given about the use of 'p_k' and 'f_k' which we need in order to fix the truth value of sentences containing them. For 'p_k' the relevant facts concern the extension of the predicate – what objects the predicate *applies to* – for it is this which affects the truth value of all utterances containing 'p_k'. For 'f_k', the relevant facts concern what pairs of objects *fulfill* that function symbol – in the sense that the pair <John Adams, John Quincy Adams> and every other father-son pair fulfill the function symbol 'father of'.

With these points in mind it is now easy to give an inductive characterization of denotation$_s$:

T1 (A) 1. 'x_k' denotes$_s$ s_k.
2. 'c_k' denotes$_s$ what it denotes.
3. $\ulcorner f_k(e) \urcorner$ denotes$_s$ an object a if and only if
(i) there is an object b that e denotes,
and (ii) 'f_k' is fulfilled by $<a,b>$.

(Here 'e' is a variable ranging over expressions of L.) Similarly we define 'true$_s$' for formulas – what Tarski calls satisfaction of a formula by s:

(B) 1. $\ulcorner p_k(e) \urcorner$ is true$_s$ if and only if
(i) there is an object a that e denotes$_s$
and (ii) 'p_k' applies to a.
2. $\ulcorner \sim e \urcorner$ is true$_s$ if and only if e is not true$_s$.
3. $\ulcorner e_1 \wedge e_2 \urcorner$ is true$_s$ if and only if e_1 is true$_s$ and so is e_2.
4. $\ulcorner \forall x_k(e) \urcorner$ is true$_s$ if and only if for each sequence s^* that differs from s at the kth place at most, e is true$_{s^*}$.

This completes the characterization of truth relative to an assignment of objects to the variables. In the case of sentences it is easily seen that we may get the same results whatever such assignment we pick; we can say

(C) A sentence is true if and only if it is true$_s$ for some (or all) s.

This completes my elaboration of Tarski*s 'truth definition' T1 for L – or his *truth characterization* (TC), as I prefer to call it. What is its philosophical significance? The obvious answer, and the correct one, I think, is that the

TC reduces one semantic notion to three others. It explains what it is for a sentence to be true in terms of certain semantic features of the primitive components of the sentence: in terms of what it is for a name to denote something, what it is for a predicate to apply to something, and what it is for a function symbol to be fulfilled by some pair of things. It is convenient to introduce the expression 'primitively denotes' as follows: every name *primitively denotes* what it denotes; every predicate and every function symbol *primitively denotes* what it applies to or is fulfilled by; and no complex expression primitively denotes anything. In this terminology, what T1 does is to explain truth in terms of primitive denotation. Similarly we can explain denotation for arbitrary closed singular terms [such as '$f_1(c_1)$'] in terms of primitive denotation, i.e., in terms of the semantic features of the names and function symbols from which the complex singular term is composed – we merely say that a closed singular term denotes an object a if it denotes$_s$ a for some (or all) s, where denotation$_s$ is defined as before. We see then that *Tarski*s semantics explains the semantic properties of complex expressions* (e.g., truth value for sentences, denotation for complex singular terms) *in terms of semantic properties of their primitive components.*

To explain truth in terms of primitive denotation is, I think, an important task. It certainly doesn't answer *every* question that anyone would ever want answered about truth, but for many purposes it is precisely what we need. For instance, in model theory we are interested in such questions as: given a set Γ of sentences, is there any way to choose the denotations of the primitives of the language so that every sentence of Γ will come out true given the usual semantics for the logical connectives?[5] For questions such as this, what we need to know is how the truth value of a whole sentence depends on the denotations of its primitive nonlogical parts, and that is precisely what T1 tells us. So *at least for model-theoretic purposes*, Tarski*s TC is precisely the kind of explication of truth we need.

I want now to return to a point I mentioned earlier, about Tarski's restriction to languages in which 'the sense of every expression is unambiguously determined by its form.' Natural languages are full of expressions that do not meet this requirement. For instance, different tokens of 'John takes grass' can differ in 'sense' – e.g., one token may be uttered in saying that John Smith smokes marijuana, and another may be uttered in saying that John Jones steals lawn material, and these differences may give rise to differences of truth value in the tokens. (I say that a complete[6] token of a sentence is true if the person who spoke or wrote that token said something true by so doing; I also say that a name token denotes an object if the person who spoke or wrote the token referred to the object by so doing.) The prevalence of such examples in natural languages raises the question of whether Tarski's type of semantic theory is applicable to languages in which the sense is *not* determined by the form; for if the answer is no, then Davidson's very worthwhile project[7] of giving truth characterizations for natural languages seems doomed from the start.

It seems clear that if we stick to the kind of TC that Tarski actually gave (see next section), there is no remotely palatable way of extending TC's to sentences like 'John takes grass'. But if we use TC's like T1 there is no difficulty at all. The only point about languages containing 'John' or 'grass' or 'I' or 'you' is that for such languages 'true', 'denotes', and other semantic terms make no clear sense as applied to expression types; they make sense only as applied to tokens. For this reason we have to interpret clause (B)2 of T1 as meaning

> A token of $\ulcorner \sim e \urcorner$ is true$_s$ if and only if the token of e that it contains is not true$_s$,

and similarly for the other clauses. Once we interpret our TC in this way in terms of tokens, i.e., individual occasions of utterance, that TC works perfectly: someone who utters 'John is sick' (or 'I am sick') says something true if and only if his token of 'sick' applies to the person he refers to by 'John' (or by 'I'); and the fact that other speakers (or this speaker on other occasions) sometimes refer to different things when they use 'John' (or 'I') is beside the point.

This analysis leaves entirely out of account the ways in which 'I' and 'John' differ: it leaves out of account, for instance, the fact that a token of 'I' always denotes the speaker who produced it. But that is no objection to the analysis, for the analysis purports merely to explain truth in terms of primitive denotation; it does not purport to say anything about primitive denotation, and the differences between 'I' and 'John' (or their analogues in a language like L) are purely differences of how they denote. (The word 'I' denotes according to the simple rule mentioned two sentences back; 'John' denotes according to much more complex rules that I have no idea how to formulate.)

Of course, the fact that a theory of denotation for a word like 'I' is so simple and obvious, makes it possible to alter the TC so that the theory of denotation for such a word is built into the TC itself – such a course is adopted, for instance, by Davidson at the end of 'Truth and Meaning.' I myself prefer to preserve the analogies of the word 'I' to words that function less systematically, e.g., 'we', 'she', and 'John'. How one treats 'I' is more or less a matter of taste; but the less systematic words I've just mentioned cannot be handled in the way that Davidson handles 'I', and the only reasonable way I can see to handle them is the way I have suggested: use a truth characterization like T1 (except stated in terms of tokens rather than types), and leave it to a separate theory of primitive denotation to explain the relevant differences between tokens of 'John' that denote John Adams and tokens of 'John' that denote John Lennon, and between tokens of 'bank' that apply to things along rivers and tokens of 'bank' that apply to the Chase Manhattan.[8]

There are other advantages to T1 besides its ability to handle ambiguous sentences, i.e., sentences for which the sense is not determined by the form. For instance, Tarski required that the vocabulary of the language be fixed once and for all; but if we decide to give truth characterizations of type T1, this is unnecessary: all that is required is that the general structure of the language be fixed, e.g., that the semantic categories[9] (name, one-place predicate, etc.) be held constant. In other words, if a language already contained proper names, the invention of a new name to baptize an object will not invalidate the old TC; though introduction of a name into a hitherto nameless language will.

To show this, we have merely to reformulate the given TC so that it does not rely on the actual vocabulary that the language contains at a given time, but works also for sentences containing new names, one-place predicates, etc., that speakers of the language might later introduce. To do this is trivial: we define denotation$_s$ by

1. The *k*th variable denotes$_s$ s_k.
2. If e_1 is a name, it denotes$_s$ what it denotes.
3. If e_1 is a singular term and e_2 is a function symbol, then $\ulcorner e_2(e_1)\urcorner$ denotes$_s$ *a* if and only if
   (i) as before,
   and (ii) e_2 is fulfilled by $\langle a,b \rangle$.

and we can generalize the definition of truth$_s$ in a similar manner.[10] This shows that, in giving a TC, there is no need to utilize the particular vocabulary used at one temporal stage of a language, for we can instead give a more general TC which can be incorporated into a diachronic theory of the language (and can also be applied directly to other languages of a similar structure). *If*, that is, we accept the modification of Tarski proposed in this section.

II

The kind of truth characterization advocated in the previous section differs from the kind of TC Tarski offered in one important respect. Tarski stated the policy 'I shall not make use of any semantical concept if I am not able previously to reduce it to other concepts' (CTFL 152/3), and this policy is flagrantly violated by T1 : T1 utilizes unreduced notions of proper names denoting things, predicates applying to things, and function symbols being fulfilled by things.

Tarski's truth characterizations, unlike T1, accorded with his stated policy: they did not contain any semantic terms like 'applies to' or 'denotes'. How did Tarski achieve this result? Very simply: first, he translated every name, predicate, and function symbol of L into English; then he utilized these translations in order to reformulate clauses 2 and 3(ii) of part (A) of the definition and clause 1(ii) of part (B). For simplicity, let's use '$\bar{c}_1$', '$\bar{c}_2$', etc. as abbreviations for the English expressions that are the translations of the words 'c_1', 'c_2', . . . of L: e.g.: if L is simplified German and 'c_1' is 'Deutschland', then '$\bar{c}_1$' is an abbreviation for 'Germany'. Similarly, let '$\bar{f}_1$' abbreviate the translation into English of the word 'f_1' of L, and let '$\bar{p}_1$' abbreviate the translation of 'p_1' into English. Then Tarski's reformulated truth definition will read as follows:

T2 (A) 1. as before
2. 'c_k' denotes$_s$ $\bar{c}_k$
3. $\ulcorner f_k(e) \urcorner$ denotes$_s$ a if and only if
(i) as before
(ii) a is $\bar{f}_k(b)$
(B) 1. $\ulcorner p_k(e) \urcorner$ is true$_s$ if and only if
(i) as before
(ii) $\bar{p}_k(a)$
2–4. as before.
(C) as before.

What T2 is like depends of course on the precise character of the translations of the primitives that are utilized. For instance, if we translate 'c_1' as 'the denotation of "c_1"', translate 'p_1' as 'is something that "p_1" applies to', etc., then T2 becomes identical with T1. This of course is *not* what Tarski intended. What Tarski intended is that T2 not contain unexplicated semantic terms, and if we are to get this result we must not employ any semantic terms in our translations.[11]

But other restrictions on translations are also necessary: if we were to translate 'Deutschland' as 'Bertrand Russell', a truth characterization T2 that was based on this translation would grossly misrepresent L. In order to state the matter more generally, I introduce the term 'coreferential': two singular terms are coreferential if they denote the same thing; two predicative expressions are coreferential if they have the same extension, i.e., if they apply to the same things; and two functional expressions are coreferential if they are fulfilled by the same pairs. It is then easily seen that any departure from coreferentiality in translation will bring errors into T2. for instance, suppose we translate foreign predicate 'glub' as 'yellow', and suppose 'glub' and yellow are not *precisely* coreferential; then clause (B)$_1$ will say falsely that 'glub(x)' is true of just those objects which are yellow.

Let us say, then, that

(1) An adequate translation of a primitive e_1 of L into English is an expression e_2 of English such that
(i) e_1 and e_2 are coreferential, and
(ii) e_2 contains no semantic terms.

This notion of an adequate translation is of course a semantic notion that Tarski did not reduce to nonsemantic terms. But that is no objection to his characterization T2 (at least, it isn't obviously an objection), for the notion of an adequate translation is never built into the truth characterization and is not, properly speaking, part of a theory of truth. On Tarski's view we need to adequately translate the object language into the metalanguage in order to give an adequate theory of truth for the object language; this means that the notion of an adequate translation is employed in the methodology of giving truth theories, but it is not employed in the truth theories themselves.

In what follows I shall assume that the language L with which we are dealing is so related to English that all its primitives *can* be adequately translated into English, according to the standards of adequacy set forth in (1). (This is another restriction that we avoid if we give TC's of the type T1; quite a significant restriction, I think.) If we then suppose that the translation given ('$\bar{c}_1$' for 'c_1', etc.) is one of the adequate translations, then T2, like T1, is a correct recursive characterization of truth for the language L. There is, of course, a simple procedure for transforming recursive characterizations such as these into explicit characterizations. To carry the procedure through in these cases would be pretty complicated, but it could be done; so we could regard T1 (or T2) as implicitly specifying a metalinguistic formula '$A_1(e)$' (or '$A_2(e)$'), and saying that an utterance e of L is true if and only if $A_1(e)$ (or $A_2(e)$). If we regard T1 and T2 as written in this form, then the key difference between them is that '$A_1(e)$' *contains semantic terms and* '$A_2(e)$' *does not*. The question then arises: is the fact that '$A_2(e)$' does not contain semantic terms an advantage of T2 over T1? If so, then *why* is it an advantage?

In order to discuss the possible advantages of T2 over T1, I think we have to go beyond mathematical considerations and focus instead on linguistic and other 'philosophical' matters. It is not enough to say that T2 *defines* truth without utilizing semantic terms, whereas T1 defines it only in other semantic terms: this is not enough until we say something more about the purpose of definition. If the purpose of giving a 'definition' of truth is to enable you to do model theory, then the elimination of semantic terms from T1 gives no advantage. For what purpose do we want definitions for which the elimination of semantic terms is useful?

One purpose to which definitions are sometimes put is in explaining the meaning of a word. This of course is very vague, but I think it is clear enough to enable us to recognize that neither T1 nor T2 has very much to do with explaining the meaning of the word 'true'. This is especially obvious for T2: a T2-type truth definition works for a single language only, and so if it 'explains the meaning of' the word 'true' as applied to that language, then for *any* two languages L_1 and L_2, the word 'true' means something different when applied to utterances of L_1 than it means when applied to utterances of L_2! I make this point not in criticism of T2, but in criticism of the idea that the significance of T2 can be explained by saying that it 'gives the meaning of' the word 'true'.

We still need to know what purpose a truth characterization like T1 or T2 could serve that would give someone reason to think that a TC without unexplicated semantic terms would be better than a TC with unexplicated semantic terms. Tarski hints at such a purpose in one place in his writings, where he is discussing the importance of being able to define the word 'true', as opposed to merely introducing axioms to establish the basic properties of truth. If a definition of semantic notions such as truth could not be given, Tarski writes,

> . . . it would then be difficult to bring [semantics] into harmony with the postulates of the unity of science of of physicalism (since the concepts of semantics would be neither logical nor physical concepts).[12]

This remark seems to me to be of utmost importance in evaluating the philosophical significance of Tarski's work, and so I will now say something about the general philosophical issues it raises. When this is done we will be in a better position to understand Tarski's choice of T2 over T1.

III

In the early 1930s many philosophers believed that the notion of truth could not be incorporated into a scientific conception of the world. I think that the main rationale for this view is hinted at in the remark of Tarski's that I quoted at the end of the last section, and what I want to do now is to elaborate a bit on Tarski's hint.

In the remark I have quoted, Tarski put a heavy stress on the doctrine of physicalism: the doctrine that chemical facts, biological facts, psychological facts, and semantical facts, are all explicable (in principle) in terms of physical facts. The doctrine of physicalism functions as a high-level empirical hypothesis, a hypothesis that no small number of experiments can force us to give up. It functions, in other words, in much the same way as the doctrine of mechanism (that all facts are explicable in terms of *mechanical* facts) once functioned: this latter doctrine has now been universally rejected, but it was given up only by the development of a well-accepted theory (Maxwell's) which described phenomena (electromagnetic radiation and the electromagnetic field) that were very difficult to account for mechanically, and by amassing a great deal of experiment and theory that together made it quite conclusive that mechanical explanations of these phenomena (e.g., by positing 'the ether') would never get off the ground. Mechanism has been empirically refuted; its heir is physicalism, which allows as 'basic' not only facts about mechanics, but facts about other branches of physics as well.[13] I believe that physicists a hundred years ago were justified in accepting mechanism, and that, similarly, physicalism should be accepted until we have convincing evidence that there is a realm of phenomena it leaves out of account. Even if there *does* turn out to be such a realm of phenomena, the only way we'll ever come to know that there is, is by repeated efforts and repeated failures to explain these phenomena in physical terms.

That's my view, anyway, but there are philosophers who think that it is in order to reject physicalism now. One way of rejecting physicalism is called 'vitalism': it is the view that there are irreducibly biological facts, i.e., biological facts that aren't explicable in nonbiological terms (and hence, not in physical terms). Physicalism and vitalism are incompatible, and it is because of this incompatibility that the doctrine of physicalism has the methodological importance it has for biology. Suppose, for instance, that a certain woman has two sons, one hemophilic and one not. Then, according to standard genetic accounts of hemophilia, the ovum from which one of these sons was produced must have contained a gene for hemophilia, and the ovum from which the other son was produced must not have contained such a gene. But now the doctrine of physicalism tells us that there must have been a *physical* difference between the two ova that explains why the first son had hemophilia and the second one didn't, if the standard genetic account is to be accepted. We should not rest content with a special biological predicate 'has-a-hemophilic-gene' – rather, we should look for nonbiological facts (chemical facts; and ultimately, physical facts) that underlie the correct application of this predicate. That at least is what the principle of physicalism tells us, and it can hardly be doubted that this principle has motivated a great deal of very profitable research into the chemical foundations of genetics.

So much for vitalism; now let us turn to other irreducibility doctrines that are opposed to physicalism. One such irreducibility doctrine is Cartesianism: it is the doctrine that there are irreducibly mental facts. Another irreducibility doctrine has received much less attention than either vitalism or Cartesianism, but it is central to our present concerns: this doctrine, which might be called 'semanticalism,' is the doctrine that there are irreducibly semantic facts. The semanticalist claims, in other words, that semantic phenomena (such as the fact that 'Schnee' refers to snow) must be accepted as primitive, in precisely the way that electromagnetic phenomena are accepted as primitive (by those who accept Maxwell's equations and reject the ether); and in precisely the way that biological phenomena and mental phenomena are accepted as primitive by vitalists and Cartesians. Semanticalism, like Cartesianism and vitalism, posits nonphysical primitives, and as a physicalist I believe that all three doctrines must be rejected.

There are two general sorts of strategy that can be taken in rejecting semanticalism, or Cartesianism, or vitalism. One strategy, illustrated two paragraphs back in discussing vitalism, is to try to explicate the terms of a biological theory in nonbiological terms. But there is another possible strategy, which is to argue that the biological terms are illegitimate. The second strategy seems reasonable to adopt in dealing with the following predicate of (reincarnationist) biology: '*x* has the same soul as *y*'. A physicalist would never try to find physical or chemical facts that underlie reincarnation; rather, he would reject reincarnation as a myth.

Since biological theory is as well developed as it is, we usually have a pretty good idea which biological terms require explication and which require elimination. When we turn to psychology and semantics, however, it is often not so obvious which strategy is the more promising. Thus in semantics, physicalists agree that all *legitimate* semantic terms must be explicable nonsemantically – they think in other words that there are no irreducibly semantic facts – but they disagree as to which semantic terms are legitimate. That disagreement has become fairly clear in recent years in the theory of meaning, with the work of Quine: the disagreement is between those physicalists who would look for a nonsemantic basis for terms in the theory of meaning, and those who would follow Quine in simply throwing out those terms. Our concern, however, is not with the theory of meaning, but with the theory of reference, and here the disagreement has been less clear, since there haven't been many physicalists who openly advocate getting rid of terms like 'true' and 'denotes'. There were such physicalists in the early 1930s; part of the importance of Tarski's work was to persuade them that they were on the wrong track, to persuade them that we should explicate notions in the theory of reference nonsemantically rather than simply get rid of them.

The view that we should just stop using semantic terms (here and in the rest of this paper, I mean terms in the theory of reference, such as 'true' and 'denotes' and 'applies to') draws its plausibility from the apparent difficulty of explicating these terms nonsemantically. People utter the sounds 'Electrons have rest mass but photons don't', or 'Schnee ist weiss und Gras ist grün', and we apply the word 'true' to their utterances. We don't want to say that it is a primitive and inexplicable fact about these utterances that they are true, a fact that cannot be explicated in nonsemantic terms; this is as unattractive to a physicalist as supposing that it is a primitive and inexplicable fact about an organism at a certain time that it is in pain. But how could we ever explicate in nonsemantic terms the alleged fact that these utterances are true? *Part* of the explication of the truth of 'Schnee ist weiss und Gras ist grün', presumably, would be that snow is white and grass is green. But this would only be part of the explanation, for still missing is the connection between snow being white and grass being green on the one hand, and the German utterance being true on the other hand. It is this connection that seems so difficult to explicate in a way that would satisfy a physicalist, i.e., in a way that does not involve the use of semantic terms.

If, in face of these difficulties, we were ever to conclude that it was *impossible* to explicate the notions of truth and denotation in non-semantic terms, we would have either to give up these semantic terms or else to reject physicalism. It seems to me that that is essentially what Tarski is saying in the quotation at the end of the last section, and I have tried to make it plausible by sketching analogies to areas other than semantics. Tarski's view, however, was that, for certain languages at least, semantic terms *are* explicable nonsemantically, and that truth definitions like T2 provide the required explication. It is understandable that as far as *philosophical* purposes go Tarski should think that T1 leaves something to be desired: after all, it merely explicates truth in terms of other semantic concepts; but what good does that do if those other concepts can't be explicated nonsemantically? T2, then, has a strong prima facie advantage over T1. In the next section I will show that it is not a genuine advantage.

IV

The apparent advantage of T2 over T1, I have stressed, is that it appears to reduce truth to nonsemantic terms; and I *think* this is why Tarski wanted to give a truth definition like T2 rather than like T1. This interpretation makes sense of Tarski's remark about physicalism, and it also explains why someone who was certainly not interested in 'meaning analysis' as that is usually conceived would have wanted to give 'definitions' of truth and would emphasize that, in these 'definitions,' 'I will not make use of any semantical concept if I am not able previously to reduce it to other concepts.' In any case, the problem of reducing truth is a very important problem, one which T1 and T2 provide a partial solution to, and one which T2 *might* be thought to provide a full solution to; and it is not at all clear what *other* interesting problems T2 could be thought to solve better than T1.

In Tarski's own exposition of his theory of truth, Tarski put very little stress on the problem of reduction or on any other problem with a clear philosophical or mathematical motivation; instead, he set up a formal criterion of adequacy for theories of truth without any serious discussion of whether or why this formal criterion is reasonable. Roughly, the criterion was this:[14]

(**M**) Any condition of the form

(2) $(\forall e)[e \text{ is true} \equiv B(e)]$

should be accepted as an adequate definition of truth if and only if it is correct and '$B(e)$' is a well-formed formula containing no semantic terms. (The quantifiers are to be taken as ranging over expressions of one particular language only.)

The 'only if' part of condition M is not something I will contest. It rules out the possibility of T1 *by itself* being an adequate truth definition; and it is right to do so, if the task of a truth definition is to reduce truth to nonsemantic terms, for T1 provides only a *partial* reduction. (To complete the reduction we need to reduce primitive denotation to nonsemantic terms.) T2, on the other hand, meets condition M; so either T2 is superior to T1 as a reduction, or else condition M is too weak and the 'if' part of it must be rejected. My own diagnosis is the latter, but the other possibility seems initially reasonable. After all, how could condition M be strengthened? We might try requiring that '$B(e)$' be not only *extensionally* equivalent to 'e is true', but *intensionally* equivalent to it; but this clearly won't do, for even if we grant that there is an intelligible notion of intensional equivalence, our concern is not with analyzing the meaning of the word 'true' but with performing a reduction. A clear and useful standard of equivalence that is stronger than extensional equivalence but not so strong as to rule out acceptable reductions is unknown at the present time, so I know no way to improve on condition M. My view is that we have a rough but useful concept of reduction which we are unable to formulate precisely; but I must admit that the alternative view, that extensional equivalence is adequate, has an initial appeal.

A closer look, however, will reveal quite conclusively that extensional equivalence is not a sufficient standard of reduction. This can be seen by looking at the concept of valence. The valence of a chemical element is an integer that is associated with that element, which represents the sort of chemical combinations that the element will enter into. What I mean by the last phrase is that it is possible – roughly, at least – to characterize which elements will combine with which others, and in what proportions they will combine, merely in terms of their valences. Because of this fact, the concept of valence is a physically important concept, and so if physicalism is correct it ought to be possible to explicate this concept in physical terms – e.g., it ought to be possible to find structural properties of the atoms of each element that determine what the valence of that element will be. Early in the twentieth century (long after the notion of valence had proved its value in enabling chemists to predict what chemical combinations there would be) this reduction of the concept of valence to the physical properties of atoms was established; the notion of valence was thus shown to be a physicalistically acceptable notion.

Now, it would have been easy for a chemist, late in the last century, to have given a 'valence definition' of the following form:

(3) $(\forall E)(\forall n)(E$ has valence $n \equiv E$ is potassium and n is $+1$, or . . . or E is sulphur and n is $-2)$

where in the blanks go a list of similar clauses, one for each element. But, though this is an extensionally correct definition of valence, it would not have been an acceptable reduction; and had it turned out that nothing else was possible – had all efforts to explain valence in terms of the structural properties of atoms proved futile – scientists would have eventually had to decide either (a) to give up valence theory, or else (b) to replace the hypothesis of physicalism by another hypothesis (chemicalism?). It is part of scientific methodology to resist doing (b); and I also think it is part of scientific methodology to resist doing (a) as long as the notion of valence is serving the purposes for which it was designed (i.e., as long as it is proving useful in helping us characterize chemical compounds in terms of their valences). But the methodology is not to resist (a) and (b) by giving lists like (3); the methodology is to look for a real reduction. This is a methodology that has proved extremely fruitful in science, and I think we'd be crazy to give it up in linguistics. *And I think we are giving up this fruitful methodology, unless we realize that we need to add theories of primitive reference to* T1 *or* T2 *if we are to establish the notion of truth as a physicalistically acceptable notion.*

I certainly haven't yet given much argument for this last claim. I *have* argued that the standard of extensional equivalence doesn't guarantee an acceptable reduction; but T2 is obviously not trivial to the extent that (3) is. What *is* true, however, is roughly that T2 minus T1 is as trivial as (3) is. One way in which this last claim can be made more precise is by remembering that really we often apply the term 'valence' not only to elements, but also to configurations of elements (at least to stable configurations that are not compounds, i.e., to radicals). Thus, if we abstract from certain physical limitations on the size of possible configurations of elements (as, in linguistics, we usually abstract from the limitations that memory, etc., impose on the lengths of possible utterances), there is an infinite number of entities to which the term 'valence' is applied. But it is an important fact about valence that the valence of a configuration of elements is determined from the valences of the elements that make it up, and from the way they're put together. Because of this, we might try to give a recursive characterization of valence. First of all, we would try to characterize all the different *structures* that configurations of elements can have (much as we try to characterize all the different grammatical structures before we give a truth definition like T1 or T2). We would then try to find rules that would enable us to determine what the valence of a complicated configuration would be, given the valences of certain less complicated configurations that make it up and the way they're put together. If we had enough such rules, we could determine the valence of a given configuration given only its structure and the valences of the elements that make it up. And if we like, we can transform our recursive characterization of valence into an explicit characterization, getting

$$\text{V1}\ (\forall c)(\forall n)\ (c \text{ has valence } n \equiv B(c,n))$$

The formula '$B(c,n)$' here employed will still contain the term 'valence', but it will contain that term only as applied to elements, not as applied to configurations. Thus our 'valence definition' V1 would characterize the valence of the complex *in terms of the valences of the simple.*

It would now be possible to eliminate the term 'valence' from '$B(c,n)$', in either of two ways. One way would be to employ a genuine reduction of the notion of valence for elements to the structural properties of atoms. The other way would be to employ the pseudo-reduction (3). It is clear that we could use (3) to give a trivial reformulation V2 of V1, which would have precisely the 'advantages' as a reduction that T2 has over T1. (V2, incidentally, would also have one of the disadvantages over V1 that T2 has over T1: V1 does not need to be overhauled when you discover or synthesize new elements, whereas V2 does.)

That is a sketch of one way that the remark I made two paragraphs back about 'T2 minus T1' could be made more precise. But it is somewhat more fruitful to develop the point slightly differently: doing this will enable me to make clearer that there is unlikely to be *any* purpose that T2 serves better than T1 (not merely that T2 is no better at reduction).

To get this result I'll go back to my original use of the term 'valence', where it applies to elements only and not to configurations. And what I will do is compare (3) not to Tarski's theory of *truth*, but to Tarski's theory of *denotation* for names; the effect of this on his theory of truth will then be considered. Tarski states his theory of denotation for names in a footnote, as follows:

> To say that the name *x* denotes a given object *a* is the same as to stipulate that the object *a* . . . satisfies a sentential function of a particular type. In colloquial language it would be a function which consists of three parts in the following order: a variable, the word 'is' and the given name *x* (CTFL 194).

This is actually only part of the theory, the part that defines denotation in terms of satisfaction; to see what the theory looks like when all semantic terms are eliminated, we must see how satisfaction is defined. The definition is given by the (A) and (B) clauses of T2, for, as I've remarked, 'satisfaction' is Tarski's name for what I've called 'truth$_s$'. What Tarski's definition of satisfaction tells us is this: for any name *N*, an object *a* satisfies the sentential function $\ulcorner x_1$ is $N\urcorner$ if and only if *a* is France and *N* is 'France' or . . . or *a* is Germany and *N* is 'Germany'. Combining this definition of satisfaction (for sentential functions of form $\ulcorner x_1$ is $N\urcorner$) with the earlier account of denotation in terms of satisfaction, we get:

(DE): To say that the name *N* denotes a given object *a* is the same as to stipulate that either *a* is France and *N* is 'France', or . . . or *a* is Germany and *N* is 'Germany'.

This is Tarski's account of denotation for English proper names. For foreign proper names, the definition of denotation in terms of satisfaction needs no modification (except that the 'is' must be replaced by a name of a foreign word, say 'ist' for German). Combining this with the definition (again given by T2) of satisfaction for foreign sentential functions like ⌜x_1 ist N⌝, we get:

(DG): To say that the name *N* denotes a given object *a* is the same as to stipulate that either *a* is France and *N* is 'Frankreich', or . . . , or *a* is Germany and *N* is 'Deutschland'.

DE and DG have not received much attention in commentaries on Tarski, but in fact they play a key role in his semantic theory; and it was no aberration on Tarski's part that he offered them as theories of denotation for English and German names, for *they satisfy criteria of adequacy exactly analogous to the criteria of adequacy that Tarski accepted for theories of truth.*[15] Nevertheless, it seems clear that DE and DG do not really reduce denotation to nonsemantic terms, any more than (3) reduces valence to nonchemical terms. What would a real explication of denotation in nonsemantic terms be like? The 'classical' answer to this question (Russell's) is that a name like 'Cicero' is 'analytically linked' to a certain description (such as 'the denouncer of Catiline'); so to explain how the name 'Cicero' denotes what it does you merely have to explain

1. the process by which it is linked to the description (presumably you bring in facts about how it was learned by its user, or facts about what is going on in the user's brain at the time of the using)
2. how the description refers to what it does

Because of (2), of course, the project threatens circularity: the project is to explain how names refer in terms of how descriptions refer; but the natural way to explain how descriptions refer is in terms of how they're built up from their significant parts,[16] and how those significant parts refer (or apply, or are fulfilled), and those significant parts will usually include names. But Russell recognized this threat of circularity, and carefully avoided it: he assumed that the primitives of the language were to be partially ordered by a relation of 'basicness,' and that each name except a most basic ('logically proper') name was to be analytically linked to a formula containing only primitives more basic than it. The most basic primitives were to be linked to the world without the intervention of other words, by the relation of acquaintance.

This classical view of how names (and other primitives) latch onto their denotations is extremely implausible in many ways (e.g., it says you can refer only to things that are definable from 'logically proper' primitives; it requires that there be certain statements, such as 'If Cicero existed then Cicero denounced Catiline', which are analytic in the sense that they are guaranteed by linguistic rules and are immune to revision by future discoveries). I conjecture that it is because of the difficulties with this classical theory, which was the only theory available at the time that Tarski wrote, that Tarski's pseudo-theories

DE and DG seemed reasonable – they weren't exciting, but if you wanted something exciting you got logically proper names. The diagnosis that any attempt to explain the relation between words and the things they are about must inevitably lead to either a wildly implausible theory (like Russell's) or a trivial theory (like Tarski's) seems to be widely accepted still; but I think that the diagnosis has become less plausible in recent years through the development of *causal* theories of denotation by Saul Kripke[17] and others. According to such theories, the facts that 'Cicero' denotes Cicero and that 'muon' applies to muons are to be explained in terms of certain kinds of causal networks between Cicero (muons) and our uses of 'Cicero' ('muon'): causal connections both of a social sort (the passing of the word 'Cicero' down to us from the original users of the name, or the passing of the word 'muon' to laymen from physicists) and of other sorts (the evidential causal connections that gave the original users of the name 'access' to Cicero and give physicists 'access' to muons). I don't think that Kripke or anyone else thinks that *purely* causal theories of primitive denotation can be developed (even for proper names of past physical objects and for natural-kind predicates); this however should not blind us to the fact that he has suggested a kind of factor involved in denotation that gives new hope to the idea of explaining the connection between language and the things it is about. It seems to me that the possibility of *some such* theory of denotation (to be deliberately very vague) is essential to the joint acceptability of physicalism and the semantic term 'denotes', and that denotation definitions like DE and DG merely obscure the need for this.

It might be objected that the purpose of DE and DG was not reduction; but what was their purpose? One answer might be that (DE) and (DG) enable us to eliminate the word 'denote' whenever it occurs. ('To explain is to show how to eliminate.') For instance,

(4) No German name now in use denotes something that does not yet exist.

would become

(4′) For any name N now in use, if N is 'Frankreich' then France already exists, and . . ., and if N is 'Deutschland' then Germany already exists.

provided that (DG) is a correct and complete list of the denotations of all those German proper names that have denotations. It seems reasonably clear that we could specify a detailed procedure for transforming sentences like (4) into materially equivalent sentences like (4′). A similar claim could be made for the 'valence definition' (3). Such a valence definition makes it possible to eliminate the word 'valence' from a large class of sentences containing it, and in a uniform way. For instance,

(5) For any elements A and B, if one atom of A combines with two of B, then the valence of A is -2 times that of B.

is materially equivalent to

> (5′) For any elements *A* and *B*, if one atom of *A* combines with two of *B*, then either *A* is sodium and *B* is sodium and +1 = −2 (+1), or . . ., or *A* is sulphur and *B* is sodium and −2 = −2 (+1), or . . .

provided that (3) is a correct and complete list of valences. So if anyone ever wants to eliminate the word 'denote' or the word 'valence' from a large class of English sentences by a uniform procedure, denotation definitions and valence definitions are just the thing he needs. There are, however, sentences from which these words are not eliminable by the sketched procedure. For instance, in semantics and possibly in chemistry there are problems with counterfactuals, e.g., 'If "Germany" had been used to denote France, then . . .'. Moreover, there are special problems affecting the case of semantics, arising from the facts

1. That the elimination procedure works only for languages in which nothing is denoted that cannot be denoted (without using semantic terms) in one's own language;
2. That it works only for languages that contain no ambiguous names;

and

3. that the denotation definitions provide no procedure for eliminating 'denote' from sentences where it is applied to more than one language; e.g., it gives no way of handling sentences like '"Glub" denotes different things in different languages.'

But, subject to these three qualifications (plus perhaps that involving counterfactuals), the elimination procedure for 'denote' is every bit as good as that for 'valence'.

What value did Tarski attach to such transformations? Unfortunately he did not discuss the one about valences, but he did discuss the one that transforms 'Smith used a proper name to denote Germany' into something logically equivalent to 'Smith uttered "Deutschland".' And it is clear that to this definition he attached great philosophical importance. After defining semantics as 'the totality of considerations concerning those concepts which, roughly speaking, express certain connexions between the expressions of a language and the objects and states of affairs referred to by those expressions' (ESS 401), he says that with his definitions, 'the problem of establishing semantics on a scientific basis is completely solved' (ESS 407). In other places his claims are almost as extravagant. For instance, the remark about physicalism that I quoted at the end of section II is intended to apply to denotation as well as to truth: if definitions of denotation like DE and DG could not be given, 'it would . . . be impossible to bring [semantics] into harmony with . . . physicalism' (ESS 406); but because of these definitions, the compatibility of the semantic concept of denotation with physicalism is established. By similar standards of reduction, one might prove that witchcraft is compatible with physicalism, as long as witches cast only a finite number of spells: for then 'cast a spell' can be defined without use of any of the terms of witchcraft theory, merely by listing all the witch-and-victim pairs.

In other places Tarski makes quite different claims for the value of his denotation definitions. For example:

> We desire semantic terms (referring to the object language) to be introduced into the meta-language only by definition. For, if this postulate is satisfied, the definition of truth, or of any other semantic concept [including denotation, which Tarski had already specifically mentioned to be definable], will fulfill what we intuitively expect from every definition; that is, it will explain the meaning of the term being defined in terms whose meaning appears to be completely clear and unequivocal.[18]

But it is no more plausible that DE 'explains the meaning of' 'denote' as applied to English, or that DG 'explains the meaning of' 'denote' as applied to German, than that (3) 'explains the meaning of' 'valence' – considerably *less* so in fact, since for 'valence' there is no analogue to the conclusions that 'denote' means something different when applied to English than it means when applied to German. In fact, it seems pretty clear that denotation definitions like DE and DG have no philosophical interest whatever. But what conclusions can we draw from this about Tarski's *truth* definitions like T2? I think the conclusion to draw is that *T2 has no philosophical interest whatever that is not shared by T1*. How this follows I will now explain.

We have seen that Tarski advocated theories of denotation for names that had the form of mere lists: examples of his denotation definitions were DE and DG, and for language L his denotation definition would take the following form:

D2 $(\forall e)(\forall a)$ [e is a name that denotes $a \equiv$ (e is 'c_1' and a is $\bar{c}_1$) or (e is 'c_2' and a is $\bar{c}_2$ or . . .]

where into the dots go analogous clauses for every name of L. Similarly, we can come up with definitions of application and fulfillment which are acceptable according to Tarski's standards, and which also have the form of mere lists. The definition of application runs:

A2 $(\forall e)(\forall a)$ [e is a predicate that applies to $a \equiv$ (e is 'p_1' and $\bar{p}_1(a)$) or (e is 'p_2' and $\bar{p}_2(a)$) or . . .].

Similarly, we can formulate a list-like characterization F2 of fulfillment for the function symbols. Clearly neither A2 nor F2 is of any more theoretical interest than D2.

Tarski, I have stressed, accepted D2 as part of his semantic theory, and would also have accepted A2 and F2; and this fact is quite important, since D2, A2, and F2 together with T2 imply T1. In other words, T1 is simply a weaker version of Tarski's semantic theory; it is a logical consequence of Tarski's theory. Now, an interesting question is what you have to add to T1 to get the rest of Tarski's semantic theory. Suppose we can find a formula R that we can argue to be of no interest whatever, such that Tarski's semantic theory (T2 $\wedge$ D2 $\wedge$ A2 $\wedge$ F2) is logically equivalent to T1 $\wedge$ R. It will then follow that the whole interest of Tarski's semantic theory lies in T1 – the rest of his semantic theory results simply by adding to it the formula R, which (I have assumed) has no interest whatever. And if there is nothing of interest in the conjunction T2 $\wedge$ D2 $\wedge$ A2 $\wedge$ F2 beyond T1, certainly there can be nothing of interest in T2 alone beyond T1.

An example of such a formula R is D2 $\wedge$ A2 $\wedge$ F2: it is obvious that Tarski's semantic theory is logically equivalent to T1 $\wedge$ D2 $\wedge$ A2 $\wedge$ F2. Because of this, *any interest in Tarski's semantic theory over* T1 *must be due to an interest in* D2 *or* A2 *or* F2 (*or to confusion*): *in this sense* D2 $\wedge$ A2 $\wedge$ F2 *is* 'T2 *minus* T1'. But I've already argued that D2, A2, and F2 have no theoretical interest whatever, and so that establishes that T2 has no theoretical interest whatever that is not shared by T1.

V

Much of what I've said in this paper gains plausibility by being put in a wider perspective, and so I now want to say a little bit about why we want a notion of truth. The notion of truth serves a great many purposes, but I suspect that its original purpose – the purpose for which it was first developed – was to aid us in utilizing the utterances of others in drawing conclusions about the world. To take an extremely simple example, suppose that a friend reports that he's just come back from Alabama and there was a foot of snow on the ground there. Were it not for his report we would have considered it extremely unlikely that there was a foot of snow on the ground in Alabama – but the friend knows snow when he sees it and is not prone to telling us lies for no apparent reason, and so after brief deliberation we conclude that probably there *was* a foot of snow in Alabama. What we did here was first to use our evidence about the person and his situation to decide that he probably said something true when he made a certain utterance, and then to draw a conclusion from the truth of his utterance to the existence of snow in Alabama. In order to make such inferences, we have to have a pretty good grasp of (i) the circumstances under which what another says is likely to be true, and (ii) how to get from a belief in the truth of what he says to a belief about the extralinguistic world.

If this idea is right, then two features of truth that are intimately bound up with the purposes to which the notion of truth are put are (I) the role that the attempt to tell the truth and the success in doing so play in social institutions, and (II) the fact that normally one is in a position to assert of a sentence that it is true in just those cases where one is in a position to assert the sentence or a paraphrase of it. It would then be natural to expect that what is involved in communicating the meaning of the word 'true' to a child or to a philosopher is getting across to him the sorts of facts listed under (I) and (II); for those are the facts that it is essential for him to have an awareness of if he is to put the notion of truth to its primary use (child) or if he is to get a clear grasp of what its primary use is (philosopher).

I think that this natural expectation is correct, and that it gives more insight than was given in sections II and IV into why it is that neither T1 nor T2 can reasonably be said to explain the meaning of the term 'true' – even when a theory of primitive reference is added to them. First consider (I). The need of understanding the sort of thing alluded to in (I), if we are to grasp the notion of truth, has been presented quite forcefully in Michael Dummett's article 'Truth,'[19] in his analogy between speaking the truth and winning at a game. It is obvious that T1 and T2 don't explain anything like this (and in fact Dummett's fourth paragraph, on Frege-style truth definitions, can be carried over directly to T1 and T2).

The matter might perhaps be expressed in terms of assertibility conditions that one learns in learning to use the word 'true': part of what we learn, in learning to use this word, is that in cases like that involving the friend from Alabama there is some prima facie weight to be attached to the claim that the other person is saying something true. But there are also *other* assertibility conditions that one learns in learning the word 'true', assertibility conditions which have received considerable attention in the philosophical literature on truth. To begin with, let's note one obvious fact about how the word 'true' is standardly learned: we learn how to apply it to utterances of our own language first, and when we later learn to apply it to other languages it is by conceiving the utterances of another language more or less on the model of utterances of our own language. The obvious model of the first stage of this process is that we learn to accept all instances of the schema

(T) X is true if and only if p.

where 'X' is replaced by a quotation-mark name of an English sentence S and 'p' is replaced by S. This must be complicated to deal with ambiguous and truth-value-less sentences, but let's ignore them. Also let's ignore the fact that certain pathological instances of (T) – the Epimenides-type paradoxical sentences – are logically refutable. Then there is a sense in which the instances of (T) that we've learned to assert determine a unique extension for the predicate 'true' as applied to sentences of our own language.[20] Our views about what English sentences belong to this unique extension may be altered, but as long as we stick to the instances of (T) they cannot consistently be altered without also altering our beliefs in what those sentences express. This fact is extremely important to the functions that the word 'true' serves (as the Alabama example illustrates).

In stressing the assertibility conditions for simple sentences containing the word 'true', I have followed Quine (*ibid.* 138); for, like him, I believe that such assertibility conditions are enough to make the term 'true' reasonably clear. But now it might be asked, 'Then why do we need causal (etc.) theories of reference? The words 'true' and 'denotes' are made perfectly clear by schemas like (T). To ask for more than these schemas – to ask for causal theories of reference to nail language to reality – is to fail to recognize that we are at sea on Neurath's boat: we have to work *within* our conceptual scheme, we can't glue it to reality from the outside.'

I suspect that this would be Quine's diagnosis – it is strongly suggested by §6 of *Word and Object*, especially when that is taken in conjunction with some of Quine's remarks about the inscrutibility of reference and truth value, the underdetermination of theories, and the relativity of ontology. It seems to me, however, that the diagnosis is quite wrong. In looking for a theory of truth and a theory of primitive reference we *are* trying to explain the connection between language and (extralinguistic) reality, but we are *not* trying to step outside of our theories of the world in order to do so. Our accounts of primitive reference and of truth are not to be thought of as something that could be given by philosophical reflection prior to scientific information – on the contrary, it seems likely that such things as psychological models of human beings and investigations of neurophysiology will be very relevant to discovering the mechanisms involved in reference. *The reason why accounts of truth and primitive reference are needed is not to tack our conceptual scheme onto reality from the outside; the reason, rather, is that without such accounts our conceptual scheme breaks down from the inside.* On our theory of the world it would be extremely surprising if there were some non-physical connection between words and things. Thus if we could argue from our theory of the world that the notion of an utterer's saying something true, or referring to a particular thing, cannot be made sense of in physicalist terms (say, by arguing that any semantic notion that makes physicalist sense *can* be explicated in Skinnerian terms, and that the notions of truth and reference *can't* be explicated in Skinnerian terms), then to the extent that such an argument is convincing we ought to be led to conclude that, if we are to remain physicalists, the notions of truth and reference must be abandoned. No amount of pointing out the clarity of these terms helps enable us to escape this conclusion: 'valence' and 'gene' were perfectly clear long before anyone succeeded in reducing them, but it was their reducibility and not their clarity before reduction that showed them to be compatible with physicalism.

The clarity of 'valence' and 'gene' before reduction – and even more, their *utility* before reduction – did provide physicalists with substantial reason to think that a reduction of these terms was possible, and, as I remarked earlier, a great deal of fruitful work in physical chemistry and chemical genetics was motivated by the fact. Similarly, insofar as semantic notions like 'true' are useful, we have every reason to suspect that they will be reducible to non-semantic terms, and it is likely that progress in linguistic theory will come by looking for such reductions. (In fact, the fruitfulness of Tarski's work in aiding us to understand language is already some sign of this, even though it represents only a partial reduction.) Of course, this sort of argument for the prospects of reducing semantic notions is only as powerful as our arguments for the utility of semantic terms; and it is clear that the question of the utility of the term 'true' – the purposes it serves, and the extent to which those purposes could be served by less pretentious notions such as warranted assertibility – needs much closer investigation.

All these remarks require one important qualification. The notion of valence, it must be admitted, is *not* reducible to nonchemical terms on the *strictest* standards of reduction, but is only *approximately* reducible; yet, in spite of this, we don't want to get rid of the notion, since it is still extremely useful in those contexts where its approximate character isn't too likely to get in the way and where if we did not approximate we'd get into quantum-mechanical problems far too complex for anyone to solve. (Moreover, considerations about the purposes of the notion of valence were sufficient to show that the notion of valence would only be approximately reducible: for the utility of the notion of valence is that it aids us in approximately characterizing which elements will combine with which and in what proportions; yet it is obvious that no *precise* such characterization is possible.)

Similarly, it may well be that a detailed investigation into the purposes of the notion of truth might show that these purposes require only an approximation reduction of the notion of truth. Still, to require an approximate reduction is to require quite a bit; after all, 'is a reincarnation of' isn't even approximately reducible to respectable biology, and 'electromagnetic field' is not approximately reducible to mechanics. Obviously the notion of approximate reduction needs to be made more precise (as in fact does the notion of strict, or nonapproximate, reduction); but even without making it so, I think we can see that T2 is no more of an approximate reduction than is V2, since D2 $\wedge$ A2 $\wedge$ F2 is no more of an approximate reduction than is (3). In other words, the main point of the paper survives when we replace the ideal of strict reduction by the ideal of approximate reduction.

It should be kept carefully in mind that the Quinean view that all we need do is clarify the term 'true', in the sense that this term is clarified by schema T (or by schema T plus a theory of translation to handle foreign languages; or by schema T plus the sort of thing alluded to in connection with Dummett), is *not* Tarski's view. Tarski's view is that we have to provide a truth characterization like T2 (which, when we choose as our object language L a 'nice' fragment of our own language, can be shown correct merely by assuming that all instances of schema T are valid – cf. fn 14, p. 361); and such a truth characterization does much more than schema T does. It does not do anything that Tarski ever claimed for it, for Tarski attached much too much importance to the pseudo-theories D2, A2, and F2; but even when we 'subtract' such trivialities from his truth characterization T2, we still get the very interesting and important truth characterization T1. T1, I believe, adequately represents Tarski's real contribution to the theory of truth, and in doing this it has a number of positive advantages over T2 (in addition to the important negative advantage I've been stressing, of preventing extravagant claims based on the fact that T2 contains no semantic terms). First of all, T1, unlike T2, is applicable to languages that contain ambiguities and languages that contain terms not adequately translatable into English. Second, T1, unlike T2, can be used in diachronic linguistics: it doesn't need overhauling as you add new words to the language, provided those new words belong to the same semantic category as words already in the language. Third, I think that the reason why Tarski's theory of truth T2 has seemed so uninteresting to so many people is that it contains the vacuous semantic theories D2, A2, and F2 for the primitives of the language. By expressing the really important features of Tarski's results on truth, and leaving out the inessential and uninteresting 'theories' of the semantics of the primitives, T1 should make the philosophical importance of Tarski's work more universally recognized.

Notes

* This paper grew out of a talk I gave at Princeton in the fall of 1970, where I defended T1 over T2. Donald Davidson and Gilbert Harman – and later, in private conversation, John Wallace – all came to the defense of T2, and their remarks have all been of help to me in writing the paper. I have also benefited from advice given by Michael Devitt, Paul Benacerraf, and especially David Hills.

1. *Logic of Scientific Discovery* (New York: Basic Books, 1968), p. 274.
2. Cf. Carnap's 'Autobiography,' in P. A. Schilpp, ed., *The Philosophy of Rudolf Carnap* (Lasalle, Ill.: Open Court, 1963), p. 61.
3. It is sometimes claimed that Tarski was interested in languages considered in abstraction from all speakers and writers of the language; that the languages he was dealing with are abstract entities to be specified by giving their rules. This seems incorrect: Tarski was interested in giving the semantics of languages that

mathematicians had been writing for years; and only as a result of Tarski's work was it then possible for philosophers like Carnap to propose that the clauses of a Tarski-type truth definition for such languages be called rules of the languages and be used in defining the languages as abstract entities.

4. 'The Concept of Truth in Formalized Languages' (CTFL), in *Logic, Semantics, and Metamathematics (LSM)* (New York: Oxford, 1956), p. 166.
5. Actually in model theory we are interested in allowing a slightly unusual semantics for the quantifiers: we are willing to allow that the quantifier not range over everything. We could build this generalization into our truth definition, by stipulating that in addition to the denotations of the nonlogical symbols we specify a universe U, and then reformulating clause (B)4 by requiring that the *k*th member of s^* belong to U. If we did this, then it would be the range of the quantifiers as well as the denotations of the nonlogical primitives that we would have explained truth in terms of.
6. An *incomplete* sentence token is a sentence token which [like the occurrence of '2 + 2 = 4' inside '~(2 + 2 = 4)'] is part of a larger sentence token.
7. 'Truth and Meaning,' *Synthese*, XVII, 3 (September, 1967): 304–323, pp. 314/5.
8. Note that the claims I've been making are intended to apply only to cases where different tokens have different semantic features; they are not intended to apply to cases of indeterminacy, i.e., to cases where a particular name token or predicate token has no determinate denotation or extension. To deal with indeterminacy requires more complex devices than I employ in this paper.
9. The notion of a semantic category is Tarski's: cf. CTFL, p. 215.
10. To do so in the obvious way requires that we introduce semantic categories of negation symbol, conjunction symbol, and universal-quantification symbol; though by utilizing some ideas of Frege it could be shown that there is really no need of a separate semantic category for each logical operator. The use of semantic categories in the generalized truth characterization raises important problems which I have had to suppress for lack of space in this paper.
11. For simplicity, I have assumed that L itself contains no semantic terms.
12. 'The Establishment of Scientific Semantics' (ESS) in *LSM*, p. 406.
13. This, of course, is very vague, but most attempts to explicate the doctrine of physicalism more precisely result in doctrines that are very hard to take seriously [e.g., the doctrine that for every acceptable predicate '$P(x)$' there is a formula '$B(x)$' containing only terminology from physics, such that '$\forall x(P(x) \equiv B(x))$' is true]. Physicalism should be understood as the doctrine (however precisely it is to be characterized) that guides science in the way I describe.
14. Tarski actually gives a different formulation, the famous Convention T, evidently because he does not think that the word 'correct' ought to be employed in stating a criterion of adequacy. First of all Tarski writes

> . . . we shall accept as valid every sentence of the form
> [T] the sentence x is true if and only if p
> where 'p' is to be replaced by any sentence of the language under investigation and 'x' by any individual name of that sentence provided this name occurs in the metalanguage (ESS 404).

Is Tarski's policy of accepting these sentences as 'valid' (i.e., true) legitimate? It seems to me that it is, in a certain special case. The special case is where

1. The object language is a proper part of the metalanguage (here, English).
2. The object language contains no paradoxical or ambiguous or truth-valueless sentences.

In this special case – and it was the case the Tarski was primarily concerned with – I think it will be generally agreed that all instances of Schema T hold. From this, together with the fact that only grammatical sentences are true, we can argue that, if a necessary and sufficient condition of form (2) has the following consequences:

(a) Every instance of Schema T
(b) The sentence '$(\forall x)(x$ is true $\supset S(x))$', where '$S(x)$' formulates (correct) conditions for an utterance of L to be a sentence

then that necessary and sufficient condition is correct. Let's say that a 'truth definition' for L (a necessary and sufficient condition of truth in L) *satisfies Convention T* if it has all the consequences listed under (a) and (b). Then, restating: when L is a language for which 1 and 2 hold, then any truth definition satisfying Convention T is correct; and since only quite uncontroversial assumptions about truth are used in getting this result, anyone will admit to the correctness of a truth characterization satisfying Convention T. If we use the term 'formally correct definition' for a sentence of form (2) in which '$B(e)$' contains no semantic terms, this means that a formally correct definition that satisfies Convention T is bound to satisfy Condition M (when the language L satisfies 1 and 2). As far as I can see, this is the only motivation for Convention T; if so, then we can discredit Convention T by discrediting Condition M.

Tarski sometimes states a more general form of Convention T, which applies to languages that do not meet restriction 1: it is what results when one allows as instances of Schema T the results of replacing 'p' by a *correct translation* of the sentence that the name substituted for 'x' denotes (in some sense of 'correct translation' in which correctness requires preservation of truth value). But then the advantage of the ungeneralized form of Convention T (viz., that anything satisfying it wears its correctness on its face, or more accurately, on the faces of its logical consequences) is lost.

15. A sentence of the form ('$(\forall N)(\forall x)[N$ denotes $x \equiv B(N, x]$' *satisfies convention* D if it has as consequences every instance of the schema 'y denotes z', in which 'y' is to be replaced by a quotation-mark name for a name N, and 'z' is to be replaced by (an adequate translation of N into English, i.e.) a singular term of English that contains no semantic terms and that denotes the same thing that N denotes. Clearly DE and DG are not only extensionally correct, they also satisfy Convention D. Presumably philosophers who are especially impressed with Convention T will be equally impressed with this fact, but they owe us a reason why satisfying Convention D is of any interest.

16. For example, by extending our definition of denotation$_s$ to descriptions by:

    $\ulcorner \iota x_k(e) \urcorner$ denotes$_s$ a if and only if [for each sequence s^* which differs from s at the kth place at most, e is true$_s{}^*$ if and only if the kth member of s^* is a].

    and then defining denotation in terms of denotation$_s$ by stipulating that a closed term denotes an object if and only if it denotes$_s$ that object for some (or all) s.

17. Some of Kripke's work on names will be published shortly in Davidson and Harman, eds., *Semantics of Natural Language* (Dordrecht: Reidel, 1971). What

I've said about Russell's view is influenced by some of Kripke's lectures on which his paper there is based.

18. 'The Semantic Conception of Truth and the Foundations of Semantics,' *Philosophy and Phenomenological Research*, IV, 3 (March 1944): 341–375, p. 351.
19. *Proceedings of the Aristotelian Society*, LIX (1958/9): 141–162.
20. Cf. W. V. Quine, *From a Logical Point of View* (New York: Harper & Row, 1961), p. 136.

Chapter 20

Truth and Meaning

D. Davidson

It is conceded by most philosophers of language, and recently even by some linguists, that a satisfactory theory of meaning must give an account of how the meanings of sentences depend upon the meanings of words. Unless such an account could be supplied for a particular language, it is argued, there would be no explaining the fact that we can learn the language: no explaining the fact that, on mastering a finite vocabulary and a finitely stated set of rules, we are prepared to produce and to understand any of a potential infinitude of sentences. I do not dispute these vague claims, in which I sense more than a kernel of truth.[1] Instead I want to ask what it is for a theory to give an account of the kind adumbrated.

One proposal is to begin by assigning some entity as meaning to each word (or other significant syntactical feature) of the sentence; thus we might assign Theaetetus to 'Theaetetus' and the property of flying to 'flies' in the sentence 'Theaetetus flies'. The problem then arises how the meaning of the sentence is generated from these meanings. Viewing concatenation as a significant piece of syntax, we may assign to it the relation of participating in or instantiating; however, it is obvious that we have here the start of an infinite regress. Frege sought to avoid the regress by saying that the entities corresponding to predicates (for example) are 'unsaturated' or 'incomplete' in contrast to the entities that correspond to names, but this doctrine seems to label a difficulty rather than solve it.

The point will emerge if we think for a moment of complex singular terms, to which Frege's theory applies along with sentences. Consider the expression 'the father of Annette'; how does the meaning of the whole depend on the meaning of the parts? The answer would seem to be that the meaning of 'the father of' is such that when this expression is prefixed to a singular

Source: SYNTHESE, Vol. 17, 1967, Dordrecht: Reidel.

term the result refers to the father of the person to whom the singular term refers. What part is played, in this account, by the unsaturated or incomplete entity for which 'the father of' stands? All we can think to say is that this entity 'yields' or 'gives' the father of x as value when the argument is x, or perhaps that this entity maps people onto their fathers. It may not be clear whether the entity for which 'the father of' is said to stand performs any genuine explanatory function as long as we stick to individual expressions; so think instead of the infinite class of expressions formed by writing 'the father of' zero or more times in front of 'Annette'. It is easy to supply a theory that tells, for an arbitrary one of these singular terms, what it refers to: if the term is 'Annette' it refers to Annette, while if the term is complex, consisting of 'the father of' prefixed to a singular term t, then it refers to the father of the person to whom t refers. It is obvious that no entity corresponding to 'the father of' is, or needs to be, mentioned in stating this theory.

It would be inappropriate to complain that this little theory *uses* the words 'the father of' in giving the reference of expressions containing those words. For the task was to give the meaning of all expressions in a certain infinite set on the basis of the meaning of the parts; it was not in the bargain also to give the meanings of the atomic parts. On the other hand, it is now evident that a satisfactory theory of the meanings of complex expressions may not require entities as meanings of all the parts. It behooves us then to rephrase our demand on a satisfactory theory of meaning so as not to suggest that individual words must have meanings at all, in any sense that transcends the fact that they have a systematic effect on the meanings of the sentences in which they occur. Actually, for the case at hand we can do better still in stating the criterion of success: what we wanted, and what we got, is a theory that entails every sentence of the form 't refers to x' where 't' is replaced by a structural description[2] of a singular term, and 'x' is replaced by that term itself. Further, our theory accomplishes this without appeal to any semantical concepts beyond the basic 'refers to'. Finally, the theory clearly suggests an effective procedure for determining, for any singular term in its universe, what that term refers to.

A theory with such evident merits deserves wider application. The device proposed by Frege to this end has a brilliant simplicity: count predicates as a special case of functional expressions, and sentences as a special case of complex singular terms. Now, however, a difficulty looms if we want to continue in our present (implicit) course of identifying the meaning of a singular term with its reference. The difficulty follows upon making two reasonable assumptions: that logically equivalent singular terms have the same reference; and that a singular term does not change its reference if a contained singular term is replaced by another with the same reference. But now suppose that 'R' and 'S' abbreviate any two sentences alike in truth value. Then the following four sentences have the same reference:

(1) R
(2) $\hat{x}(x=x.R)=\hat{x}(x=x)$
(3) $\hat{x}(x=x.S)=\hat{x}(x=x)$
(4) S

For (1) and (2) are logically equivalent, as are (3) and (4), while (3) differs from (2) only in containing the singular term '$\hat{x}(x=x.S)$' where (2) contains '$\hat{x}(x=x.R)$' and these refer to the same thing if S and R are alike in truth value. Hence any two sentences have the same reference if they have the same truth value.[3] And if the meaning of a sentence is what it refers to, all sentences alike in truth value must be synonymous – an intolerable result.

Apparently we must abandon the present approach as leading to a theory of meaning. This is the natural point at which to turn for help to the distinction between meaning and reference. The trouble, we are told, is that questions of reference are, in general, settled by extra-linguistic facts, questions of meaning not, and the facts can conflate the references of expressions that are not synonymous. If we want a theory that gives the meaning (as distinct from reference) of each sentence, we must start with the meaning (as distinct from reference) of the parts.

Up to here we have been following in Frege's footsteps; thanks to him the path is well known and even well worn. But now, I would like to suggest, we have reached an impasse: the switch from reference to meaning leads to no useful account of how the meanings of sentences depend upon the meanings of the words (or other structural features) that compose them. Ask, for example, for the meaning of 'Theaetetus flies'. A Fregean answer might go something like this: given the meaning of 'Theaetetus' as argument, the meaning of 'flies' yields the meaning of 'Theaetetus flies' as value. The vacuity of this answer is obvious. We wanted to know what the meaning of 'Theaetetus flies' is; it is no progress to be told that it is the meaning of 'Theaetetus flies'. This much we knew before any theory was in sight. In the bogus account just given, talk of the structure of the sentence and of the meanings of words was idle, for it played no role in producing the given description of the meaning of the sentence.

The contrast here between a real and pretended account will be plainer still if we ask for a theory, analogous to the miniature theory of reference of singular terms just sketched, but different in dealing with meanings in place of references. What analogy demands is a theory that has as consequences all sentences of the form '*s* means *m*' where '*s*' is replaced by a structural description of a sentence and '*m*' is replaced by a singular term that refers to the meaning of that sentence; a theory, moreover, that provides an effective method for arriving at the meaning of an arbitrary sentence structurally described. Clearly some more articulate way of referring to meanings than any we have seen is essential if these criteria are to be met.[4] Meanings as entities, or the related concept of synonymy, allow us to formulate the following rule relating sentences and their parts: sentences are synonymous whose corresponding parts are synonymous ('corresponding' here needs spelling out of course). And meanings as entities may, in theories such as Frege's, do duty, on occasion as references, thus losing their status as entities distinct from references. Paradoxically, the one thing meanings do not seem to do is oil the wheels of a theory of meaning – at least as long as we require of such a theory that it non-trivially give the meaning of every sentence in the language. My objection to meanings in the theory of meaning is not that they are abstract or that their identity conditions are obscure, but that they have no demonstrated use.

This is the place to scotch another hopeful thought. Suppose we have a satisfactory theory of syntax for our language, consisting of an effective method of telling, for an arbitrary expression, whether or not it is independently meaningful (i.e., a sentence), and assume as usual that this involves viewing each sentence as composed, in allowable ways, out of elements drawn from a fixed finite stock of atomic syntactical elements (roughly, words). The hopeful thought is that syntax, so conceived, will yield semantics when a dictionary giving the meaning of each syntactic atom is added. Hopes will be dashed, however, if semantics is to comprise a theory of meaning in our sense, for knowledge of the structural characteristics that make for meaningfulness in a sentence, plus knowledge of the meanings of the ultimate parts, does not add up to knowledge of what a sentence means. The point is easily illustrated by belief sentences. Their syntax is relatively unproblematic. Yet, adding a dictionary does not touch the standard semantic problem, which is that we cannot account for even as much as the truth conditions of such sentences on the basis of what we know of the meanings of the words in them. The situation is not radically altered by refining the dictionary to indicate which meaning or meanings an ambiguous expression bears in each of its possible contexts; the problem of belief sentences persists after ambiguities are resolved.

The fact that recursive syntax with dictionary added is not necessarily recursive semantics has been obscured in some recent writing on linguistics by the intrusion of semantic criteria into the discussion of purportedly syntactic theories. The matter would boil down to a harmless difference over terminology if the semantic criteria were clear; but they are not. While there is agreement that it is the central task of semantics to give the semantic interpretation (the meaning) of every sentence in the language, nowhere in the linguistic literature will one find, so far as I know, a straightforward account of how a theory performs this task, or how to tell when it has been accomplished. The contrast with syntax is striking. The main job of a modest syntax is to characterize *meaningfulness* (or sentencehood). We may have as much confidence in the correctness of such a characterization as we have in the representativeness of our sample and our ability to say when particular expressions are meaningful (sentences). What clear and analogous task and test exist for semantics?[5]

We decided a while back not to assume that parts of sentences have meanings except in the ontologically neutral sense of making a systematic contribution to the meaning of the sentences in which they occur. Since postulating meanings has netted nothing, let us return to that insight. One direction in which it points is a certain holistic view of meaning. If sentences depend for their meaning on their structure, and we understand the meaning of each item in the structure only as an abstraction from the totality of sentences in which it features, then we can give the meaning of any sentence (or word) only by giving the meaning of every sentence (and word) in the language. Frege said that only in the context of a sentence does a word have meaning; in the same vein he might have added that only in the context of the language does a sentence (and therefore a word) have meaning.

This degree of holism was already implicit in the suggestion that an adequate theory of meaning must entail *all* sentences of the form '*s* means *m*'. But now, having found no more help in meanings of sentences than in meanings of words, let us ask whether we can get rid of the troublesome singular terms supposed to replace '*m*' and to refer to meanings. In a way, nothing could be easier: just write '*s* means that *p*', and imagine '*p*' replaced by a sentence. Sentences, as we have seen, cannot name meanings, and sentences with 'that' prefixed are not names at all, unless we decide so. It looks as though we are in trouble on another count, however, for it is reasonable to expect that in wrestling with the logic of the apparently non-extensional 'means that' we will encounter problems as hard as, or perhaps identical with, the problems our theory is out to solve.

The only way I know to deal with this difficulty is simple, and radical. Anxiety that we are enmeshed in the intensional springs from using the words 'means that' as filling between description of sentence and sentence, but it may be that the success of our venture depends not on the filling but on what it fills. The theory will have done its work if it provides, for every sentence *s* in the language under study, a matching sentence (to replace '*p*) that, in some way yet to be made clear, 'gives the meaning' of *s*. One obvious candidate for matching sentence is just *s* itself, if the object language is contained in the metalanguage; otherwise a translation of *s* in the metalanguage. As a final bold step, let us try treating the position occupied by '*p*' extensionally: to implement this, sweep away the obscure 'means that', provide the sentence that replaces '*p*' with a proper sentential connective, and supply the description that replaces '*s*' with its own predicate. The plausible result is

(T) *s* is *T* if and only if *p*.

What we require of a theory of meaning for a language *L* is that without appeal to any (further) semantical notions it place enough restrictions on the predicate 'is *T*' to entail all sentences got from schema *T* when '*s*' is replaced by a structural description of a sentence of *L* and '*p*' by that sentence.

Any two predicates satisfying this condition have the same extension,[6] so if the metalanguage is rich enough, nothing stands in the way of putting what I am calling a theory of meaning into the form of an explicit definition of a predicate 'is *T*'. But whether explicitly defined or recursively characterized, it is clear that the sentences to which the predicate 'is *T*' applies will be just the true sentences of *L*, for the condition we have placed on satisfactory theories of meaning is in essence Tarski's Convention *T* that tests the adequacy of a formal semantical definition of truth.[7]

The path to this point has been tortuous, but the conclusion may be stated simply: a theory of meaning for a language *L* shows 'how the meanings of sentences depend upon the meanings of words' if it contains a (recursive) definition of truth-in-L. And, so far at least, we have no other idea how to turn the trick. It is worth emphasizing that the concept of truth played no ostensible role in stating our original problem. That problem, upon refinement, led to the view that an adequate theory of meaning must characterize a predicate meeting certain conditions. It was in the nature of a discovery that such a predicate would apply exactly to the true sentences. I hope that what I am doing may be described in part as defending the philosophical importance of Tarski's semantical concept of truth. But my defense is only distantly related, if at all, to the question whether the concept Tarski has shown how to define is the (or a) philosophically interesting conception of truth, or the question whether Tarski has cast any light on the ordinary use of such words as 'true' and 'truth'. It is a misfortune that dust from futile and confused battles over these questions has prevented those with a theoretical interest in language – philosophers, logicians, psychologists, and linguists alike – from recognizing in the semantical concept of truth (under whatever name) the sophisticated and powerful foundation of a competent theory of meaning.

There is no need to suppress, of course, the obvious connection between a definition of truth of the kind Tarski has shown how to construct, and the concept of meaning. It is this: the definition works by giving necessary and sufficient conditions for the truth of every sentence, and to give truth conditions is a way of giving the meaning of a sentence. To know the semantic concept of truth for a language is to know what it is for a sentence – any sentence – to be true, and this amounts, in one good sense we can give to the phrase, to understanding the language. This at any rate is my excuse for a feature of the present discussion that is apt to shock old hands: my freewheeling use of the word 'meaning', for what I call a theory of meaning has after all turned out to make no use of meanings, whether of sentences or of words. Indeed since a Tarski-type truth definition supplies all we have asked so far of a theory of meaning, it is clear that such a theory falls comfortably within what Quine terms the 'theory of reference' as distinguished from what he terms the 'theory of meaning'. So much to the good for what I call a theory of meaning, and so much, perhaps, against my so calling it.[8]

A theory of meaning (in my mildly perverse sense) is an empirical theory, and its ambition is to account for the workings of a natural language. Like any theory, it may be tested by comparing some of its consequences with the facts. In the present case this is easy, for the theory has been characterized as issuing in an infinite flood of sentences each giving the truth conditions of a sentence; we only need to ask, in selected cases, whether what the theory avers to be the truth conditions for a sentence really are. A typical test case might involve deciding whether the sentence 'Snow is white' *is* true if and only if snow is white. Not all cases will be so simple (for reasons to be sketched), but it is evident that this sort of test does not invite counting noses. A sharp conception of what constitutes a theory in this domain furnishes an exciting context for raising deep questions about when a theory of language is correct and how it is to be tried. But the difficulties are theoretical, not practical. In application, the trouble is to get a theory that comes close to working; anyone can tell whether it is right.[9] One can see why this is so. The theory reveals nothing new about the conditions under which an individual sentence is true; it does not make those conditions any clearer than the sentence itself does. The work of the theory is in relating the known truth conditions of each sentence to those aspects ('words') of the sentence that recur in other sentences, and can be assigned identical roles in other sentences. Empirical power in such a theory depends on success in recovering the structure of a very complicated ability – the ability to speak and understand a language. We can tell easily enough when particular pronouncements of the theory comport with our understanding of the language; this is consistent with a feeble insight into the design of the machinery of our linguistic accomplishments.

The remarks of the last paragraph apply directly only to the special case where it is assumed that the language for which truth is being characterized is part of the language used and understood by the characterizer. Under these circumstances, the framer of a theory will as a matter of course avail himself when he can of the built-in convenience of a metalanguage with a sentence guaranteed equivalent to each sentence in the object language. Still, this fact ought not to con us into thinking a theory any more correct that entails '"Snow is white" is true if and only if snow is white' than one that entails instead:

(*S*) 'Snow is white' is true if and only if grass is green,

provided, of course, we are as sure of the truth of (*S*) as we are of that of its more celebrated predecessor. Yet (*S*) may not encourage the same confidence that a theory that entails it deserves to be called a theory of meaning.

The threatened failure of nerve may be counteracted as follows. The grotesqueness of (*S*) is in itself nothing against a theory of which it is a consequence, provided the theory gives the correct results for every sentence (on the basis of its structure, there being no other way). It is not easy to see how (*S*) could be party to such an enterprise, but if it were – if, that is, (*S*) followed from a characterization of the predicate 'is true' that led to the invariable pairing of truths with truths and falsehoods with falsehoods – then there would not, I think, be anything essential to the idea of meaning that remained to be captured.

What appears to the right of the biconditional in sentences of the form '*s* is true if and only if *p*' when such sentences are consequences of a theory of truth plays its role in determining the meaning of *s* not by pretending synonymy but by adding one more brush-stroke to the picture which, taken as a whole, tells what there is to know of the meaning of *s*; this stroke is added by virtue of the fact that the sentence that replaced '*p*' is true if and only if *s* is.

It may help to reflect that (*S*) is acceptable, if it is, because we are independently sure of the truth of 'Snow is white' and 'Grass is green'; but in cases where we are unsure of the truth of a sentence, we can have confidence in a characterization of the truth predicate only if it pairs that sentence with one we have good reason to believe equivalent. It would be ill advised for someone who had any doubts about the color of snow or grass to accept a theory that yielded (*S*), even if his doubts were of equal degree, unless he thought the color of the one was tied to the color of the other. Omniscience can obviously afford more bizarre theories of meaning than ignorance; but then, omniscience has less need of communication.

It must be possible, of course, for the speaker of one language to construct a theory of meaning for the speaker of another, though in this case the empirical test of the correctness of the theory will no longer be trivial. As before, the aim of theory will be an infinite correlation of sentences alike in truth. But this time the theory-builder must not be assumed to have direct insight into likely equivalences between his own tongue and the alien. What he must do is find out, however he can, what sentences the alien holds true in his own tongue (or better, to what degree he holds them true). The linguist then will attempt to construct a characterization of truth-for-the-alien which yields, so far as possible, a mapping of sentences held true (or false) by the alien onto sentences held true (or false) by the linguist. Supposing no perfect fit is found, the residue of sentences held true translated by sentences held false (and vice versa) is the margin for error (foreign or domestic). Charity in interpreting the words and thoughts of others is unavoidable in another direction as well: just as we must maximize agreement, or risk not making sense of what the alien is talking about, so we must maximize the self-consistency we attribute to him, on pain of not understanding *him*. No single principle of optimum charity emerges; the constraints therefore determine no single theory. In a theory of radical translation (as Quine calls it) there is no completely disentangling questions of what the alien means from questions of what he believes. We do not know what someone means unless we know what he believes; we do not know what someone believes unless we know what he means. In radical translation we are able to break into this circle, if only incompletely, because we can sometimes tell that a person accedes to a sentence we do not understand.[10]

In the past few pages I have been asking how a theory of meaning that takes the form of a truth definition can be empirically tested, and have blithely ignored the prior question whether there is any serious chance such a theory can be given for a natural language. What are the prospects for a formal semantical theory of a natural language? Very poor, according to Tarski; and I believe most logicians, philosophers of language and linguists agree.[11] Let me do what I can to dispel the pessimism. What I can in a general and programmatic way, of course; for here the proof of the pudding will certainly be in the proof of the right theorems.

Tarski concludes the first section of his classic essay on the concept of truth in formalized languages with the following remarks, which he italicizes:

> *The very possibility of a consistent use of the expression 'true sentence' which is in harmony with the laws of logic and the spirit of everyday language seems to be very questionable, and consequently the same doubt attaches to the possibility of constructing a correct definition of this expression.*[12]

Late in the same essay, he returns to the subject:

> the concept of truth (as well as other semantical concepts) when applied to colloquial language in conjunction with the normal laws of logic leads inevitably to confusions and contradictions. Whoever wishes, in spite of all difficulties, to pursue the semantics of colloquial language with the help of exact methods will be driven first to undertake the thankless task of a reform of this language. He will find it necessary to define its structure, to overcome the ambiguity of the terms which occur in it, and finally to split the language into a series of languages of greater and greater extent, each of which stands in the same relation to the next in which a formalized language stands to its metalanguage. It may, however be doubted whether the language of everyday life, after being 'rationalized' in this way, would still preserve its naturalness and whether it would not rather take on the characteristic features of the formalized languages.[13]

Two themes emerge: that the universal character of natural languages leads to contradiction (the semantic paradoxes), and that natural languages are too confused and amorphous to permit the direct application of formal methods. The first point deserves a serious answer, and I wish I had one. As it is, I will say only why I think we are justified in carrying on without having disinfected this particular source of conceptual anxiety. The semantic paradoxes arise when the range of the quantifiers in the object language is too generous in certain ways. But it is not really clear how unfair to Urdu or to Hindi it would be to view the range of their quantifiers as insufficient to yield an explicit definition of 'true-in-Urdu' or 'true-in-Hindi'. Or, to put the matter in another, if not more serious way, there may in the nature of the case always be something we grasp in understanding the language of another (the concept of truth) that we cannot communicate to him. In any case, most of the problems of general philosophical interest arise within a fragment of the relevant natural language that may be conceived as containing very little set theory. Of course these comments do not meet the claim that natural languages are universal. But it seems to me this claim, now that we know such universality leads to paradox, is suspect.

Tarski's second point is that we would have to reform a natural language out of all recognition before we could apply formal semantical methods. If this is true, it is fatal to my project, for the task of a theory of meaning as I conceive it is not to change, improve or reform a language, but to describe and understand it. Let us look at the positive side. Tarski has shown the way to giving a theory for interpreted formal languages of various kinds; pick one as much like English as possible. Since this new language has been explained in English and contains much English we not only may, but I think must, view it as part of English for those who understand it. For this fragment of English we have, *ex hypothesi*, a theory of the required sort. Not only that, but in interpreting this adjunct of English in old English we necessarily gave hints connecting old and new. Wherever there are sentences of old English with the same truth conditions as sentences in the adjunct we may extend the theory to cover them. Much of what is called for is just to mechanize as far as possible what we now do by art when we put ordinary English into one or another canonical notation. The point is not that canonical notation is better than the rough original idiom, but rather that if we know what idiom the canonical notation is canonical *for*, we have as good a theory for the idiom as for its kept companion.

Philosophers have long been at the hard work of applying theory to ordinary language by the device of matching sentences in the vernacular with sentences for which they have a theory. Frege's massive contribution was to show how 'all', 'some', 'every', 'each', 'none', and associated pronouns, in some of their uses, could be tamed; for the first time, it was possible to dream of a formal semantics for a significant part of a natural language. This dream came true in a sharp way with the work of Tarski. It would be a shame to miss the fact that as a result of these two magnificent achievements, Frege's and Tarski's, we have gained a deep insight into the structure of our mother tongues. Philosophers of a logical bent have tended to start where the theory was and work out towards the complications of natural language. Contemporary linguists, with an aim that cannot easily be seen to be different, start with the ordinary and work toward a general theory. If either party is successful, there must be a meeting. Recent work by Chomsky and others is doing much to bring the complexities of natural languages within the scope of serious semantic theory. To give an example: suppose success in giving the truth conditions for some significant range of sentences in the active voice. Then with a formal procedure for transforming each such sentence into a corresponding sentence in the passive voice, the theory of truth could be extended in an obvious way to this new set of sentences.[14]

One problem touched on in passing by Tarski does not, at least in all its manifestations, have to be solved to get ahead with theory: the existence in natural languages of 'ambiguous terms'. As long as ambiguity does not affect grammatical form, and can be translated, ambiguity for ambiguity, into the metalanguage, a truth definition will not tell us any lies. The trouble, for systematic semantics, with the phrase 'believes that' in English is not its vagueness, ambiguity, or unsuitability for incorporation in a serious science: let our metalanguage be English, and all *these* problems will be translated without loss or gain into the metalanguage. But the central problem of the logical grammar of 'believes that' will remain to haunt us.

The example is suited to illustrating another, and related, point, for the discussion of belief sentences has been plagued by failure to observe a fundamental distinction between tasks: uncovering the logical grammar or form of sentences (which is in the province of a theory of meaning as I construe it), and the analysis of individual words or expressions (which are treated as primitive by the theory). Thus Carnap, in the first edition of *Meaning and Necessity*, suggested we render 'John believes that the earth is round' as 'John responds affirmatively to "the earth is round" as an English sentence'. He gave this up when Mates pointed out that John might respond affirmatively to one sentence and not to another no matter how close in meaning. But there is a confusion here from the start. The semantic structure of a belief sentence, according to this idea of Carnap's, is given by a three-place predicate with places reserved for expressions referring to a person, a sentence, and a language. It is a different sort of problem entirely to attempt an analysis of this predicate, perhaps along behavioristic lines. Not least among the merits of Tarski's conception of a theory of truth is that the purity of method it demands of us follows from the formulation of the problem itself, not from the self-imposed restraint of some adventitious philosophical puritanism.

I think it is hard to exaggerate the advantages to philosophy of language of bearing in mind this distinction between questions of logical form or grammar, and the analysis of individual concepts. Another example may help advertise the point.

If we suppose questions of logical grammar settled, sentences like 'Bardot is good' raise no special problems for a truth definition. The deep differences between descriptive and evaluative (emotive, expressive, etc.) terms do not show here. Even if we hold there is some important sense in which moral or evaluative sentences do not have a truth value (for example, because they cannot be 'verified'), we ought not to boggle at '"Bardot is good" is true if and only if Bardot is good'; in a theory of truth, this consequence should follow with the rest, keeping track, as must be done, of the semantic location of such sentences in the language as a whole – of their relation to generalizations, their role in such compound sentences as 'Bardot is good and Bardot is foolish', and so on. What is special to evaluative words is simply not touched: the mystery is transferred from the word 'good' in the object-language to its translation in the metalanguage.

But 'good' as it features in 'Bardot is a good actress' is another matter. The problem is not that the translation of this sentence is not in the metalanguage – let us suppose it is. The problem is to frame a truth definition such that '"Bardot is a good actress" is true if and only if Bardot is a good actress' – and all other sentences like it – are consequences. Obviously 'good actress' does not mean 'good and an actress'. We might think of taking 'is a good actress' as an unanalyzed predicate. This would obliterate all connection between 'is a good actress' and 'is a good mother', and it would give us no excuse to think of 'good', in these uses, as a word or semantic element. But worse, it would bar us from framing a truth definition at all, for there is no end to the predicates we would have to treat as logically simple (and hence accommodate in separate clauses in the definition of satisfaction): 'is a good companion to dogs', 'is a good 28-years old conversationalist', and so forth. The problem is not peculiar to the case: it is the problem of attributive adjectives generally.

It is consistent with the attitude taken here to deem it usually a strategic error to undertake philosophical analysis of words or expressions which is not preceded by or at any rate accompanied by the attempt to get the logical grammar straight. For how can we have any confidence in our analyses of words like 'right', 'ought', 'can', and 'obliged', or the phrases we use to talk of actions, events and causes, when we do not know what (logical, semantical) parts of speech we have to deal with? I would say much the same about studies of the 'logic' of these and other words, and the sentences containing them. Whether the effort and ingenuity that has gone into the study of deontic logics, modal logics, imperative and erotetic logics has been largely futile or not cannot be known until we have acceptable semantic analyses of the sentences such systems purport to treat. Philosophers and logicians sometimes talk or work as if they were free to choose between, say, the truth-functional conditional and others, or free to introduce non-truth-functional sentential operators like 'Let it be the case that' or 'It ought to be the case that'. But in fact the decision is crucial. When we depart from idioms we can accommodate in a truth definition, we lapse into (or create) language for which we have no coherent semantical account – that is, no account at all of how such talk can be integrated into the language as a whole.

To return to our main theme: we have recognized that a theory of the kind proposed leaves the whole matter of what individual words mean exactly where it was. Even when the metalanguage is different from the object language, the theory exerts no pressure for improvement, clarification or analysis of individual words, except when, by accident of vocabulary, straightforward translation fails. Just as synonomy, as between expressions, goes generally untreated, so also synonomy of sentences, and analyticity. Even such sentences as 'A vixen is a female fox' bear no special tag unless it is our pleasure to provide it. A truth definition does not distinguish between analytic sentences and others, except for sentences that owe their truth to the presence alone of the constants that give the theory its grip on structure: the theory entails not only that these sentences are true but that they will remain true under all significant rewritings of their non-logical parts. A notion of logical truth thus given limited application, related notions of logical equivalence and entailment will tag along. It is hard to imagine how a theory of meaning could fail to read a logic into its object language to this degree; and to the extent that it does, our intuitions of logical truth, equivalence and entailment may be called upon in constructing and testing the theory.

I turn now to one more, and very large, fly in the ointment: the fact that the same sentence may at one time or in one mouth be true and at another time or in another mouth be false. Both logicians and those critical of formal methods here seem largely (though by no means universally) agreed that formal semantics and logic are incompetent to deal with the disturbances caused by demonstratives. Logicians have often reacted by downgrading natural language and trying to show how to get along without demonstratives; their critics react by downgrading logic and formal semantics. None of this can make me happy: clearly demonstratives cannot be eliminated from a natural language without loss or radical change, so there is no choice but to accommodate theory to them.

No logical errors result if we simply treat demonstratives as constants;[15] neither do any problems arise for giving a semantic truth definition. '"I am wise" is true if and only if I am wise', with its bland ignoring of the demonstrative element in 'I' comes off the assembly line along with '"Socrates is wise" is true if and only if Socrates is wise' with *its* bland indifference to the demonstrative element in 'is wise' (the tense).

What suffers in this treatment of demonstratives is not the definition of a truth predicate, but the plausibility of the claim that what has been defined is truth. For this claim is acceptable only if the speaker and circumstances of utterance of each sentence mentioned in the definition is matched by the speaker and circumstances of utterance of the truth definition itself. It could also be fairly pointed out that part of understanding demonstratives is knowing the rules by which they adjust their reference to circumstance; assimilating demonstratives to constant terms obliterates this feature. These complaints can be met, I think, though only by a fairly far-reaching revision in the theory of truth. I shall barely suggest how this could be done, but bare suggestion is all that is needed: the idea is technically trivial, and quite in line with work being done on the logic of the tenses.[16]

We could take truth to be a property, not of sentences, but of utterances, or speech acts, or ordered triples of sentences, times and persons; but it is simplest just to view truth as a relation between a sentence, a person, and a time. Under such treatment, ordinary logic as now read applies as usual, but only to sets of sentences relativized to the same speaker and time; further logical relations between sentences spoken at different times and by different speakers may be articulated by new axioms. Such is not my concern. The theory of meaning undergoes a systematic but not puzzling change: corresponding to each expression with a demonstrative element there must in the theory be a phrase that relates the truth conditions of sentences in which the expression occurs to changing times and speakers. Thus the theory will entail sentences like the following:

> 'I am tired' is true as (potentially) spoken by p at t if and only if p is tired at t.
> 'That book was stolen' is true as (potentially) spoken by p at t if and only if the book demonstrated by p at t is stolen prior to t.[17]

Plainly, this course does not show how to eliminate demonstratives; for example, there is no suggestion that 'the book demonstrated by the speaker' can be substituted ubiquitously for 'that book' *salva veritate*. The fact that demonstratives are amenable to formal treatment ought greatly to improve hopes for a serious semantics of natural language, for it is likely that many outstanding puzzles, such as the analysis of quotations or sentences about propositional attitudes, can be solved if we recognize a concealed demonstrative construction.

Now that we have relativized truth to times and speakers, it is appropriate to glance back at the problem of empirically testing a theory of meaning for an alien tongue. The essence of the method was, it will be remembered, to correlate held-true sentences with held-true sentences by way of a truth definition, and within the bounds of intelligible error. Now the picture must be elaborated to allow for the fact that sentences are true, and held true, only relative to a speaker and a time. The real task is therefore to translate each sentence by another that is true for the same speakers at the same times. Sentences with demonstratives obviously yield a very sensitive test of the correctness of a theory of meaning, and constitute the most direct link between language and the recurrent macroscopic objects of human interest and attention.[18]

In this paper I have assumed that the speakers of a language can effectively determine the meaning or meanings of an arbitrary expression (if it has a meaning), and that it is the central task of a theory of meaning to show how this is possible. I have argued that a characterization of a truth predicate describes the required kind of structure, and provides a clear and testable criterion of an adequate semantics for a natural language. No doubt there are other reasonable demands that may be put on a theory of meaning. But a theory that does no more than define truth for a language comes far closer to constituting a complete theory of meaning than superficial analysis might suggest; so, at least, I have urged.

Since I think there is no alternative, I have taken an optimistic and programmatic view of the possibilities for a formal characterization of a truth predicate for a natural language. But it must be allowed that a staggering list of difficulties and conundrums remains. To name a few: we do not know the logical form of counterfactual or subjunctive sentences; nor of sentences about probabilities and about causal relations; we have no good idea what the logical role of adverbs is, nor the role of attributive adjectives; we have no theory for mass terms like 'fire', 'water' and 'snow', nor for sentences about belief, perception and intention, nor for verbs of action that imply purpose. And finally, there are all the sentences that seem not to have truth values at all: the imperatives, optatives, interrogatives, and a host more. A comprehensive theory of meaning for a natural language must cope successfully with each of these problems.

Notes

1. Elsewhere I have urged that it is a necessary condition, if a language is to be learnable, that it have only a finite number of semantical primitives: see 'Theories of Meaning and Learnable Languages', in *Proceedings of the 1964 International Congress for Logic, Methodology and Philosophy of Science*, North-Holland Publishing Company, Amsterdam, 1965, pp. 383–394.
2. A 'structural description' of an expression describes the expression as a concatenation of elements drawn from a fixed finite list (for example of words or letters).
3. The argument is essentially Frege's. See A. Church, *Introduction to Mathematical Logic*, Vol. I, Princeton 1956, pp. 24–25. It is perhaps worth mentioning that the argument does not depend on any particular identification of the entities to which sentences are supposed to refer.
4. It may be thought that Church, in 'A Formulation of the Logic of Sense and Denotation', in *Structure, Method and Meaning: Essays in Honor of H. M. Sheffer* (ed. by Henle, Kallen and Langer), Liberal Arts Press, New York, 1951, pp. 3–24, has given a theory of meaning that makes essential use of meanings as entities. But this is not the case: Church's logics of sense and denotation are interpreted as being about meanings, but they do not mention expressions and so cannot of course be theories of meaning in the sense now under discussion.
5. For a recent and instructive statement of the role of semantics in linguistics, see Noam Chomsky, 'Topics in the Theory of Generative Grammar', in *Current Trends in Linguistics* (ed. by Thomas A. Sebeok), Vol. III, The Hague 1966. In this article, Chomsky (1) emphasizes the central importance of semantics in linguistic theory, (2) argues for the superiority of transformational grammars over phrase structure grammars largely on the grounds that, although phrase structure grammars may be adequate to define sentencehood for (at least) some natural languages, they are inadequate as a foundation for semantics, and (3) comments

repeatedly on the 'rather primitive state' of the concepts of semantics and remarks that the notion of semantic interpretation 'still resists any deep analysis'.

6. Assuming, of course, that the extension of these predicates is limited to the sentences of *L*.
7. Alfred Tarski, 'The Concept of Truth in Formalized Languages', in *Logic, Semantics, Metamathematics*, Oxford 1956, pp. 152–278.
8. But Quine may be quoted in support of my usage: '. . . in point of *meaning* . . . a word may be said to be determined to whatever extent the truth or falsehood of its contexts is determined.' 'Truth by Convention', first published in 1936; now in *The Ways of Paradox*, New York 1966, p. 82. Since a truth definition determines the truth value of every sentence in the object language (relative to a sentence in the metalanguage), it determines the meaning of every word and sentence. This would seem to justify the title Theory of Meaning.
9. To give a single example: it is clearly a count in favor of a theory that it entails '"Snow is white" is true if and only if snow is white'. But to contrive a theory that entails this (and works for all related sentences) is not trivial. I do not know a theory that succeeds with this very case (the problem of 'mass terms').
10. This sketch of how a theory of meaning for an alien tongue can be tested obviously owes its inspiration to Quine's account of radical translation in Chapter II of *Word and Object*, New York 1960. In suggesting that an acceptable theory of radical translation take the form of a recursive characterization of truth, I go beyond anything explicit in Quine. Toward the end of this paper, in the discussion of demonstratives, another strong point of agreement will turn up.
11. So far as I am aware, there has been very little discussion of whether a formal truth definition can be given for a natural language. But in a more general vein, several people have urged that the concepts of formal semantics be applied to natural language. See, for example, the contributions of Yehoshua Bar-Hillel and Evert Beth to *The Philosophy of Rudolph Carnap* (ed. by Paul A. Schilpp), La Salle, Ill., 1963, and Bar-Hillel's 'Logical Syntax and Semantics', *Language* **30**, 230–237.
12. Tarski, *ibid.*, p. 165.
13. *Ibid.*, p. 267.
14. The rapprochement I prospectively imagine between transformational grammar and a sound theory of meaning has been much advanced by a recent change in the conception of transformational grammar described by Chomsky in the article referred to above (note 5). The structures generated by the phrase-structure part of the grammar, it has been realized for some time, are those suited to semantic interpretation; but this view is inconsistent with the idea, held by Chomsky until recently, that recursive operations are introduced only by the transformation rules. Chomsky now believes the phrase-structure rules are recursive. Since languages to which formal semantic methods directly and naturally apply are ones for which a (recursive) phrase-structure grammar is appropriate, it is clear that Chomsky's present picture of the relation between the structures generated by the phrase-structure part of the grammar, and the sentences of the language, is very much like the picture many logicians and philosophers have had of the relation between the richer formalized languages and ordinary language. (In these remarks I am indebted to Bruce Vermazen.)

15. Quine has good things to say about this in *Methods of Logic*, New York 1950, See §8.
16. For an up-to-date bibliography, and discussion, see A. N. Prior, *Past, Present, and Future*, Oxford 1967.
17. There is more than an intimation of this approach to demonstratives and truth in Austin's 1950 article 'Truth', reprinted in *Philosophical Papers*, Oxford 1961. See pp. 89–90.
18. These remarks clearly derive from Quine's idea that 'occasion sentences' (those with a demonstrative element) must play a central role in constructing a translation manual.

Afterword

Truth and Paradox

Vann McGee

Semantics is the branch of linguistics which studies the connection between the expressions of a language and the objects or states of affairs those expressions refer to.[1] The *semantic conception of truth*, as traditionally formulated, has it that the truth of a sentence consists in a correspondence between the sentence and an existing state of affairs.

As a definition of truth, this formulation suffers from two serious defects. First, the phrase 'corresponds to an existing state of affairs' is too vague for the definition to be much use in trying to figure out whether a particular sentence is true. Second, one wants to define a new notion in terms of old notions that already understood, and the notion of correspondence is likely to be no better understood than the notion of truth. In particular, we ask about truth because we want to understand the connection between language and the world, but, since correspondence is a semantic notion, we will only understand the phrase 'corresponds to an existing state of affairs' if we already have a theoretical understanding of the connection between language and the world. To be really helpful, a definition should define 'true' in non-semantical terms.

Alfred Tarski[2] showed how, for a wide range of languages (though not for all languages), it is possible to give a definition of 'true' which is entirely free of both these defects. Before he gave his definition, Tarski solved a preliminary problem whose solution has turned out to be nearly as important as the definition itself. The preliminary problem was to give a criterion by which to judge when a proposed definition of truth is satisfactory. When we are defining a new term, we are free to let the new term mean whatever we like. But if the term we are 'defining' is a world like 'true,' which is already in common use, we need to make sure that our new definition does not conflict with pre-existing usage.

Tarski's solution to the preliminary problem is as simple as it is elegant.

Being the sort of people they are, philosophers are sure to disagree wildly about any general theoretical claim you might want to make about truth. On the other hand, there are some very simple observations about truth that virtually anyone is sure to accept, for example:

> 'Snow is white' is true if and only if snow is white.
> 'Grass is green' is true if and only if grass is green.
> 'Flounders snore' is true if and only if flounders snore.

Let us refer to sentences of the form

> *x* is true if and only if *S*

where '*S*' is replaced by a sentence and '*x*' is replaced by a quotation name of the same sentence, as *T-sentences*. Tarski's criterion was that a proposed definition of truth be considered adequate just in case it entails all the T-sentences.

Tarski's criterion is a test for material adequacy. A proposed definition is said to be *materially adequate* if it picks out the right things. An example in constant use since Aristotle is 'featherless biped' as a definition of 'human being.' This definition is in many ways unsatisfactory, for it has not told us anything essential about what it is to be a human being; nevertheless, it is a materially adequate definition, for it picks out the right things. Similarly, a definition of truth that implies the T-sentences may well be unfit for many uses, but it will, at least, pick out the right things.

A couple of caveats need to be voiced at once. First,

> 'Are we having fun yet?' is true if and only if are we having fun yet?

is nonsensical. Sentences used to issue orders or ask questions aren't either true or false. Tarski's criterion can only be applied to declarative sentences.

Even declarative sentences cannot generally be said to be either true or false. The sentence (ie. the sentence *type*) 'I am having fun now' is neither true nor false. Whether an utterance of the sentence is true or false depends on when it's said and by whom. The appropriate T-sentence should be, not

> 'I am having fun now' is true if and only if I am having fun now

but rather,

> An utterance of 'I am having fun now' is true if and only if the speaker is having fun at the time of utterance.[3]

Tarski ignored such problems, for the sentences he was interested in were those occurring in mathematics or other theoretical sciences. For such sentences, we find that the truth or falsity of an utterance of the sentence is unlikely to depend upon the circumstances of utterance. If we restrict our attention to such sentences, we can uphold the pretense that it is sentences (rather than utterances or propositions or sentence-context pairs) that are either true or false.

Finally, we need to note that Tarski's criterion, as we've described it, only applies to sentences of English. Try applying it to the German sentence '*Schnee ist weiss*' and you get a jumble of words that is neither intelligible English nor intelligible German:

> '*Schnee ist weiss*' is true if and only if *Schnee ist weiss.*

Tarski gave a more general version of his criterion that applies to sentences from outside English: A materially adequate definition of truth for a language $\mathscr{L}$ should imply each sentence,

> x is true if and only if S

where 'x' is replaced by the name of a sentence of $\mathscr{L}$ and 'S' is replaced by its English translation.

There is now a problem about languages that overlap. If it should turn out that the English sentence 'Snow is white' should also appear as a Froggish sentence meaning 'Peanuts are puce,' we shall be forced to accept both these T-sentences:

> 'Snow is white' is true if and only if Snow is white
> 'Snow is white' is true if and only if peanuts are puce

leading to the absurd conclusion,

> Snow is white if and only if peanuts are puce.

To avoid this absurdity, we must acknowledge that truth is a relative notion. A sentence is not simply true or false, but true or false in a particular context within a particular language. Thus,

> 'Snow is white' is true in English if and only if snow is white
> 'Snow is white' is true in Froggish if and only if peanuts are puce.

Thus Tarski's criterion takes the general form:

> A theory of truth for a language $\mathscr{L}$ is *materially adequate* if it entails each sentence of the form
> x is true in $\mathscr{L}$ if and only if S,
> where 'x' is replaced by the quotation name of a sentence of $\mathscr{L}$ and 'S' is replaced by its English translation.

The question what constitutes a correct translation is fiercely embattled among philosophers. We shall have to discuss it a little bit eventually, but, for now, we can set it aside by restricting our attention to cases in which the language $\mathscr{L}$ is either English or a fragment of English.

Now that we know what would count as an adequate definition of truth, how do we go about finding one? Tarski's solution begins by noticing how the truth or falsity of a compound sentence depends upon the truth or falsity of its simple components. 'Snow is white or grass is green' is true if and only if 'Snow is white' is true or 'Grass is green' true. Having this observation in hand, we can reduce the problem of defining truth to the problem of specifying when a simple sentence is true. This isn't as much help as we had hoped, because there are infinitely many simple sentences ('There are at least two stars,' 'There are at least three stars,' etc.).

To make real progress, we need to be able to get inside the structure of simple sentences. Consider the simple sentence:

> Some fish fly.

If everything had a name, we could readily describe the sentence's truth conditions, by saying that the sentence is true just in case there is some way of filling in the blanks in

> ____________ is a fish

and in

> ____________ flies

so as to make both simple sentences true. However, not everything has a name, so we have to worry about the possibility that some fish fly but no named fish fly. To get the correct truth conditions for 'Some fish fly,' we need the notion of *satisfaction*. The open sentence 'x is a fish' is satisfied by fish and by nothing else; 'x flies' is satisfied by all and only the things that fly. We have

> Some fish fly

is true if and only if there is something that satisfies both the open sentence

> *x* is a fish

and

> *x* flies.

Once we have the notion of satisfaction, we easily get truth conditions for simple sentences of the form

> Theaetetus flies

by introducing the further notion of *denotation*. 'Theaetetus flies' is true if and only if the individual denoted by 'Theaetetus' satisfies '*x* flies.'[4] The notions of denotation and satisfaction are connected;

> The man who discovered the five perfect solids

denotes the unique individual (provided there is one) who satisfies

> *x* is a man and *x* discovered the five perfect solids.

Let me use *reference* as a comprehensive term comprising both denotation and satisfaction.

When we go beyond the very simplest sentences, things get more complicated. For the truth conditions for

> Every fish has a brother

we need: For every individual *a*, there exists an individual *b* such that the ordered pair $\langle a,b \rangle$ satisfies

> If *x* is a fish, *y* is *x*'s brother.

So we need to talk, not about the satisfaction of an open sentence by an individual but about the satisfaction of an open sentence by a sequence of individuals.

Complications aside, the strategy is clear. Explain the truth conditions of sentences in terms of the satisfaction conditions of very simple open sentences. The English language is exceedingly complex and not at all well understood, so there are a great many English locutions that do not readily submit to this procedure. Modal statements, indirect discourse, attributions of mental attitudes, and counterfactual conditionals, among many others. But there is a sizeable fragment of English which responds to the treatment quite well, so that there is a sizeable body of English sentences for which we are able to give truth conditions in terms of the satisfaction conditions of such very simple sentences as '*x* is a fish,' '*x* flies,' and '*y* is *x*'s brother.'

How do we give satisfaction conditions for the simplest open sentences? Tarski's answer is effective, but crude. We say:

> An individual satisfies '*x* is a fish' if and only if it is a fish
> An individual satisfies '*x* flies' if and only if it flies
> An ordered pair satisfies '*y* is *x*'s brother' if and only if its second component is a brother of its first component

and so on. Since English has a finite vocabulary, there will be only finitely many such simple open sentences to deal with.

In the end, we are able to fully specify satisfaction conditions for our fragment of English. We give the satisfaction conditions for the simplest open sentences by listing the open sentences one by one, giving satisfaction conditions for each. Then the satisfaction conditions for compound open sentences are given in terms of those for their simpler components. This gives us what is called a *recursive definition* of satisfaction. It is almost circular, defining satisfaction in terms of satisfaction. It specifies what 'satisfies' means when applied to compound sentences in terms of what 'satisfies' means when applied to simpler open sentences. Another example of a recursive definition is the definition of exponentiation:

$$m^0 = 1$$
$$m^{n+1} = m^n \cdot m$$

which defines one value of the exponent function in terms of earlier values of the exponent function. Recursive definitions should be contrasted with *explicit definitions*, like

> *x* is a rhombus if and only if *x* is an equilateral parallelogram

in which the term to be defined appears on the left but not on the right. There are standard mathematical techniques[5] for converting recursive definitions into explicit definitions. Applying them, Tarski was able to give an explicit definition of 'satisfies'. Going on to define 'true' in terms of 'satisfies,' Tarski was able to get a materially adequate explicit definition of the form

> *x* is true if and only if *x* is ____________

where no semantic terms occur within the blank.

Though it gives a materially adequate definition, Tarski's treatment of the simplest open sentences is disappointing. There is some connection between the people who live in English-speaking countries and the animals that live under water in virtue of which '*x* is a fish' is satisfied by fish. By observing that, for any *a*,

a satisfies '*x* is a fish' if and only *a* is a fish.

Tarski has described the connection, but he hasn't in any way explained it. And, as Aristotle noticed,[6] the mark of genuine scientific understanding is to know why as well as what.

Another way to express the complaint is this: Tarski has advertised his theory as the semantic conception of truth, the modern, scientific heir to the traditional correspondence theory. Yet he hasn't really located a connection between language and the world, because an arbitrary pairing of words with objects doesn't constitute a connection. If I pair off planets with baseball positions, enumerating <Mercury, pitcher>, <Venus, catcher>, <Earth, first base>, and so on, I haven't exhibited a genuine connection between Saturn and shortstops. In the same way, Tarski's theory isn't genuinely semantical.

Hartry Field,[7] who gave eloquent voice to our dissatisfaction here, has recommended that Tarski's treatment of the simplest sentences be replaced by a causal account. Some ancient Saxon held a fish in his hands and grunted 'fish,' and, via the complex pathways by which customs are handed down, we have inherited his usage.

As illuminating as it might be, it is hard to see how such a causal account could accomplish Tarski's purpose. Tarski intended explicitly to write down a definition of truth that yielded the T-sentences. For this purpose, it does not suffice to know a general outline of the origins and history of the language. One requires specific details, for one need to know the meaning of every single word in the language. Since any particular word might have meant something different without much else changing, our causal history would have to specify the origin of every single word. It must also take account of the winding patterns by which 'egregious,' derived from a Latin word meaning 'outstandingly good,' has come to mean 'outstandingly bad.' Such an intricate and voluminuous account might be possible in principle, and possibility in principle is what Field, for metaphysical purposes, is primarily interested in. But one would hardly expect to be able actually to write down such an account, or even to describe it, except in a loose and general way. So a causal account would not be practicable for Tarski's purpose.

To get the T-sentences, we need to describe the language in complete detail. We need to discern that, whereas 'inedible' means 'not edible,' 'inflammable' means 'flammable.' There is no reason to suppose that a causal account would give us such exhaustive detail. Tarski's account does give us the details, but it does so by resorting to a word-by-word vocabulary list. Now there is nothing inherently disreputable about a scientific theory that gives us a list. A lepidoptery text consists largely of an illustrated list of the kinds of butterflies there are, but no one supposes that lepidoptery is bad science on that account. Precisely what species of butterflies there are is a matter of accident, just as it is an accident precisely what vocabulary we use. We do not generally suppose that it is either possible or necessary to explain accidents; we are often content merely to describe them. Even so, apart from the innumerable specific details, one would like a general understanding of how our conventions, intentions, and practices forge a link between language and the world, and Tarski's theory does not offer us such an understanding.

We discern two separate aims one might have in developing a theory of truth. One is to explain the processes by which language is linked with the world. The other is to describe the language in sufficient detail to get the T-sentences. there is no good reason to suppose that a theory that fulfills one of these aims will fulfill the other.

Indeed, there is some reason to think that the two aims are not merely separate but incompatible. Currently the most prominent alternative to the semantic conception of truth is what we may call the *disquotational conception of truth*, according to which, more than merely materially adequate, Tarski's definition tells us the nature of truth. Contrary to Field's hopes, underlying Tarski's list there is no deep explanation of the connection between language and the world.

According to the disquotational conception, after one has learned the bulk of one's language, one learns the notions of denotation and satisfaction by learning the algorithm that lets us assert:

> 'Adam' denotes Adam
> 'Eve' denotes Eve
> 'Cain' denotes Cain
> 'Abel' denotes Abel

and so on. When we learn this algorithm, we learn the meaning of the word 'denotes,' and a similar algorithm teaches us the meaning of 'satisfies.' Questions about how and why 'Adam' refers to Adam or about how an individual or a culture acquires a language are interesting questions, but they are not questions a theory of truth and reference undertakes to answer.[8]

According to disquotationalism, it is not the task of a theory of truth and reference to explain the role of language in human affairs. Instead, the notion of truth serves a peculiar logical purpose. When I tell you,

> Everything the Pope says is true.

I have, in effect, given you the conjunction of infinitely many sentences:

If the Pope says 'Aardvarks are amorous,' then aardvarks are amorous
If the Pope says 'Aaron is ambidextrous,' then Aaron is ambidextrous
If the Pope says 'Abigail is ambitious,' then Abigail is ambitious

and so on. Without employing the notion of truth, we can conjoin sentences two at a time, by inserting the word 'and' between them. With the notion of truth, we can conjoin infinitely many sentences at once. Thus truth serves a mightily important purpose, for without it we could only describe local, sentence-by-sentence features of systems of statements and beliefs; global properties would escape us. But, for all its power, the use of the word 'true' no more signifies a deep connection between language and the world than the use of 'and' does.

To serve as a mechanism for infinite conjunction, one's notion of truth will have to yield the T-sentences. And there are good reasons to doubt that a semantical conception of truth will invariably yield the T-sentences.

One such reason has to do with vague terms. Among the T-sentences are these:

'Harry is bald' is true if and only if Harry is bald
'Harry is not bald' is true if and only if Harry is not bald.

Together these yield, by logic,

Either 'Harry is bald' is true or 'Harry is not bald' is true.

On a semantical conception of truth, when a sentence is true, then our conventions, intentions, and practices, together with the non-semantic facts, make it true. Hence,

Our conventions, intentions, and practices, together with the non-semantic facts, determine either that 'Harry is bald' is true or that 'Harry is not bald' is true.

But, if Harry is a borderline case for 'bald,' such a contention is implausible.

Another problem has to do with translations. Donald Davidson[9] has argued persuasively that the most our conventions, intentions, and practices can establish are the truth conditions for the sentences of a language. But truth conditions drastically underdetermine reference and meaning. Davidson's example:[10] Taking 'Wilt' to refer to Wilt's shadow and '*x* is tall' to be satisfied by all and only the shadows of tall things will give us the same truth conditions for 'Wilt is tall' that we get by taking 'Wilt' to refer to Wilt and '*x* is tall' to be satisfied by tall things; so our conventions, intentions, and practices don't determine whether 'Wilt' refers to Wilt or his shadow. Quine's example:[11] With suitable changes all around, 'rabbit' could be taken to refer either to rabbits or to undetached living rabbit parts.

Perhaps if the language we are dealing with is that of a tribe so distant from us that we are not willing to posit any hypotheses about their psychological makeup, this is where we must leave the matter. (Trying to fix meaning without venturing any psychological hypotheses is the program of *radical translation*, introduced as an artificial methodology in order to isolate linguistic hypotheses from psychological hypotheses.)[12] But, for one's own language, it sounds hopelessly paradoxical to assert 'I don't know – indeed there is no fact of the matter there to be known – whether, when I use the word "rabbit" I am referring to rabbits or rabbit parts.'

The disquotationalist has an easy way out of this puzzle. Reference conditions for one's own language are fixed disquotationally – 'Adam' refers to Adam, etc. Reference conditions for somebody else's language are determined by translating that person's language into one's own, determining correctness of translation by appropriate similarity of conceptual roles. Much more needs to be said here, both about what constitutes appropriate similarity and about what to do with languages that can't be translated into one's own. But it is a promising program.

The main problem with disquotationalism is not with what it tells us but with what it doesn't tell us. The regular relations between language and the world, in virtue of which acoustical emanations from a speaker's lips routinely produce reliable expectations about parts of the world far removed from the immediate experience of either speaker or listener, is one of the central organizing features of the social life of mankind, without which much of human behavior would be simply incomprehensible. Such an important phenomenon demands an explanation. The semantic conception attempts to give such an explanation, albeit in a vague and sketchy way, in terms of a causal theory of reference. For the disquotationalist, truth and reference do not function as explanatory terms, so that the disquotationalist needs some other approach to explaining the role of language in human affairs, with some other central notion, perhaps something like warranted assertability. But, as faintly sketched as the causal theory of language may be, our understanding of warranted assertability is ever so much fainter.

Until the sketches have been filled in a great deal better than they are at present, one would, if forced to decide, choose between the semantic and disquotational conceptions of truth, not by comparing their successes, but by comparing the cheeriness of their promises.

So far, I have been speaking as if it were possible to use Tarski's methods to give a theory of truth for English. This pretense is contrary to the facts, for Tarski's methods cannot be applied to sentences outside a core of straightforward, 'just-the-facts-ma'am' reports. For example, if we try to use Tarski's technique to get the truth conditions for belief reports we get this:

> 'Clark Kent is believed by Lois Lane to be a mild-mannered reporter' is true if and only if
> the individual denoted by 'Clark Kent' satisfies 'x is believed by Lois Lane to be a mild-mannered reporter' if and only if
> the individual denoted by 'Superman' satisfies 'x is believed by Lois Lane to be a mild-mannered reporter' [because the individual named by 'Clark Kent' and the individual named by 'Superman' are one and the same] if and only if
> 'Superman is believed by Lois Lane to be a mild-mannered reporter' is true

But this is absurd. Clark Kent is believed by Lois Lane to be a mild-mannered reporter, but Superman is not. To give the correct truth conditions for belief attributions would require methods considerably more subtle than those Tarski employs.

To some extent, pretending that Tarski's methods can yield a theory of truth for English merely reflects a hearty optimism. We may hope that such utterances as belief attributions, indirect speech reports, counterfactual conditionals, and sentences containing indexical terms, though they don't submit directly to a Tarskian analysis, can be tamed, once we understand them better, by some sophisticated variation on a Tarskian theme.

There is another problem lurking about which is altogether more serious, for it shows that, no matter how sophisticated we become, we shall never get a consistent theory of truth for English which yields the T-sentences. The problem has several versions, the simplest of which involves the following sentence, which we call the *Simple Liar Sentence*:

> The Simple Liar Sentence is false.

The relevant T-sentence is this:

> 'The Simple Liar Sentence is false' is true if and only if the Simple Liar Sentence is false.

Substituting equals for equals, we get:

> The Simple Liar Sentence is true if and only if the Simple Liar Sentence is false.

So far, things are not so bad. We may say that the Simple Liar Sentence has failed to attach itself onto the world properly, so that it is neither true nor false. Indeed, Saul Kripke[13] has shown how, in a language with a non-classical logic that allows truth-value gaps, we can arrange things so that, whenever x is a quotation name of the sentence S, we have:

> 'x is true' is true if and only if S is true.

'x is true' is false if and only if S is false.
'x is true' is neither true nor false if and only if S is neither true nor false.

Our relief at escaping from the paradox is short-lived. For consider the *Strengthened Liar Sentence*:

The Strengthened Liar Sentence is not true.

On the analysis in terms of truth-value gaps, the Strengthened Liar Sentence is neither true nor false. But, if it is neither true nor false, it is not true. But that it is not true is what the Strengthened Liar Sentence says, so that what the sentence says is true after all. More directly, we see the problem by looking at the T-sentence:

'The Strengthened Liar Sentence is not true' is true if and only if the Strengthened Liar Sentence is not true.

Substituting equals for equals, we get:

The Strengthened Liar Sentence is true if and only if the Strengthened Liar Sentence is not true

an outright contradiction.

Whatever the source of the problem is, it afflicts all our attempts to link language and thought with the world. Thus our intuitive understanding of satisfaction follows the paradigm:

Theaetetus satisfies 'x is a fish' if and only if Theaetetus is a fish.

Applying this paradigm to the open sentence 'x does not satisfy itself,' we get, absurdly,

'x does not satisfy itself' satisfies 'x does not satisfy itself' if and only if 'x does not satisfy itself' does not satisfy itself.[14]

A similar problem with denotation:[15] Only finitely many natural numbers are named by English expressions of fewer than thirty syllables, so there must exist a least natural number not nameable in fewer than thirty syllables. But the phrase 'the least natural number not nameable in fewer than thirty syllables' names that number in twenty syllables.

A similar problem arises with knowledge.[16] For simplicity, let us say that a sentence is known when we mean that the sentence expresses a proposition that is known. Now consider the *Unknown Sentence*:

The Unknown Sentence is not known.

Clearly,

> If 'The Unknown Sentence is not known' is not known, then the Unknown Sentence is not known.

On the other hand, the first principle of epistemology – if it is known that *P*, then *P* – gives us:

> If 'The Unknown Sentence is not known' is known, then the Unknown Sentence is not known.

Whence we derive,

> The Unknown Sentence is not known.

Now we reflect that we have got this result by careful, correct, and explicit deduction from known premises, and that anything got in this way is known. Hence,

> 'The Unknown Sentence is not known' is known.

This yields:

> The Unknown Sentence is known.

Contradiction. Richard Montague[17] derives an analogous problem for necessity.

The problem is everywhere. Even such an apparently innocuous notion as eligibility to join a club falls prey to it. Thus Charles Chihara[18] considers the Secretaries' Liberation Club, whose rules offer membership to those who are secretaries of clubs they are not permitted to join. Is the Secretaries' Liberation Club's secretary eligible to join Secretaries' Liberation?

To solve this budget of paradoxes, Tarski recommended a drastic measure. Distinguishing the language one is speaking when discussing a language – the *metalanguage* – from the language one is speaking about – the *object language* – Tarski proposed this:

> One should never attempt to develop a theory of truth for a language within the language itself, but always with a metalanguage essentially richer in expressive power.

The same restriction applies to a theory of denotation or of satisfaction or of what sentences express things that are known or of what sentences express necessary truths.

Tarski concluded that it would not be possible to give a theory of truth for English. He based this conclusion of the premise that English, like any natural language, is a *universal language*, so that anything you can express in any language at all you can express in English. But to reach the conclusion, we do not require such a strong premiss. It is enough to observe that natural languages are all roughly equal in expressive power, while known artificial languages are vastly weaker in expressive power than English. Thus any language essentially richer than English would have to be of entirely different character from any language now known. If we somehow developed such a superlanguage, we would immediately want to know what were the true sentences of the superlanguage, and, to answer that, we would have to create a super-superlanguage, so we would never find ourselves in the happy state of having a theory of truth for the very language we speak.

Tarski's principal concerns were mathematical and methodological, rather than metaphysical, linguistic, or sociological. He wanted to develop theories of truth for artificial languages for use in mathematics and in the most highly developed of the empirical sciences. For him, the conclusion that one could not obtain a theory of truth for a natural language was not a cause of great alarm.

If our interests are broader, we shall not be able to afford such a complacent attitude. The use of natural language is one of the central organizing features of the social life of mankind, and if we can't give a linguistic theory that describes natural languages (or if the theory of natural language we can give is so restricted that it can talk about the internal structure of a language – its syntax – but not about what it means), much of human social life must remain incomprehensible to us. Similarly, we cannot adequately understand human psychology unless we can see how people use language to express beliefs; and an adequate understanding must describe not only the internal structure of beliefs but what the beliefs are about. Thus, if we accept Tarski's restriction, we shall find that both people and society lie, to a large extent, beyond the reach of scientific understanding. We may, if we like, employ Tarski's methods to give a theory of truth for a restricted fragment of English, a fragment from which words like 'true,' 'refers,' 'satisfies,' 'knows,' and 'necessarily' have been excised. But the language we use to talk about language and the thoughts we employ in thinking about thought will remain outside the reach of science.

A central tendency of twentieth century thought has been what we may call *naturalism*, the belief that human beings are products of nature and the lives of human beings are amenable to scientific understanding no less than geological or astronomical phenomena. To accept the restriction Tarski proposes, we must repudiate naturalism, for we reject the possibility of a comprehensive scientific understanding of human thought and language.

If this price seems too dear, we must find a way to overcome Tarski's restriction, so that we give a theory of the very language we speak, even though we have no recourse to an essentially richer metalanguage. This means we must somehow limit our acceptance of the T-sentences, for we have seen that the T-sentences are inconsistent with manifest facts, specifically the fact that

> 'The Strengthened Liar Sentence is not true' = the Strengthened Liar Sentence.

One can say more; by applying methods of Kurt Gödel,[19] Tarski[20] constructed a more subtle version of the liar paradox which shows that the T-sentences are inconsistent with the basic laws of syntax. Let me emphasize what this shows. It does not show merely that it is impossible for us to give a consistent theory that includes basic syntax and entails the T-sentences. If that were all we had, a satisfactory explanation would be that a natural language is so intricate that it is not possible for us to describe it in enough detail to get the T-sentences. But Tarski showed something much stronger: it is not possible to get a theory which includes the simple, basic laws of syntax and is *consistent* with the T-sentences.

To get a theory of truth for English, we have to somehow restrict the T-sentences. There are two possibilities. Either accept all the T-sentences and restrict classical logic somehow so that we can no longer derive absurd consequences, or repudiate some of the T-sentences. The first alternative is not very promising, for an exceedingly weak logic will suffice to derive preposterous consequences from the T-sentences together with the basic laws of syntax.[21] So the remaining alternative is that, in spite of their extreme obviousness and naturalness, we relinquish some of the T-sentences, giving up enough of our intuitive understanding of truth to avoid paradoxes, yet retaining enough so that what is left is still recognizably and usefully a notion of truth.

There are two problems here, connected but distinct. The first arises from the observation that, in spite of the paradoxes, ordinary speakers of English do not stumble all over themselves when trying to employ the notion of truth. In fact, even after they have seen the paradoxes, ordinary speakers have such clear and reliable intuitions about when the word 'true' ought to be applied that the paradoxes scarcely impair the notion's usefulness, even in contexts in which there is convoluted self-reference. So the first problem is to describe how ordinary speakers apply the world 'true.' For example, suppose A says:

(a1) Two plus two is three
(a2) Snow is always black
(a3) Everything B says is true
(a4) Something B says is not true

while B says:

(b1) One plus one is two
(b2) Snow is sometimes white
(b3) At most one thing A says is true.

Ordinary speakers have unmistakable intuitions that (b3) and (a3) are both true.[22] One wants to describe and explain these intuitions.

Quite a bit of progress has been made in describing the intuitions, by presenting classificatory schemes that concur with the practices of ordinary speakers in classifying sentences as true, false, or neither.[23] Rather less progress has been made in explaining the intuitions, since, in describing the classificatory scheme, one invariably takes a formal language, intended as a model of a fragment of English, and one presents the classificatory scheme for that language within an essentially richer metalanguage. This leaves us wondering how speakers of English, who have no essentially richer metalanguage, are able to classify sentences of English.

The second problem seems to me altogether more urgent. The notions of truth and reference are the principal links by which we try to understand the connection of human language and thought with the world around us. Until we have a satisfactory understanding of truth and reference, we cannot hope to have even the beginning of an adequate understanding of human language and thought, and we do not have, at present, even the beginning of a satisfactory understanding of truth and reference. Our present-day understanding of truth and reference is governed by the T-sentences, and, as an account of truth and reference, the T-sentences fail in the worst way possible: they are inconsistent. So, before we can adequately understand language and thought, we need to develop an understanding of truth that is not governed by the T-sentences and does not lapse into contradiction. This new understanding of truth might be obtained by making explicit our ordinary practices in applying the word 'true'; or it might involve replacing our ordinary notion of truth by a scientifically reconstructed notion, in the way science reconstructs our ordinary notions of space and time. One way or another, if we want a theoretical understanding of language and thought, we badly need a consistent theory of truth and reference; indeed, it is hard to imagine a more pressing philosophical problem.

A radical alternative to the program of restricting the T-sentences to obtain a consistent theory of truth would be to completely relinquish the notions of truth and reference as vehicles for theoretical understanding. Truth, as we naively conceive it, is characterized by the T-sentences, but the notion of truth described by the T-sentences is riddled with paradox. Moreover, as we saw in our discussion of disquotationalism, even within the fragments of English in which the paradoxes do not appear, the notion of truth described by the T-sentences does not suffice to give us a causally explanatory account of the use of language. So we are best off abandoning the disgraced notion of truth altogether, and employing some other notion – warranted assertability, or some such – in trying to understand the connection between language and the world.

One reason for not rushing to adopt the radical alternative is that, even if we do not intend to use the notion of truth for causal explanatory purposes, we shall still need it to effect infinite conjunctions. Another, more pressing, concern is that there is reason to fear that the notions we employ in place of truth in trying to understand the link between language and the world will fall prey to paradox as well. Thus, if we accept the extremely plausible principle that one is never warranted in making an assertion of the form

> *P*, but I am not warranted in asserting that *P*

we can use the Unassertable Sentence –

> I am not warranted in asserting the Unassertable Sentence

– to get a paradox much like the Unknown Sentence paradox.

Around 270 BC, the Stoic philosopher and poet Philetas of Cos died, we are told, from the sleepless nights he spent fretting about the liar paradox. The ingenious work of Tarski, Kripke, and others has been extremely illuminating, yet what we know about truth remains so vastly overshadowed by what we do not know that, even today, we aren't that much better off than Philetas was.

Notes

1. This definition of semantics is taken from p. 345 of Alfred Tarski's 'The semantic conception of truth,' *Philosophy and Phenomenological Research*, 4: 341–76.
2. Tarski (1956), 'Der Warheitsbegriff in den formalisierten Sprachen,' *Studia Logica 1*: 261–405. English translation by J. H. Woodger, 'The concept of truth in formalized languages,' in Tarski's *Logic, Semantics, Metamathematics* (Oxford: Oxford University Press), pp 152–278. See also 'The semantic conception of truth.'
3. Cf pp 33–5 of Donald Davidson's 'Truth and meaning' in his (1984) *Inquiries in Truth and Interpretation* (Oxford: Clarendon Press), pp 17–36.
4. This account of the simplest sentences was already given by Plato. See section 263 of the *Sophist*.
5. Due to Gottlob Frege, (1879), *Begriffsschrift* (Halle: Nebert).
6. *Metaphysics* B.
7. Field, H. (1972), 'Tarski's theory of truth,' *Journal of Philosophy*, 69: 347–75.
8. The disquotationalist program I am describing here is to define the reference conditions for simple terms disquotationally, then to use Tarski's methods to get the reference conditions for complex terms and the truth conditions for sentences.

A better known version of disquotationalism is to take the notion of truth to be characterized directly by the T-sentences; this is Paul Horwich's (1990) proposal (*Truth*, Oxford and Cambridge, Mass.: Basil Blackwell). An objection to this more direct procedure was voiced by Tarski (pp. 257f of 'The concept of truth in formalized languages'). From the T-sentences, you can derive each particular sentence that follows the paradigm:

> 'Snow is white and grass is green' is true if and only if 'Snow is white' is true and 'Grass is green' is true.

But the T-sentences do not give us the resources to put infinitely many such separate observations together to get the generalization:

> A conjunction is true if and only if both conjuncts are true.

9. *Op. cit.*
10. From 'The inscrutability of reference,' pp 227–41 of *Inquiries into Truth and Understanding*. The example cannot be taken literally, since it would require that every object have a unique shadow, but it is not hard to repair the example.
11. From Chapter 2 of *Word and Object* (1960), (Cambridge, Mass.: MIT Press).
12. See Davidson, 'Truth and meaning.'
13. Kripke, S. (1975), 'Outline of a theory of truth,' *Journal of Philosophy*, 72: 690–716. Reprinted on pp 53–81 of Robert L. Martin, (ed.) (1984), *Recent Essays on Truth and the Liar Paradox* (Oxford: Oxford University Press). The mathematical construction Kripke develops is quite versatile, so that, even though the most direct application of Kripke's construction is unable to cope with the paradox posed by the Strengthened Liar Sentence, there is hope that some more sophisticated application of his construction will prove more successful. See, for example, my (1989), 'Applying Kripke's theory of truth,' *Journal of Philosophy*, 86: 530–9.
14. This paradox is due to Kurt Grelling and L. Nelson, 'Bemerkungen zu den Paradoxien von Russell und Burali-Forti (1908),' *Abhandlungen der Fries'schen Schule neue Folge*, 2: 301–34.
15. Due to G. G. Berry. See Bertrand Russell and Alfred North Whitehead, (1927), *Principia Mathematica*, Vol. 1 (2nd ed., Cambridge: Cambridge University Press), p. 61.
16. See Richard Montague and David Kaplan, (1960), 'A paradox regained,' *Notre Dame Journal of Formal Logic*, 1: 79–90. Reprinted in Montague's (1974), *Formal Philosophy* (New Haven and London: Yale University Press), pp 271–85.
17. Montague, R. (1963), 'Syntactic treatments of modality, with corollaries on reflexion principles and finite axiomatizability,' *Acta Philosophica Fennica*, 16: 153–67. Reprinted in *Formal Philosophy*, pp 286–302.
18. Chihara, C. (1979), 'The semantic paradoxes: A diagnosis,' *Philosophical Review*, 88: 590–618.
19. Gödel, K. (1931), 'Über formal unentscheidbare Sätze der *Principia mathematica* und verwander Systeme I,' *Monatschefte für Mathematik und Physik*, 38: 173–98. English translation by Jean van Heijenoort, 'On formally undecidable

propositions of *Principia Mathematica* and related systems I,' in van Heijenoort, (ed.) (1967), *From Frege to Gödel* (Cambridge, Mass.: Harvard University Press), pp 596–616.

20. 'The concept of truth in formalized languages,' pp 247–51.
21. See Solomon Feferman, 'Toward useful type-free theories I,' *Journal of Symbolic Logic*, 49: 75–111. Reprinted in Martin (1984), pp 237–87.
22. This example is from Anil Gupta's (1982), 'Truth and paradox,' *Journal of Philosophical Logic*, 11: 1–60. Reprinted in Martin (1984), pp 175–235.
23. The most prominent results here can be found in the Martin (1984) volume.